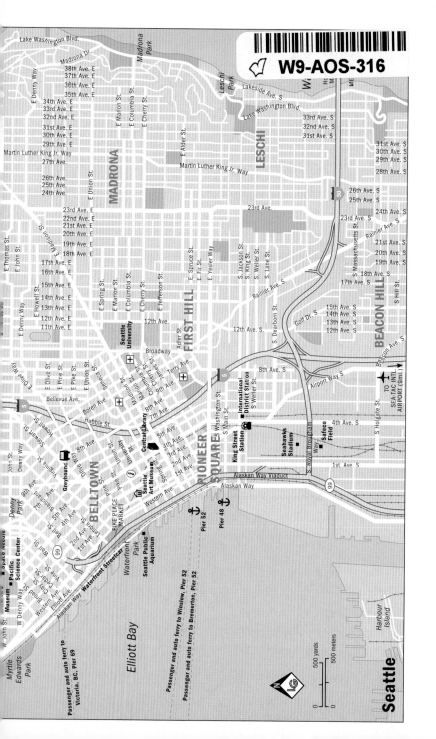

W9-AOS-316

Seattle

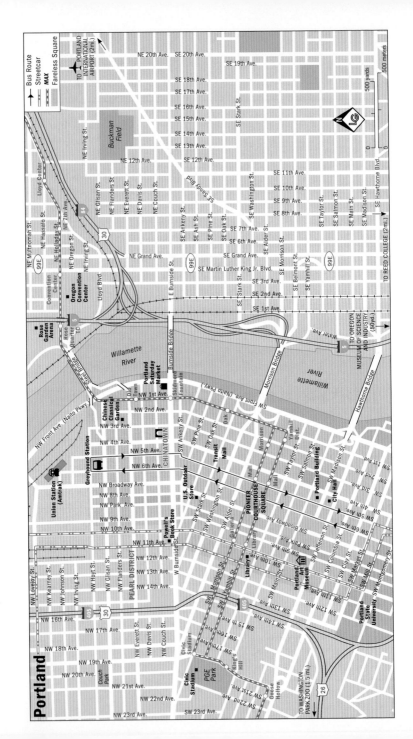

Portland

Legend
- → Bus Route
- Streetcar
- MAX
- Fareless Square

TO PORTLAND INTERNATIONAL AIRPORT (2mi.)

500 meters
500 yards

NE 20th Ave.
SE 20th Ave.
SE 19th Ave.
SE 18th Ave.
SE 17th Ave.
SE 16th Ave.
SE Stark St.
SE 15th Ave.
SE 14th Ave.
SE 13th Ave.
NE 12th Ave.
SE 12th Ave.

Buckman Field

NE Irving St.

NE Multnomah St.
Lloyd Center
NE Hassalo St.
NE Holladay St.
NE 7th Ave.
NE Oregon St.
NE Glisan St.
NE Flanders St.
NE Everett St.
NE Davis St.
NE Couch St.
NE Irving St.
SE Sandy Blvd.

SE 11th Ave.
SE 10th Ave.
SE 9th Ave.
SE 8th Ave.
SE Washington St.

SE Ankeny St.
SE Ash St.
SE Pine St.
SE Oak St.
SE 7th Ave.
SE Alder St.
SE 6th Ave.
SE Morrison St.
SE Taylor St.
SE Salmon St.
SE Main St.
SE Madison St.
SE Hawthorne Blvd.

Convention Center
Oregon Convention Center
Lloyd Blvd.

SE Grand Ave.
NE Grand Ave.
E Burnside St.
SE Martin Luther King Jr. Blvd.

SE Stark St.
SE Belmont St.
SE Yamhill St.

SE 3rd Ave.
SE 2nd Ave.
SE 1st Ave.

TO REED COLLEGE (2mi.)

Rose Garden Arena
Rose Quarter TC

Willamette River

Steel Bridge

Burnside Bridge

Portland Saturday Market

Water Ave.

TO OREGON MUSEUM OF SCIENCE AND INDUSTRY (.50vd.)

Old Town
NW 1st Ave.
Skidmore Fountain
Chinese Classical Garden
NW 2nd Ave.
NW 3rd Ave.
NW 4th Ave.

SW Front Ave. (Naito Pkwy.)

Morrison Bridge

Willamette River

Hawthorne Bridge

Greyhound Station
NW 5th Ave.
NW 6th Ave.
CHINATOWN

SW Ankeny St.
SW Pine St.
SW Oak St.
Oak
Morrison
Mall
Yamhill St.

Union Station (Amtrak)
NW Broadway Ave.
NW 8th Ave.
NW Park Ave.
NW 9th Ave.
NW 10th Ave.

U.S. Outdoor Store
Transit Mall
SW Stark St.
SW Washington St.
SW Alder St.
Galleria
Mall
PIONEER COURTHOUSE SQUARE
SW Taylor St.
SW Salmon St.
Portland Building
City Hall
SW Madison St.

SW 1st Ave.
SW 2nd Ave.
SW 3rd Ave.
SW 4th Ave.
SW 5th Ave.
SW 6th Ave.

Powell's Book Store
NW 11th Ave.
W Burnside St.
NW 12th Ave.
NW 13th Ave.
NW 14th Ave.

Library
SW Morrison St.
SW Yamhill St.
SW Broadway Ave.
SW Park Ave.
SW 9th Ave.
SW Main St.
SW Jefferson St.
SW Columbia St.
SW Clay St.
SW Market St.
SW Mill St.
SW Montgomery St.

PEARL DISTRICT
NW Lovejoy St.
NW Kearney St.
NW Johnson St.
NW Irving St.
NW Hoyt St.
NW Glisan St.
NW Flanders St.
NW Everett St.
NW Davis St.
NW Couch St.

Portland Art Museum
Library
SW 10th Ave.
SW 11th Ave.
SW 12th Ave.
SW 13th Ave.
SW 14th Ave.
SW 15th Ave.
SW 16th Ave.

Portland State University

Couch Park
NW 16th Ave.
NW 17th Ave.
NW 18th Ave.
NW 19th Ave.
NW 20th Ave.
NW 21st Ave.
NW 22nd Ave.
NW 23rd Ave.

Civic Stadium
PGE Park
Goose Hollow
King's Hill
SW 17th Ave.
SW 18th Ave.
SW 21st Ave.
SW 22nd Ave.
SW 23rd Ave.

TO WASHINGTON PARK ZOO (1.5 mi.)

30
84
5
99E
26
405

DISCOVER THE PACIFIC NORTHWEST

From the dense, misty rainforests of Oregon to the last desolate, treeless island in northern BC, North America's northwest coast is a land of staggering natural beauty. Along the coast, sharp young peaks soar skyward from the water's edge, spilling glaciers into the ocean at their bases. Human settlements of varying sizes and degrees of glamour mark the spots where rivers meet the coast, pointing the way to the region's interior. There, peaks give way to arable land, desert, and more mountains, peppered with cities and towns.

For thousands of years, human settlement in the region has relied on natural resources. In the last two hundred years, human activities have significantly impacted the land—enthusiastic logging, mining, and fishing proved the land isn't inexhaustible—but the birth of the environmental spirit in the late 20th century is revitalizing the region's natural charm. That spirit (visible in the adoption of sustainable practices by resource-based industries) and the explosive growth of tourism (dependent on the beauty of the region's forests) have helped modern governments see old-growth forests as something more than raw lumber.

While you are assured of seeing visitors wherever you go, with a minimum of effort you are easily able to lose the crowds. For example, while Banff National Park, in the Rockies, welcomes five million visitors a year, the right day hike—or a visit to one of the park's lesser-known neighbors—is all it takes to find solitude. For those overwhelmed by the boundless backcountry, welcoming hostels, quirky communities, and laid-back cities anchor the wilderness.

Winter visits promise hundreds of miles of skiing, snowboarding, snowshoeing, and snowmobiling out of snow-bound cities. Farther south along the coast, winter is more wet than white, and the litany of snow sports is restricted to higher elevations. Still, all it takes to find perfect powder is a couple hours (or less) on the highway out of town.

However audacious it is to cram this many miles of coast and this deep an interior into a single book, the present attempt is culled from what our researchers insisted they would do again if they could turn around and do their trips over. The guide has been made over for this edition as an Adventure Guide, which means an even greater focus on hiking, camping, and other wilderness and recreation activities. The sample itineraries that follow are intended to help you picture what your own personal Northwest adventure might look like. For practical trip-planning resources, including campground reservation numbers, road reports, climate charts, and Internet resources, see the **Essentials** (p. 18) chapter, and begin thumbing through the rest of *Let's Go: Pacific Northwest Adventure Guide*.

WHEN TO GO

Tourist season in the Pacific Northwest runs from late May to early September, from Victoria Day (Canada) and Memorial Day (US) to Labour/Labor Day. Low-season accommodations may be cheaper and much less crowded, but the sights you traveled so far to see may also be closed, and camping is not nearly as pleasant in the colder, damper winter conditions (lows of 10°F/-12°C). The

FACTS AND FIGURES

OREGON (OR): THE DRIVE DOWN I-5
Best place for a cold one: Portland, the microbrewery capital of the US.
Best place to windsurf: the Columbia River Gorge, home to some of the world's best.
Deepest river gorge in North America: the 8000 ft. deep Hells Canyon.

WASHINGTON (WA): EVERGREEN, EVER-CAFFEINATED
Number of wineries in 1981: 19. Number of wineries in 2004: 260.
Rank in US apple production: 1.
Highest peak: Mt. Rainier, 14,410 ft., the tallest in the Pacific Northwest.

BRITISH COLUMBIA (BC): "HOLLYWOOD NORTH"
British Columbia's rank among the film and TV production centers in the world: 3.
Number of films/shows shot in British Columbia in year 2002: 205.
Best place to spot a mythological creature: at Okanagan Lake, where the sea creature "Ogopogo" is said to reside.

ALBERTA (AB): WHERE THE ROCKIES MEET THE PRAIRIES
Hours of sunlight per year: approximately 2400, the most in Canada.
Home of world's largest shopping/entertainment complex: the West Edmonton Mall.
Kilometers of road: 180,000. Kilometers of paved roads: 31,000. Kilometers of pipelines for oil: 184,000.

coastal cities are justly famous for rain, which pours down 10 months of the year. The ocean keeps coastal temperatures moderate year-round. In Portland, Seattle, and Vancouver, a few snow days a year are the norm, but the white stuff doesn't stick around for long. To the east of the coastal mountains, expect less precipitation, warmer summers (highs of 100°F/38°C), and colder winters. Don't be surprised to see snow September through June at some spots in the Cascades, where the mountains push moist ocean air up into the chilly atmosphere. The same variation occurs up north, only on a shifted scale—interior winters are bitterly cold, while summers are decidedly cool. As in the south, things even out on the coast, with plenty of rain (called liquid sunshine by some coastal residents).

GOVERNMENT HOLIDAYS

On official government holidays, many sights and all banks and government offices will be closed, and transportation may run on restricted schedules.

2005	2006	US HOLIDAY	2005	2006	CANADIAN HOLIDAY
Jan. 1	Jan. 1	New Year's Day	Jan. 1	Jan. 1	New Year's Day
Jan. 17	Jan. 16	Martin Luther King, Jr. Day	Mar. 25	Apr. 14	Good Friday
Feb. 21	Feb. 20	Washington's Birthday	Mar. 28	Apr. 17	Easter Monday
May 30	May 29	Memorial Day	May 23	May 22	Victoria Day
July 4	July 4	Independence Day	July 1	July 1	Canada Day
Sept. 5	Sep. 4	Labor Day	Aug. 1	Aug. 7	BC Day (BC only)
Oct. 10	Oct. 9	Columbus Day	Sep. 5	Sep. 4	Labour Day
Nov. 11	Nov. 11	Veterans Day	Oct. 10	Oct. 9	Thanksgiving
Nov. 24	Nov. 23	Thanksgiving	Nov. 11	Nov. 11	Remembrance Day

THINGS TO DO

ON FOOT

The vast scenic lands of the Pacific Northwest provide hikers with limitless opportunities. Known for its natural beauty, this region is arguably the most desirable place in North America to hit the trails. The national, provincial, and state parks provide some of the best and most varied hiking anywhere and are well staffed, well maintained, and well worth it. For a starting point, be sure to check out **The Great Outdoors**, p. 59, or contact the relevant visitors center for more info on how to break fresh ground. Reading the **Outdoor Activities** sections of a few parks should give a sense of the possibilities. Popular destinations often limit the number of visitors, but even though campsites may be hard to secure and crowds will surely be on hand, one need not be in a designated park to enjoy the outdoors in the Northwest. Trails through unimaginably beautiful virgin lands abound. Experienced hikers may wish to consider the following multi-day or many-month-long hikes:

PACIFIC CREST TRAIL. This 2650 mi. trail stretches from California's border with Mexico to Washington's border with Canada. First explored in the 1930s, the system of trails is now a federally protected Scenic Trail that takes five to six months to hike. Pick up the trail in any of the national parks along the Cascade Range (such as the **North Cascades National Park,** p. 252) or in the **Columbia River Gorge** (p. 99). The **Pacific Crest Trail Association** (PCTA) maintains the trail and sells comprehensive trail guides and videos on its website. (☎916-349-2109; www.pcta.org. Call 888-728-7245 for a free info pack or trail condition report.)

WEST COAST TRAIL. This spectacular trail winds through 75km (6-8 days) of coastal forest and beach along the Pacific Ocean in the Pacific Rim National Park on the west coast of Vancouver Island. Reservations are necessary to hike the trail during the peak summer season; book several months in advance to secure a spot in July and August. (See p. 332 for info.)

TRANS-CANADA TRAIL. In 1992, in celebration of its 125th year of confederation, Canada set out to build the longest recreation trail in the world. Covering approximately 17,244km, the proposed path would be open to hikers, bikers, horseback riders, and cross country skiers. The trail was to cross the entire country dipping and curving throughout every province and territory and incorporating as much of the population as possible. Although it was not com-

TOP 10 TOWNS THAT DESERVE A VISIT

1. Hood River, OR. (p. 99) Geared toward a young crowd and just spitting distance from Portland, Hood River combines wilderness adventure with incredible scenic beauty, a small town feel, and a friendly local population.

2. Stehekin, WA. (p. 260) Surrounded by the clear waters of Lake Chelan, lush wilderness, and the towering Cascade mountain range, this isolated town is accessible only by boat, float plane, or foot.

3. Salt Spring Island, BC. (p. 330) A small island populated by friendly former hippies living in their own groovy world. Low-key bars boast live music every night in summer, and top-notch hiking, kayaking, and vistas are all within easy reach.

4. Polebridge, MT. (p. 437) The perfect place for the tourist-loathing traveler who is there not for shopping or espresso but for a pure unadulterated wilderness jumping-off point. No electricity in town, but a good hostel, cheap pub, bakery, and most importantly, access to the only non-RVed part of Glacier National Park.

5. Nelson, BC. (p. 368) This less commercialized alternative to Penticton and Kelowna is home to a thriving counterculture, complete with authentic (i.e., aging) hippies.

6. Ashland, OR. (p. 140) The home of the Oregon Shakespeare Festival, which lasts half the year. Don't be put off by the theater-going crowds: Ashland has an unusually vibrant community even after the summer visitors go home.

7. Tofino, BC. (p. 335) Plan your visit to this town in Pacific Rim National Park Reserve to coincide with the summer solstice or Canada Day for guaranteed rockin' parties; then spend the night at one of the Northwest's nicest hostels before exploring the local hot springs, surfing, whale watching, and hiking.

8. Twisp, WA. (p. 282) Tucked into the lush Methow Valley, this hamlet is home to both a thriving arts population and hiking, biking, and other wilderness opportunities galore. If that's not enough to sell you, maybe the lure of Twisp's very own cowboy poet will.

9. Alert Bay, BC. (p. 348) The east side of Vancouver Island hides this tiny town, home to first-class whale watching, the world's tallest totem pole, a unique Cultural Center, and a beautiful hostel that makes you feel right at home.

10. Joseph, OR. (p. 159) Bet you thought all of the Northwest was damp and rainy. The awesome Wallowa Mountains rise up sharply all around this small but beautiful town in Oregon's hot and dry southeastern corner.

pleted by the hoped for 2000 deadline and will probably not be done by the new 2005 one, much of the trail is open, and travelers throughout the world have taken to its seemingly endless paths. The majority of the route is made up of existing trails to be incorporated into the larger one, such as the **Galloping Goose** trail that covers much of Vancouver Island. (☎514-485-3959 or 800-465-3636; www.tctrail.ca.)

ON WATER

Rivers, lakes, and ocean throughout the Northwest provide kayakers, canoers, surfers, and rafters with more than enough opportunity to exercise their paddling urges. **Rafting** is the most accessible water sport to novices and is wildly popular in both the US and Canada. Most of Oregon's commercial trips float on the beautiful **Rogue** (see Grants Pass, p. 138) and **Deschutes** (see Bend, p. 148) rivers. Interior BC offers adrenaline-rushing runs on **Adam's River** (p. 356), in the Shuswap. In Jasper, two rivers present prime rafting: the **Athabasca** and the faster **Sunwapta** (p. 448). Expect professionalism from a rafting outfit. If the rafts are patched or the paddles are different shapes and sizes, you may want to take your business elsewhere.

Kayaking in the region's rivers and oceans couldn't be finer (unless the water were a little warmer). The small boat allows almost unlimited access to the coastline and is perfect for investigating small coves and inlets, as well as escaping the cruise ship crowd. The west coast of Vancouver Island, particularly **The Broken Islands** (p. 334), is a popular place to explore by kayak.

Long Beach and **Cox Beach,** in Pacific Rim National Park Reserve on Vancouver Island (p. 332), offer sweet surf rides. The best medicine for the icy Pacific is to bear inland to the many **hot springs.** An ideal place to warm up or to soothe aching muscles, this natural phenomenon is a favorite pastime. For a start, try **Cougar Hot Springs** in Eugene, OR (p. 131), **Canyon Hot Springs** in Revelstoke, BC (p. 375), or **Hot Springs Cove** in the Pacific Rim National Park in BC (p. 332).

Nothing makes a better combination in the Northwest than water and wind. The gods smiled fondly on **Columbia River Gorge** (p. 99), blessing it with a river, gracing it with steep canyons, and consecrating it with a howling wind. Out of this arose the **windsurfing** cult, spawning the **Gorge Games** which draw hundreds of enthusiasts each July. Although the Gorge is eminent in the minds of windsurfers, other sites abound by virtue of good breeze off the Pacific and moderate weather.

DUDE, I HIT A CLASS V: KNOWING YOUR RAPIDS CLASSES

Knowing whether the river you're about to hit is a smooth stream or a 30 ft. waterfall is vital information for any would-be rapids runner. This chart covers the basics, but the classification of rapids is an art, not a science. A stretch of water is often classified differently by different people, and tides, dam releases, or seasonal thaws can make all the difference in a rapid's difficulty. Rapids can also be designated with + or - signs—a Class III+ is a bit tougher than your regular Class III, whereas a II- is an easy Class II.

CLASS I: Not something your hardcore kayaker will brag about. Class I rapids may have a few small waves and some rocks near the banks, but are rarely given a name. However, their presence may be an indication of upcoming larger rapids.

CLASS II: More obstacles, some eddies and bends in the river's course. Waves may reach up to 3 ft. high—you can get wet!—but still suitable for novices. Like Class Is, Class IIs are rarely named.

CLASS III: The playground of intermediate rafters and kayakers, Class IIIs will require maneuvering and may include a small falls and large rocks or other obstacles. You will definitely experience high, irregular waves splashing over the sides of your vessel.

CLASS IV: Very difficult, advanced, longer rapids which require deft maneuvering. Class IVs may include a strong current, large rocks, and even larger waves. You will most likely need to scout ahead from the bank.

CLASS V: The Holy Grail of expert whitewater enthusiasts. Extremely difficult, long courses with huge waves, large rocks, deceptive currents, and sudden drops.

CLASS VI: Otherwise known as "waterfalls," Class VIs were once thought to be unrunnable; however, experts have been known to occasionally cheat death on these roller coasters. Many rocks, many stomach-lurching drops. Do not attempt.

ON SNOW

The skiing and snowboarding in the northern Rockies, the Cascades, the Olympics, and Coast range are some of North America's best. The biggest and best mega-resort is **Whistler Blackcomb** (p. 318), a 1½hr. drive north of Vancouver, BC, which draws nearly two million international visitors per year. Most remarkable about the skiing, though, is that many great areas are only minutes from urban centers. Hostels in Washington, Oregon, Alberta, and BC all offer ski-and-stay packages. **Fernie Alpine Resort** (p. 374) is working to gain the title of skiing behemoth; the resort covers more than 2400 acres and gets an average of 29 ft. (9 m) of snowfall per year. The sleeper resort to watch is **Powder Springs** (p. 375), in Revelstoke. With the largest vertical drop in North America, it may only be a matter of time until Powder Springs becomes another Whistler. Other local ski havens include **Crystal Mountain** and **Stevens Pass** in Washington, **Mount Bachelor** and **Mount Hood Meadows** in Oregon, and **Sun Peaks** in BC. Good news for snowboarders across North America: ski hills have finally accepted that riders are here to stay, and most resorts maintain meticulously-crafted snowboard parks for their riding patrons. Riders can make a pilgrimage to the self-proclaimed birthplace of snowboarding at **Mount Baker** (p. 220). While **cross-country skiing** tends to get overshadowed by its vertical counterpart in the Northwest, plentiful snow covering beautiful hiking trails grants the region miles and miles of pristine skiing trails.

ON CRACK

In the past decade, outdoor sports have battled to top the thrill that plain old Mother Nature provides. Pain often seems to be a requisite for the rating of extreme. The **Ski to Sea Race** (p. 217) in Bellingham, WA, on Memorial Day weekend, is the mother of all relays, with skiing, running, canoeing, and kayaking stages covering the terrain from Mt. Baker to Bellingham Bay. Scope out the kiteboarders (yes, "kiteboarders"—see p. 102) at the **Gorge Games** on the Columbia River Gorge. Defy gravity in Nanaimo, BC, at the **Bungy Zone** (p. 339), and defy it again climbing the phenomenal **Skaha Bluffs, BC** (p. 364). Firefighters train to sky-dive into forest fires at the **North Cascades Smokejumpers Base** (p. 280), between Winthrop and Twisp, WA. You can off-road on the **Oregon Sand Dunes** (p. 119) along the coast or **ski sans snow** (p. 391) in August on the sandy bluffs of the Nechako Cutbanks, in Prince George, BC.

CULTURAL HIGHLIGHTS

NATIVE CULTURE

The Northwest is home to some of the finest exhibits of Native American and First Nation (the indigenous people of the US and Canada, respectively) culture on the continent, and is the birthplace of some of their most popular traditions, such as potlatch, cedar carving, and longhouses. While native cultures in the Northwest have not entirely escaped the persecution endemic to First Nation peoples the continent over, many tribes and customs still thrive. Major museums in the region are the **Royal British Columbia Museum** in Victoria, BC (p. 322); the **Museum of Anthropology** in Vancouver, BC (p. 309); and the **Museum at Warm Springs,** OR (p. 154).

VINEYARDS AND BREWERIES

Up and down the coast of Washington and Oregon, small companies turn out unique beverages that have won more awards per liter than any state in the Union. The wine counter-culture is on the upswing—wine bars are cropping up and wine tastings are becoming an institution. In Washington and Oregon, **Spokane** (p. 290), **Salem** (p. 127), and **Lopez Island** (p. 229), have more than their fair share of vintners. In the fertile crescent of Interior BC, **Kelowna** (p. 359) and **Penticton** (p. 364), harbor prize-winning vintages. Stop by Kelowna for the **Okanagan Wine Festival** in October. A must-see for true connoisseurs is the **Shallon winery** in Astoria (p. 104), where you can sample rarities such as lemon meringue pie wine. Beer rules the roost in Oregon, especially at the **Oregon Brewers Guild** (p. 79) in Portland (the city with the highest number of microbreweries in the United States) and the **Rogue Ale Brewery** (p. 118), in Newport.

LET'S GO PICKS

BEST RACE: The annual **Bathtub Race** in Nanaimo, BC, with a Silver Plunger awarded to the first tub to sink (p. 341).

BEST BICYCLE RIDE: Through breathtaking glaciers from Jasper to Banff along the **Icefields Parkway** (p. 447).

BEST BOOKSTORE: Cavernous **Powell's City of Books** in Portland swallows patrons in its book-lined walls (p. 89).

BEST ANIMAL ENCOUNTERS: Get intimate with buffalo skeletons at **Head-Smashed-in Buffalo Jump,** AB (p. 430) and learn how a native tribe could destroy a herd of buffalo in an afternoon.

BEST PLACE TO FIND ALLIGATOR SKIN BOOTS: Undoubtedly The **Stampede** in chilly Calgary, AB, where locals celebrate their rough-and-tumble heritage (p. 421).

SUGGESTED ITINERARIES

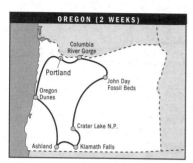

OREGON (2 WEEKS)

OREGON (2 WEEKS) Any trip through Oregon should begin and end in **Portland** (p. 79). Visitors could while away weeks in this phenomenal city that combines cosmopolitan flare, crunchy outdoors, and youthful money. After satisfying the city dweller in you, embark on the open road to venture into the **Columbia River Gorge** (p. 99), where you can trade the car in for a surfboard and let loose on windsurfing heaven. Venture into the hot interior, visiting the **John Day Fossil Beds** (p. 170), where fossilized remains of tropical rainforests defy the naked eye. The unusual landscape continues at **Klamath Falls,** where **Crater Lake** plunges to a depth of 1932 feet (p. 155). Unfortunately, it's forbidden to swim in the lake. Withdrawing from the rugged outdoors, stop in at **Ashland** (p. 140) to sample some of the country's best Shakespeare. Gradually meander back up the coast to Portland on US 101, with stops to play in the sand and surf, making sure to ride the waves at **Oregon Dunes** (p. 119), a mecca for sand-surfing.

WASHINGTON (3 WEEKS) The jewel in Washington's crown is undoubtedly the Emerald City—misty, alt-rocking **Seattle** (p. 173). Head south to **Mount Rainier National Park** (p. 273), home to the most technical alpine climb in the continental US and a multitude of fantastic views and day hikes. Jump on a ferry and plan for several days hopping between the **San Juan Islands** (p. 222) and their many beautiful beaches. This archipelago is perfect for kayaking. Touch base in Seattle to provision for a journey to **Mount Baker** (p. 221). A mecca for skiing in the winter, it provides gorgeous vistas, challenging hikes, and breathtaking drives for summer visitors. A final must-see stop is the **Olympic National Park** (p. 231), an outdoor-lover's playground; solace from civilization can be found within its rugged boundaries.

WASHINGTON (3 WEEKS)

BRITISH COLUMBIA (4 WEEKS) Fly into Vancouver and head straight for the slopes of **Whistler** (p. 318), one of the premier ski resorts in the world, where the glacier atop sister mountain Blackcomb is ski- and snowboard-accessible through August. Non-skiers will find plenty of hiking, rafting, and mountain biking action in the vicinity. After you've tackled the chutes and bowls, drive back along the winding Sea to Sky Hwy. (Hwy. 99) to BC's biggest metropolis, **Vancouver** (p. 298), a cultural whirlwind of sights, nightlife, and international cuisine. Hop a ferry over to **Victoria** (p. 322) for a spot of high tea at the most British-feeling city in the province. Head up

BRITISH COLUMBIA (4 WEEKS)

island to **Nanaimo** (p. 339), the gateway to breathtaking Vancouver Island wilderness and naked bungee jumping. Next up is **Pacific Rim National Park Reserve** (p. 332) and the infamous West Coast Trail, a rugged 75km trek through mossy evergreen forests and windswept coastline. Finally, cap off your wilderness travels at **Strathcona Provincial Park** (p. 347), the oldest provincial park in British Columbia. Over 2000 sq. km of trails and backcountry await you in one of the best preserved wilderness areas on the Island.

CANADIAN ROCKIES (3 WEEKS)

Start the National Parks escapade in **Waterton-Glacier International Peace Park** (p. 431), one million acres of forests, lakes, and alpine wilderness spanning the Alberta-Montana border. Drive north to BC's **Kootenay** (p. 382) and fight the crowds in popular **Banff National Park** (p. 440) before moving to the less crowded **Kanaskis Country** (p. 429), a 4200 sq. km stretch of free parks and recreation areas between Banff and Calgary that provide opportunities for unrestricted snowmobiling and fishing. Continue the national park crusade in **Yoho National Park** (p. 380), Banff's less touristy but no less action-packed neighbor. Next, head to

Jasper National Park (p. 448), where dazzling vistas and plentiful wildlife compete for attention. While hiking is the premier activity, climbing, kayaking, and rafting also keep the outdoor-lover satisfied. Afterwards, take the Icefields Parkway down to Clearwater, the gateway to **Wells Gray Provincial Park** (p. 355). Dotted with clear lakes, plunging waterfalls, and unspoiled wildflower meadows, Wells Gray is 5000 sq. km of wilderness paradise. Finally, conclude your trip by hiking through the virtually untouched wilderness of **Glacier National Park** (p. 378).

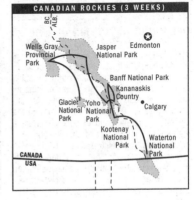

CANADIAN ROCKIES (3 WEEKS)

LIFE AND TIMES

Since prehistoric times, several groups have had the good fortune to discover the sparkling waters, lush forests, unconquered mountains, and virgin wilderness that make up the Pacific Northwest. Oregon, Washington, British Columbia, and Alberta have captivated all visitors—from the earliest indigenous coastal communities to the first waves of European traders, from the Lewis and Clark expedition to contemporary conservationists, and from snow bums to coffee addicts. Looking for adventure? Start with the region's dynamic history—over the years, the area has been explored, trekked, skied, camped, biked, kayaked, logged, and waterlogged. Nevertheless, the Northwest remains for the most part pristine, full of promise, and just waiting for you to seize that pack and paddle and hit the trail.

HISTORY

THE INDIGENOUS PEOPLE

Between 12,000 and 16,000 years ago, a group of nomadic hunters traveled across the (frozen) Bering Strait from Siberia into present-day Alaska and the region now called the Pacific Northwest. True to popular imagination, many lived in igloos, used dogsleds for transport, and sustained themselves by hunting whales and other sea life.

Native communities were sustained by a rich supply of salmon and halibut, and daily life centered around fishing. The economy of coastal groups focused around three main subsystems, all related to fish: fishing, construction of plank houses for smoking and drying fish, and later transportation, which provided access to the fish. Almost all native groups adjusted their lifestyles according to the season, moving between different settlements that favored the harvesting of available game, fish, and living materials. The coastal culture, prevalent throughout much of the Northwest, was one of waterside villages of cedar plank houses, wooden sculptures, massive dugout canoes, and potlatch festivals.

Although large-scale potlatch festivals no longer occur, another remnant of the native culture remains a defining aspect of the Pacific Northwest: the totem pole. Particularly noticeable in British Columbia, the totem pole peppers parks, sites, and tourist shops.

EUROPEAN ARRIVAL

The next arrivals in the Pacific Northwest were Europeans, who came in from a variety of Old World countries. The most famous European figures include:

EXPLORER	YEAR	NATIONALITY	CLAIM TO FAME
Francis Drake	16th century	English	Circumnavigated the globe; claimed Oregon for the English and affectionately described the coast as wrapped in "vile, thicke, and stinking fogges."
Juan de Fuca	1592	Greek, working for Spain	Sought Northwest Passage; claimed to find inland sea between Vancouver Island and BC which now bears his name.

EXPLORER	YEAR	NATIONALITY	CLAIM TO FAME
Martin Aquilar	1603	Spanish	Sailed north from California along Pacific coast; discovered a "great river," probably the Columbia.
James Cook	1778	English	Searched for a polar trade route; voyaged from Oregon to Alaska's westernmost tip.
Estivan Martinez	1789	Spanish	Claimed Nootka Sound for Spain and re-initiated European interest in the region.
George Vancouver	1792	English	Cartographer who followed Cook's route and mapped out the Pacific Northwest. Island and big city in BC named after him. Vancouver named Mt. Rainier after his friend Rear Admiral Peter Rainier, who in fact never saw the mountain.
Alexander Mackenzie	1793	English	Completed an overland exploration of Alberta and British Columbia, reaching the Pacific Ocean.

Prior to an intense trading conflict in 1802 between Russia and the Tlingit people of Alaska, the Europeans considered the indigenous nations to be autonomous and profitable trading partners. By the 19th century, however, the coast had become a lucrative asset for a number of well-armed and well-organized outsiders. During the coming decades, the valuable resources of the Pacific Northwest coast would be bargained for among England, Russia, and the US, while indigenous people would be forced out of partnerships in the coastal economy.

HOW THE WEST WAS WON

Trade, according to most Europeans, was mutually beneficial: Europeans took valuable furs and pelts, and natives received weapons with which they could defend themselves and their property. The Hudson Bay Company was instrumental in both setting up trade networks with native communities and bringing in European and later US and Canadian settlers into the Pacific Northwest. Sadly, the Europeans also brought less welcome gifts with them: smallpox, venereal infections, and other contagious diseases. Ultimately, the influx of diseases and increasing waves of new settlers crippled the indigenous people's power.

LEWIS AND CLARK. As more people streamed into western Washington and Oregon in the middle of the 19th century, Europeans and natives had to compete not only against one another, but also against the United States. In 1803, Thomas Jefferson negotiated the **Louisiana Purchase,** in which the US bought a huge swath of land, constituting most of the modern-day Midwest, from the French. After the Purchase, Jefferson organized the first US overland exploration of the West, headed by **Meriwether Lewis** and **William Clark.** Jefferson sent out the Lewis and Clark expedition in 1804 with political, scientific, and commercial goals (including the declaration of American sovereignty in the uncharted region), believing that the nation that controlled the fabled **Northwest Passage**—a water route between the Atlantic and Pacific oceans that would allow the Eastern US to trade more quickly with Asia—would control the continent's destiny. The team traveled from St. Louis to the Pacific Ocean near **Seaside** (p. 108) and back, returning in 1806 with information about plants, animals, rivers, mountains, and native cultures. While the team did not find a northwest passage, its safe return and promising discoveries encouraged many families to migrate west. You can see the expedition's winter headquarters reconstructed at the **Fort Clatsop National Memorial** (p. 107).

BORDER PATROL. Though the Louisiana Purchase granted the US possession of part of Oregon, the remainder of the territory was technically still under joint US and British occupancy, while the rest of the northern Pacific Northwest remained under British control. A growing tide of US migration to the region, combined with an ongoing dispute over the boundary between US and British (now Canadian) lands, finally led US President James K. Polk to sign a treaty in 1846 that established the border at the **49th parallel.** This designation remains the current boundary between the US and Canada in the Pacific Northwest. While the boundary line through the San Juan Islands was disputed until 1872, the signing of the treaty opened the floodgates for travelers on the **Oregon Trail** (today's I-84).

GO WEST, YOUNG MAN. Hundreds departed for the West along the famed Oregon Trail. The trail extended from Independence, Missouri to the mouth of the Columbia River and took four to six months to travel. While the Trail offered settlers the opportunity to stake claims in unexplored lands, it also posed great risks. The journey was often filled with hardships caused by poor equipment, illness, and attacks from natives. To provide for families on the frontier and to foster the establishment of communities, the **1862 Homestead Act** made 160 acres of land available for free to any married man who would live on and cultivate the land for five years. The same act barred the ownership of land by non-whites, although the **Dawes Act of 1887** allocated Native Americans their own plots in an attempt to Westernize them by encouraging them to establish private homes. Settlers created a provisional government in 1843, lobbied for territorial status in 1848, and joined the Union as Oregon 11 years later.

BOW DOWN TO WASHINGTON. In the early 1850s, residents of what is now Washington State asked Congress to create a new territory separate from Southern Oregon, citing that the capital of Oregon Territory (Oregon City) was too far away to represent its citizens to the north. In 1853 Congress passed a bill creating **Washington Territory,** which at the time encompassed present-day Washington, western Idaho, and Western Montana. The transcontinental railroad reached Puget Sound in 1883 and Washington eventually was admitted as a state in 1889.

GOLD! IT'S GOLD! Gold and oil discoveries along the West Coast in the late 19th century also supported settlement in the Pacific Northwest. These finds not only encouraged the development of cities surrounding the gold and oil but also helped supplying towns grow. When gold was discovered in the Fraser River Valley in 1857, hordes of eager opportunists entered the area. The 1897 **Yukon Gold Rush,** prompted by the discovery of gold in the Klondike, swelled Seattle, Vancouver, Edmonton, and other nearby cities with fortune-seekers rich and dispirited alike, as well as merchants eager to outfit the prospectors at exorbitant prices. The British government established the official colony of **British Columbia** one year later in an attempt to regulate the booming new population. In 1866, Vancouver Island—site of Victoria, the first permanent colony in the region and the current capital—joined BC. Despite its rapid development and plentiful natural resources, the young colony was virtually isolated from the rest of British North America by distance and rugged terrain. In order to gain both a railway and patriotic link to Canada, British Columbia joined the Confederation as a province in 1871.

ALBERTA ARRIVES. The wild and undeveloped land that would become the province of **Alberta** was a latecomer to the Pacific Northwest's trend of 19th century development. In 1870 the **Hudson Bay Company** sold the territory to the Confederation of Canada, and the Canadian Pacific Railway passed through in the 1880s, but migration to the region remained slow. In the 1890s the Canadian government offered free land to encourage settlement to the fertile but empty territory. This, combined with a dwindling amount of farmland in the rest of the West, finally led to increased population growth. Alberta became a province in 1905.

POLICY TOWARD NATIVE PEOPLE

UNITED STATES. From the birth of the United States until 1924, when Congress granted Native Americans citizenship, US policy consisted of a series of broken promises of land. Laws such as the Indian Removal Act (1830) left little doubt of the government's intentions. Conditions improved slightly with President Roosevelt's Indian Reorganization Act (1934), by which indigenous communities were recognized as tribes and directed to create their own constitutions. The effect of this policy was mitigated by a subsequent reversal of policy in Operation Relocation (1952), in which large groups of Native Americans were relocated from reservations into cities. The gesture had an unexpected effect as, for the first time in generations, Native Americans who lived off reservations began to recognize themselves as an ethnic group against the backdrop of mainstream society. This marked the beginning of a modern native revival.

CANADA. The Canadian policy toward the First Nations (the Canadian term for Native Canadian peoples) was not any more hospitable. The **1876 Indian Act** gave the government complete control over every person that it declared to be Indian. Children were separated from their families, forbidden to speak with their siblings, and even prohibited from speaking their native language. Those who refused to submit to these policies were severely punished, and many children were physically and sexually abused. Adults were taught methods of farming untenable in many of the regions where they were attempted, and traditions of community life were disallowed. A few rights were granted after World War II, but by the time residential schools were closed, some as late as the 1970s, an entire generation had been raised in isolation from their land and weakened by alcoholism and poverty.

Since the 1970s, tribes in both countries have been making slow gains as the descendants of their conquerors grant them more autonomy. Much of their culture is gone forever, as are most native tongues, but for many tribes in the Pacific Northwest, now is a time of renewal.

NEGOTIATING. Native American and Native Canadian tribes have once again begun to flourish as independent communities. Some indigenous people live on reservations within sight of cities; others have settled land claim negotiations and are living on their traditional territory and resurrecting their customs. Most indigenous communities that are federally recognized reservation tribes in the US, or administered under the 1876 Indian Act in Canada, are allowed hunting and fishing rights, as well as the right to use specified lands for ceremonial purposes. Some communities seek first and foremost to preserve the cultural heritage of their traditional lands. In British Columbia, for example, Haida tribesmen oversaw the use of ancient village sites in the disputed territory of the Queen Charlotte Islands and lobbied heavily for its preservation from logging. After the federal government purchased the land, the Haida's role in the stewardship of the spectacular **Gwaii Haanas National Park Reserve** (p. 411) became officially recognized.

CONTEMPORARY CULTURE

CONSERVATION AND HARVEST

Political entities in the Northwest strive to protect their independent interests within the framework of federal legislation. Inevitably, negotiations don't go smoothly. The central political tensions are between conservation and harvest. Conservation leads to the preservation of breathtaking forests and endangered animals, but harvest leads to jobs in logging and fishing, two of the Pacific Northwest's primary industries. These are particularly difficult to balance in Oregon and Washington, home to the most federally- and state-protected land in the United States. The challenge of co-managing renewable resources is exacerbated in British Columbia by territorial disputes with First Nations. The work of co-managing the resources that these states and provinces share—like the Pacific salmon fishery—has been the most dramatic and drawn-out subject of reconciliation.

Policies of environmental stewardship emerged in response to a variety of pressures, from civic consciousness to political activism. Oregon has led the pack in reform, beginning in 1967, when the **Oregon coast** was preserved for free and uninterrupted use by the public. Moreover, Oregon's 1971 **Bottle Bill** was the first recycling refund program in the US.

On the animal front, Washington and Oregon's **spotted owl** has remained a symbol of conflict between conservationists and industrialists after vast tracts of the endangered bird's old-growth forest habitat were protected. On Vancouver Island, residents rallied to save the endangered marmot; efforts culminated with a **"Marmot-aid"** benefit concert. A vociferous battle has also been fought over the gray whale, culminating in a 1937 commercial harvesting ban. In many cases, indigenous communities lead conservation efforts, suspending their hunting and trapping before sluggish government wheels begin to roll toward curbing industries. A twist on this situation occurred with the **Makah whale controversy.** In the 1990s, the Makah people applied to the International Whaling Commission, with US support, for a cultural exemption to the continuing ban. The five-whale allowance granted to the Makah enraged conservationists, but the Makah returned to the ceremonial and subsistence hunt in 1999 among protest and publicity.

FOOD AND DRINK

The Pacific Northwest has tastes that vary drastically from one region to another, but in all cases, cities and cultures cling tenaciously to their distinctive flavors. Here are some of the foods and drinks you'll find in your travels:

BANNOCK IN BRITISH COLUMBIA. Though there's no single traditional recipe, bannock generally takes the form of a biscuit-like cake made from flour, lard, and honey. Some varieties incorporate local delicacies such as salmon. Invariably, everyone who makes it considers theirs the best.

HALIBUT AND SALMON. In close proximity to the arctic waters these fish frequent, many cities in the Pacific Northwest are known for superior seafood. Halibut and salmon in particular are in everything from chowder to tacos.

MICROBREWS IN OREGON. Portland is the microbrewery capital of North America and has the beer to prove it. One establishment in Seaside tries to cram as much alcohol as they can into the largest possible beer (p. 118).

FRESH PRODUCE. The fertile inland farmland produces fruits and vegetables of all varieties, which are often sold at farmers' markets. The Northwest is also home to several wild berry species like huckleberries, marionberries, and lingonberries, not to mention classics like blueberries, blackberries, and strawberries.

CULTURE AND THE ARTS

Years ago, cities like Vancouver were middle-class port towns with burgeoning counter-cultures. In the years since, their popularity has exploded and the entire region seems to have escaped its humdrum roots: tourists have poured in, technological industries have expanded, and resource-driven industries are grinding to a

LIFE AND TIMES

halt under environmental pressures. Yet none of the communities of the Northwest stray far from their origins—port towns remain port towns, and the festivals that first brought communities together continue to do so. The laid-back lifestyle of the Northwest results from the seamless blending of old and new, and residents' love for the land is expressed in its aggressive defense.

MUSIC AND THEATER. Music lovers wouldn't hesitate to say that **Seattle** stole the show from California at the close of the millennium. It's undeniable that many of rock's greatest influences emanate from the Pacific Northwest, the birthplace of **Jimi Hendrix** (p. 203) and the cradle of grunge. Artists who hit it big in the 90s included **Pearl Jam, Nirvana, Alice in Chains,** and **Soundgarden,** all of whom pioneered the **grunge** sound and its studied flannel-and-fussed-hair look. Today, rock still reigns supreme in Seattle at the **Experience Music Project** (p. 191), which opened in 2000. Although prowling record executives signing garage bands to contracts have departed Seattle, the Northwest has been has been identified as a breeding ground for **riot-grrrl rock** and **alternative/indie-rock.** More recent local flavor getting national airtime includes **Modest Mouse, Death Cab for Cutie,** and the recently-reunited **Presidents of the United States of America.** Seattle also has a **repertory theater** community third in size only to those of Chicago and New York, and its internationally-renowned **opera** company moved into the world-class McCaw Hall in June 2003. While Vancouver and Portland can't quite rival Seattle's rock music heritage, both have opera companies and established theater communities—the **Portland Center for the Performing Arts** is one of the largest in the US—as well as thriving live music scenes.

VISUAL ARTS. Some of the continent's oldest art forms can be found in the Pacific Northwest, and the cedar **masks, totems,** and **longhouses** of indigenous coastal nations have long been recognized as some of the world's most notable artistic achievements. Native carving is a versatile art that entwines religious and cultural heritage. **Bill Reid** (1920-1998), a Haida carver and Vancouver native, was one of many artists celebrated for revitalizing communities through carving, dance, song, and potlatch, all forms suppressed during the last hundred years.

Several major **films** have used the Pacific Northwest as a (usually-unacknowledged) backdrop. British Columbia in particular is known as "Hollywood North" and is the third-largest film and television production center in North America behind Los Angeles and New York.

MOVIE	DIRECTOR	YEAR	LOCATION
Insomnia	Christopher Nolan	2002	Port Alberni, BC (p. 334)
X-Men 2	Bryan Singer	2002	Kananaskis Country, AB (p. 429)
Best in Show	Christopher Guest	2000	Vancouver, BC (p. 298)
Mystery, Alaska	Jay Roach	1999	Banff National Park, AB (p. 440)
Independence Day	Roland Emmerich	1996	Grants Pass, OR (p. 138)
Free Willy	Simon Wincer	1993	Cannon Beach, OR (p. 109)
Singles	Cameron Crowe	1992	Seattle, WA (p. 173)
The Goonies	Richard Donner	1985	Astoria, OR (p. 104)
Indiana Jones and the Temple of Doom	Steven Spielberg	1984	Grand Coulee Dam, WA (p. 260)
The Shining	Stanley Kubrick	1980	Timberline Lodge, OR (p. 98)
One Flew Over the Cuckoo's Nest	Milos Forman	1975	Salem, OR (p. 127)

ARCHITECTURE AND PUBLIC ART. Although **Frank Gehry's** inventive design of the **Experience Music Project** (p. 191) in Seattle has drawn both raves and rants for its flashy multi-colored sinuosity, most Pacific Northwest architecture is less incendiary. For a futuristic way to scope out the view, Vancouver, Seattle, and Calgary all boast sky-scraping structures—the 581 ft. **Harbour Centre Tower,** the 520 ft. **Space Needle** (p. 191), and the 626 ft. **Calgary Tower.** As befits the Northwest, some of its most beautiful "architecture" is found not in steel and concrete but in the mossy slopes and trickling streams of its city parks. Ashland's sunlight-filled **Lithia Park** was designed by **John McLaren,** landscape architect of San Francisco's Golden Gate Park. The Seattle park system is based on the **Olmsted Plan,** which translates to interconnected parks, innumerable playgrounds and playfields, and awe-inspiring vistas that spring up at seemingly every turn in the road.

Government support reflects the public's commitment to the arts. Portland and Seattle, for example, funnel a 1% tax on capital improvements into the acquisition and creation of public art. While government cutbacks have compromised the health of famed centers for arts in western Canada, artist communities and colonies are alive and thriving among the San Juan and Gulf Islands of Washington and British Columbia. Where government comes up short, philanthropists step in: in 2002-2003, the Patrons of Northwest Civic, Cultural, and Charitable Organizations, or **PONCHO,** dispensed almost $2 million in the Puget Sound area. (Since 1962, the group has poured almost $30 million into the region's arts organizations.)

BOOKS AND LITERATURE. While most people in the environmentally-conscious Pacific Northwest will decry the over-harvesting of forests, that doesn't mean that certain processed tree products are in short supply. Many authors find inspiration in the smog-free horizons, isolated islands, and even in the persistent drizzle. **Sherman Alexie** has published many books of literature and poetry taken from his experiences growing up on the Spokane Indian reservation, including *The Business of Fancydancing.* A fictional Puget Sound island is the setting for World War II era Japanese internment in **David Guterson's** critically-acclaimed novel *Snow Falling on Cedars,* which was also made into a film. Oregon can claim ownership of children's literature icon **Beverly Cleary,** author of the popular Ramona Quimby books; **Chuck Palahniuk,** author of provocative cult novels such as the screen-adapted *Fight Club;* and fantasy/sci-fi legend **Ursula K. Le Guin,** creator of the *Earthsea* books. Other Northwest writers include the quirkily articulate **Tom Robbins; Jon Krakauer,** chronicler of the disastrous Mt. Everest expedition *Into Thin Air;* poets **Gary Snyder** and **Theodore Roethke;** and short-story writer **Raymond Carver.** To find these texts, look no further than Portland's **Powell's City of Books** (p. 89), the world's largest independent bookstore.

FESTIVALS

DATE	NAME & LOCATION	DESCRIPTION
Late Feb. to Late Oct.	Oregon Shakespeare Festival Ashland, OR (p. 145)	That's a lot of drama. Enough that accommodations fill up a year in advance, and tickets are often sold for more than three times face value. Reserve your summer tickets several months in advance.
Memorial Day Weekend	Northwest Folklife Festival Seattle, WA (p. 195)	Seattle Center plays host to a free celebration of ethnic, folk, and traditional art, music, and dance. The annual festival draws 250,000 visitors and 6000 performers.
July 1	Canada Day All over Canada	Canada celebrates the anniversary of Confederation with fireworks, BBQ, and joyful choruses of "O Canada"; Vancouver's festivities are the largest west of Ottawa.
July 4	Independence Day All over the US	The old classics of beer, hot dogs, and fireworks; go out onto practically any body of water (and pray for clear skies) to see professional fireworks displays.
3 days in mid-July	Oregon Country Fair Veneta, OR (p. 137)	Artsy-craftsy folk and crystal-worshippers converge near Eugene to eat, play, discuss sustainable energy, and hug.

DATE	NAME & LOCATION	DESCRIPTION
1 week in mid-July	**Calgary Stampede** Calgary, AB (p. 425)	One of the biggest rodeos in the world; international contestants, hundreds of thousands of visitors, and many cows.
1 week in mid-July	**Gorge Games** Columbia River Gorge, OR (p. 99)	A hard-core week of windsurfing, sailing, biking, kayaking, running, canoeing, skateboarding, and even kiteboarding (a sport that combines water skiing and sailing).
3 days in mid-July	**Folk Music Festival** Vancouver, BC (p. 311)	The Woodstock of the West. Folkies from around the world strap on their Birkenstocks and jam.
3 days in mid-July	**Rhythm & Blues Festival** Winthrop, WA (p. 280)	Just what its name says. Ample rhythm and plentiful blues invade a self-proclaimed wild Western town.
Last full weekend in July	**Oregon Brewers Festival** Portland, OR (p. 94)	The continent's largest gathering of independent brewers brings together 72 breweries and 80,000 people to drink and groove to live music—but mostly to drink.
First weekend in Aug.	**Folk Music Festival** Edmonton, AB (p. 420)	Bills itself as the top folk music festival in North America (Vancouver's claim to the title notwithstanding.) Join hands and sing along to blues, Celtic, world music, and bluegrass.
Labor Day weekend	**Bumbershoot** Seattle, WA (p. 196)	Seattle's block party for the arts draws hundreds of thousands of groovesters to watch every sort of big-name act, from the Pixies to Naz to Liz Phair.

An Introduction to the Indigenous People of the Northwest Coast

The Native culture of the Pacific Northwest is composed of many extremely diverse groups of people, sharing ceremonial, social, and economic similarities while speaking over 40 different languages. This does not mean, however, that there was no interaction between groups in the past or in present day. There has always been trading, cultural exchange, and even warfare between coastal groups. Trading was facilitated by the use of "Chinook jargon," a new language consisting of words from many native languages, which came to include French and English words as well in the 19th and 20th centuries.

While each tribe or band had its own origin stories, kinship structure, and religious practices, there were some institutions and resources shared by all the coastal groups. Life on the Northwest Coast was centered around maritime activities. The sea provided the vast majority of foodstuffs, from fish to kelp to octopus. Salmon was especially important; the return of the salmon to their spawning streams was greeted each year with First Salmon Ceremonies in which the bones of the first harvested fish were respectfully returned to the river in order to ensure a plentiful bounty in years to come.

Another important anadromous fish—one that returns to spawning streams along the coast—was the euchalon, or candlefish. These small fish were caught by the thousands and rendered into oil, a symbol of wealth and key trade good along the coast. The Haida of the Queen Charlotte Islands were expert canoe makers and traded their canoes with the Tsimshian on British Columbia coast for euchalon oil and mountain goat wool and horns, none of which were available to them on their isolated island chain.

Herring roe was cultivated by placing tree branches in a protected harbor where the fish were known to spawn. The roe could then be harvested and eaten in small, popcorn-like bunches directly from the branches. Fishing was supplemented by the hunting of marine mammals. Seal hunting was commonplace and a few groups from the West coast of Vancouver Island and the Olympic Peninsula in Washington even went whaling in their canoes.

A canoe was the single most important piece of equipment a family could own on the Northwest Coast. Most groups used dug-out, steam-bent canoes made from the Western red cedar tree. Canoes ranged from two-person fishing canoes to huge traveling canoes, holding dozens of people. A Haida canoe in the collection of the American Museum of Natural History in New York is approximately 65 ft. long and six feet across at the beam, with an inch-thick hull. The seas were the highway on the Northwest Coast, as travel over water was much easier than slogging through the dense old-growth forests. Villages were arranged between forest and sea; houses faced the water so their inhabitants could welcome family home, greet guests and keep a look out for enemies.

In northern British Columbia, villages were filled with totem poles and painted house fronts. These traditions made their way down the coast in the 19th and 20th centuries, spreading from the Haida and Tsimshian to their southern neighbors. Today, totem poles are ubiquitous on the coast and can be seen as far south as Washington in Salish lands.

Canoes, houses, and poles were all made from the red cedar tree. Besides providing wood for monumental pieces, cedar had innumerable other uses. Cedar bark clothing, including rain capes and hats, was woven by Native women. Shredded cedar bark was used to make everything from diapers to twine to ceremonial regalia.

Along with a reliance on the sea and forest, all the Northwest Coast groups had a shared cultural institution in the potlatch. While the protocol and procedures of potlatching varied from group to group, it had a similar function throughout the Northwest Coast: the public display of inherited privileges and the payment of witnesses to that display.

In contrast to the communal nature of many Native American nations, everything on the Northwest Coast was owned by an individual or family. This included tangible items like houses, canoes, and tools; resource areas such as berry bushes, salmon spawning streams, and fishing spots; and intangible items such as names, songs, and dances. The rights to these items were often embodied in the masks worn at potlatches.

In a culture without written language, oral history preserved the traditions and knowledge of the tribe. Business such as weddings, namings, the opening of a new house, the raising of a pole or the transfer of any of privileges and rights were conducted at a potlatch. Guests were paid for their role as witnesses and were expected to remember the business that was conducted. Payments included foodstuffs, euchalon oil, bentwood boxes, silver bracelets, household items, blankets, and cash. In the 19th and early 20th centuries, Hudson's Bay Company blankets were given away by the hundreds at some Kwakwaka'wakw potlatches. Despite being outlawed in Canada and persecuted in the United States in the early 20th century, potlatches survived and flourish among Native people today.

Kathryn Bunn-Marcuse is a a Ph.D. candidate in Art History at the University of Washington. She has previously contributed to American Indian Art Magazine *and is writing her dissertation on Northwest Coast silver jewelry.*

ESSENTIALS

PLANNING YOUR TRIP

ENTRANCE REQUIREMENTS
Passport (p. 19). Required for all visitors who are not citizens of the US or Canada.
Visa (p. 21). Generally required for all visitors who are not citizens of the US or Canada, but requirement can be waived for residents of certain countries if staying less than 90 days.
Work Permit (p. 21). Required for all those planning to work in the US or Canada.
Driving Permit (p. 37). Required for all those planning to drive.

EMBASSIES AND CONSULATES

US AND CANADIAN CONSULAR SERVICES ABROAD

Contact the nearest embassy or consulate to obtain information regarding the visas and permits necessary to travel to the United States and Canada. Listings of foreign embassies within the US as well as US embassies abroad can be found at www.embassyworld.com. A US **State Department** website provides contact info for key officers at US overseas stations: http://foia.state.gov/MMS/KOH/key-offcity.asp. The Canadian Ministry of Foreign Affairs lists the websites of its overseas embassies and consulates at www.dfait-maeci.gc.ca/dfait/missions/menu-e.asp. A useful website overseen by the US embassy in Ottawa at www.amcits.com provides general information for travelers to the US and Canada, particularly for US citizens traveling to Canada.

US CONSULATES AND EMBASSIES

Australia: Moonah Pl., Yarralumla (Canberra), ACT 2600 (☎61 02 6214 5600; http://usembassy-australia.state.gov). **Consulates:** MLC Centre, Level 59, 19-29 Martin Pl., Sydney, NSW 2000 (☎61 02 9373 9200; fax 9373 9184); 553 St. Kilda Rd., Melbourne, VIC 3004 (☎61 03 9526 5900; fax 9525 0769); 16 St. George's Terr., 13th fl., Perth, WA 6000 (☎61 08 9202 1224; fax 9231 9444).

Canada: 490 Sussex Dr., Ottawa, ON K1N 1G8 (☎1-613-688-5335; www.usembassy-canada.gov). **Consulates:** 615 Macleod Trail SE, ste. 1000, Calgary, AB T2G 4T8 (☎1-403-266-8962; fax 264-6630); Ste. 904, Purdy's Wharf Tower II, 1969 Upper Water St., Halifax, NS B3J 3R7 (☎1-902-429-2480; fax 423-6861); 1155 St. Alexandre St., Montréal, QC H2Z 1Z2 (mailing address: P.O. Box 65, Station Desjardins, Montréal, QC H5B 1G1. ☎1-514-398-9695; fax 398-0702); 2 Place Terrasse Dufferin, B.P. 939, Québec City, QC G1R 4T9 (☎1-418-692-2095; fax 692-4640); 360 University Ave., Toronto, ON M5G 1S4 (☎1-416-595-1700; fax 595-6501); 1095 W. Pender St., Vancouver, BC V6E 2M6 (☎1-604-685-4311; 685-7175).

Ireland: 42 Elgin Rd., Ballsbridge, Dublin 4 (☎353 01 668 8777; www.dublin.usembassy.gov).

New Zealand: 29 Fitzherbert Terr., Thorndon, Wellington (☎644 462 6000; www.usembassy.org.nz). **Consulate:** 23 Customs St., Citibank Building, 3rd fl., Auckland (☎649 303 2724; fax 366 0870).

UK: 24 Grosvenor Sq., London W1A 1AE (☎44 0207 499 9000; www.usembassy.org.uk). **Consulates:** Danesfort House, 223 Stranmillis Rd., Belfast, N. Ireland BT9 5GR (☎44 0289 038 6100; fax 068 1301); 3 Regent Terr., Edinburgh, Scotland EH7 5BW (☎44 0131 556 8315; fax 557 6023).

CANADIAN CONSULATES AND EMBASSIES

Australia: Commonwealth Ave., Canberra ACT 2600 (☎61 02 6270 4000; www.dfait-maeci.gc.ca/australia). **Consulate:** 111 Harrington St., Level 5, Sydney NSW 2000 (☎61 02 9364 3000; fax 9364 3098);

Ireland: 65 St. Stephen's Green, Dublin 2 (☎353 01 417 4100; www.dfait-maeci.gc.ca/canadaeuropa/menu-en.asp?mid=28).

New Zealand: 61 Molesworth St., 3rd fl., Thorndon, Wellington (☎644 473 9577; www.dfait-maeci.gc.ca/newzealand).

UK: 1 Grosvenor Sq., London, SW1K 4AB (☎44 0207 258 6600; www.dfait-maeci.gc.ca/canadaeuropa/united_kingdom). **Consulates:** 8 Cromac Ave., Belfast, N. Ireland BT7 2JA (☎, fax 44 0289 127 2060); 30 Lothian Rd., **Edinburgh,** Scotland EH2 2XZ (☎44 0131 220 4333; fax 245 6010).

US: 501 Pennsylvania Ave. NW, Washington, D.C. 20001 (☎1-202-682-1740; http://canadianembassy.org). **Consulates:** 2 Prudential Plaza, 180 N. Stetson Ave., Ste. 2400, Chicago, IL 60601 (☎1-312-616-1860; fax 616-1878); 550 S. Hope St. 9th fl., Los Angeles, CA 90071 (☎1-213-346-2700; fax 346-2767); 1251 Ave. of the Americas, New York, NY 10020 (☎1-212-596-1628; fax 596-1793).

CONSULAR SERVICES IN THE US AND CANADA

IN WASHINGTON, D.C. (US)

Australia: 1601 Mass. Ave. NW, 20036 (☎1-202-797-3000; www.austemb.org).

Canada: 501 Penn. Ave., 20001 (☎1-202-682-1740; www.canadianembassy.org).

Ireland: 2234 Mass. Ave. NW, 20008 (☎1-202-462-3939; www.irelandemb.org).

New Zealand: 37 Observatory Circle, 20008 (☎1-202-328-4800; www.nzemb.org).

UK: 3100 Mass. Ave., 20008 (☎1-202-588-7800; www.britainusa.com/consular/embassy).

IN OTTAWA, ONTARIO (CANADA)

Australia: 50 O'Connor St., Suite 710, K1P 6L2 (☎1-613-236-0841; www.ahc-ottawa.org).

Ireland: 130 Albert St., Ste. 1105, K1P 5G4 (☎1-613-233-6281; fax 233-5835).

New Zealand: 99 Bank St., Ste. 727, K1P 6G3 (☎1-613-238-5991; www.nzhcottawa.org).

UK: 80 Elgin St., K1P 5K7 (☎1-613-237-1530; www.britain-in-canada.org).

US: 490 Sussex Dr., K1N 1G8 (☎1-613-238-5335; www.usembassycanada.gov).

DOCUMENTS AND FORMALITIES

PASSPORTS

REQUIREMENTS

All non-Canadian and non-American citizens need valid passports to enter the US and Canada and to re-enter their countries. Returning home with an expired passport is usually illegal and may result in a **fine,** and often it may not be possible at all.

ESSENTIALS

Moreover, travelers who normally require a passport to enter the region must have a passport valid for at least six months (for visitors to the US) or one day (for visitors to Canada) beyond their intended stays. Canadians can enter the US (and vice versa) with proof of citizenship along with a photo ID—a driver's license and birth certificate should suffice. Your passport, however, is the most convenient and hassle-free method of identification. Minors (those under 18) who are crossing the border without both parents should bring notarized letters of travel consent from any parents not traveling with them and/or a custody document or death certificate.

NEW PASSPORTS

Citizens of Australia, Canada, Ireland, New Zealand, the United Kingdom, and the United States can apply for a passport at any passport office or court of law or at many post offices. Any new passport or renewal applications must be filed well in advance of the departure date (at least six weeks for most countries), although most passport offices offer rush services that will get your passport to you in about two weeks for a fee (typically $60). A number of third-party agencies can get you your passport within a week or even a day but charge fees of up to $200.

PASSPORT MAINTENANCE

Photocopy the page of your passport with your photo, as well as your visas, travelers check serial numbers, and any other important documents. Carry one set of copies in a safe place, apart from the originals, and leave another set at home. Consulates also recommend that you carry an expired passport or an official copy of your birth certificate in a part of your baggage separate from other documents.

If you lose your passport, immediately notify the local police and the nearest embassy or consulate of your home government. To expedite its replacement, you will need to know all information previously recorded and show ID and proof of citizenship, as well as pay a fee and possibly include a police report. Replacements take approximately 10 days to process, but some consulates offer three-day rush service for an additional fee. A replacement may be valid only for a limited time. Any visas stamped in your old passport will be irretrievably lost. In an emergency, some consulates provide immediate temporary traveling papers that will permit you to re-enter your home country. Call the nearest embassy or consulate of your home government for information on their specific policies.

VISAS AND WORK PERMITS

VISAS

Citizens of some non-English speaking countries need a visa—a stamp, sticker, or insert in your passport specifying the purpose of your travel and the duration of your stay—in addition to a valid passport for entrance to the US. Canadian citizens do not need to obtain a visa for admission to the US; citizens of Australia, New Zealand, and most European countries (including the UK and Ireland) can waive US visas through the **Visa Waiver Program (VWP).** Visitors qualify if they are traveling only for business or pleasure (*not* work or study), are staying for fewer than **90 days,** have proof of intent to leave (e.g., a return plane ticket), possess an I-94W form (arrival/departure certificate issued upon arrival), are traveling on particular air or sea carriers (most major carriers qualify—contact the carrier for details), and have no visa ineligiblities (e.g., a criminal record). As of October 2004, visitors in the VWP must possess a **machine-readable passport** to be admitted to the US without a visa, although most countries in the VWP have already been issuing such passports for some time and many travelers will not need new passports. **Children** from these countries who normally travel on a parent's passport will also need to obtain their own machine-readable passports. Additionally, as of August 2004, travelers in the VWP may travel on regular machine-readable passports issued before October 26 2004, but all passports issued after that date must have **biometric** identifiers, such as encoded fingerprints and iris scans, to be used as visa waivers. Most countries in the VWP are not expected to be able to convert to biometric passports by the deadline, however, so **even VWP travelers to the US with recently-issued passports may have to apply for a visa.** Legislation to extend the biometric deadline to 2006 is under consideration by Congress but has not been passed. See http://travel.state.gov/visa/tempvisitors_novisa_waiver.html or contact your local consulate for a list of countries participating in the VWP and the latest information on biometric deadline extensions.

For stays of longer than 90 days in the US, all foreign travelers (except Canadians) must obtain a visa. Visitors to the US under the VWP are allowed to leave and re-enter the US to visit Canada, Mexico, and some neighboring islands, but time spent in those areas counts toward the total 90-day limit. Travelers eligible to waive their visas and who wish to stay for more than 90 days must receive a visa **before** entering the US.

In Canada, citizens of some non-English speaking countries also need a visitor's visa if they're not traveling with a valid green card. Citizens of Australia, Ireland, New Zealand, the UK, and the US, as well as many other countries, do not need a visa for tourism. See www.cic.gc.ca/english/visit/visas.html for a list of countries whose citizens are required to hold visas, or call your local Canadian consulate. Visitor's visas cost CDN$75 and can be purchased from the **Canadian Embassy** in Washington, D.C. Monday to Friday between 9am and noon. US citizens can take advantage of the **Center for International Business and Travel (CIBT),** which secures visas to almost all countries for a varying service charge depending on how soon the documents are required (☎800-929-2428; www.cibt.com). Travelers may leave and re-enter Canada, but those who need a visa to visit Canada may only leave and re-enter if leaving to visit the US or St-Pierre and Miquelon.

Double-check entrance requirements at the nearest embassy or consulate of the US and Canada (p. 18) for up-to-date info before departure. US citizens can also consult www.pueblo.gsa.gov/cic_text/travel/foreign/foreignentryreqs.html.

WORK PERMITS

Admission as a visitor does not include the right to work, which is authorized only by a work permit. Entering the US to study requires a special visa; for Canada, a student visa is needed for studies longer than six months. Be prepared for long processing times for work permits, especially. For more information, see **Alternatives to Tourism** (p. 58).

IDENTIFICATION

When you travel, always carry at least two forms of identification on your person, including at least one photo ID. A passport and a driver's license or birth certificate are usually adequate. Never carry all of your IDs together; split them up in case of theft or loss, and keep photocopies of all of them in your luggage and at home.

STUDENT, TEACHER, AND YOUTH IDENTIFICATION

The **International Student Identity Card (ISIC)** provides discounts on some sights, accommodations (20% or more off rooms many chain hotels), food, and transport (e.g., 5-15% off Alamo Car rentals); access to a 24hr. emergency helpline; and insurance benefits for US cardholders (see **Insurance,** p. 30). Applicants must be full-time secondary or post-secondary school students at least 12 years of age. Because of the proliferation of fake ISICs, some services (particularly airlines) require additional proof of student identity. Particularly in the US and Canada, ISIC cards are less well-recognized than they are abroad, so travelers are advised to have another form of student ID.

For travelers who are 25 years old or under but are not students, the **International Youth Travel Card (IYTC)** also offers many of the same benefits as the ISIC. The **International Teacher Identity Card (ITIC)** offers teachers the same insurance coverage as the ISIC and similar but limited discounts.

Each of these identity cards costs $22. ISIC and ITIC cards are valid until the new academic year (plus extra months for travel) up to 16 months; IYTC cards are valid for one year from the date of issue. Many student travel agencies (p. 33) issue the cards; for a list of issuing agencies or more information, see the **International Student Travel Confederation (ISTC)** website (www.istc.org).

The **International Student Exchange Card (ISE)** is a similar identification card available to students, faculty, and youth aged 12 to 26. The card provides discounts, medical benefits, access to a 24hr. emergency helpline, and the ability to purchase student airfares. The card costs $25; call ☎800-255-8000 for more info, or visit www.isecard.com.

CUSTOMS

Upon entering the US or Canada, you must declare certain items from abroad and pay a duty on the value of those articles if they exceed the allowance established by the US or Canada's customs service. Goods and gifts purchased at **duty-free** shops abroad are not exempt from duty or sales tax; "duty-free" merely means that you need not pay a tax in the country of purchase. Upon returning home, you must likewise declare all articles acquired abroad and pay a duty on the value of articles in excess of your home country's allowance. In order to expedite your return, make a list of any valuables brought from home and register them with customs before traveling abroad, and be sure to keep receipts for all goods acquired abroad.

The US does not refund sales tax to foreign visitors. Travelers leaving Canada may receive a tax refund on goods purchased in Canada if they provide customs-validated receipts totalling over CDN$200 before taxes. See **Taxes** (p. 25).

If driving across the US-Canada border, make sure to bring plenty of gas so that you won't run out while waiting to reach the Border Patrol. Co-operate with the customs officers in order to get through as quickly as possible. Try to resolve any questions you may have about transporting items across the border with your local embassy or consulate before making your trip. Car searches are likely, especially for young travelers; having a clean and orderly car will make the search go more quickly. Your appearance can also have an effect on customs officers; try to look clean-cut and respectable.

MONEY

CURRENCY AND EXCHANGE

The currency chart below is based on August 2004 exchange rates between local currency and Australian dollars (AUS$), Canadian dollars (CDN$), European Union euros (EUR€), New Zealand dollars (NZ$), British pounds (UK£), and US dollars (US$). Check the currency converter on websites like www.xe.com or www.bloomberg.com or a large newspaper for the latest exchange rates.

US DOLLARS		CANADIAN DOLLARS	
CDN$1 = US$0.76	US$1 = CDN$1.32	US$1 = CDN$1.32	CDN$1 = US$0.76
UK£1 = US$1.83	US$1 = UK£0.55	UK£1 = CDN$2.40	CDN$1 = UK£0.42
EUR€1 = US$1.21	US$1 = EUR€0.83	EUR€1 = CDN$1.59	CDN$1 = EUR€0.63
AUS$1 = US$0.70	US$1= AUS$1.42	AUS$1 = CDN$0.93	CDN$1=AUS$1.08
NZ$1 = US$0.64	US$1 = NZ$1.55	NZ$1 = CDN$0.85	CDN$1 = NZ$1.18

As a general rule, it's cheaper to convert money in the US or Canada than at home. Nevertheless, while currency exchange will probably be available in your arrival airport, it's wise to bring enough foreign currency to last for the first 24 to 72 hours of your trip.

When changing money out of your home country, try to go only to banks that have at most a 5% margin between their buy and sell prices. Since you lose money with every transaction, **convert large sums but no more than you'll need.**

If you use travelers checks or bills, carry some in small denominations ($50 or less) for times when you are forced to exchange money at disadvantageous rates, but bring a range of denominations since charges may be levied per check cashed. Store your money in a variety of forms; ideally, at any given time you will be carrying some cash, some travelers checks, an ATM card, and a credit and/or debit card.

TRAVELERS CHECKS

Travelers checks are one of the safest and least-troublesome means of carrying funds. American Express and Visa are the most recognized brands. Many banks and agencies sell them for a small commission. Check issuers provide refunds if the checks are lost or stolen, and many provide additional services, such as toll-free refund hotlines abroad, emergency message services, and stolen credit card assistance. Travelers checks are readily accepted in the Pacific Northwest. Ask about toll-free refund hotlines and the location of refund centers when purchasing checks, and always carry emergency cash.

American Express: Checks available with commission at select banks, at all AmEx offices, and online (www.americanexpress.com; US residents only). American Express cardholders can also purchase checks by phone (☎800-721-9768). Checks available in Australian, Canadian, Japanese, euro, British, and US currencies. For purchase locations or more information contact AmEx's service centers: in Australia ☎61 800 68 80 22; in New Zealand 64 050 855 5358; in the UK 44 080 587 6023; in the US and Canada 800-221-7282; elsewhere, call the US collect at 1-801-964-6665.

Visa: Checks available (generally with commission) at banks worldwide. AAA (p. 37) offers commission-free checks to its members. For the location of the nearest office, call Visa's service centers: in the UK ☎0800 89 5078; in the US 800-227-6811; elsewhere, call the UK collect at 44 173 331 8949. Checks available in Canadian, Japanese, Euro, British, and US currencies.

Travelex/Thomas Cook: In the US and Canada call ☎800-287-7362; in the UK call 0800 62 2101; elsewhere call the UK collect at 44 1733 31 89 50. Also available online at www.travelex.com/usa/personal/TC_default.asp. Members of AAA and affiliated automobile associations receive a 25% commission discount on check purchases.

CREDIT, DEBIT, AND ATM CARDS

Where they are accepted, credit cards often offer superior exchange rates—up to 5% better than the retail rate used by banks and other currency exchange establishments. Credit cards may also offer services such as insurance or emergency help, and are sometimes required to reserve hotel rooms or rental cars. Mastercard and Visa are the most welcomed; American Express cards work at some ATMs and at AmEx offices and major airports.

ATMs are widespread in the US and Canada, but they may be difficult to locate in rural or far-flung areas. Depending on your home bank, you can most likely access your personal bank account from abroad. ATMs get the same exchange rate as credit cards, but there is often a limit on the amount of money you can withdraw per day (usually around $500). There is typically also a surcharge of $1-5 per with-

ESSENTIALS

drawal from an ATM not owned by your bank. Some banks reimburse this surcharge under certain conditions; check with your bank for details. **Internet banks** (which have no ATMs of their own) are particularly likely to offer reimbursements.

Debit cards are a form of purchasing power that are as convenient as credit cards but have a more immediate impact on your funds. A debit card can be used wherever its associated credit card company (usually Mastercard or Visa) is accepted, yet the money is withdrawn directly from the holder's checking account. Debit cards often also function as ATM cards and can be used to withdraw cash from associated banks and ATMs throughout the US and Canada. Ask your local bank about obtaining one.

GETTING MONEY FROM HOME

If you run out of money while traveling, the easiest and cheapest solution is to have someone back home make a deposit to your bank account. Failing that, consider one of the following options. The online **International Money Transfer Consumer Guide** (http://international-money-transfer-consumer-guide.info) may also be of help.

WIRING MONEY

It is possible to arrange a **bank money transfer** asking a bank back home to wire money to a local bank for a small fee (usually $10 to receive and $20-40 to send; sending fees are lower from within the country). This is the cheapest way to transfer cash but also the slowest, taking two days from most English-speaking countries, such as the UK and Australia, or four to six days for Italy and France. Some banks may only release your funds in local currency, potentially sticking you with a poor exchange rate; inquire about this in advance. Money transfer services like **Western Union** can send money almost instantly but charge a commission (about 10%) instead of the flat fee of banks. Western Union has many locations worldwide. To wire money via Western Union, visit www.westernunion.com, or call in the US ☎ 800-325-6000, in Canada 800-235-0000, in Australia 800 501 500, in the UK 0800 83 38 33, or in New Zealand 800 005 253. To wire money within the US or Canada using a credit card (Visa, MasterCard, Discover), call 800-225-5227. Money transfer services are also available at **American Express** and **Thomas Cook** offices.

COSTS

The cost of your trip will vary considerably, depending on where you go, how you travel, and where you stay. The most significant expenses will probably be your round-trip (return) **airfare** to the Pacific Northwest. (see **Getting to the Pacific Northwest: By Plane,** p. 32). Make sure to factor in gas, which costs about $2 per gallon in the US and CDN$0.85 per liter ($2.50 per gallon) in Canada. Before you go, spend some time calculating a reasonable daily **budget.**

STAYING ON A BUDGET

A bare-bones day in the Pacific Northwest (camping or sleeping in hostels/guesthouses, buying food at supermarkets) costs about $30, not including gas; a slightly more comfortable day (sleeping in hostels/guesthouses and the occasional budget hotel, eating one meal per day at a restaurant, going out at night) runs around $60; and for a luxurious day, the sky's the limit. Don't forget to factor in emergency reserve funds (at least $200) when planning how much money you'll need.

TIPS FOR SAVING MONEY

Some simpler ways include searching out opportunities for free entertainment, splitting accommodation and food costs with trustworthy fellow travelers, and buying food in supermarkets rather than eating out. Bring a **sleepsack** (p. 25) to save on sheet charges, and do your **laundry** in the sink (unless you're explicitly prohibited from doing so). That said, don't go overboard. Though staying within your budget is important, don't do so at the expense of your health or a great travel experience.

TIPPING AND BARGAINING

In the US and Canada, it is customary to tip waitstaff and cab drivers 15-20%, but do so at your discretion. Tips are usually not included in restaurant bills. At the airport and in hotels, porters expect a tip of at least $1 per bag to carry your baggage. Bargaining is generally frowned upon and fruitless in the Pacific Northwest.

TAXES

Washington state sales tax is 6.5%, while Oregon has no sales tax. There is no tax on groceries in Washington or Oregon. Usually sales taxes are not included in the prices of items listed in *Let's Go*.

Canada has a 7% goods and services tax (GST) and an additional sales tax in some provinces. The provincial sales tax (PST) in British Columbia is 7.5%; Alberta has no sales tax. Visitors can claim a rebate of the GST they pay on accommodations of less than one month and on most goods they buy and take home, so be sure to save your receipts and pick up a GST rebate form either at a hotel, gift shop, or duty-free store, or online at www.cra-arc.gc.ca/E/pbg/gf/gst176/README.html. Total purchases must be at least CDN$200 and individual receipts at least CDN$50. A brochure detailing restrictions is available from local tourist offices or through Revenue Canada, Visitor's Rebate Program, 275 Pope Rd. Ste. 104, Summerside, PE C1N 6C6 (☎1-902-432-5608 or 800-668-4748; www.ccra-adrc.gc.ca/visitors).

PACKING

Pack lightly: Lay out only what you absolutely need, then take half the clothes and twice the money. The Travelite FAQ (www.travelite.org) is a good resource for tips on traveling light. The online **Universal Packing List** (http://upl.codeq.info) will generate a customized list of suggested items based on your trip length, the expected climate, your planned activities, and other factors. If you plan to do a lot of hiking, see **Camping** (p. 44 and p. 66).

Luggage: If you plan to cover most of your itinerary by foot, a sturdy **frame backpack** is essential. (For the basics on buying a pack, see p. 68.) Toting a **suitcase** or **trunk** is fine if you plan to live in one or two cities and explore from there, but not a great idea if you plan to move around frequently. In addition to your main piece of luggage, a **daypack** (a small backpack or courier bag) is useful.

Clothing: Dressing in layers is the best way to handle the variable climate in the Pacific Northwest. No matter when you're traveling, it's a good idea to bring a **warm jacket** or wool sweater, a **rain jacket** (Gore-Tex® is both waterproof and breathable), **sturdy shoes** or hiking boots, and thick **socks**. Flip-flops or waterproof sandals are must-haves for grubby hostel showers. You may also want one outfit for going out, and maybe a nicer pair of shoes.

Sleepsack: Some hostels require that you either provide your own linen or rent sheets from them. Save cash by making your own **sleepsack**: fold a full-size sheet in half the long way, then sew it closed along the long side and one of the short sides.

Converters and Adapters: In the US and Canada, electricity is 220 volts AC, which is incompatible with the 220/240V AC appliances found in most other countries. Appliances from anywhere outside North America will need to be used with an **adapter** (which changes the shape of the plug, $5) and a **converter** (which changes the voltage, $20-30). New Zealanders, Australians, and UK residents (who use 230V at home) won't need a converter but will need a set of adapters to use anything electrical. For more on all things adaptable, check out http://kropla.com/electric.htm.

Toiletries: Contact lenses are likely to be expensive and difficult to find, so bring enough extra pairs and solution for your entire trip. Also bring your glasses and a copy of your prescription in case you need emergency replacements.

First-Aid Kit: Pack bandages, a pain reliever, antibiotic cream, a thermometer, a Swiss Army knife, tweezers, moleskin (for blisters), decongestant, motion-sickness remedy, diarrhea or upset-stomach medication (Pepto Bismol or Imodium), an antihistamine, sunscreen, insect repellent (preferably DEET-based), and burn ointment.

Film: Camera stores are common in the Pacific Northwest, and supplies should be readily available. Less serious photographers may want to bring a **disposable camera** or two. Despite disclaimers, airport security X-rays can fog film, so buy a lead-lined pouch at a camera store or ask security to hand-inspect it. Always pack film in your carry-on luggage, since higher-intensity X-rays are used on checked luggage.

Other Useful Items: For safety purposes, you should bring a **money belt** and small **padlock.** Basic **outdoors equipment** (plastic water bottle, compass, waterproof matches, pocketknife, sunglasses, sunscreen, hat) may also prove useful (for more on outdoors equipment, see **The Great Outdoors,** p. 68). **Quick repairs** of torn garments can be done on the road with a needle and thread; also consider bringing electrical tape for patching tears. If you want to do laundry by hand, bring detergent, a small rubber ball to stop up the sink, and string for a makeshift clothes line. **Other things** you're liable to forget are an umbrella; sealable **plastic bags** (for damp clothes, soap, food, shampoo, and other spillables); an **alarm clock;** safety pins; rubber bands; a flashlight; earplugs; garbage bags; and a small **calculator.** A **cell phone** can be a lifesaver (literally) on the road; see p. 41 for information on acquiring one that will work at your destination.

Important Documents: Don't forget your **passport, travelers checks, ATM** and/or **credit cards,** adequate **ID,** and **photocopies** of all of the aforementioned in case these documents are lost or stolen (p. 21). Also check that you have any of the following that might apply to you: a hosteling membership card (p. 43); driver's license (p. 21); travel insurance forms; and/or ISIC card (p. 21).

SAFETY AND HEALTH

GENERAL ADVICE

In any type of crisis situation, the most important thing to do is **stay calm.** Your country's embassy abroad (p. 19) is usually your best resource when things go wrong; registering with that embassy upon arrival in the country is often a good idea. The government offices listed in the **Travel Advisories** box below can provide information on the services they offer their citizens in case of emergencies abroad.

LOCAL LAWS AND POLICE

DRUGS AND ALCOHOL

If you carry **prescription drugs** while traveling, it is vital to have a copy of the prescriptions to present at US and Canadian borders. Border guards of both countries have unlimited rights to search your baggage, your person, and your vehicle. In the wake of the September 11 terrorist attacks, vehicle searches have increased in frequency. Customs officers will seize vehicles on the spot that are found to be involved in smuggling even small quantities of illegal substances. US border guards can also ban you on the spot from re-entering the country for years. If you are not a US citizen, you may have no right to appeal such decisions. Away from borders, police attitudes vary widely, but the old standards—marijuana, LSD, heroin, cocaine—are illegal in every province and state. Medical marijuana exemptions in Canada, Washington, and Oregon apply only to in-state (or in-country, in the case of Canada) residents.

In the US, the drinking age is 21; in Canada it is 19, except in Alberta, Manitoba, and Québec, where it is 18. Drinking restrictions are strict; expect to be asked to show government-issued identification when purchasing any alcoholic beverage. Drinking and driving is prohibited everywhere. It is also dangerous and ill-advised. Open beverage containers in your car will incur heavy fines; a failed breathalyzer test will mean fines, a suspended license, and possible imprisonment. Drunk driving laws are very strictly enforced against drivers under the legal drinking age; such drivers are also held to a lower minimum blood alcohol content and can receive harsher sentences. Carrying open containers of alcohol on the street is illegal in some areas. Most localities restrict where and when alcohol can be sold under restrictions known as "blue laws." Sales usually stop at a certain time at night and are often prohibited entirely on Sundays.

GAMBLING
Gambling is highly regulated in the US and Canada. Many casinos operate on Native American land, which enforce their own gambling laws. The minimum age to gamble in a casino is 18 in Washington, but 21 if alcohol is served in the casino. In Oregon, 18 is the minimum age for lottery, bingo, and blackjack but 21 for other forms of gambling, including Native American casino gambling. The gambling age is 18 in Alberta and 19 in British Columbia.

FIREARMS
Most ordinary shotguns and rifles are allowed in the US and Canada for hunting and personal protection at the discretion of the customs officer. Importing more dangerous weapons into Canada requires you to declare the weapon at a cost of CDN$50 and to acquire an Authorization to Transport (ATT), which is difficult to obtain unless you are bringing the firearm for a specific event (such as a gun show or shooting contest). Many firearms are prohibited altogether. If you are bringing firearms from the US to Canada, be sure to declare the firearms to US customs officers upon leaving the US to prove that you did not obtain the gun in Canada. See www.cfc-ccaf.gc.ca/en/owners_users/ fact_sheets/visitin.asp or call ☎800-731-4000 for details. To import firearms into the US, you need to submit a valid hunting license for a US state (not necessarily the state you are visiting) or an invitation to a shooting event to the Bureau of Alcohol, Tobacco, and Firearms, along with an ATF form 6NIA. Make sure to submit all forms well before your visit; it can take up to three months for applications to be approved. See www.atf.gov/firearms/form6nia/ faqs.htm or call ☎202-927-8330 for forms and details.

SPECIFIC CONCERNS

TERRORISM
In light of the September 11th, 2001 terrorist attacks, there is an elevated threat of further attacks throughout the US and Canada. A terrorist attack would likely target a popular landmark; however, the threat is neither specific enough nor of great enough magnitude to warrant avoiding tourist attractions or certain regions. Monitor developments in the news and stay on top of any local, state, or federal terrorist warnings. In addition, prepare yourself for additional security checks in airports and avoid packing any sharp or dangerous objects in your carry-on luggage—they will be confiscated and not returned.

TRAVEL ADVISORIES. The following government offices provide travel information and advisories by telephone, by fax, or via the web:

Australian Department of Foreign Affairs and Trade: ☎130 055 5135; www.dfat.gov.au.

Canadian Department of Foreign Affairs and International Trade (DFAIT): In Canada and the US call ☎800-267-8376, elsewhere call ☎1-613-944-4000; www.dfait-maeci.gc.ca. Call for their free booklet, *Bon Voyage...But.*

New Zealand Ministry of Foreign Affairs: ☎04 439 8000; www.mft.govt.nz/travel/index.html.

United Kingdom Foreign and Commonwealth Office: ☎020 7008 0232; www.fco.gov.uk.

US Department of State: ☎202-647-5225; http://travel.state.gov. For *A Safe Trip Abroad*, call 1-202-512-1800.

PERSONAL SAFETY

EXPLORING AND TRAVELING

What crime there is in the Pacific Northwest is concentrated in urban areas. To avoid unwanted attention, try to blend in. Familiarize yourself with your surroundings before setting out, and carry yourself with confidence. Check maps in shops and restaurants rather than on the street. If you are traveling alone, be sure someone at home knows your itinerary, and never admit that you're by yourself. When walking at night, stick to busy, well-lit streets and avoid dark alleyways. If you ever feel uncomfortable, leave the area as quickly and directly as you can.

There is no sure-fire way to avoid all the threatening situations you might encounter while traveling, but a good **self-defense course** will give you concrete ways to react to unwanted advances. **Impact, Prepare, and Model Mugging** can refer you to local self-defense courses in the US (☎800-345-5425). Visit the website at www.impactsafety.org for a list of nearby chapters. Workshops (1½-3hr.) start at $75; full courses (20-25hr.) run $350-400.

EMERGENCY = 911. For emergencies in the US and Canada, dial **911.** This number is toll-free from all phones, including coin phones. In a very few remote communities, 911 may not work. If it does not, dial 0 for the operator and ask to be connected with the appropriate emergency service. In national, state, or provincial parks, it is usually best to call the **park warden** in case of emergency. Other places in the Pacific Northwest where 911 is not the emergency number include the Queen Charlotte Islands and several national parks. *Let's Go* always lists emergency contact numbers.

If you are using a **car,** learn local driving signals and wear a seatbelt. Children under 40 lbs. should ride only in specially-designed carseats, available for a small fee from most car rental agencies. Study route maps before you hit the road, and if you plan on spending a lot of time driving, consider bringing spare parts. For more on how to keep your car up and running, see **Getting Around the Pacific Northwest: By Car** (p. 35). If your car breaks down, wait for the police to assist you. For long drives in desolate areas, invest in a cellular phone and a roadside assistance program (p. 37). Park your vehicle in a garage or well traveled area, and use a steering wheel locking device in larger cities. **Sleeping in your car** by the side of the road is one of the most dangerous (and often illegal) ways to get your rest. For info on the perils of **hitchhiking,** see p. 39.

POSSESSIONS AND VALUABLES

Never leave your belongings unattended; crime occurs in even the most demure-looking hostel or hotel. Bring your own **padlock** for hostel lockers, and don't ever store valuables in any locker. Be particularly careful on **buses** and **trains;** horror stories abound about determined thieves who wait for travelers to fall asleep. Carry your backpack in front of you where you can see it. When traveling with others, sleep in alternate shifts. When alone, use good judgment in selecting a train compartment: never stay in an empty one, and use a lock to secure your pack to the luggage rack. Try to sleep on top bunks with your luggage stored above you (if not in bed with you), and keep important documents and other valuables on your person. If traveling by **car,** don't leave valuables (such as radios or luggage) in it while you are away, or if you must, be sure to lock them in the trunk.

There are a few steps you can take to minimize the financial risk associated with traveling. First, **bring as little with you as possible.** Second, buy a few combination **padlocks** to secure your belongings either in your pack or in a hostel or bus station locker. Third, **carry as little cash as possible.** Keep your travelers checks and ATM/ credit cards in a **money belt**—not a "fanny pack"—along with your passport and ID cards. Fourth, **keep a small cash reserve separate from your primary stash.** This should be about $50 sewn into or stored in the depths of your pack, along with your travelers check numbers and important photocopies.

In large cities **con artists** often work in groups and may involve children. Beware of certain classics: sob stories that require money, rolls of bills "found" on the street, mustard spilled (or saliva spit) onto your shoulder to distract you while they snatch your bag. **Never let your passport and your bags out of your sight.** Beware of **pickpockets** in city crowds, especially on public transportation. Also, be alert in public telephone booths: If you must say your calling card number, do so very quietly; if you punch it in, make sure no one can look over your shoulder.

If you will be traveling with electronic devices, such as a laptop computer or a PDA, check whether your homeowner's insurance covers loss, theft, or damage when you travel. If not, you might consider purchasing a low-cost separate insurance policy. **Safeware** (☎ 800-800-1492; www.safeware.com) specializes in covering computers and charges $90 for 90-day comprehensive international travel coverage up to $4000.

PRE-DEPARTURE HEALTH

In your **passport,** write the names of any people you wish to be contacted in case of a medical emergency, and list any allergies or medical conditions. Matching a prescription to a foreign equivalent is not always easy, safe, or possible, so if you take prescription drugs, consider carrying up-to-date, legible prescriptions or a statement from your doctor stating the medication's trade name, manufacturer, chemical name, and dosage. While traveling, be sure to keep all medication with you in your carry-on luggage. For tips on packing a basic **first-aid kit** and other health essentials, see p. 26.

IMMUNIZATIONS AND PRECAUTIONS

Travelers over two years old should make sure that the following vaccines are up to date: MMR (for measles, mumps, and rubella); DTaP or Td (for diphtheria, tetanus, and pertussis); IPV (for polio); Hib (for *haemophilus* influenza B); and HBV (for Hepatitis B). For recommendations on immunizations and prophylaxis, consult the CDC (see below) in the US or the equivalent in your home country, and check with a doctor for guidance.

ESSENTIALS

INSURANCE

Travel insurance covers four basic areas: medical/health problems, property loss, trip cancellation/interruption, and emergency evacuation. Though regular insurance policies may well extend to travel-related accidents, you may consider purchasing separate travel insurance if the cost of potential trip cancellation, interruption, or emergency medical evacuation is greater than you can absorb. Prices for travel insurance purchased separately generally run about $50 per week for full coverage, while trip cancellation/interruption may be purchased separately at a rate of $3-5 per day depending on length of stay.

Medical insurance (especially university policies) often covers costs incurred abroad; check with your provider. **US Medicare** does not cover foreign travel. In rare circumstances, it pays for care in Canada; see www.medicare.gov for specifics. **Canadian** provincial health insurance plans increasingly do not cover foreign travel; check with the provincial Ministry of Health or Health Plan Headquarters for details. **Homeowners' insurance** (or your family's coverage) often covers theft during travel and loss of travel documents (passport, plane/train tickets etc.) up to $500.

ISIC and **ITIC** (p. 21) provide basic insurance benefits to US cardholders, including $100 per day of in-hospital sickness for up to 60 days, $5000 of accident-related medical reimbursement, and $250,000 for emergency evacuation (see www.isicus.com). Cardholders have access to a toll-free 24hr. helpline for medical, legal, and financial emergencies overseas. **American Express** (☎800-528-4800) grants most cardholders automatic collision and theft car rental insurance and ground travel accident coverage of $100,000 on flight purchases made with the card.

INSURANCE PROVIDERS

STA (p. 33) offers a range of plans that can supplement your basic coverage. Other private insurance providers in the US and Canada include: **Access America** (☎800-284-8300; www.accessamerica.com); **Berkely Group** (☎800-797-4514; www.berkely.com); **Globalcare Travel Insurance** (☎800-821-2488; www.globalcare-cocco.com); **Travel Assistance International** (☎800-821-2828; www.europ-assistance.com); and **Travel Guard** (☎800-826-4919; www.travelguard.com). **Columbus Direct** (☎020 7375 0011; www.columbusdirect.co.uk) operates in the UK and **AFTA** (☎02 9264 3299; www.afta.com.au) in Australia.

USEFUL ORGANIZATIONS AND PUBLICATIONS

The US **Centers for Disease Control and Prevention (CDC;** ☎877-FYI-TRIP; www.cdc.gov/travel) maintains an international travelers' hotline and an informative website. The CDC's comprehensive booklet *Health Information for International Travel* (The Yellow Book), an annual rundown of disease, immunization, and general health advice, is free online or $29-40 via the Public Health Foundation (☎877-252-1200; http://bookstore.phf.org). Consult the appropriate government agency of your home country for consular information sheets on health, entry requirements, and other issues for various countries (see the listings in the box on **Travel Advisories**, p. 28). For information on medical evacuation services and travel insurance firms, see the US government's website at http://travel.state.gov/medical.html or the **British Foreign and Commonwealth Office** (www.fco.gov.uk). For general health info, contact the **American Red Cross** (☎800-564-1234; www.redcross.org).

STAYING HEALTHY

Common sense is the simplest prescription for good health while you travel. Drink fluids to prevent dehydration and constipation, and wear sturdy, broken-in shoes and thick, clean socks. Fortunately, both the US and Canada have excellent health care systems, although medical facilities may be sparse in remote areas. See **The Northwest and You** (p. 72) for information on health hazards related to the outdoors.

MEDICAL CARE ON THE ROAD

Medical care in both the US and Canada is world-class and widespread. In more remote regions, however, finding doctors can be difficult and expensive. If you are concerned about obtaining medical assistance while traveling, you may wish to employ special support services. The *MedPass* from **GlobalCare, Inc.,** 6875 Shiloh Rd. East, Alpharetta, GA, 30005-8372. (☎800-860-1111; www.globalcare.net), provides 24hr. international medical assistance and medical evacuation resources. If your regular **insurance** policy does not cover travel abroad, you may wish to purchase additional coverage.

Those with medical conditions (such as diabetes, allergies to antibiotics, epilepsy, heart conditions) may want to obtain a **Medic Alert** membership (first year $35, annually thereafter $20), which includes a stainless steel ID tag, among other benefits, such as a 24hr. collect-call number. Contact the Medic Alert Foundation, 2323 Colorado Ave, Turlock, CA 95382 (☎888-633-4298; outside US 209-668-3333; www.medicalert.org).

WOMEN'S HEALTH

Tampons, pads, and **contraceptive devices** are widely available, though your favorite brand may not be stocked—bring extras of anything you can't live without. **Abortion** is legal in the US and Canada; for medical questions or the nearest family planning center, contact Planned Parenthood (☎800-230-7526 in the US; www.plannedparenthood.org; in Canada call 613-241-4474; www.ppfc.ca).

GETTING TO THE PACIFIC NORTHWEST

BY PLANE

When it comes to airfare, a little effort can save you a bundle. Tickets bought from consolidators and standby seating are usually good deals, but last-minute specials, airfare wars, and charter flights often beat these fares. The key is to hunt around, to be flexible, and to ask persistently about discounts.

AIRFARES

Airfares to the US and Canada peak during the summer; holidays are also expensive. Otherwise, flight prices remain steady throughout the year. Midweek (M-Th morning) round-trip flights run $40-50 cheaper than weekend flights, but they are generally more crowded and less likely to permit frequent-flier upgrades. Not fixing a return date ("open return") or arriving in and departing from different cities ("open-jaw") can be pricier than round-trip flights. Patching one-way flights together is the most expensive way to travel. Flights between capitals or regional hubs in the Pacific Northwest—such as Portland (OR), Seattle (WA), and Calgary (AB)—will tend to be cheaper.

If the Pacific Northwest is only one stop on a more extensive globe-hop, consider a round-the-world (RTW) ticket. Tickets usually include at least five stops and are valid for about a year; prices range $3400-5000. Try **Northwest Airlines/KLM** (US ☎ 800-447-4747; www.nwa.com) or **Star Alliance,** a consortium of 22 airlines including United Airlines (US ☎ 800-241-6522; www.star-alliance.com).

BUDGET AND STUDENT TRAVEL AGENCIES

While knowledgeable agents specializing in flights to the Pacific Northwest can make your life easy and help you save, they may not spend the time to find you the lowest possible fare—they get paid on commission. Travelers holding **ISIC** and **IYTC cards** (p. 21) qualify for big discounts from student travel agencies. Most flights from budget agencies are on major airlines, but in peak season some may sell seats on less reliable chartered aircraft.

STA Travel, 5900 Wilshire Blvd., ste. 900, Los Angeles, CA 90036 (24hr. reservations and info ☎ 800-781-4040; www.sta-travel.com). A student and youth travel organization with over 150 offices worldwide (check their website for a listing of all their offices), including US offices in Boston, Chicago, L.A., New York, San Francisco, Seattle, and Washington, D.C. Ticket booking, travel insurance, railpasses, and more. Walk-in offices are located throughout Australia (☎ 03 9349 4344), New Zealand (☎ 09 309 9723), and the UK (☎ 0870 1 600 599).

CTS Travel, 30 Rathbone Pl., London W1T 1GQ, UK (☎ 0207 209 0630; www.ctstravel.co.uk). A British student travel agent with offices in 39 countries including the US, Empire State Building, 350 Fifth Ave., ste. 7813, New York, NY 10118 (☎ 877-287-6665; www.ctstravelusa.com).

Travel CUTS (Canadian Universities Travel Services Limited), 187 College St., Toronto, ON M5T 1P7 Canada (☎ 416-979-2406; www.travelcuts.com). Offices across Canada and the US including Los Angeles, New York, Seattle, and San Francisco.

USIT, 19-21 Aston Quay, Dublin 2 Ireland (☎ 01 602 1777; www.usitworld.com), Ireland's leading student/budget travel agency has 22 offices throughout Northern Ireland and the Republic of Ireland. Offers programs to work in North America.

 FLIGHT PLANNING ON THE INTERNET. The Internet may be the budget traveler's dream when it comes to finding and booking bargain fares, but the array of options can be overwhelming. Many airline sites offer special last-minute deals on the web; the Seattle-based Alaska Airlines and Horizon Air (www.alaska-air.com) is a good place to check for flights to the Pacific Northwest. **STA** (www.sta-travel.com) and **StudentUniverse** (www.studentuniverse.com) provide quotes on student tickets, while **Orbitz** (www.orbitz.com), **Expedia** (www.expedia.com), and **Travelocity** (www.travelocity.com) offer full travel services and are the most user-friendly sites. If you are willing to sacrifice flexibility for lower fares, try **Priceline** (www.priceline.com), which lets you specify a price, and obligates you to buy any ticket that meets or beats it. A similar option is **Hotwire** (www.hotwire.com), which offers bargain fares but won't reveal the airline or flight times until you buy. Other sites of about the same caliber that compile deals for you include www.bestfares.com, www.flights.com, www.lowestfare.com, www.onetravel.com, and www.travelzoo.com. Increasingly, there are online tools available to help sift through multiple offers; **SideStep** (www.sidestep.com; download required) and **Booking Buddy** (www.bookingbuddy.com) let you enter your trip information once and search multiple sites. An indispensable resource on the Internet is the **Air Traveler's Handbook** (www.faqs.org/faqs/travel/air/handbook), a comprehensive listing of links to everything you need to know before you board a plane.

COMMERCIAL AIRLINES

The commercial airlines' lowest regular offer is the **APEX** (Advance Purchase Excursion) fare, which provides confirmed reservations and allows "open-jaw" tickets. Generally, reservations must be made seven to 21 days ahead of departure, with seven- to 14-day minimum-stay and up to 90-day maximum-stay restrictions. These fares carry hefty cancellation and change penalties (fees rise in summer). Book peak-season APEX fares early. Use **Expedia** (www.expedia.com) or **Travelocity** (www.travelocity.com) to get an idea of the lowest published fares, then use the resources outlined here to try and beat those fares. Low-season fares should be appreciably cheaper than the **high-season** (mid-June to Aug.) ones listed here.

The following chart shows a range of sample round-trip fares between various destinations and some major airport hubs in the Pacific Northwest, with origins listed on the left and destinations listed on top. Be forewarned that airline prices change frequently; these are just guidelines.

(ALL PRICES IN US$)	PORTLAND	SEATTLE	CALGARY
Most North American Locations	$250-650	$250-650	$300-750
UK and Ireland	$600-1000	$550-950	$650-1100
Sydney, Australia	$1100-1500	$1000-1400	$1300-1700
Auckland, New Zealand	$1250-1600	$1200-1600	$1300-1700

STANDBY FLIGHTS

Traveling standby requires considerable flexibility in arrival and departure dates and cities. Companies dealing in standby flights sell vouchers rather than tickets, along with the promise to get you to your destination (or near your destination) within a certain window of time (typically 1-5 days). You call in before your specific window of time to hear your flight options and the probability that you will be able to board each flight. You can then decide which flights you want to try to make, show up at the appropriate airport at the appropriate time, present your voucher, and board if space is available. Vouchers can usually be bought for both one-way and round-trip travel. You may receive a monetary refund only if every available flight within your date range is full; if you opt not to take an available (but perhaps less convenient) flight, you can only get credit toward future travel. Carefully read agreements with any company offering standby flights as tricky fine print can leave you in the lurch. To check on a company's service record in the US, call the **Better Business Bureau** (☎703-276-0100; www.bbb.org). It is difficult to receive refunds, and clients' vouchers will not be honored when an airline fails to receive payment in time.

TICKET CONSOLIDATORS

Ticket consolidators, or **"bucket shops,"** buy unsold tickets in bulk from commercial airlines and sell them at discounted rates. Not all bucket shops are reliable, so insist on a receipt that gives full details of restrictions, refunds, and tickets, and pay by credit card (in spite of the 2-5% fee) so you can stop payment if you never receive your tickets. For more info, see www.travel-library.com/air-travel/consolidators.html. Most of the consolidators below will only sell tickets on flights departing from the US, Canada, and the UK. If you are flying from elsewhere, the best place to look is in the Sunday travel section of any major newspaper, where many bucket shops place tiny ads. Call quickly, as availability is typically extremely limited. Keep in mind that these are just suggestions to get you started in your research; *Let's Go* does not endorse any of these agencies. As always, be cautious, and research companies before you hand over your credit card number. **Travel Avenue** (☎800-333-3335; www.travelavenue.com) searches for best available published fares and then uses your hood is a universal signal of distress, though you may care not to do this during hail or heavy precipitation. If you don't want to depend on the kindness of strangers, membership in an auto club like **AAA** or **CAA** (p. 70) is invaluable in case of a breakdown; they can come to your aid in all but the most remote areas. For more info on car care, see **The Great Outdoors,** p. 70.

RENTING

Four-wheel drive (4WD) is about $20 per day more expensive than two-wheel drive, but some access roads and parts of certain parks may be inaccessible without it. Cheaper cars tend to be less reliable and harder to handle on difficult terrain. Less expensive 4WD vehicles in particular tend to be more top-heavy and prone to flipping, and are more dangerous when navigating particularly bumpy roads.

RENTAL AGENCIES

You can generally make reservations before you leave by calling major international offices in your home country. Occasionally, however, the price and availability information they give doesn't jive with what the local offices in your country will tell you. Try checking with both numbers to make sure you get the best price and accurate information. Local desk numbers are included in town listings; for home-country numbers, call your toll-free directory.

To rent a car from most establishments in the Pacific Northwest, you need to be at least 21 years old. Many agencies require renters to be 25, and most charge those aged 21-24 an additional insurance fee (minimum around $5 per day). Policies and prices vary from agency to agency. Small local operations occasionally rent to people under 21, but be sure to ask about the insurance coverage and deductible, and always check the fine print. Most agencies offer special internet-only and last-minute deals. Rental agencies in the Pacific Northwest include:

Alamo (☎800-462-5266; www.alamo.com). Less widespread in Canada; only locations in Edmonton and Calgary.

Budget (☎800-527-0700 in the US, 800-268-8900 in Canada; www.budget.com). Many locations throughout the Pacific Northwest.

Dollar (☎800-800-4000; www.dollar.com). Located in major Pacific Northwest cities as well as in some surprisingly remote locations in British Columbia.

Enterprise (☎800-261-7331; www.enterprise.com). Many locations throughout the Pacific Northwest, including multiple centers in major urban centers.

Hertz (☎800-654-3131; www.hertz.com). Plentiful throughout the region, in all major and minor cities.

Thrifty (☎800-367-2277; www.thrifty.com). Extensively located throughout the Pacific Northwest, including remote locales such as the Queen Charlotte Islands.

COSTS AND INSURANCE

Rental car prices start at around $15 a day on the weekend and around $30 during the week from national companies. Expect to pay more for larger cars and for 4WD.

Many rental packages offer unlimited mileage, while others allow you a certain number of miles with a surcharge of approximately $0.25-0.40 per mile after that. Return the car with a full tank of gas to avoid high fuel charges at the end. Be sure to ask whether the price includes **insurance** against theft and collision. There may be an additional charge for a **collision and damage waiver (CDW),** which usually comes to about $12-15 per day. Major credit cards (including MasterCard and American Express) will sometimes cover the CDW if you use their card to rent a car; call your credit card company for specifics. Remember that if you are driving a conventional vehicle on an **unpaved road** in a rental car, you are almost never covered by insurance; ask about this before leaving the rental agency.

several consolidators to attempt to beat that fare. Other consolidators
include **Cheap Tickets** (☎ 800-652-4327; www.cheaptickets.com), **Hotwire**
wire.com), **Flights.com** (www.flights.com) and **TravelHUB** (www.travelhu
London, the **Air Travel Advisory Bureau** (☎ 0207 306 5000; www.atab.co.uk) c
names of reliable consolidators and discount flight specialists.

BORDER CROSSINGS

ENTERING CANADA FROM THE US. Though a passport is not spec
required to cross the Canadian border, proof of citizenship along with pl
are, and so it pays to bring identification (p. 21) to avoid annoying delays. D
surprised if authorities ask to search your car.

ENTERING THE US FROM CANADA. In the wake of September 11, count
search of your car and a thorough examination of your identification papers. It
to have your passport handy, as well as any other identification you can muste

GETTING AROUND THE PACIFIC NORTHWEST

BY CAR

Carry emergency **food and water** if there's a chance you may be stranded in a remote
area. A cell phone is the perfect companion on a road trip, but beware of spotty
coverage in rural or remote areas. Always have plenty of **gas** and check road conditions ahead of time (see **Road Conditions,** below), particularly during winter. To
burn less fuel, make sure your tires have enough air. If you are driving long distances, gas will be one of your major expenses, and on some remote roads may not
be readily available. If you are headed away from major highways, consider carrying **additional gas** along with you. If you carry extra gas, it is extremely important
that you store it carefully—use a **metal safety can** and secure it down in your trunk
so that it does not slosh around while you drive. Plastic cans are cheaper, but they
are also more apt to spill, which creates both noxious fumes and a fire hazard.

> **ROAD CONDITIONS.** Both **Oregon** (☎ 800-977-6368 or 503-588-2941;
> www.tripcheck.com) and **Washington** (☎ 800-695-7623 or 206-368-4499;
> www.smarttrek.org) have comprehensive websites with live traffic cameras and
> up-to-date reports on construction and snow conditions in mountain passes.
> Within the states, dialing ☎ 511 provides automated alerts of current condi-
> tions. In **British Columbia,** check the website www.th.gov.bc.ca for road reports,
> weather conditions, and footage from highway cameras. The government of
> **Alberta** has a website www.tu.gov.ab.ca, and the Alberta Motor Association
> (AMA) has an information line available within the province (☎ 800-550-4997).

The cost of being towed can be quite pricey, particularly the further away you
are from a major city. One of the simplest ways to get yourself stalled out in the
midst of nowhere is to overlook your **battery**—if it is at all old or corroded, get a
new one before hitting the road.

If your vehicle breaks down, it is generally best to stay with it, particularly in the
winter. Some Northwest highways have dramatic distances between towns, but it
is likely that you will eventually be discovered by another passer-by. Putting up

National chains often allow one-way rentals, picking up in one city and dropping off in another. There is usually a minimum hire period and sometimes an extra drop-off charge of several hundred dollars.

ON THE ROAD

Be sure to **buckle up**—seat belts are required by law in all parts of the Pacific Northwest. The **speed limit in the US** varies considerably from region to region and road to road. Most urban highways have a limit of 55 mph (88km per hr.), while the limit on rural routes ranges from 60-80 mph (97-128km per hr.). The **speed limit in Canada** is generally 50km per hr. in urban areas, and 80-110km per hr. (50-68 mph) on highways. For more on driving, see **On the Road in the Pacific Northwest,** p. 70.

DRIVING PERMITS AND CAR INSURANCE

INTERNATIONAL DRIVING PERMIT (IDP)

If you do not have a license issued by a US state or Canadian province or territory, you might want an **International Driving Permit (IDP).** While the US allows you to drive with a foreign license for up to a year and Canada allows it for six months, the IDP may facilitate things with police if your license is not in English. You must carry your home license with your IDP at all times. It is valid for a year and must be issued in the country of your license, and you must be 18 to obtain one. An application for an IDP usually requires one or two photos, a current local license, an additional form of identification, and a fee. To apply, contact the national or local branch of your home country's automobile association. Be careful when purchasing an IDP online or anywhere other than your home automobile association. Many vendors sell permits of questionable legitimacy for higher prices.

Australia: Contact your local Royal Automobile Club (RAC) or the National Royal Motorist Association (NRMA) if in NSW or the ACT (☎08 9421 4444; www.rac.com.au/travel). Permits AUS$20.

Ireland: Contact the Irish Automobile Association (☎01 677 9481; www.theaa.ie) which honors most foreign automobile club memberships (24hr. breakdown and road service ☎800 667 788; toll-free in Ireland). Permits EUR€5.

New Zealand: Contact your local Automobile Association (AA) or their main office (☎ 9 377 4660; www.nzaa.co.nz). Permits NZ$15 in person, more by mail or online.

UK: To visit your local AA Shop, contact the AA Headquarters (☎0870 600 0371; www.theaa.com). Permits UK£4.

CAR INSURANCE

Most credit cards cover standard insurance. If you rent, lease, or borrow a car, you will need a **green card,** or **International Insurance Certificate,** to certify that you have liability insurance. Green cards can be obtained at rental agencies, car dealers (for those leasing cars), some travel agents, and some border crossings.

BY BUS

Buses generally offer the most frequent and complete service between the cities and towns of the US and Canada. Often a bus is the only way to reach smaller locales without a car. *Russell's Official National Motor Coach Guide* ($18) is an invaluable tool for constructing an itinerary. Updated each month, *Russell's Guide* has schedules of every bus route (including Greyhound and other budget options) between any two towns in the US and Canada. Russell's also publishes two semiannual supplements that are free when ordered with the May and December issues; a *Directory of Bus Lines and Bus Stations;* and a series of route maps (both $8.40 if ordered separately). To order any of the above, write Russell's Guides, Inc., P.O. Box 278, Cedar Rapids, IA 52406 (☎319-364-6138; fax 365-8728).

GREYHOUND

Greyhound (☎800-231-2222; www.greyhound.com) operates the most routes in the US. Schedule information is available at any Greyhound terminal or agency, on their web page, or by calling them toll-free.

Advance purchase fares: Reserving space far ahead of time usually ensures a lower fare, but expect a smaller discount during the busy summer months. For tickets purchased more than 7 days in advance, fares anywhere in the US will be no more than $119 one-way. Fares are often reduced even more for 21-day advance purchases on many popular routes; call for up to the date pricing or consult their web page.

Discounts on full fares: Available for senior citizens 62+ (5% off); children ages 2-11 (40% off); students with a Student Advantage card (up to 15% off); the companions of travelers with disabilities and/or special needs (50% off). Active and retired US military personnel and National Guard Reserves (10% off with valid ID) and their spouses and dependents may take a round-trip between any 2 points in the US for $198.

Discovery Pass: Call ☎888-454-7277 or visit www.greyhound.ca/en/passes/description.shtml. Ameripass allows adults unlimited travel through the US for 7 days ($239, $215 senior citizens and students with valid ID); 10 days ($289, $260); 15 days ($359/$323); 21 days ($419/$377); 30 days ($479/$431); 45 days ($539/$485); or 60 days ($669/$602). Passes that allow travel through the US and Canada (Domestic CanAm Pass) are for 15 days ($439, seniors and students $395; 21 days ($479/$431); 30 days ($549/$494); 45 days ($619/$557); 60 days ($719/$647). For travel exclusively through the western US and Canada, there is a Domestic West Coast CanAm Pass for 10 days ($299/$269) or 21 days ($399/$359). Children's passes are half the price of adult passes. The pass takes effect the first day used.

International Discovery Pass: For travelers from outside the US. A 4-day pass to travel through the US is $169; a 7-day pass ($229, $206 seniors and students); a 10-day pass ($279/$251); 15-day pass ($339/$305); 21-day pass ($399/$359); 30-day pass ($459/$413); 45-day pass ($509/$458); 60-day pass ($617/$557). Travel through the US and Canada for 15 days runs ($419/$377); 21 days ($459/$413); 30 days ($519/$467); 45 days ($599/$539); 60 days ($679/$611). The western US and Canada pass is available for 10 days ($299/$269); or 21 days ($399/$359). Call ☎888-454-7277 for info. International Ameripasses are not sold at the terminal; they can be purchased in foreign countries at Greyhound-affiliated agencies. Telephone numbers vary by country and are listed online. Passes can also be ordered online or purchased in Greyhound's International Office in Port Authority Bus Station, 625 Eighth Ave., New York, NY 10018 (☎800-246-8572 or 212-971-0492; intlameripass@greyhound.com).

GREYHOUND CANADA TRANSPORTATION

Greyhound Canada Transportation, 877 Greyhound Way, Calgary, AB T3C 3V8 (☎800-661-8747; www.greyhound.ca) is Canada's main intercity bus company. The web page has full schedule info. Discounts are available for those ages 62 and older (10% off); 5-11 (50%), under 4 free; students (25% off with an ISIC; 10% off with other student cards); a companion of a disabled person free. If reservations are made at least 3 days in advance, a friend travels for CDN$15. A child under 16 rides free with an adult. **Canada Pass** can provide 7, 10, 15, 21, 30, 45, and 60-day unlimited travel from the western border of Canada to Montreal on all routes for North American residents, including limited links to northern US cities. 7-day advance purchase required. (7-day pass CDN$309/

$278 for seniors and students; 10-day pass CDN\$389/\$350; 15-day pass CDN\$459/\$413; 21-day pass CDN\$499/\$449; 30-day pass CDN\$579/\$521; 45-day pass CDN\$639/\$575; 60-day pass CDN\$719/\$647).

BY TRAIN

One of the most scenic ways to tour the Pacific Northwest is by locomotive, but keep in mind that bus travel is much faster—and often much cheaper—than train travel. As with bus lines, you can save money by purchasing your tickets as far in advance as possible, so plan ahead and make reservations early. It is essential to travel light on trains; not all stations will check your baggage. Note that Amtrak and VIA Rail have recently separated; however, the North America pass is still being offered. Call ahead to check before making travel plans.

AMTRAK. (☎800-872-7245; www.amtrak.com.) The only provider of intercity passenger train service in most of the US. Their informative web page lists schedules, fares, arrival and departure info, and takes reservations. Discounts on full rail fares are given to: senior citizens (15% off), students with a Student Advantage card (15% off), travelers with disabilities (15% off), children ages 2-15 accompanied by an adult (50% off up to two children), children under two (free for one child), and US veterans (15% off with a VeteransAdvantage membership card). "Rail SALE" offers online discounts up to 90%; visit the website for details and reservations. Amtrak also offers a 30-day **North America pass** in conjunction with Via Rail (Jun. 1-Oct. 15 \$699; other times \$495), a **National Rail Pass** for 15 days (May 28-Sept. 6 \$440; other times \$295) or 30 days (May 28-Sept. 6 \$550; other times \$385), and a **West Rail Pass** for 15 days (May 28-Sept. 6 \$325/\$210) or 30 days (May 28-Sept. 6 \$270/\$405).

VIA RAIL. (☎888-842-7245; www.viarail.ca.) Formerly united with Amtrak and now the Canadian answer to railroad travel, VIA Rail offers **discounts** on full fares: ages 18-24 with ISIC card (35% off full fare); ages 12-17 (35% off full fare); seniors 60 and older (10% off); ages 11 and under accompanied by an adult (free). Advance purchase discounts are often available, typically for purchases one week in advance. Reservations are required for first-class seats and sleepers. "Supersaver" fares offer discounts between 25-35%. The **Canrail Pass** allows unlimited travel on 12 days within a 30-day period on VIA trains. Between early June and mid-October, a 12-day pass costs CDN\$748 (seniors and youths CDN \$667). Low-season passes cost CDN\$461 (CDN\$415). Add CDN\$36-63 for additional days of travel. Call for information on seasonal promotions such as discounts on Grayline Sightseeing Tours.

BY THUMB

Let's Go urges you to consider the risks and disadvantages of hitchhiking before thumbing it. Hitching means entrusting your life to a stranger who happens to stop beside you on the road. While this may be comparatively safe in some areas of Europe and Australia, it is **NOT** in most of North America. We do **NOT** recommend it. Don't put yourself in a situation where hitching is the only option.

That said, if you decide to hitchhike, there are precautions you should take. **Women traveling alone should never hitch in the United States.** Refuse a ride if you feel in any way uncomfortable with the driver. If at all threatened or intimidated, ask to be let out no matter how uncompromising the road looks. Have a **back-up plan** in case you get stranded. Carrying a cellular phone for emergency use is a good idea, although coverage is spotty in some rural areas. Many areas prohibit hitchhiking while standing on the roadway itself or behind a freeway entrance sign; hitchers more commonly find rides near intersections where many cars converge and well-lit areas where drivers can see their prospective rider and stop safely. If hitching across the **USA-Canada border,** be prepared for a series of queries about citizenship, insurance, contraband, and finances, and for an auto inspection. Walking across the border avoids some of the hassle.

KEEPING IN TOUCH

BY MAIL

SENDING MAIL FROM THE US AND CANADA

Airmail is the best way to send mail abroad from the US and Canada. **Aerogrammes,** printed sheets that fold into envelopes and travel via airmail, are available at post offices. Write "airmail" or "par avion" on the front. Most post offices will charge exorbitant fees or simply refuse to send aerogrammes with enclosures. **Surface mail** is by far the cheapest and slowest way to send mail. It takes one to two months to cross the Atlantic and one to three to cross the Pacific. Check with the closest post office to find out about postage rates to your country.

SENDING MAIL TO THE US AND CANADA

To ensure timely delivery, mark envelopes "airmail" or "par avion." In addition to the standard postage system whose rates are listed below, **Federal Express** (www.fedex.com; Australia ☎ 13 26 10; Canada and US 800-463-3339; Ireland 1800 535 800; New Zealand 0800 733 339; UK 0800 123 800) handles express mail services from most countries to the US and Canada; they can get a letter from New York to Seattle in two days for $12 and from London to Seattle in one to two days for UK£30. Sending a postcard within the US costs $0.23, while sending letters (up to 13oz) domestically requires $0.37 for the first ounce and $0.23 for each additional ounce. In Canada, postcards and letters up to 30g cost CDN$0.49 or $0.80 between 30g and 50g.

RECEIVING MAIL IN THE US AND CANADA

Mail can be sent via **General Delivery** to almost any city or town in the US or Canada with a post office. Address General Delivery letters like so:

Louis ENCLARK
General Delivery
Seattle, WA 98144 USA

The mail will go to a special desk in the central post office, unless you specify a post office by street address or postal code. It's best to use the largest post office, since mail may be sent there regardless. Bring your passport or other photo ID for pick-up. If the clerks insist that there is nothing for you, have them check under your first name as well. *Let's Go* lists post offices in the **Practical Information** section for each city and most towns.

BY TELEPHONE

CALLING HOME FROM THE US AND CANADA

A **calling card** is probably your cheapest bet. Calls are billed collect or to your account. You can frequently call collect without even possessing a company's calling card just by calling their access number and following the instructions. **To obtain a calling card** before leaving home, contact a communications company that provides service in the US and Canada. Before settling on a calling card plan, be sure to research your options in order to pick the one that best fits both your needs and your destination.

You can usually also make **direct international calls** from pay phones, but if you aren't using a calling card, you may need to drop your coins as quickly as your words. Prepaid phone cards and occasionally major credit cards can be used for direct international calls, but they are generally less cost-efficient. Placing a **collect call** through an operator (by dialing 0) will be very expensive, but may be necessary in case of emergency. You can also place collect calls through a service provider even if you don't have a phone card from that company.

 PLACING INTERNATIONAL CALLS. To call the US or Canada from home or to call home from the US or Canada, dial:

1. The **international dialing prefix.** To call from **Australia**, dial 0011; **Canada** or the **US**, 011; **Ireland, New Zealand,** or the **UK,** 00.
2. The **country code** of the country you want to call. To call **Australia,** dial 61; **Canada** or the **US,** 1; **Ireland,** 353; **New Zealand,** 64; the **UK,** 44.
3. The **area code.** *Let's Go* lists the area codes for cities and towns in the Pacific Northwest opposite the city or town name, next to a ☎.
4. The **local number.**

CALLING WITHIN THE US AND CANADA

The simplest way to call within the country is to use a coin-operated phone; local calls typically cost $0.35 in the United States and CDN$0.25 in Canada. **Prepaid phone cards,** which carry a certain amount of phone time depending on the card's denomination, usually save time and money in the long run, although they often require a $0.25 surcharge from pay phones. The computerized phone will tell you how much time you have left on your card. Another kind of prepaid telephone card comes with a Personal Identification Number (PIN) and a toll-free access number. Instead of inserting the card into the phone, you call the access number and follow the directions on the card. These cards can be used to make international as well as domestic calls. Phone rates typically tend to be highest in the morning, lower in the evening, and lowest on Sunday and late at night.

CELLULAR PHONES

While pay phones can be found in almost every city and town in the Pacific Northwest, if you own a cell phone you can avoid much of the hassle of scrounging up change or buying a phone card. Cell phone reception is clear and reliable in most of the region, although in remote areas or in the mountains, reception can be spotty; your provider may also slap on roaming or extended area fees of up to $1.25/min. Call your service provider to check their coverage policies in your destination.

The international standard for cell phones is **GSM**, a system that began in Europe and has spread to much of the rest of the world. Some cell phone companies in the US and Canada use GSM in certain regions (e.g., T-Mobile and AT&T), but most employ other services such as **TDMA, CDMA, I-den,** and **AMPS.** You can make and receive calls in the US and Canada with a GSM or GSM-compatible phone, but you will only get coverage in relatively populated areas, and your phone will only work if it is from North America or if it is a **tri-band** phone. American GSM networks use different frequencies from those used in Europe; a tri-band phone allows you to use both the European 900MHz and 1800MHz frequencies as well as the North American 1900 MHz frequency. If you are using a GSM phone in the Pacific Northwest, you will need a **SIM (subscriber identity module) card,** a country-specific, thumbnail-sized chip that gives you a local phone number and plugs you into the local network. You may need to **unlock** your phone in order to insert a SIM card. Many companies will offer to unlock your phone for fees from $5-50, but call your provider ahead of time; some will unlock your phone for free upon request. If your provider won't unlock your phone, your best bet is to look online for an unlocking service, but bear in mind that getting your phone unlocked may violate your service agreement. Many SIM cards are prepaid, meaning that they come with calling time included and you don't need to sign up for a monthly service plan. Incoming calls are frequently free. When you use up the prepaid time, you can buy additional cards or vouchers. For more information on GSM phones, check out www.telestial.com, www.orange.co.uk, www.roadpost.com, or www.t-mobile.com.

   Renting a cell phone is possible but usually more expensive than getting a short-term prepaid contract. A good option, especially if you want to make occasional calls over a short period, is to buy a cell phone with a **prepaid contract** such as those provided by **Ecallplus** (www.ecallplus.com), **AT&T** (www.att.com), or **Verizon** (www.verizon.com). If you elect to buy a used cell phone, make sure it is compatible with the service you want to use.

EMERGENCY CALLS.
If you only want a cell phone for emergencies, you may not need to buy a cell phone plan or a calling card. All working cell phones in the US and Canada are required to be able to call 911 if they are within service range.

TIME DIFFERENCES

The Pacific Northwest covers several time zones, anywhere from 7 to 9 hours ahead of **Greenwich Mean Time (GMT).** Both the US and Canada observe Daylight Saving Time, so clocks are set forward one hour in the spring and backward one hour in the fall.

3AM	4AM	5AM	7AM	NOON	10PM
Anchorage, AK	Vancouver	Calgary	Toronto	London	Sydney
	Seattle	Edmonton	Ottawa	(GMT)	Canberra
	Portland	Denver	New York		Melbourne
	Los Angeles				

BY EMAIL AND INTERNET

If your email provider won't let you check your email from the web, your best bet for reading email from the road is to use a free **web-based email account** (e.g., www.hotmail.com and www.yahoo.com). **Internet cafes** and the occasional free Internet terminal at a public library or university are listed in the **Practical Information** sections of major cities. For lists of additional cybercafes in the Pacific Northwest, check out www.cypercaptive.com or www.netcafeguide.com.

   Increasingly, travelers find that taking their **laptop computers** on the road with them can be a convenient option for staying connected. Laptop users can call an Internet service provider via a modem using long-distance phone cards specifically intended for such calls. They may also find Internet cafes that allow them to connect their laptops to the Internet. And most excitingly, travelers with wireless-enabled laptops can take advantage of an increasing number of Internet "hotspots," where they can get online for free or a small fee. Websites like www.ww.jiwire.com, www.wi-fihotspotlist.com, and www.locfinder.net can help you find a nearby hotspot. In the Pacific Northwest, **Starbucks** is a widespread coffee chain that provides hotspots at virtually every location. Many truckstops also have wireless Internet access. For information on insuring your laptop while traveling, see p. 29.

ACCOMMODATIONS

HOSTELS

Many hostels are laid out dorm-style, often with large single-sex rooms and bunk beds, although private rooms that sleep two to four are becoming more common. They sometimes have kitchens and utensils for your use, bike rentals, storage areas, transportation to airports, breakfast and other meals, laundry facilities, and Internet access. There can be drawbacks: some hostels close during certain daytime "lockout" hours, have a curfew, don't accept reservations, impose a maximum stay, or, less frequently, require that you do chores. In the Pacific Northwest, a dorm bed in a hostel will average around $15-25 and a private room around $50.

 A HOSTELER'S BILL OF RIGHTS. There are certain standard features that we do not include in our hostel listings. Unless we state otherwise, you can expect that every hostel has no lockout, no curfew, a kitchen, free hot showers, some system of secure luggage storage, no minimum/maximum stay, and no key deposit.

HOSTELLING INTERNATIONAL

Joining the youth hostel association in your own country (listed below) automatically grants you membership in **Hostelling International (HI),** a federation of national hosteling associations; members receive discounts of approximately 15% in HI hostels. Many hostels in the Pacific Northwest are part of HI, and several non-HI hostels still provide discounts to HI members. HI's umbrella organization's web page (www.hihostels.com), which lists the web addresses and phone numbers of all national associations, can be a great place to begin researching hostelling in a specific region. The site also allows you to book some hostels online.

Most student travel agencies (p. 33) sell HI cards, as do the national hosteling organizations listed below. All prices listed below are valid for **one-year memberships** unless otherwise noted.

Australian Youth Hostels Association (AYHA), 422 Kent St., Sydney, NSW 200 (☎02 9261 1111; www.yha.com.au). AUS$52, under 18 AUS$19.

Hostelling International-Canada (HI-C), 205 Catherine St. #400, Ottawa, ON K2P 1C3 (☎613-237-7884; www.hihostels.ca). CDN$35, under 18 free.

An Óige (Irish Youth Hostel Association), 61 Mountjoy St., Dublin 7 (☎830 4555; www.irelandyha.org). €20, under 18 €10.

Hostelling International Northern Ireland (HINI), 22 Donegal Rd., Belfast BT12 5JN (☎02890 31 54 35; www.hini.org.uk). UK£13, under 18 UK£6.

Youth Hostels Association of New Zealand (YHANZ), Level 1, Moorhouse City, 166 Moorhouse Ave., P.O. Box 436, Christchurch (☎0800 278 299 (NZ only) or 03 379 9970; www.yha.org.nz). NZ$40, under 18 free.

Scottish Youth Hostels Association (SYHA), 7 Glebe Cres., Stirling FK8 2JA (☎01786 89 14 00; www.syha.org.uk). UK£6, under 17 £2.50.

Youth Hostels Association (England and Wales), Trevelyan House, Dimple Rd., Matlock, Derbyshire DE4 3YH, UK (☎0870 770 8868; www.yha.org.uk). UK£14, under 18 UK£7.

Hostelling International-USA, 8401 Colesville Rd., ste. 600, Silver Spring, MD 20910 (☎301-495-1240; www.hiayh.org). $28, under 18 free.

BOOKING HOSTELS ONLINE. One of the easiest ways to ensure you've got a bed for the night is by reserving online. Click to the **Hostelworld** booking engine through **www.letsgo.com,** and you'll have access to bargain accommodations from Ashland to Zillah with no added commission.

OTHER TYPES OF ACCOMMODATIONS

HOTELS

Hotel singles in the Pacific Northwest cost about $45-70 per night, doubles $65-95. You'll typically have a private bathroom and shower with hot water, although cheaper places may offer shared bath. If you make **reservations** in writing, indicate your night of arrival and the number of nights you plan to stay. The hotel will send you a confirmation and may request payment for the first night. Often it is easiest to make reservations over the phone with a credit card.

BED AND BREAKFASTS (B&BS)

For a cozy alternative to impersonal hotel rooms, B&Bs (private homes with rooms available to travelers) range from the acceptable to the sublime. Rooms in B&Bs generally cost $40-70 for a single and $60-90 for a double in the Pacific Northwest. Any number of websites provide listings for B&Bs. For more information, check out **Bed & Breakfast Inns Online** (www.bbonline.com), **InnFinder** (www.inncrawler.com), **InnSite** (www.innsite.com), **BedandBreakfast.com** (www.bedandbreakfast.com), **Pamela Lanier's Bed & Breakfast Guide Online** (www.lanierbb.com), or **BNBFinder.com** (www.bnbfinder.com).

CAMPING AND THE OUTDOORS

For those with the proper equipment, camping is one of the least expensive and most enjoyable ways to travel through the Pacific Northwest. Camping opportunities in this predominantly rural region are boundless, and many are accessible to inexperienced travelers. Generally, private campgrounds have sites for a small fee and offer even the most inexperienced campers safety and security. Campsites in national parks and other scenic areas vary widely in price (some are free, others as much as private campgrounds) but require more experience than camping at a campground, since there are rarely as many people around. The **Great Outdoor Recreation Pages** (www.gorp.com) pro-

vides excellent general information for travelers planning on camping or spending time in the outdoors. For more on camping reservations, supplies, tips, and safety, see **The Great Outdoors,** p. 66.

SPECIFIC CONCERNS

TRAVELING ALONE

There are many benefits to traveling alone, including independence and greater interaction with locals. On the other hand, any solo traveler is a more vulnerable target of harassment and street theft. As a lone traveler, try not to stand out as a tourist, look confident, and be especially careful in deserted or very crowded areas. If questioned, never admit that you are traveling alone. Maintain regular contact with someone at home who knows your itinerary. For more tips, pick up *Traveling Solo* by Eleanor Berman (Globe Pequot Press, $18), visit www.travelaloneandloveit.com, or subscribe to **Connecting: Solo Travel Network,** 689 Park Rd., Unit 6, Gibsons, BC V0N 1V7, Canada (☎604-886-9099; www.cstn.org; membership $28-45).

WOMEN TRAVELERS

Women exploring on their own inevitably face some additional safety concerns, but it's easy to be adventurous without taking undue risks. If you are concerned, consider staying in hostels which offer single rooms that lock from the inside or in religious organizations with rooms for women only. Stick to centrally located accommodations and avoid solitary late-night treks or metro rides.

Always carry extra money for a phone call, bus, or taxi. **Hitchhiking** is never safe for lone women, or even for two women traveling together. Look as if you know where you're going and approach older women or couples for directions if you're lost or uncomfortable.

Don't hesitate to seek out a police officer or a passerby if you are being harassed. A self-defense course will both prepare you for a potential attack and raise your level of awareness of your surroundings (see **Self Defense,** p. 29). Also be sure you are aware of the health concerns that women may face when traveling (p. 32).

GLBT TRAVELERS

Attitudes in the Pacific Northwest are generally very accepting toward gay, lesbian, bisexual, and transgendered (GLBT) travelers. More populated areas tend to be more gay-friendly: cities in the western regions of Washington and Oregon frequently have thriving gay communities, whereas the eastern regions are more conservative. Canada is generally welcoming toward gays; as of June 2004, British Columbia is one of two Canadian provinces to allow gay marriage. Alberta, however, is considered more conservative than the rest of the country.

To avoid hassles at airports and border crossings, **transgendered** travelers should make sure that all of their travel documents consistently report the same gender. Many countries (including the US, the UK, Canada, Ireland, Australia, and New Zealand) will amend the passports of post-operative transsexuals to reflect their true gender, although governments are generally less willing to amend documents for pre-operative transsexuals and other transgendered individuals.

> **FURTHER READING: GLBT TRAVEL.**
> *Spartacus 2003-2004: International Gay Guide.* Bruno Gmunder Verlag ($33).
> *Damron Men's Travel Guide, Damron Road Atlas, Damron Accommodations Guide, Damron City Guide,* and *Damron Women's Traveller.* Damron Travel Guides ($11-19). For info, call ☎800-462-6654 or visit www.damron.com.
> *Ferrari Guides' Gay Travel A to Z, Ferrari Guides' Men's Travel in Your Pocket, Ferrari Guides' Women's Travel in Your Pocket,* and *Ferrari Guides' Inn Places.* Ferrari Publications ($16-20).
> *The Gay Vacation Guide: The Best Trips and How to Plan Them,* Mark Chesnut. Kensington Books ($15).
> *Gayellow Pages USA/Canada,* Frances Green. Gayellow Pages ($16). Visit Gayellow pages online at www.gayellowpages.com.

Out and About (www.planetout.com/travel) offers a bi-weekly newsletter as well as a comprehensive site addressing gay travel concerns. The online newspaper **365gay.com** also has a travel section (www.365gay.com/travel/travelchannel.htm). The **International Lesbian and Gay Association (ILGA)** (www.ilga.org), provides political information, such as homosexuality laws of various countries (but not the US).

TRAVELERS WITH DISABILITIES

Those with disabilities should inform airlines and hotels of their disabilities when making reservations; time may be needed to prepare special accommodations. Call ahead to restaurants, museums, and other facilities to find out if they are wheelchair-accessible. Visiting more rugged parks may be difficult or impossible if you have severe disabilities, but some parks, especially popular ones, have wheelchair-accessible trails. *Let's Go* tries to list wheelchair accessibility whenever possible.

Certified **guide dogs** are allowed into Canada without restriction. Dogs entering the US must either have originated from or lived for six months in an area that is free from rabies (including Australia, Canada, Ireland, New Zealand, and the UK) or they must have unexpired vaccination certificates. For a complete list of rabies-free areas, see www.cdc.gov/travel/diseases/rabies.htm. In all areas in the Pacific Northwest, guide dogs are legally allowed, free of charge, on public transportation and in all "public establishments," including hotels, restaurants, and stores.

In the US, both Amtrak and major airlines will accommodate disabled passengers if notified at least 72 hours in advance. Amtrak offers a 15% discount to physically disabled travelers (☎800-872-7245). Greyhound buses will provide a 50% discount for a companion if the ticket is purchased at least three days in advance. if you are without a fellow traveler, call Greyhound (☎800-752-4841, TDD ☎800-345-3109) at least two days before you plan to leave, and they will make arrangements to assist you. For information on transportation availability in individual US cities, contact the local chapter of the **Easter Seal Society** (☎800-221-6827; www.easter-seals.org).

If you are planning to visit a national park or attraction in the US run by the National Park Service, obtain a free **Golden Access Passport,** which is available at all park entrances and from federal offices whose functions relate to land, forests, or wildlife. The Passport entitles disabled travelers and their families to free park admission and provides a lifetime 50% discount on all campsite and parking fees.

USEFUL ORGANIZATIONS

Directions Unlimited, 123 Green Ln., Bedford Hills, NY 10507 (☎800-533-5343). Books individual vacations for the physically disabled; not an info service.

Mobility International USA (MIUSA), P.O. Box 10767, Eugene, OR 97440 (☎541-343-1284; www.miusa.org). Provides a variety of books and other publications containing information for travelers with disabilities, as well as general listings of exchange programs.

Society for Accessible Travel & Hospitality (SATH), 347 Fifth Ave., #610, New York, NY 10016 (☎212-447-7284; www.sath.org). An advocacy group that publishes free online travel information. Annual membership $45, students and seniors $30.

MINORITY TRAVELERS

Harassment of racial or religious minorities in the Pacific Northwest is rare. Report individuals to a supervisor and establishments to the **Better Business Bureau** for the region (www.bbb.org, or call the operator for local listings); contact the police in extreme situations. *Let's Go* always welcomes reader input regarding discriminatory establishments.

DIETARY CONCERNS

The vegetarian or vegan traveler should find plenty of options in the Pacific Northwest. On account of the environmentally-conscious nature of the region, even establishments in smaller towns often offer organic or vegetarian options. The travel section of the Vegetarian Resource Group's website, at www.vrg.org/travel, has a comprehensive list of organizations and websites geared toward helping vegetarians and vegans traveling abroad. For more information, visit your local bookstore or health food store and consult *The Vegetarian Traveler: Where to Stay if You're Vegetarian, Vegan, Environmentally Sensitive*, by Jed and Susan Civic (Larson Publications; $16) or *Vegetarian United States*, by John Howley (Vegetarian Guides Ltd.; UK£17). Vegetarians will also find numerous resources on the web, including www.vegeats.com, www.vegdining.com, and www.happycow.net.

Travelers who keep kosher should contact synagogues for information on kosher restaurants. Your own synagogue or college Hillel should have access to lists of Jewish institutions across the nation. **Jewish Celebrations** also has a searchable directory of Kosher restaurants at www.jewishcelebrations.com/restaurants. If you are strict in your observance, you may have to prepare your own food on the road, especially outside major metropolitan areas. A good resource is the *Jewish Travel Guide*, edited by Michael Zaidner (Vallentine Mitchell; $18). Travelers looking for halal restaurants may find www.zabihah.com a useful resource.

OTHER RESOURCES

Let's Go tries to cover all aspects of budget travel, but we can't put *everything* in our guides. Listed below are books and websites that can serve as jumping-off points for your own research.

TRAVEL PUBLISHERS AND BOOKSTORES

Also see Outdoor Travel Publications in **The Great Outdoors** (p. 59).

Hunter Publishing, P.O. Box 746, Walpole, MA 02081 (☎800-255-0343; www.hunterpublishing.com). Has an extensive catalog of travel guides and diving and adventure travel books.

Rand McNally, P.O. Box 7600, Chicago, IL 60680 (☎847-329-8100; www.randmcnally.com), publishes road atlases.

Travel Books & Language Center, Inc., 4437 Wisconsin Ave. NW, Washington, D.C. 20016 (☎800-220-2665). Over 60,000 titles from around the world.

WORLD WIDE WEB

Almost every aspect of budget travel is accessible via the web. In 10min. at the keyboard, you can make a hostel reservation, get advice on travel hotspots from other travelers, or find out how much a train from Vancouver to Banff costs.

Listed here are some regional and travel-related sites to start off your surfing; other relevant websites are listed throughout the book. Because website turnover is high, use search engines (such as www.google.com) to strike out on your own.

WWW.LETSGO.COM Our freshly redesigned website features extensive content from our guides; community forums where travelers can connect with each other and ask questions or advice—as well as share stories and tips; and expanded resources to help you plan your trip. Visit us soon to browse by destination, find information about ordering our titles, and sign up for our e-newsletter!

Atevo Travel: www.atevo.com/guides/destinations. Detailed introductions, travel tips, and suggested itineraries.

BootsnAll.com: www.bootsnall.com. Numerous resources for independent travelers, from planning your trip to reporting on it when you get back.

Travel Intelligence: www.travelintelligence.net. A large collection of travel writing by distinguished travel writers, categorized by location.

INFORMATION ON THE PACIFIC NORTHWEST

CIA World Factbook: www.odci.gov/cia/publications/factbook/index.html. Tons of vital statistics on the geography, government, economy, and people of the US and Canada.

Go Northwest: www.gonorthwest.com. A collection of tourism information on the Pacific Northwest (not including Alberta).

Information USA: http://usinfo.state.gov/usa/infousa. An exhaustive database of links on all aspects of the US.

Oh, Canada!: www.ualberta.ca/%7Ebleeck/canada. A voluminous resource and database of useful links on all things Canadian, from history to wildlife to education.

Travel Library: www.travel-library.com. A fantastic set of links for specialized guides (information on visiting the Canadian Rockies, a wine guide to Washington, etc.) and personal travelogues.

TravelPage: www.travelpage.com. Links to official tourist office sites in the Pacific Northwest.

ALTERNATIVES TO TOURISM

A PHILOSOPHY FOR TRAVELERS

Let's Go believes that the connection between travelers and their destinations is an important one. We've watched the growth of the 'ignorant tourist' stereotype with dismay, knowing that many travelers care passionately about the communities and environments they explore—but also knowing that even conscientious tourists can inadvertently damage natural wonders and harm cultural environments. With this "Alternatives to Tourism" chapter, *Let's Go* hopes to promote a better understanding of the Pacific Northwest and enhance your experience there.

When we started out in 1961, 1.7 million people in the world were traveling internationally; in 2002, nearly 700 million trips were made, projected to be up to a billion by 2010. The dramatic rise in tourism has created an interdependence between the economy, environment, and culture of many destinations.

Conservationists are concerned over the impact of increased use on once-isolated national parks, forests, and wildlife refuges, and many park areas have quotas on the number of visitors allowed per day. Those looking to **volunteer** in the efforts to resolve these issues have many options. You can participate in projects from maintaining trails in old-growth forests of spruce to working with scientists to study the habits of local wildlife. Later in this section, we recommend organizations that can help you find the opportunities that best suit your interests, whether you're looking to pitch in for a day or a year.

There are any number of other ways that you can integrate yourself with the communities you visit. **Studying** at a college or language program is one option. Some schools even have programs that allow you to earn academic credits or certificates by learning outdoors skills. Many travelers also structure their trips by the **work** that they can do along the way—either odd jobs as they go or full-time stints in cities where they plan to stay for some time. Other possibilities abound in the major cities, such as Portland (OR), Seattle (WA), and Vancouver (BC).

 Start your search at **www.beyondtourism.com,** Let's Go's brand-new searchable database of Alternatives to Tourism, where you can find exciting feature articles and helpful program listings divided by country, continent, and program type.

VOLUNTEERING

Though the US and Canada are considered wealthy in worldwide terms, they are not immune to the universal problems of poverty and hunger, and a large number of organizations exist to deal with these issues. Conservation and environmental issues are also concerns addressed by park services and private organizations.

Volunteering can be one of the most fulfilling experiences you have in life, especially if you combine it with the thrill of traveling in a new place. Most people who volunteer in the region do so on a short-term basis, at organizations that make use of drop-in or once-a-week volunteers. These can be found in virtually every city, and are referenced both in this section and in our town and city write-ups themselves. The best way to find opportunities that match up with your interests and schedule may be to check with organizations such as **United Way** or **Americorps** (a domestic version of the Peace Corps, open only to US citizens, nationals, and residents), which both work with local organizations to promote community service at the grassroots level (see below). Visit websites such as www.voe-reb.org (Canada only), www.networkforgood.org, www.planetedu.com, www.volunteermatch.com, and www.volunteer-abroad.com, as well as the ones listed below to begin your search.

More intensive volunteer services may charge you a fee to participate. These costs can be surprisingly hefty (although they frequently cover airfare and most living expenses). Most people choose to go through a parent organization that takes care of logistical details and often provides a group environment and support system. There are two main types of organizations—religious and non-sectarian—although there are rarely restrictions on participation for either.

PARK PROGRAMS

Many park systems provide host programs that allow long-term visitors to work at the park in lieu of paying campground fees. You can also contact individual parks for volunteer information, particularly in British Columbia, where park management is frequently decentralized and performed by private contractors. The following organizations all offer volunteer opportunities within the parks of the Pacific Northwest:

National Park Service, 1849 C St., NW, Washington, D.C., 20240 (☎202-208-6843; www.nps.gov/volunteer). **Volunteers-in-Parks** program participants work in National Parks and all other national lands in a range of capacities, from nature guide to maintenance. A list of parks currently seeking volunteers is on the website. National Parks that are part of the **Artists-in-Residence** program offer a chance for artists, writers, and composers to live and work inside the park.

Oregon State Parks, 725 Summer St. NE, Suite C, Salem, OR 97301 (☎503-986-0707; www.prd.state.or.us/volunteering.php). Oregon State Parks provides a Host Program similar to Washington's.

Parks and Protected Areas Division, 2nd fl., Oxbridge Place, 9820-106 St., Edmonton, AB T5K 2J6, Canada (☎780-427-9017; www.cd.gov.ab.ca/involved/parks/volunteer/index.asp). Alberta Parks also has information on a number of Alberta organizations dedicated to improving parks and protected areas.

Parks Canada National Volunteer Program, 25 Eddy St., 4th fl., Hull, QC, K1A 0M5, Canada (www.pc.gc.ca/agen/empl/index_e.asp). The Canadian equivalent of the National Park Service accepts volunteers for parks, historical sites, and marine conservation areas. Canadian applicants should contact the specific parks in which they are interested. Foreign applicants should write to the address above or email to obtain a questionnaire. Deadline for summer and autumn placement is Dec. 1 of the preceding year; deadline for winter and spring placement is June 30.

Washington State Parks, 7150 Cleanwater Ln., P.O. Box 42650, Olympia, WA 98504 (☎360-902-8583; www.parks.wa.gov/volunteer.asp). Volunteers perform routine park tasks in exchange for free camping or boat moorage (minimum stays are 30 days for camping, 14 days for moorage). Other volunteer opportunities are also available for both long and short terms.

ALTERNATIVES TO TOURISM

> **BEFORE YOU GO** Before handing your money over to any volunteer or study abroad program, make sure you know exactly what you're getting into. It's wise to get the names of **previous participants** and ask them about their experience, as some programs sound much better on paper than in reality. Also, make sure the program itself is able to answer the following **questions:**
> -Will you be the only person in the program? If not, what are the other participants like? How old are they? Will you interact with them?
> -Is room and board included? If so, what is the arrangement?
> -Is transportation included? Are there any additional expenses?
> -How much free time will you have? Will you be able to travel?
> -What kind of safety network is set up? Will you still be covered by your home insurance? Does the program have an emergency plan?

ENVIRONMENTAL CONSERVATION

Your conservation experience doesn't have to be confined to a park. Many organizations in the Pacific Northwest will place you in the city or in a rural setting to work with locals on issues concerning the environment. While some programs charge a fee, the program price almost always includes room and board.

Earthshare, 7735 Old Georgetown Rd., Suite 900, Bethesda, MD 20814 (☎240-333-0300; www.earthshare.org). This umbrella organization of environmental groups has chapters in both Washington and Oregon. Members range from the Sierra Club to the Bicycle Alliance of Washington.

Earthwatch, 3 Clock Tower Pl., Suite 100, Box 75, Maynard, MA 01754 (☎978-461-0081; www.earthwatch.org/region/namerica.html). Places volunteers in 1-3 week research programs with scientists to promote conservation of natural environments. Typical program cost is $1000 per week.

Student Conservation Association, 689 River Rd., P.O. Box 550, Charlestown, NH 03603 (☎603-543-1700; www.thesca.org). Begun in Olympic National Park, the SCA allows you to live and work in public lands for 3-12 months. Projects include conservation, archaeology, backcountry management, forestry, and more. All expenses paid internship; possible scholarship. Contact the **SCA Northwest Office,** 1265 S Main St., #210, Seattle, WA 98144 (☎206-324-4649, fax 324-4998).

USDA Forest Service: Pacific NW Region, P.O. Box 3623, 333 SW First Ave., Portland, OR 97208-3623 (☎503-808-2468; www.fs.fed.us/r6). Volunteer in a range of capacities, from desk jobs to more exciting tasks in the outdoors. Flexible duration, ranging from one-time to full year; part-time or full-time. Option to live in national forest in summers. Part-time and full-time jobs also available.

STUDYING

Studying in the Pacific Northwest can mean anything from intensive English language classes to a snowshoeing course. In order to choose a program that best fits your needs, you will want to research all you can before making your decision—determine costs and duration, as well as what kind of students participate in the program and what sort of accommodations are provided. International students studying in the US and Canada must have student visas. See **Visa and Work Permit Information,** p. 20, for more info. Students must prove sufficient financial support and be in good health (see **Entrance Requirements,** p. 19).

CLASSROOM OUTDOORS

Studying in the Pacific Northwest is not just about poring over books, attending lectures, and typing away at papers. The region gives you the chance to learn through doing, and adventure can be just as educational as that heavy textbook you never opened. Programs here are operated by universities or offer certifications; see **Organized Trips and Outfitters** (p. 74) for a listing of similar programs with less of a focus on providing educational credentials.

Canadian Outdoor Leadership Training, P.O. Box 2160, Campbell River, BC V9W 5C5, Canada (☎250-286-3122; www.colt.bc.ca). Based in Vancouver Island's Strathcona Park, COLT offers three-month programs that provide training and certification in a variety of outdoor activities, including canoeing, kayaking, rock climbing, and first aid. Program cost CDN$8000-10,000; includes food and some equipment.

Capilano College Wilderness Leadership Program, Box 1538, Squamish, BC V0N 3G0, Canada (☎604-986-1911 ext. 5801; www.capcollege.bc.ca/programs/wilderness/index.xhtml). Offers certificate programs combining classes such as Natural History for Outdoors Leaders with more hands-on courses like sailing, cross-country skiing, and mountain biking. Offers wilderness travel, water travel, and winter travel programs. CDN$3000-4000 for Canadian students; CDN$9000-1100 for international students. Fee does not include food but does include equipment use.

IslandWood, 4450 Blakely Ave. NE, Bainbridge Island, WA 98110 (☎206-855-4300; www.islandwood.org). This sustainably-designed 255-acre campus in Puget Sound provides summer and weekend programs for children and adults about nature education and community/environmental stewardship. They offer a 10-month on-site intensive education and community certification for graduate students ($14,000; includes room and some board) and educators ($11,250).

University of Calgary Outdoor Programs, Outdoor Centre, Campus Recreation, Faculty of Kinesiology, University of Calgary, 2500 University Dr. NW, Calgary, AB T2N 1N4 (☎403-220-5038; www.kin.ucalgary.ca/campusrec/outdoors/programs.aspx). The University offers day- or weekend-long courses in activities ranging from fly-fishing to snowshoeing. Classes CDN$30-400.

UNIVERSITIES

If you are currently studying as an undergraduate and would like to get credit for schoolwork completed in the US or Canada, check with universities in your home country to see if they offer exchanges with particular North American schools. Most university-level study-abroad programs are meant as language and culture enrichment opportunities, and therefore are conducted in the native language of the country. Those relatively fluent in English may find it cheaper to enroll directly full-time in a university, although getting college credit may be more difficult. Financial aid is frequently available for international students. For non-English speaking students, many colleges and schools offer courses on English as a second language.

A good resource for finding programs that cater to your particular interests is www.studyabroadlinks.com which has links to various semester abroad programs categorized by location and area of study. The following is a list of organizations that can help place students in university programs abroad, or have their own branch in the Pacific Northwest.

PROGRAMS IN THE PACIFIC NORTHWEST

Thanks to government subsidies, tuition at Canadian schools is generally affordable. Although foreign students pay more than Canadian citizens, the total cost can be less than half of the tuition for American schools.

Oregon and Washington have innumerable liberal arts, community, profes-sional, and technical colleges. Unfortunately, tuition costs are high in the United States and a full course of undergraduate study often entails a four-year commit-ment. The state university systems are usually very affordable for residents of those states, but expensive to outsiders. Community and technical colleges cost less, but may only offer two-year programs. Unless otherwise specified, tuitions below do not include room and board and all programs are full-time, full-year.

Many institutions of higher learning in the Pacific Northwest belong to the **National Student Exchange,** a network of universities in the US, Canada, and Puerto Rico. (Check the website for a list of all participating universities.) It allows stu-dents of member institutions to spend up to one year at any other member school. Policies may vary depending on your home institution, but usually students pay the same tuition that they would at their resident university, and all credits are transferable. (☎800-478-1823; www.nse.org.)

Association of Commonwealth Universities (ACU), John Foster House, 36 Gordon Sq., London WC1H OPF UK (☎020 7380 6700; www.acu.ac.uk). Publishes info about Com-monwealth Universities, including most public universities in BC and Alberta.

International Student Exchange Program (ISEP), 1616 P St. NW, Suite 150, Washing-ton, D.C., 20036 (☎202-667-8027; www.isep.org). A network of over 230 universities in 35 countries, ISEP allows students of participating institutions to study affordably internationally at member universities. Students pay their normal tuition and board to their home university and study full-time at their host school from one term to two years.

University of Alberta Faculty of Graduate Students and Research (FGSR), Edmonton, AB, Canada (see website for phone contact information and correct street address, which varies with department: http://gradfile.fgsro.ualberta.ca/international). Tuition ranges from CDN$2220 (part-time) to CDN$4150 (full-time) per term.

University of Oregon Office of International Programs (OIP), Room 330 Oregon Hall, 5209 University of Oregon, Eugene, OR 97403-520 (☎541-346-3206, http://oip.uore-gon.edu). International students with F-1 or J-1 visas can enroll in one of the many pro-grams offered. Check the website for admissions information. Tuition is $16,400.

University of Washington, 1410 NE Campus Parkway, Box 355852, Seattle, WA 98195 (☎206-543-9686; www.washington.edu/students/uga/in). Website offers information for international students seeking to apply. Tuition is $17,000.

LANGUAGE SCHOOLS

Language schools are a good alternative to university study if you desire a deeper focus on the language or a slightly less rigorous courseload. These programs are also good for younger high school students who might not feel comfortable in a university program. Many universities offer **English as a Second Language (ESL)** classes for non-native speakers of English as part of their courses, though these may be limited to certain campuses. Some good programs include:

Oregon State University English Language Institute (ELI), 301 Snell Hall, Corvallis, OR 97331 (☎541-737-2464; www.orst.edu/dept/eli). Specifically addresses the needs of both teens and adults. Tuition $2500 per trimester.

University of British Columbia English Language Institute (ELI), 2121 West Mall, Vancouver, BC V6T 1Z4, Canada (☎604-822-1555; www.eli.ubc.ca). Services include both long- and short-term programs; ELI can also set visiting students up with accommodations. Intensive 10-12 week English programs $3500-4000; 3-4 week language and culture programs $1000-2000.

University of Washington International and English Language Programs, 5001 25th Ave. NE, Seattle, WA 98105 (☎206-543-6242; http://depts.washington.edu/uwelp). Offers certificate programs for international students with the proper visa credentials. Not all classes are for credit, see website for details. Fees vary with program duration.

WORKING

As with volunteering, work opportunities tend to fall into two categories. Some travelers want long-term jobs that allow them to get to know another part of the world as a member of the community, while other travelers seek out short-term jobs to finance the next leg of their travels. In the Pacific Northwest, short-term jobs are easier to find and more abundant than long-term jobs. With the arrival of summer comes tourists and hundreds of tourism-related jobs in hotels, lodges, tour operations, outfitters, cruise ships, and restaurants. Summer also brings the salmon runs, creating a huge labor demand in fishing and seafood processing, though these jobs could potentially be long-term as well. Some other long-term jobs to consider are in the service industry, one of the fastest growing industries in the state, but with comparatively low wages. Other options are in the transportation industry and business. Work side by side with experienced fishermen to bring in the latest run of salmon, guide kayak excursions through narrow fjords, or help run a campground (p. 66). Minimum wage is around $7 in the Oregon and Washington, CDN$8 in British Columbia, and around CDN$6 in Alberta.

All foreign visitors intending to work in the US and Canada must first obtain a work permit (see p. 56). To apply, you must first find a job and be sponsored by an employer, but several organizations such as Council Exchanges or BUNAC will help you obtain a work permit without having a job (see below).

Even if you already have a job lined up before arriving in the region, it is wise to have access to at least $1000 cash, more if you still need to find employment. The cost of living in the Pacific Northwest can be high compared to other regions of the US and Canada, such as the American South and Midwest; prices are similar to those found in the Northeast US. Living in Alberta is slightly cheaper than in British Columbia; likewise, Oregon is marginally less expensive than Washington.

A good option is to read the classified sections of major newspapers. In Canada, you can visit www.jobsetc.ca, which provides job listings, techniques on finding a job, advice, and various links. Other Canada-oriented possibilities are **NiceJob** (☎888-907-1111; http://actijob.nicejob.ca), where job-hopefuls can post and update their resumes, search for employers, and browse a frequently-updated list of openings, and **Cool Jobs Canada** (www.cooljobscanada.com). **Craigslist** (http://portland.craigslist.org; http://seattle.craigslist.org; http://vancouver.craigslist.org) is a popular site with employment and housing postings for major cities. **Monster.com** (www.monster.com) is a site with searchable job listings all over the world; it also has a separate section for those looking for a job overseas. **BestJobsUsa.com** (www.bestjobsusa.com) is another searchable site for jobs in the US.

SUMMER CAMP COUNSELING

Working as a camp counselor is a popular way for college or graduate students to see the world on their summer vacations. Many camps also give you the opportunity to spend serious time outdoors and teach children to enjoy the wilderness. Camp counselors typically receive room (sometimes without electricity or plumbing; check ahead), board, and poor pay. An inexperienced counselor should expect to earn around $800-1500, and international counselors frequently receive less. Counselors at a day camp typically receive slightly above minimum wage but no room or board.

Placement programs such as **Camp America** (www.campamerica.co.uk), **International Counselor Exchange Program** (☎212-787-7706; www.international-counselors.org), and **InterExchange** (☎212-924-0446; www.interexchange.org) generally pay less than a camp would but can help you obtain a job and visa. The **YMCA** runs a number of camps throughout the US and Canada; see www.stwmd.com/y-camps.php for listings by state

VISA AND WORK PERMIT INFORMATION

All foreign visitors to the US are required to have a **visa** if they are planning a stay of more than 90 days (180 days for Canadians) or if they intend to work or study. In general, visitors cannot change visa status once in the US or Canada; if you intend to work or study, make the relevant arrangements before your trip. Travelers must provide proof of intent to leave, such as a return plane ticket or an **I-94** card. To obtain a visa, contact a US embassy or consulate. Foreign students who wish to study in the US must first be admitted to a school, then apply for either an **M-1 visa** (vocational studies), an **F-1 visa** (for students enrolled full-time in an academic or language program), or a **J-1 visa** (for students participating in exchange programs). Students who wish to study in Canada need a student authorization (IMM 1208) plus the appropriate tourist visa. **To obtain a visa,** contact a US or Canadian embassy or consulate. See **Essentials,** p. 18, for a list of US and Canadian consulates in English-speaking nations, and see p. 20 for more on obtaining visas. Or, check http://travel.state.gov/links.html for US listings and www.dfait-maeci.gc.ca/world/embassies/menu-en.asp for Canadian listings worldwide. **US visa extensions** are sometimes attainable with a completed I-539 form; call the Bureau of Citizenship and Immigration Service's (BCIS) forms request line (☎800-870-3676) or get it online at www.immigration.gov. See http://travel.state.gov/visa_services.html for more information.

A **work permit** (or "green card" in the US) is also required of all foreigners planning to work in the US or Canada. Your employer must obtain this document, usually by demonstrating that you have skills that locals lack. Friends in the country can sometimes help expedite work permits or arrange work-for-accommodations exchanges. **To obtain a work permit in the US,** fill out the I-765 form from the BCIS, follow all other instructions, and return it to your regional BCIS service center. Processing may take up to 90 days. Recent security measures have made the visa application process more rigorous, and therefore lengthy. **Apply well in advance of your travel date.** In Canada, you can obtain form IMM 1295 online at www.cic.gc.ca/english/applications/work.html or at the visa office and return it to your local visa office at a Canadian high commission or consulate. The process may be complex, but it's critical that you go through the proper channels—the alternative is potential deportation.

and country. A number of websites provide listings of summer camps, including **Allen's Guide** (www.allensguide.com), **Camp Page** (www.camppage.com), **Camp Channel** (www.campchannel.com), and **Adventure-Camp.com** (www.adventure-camp.com).

SHORT-TERM WORK

Traveling for long periods of time can get expensive; therefore, many travelers try their hand at odd jobs for a few weeks at a time to make some extra cash to carry them through another month or two of touring around. Potential odd jobs include working at a small cafe or restaurant, adventure outfitters, tour operators, or working in a fish cannery or processing plant. Another favorite is to work at a hostel in exchange for free or discounted room and/or board. Most often, these short-term jobs are found by word of mouth; many places are always eager for help, even if only temporary. *Let's Go* tries to list temporary jobs when possible; look in the practical information sections of larger cities, or check out the list below for some short-term jobs in popular destinations.

InterExchange, 161 Sixth Ave., New York, NY 10013 (☎212-924-0446; www.interexchange.org), helps place international students in seasonal entry-level jobs in US service and summer camps, as well as au pair jobs.

SIGNING ON
The Chimpanzee-Human Communications Institute

Ellensburg, WA, is a small college town in the middle of the state. Tucked away on the Central Washington University campus, however, is the renowned Chimpanzee-Human Communications Institute (CHCI). For the past twenty-five years, Dr. Roger Fouts, his wife Debbi Fouts, and a team of researchers have studied the language abilities of Washoe, her adopted son Loulis, and three other chimpanzees, Dar, Tatu and the recently deceased Moja. Today, much of the work concentrates on finding better means of caring for chimpanzees. When I attended CHCI for two weeks as part of an Earthwatch program, my team helped track the objects that each chimpanzee used. While this might not seem like glamorous work, the unfortunate truth is that many captive chimpanzees locked in five by five foot cages are given almost nothing to do. By studying object use, CHCI will provide a better understanding of what toys chimpanzees will find most enriching and help demonstrate that providing toys is important for maintaining a healthy habitat.

But CHCI is much more than a research institute. The Fouts have devoted their lives to protecting Washoe and her family and to educating humans on the close genetic bond between chimpanzees and humans. The first week of the two-week Earthwatch program focused on education: general—the history of animal language experiments, the biological characteristics of chimpanzees and other great apes; humanitarian—the status of chimpanzees as a protected species, the state of medical experiments on chimpanzees in the US, and the dangers to chimpanzees in Africa, including bushmeat and habitat loss; and practical—safety, cooking for chimpanzees, and recognition. The last is not as easy as you might think: try telling the difference between four chimpanzees the first time you meet them. Of course, we didn't learn enough to operate on our own with chimps; everyone at CHCI is quick to point out that two weeks is not nearly enough time to learn all the intricacies of interacting with chimps or to earn their trust.

Indeed, I found one of the most rewarding aspects of the program to be watching people who have worked with chimpanzees for months and years interact in meaningful ways with their chim-

panzee friends. Even for us, as visitors, our own interactions were fascinating: much of our relatively brief interactions took the form of being teased by Washoe, who demanded that we take off our shoes for her amusement. The stories the staff told were equally engaging. Once, Tatu asked a new research assistant for ice cream. The assistant, knowing that Tatu was lactose-intolerant, told her she couldn't have any. Tatu replied that Roger had said that it was OK. The assistant, accepting Tatu's word, prepared a bowl of ice cream, only to run into Dr. Fouts, who, upon hearing the story, informed the assistant that he had said no such thing. Tatu's deviousness is an example of the advanced and individual personalities of each chimp. Washoe is the family matriarch and tends to resolve conflicts. Dar, a male, appears more laid-back even though he is by far the largest and seemingly should dominate the group. Loulis, the other male, often acts like a teenager, but we're told he has mellowed with age. Moja was fond of dressing up in clothing, wearing masks, and looking at herself in the mirror.

Of course, we couldn't spend all of our time interacting with the chimps—in fact, one of the primary tenets of CHCI is that we are the guests of the chimps in their habitat, and we must respect their privacy. Even the rooms next to the enclosure have blinds that allow the chimps to see in rather than the humans to see out. But we were also there to collect data. Over the course of several hours, divided into 15 minute intervals, groups of four of us would rotate in to observe the chimps. Every 15 seconds, we would record what our assigned chimp was doing. Prior to taking these observations, we all had to achieve high scores for reliability based on sample observation sessions with known results.

Though we only spent two weeks at CHCI, our team was able to contribute both to the research and day-to-day running of the program; in addition to observing the chimpanzees, we also cleaned cages and cooked their dinner. We may not have been writing scientific reports on the chimps, but our volunteer experience, if short-lived, still taught us a great deal about working with chimps and allowed us to contribute to the program.

F. Alexander Allain is studying Psychology and Computer Science at Harvard University and runs the website Cprogramming.com.

International Association for the Exchange of Students for Technical Experience (IAESTE), 10400 Little Patuxent Pkwy. Suite 250, Columbia, MD 21044-3519 (☎410-997-2200, www.aipt.org). IAESTE provides assistance in finding jobs in the US lasting up to 4 months for students from Argentina, Australia, Brazil, the Netherlands, and Uruguay, as well as 8- to 12-week programs in Canada for US students who have completed 2 years of technical study. IAESTE can also help provide housing, tax advice, insurance, and visas. $25-100 application fee. Program or service fees range from about $800-2000.

NW Hospitality.net (www.nwhospitality.net). An online database of hospitality (mostly restaurant) jobs in the region.

FOR FURTHER READING ON ALTERNATIVES TO TOURISM

Alternatives to the Peace Corps: A Directory of Third World and U.S. Volunteer Opportunities, by Joan Powell. Food First Books, 2000 ($10).

International Directory of Voluntary Work, by Whetter and Pybus. Peterson's Guides and Vacation Work, 2000 ($16).

Overseas Summer Jobs 2002, by Collier and Woodworth. Peterson's Guides and Vacation Work, 2002 ($18).

Work Abroad: The Complete Guide to Finding a Job Overseas, by Hubbs, Griffith, and Nolting. Transitions Abroad Publishing, 2000 ($16).

Work Your Way Around the World, by Susan Griffith. Worldview Publishing Services, 2001 ($18).

Invest Yourself: The Catalogue of Volunteer Opportunities, published by the Commission on Voluntary Service and Action (☎718-638-8487).

ALTERNATIVES TO TOURISM

ESSAY CONTEST WINNER!

beyondtourism.com

Last year's winner, Eleanor Glass, spent a summer volunteering with children on an island off the Yucatan Peninsula. Read the rest of her story and find your own once-in-a-lifetime experience at **www.beyondtourism.com!**

"... I was discovering elements of life in Mexico that I had never even dreamt of. I regularly had meals at my students' houses, as their fisherman fathers would instruct them to invite the nice gringa to lunch after a lucky day's catch. Downtown, tourists wandered the streets and spent too much on cheap necklaces, while I played with a friend's baby niece, or took my new kitten to the local vet for her shots, or picked up tortillas at the tortilleria, or vegetables in the mercado. ... I was lucky that I found a great place to volunteer and a community to adopt me. ... Just being there, listening to stories, hearing the young men talk of cousins who had crossed the border, I know I went beyond tourism." - Eleanor Glass, 2004

LET'S GO

THE GREAT OUTDOORS

While the Pacific Northwest has its share of teeming urban centers, you'll find it hard to forget that you are in nature's domain. Just look up to see jagged snow-capped mountain peaks on the horizon in every direction. Or drive 10 minutes out of the city to find yourself surrounded by forests. With national, state, and provincial parks covering huge spans of the region, not to mention four colossal mountain ranges dominating the landscape, the outdoors adventure of your dreams is within easy grasp.

GREAT OUTDOORS FACTS AND FIGURES

OREGON
Wilderness areas: 35, covering over 2 million acres.
National Forests: 14, covering more than 15 million acres.
Number of yurts in state parks: 159, to service all your camping needs.

WASHINGTON
Largest glacier in the lower 48: Emmons Glacier on Mt. Rainier.
Largest wilderness area in the lower 48: in Olympic National Park.
Acres of public land: 9 million, including 3 million without roads or development.

BRITISH COLUMBIA
Number of provincial parks and protected areas: more than 800.
Hectares of protected land: 11.9 million, accounting for over 12% of the province.
Species of invertebrates: 1138, including 24 unique to British Columbia.

ALBERTA
Land covered by forests: over half of the province, approximately 350,000 sq. km.
Size of Jasper National Park: 6750 sq. km, Canada's largest mountain national park.
Age of Banff National Park: 120 years old; founded in 1885, it is Canada's oldest.

FLORA AND FAUNA

The Pacific Northwest's size and geographical diversity results in a range of environments, wildlife, and vegetation throughout the region. As you traverse the windswept coastline or blaze a trail through a tangled forest, it's not uncommon to see a whale casually surface or spy a foraging black bear lumbering by. But as isolated as much of the wilderness and its creatures may seem, keep in mind that human actions often have lasting, unpredictable effects on the outdoors environment. Never feed the wildlife, no matter how much you want them to come closer to you and your camera. Animals accustomed to being fed may lose their fear of humans and harass hikers; the high content of grease, sodium, and other chemicals present in processed foods can harm the digestive systems of many animals.

PLANTS

TEMPERATE RAINFORESTS. The coasts of Oregon, Washington, and British Columbia are a verdant paradise, sheltering the native tribes like Haida, Kwakiutl, Skagit, Makah, and Tillamook for generations. **Spruce** and **western red cedars**—the official tree of British Columbia—challenge the skies, lifting up evergreen boughs to meet the rain. Upon mountain slopes, alpine meadows filled with grasses and wildflowers predominate above the treeline.

TAIGA. In the interior the climate becomes colder and drier, and trees become shorter and more sparse. **White spruce, birches, aspen, firs,** and **cottonwood** grow in the boreal forest (the English translation of the Russian word "taiga"), while farther north trees become scattered. You can also find the **Douglas-fir** (the Oregon state tree) and the **western hemlock,** the state tree of Washington. The **lodgepole pine,** the provincial tree of Alberta, is profuse throughout the Canadian Rockies.

WILDFLOWERS. The meadows, bogs, forests, and subalpine meadows of the Pacific Northwest hold wildflowers of every possible color and species. In moist forest areas the rose-colored **Pacific bleeding heart** makes an appearance; in early spring and summer you can find the **avalanche lily** blooming at the edge of snowfields. Some of these flowers are even edible, like the bulbs of the orange freckled **Columbia tiger lily,** harvested by aboriginal tribes for their peppery taste.

BERRIES. The Pacific Northwest's abundance of berries once fed the region's earliest native inhabitants, and now can provide an earthy, free snack for the hungry hiker or backpacker. From the mundane **strawberries, blueberries,** and **blackberries** to local specialties like **salmonberries, huckleberries,** and **marionberries,** the forests and meadows offer a veritable feast in late summertime. As tantalizing as this may sound, be careful; you should never eat anything that you can't identify. Be advised that bears are gluttons for these sweet berries, so take care you're not intruding on some grizzly's favorite berry patch.

POISON OAK. While poison ivy and poison sumac are rare or nonexistent in the Pacific Northwest, **poison oak** is still a plant to watch out for. In the Pacific Northwest, poison oak manifests itself as a shrub-like plant or a climbing vine, with three leaves on a stem (one to each side and one in the front). The berries of poison oak are small and whitish or brown, and its leaves are typically shiny and lobed like oak leaves. All parts of poison oak can cause nasty rashes and blisters upon contact. If you get poison oak, try to avoid scratching, which can spread the rash. Wash off the affected area with water as soon as possible, and clean your clothes along with anything else that came into contact with the plants. Itching creams, such as **hydrocortisone** or **calamine,** and **antihistamines,** such as Benadryl, can help calm the itching. The rash usually goes away by itself within two weeks. In severe cases, see a doctor.

ANIMALS

CARIBOU. Better known in the popular imagination as reindeer, the caribou were made to travel over land. These animals cover more ground each year (3000 mi.) than any other mammal, swimming across rivers and reaching land speeds of up to 50 mph. Caribou can be found in the forests of northern British Columbia and northern and western Alberta.

MOUNTAIN GOATS. Unlike the fast-moving caribou, mountain goats move at a more deliberate pace. This can cause problems in the **Canadian Rockies** (see p. 414), where traffic stands still every time a tour bus sights one. Male goats (billies) crawl on their bellies when they are pursuing a female goat (nannies). The goats can be found along the British Columbia coastline, in the Rocky Mountains, and in north-central Washington.

GRAY WOLVES (A.K.A. TUNDRA WOLVES OR TIMBER WOLVES). If the billies spent less time on their bellies, they might have better luck evading the gray wolves, who are their natural predators. To catch a glimpse of these elusive and cunning creatures, check out **Wolf Haven International** in Olympia (see p. 214). The wolves can be found throughout British Columbia and Alberta, particularly in the Rockies, but are considered endangered in all US states except Montana.

MOOSE. These peculiar-looking creatures, with their massive, drooping heads and barrel-like bodies balanced upon long spindly legs, retain a sense of majesty from their regal crown of horns. Moose can be found throughout the Pacific Northwest wilderness, particularly in northern forests. They occasionally leave their woody river habitats and wander into town to munch on garbage, preen for tourist cameras, and hinder traffic. Bad-tempered moose can present as much of a danger as an irritated bear. Bulls in mating season (late September to early October) are very grouchy. Ask park rangers about moose territory, and never come between a cow and her calves. If attacked by a moose, run away. Get behind a tree if possible. Remember that moose can kick with both their front and back feet.

BEARS. The Pacific Northwest is home to both brown (grizzly) and black bears. These curious and highly intelligent animals are found throughout the region, primarily in forests, but their wide range of habitat and omnivorous nature means that they can occasionally be found rummaging through trash cans in suburbia as well. One of the best places to see bears in the Pacific Northwest is in Banff National Park (p. 440), where rangers keep a running tally of sightings in the area. For information on unwanted ursine encounters, see **bear safety** (p. 62).

BALD EAGLES. The emblem of the United States, this majestic bird is unique to North America. Though the population once dwindled due to hunting and pesticides, the bald eagle has staged a promising comeback. Bald eagles can be found in all of the Pacific Northwest, particularly in coastal British Columbia and the Puget Sound area. The best time to spot a bald eagle in the region is during the summer, since the birds migrate south in the winter.

SOMETHING IN THE WATER. There's a reason the region takes half its name from the largest ocean on earth—from massive whales to tiny sea anemones, the waters of the Pacific Northwest are positively teeming with sea life. **Sea otters** cavort through the blue-green waters, while each spring, **gray whales** migrate north from Baja California along with **humpback whales** from Hawaii. **Orcas**, made famous under their misnomer killer whale, are not really whales but the largest of the dolphin species. While these relatively-small (15-35 ft.) black-and-white tourist attractions can be found in oceans all over the world, the Vancouver Island and Puget Sound region is one of the few areas where they are concentrated enough to be seen with any frequency. But even orcas in this area are threatened by overfishing, water pollutants, and boat traffic and have recently been classified as endangered in Washington. Other whales and sea mammals include the **beluga whale, blue whale, harbor seal, bearded seal, northern fur seal, walrus,** and the **sea lion.**

And of course, there's the famed **salmon** and **halibut** for which avid fishing-fanatics come flocking to the coastal waters off British Columbia. Salmon come in five varieties, each of them with its own charm: **chinook,** or king salmon, is the largest; many consider **chum,** or dog salmon, the least edible of the five, though some say it's underrated; the bright silver **coho** is the swiftest and the most popular sport fish; despite being the smallest, **humpback** salmon, also known as pink salmon for the color of its flesh, is important to commercial fishing; **sockeye** salmon has a distinctive red flesh and is acclaimed as the best tasting.

INSECTS AND REPTILES

MOSQUITOES WILL SAVAGE YOU. In the summer, **mosquitoes** will almost certainly be a hassle in most non-urban areas and in northern British Columbia especially. Perfume, scented shampoos and soaps, hairspray, and cologne will attract mosquitoes as well as bears and should be left at home. Mosquitoes can bite through thin fabric, so cover up as much as possible with thicker ones. Covering all exposed skin is the best way of keeping off bugs. **DEET** is the most effective repellent out there, but there's no need to use a solution that's more than 30% DEET. **OFF! Deep Woods** and **Cutter Outdoorsman** are two widely-available repellents with 30% concentrations. If you do use DEET, be careful; while it's the most effective repellent out there, it can also damage rayon, spandex, leather, and plastics (including glasses frames). **Vitamin B$_{12}$ pills** or **garlic tablets** are sometimes used by travelers worried about the damaging effects of DEET, although garlic may repel people as well as insects.

RATTLESNAKES WILL BITE YOU. While not snakes do not pose much of a threat in most of the water-logged Northwest, you may encounter them in the drier areas east of the mountains, particularly in southeastern Oregon. **Rattlesnakes** have broad, triangular heads and rattles on the end of their tails, and are typically found in dry areas below 6000 ft., but have been known to range as high as 8000 ft. Exercise common sense by watching where you step, sit, reach, and poke. Wear long pants and thick boots when exploring the outdoors. If you encounter a snake, stand still until it slithers away. If the snake is backed into a corner, stay still for a while and then back away slowly, stepping gently. Unless it is surprised and bites reflexively, a rattlesnake will coil defensively and shake its rattle before it strikes. If bitten, get to a medical facility as quickly as possible.

BANANA SLUGS WILL NUMB YOU. The second-largest slug in the world, this up to 10 in. slimy critter gets its name from its bright yellow coloring and black spots. It is native to the Pacific coast and can be found on the moist temperate forest floor. Hard-core Northwest natives have been known to lick banana slugs when they come across them while hiking, as the slime is reported to numb your tongue.

BEAR SAFETY

BEARS WILL EAT YOU. The national parks and forests of the Pacific Northwest are the habitat of **bears,** who—besides believing themselves to have a previous claim to your campsite—are bigger and stronger than you. While hiking or camping remember: bear avoidance is far easier and safer than bear evasion.

ON THE TRAIL. If you're close enough for a bear to be observing you, you're too close. If you see a bear at a distance, calmly walk (don't run) in the other direction. If it seems interested, back away slowly while speaking to the bear in firm, low tones and head in the opposite direction or toward a settled area. In all situations, remain calm, as loud noises and sudden movements can trigger an attack.

Whenever you are walking along a trail, especially in forested or hilly areas where a bear may not have complete visibility, you should make noise. You can **sing, whistle,** or tie **bells** to your shoes or clothes, but make sure to let the bears up ahead know that you are on the way and aren't part of an ambush. At the same time, don't make too much noise. Bears are curious and will investigate very loud sounds or novel noises. **Binoculars** allow you to scrutinize suspicious forms in the distance, and to stay away from potential bears. Remember that when hiking in a group it is safer to be bunched close together than it is to be spread widely apart.

CAMPGROUND WISDOM. Though these tactics will help you successfully avoid bears on the trail, you'll also need to avoid them at camp. The first step is to choose your campsite carefully. Bears will generally avoid areas that smell like humans and will investigate areas that smell like bear food. If possible, don't choose a campsite that is exposed to the wind. The breeze will carry away your scent and make it hard for bears to know you're there. Avoid noisy areas that could obscure bear sounds or your sounds from the bears. Avoid hidden or concealed areas that bears could accidentally stumble upon.

Inspect for signs of previous bear activity. Bear scat and tracks are the most obvious indicators, but it's good to talk with locals and rangers about recent bear sightings, or about which areas are known for recent or increasing bear activity. Be wary of camping anywhere with trash or dirty firepits. This indicates that previous campers haven't taken care of their waste. Avoid areas with berries or areas near streams, and don't set up camp on areas that bears must traverse due to natural obstacles.

Try to avoid arousing the curiosity of local bears. Use muted, earthy colors as much as possible on your gear and equipment, and avoid bright or oddly-shaped tents. If you have multiple tents, set them up in a line, not in a circle—this way, it will be easier for an errant bear to exit the area.

THE MASKED MENACE. Many of the tactics you use to prevent bears from invading your campsite should also be employed against **raccoons,** who if anything are more hazardous to your garbage than bears. In some campgrounds, years of careless campers have made the local raccoons experts at stealing food. Their deft little paws can pry open tightly sealed containers and even work zippers. To prevent raccoons from snacking on your supplies, put rocks or other heavy objects on top of garbage or food containers; a hard-sided container with a tight-fitting lid will be the most effective. Never leave unsecured food unattended, as it only takes a second for a wily raccoon to nab your bag of gorp.

THE GREAT OUTDOORS

Don't leave **food** or other **scented items** (trash, toiletries, the clothes that you cooked in, lip balm, or anything with any scent at all) near your tent. Keep them at least 100m away. Bear-bagging—hanging edibles and other good-smelling objects from a tree out of reach of hungry paws—is the best way to keep your toothpaste from becoming a condiment. Bears are also attracted to any perfume, as are bugs, so cologne, scented soap, deodorant, and hairspray should stay at home.

If there are no trees in the area, hang your food off of a cliff or overhang. If the area is flat and treeless, store your food and scented items 100m away. Remember that wastewater should be treated like food—keep it away from your campsite. If you need to urinate at night, urinate into a designated bottle, and dump it in the morning. For more information, consult *How to Stay Alive in the Woods*, by Bradford Angier (Macmillan Press, $8).

WHEN BEARS ATTACK. There are two types of bear attacks: defensive and aggressive. How you should react depends on the type of threat. If a bear attack is defensive in nature, provoked by a threat to a food supply or a sow's cubs, you should let the bear know you're not a threat: lay down, curl up into a ball with your pack protecting the back of your head and neck, and pretend to be dead. Don't move until the bear goes away or unless it tries to eat you.

In an aggressive attack, the bear considers you prey. You should fight back while making noise and waving your arms to frighten the bear away. If possible, stand on a rock or a stump to make yourself look taller. A variety of commercial products can also help you in the case of an aggressive attack. **Bear spray** is carried in canisters approximately the size of an aerosol can and can be deployed against bears approaching from up to 15 ft. away, though wind can interfere. A **flare gun** or other scare device can be used to stun or distract bears, but note that the stun effect is not guaranteed to always work. You should be able to easily shift up your hiking pack to cover your head and neck in case of an attack. **Firearms** should not be employed unless the bearer is experienced in using guns. Handguns are useless for bear defense; large-bore rifles and 12 gauge shotguns are better options. If you carry a shotgun, only use slugs and keep firing until the bear stops moving.

PUBLIC LANDS IN THE PACIFIC NORTHWEST

In the Northwest, almost half of the total land area is public land. It is important to know whether the land you intend to traverse is public park land or a private holding, since different rules and standards of conduct apply to each. Important landholders in the Pacific Northwest include corporations, Native groups, individuals, and nonprofit agencies. Government agencies holding Northwestern land include the US National Forest Service, Parks Canada, the US Bureau of Land Management, the US Department of Fish and Wildlife, the Canadian Wildlife Service, and the state and provincial governments.

NATIONAL PARKS

National parks protect some of the US and Canada's most precious wildlife and spectacular scenery. The parks also offer activities such as hiking, skiing, and snowshoe expeditions, as well as hosting a variety of recreational activities such as ranger talks, marked trails, bus tours, and educational programs. Most have backcountry camping and developed campgrounds; others welcome RVs, and a few offer opulent living in grand lodges.

Entry fees vary from park to park. In US parks pedestrian and cyclist entry fees tend to range from $2-10, while vehicles cost $4-20. National parks in the US offer a number of passes. The **National Parks Pass** ($50 a year) admits the bearer and accompanying passengers in a vehicle (or family members where access is not by vehicle) into most US parks. Passes can be purchased at park entrances, online at www.nationalparks.org, or by calling ☎888-GO-PARKS/467-2757. For an additional $15, the Parks Service will affix a **Golden Eagle Pass** hologram to your card which will allow you access to sites managed by the US Fish and Wildlife Service, the US Forest Service, and the Bureau of Land Management. The **Golden Age Passport** ($10 one-time fee), available to those 62 or older, and the **Golden Access Passport,** free to travelers who are blind or permanently disabled, allow access to US national parks and 50% off camping and other park fees. Both passes can be purchased at park entrances by US citizens or permanent residents.

In Canada, pedestrian and cyclist entry costs CDN$2-10, while vehicles run CDN$5-20. The **Western Canada Annual Pass,** available for both individuals and groups, offers a similar deal to the National Parks Pass at Canadian national parks in the four western provinces (CDN$35, ages 64 and older CDN$27, 6-16 CDN$18, groups of up to seven adults CDN$70, groups of up to seven which include at least one senior $53). Passes can be purchased at park entrances.

In 2004, Parks Canada began a gradual price hike in visitor and commercial fees, to be phased in through 2007. The increase would go towards supporting park and visitor facilities. For current information, contact Parks Canada. *Let's Go* lists fees for individual parks and contact information for park visitors centers (check the index for a complete listing). All national parks in the US and Canada have a webpage listing general information, contact info, fees, and reservation policies; see the **National Park Service** (www.nps.gov) or **Parks Canada** (www.pc.gc.ca).

NATIONAL FORESTS

If national park campgrounds are too developed for your tastes, **national forests** provide a purist's alternative. While some have recreation facilities, most are equipped only for primitive camping; pit toilets and no running water are the norm. (See **Camping Reservation Numbers,** p. 66, for reservations.) For general information, including maps, contact the **US Forest Service, Outdoor Recreation Information Center,** 222 Yale Ave. N, Seattle, WA 98109 (☎206-470-4060; www.fs.fed.us). For Canadian parks contact the **Canadian Forest Service,** 530 Booth St., 8th fl., Ottawa, ON K1A 0E4 (☎613-947-7341; www.nrcan-rncan.gc.ca/cfs-scf).

Backpackers can enjoy specially designated **wilderness areas,** which are even less accessible due to regulations barring vehicles (including mountain bikes). **Wilderness permits** (generally free) are required for backcountry hiking.

Many trailhead parking lots in Oregon and Washington National Forests require a Trail Park Pass ($5 per day per vehicle; annual pass $30). Passes are available at area outfitters and convenience stores, but not at trailheads.

The US Department of the Interior's **Bureau of Land Management (BLM)** offers a variety of outdoor recreation opportunities on the 270 million acres it oversees in ten western states, including camping, hiking, mountain biking, rock climbing, river rafting, and wildlife viewing. Unless otherwise posted, all public lands are open for recreational use. Write the Washington/Oregon office (☎503-808-6002) at PO Box 2965, Portland, OR 97208 or see their website www.or.blm.gov for a guide to BLM campgrounds, many of which are free.

WILDERNESS AREAS

The **Wilderness Act of 1964** established a federal system intended to provide the maximum level of preservation to incorporated parcels of land. Wilderness areas are sprinkled throughout the Pacific Northwest and include many coastal islands. For more info on restrictions and permits in specific regions, contact the agency responsible for managing the area. The **Wilderness Information Network** maintains a very useful website on US wilderness areas at www.wilderness.net.

STATE AND PROVINCIAL PARKS

In contrast to national parks, whose focus is on preservation, the primary function of state and provincial parks is usually recreation. Prices for camping at public sites are usually better than those at private campgrounds. Usually, state parks offer opportunities for motorized recreation, which often means **all-terrain vehicle (ATV)** use (**snowmobiling** in the winter) and **boating.** Many state parks in the Pacific Northwest feature lakes and other bodies of water. Don't let swarming visitors dissuade you from seeing the larger parks—these places can be huge, and even at their most crowded they offer opportunities for quiet and solitude. Most campgrounds are first come, first served, so arrive early. Some limit your stay and/or the number of people in a group. For general information, including **detailed websites** outlining the opportunities and policies at individual parks, contact:

Alberta Parks and Protected Areas, 9820 106 St., 2nd fl., Edmonton, AB T5K 2J6 (☎866-427-3582; www.gov.ab.ca/env/parks.html).

THE GREAT OUTDOORS

BC Parks, P.O. Box 9398, Stn. Prov. Govt., Victoria, BC V8W 9M9 (☎250-387-1161; http://wlapwww.gov.bc.ca/bcparks).

Oregon State Parks and Recreation Department, 725 Summer St. NE, Suite C, Salem, OR 97301 (☎800-551-6949 or 503-378-6305; www.prd.state.or.us).

Washington State Parks and Recreation Commission, 7150 Cleanwater Lane, P.O. Box 42650, Olympia, WA 98504, info ☎360-902-8844; www.parks.wa.gov).

CAMPING

Camping is probably the most rewarding way to slash travel costs. In some areas of the Pacific Northwest, it will also often be the most convenient option. Well-equipped campsites (usually including prepared tent sites, toilets, and potable water) go for $5-20 per night. In general, the more popular the park or forest, the better-equipped and the more expensive the established campgrounds. Most campsites are first come, first served, though a few accept reservations, usually for a small fee (see below for more info). Dispersed camping (camping anywhere outside of a designated campground) is usually not permitted in developed areas such as campgrounds, trailheads, or picnic areas. **Backcountry camping,** which lacks all amenities, is often free, but permits may be required in some national parks and may cost up to $20. Dispersed backcountry camping is usually inconvenient for those traveling by car, because it requires a long hike. It is not legal or safe to camp on the side of the road, even on public lands; *Let's Go* lists areas where dispersed roadside camping is permitted.

 A CAMPER'S BILL OF RIGHTS. While campground amenities vary largely, there are some features that we do not include in our campground listings. Unless we state otherwise, you can expect that every campground has water and toilets. If a campground has RV sites, you can also expect that it will have electrical hookups at some tent sites.

LEAVE NO TRACE

The idea behind environmentally responsible camping is to leave no trace of human presence behind. A portable **stove** is a safer way to cook than using vegetation to build a campfire, but if you must make a fire, keep it small and use only dead branches or brush rather than cutting live vegetation. Make sure your **campsite** is at least 150 ft. from the nearest water, be it a spring, a stream, or a lake. If there are no toilet facilities, bury **human waste** (but not paper, which should be packed out or burned with a lighter if used) at least 6 in. deep, but not more than 10 in., and 150 ft. or more from any water source or campsite. Always pack your **trash** in a plastic bag and carry it with you until you reach a trash receptacle.

RESERVATIONS

Though many campgrounds, both in national forests and national parks, are first come, first served, reservations can make travel much more relaxed and enjoyable. The **US National Forest Service** takes reservations through the **National Recreation Reservation Center,** offering easy online bookings as well (☎518-885-3639 or 877-444-6777; www.reserveusa.com). Camping reservations require a $10 service fee for National Forest Service sites and are available for most forests, though they are often unnecessary except during high season at the most popular sites. You can email or call up to 240 days in advance to reserve individual campsites, or 360 days for cabins or group facilities. The **National Park Reservation Service** (☎800-365-2267 or 301-722-1257; http://reservations.nps.gov) takes reservations for campgrounds in Olympic and Rainier National Parks and at

Fort Clatsop National Memorial. Campgrounds are reservable starting five months in advance. There is no fee for this service. For info on USFS campgrounds, cabins, and fire lookouts in Washington and Oregon not listed with the nationwide network, contact **Nature of the Northwest**, 800 NE Oregon St. #177, Portland, OR (☎503-872-2750; www.naturenw.org).

Many **state park** campsites also take reservations. The Oregon state parks info line (☎800-452-5687; www.prd.state.or.us) and its Washington equivalent (☎800-233-0321; www.parks.wa.gov) provide info on state parks, including those not listed with the reservations center, and can refer callers to the agencies responsible for all other campsites in the state. **BC Discover Camping** (☎800-689-9025 or 604-689-9025; www.discovercamping.ca) reserves sites at many of the BC provincial parks (CDN$12-20 per night; reservation fee CDN$6.42 per night for first 3 nights). For info on other, non-reservable provincial park campsites, call ☎250-387-4550. **Supernatural British Columbia** (☎800-663-6000; www.hellobc.com) can refer you to private campgrounds throughout BC. For info on campground reservations in Alberta parks, contact the **Alberta Campsite Reservation Service** (☎866-427-3582; www.cd.gov.ab.ca/enjoying_alberta/parks/planning/camping/campres.asp).

ATTRACTION	WHERE TO FIND IT
HIKING	• The steep and untouched forest trails of tourist-free **Marble Range Provincial Park** in British Columbia (p. 321). • **Tweedsmuir Provincial Park,** wandering in solitude past waterfalls, mountain lakes, and old-growth forests (p. 387).
SKIING / SNOW-BOARDING	• **Whistler Blackcomb**'s one vertical mile of powder paradise; Blackcomb Glacier is open through Aug. (p. 318). • **Mount Baker,** arguably the birthplace of snowboarding, promises fresh powder 6 months of the year (p. 220). • **Fernie Alpine Resort,** with over 2400 acres of terrain and 9m (29 ft.) average snowfall (p. 374).
WATER SPORTS	• **Sechelt Rapids,** where the tidal flow creates churning whirlpools for only the most experienced kayakers (p. 316). • In the Columbia River Gorge at **Hood River,** whose 30 mph winds are revered by windsurfers (p. 96). • Oregon's aptly-named **Rogue River,** where expert paddlers take on Class III and IV rapids (p. 140).
VIEWS AND VISTAS	• The permanently snowcapped **Mount Rainier,** 14,411 ft. and nearly as many views on its 240 mi. of trails (p. 273). • The breathtaking jagged peaks of **Mount Washington** as seen from Rte. 126 in Oregon (p. 136).
WILDLIFE	• BC's **Okanagan Lake** area, where the sea monster "Ogopogo" is said to make periodic appearances (p. 366). • The waters off **San Juan Island,** where 3 pods of orcas make a routine passage through the Haro Strait (p. 225).
HORSE-BACK RIDING	• The lush forest trails of **Wells Gray National Park,** where you can even participate in a cattle drive (p. 355). • On the isolated, cliff-lined beaches of **Bandon** on the Southern Oregon coast (p. 125).
BIKING	• Through glaciers from Jasper to Banff along the grueling Hwy. 93, better known as the **Icefields Parkway** (p. 447). • In summer on **Calgary's** deserted alpine ski slopes, former home of 1988 Olympic glory (p. 425).
BUNGEE	• At **Nanaimo, BC's** bungee bridge, where the truly hardcore can join in the annual naked jump (p. 341).

ATTRACTION		WHERE TO FIND IT
	CAVING	• At the **Oregon Caves National Monument,** where visitors wind through glistening marble caverns (p. 140). • The former lava tube of **Ape Cave** near Mt. St. Helens, one of the longest in the world at almost 13,000 ft. (p. 269).
	CLIMBING	• On active volcano Mt. St. Helens—beat the crowds by taking the **Monitor Ridge** route at 4am, and you'll be rewarded by a glorious sunrise behind distant Mt. Adams (p. 269).

EQUIPMENT

WHAT TO BUY...

Good camping equipment is worth the investment, because a leaky tent or poorly fitting boots can be annoying, painful, and downright dangerous. North American suppliers tend to offer the most competitive prices.

Sleeping Bags: Most sleeping bags are rated by season, or the lowest outdoor temperature at which they will keep you warm; "summer" means 30-40°F (around 0°C) at night; "four-season" or "winter" often means below 0°F (-17°C). Bags are made of **down** (warm, light, and packable, but more expensive and miserable when wet) or of **synthetic** material (heavy, more durable, and warmer when wet). Prices range from $50-250 for a summer synthetic to $200-300 for a good down winter bag. **Sleeping bag pads** include foam pads ($10-30), air mattresses ($15-50), and self-inflating mats ($30-120), all of which cushion your back and neck and insulate you from the ground. Bring a **stuff sack** to store your bag and keep it dry.

Tents: The best (sturdiest) tents are free-standing (with their own frames and suspension systems), set up quickly, and only require staking in high winds. Low-profile dome tents are the best all-around; their internal space is almost entirely usable, which means little unnecessary bulk. Tent sizes can be somewhat misleading: 2 people can fit in a 2-person tent but will find life more pleasant in a 4-person. If you're traveling by car, go for the bigger tent, but if you're hiking, stick with a smaller tent that weighs no more than 4-6 lbs. (2-3kg). Worthy 2-person tents start at $100, 4-person at $160. Make sure your tent has a **rain fly,** and seal its seams with waterproofer. Other useful accessories include a **battery-operated lantern,** a plastic **groundcloth,** and a nylon **tarp. Mosquito netting** is important during the summer bug season. In any event, keep in mind that **bears** will be attracted to brightly-colored or oddly-shaped tents. For more info on bear safety, see **Bear Safety, p. 62.**

Backpacks: Internal-frame packs mold well to your back, keep a lower center of gravity, and flex enough to allow you to hike difficult trails that require a lot of bending and maneuvering, while **external-frame packs** are more comfortable for long hikes over even terrain, as they carry weight higher and distribute it more evenly. If your trip involves significant numbers of flights, consider an **"adventure travel" pack,** which is designed to weather baggage handling systems as well as wilderness. Companies such as NorthFace and Lowe-Alpine make durable models. Make sure your pack has a strong, padded hip-belt to transfer weight to your legs instead of your back. There are models designed specifically for women. Any serious backpacking requires a pack of at least 4000 cu. in. (16,000cc), plus 500 cu. in. for sleeping bags in internal-frame packs. Sturdy backpacks cost anywhere from $125-420—your pack is an area where it doesn't pay to economize, and cheaper packs may be less comfortable or durable. On your hunt for the perfect pack, fill up a prospective model with something heavy, strap it on correctly, and walk around the store to get a sense of how the pack distributes weight. Either buy a **rain cover** ($10-20) or store all of your belongings in plastic bags inside your pack.

Boots: Be sure to wear hiking boots with good **ankle support** that are appropriate for the terrain you plan to hike. **Gore-Tex** fabric and part-leather boots are appropriate for day hikes or 2- or 3-day overnight trips over moderate terrain, but for longer trips, or trips in mountainous terrain, stiffer **leather** boots are highly preferable. Your boots should fit snugly and comfortably over 1 or 2 wool socks and a thin liner sock. Breaking in boots properly before setting out requires wearing them for several weeks; doing so will spare you from painful and debilitating blisters. Waterproof your boots with wax or waterproofing treatment before going out in the woods. If they get wet, dry them slowly. Though it may feel good to rest them close to the campfire, intense heat can crack the leather and damage the adhesive bonding of the soles.

Water Purification and Transport: When venturing out from developed campgrounds that have potable water, you will need to carry water and purify any that you might find along the trail. Because **giardia** (p. 73) can wreak havoc on the digestive system, even water taken from the cleanest backcountry spring must be purified. **Boiling** water for 3-5min. is the most effective, though not the most convenient, method of purification, and works even at high altitudes. Though iodine- and chlorine-containing tablets are the cheapest method of purification, they will not rid water of its muck or its characteristic taste, and it can be unhealthy to consume iodine tablets over a long period of time. Furthermore, neither chlorine nor iodine reliably kill giardia in every case. Portable **water filters** pump out a crystal-clear product but often require careful maintenance and extra disposable filters. Do not ever pump dirty water unless you want to repeatedly clean or replace clogged filter cartridges. For transport, plastic **canteens** or water bottles keep water cooler than metal ones do, and are virtually shatter and leak proof. Large plastic **water bags** or **bladders** can hold up to several gallons and are perfect for long-haul travel. Bladders weigh practically nothing when empty, though they are bulky when full.

Other Necessities: Raingear in 2 pieces, a top and pants, is far superior to a poncho. **Gore-Tex** is the best material if you are doing aerobic activities and need breathable raingear; **rubber** raingear will keep you completely dry but will get clammy if you sweat. For warm layers, **synthetics,** like polypropylene or polyester tops, socks, and long underwear, along with a fleece or pile jacket work well because they keep you warm even when wet and dry quickly. **Wool** also stays warm (and smells awful) when wet, but is much heavier. Never rely on **cotton** for warmth. In the wild, this "death cloth" will be absolutely useless should it get wet. When camping in autumn, winter, or spring, bring along a **"space blanket,"** which helps you to retain your body heat and doubles as a groundcloth ($5-15). Though many campgrounds provide campfire sites, you will probably want to bring a **camp stove,** especially for places that forbid fires or wood gathering. Propane-powered Coleman stoves start at about $50; the more expensive **Whisperlite** stoves ($60-100), which run on cleaner-burning white gas, are lighter and more versatile. You may also want to bring a small **metal grate** or **grill** of your own. You'll need to purchase a **fuel bottle** and fill it with fuel to operate stoves. A **first-aid kit, Swiss army knife, insect repellent, calamine lotion, waterproof matches** or a **lighter, duct tape,** and **large plastic garbage bags** are other essential supplies. **Fishing gear** is a good idea even if you don't normally fish very often, just in case the many Northwest lakes and streams prove too much of a temptation or you happen to run out of food while camping.

...AND WHERE TO BUY IT

The mail-order/online companies listed below offer lower prices than many retail stores, but a visit to a local camping or outdoors store will give you a good sense of items' look and weight. Many local outdoor stores also have message boards where used equipment can be found. Keep in mind that these locations do not specialize in **fishing** or **hunting** equipment. Local **sporting goods shops** are often excellent sources of information on the outdoors scene.

THE GREAT OUTDOORS

Campmor, 28 Parkway, P.O. Box 700, Upper Saddle River, NJ 07458 (US ☎888-226-7667, outside US call 201-825-8300; www.campmor.com).

Discount Camping, 880 Main North Rd., Pooraka, SA 5095, Australia (☎08 8262 3399; www.discountcamping.com.au).

Eastern Mountain Sports (EMS), 1 Vose Farm Rd., Peterborough, NH 03458 (☎888-463-6367 or 603-924-7231; www.ems.com). Call to locate the branch nearest you.

L.L. Bean, Freeport, ME 04033 (US/Canada ☎800-441-5713; UK 0800 891 297; elsewhere, call US 207-552-3028; www.llbean.com). Refunds and replaces products that don't meet your expectations. The main store and 800 number are both open 24hr.

Mountain Designs, 51 Bishop St., Kelvin Grove QLD 4059, Australia (☎07 3856 2344; www.mountaindesigns.com).

Recreational Equipment, Inc. (REI), Sumner, WA 98352 (US/Canada ☎800-426-4840 or 253-891-2500; www.rei.com).

YHA Adventure Shop, 19 High St., Staines Middlesex, TW18, UK (☎1784 458625; www.yhaadventure.com), is one of Britain's largest equipment suppliers.

ON THE ROAD IN THE PACIFIC NORTHWEST

BEFORE YOU HIT THE ROAD

Membership in an auto club, which provides free emergency roadside assistance 24hr. per day, is the way to go for anyone planning to drive on a vacation. The **American Automobile Association (AAA)** and its Canadian branch **(CAA)** have reciprocal agreements, so a membership in either is good for road service in Canada and the US. Both organizations have the same emergency phone number: ☎800-AAA-HELP/800-222-4357. A basic annual membership is around $40-70 and includes limited free towing, travelers checks, discounts on Amtrak tickets, Hertz rentals, and certain motel chains. Call ☎800-564-6222 or visit www.aaa.com or www.caa.ca to sign up.

It is a good idea to have your car checked over by a mechanic for any potential failure points a few weeks before you depart, to allow time to fix any problems. Learning how to **change a tire** before you hit the highway is also an excellent idea.

Logging and service roads change drastically over time. Certain roads should not be attempted unless you have a **4WD vehicle**—inquire locally to find out about the condition of backroads, and also make sure that your own travels don't conflict with **active logging operations.**

In order to make minor repairs on your car, or to keep it moving after a problem, you will need to carry several tools, including a wrench, flashlights (a regular flashlight and a pen light), screwdrivers, and pliers. Other vital items include extra oil, extra coolant, a jack, a tire iron, a full-sized spare tire, extra gasoline, extra clean water, a tire pressure gauge, road flares, hose sealant, a first-aid kit (p. 26), jumper cables, fan belts, extra windshield washer fluid, plastic sheeting, string or rope, a larger tow rope, duct tape, an ice scraper, rags, a funnel, a spray bottle filled with glass cleaner, a compass, matches, and blankets and food. Even if you don't have a tow hitch, or are traveling alone, carry along a tow rope. Having one on hand will make it easier for others who find you to help get you out of your jam.

ON-ROAD DANGERS

On a long stretch of unexciting road, it's easy to zone out and not be on the lookout for crossing **elk, deer, moose, caribou,** or **bears** who call the roadside wilderness of the Pacific Northwest home. Also be aware of the potential hazards of narrow, gravel, or unpaved roads and steep grades, especially in national parks. Speeding, while never a brilliant idea, is especially inadvisable on this kind of road; the faster you are going, the harder it is to control your car should you begin to skid. Watch out for large trucks or RVs on both small roads and major highways; stones flung up from their wheels can chip or crack your windshield. Always keep your **headlights** on while driving on this kind of road—on a narrow or winding road, they will alert oncoming drivers to your presence.

OVERHEATING

Summer can bring high levels of heat during the day. Take **several gallons of clean water** with you. You should also carry a gallon of **additional coolant** along with you. Coolant needs to be mixed with water after being poured into the radiator, so don't substitute water with more coolant—take both. Turning off the A/C and turning on the heat can help prevent overheating. In case of overheating, pull over. If the radiator fluid is steaming, turn off the car for at least 30min. Otherwise, run it in neutral for a few minutes to circulate coolant.

If you open your radiator cap, always wait 45min. or more until the coolant inside of the radiator loses its heat. Even after waiting, you may still be spattered with warm coolant, so stand to the side whenever opening your radiator cap. Remember that 'topping off' your radiator does not mean filling it completely. Instead, there is probably a tank or reservoir with a filling indicator somewhere near the radiator. Pour a small amount of water and coolant into the radiator (in a 50/50 mixture) and wait for it to work its way into the system and raise the reservoir. Some vehicles need the engine to run in order to draw the coolant in.

BATTERY FAILURES AND FLUBS

To safely jump start your vehicle, position the two cars close to one another while making sure that there is no contact between them. Set the emergency brakes and turn off both engines before you open the hoods. Identify the positive posts on both batteries and attach the **red cable** to both posts. Do not let the red clips contact the clips on the black cable. Attach one clip on the **black cable** to the negative post on the working battery, and then attach the other clip to bare metal on the disabled vehicle's engine frame, as far as possible from the battery—otherwise, the battery's hydrogen gas could ignite. Start the working vehicle, and rev it for a few moments before starting the disabled vehicle. Once both vehicles are running, disconnect the cables in reverse order (do not kill the engines or allow the cables to contact one another until they are completely disconnected), starting with the black cable attached to the bare metal. Afterwards, drive around for 30min. or more to allow the alternator to recharge the battery.

WILDERNESS SAFETY

GENERAL WISDOM

Stay warm, dry, and **hydrated.** The vast majority of life-threatening wilderness situations result from a breach of this simple dictum. On any hike, however brief, you should pack enough equipment to keep you alive should disaster befall you. This includes **raingear, hat** and **mittens, a first-aid kit, a reflector, a whistle, high energy food,** and **extra water.** Be prepared for potential dramatic shifts in weather—the north is notorious for its capricious climate. On any trip of significant length, you should always carry a **compass** and a detailed **topographic map** of the area where you are hiking, preferably an official map from the US Geological Survey. Check the map's publication and update dates, though. Sometimes, private vendors will have more recent data than the USGS maps. Dress warmly and in layers (see p. 69). Weather can change suddenly anywhere in the region, and in the higher peaks it can snow any time of the year. Check **weather forecasts** and pay attention to the skies when hiking. Whenever possible, hike in groups or with a partner. Hiking alone greatly magnifies the risks of traveling in the wilderness. Always be sure to let someone know when and where you are hiking. In very

> **MY KINGDOM FOR A MAP.** One of the most neglected tenets of wilderness safety is carrying maps wherever you go. When hiking, biking, climbing, or camping, you should ALWAYS carry a compass and use a set of detailed topographical maps. The **United States Geological Survey,** 47914 252nd St., Sioux Falls, SD 57198 (☎800-252-4547; http://edc.usgs.gov/products/map.html), sells indispensable 7½min. and 15min. topo maps. **Trails Illustrated,** affiliated with National Geographic (☎800-962-1643; www.trailsillustrated.com), sells larger topo maps of the Oregon and Washington's parks and other public lands. **DeLorme** (www.delorme.com/atlasgaz) sells paper topographic maps of US states at a scale useful for larger overviews. In Canada, **Map Town,** 100-400 5th Ave SW, Calgary, AB T2P 0L6 (☎877-921-6277 or 402-266-2241; www.maptown.com) has a wide array of topographic maps in 2 scales.

remote areas, it may be advisable to carry a **GPS emergency beacon.** Be warned that once you activate the beacon, a very serious search will be launched for you that may endanger your rescuers and cost over $100,000. Make sure that any beacon you purchase works for the regions of you wish to visit.

THE NORTHWEST AND YOU

If you are planning to do extensive backcountry hiking or camping, it is important to be prepared for potential crisis situations.

ENVIRONMENTAL HAZARDS

The Pacific Northwest can be a region of extreme climates, reaching temperatures of 10°F (-12°C) the winter and 100°F (38°C) in the summer. Surprisingly unseasonable weather can be created by the combination of mountain ranges and the Pacific Ocean, leading to balmy winters or snowbanks in August. Temperature fluctuations are common in some areas, so it's important to be prepared for a variety of weather-related hazards.

Heat exhaustion and dehydration: Heat exhaustion leads to fatigue, nausea, excessive thirst, headaches, and dizziness. Avoid it by drinking plenty of fluids, eating salty foods (e.g., crackers), abstaining from dehydrating beverages (e.g., alcohol and caffeinated beverages), and always wearing sunscreen. Drinking large quantities of water to quench your thirst after physical exertion is not as effective as taking preventative measures to stay hydrated. Whether you are driving or hiking, tote **1½ gallons of water per person per day** in the summer. Designate at least 1 container as an emergency supply, and always have water at your side. In the car, keep backup containers in a cooler. When drinking sweet beverages, dilute them with water to avoid an over-reaction to high sugar content. For long-term stays, a high-quality beverage with potassium compounds and glucose, such as ERG (an industrial-strength Gatorade available from camping suppliers) will help keep your strength up. Continuous heat stress can eventually lead to heatstroke, characterized by a rising temperature, severe headache, delirium, and cessation of sweating. Victims should be cooled off with wet towels and taken to a doctor.

Sunburn: Always wear sunscreen (SPF 30 is good) when spending excessive amounts of time outdoors. If you are planning on spending time near water, in the desert, or in the snow, you are at a higher risk of getting burned, even through clouds. If you get sunburned, drink more fluids than usual and apply an aloe-based lotion. Severe sunburns can lead to sun poisoning, a condition that affects the entire body, causing fever, chills, nausea, and vomiting. Sun poisoning should always be treated by a doctor. Glare from the sun can also cause sunburn and **snow blindness,** making sunblock, a hat, and sunglasses with 100% UV protection a must when visiting glaciers or snow fields.

Hypothermia and frostbite: A rapid drop in body temperature is the clearest sign of overexposure to cold. Victims may also shiver, feel exhausted, have poor coordination or slurred speech, hallucinate, or suffer amnesia. **Do not let hypothermia victims fall asleep.** To avoid hypothermia, keep dry, wear layers, and stay out of the wind. When the temperature is below freezing, watch out for frostbite. If skin turns white or blue, waxy, and cold, do not rub the area. Drink warm beverages, stay dry, and slowly warm the area with dry fabric or steady body contact until a doctor can be found. **Do not drink alcohol.** It will make you feel warmer, but alcohol also impairs circulation and increases the risk of death from hypothermia. While the entire region gets extremely cold in the winter, Northern British Columbia and Alberta are especially frigid.

High altitude: Allow your body a couple of days to adjust to less oxygen before exerting yourself. Altitude sickness can be marked by coughing, severe headaches, nausea, and vomiting. If you experience altitude sickness, descend until it subsides and re-ascend at a slower pace. Alcohol is more potent and UV rays are stronger at high elevations.

INSECT- AND ANIMAL-BORNE DISEASES

Many diseases are transmitted by insects—mainly mosquitoes, fleas, ticks, and lice. Be aware of insects in wet or forested areas, especially while hiking and camping; wear long pants and long sleeves, tuck your pants into your socks, and use a mosquito net. Use insect repellents such as DEET and soak or spray your gear with permethrin (licensed in the US for use on clothing).

Lyme disease: A bacterial infection carried by ticks and marked by a circular bull's-eye rash of 2 in. or more. Later symptoms include fever, headache, fatigue, and aches and pains. Antibiotics are effective if administered early. Left untreated, Lyme can cause problems in joints, the heart, and the nervous system. **Ticks**—responsible for a variety of potentially fatal diseases, including Lyme disease, tick paralysis, and Rocky Mountain spotted fever—can be particularly dangerous in rural and forested regions. Be on the lookout for them while camping or hiking in any part of the Pacific Northwest. If you find a tick attached to your skin, grasp the head with tweezers as close to your skin as possible and apply slow, steady traction. Removing a tick within 24hr. greatly reduces the risk of infection. Do not try to remove ticks by burning them or coating them with nail polish remover or petroleum jelly.

Giardiasis: An intestinal disease transmitted through parasites (microbes, tapeworms, etc. in contaminated water and food) and acquired by drinking untreated water from streams or lakes. Symptoms include diarrhea, abdominal cramps, bloating, fatigue, weight loss, and nausea. If untreated it can lead to severe dehydration. (See **Water Purification and Transport,** p. 69).

Rabies: Transmitted through the saliva of infected animals; often fatal if untreated. By the time symptoms (thirst and muscle spasms) appear, the disease is in its terminal stage. If you are bitten, wash the wound thoroughly, seek immediate medical care, and try to have the animal located. A rabies vaccine, which consists of 3 shots given over a 21-day period, is available but only semi-effective. In the US and Canada, rabies is rarely found in dogs; it is usually transmitted by bats or wild carnivores.

FURTHER READING: WILDERNESS SAFETY

How to Stay Alive in the Woods, Bradford Angier. Macmillan ($10).
Everyday Wisdom: 1001 Expert Tips for Hikers, Karen Berger. Mountaineer ($17).

THE GREAT OUTDOORS

The Outdoor Survival Handbook, Paul Bryan, et al. St. Martin's Press ($15).

Making Camp, Steve Howe, et al. Mountaineer ($17).

Practical Outdoor Survival: A Modern Approach, Len McDougall. Lyons Press ($17).

NATURAL DISASTERS

AVALANCHES. Avalanches present the most commonly encountered serious natural disaster in the Pacific Northwest. There are many factors that can contribute to the onset of an avalanche, such as slope shape and steepness, depth of snow, weather, and temperature. While some avalanches are natural, many are the result of human disturbance. A loud noise, or the added weight of skis or a snowmobile could trigger an avalanche, especially if the snow is melting or light and powdery. In case of an avalanche, discard all your equipment and seek shelter behind rocks, trees, or vehicles. Cover your nose and mouth and brace for impact. When the avalanche has stopped, try to dig yourself out and call out for rescuers if you can. If your companions are caught, call ☎911 or the local emergency number, mark the place where they were last seen, and do not leave the site until help arrives. During the winter, always check with local authorities such as park rangers for avalanche conditions before setting out.

LANDSLIDES/MUDSLIDES. Heavy rain, flooding, or snow runoff combined with hilly terrain can lead to landslides or mudslides, particularly on slopes where vegetation or trees have been removed. This will most likely not be a concern in the city; however, if you are hiking after a period of extensive rainfall, be aware of the possibility of a slide. If you are caught in a mudslide or landslide, try to get out of its path and run to the nearest high ground or shelter. If escape is not possible, curl into a small ball and protect your head.

FOREST FIRES. The summer of 2004 marked the 5th consecutive year of drought for much of the West. In 2003, forest fires ravaged much of the eastern Cascades, as well as parts of eastern Oregon and British Columbia. If you are hiking or camping and smell smoke, see flames, or hear fire, leave the area immediately. To prevent forest fires, always make sure campfires are completely extinguished; during high levels of fire danger, campfires will probably be prohibited. Before you hike or camp, be sure to check with local authorities for the level of fire danger in the area.

ORGANIZED TRIPS AND OUTFITTERS

Organized adventure tours offer another way of exploring the wild. Stores and organizations specializing in camping and outdoors equipment can often provide good info on trips (p. 69). Sales reps at REI, EMS, or Sierra often know of a range of cheap, convenient trips. They may also offer training programs for travelers.

When choosing an **outfitter** for a day or multi-day trip, check into their credentials and qualifications. Check local **visitors centers** for lists of established, experienced, and credentialed guide services, and weigh your options before trusting life and limb to a person you have never met before. For a list of outdoors programs with a more academic focus, see **Classroom Outdoors** (p. 53).

BC Wilderness Tourism Association, P.O. Box 1483, Gibsons, BC V0N 1V0, Canada (☎604-886-8755; www.wilderness-tourism.bc.ca). This website provides listings of wilderness tours in BC and beyond.

G.A.P. Adventures, 335 Eglinton Ave. East, Toronto, Ontario M5H 3H1, Canada (☎800-465-5600 US and Canada only; www.gapadventures.com). Small group travel with emphasis on adventure and responsibility toward locals. Average price $1800.

Earthfoot (www.earthfoot.org). A web-based organization focused on "people to people travel" that lists small (1-6 people), local tours, including many in the Pacific Northwest. You can also use the site to contact a tour guide based on your individual interests.

The National Outdoor Leadership School (NOLS), 284 Lincoln St., Lander, WY 82520 (☎800-710-6657 or 307-332-5300; www.nols.edu/courses/locations/pacificnw). Summer sessions at their 30-acre Pacific Northwest headquarters in Conway, WA teach outdoor leadership, with a strong emphasis on skill development. Training in wilderness medicine also possible. Apply at least 3 months in advance. Programs typically last 1 month ($2200) or 3 months ($8700). Financial aid and scholarships possible. Some colleges accept credit.

Outward Bound Wilderness Expeditions, 100 Mystery Point Rd., Garrison, NY 10524 (☎866-467-7651 or 720-497-2340; www.outwardboundwilderness.com). Outward Bound courses in Washington and Oregon last from 4 days ($600) to 3 months ($9000); they sometimes provide financial aid and scholarships. Similar to NOLS but with more of an emphasis on emotional development than on skills.

The Sierra Club, 85 Second St., 2nd Fl. San Francisco, CA 94105 (☎415-977-5500; www.sierraclub.org/outings), plans many adventure outings at all of its branches throughout the US, including the Northwest.

Specialty Travel Index, 305 San Anselmo Ave., #313, San Anselmo, CA 94960 (US ☎800-442-4922, elsewhere 415-459-4900; www.specialtytravel.com), is a directory listing tour operators worldwide.

TrekAmerica, P.O. Box 189, Rockaway, NJ 07866 (☎800-221-0596; www.trekamerica.com), which recently merged with AmeriCan Adventures, operates small group active adventure tours throughout the US. These tours are for 18 to 38-year-olds and run from 1 to 9 weeks. Typical cost of $450 per week usually includes transportation and campground fees but not food.

OUTDOOR TRAVEL PUBLICATIONS

A variety of publishing companies offer outdoors guidebooks to meet the educational needs of novice or expert. For **books** about camping, hiking, biking, and climbing, write or call the publishers listed below to receive a free catalog.

Falcon Guides, Globe Pequot Press, P.O. Box 480, Guilford, CT 06437 (☎888-249-7586; www.globepequot.com). Over 1000 guides to many different outdoor-related activities. Many of the books are organized by activity and state, so they are best for the focused traveler.

The Milepost, P.O. Box 1668, Augusta, GA 30903 (☎800-726-4707; www.themilepost.com). An annual trip planning publication—best for home turf Alaska, but also useful in British Columbia and Alberta.

The Mountaineers Books, 1001 SW Klickitat Way, Ste. 201, Seattle, WA 98134 (☎206-223-6303; www.mountaineersbooks.org). Boasts over 500 titles on hiking, biking, mountaineering, natural history, and conservation.

Sierra Club Books, 85 Second St., 2nd fl., San Francisco, CA 94105 (☎415-977-5500; www.sierraclub.org/books). Publishes general resource books on hiking and camping, and provides advice for women traveling in the outdoors, as well as books on hiking in British Columbia, The Pacific, and The Rockies.

Wilderness Press, 1200 5th St., Berkeley, CA 94710 (☎800-443-7227 or 510-558-1666; www.wildernesspress.com). Carries over 100 hiking guides and maps, with dozens for destination in the Pacific Northwest.

Woodall Publications Corporation, 2575 Vista Del Mar Dr., Ventura, CA 93001 (☎877-680-6155; www.woodalls.com). Annually updates campground directories, with extensive coverage of many Pacific Northwest parks.

THE GREAT OUTDOORS

GREAT OUTDOORS GLOSSARY

Although English is the language of choice throughout the Pacific Northwest, you may find that its population of hikers, skiers, climbers, and assorted wilderness-lovers speak a dialect all their own. Let's Go provides the following glossary to help you blend in with the local adventurers and keep your scramble (as in breakfast) and scramble (as in mountain) straight.

ATV. Stands for "all-terrain vehicle"; a small motor-propelled vehicle with wheels or tractor treads for traveling over rough ground, snow, or ice. In the Northwest, you'll most likely hear these noisy jalopies before you see them at campsites near places like the Oregon Dunes.

BELAY. As a verb, to secure the climber. The belayer stands at the bottom of the climb with a rope and anchor. When the belayer is ready, he shouts "belay on," indicating that the climber is secured.

CHEMICAL TOILET. Found in certain campgrounds, this type of non-flushing toilet controls odors and sanitizes through chemicals in the retaining tank.

GORE-TEX. Waterproof and windproof fabric that is the de facto uniform for Northwest residents and visitors alike. Prides itself on being durable and breathable—don't head to the wilderness without it!

GORP. The hiker's Breakfast of Champions, made up of nuts, dried fruit, M&Ms, seeds, etc. Legend says it stands for "Good Old Raisins and Peanuts" but it is basically any type of trail mix.

LEAD/LEAD CLIMB. To ascend a climb from the bottom up, placing or clipping protection as you go along.

MORAINE. An accumulation of rocks and other debris deposited by a glacier.

PIT TOILET. Found in many campgrounds throughout the US, a pit toilet is basically an outhouse. These can be compost toilets as well, wherein the waste product naturally decomposes in a confined area (often a pit.) Both of these are "dry"—no running water involved.

SCRAMBLE. A slope steep enough to require the use of all four limbs to scale it, but not steep enough to qualify as rock climbing. Also a common breakfast offering in Eugene, OR's many organic restaurant establishments.

SCREE. Loose rocks covering a slope. Progress over scree frequently involves climbing 2 ft. up and sliding 1 ft. down.

TOP ROPE. Free climbing a route that has the safety rope attached to the top of the climb. Hands, feet, and natural holds are used to scale the climb—the rope is only used for safety, and not for climbing assistance.

YURT. Stronger and more weather-tight than a tent, a yurt is the modern adaptation of an ancient nomadic dwelling. Your basic yurt is circular-shaped, with a wooden frame and a cover made of durable fabric. Many Northwest campsites offer yurt camping.

THE GREAT OUTDOORS

OREGON

OREGON FACTS AND FIGURES
Capital: Salem. **Area:** 97,073 sq. mi. **Population:** 3,559,596.
Motto: "She flies with her own wings." **Nickname:** Beaver State.
State Animal: Beaver. **State Fish:** Chinook salmon. **State Nut:** Hazelnut.
State Rock: Thunderegg (a.k.a. geode). **State Shell:** Oregon Hairy Triton.

Discovered by Lewis and Clark on their overland expedition to the Pacific Ocean, Oregon (OR-uh-gun) soon became a hotbed of exploration and exploitation. Lured by plentiful forests and promises of gold and riches, entire families liquidated their assets and sank their life savings into covered wagons, corn meal, and oxen, hightailing it to Oregon (on the infamous "Oregon Trail") in search of prosperity and a new way of life. The resulting population of outdoors-enthusiasts and fledgling townspeople joined the Union in 1859, and has since become an eclectic mix of treehuggers and suave big-city types. Today, Oregon remains as popular a destination as ever for backpackers, cyclists, anglers, beachcrawlers, and families alike.

The wealth of space and natural resources that supported the prospectors and farmers of old continues to provide the backbone of Oregon today: close to half of Oregon's population is involved in some way with one of the most diversified agricultural centers in the US. More than half of Oregon's forests lie on federally owned land, hopefully preserving them for future generations of outdoor explorers. This obligation is constantly balanced against the needs of the 55,000 workers who depend on a timber industry that is threatened by over-logging, by the Endangered Species Act, and by disputes over ownership of the remaining land and rights. Nevertheless, Oregon deserves its environmentalist reputation, having created the country's first recycling refund program and spearheaded widescale preservation of line for public use.

The caves and cliffs of the coastline are a siren's song to Oregon's most precious non-natural resource: tourists. For those in search of big city life, Portland's laidback and idiosyncratic personality—its name was determined by a coin toss (the flip side would havve christened it "Boston, Oregon")—draws the microchip, mocha, and music crowds, while the college town of Eugene embraces hippies and Deadheads from around the West. With everything from excellent microbrews to untouched wilderness, Oregon is still worth crossing the Continental Divide for.

OREGON

HIGHLIGHTS OF OREGON

CRATER LAKE NATIONAL PARK protects a placid, azure pool in the maw of an ancient and enormous volcano (p. 155).

HIGH DESERT MUSEUM in Bend bolsters appreciation for nature (p. 148).

COLUMBIA RIVER GORGE cuts a stunning chasm on the OR-WA border (p. 99).

OREGON SHAKESPEARE FESTIVAL would make Will proud (p. 145).

CANNON BEACH with its silky soft sand is the ultimate seaside getaway (p. 109).

DUNE BUGGIES gear it up in Oregon Dunes National Recreation Area (p. 119).

PORTLAND'S ROSE GARDEN blooms high above the "City of Roses" (p. 90).

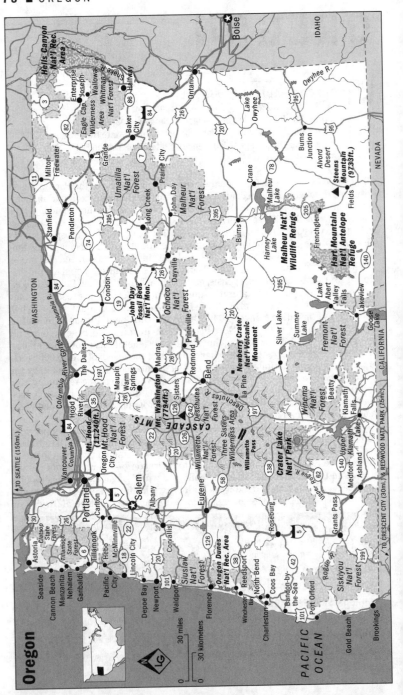

Oregon

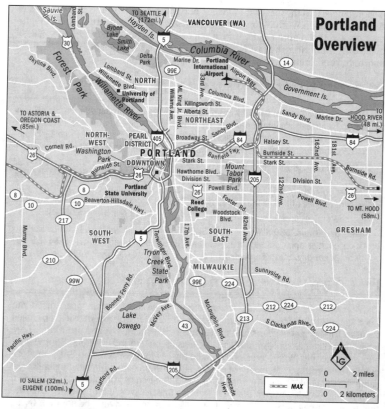

Portland Overview

PORTLAND

☎ 503

As a recent spate of "Best Places to Live" awards attests, Portland is no longer the secret it once was. With over 250 parks, the pristine Willamette River, and snow-capped Mt. Hood in the background, the City of Roses basks in natural beauty. An award-winning transit system and pedestrian-friendly streets make it feel more like a pleasantly overgrown town than a crowded metropolis. Yet with nearly two million residents, a respectable set of skyscrapers downtown, and industry giants Nike and Intel, Portland is a thriving member of the West Coast economy.

When the rain and clouds clear—and they do, in summer—lovers of the outdoors reap the visual and recreational rewards of the nearby Oregon Coast and Cascades. Closer to town, the spectacular attractions of Washington Park are a brief car or light rail ride away from downtown. Beyond natural and scenic beauty, Portland is home to dozens of galleries in the Pearl District, as well as the Portland Museum of Art and public art all over downtown.

The home of the Western Culinary Institute, Portland has many fine restaurants, some of which are easily affordable for the budget traveler. The city's orchestra, the oldest in the United States, maintains the traditional side of Portland's cultural scene. In the rainy season, Portlanders flood pubs and clubs, where musicians often strum, sing, or spin for cheap or free. In the summer, music from outdoor performances fills the air from Pioneer Courthouse Square to the concert lawn of the Oregon Zoo in Washington Park. Improvisational theaters are in constant production, and the talented and/or brave can chime in at open-mic night, in vogue all over town. And throughout it all, America's best beer pours from the taps in the microbrewery capital of the US.

⊠ INTERCITY TRANSPORTATION

Flights: Portland International Airport (☎460-4234; www.portlandairportpdx.com) is served by almost every major airline. The airport is connected to the city center by the **MAX Red Line,** an efficient light rail system (38min.; every 15min. daily 5am-11:30pm; $1.55). Taxis are also available (see **Local Transportation,** below). Airport code: PDX.

Trains: Amtrak, 800 NW 6th Ave. (☎273-4866; reservations ☎800-872-7245 or through www.amtrak.com), at Irving St. in historic Union Station, built in 1896. Ticket counter open daily 7:45am-9pm. Prices vary based on dates of departure and arrival; be sure to check the website. To: **Eugene** (2½hr.; 3 per day; $18-30); **San Francisco** (19hr.; daily; $61-118, sleeper $280-330); **Seattle** (4hr.; 4 per day; $24-38).

Buses: Greyhound, 550 NW 6th Ave. (☎800-454-2487), at NW Glisan by Union Station. Ticket counter open 5am-1am. To: **Eugene** (2½-3½hr., 9 per day, $15); **Seattle** (3-4½hr., 9 per day, $21); **Spokane** (7-11½hr., 5 per day, $40). Lockers $5 per day.

⊡ LOCAL TRANSPORTATION

The award-winning **Tri-Met bus system** is one of the most logically organized and rider-friendly public transit systems in America. The downtown **transit mall,** closed to all traffic but pedestrians and buses, lies between SW 5th and 6th Ave., where over 30 covered passenger shelters serve as stops and info centers. Southbound buses stop along SW 5th Ave., northbound buses along SW 6th Ave. Bus routes are colored according to their **service areas,** each with its own whimsical insignia: red salmon, orange deer, yellow rose, green leaf, blue snow, purple rain, and brown beaver. Most of downtown is in the **Fareless Square,** where all public transportation is free. (Anywhere north or east of I-405, west of the river, and south of Irving St.) For directions and fares outside this zone, see **Public Transportation,** below.

Most downtown streets are **one-way.** The city's **Smart Parks** are common and well marked, providing plentiful parking downtown. (Near Pioneer Sq. $0.95 per hr., $3 per hr. after 4hr., $2 after 6pm, max. $12; weekends $5 per day.) Parking is cheaper farther from city center. **Tri-Met** is the best bet for day-long excursions downtown.

Public Transportation: Tri-Met, 701 SW 6th Ave. (☎238-7433; www.tri-met.org), in Pioneer Courthouse Sq. Open M-F 8:30am-5:30pm. Several information lines available: **Call-A-Bus** info system ☎231-3199; fare info 231-3198; TDD info 238-5811. Buses generally run 5am-midnight with reduced schedules on weekends. All buses and bus stops are marked with 1 of 7 symbols (see above) and offer public bike racks. Fare $1.30-1.60, disabled, ages 65 and older or 7-18 $0.60, under 7 free. Free downtown. All-day pass $4; 10 fares for $13. **MAX** (☎228-7246), based at the Customer Service Center, is Tri-Met's light-rail train running between downtown, Hillsboro in the west, and Gresham in the east. Clean and convenient, the MAX keeps pace with technology—electronic signs tell when the next train's coming at many stops. The airport is served by a line from the main line's "Beaverton" stop. Transfers from buses can be used to ride the MAX. Runs M-F about 4:30am-1:30am, Sa 5am-12:30am, Su 5am-11:30pm.

Taxis: Radio Cab (☎227-1212). **Broadway Cab** (☎227-1234). Both $2.50 base, $1.80 per mi. Airport to downtown $25-30. 24hr.

Car Rental: Crown Auto Rental, 1315 NE Sandy Blvd. (☎230-1103; www.crownauto-rental.com). Although it has a limited selection, Crown is by far the cheapest option for anyone under 25. 18-21 must have credit card and proof of insurance. 22-25 must have credit card. Transport from airport available upon request. Open M-F 8:30am-5pm or by appointment. From $20-60 per day, $110-275 per week, $199+ per week if under 21. **Rent-a-Wreck,** 1800 SE M.L. King Blvd. (☎233-2492 or 888-499-9111; www.rentawreck.com). Older cars. Will rent to drivers under 21. Open M-F 8am-5pm, weekends by appointment only. From $28 per day, $150 per week, with 100 free mi. per day. Under 25 surcharge $5 per day. **Dollar Rent-a-Car** (☎800-800-4000; www.dollar.com), at airport. Must be 25 with credit card or be 21 with proof of insurance and pay a $20 per day surcharge. Open 24hr. From $20 per day, $140 per week, unlimited mileage. Extra 15% airport fee.

AAA: 600 SW Market St. (☎222-6777 or 800-222-4357), between Broadway and 6th Ave., near the Portland State University campus. Open M-F 8:30am-5pm.

▓ ORIENTATION

Portland lies in the northwest corner of Oregon, near the confluence of the Willamette River (wih-LAM-it) and the Columbia River. **I-5** connects Portland to San Francisco (659 mi., 11-14hr.) and Seattle (179 mi.; 3-3½hr.), while **I-84** follows the route of the Oregon Trail through the Columbia River Gorge, heading along the Oregon-Washington border toward Boise, Idaho. West of Portland, **US 30** follows the Columbia downstream to Astoria, but **US 26** is the fastest way to the coast, connecting to US 101 between Cannon Beach and Seaside. **I-405** makes the west side of a loop around Portland with I-5 and links the loop to US 30 and 26.

Most street names in Portland carry one of five prefixes: **N, NE, NW, SE,** or **SW,** indicating in which part of the city the address is located. East and west are separated by the Willamette River, and **Burnside Street** divides north from south. **Williams Avenue** marks off north from northeast. The roads are organized as a grid: in general, numbered avenues run north-south, and named streets go east-west. The first one or two digits of an address on an east-west street generally reflect its position relative to numbered streets: 3813 Killingsworth St. will be near 38th St.

Portland is organized into a series of neighborhoods. Close to the city center, Northwest Portland is home to **Chinatown** and most of **Old Town,** which holds the highest concentration of Portland's nightclubs and bars. **Nob Hill** and the **Pearl District,** a neighborhood that used to be dominated by industry and warehouses, is now home to many of the chicest shops and galleries in the city. These neighborhoods are just north of Chinatown, on the other side of the park between NW 8th Ave. and NW Park Ave. The serene greenery of **Washington Park** is farther west. **Forest Park** is a huge wooded area that stretches along the river. Southwest Portland includes downtown, the southern end of Old Town, and a slice of the wealthier **West Hills** area. **Portland State University** shares a large, if dispersed, cultural center south of the city center with museums, concert halls, and theatres. Southeast Portland contains parks, factories, local businesses, residential areas of several socio-economic brackets, and a rich array of cafes, stores, theaters, and restaurants, particularly around **Hawthorne Boulevard** east of SE 33rd St. **Reed College,** with its wide green quadrangles and brick halls, lies deep within the southeast district at the end of **Woodstock Boulevard** (some might say appropriately), which has a distinct culture of its own. Northeast Portland is highly residential, but has pockets of activity; areas around **Killingsworth** and **Alberta Street** east of 99 East are currently undergoing gentrification as "hipsters" and restaurants flock to a once seedy area. The Northeast has few budget accommodations, so venturing out is a little more

OREGON

difficult. Some of the Northeast's biggest draws are near the river and include the Lloyd Center Shopping Mall and the Oregon Convention Center. The north of Portland is mostly residential and receives next to no tourist traffic.

🔲 PRACTICAL INFORMATION

TOURIST AND FINANCIAL SERVICES

Visitor Information: Portland Oregon Visitors Association (POVA), 701 SW Morrison St. (☎275-9750; www.travelportland.com). Located in Pioneer Courthouse Sq. Walk between the fountains in the unique and beautiful amphitheater through the crowds of screaming kids and more distinctive characters to enter. All the pamphlets you could want, plus a 12min. interpretive movie. Free *Portland Book* has maps and comprehensive info on local attractions. Open M-F 8:30am-5:30pm, Sa 10am-4pm. Also houses a **Tri-Met Service Counter,** open M-F 8:30am-5:30pm.

Outdoor Information: Portland Parks and Recreation, 1120 SW 5th Ave. #1302 (☎823-2223; www.parks.ci.portland.or.us), in the Portland Building between Main and Madison St. Offers a wealth of information including maps and pamphlets on Portland's parks. Open M-F 8am-5pm. **Nature of Northwest,** 800 NE Oregon St. #117 (☎872-2750; www.naturenw.org), 2 blocks east of the Convention Center on NE 7th Ave. A multitude of hiking maps, guidebooks, and raw information is on tap at this US Forest Service-run shop. Pick up a Northwest Forest Pass here, required for parking in most National Forests in WA and OR ($5 per day, $30 annually). Open M-F 9am-5pm.

Currency Exchange: A **Travelex** can be found inside of Powell's Travel (see below) for any money-changing needs. Open M-F 9am-5:30pm, Sa 11am-2pm.

LOCAL SERVICES

Bookstore: See **Powell's City of Books,** p. 89. **Powell's Travel Store** (☎228-1108; www.powells.com), adjacent to the **Tourist Information** in Pioneer Courthouse Sq., has a vast array of road maps, hiking maps, guidebooks, and travel literature. Open M-F 9am-7pm, Sa 10am-6pm, Su 10am-5pm.

Outdoors Equipment: 🔲**US Outdoor Store,** 219 SW Broadway (☎223-5937; www.usoutdoorstore.com), between Pine and Ankeny St. This store might sound like a military surplus shop, but it has a huge selection of gear for almost any outdoor activity and a very knowledgeable staff. Open M-F 9am-8pm, Sa 10am-6pm, Su noon-5pm.

Gay and Lesbian Info: Portland's best resource for queer info is the biweekly newspaper **Just Out** (www.justout.com), available free around the city.

Tickets: Ticketmaster (☎224-4400; www.ticketmaster.com). Surcharge $1.50-7.75. **Fastixx** (☎224-8499; www.fastixx.com). Surcharge $2-3 per order plus an additional $1 per ticket ordered. Also try **Ticket Central Portland** (see **Tourist Services,** p. 82).

Laundromat: Springtime Thrifty Cleaners and Laundry, 2942 SE Hawthorne Blvd. (☎232-4353). 150 ft. from the Hawthorne hostel. Open M-F 7:30am-9pm, Sa-Su 8am-8pm. Wash $1.25, dry $0.25 per 10min.

EMERGENCY AND COMMUNICATION

Police: 1111 SW 2nd Ave. (non-emergency response ☎823-3333, info 823-4636, lost and found 823-2179), between Madison St. and Main St.

Crisis and Suicide Hotline: ☎655-8401. **Women's Crisis Line:** ☎235-5333. 24hr.

Late-Night Pharmacy: Walgreens (☎238-6053), intersection of SE 39th Ave. and Belmont St. Open 24hr.

Hospital: Legacy Good Samaritan, 1015 NW 22nd St. (☎413-8090; emergency 413-7260), between Lovejoy and Marshall.

Internet Access: Found at the elegant and distinguished **Central Library,** 801 SW 10th Ave. (☎988-5123; www.multcolib.org), between Yamhill and Taylor. 1hr. free with a guest pass from customer service. Open M-Th 9am-9pm, F-Sa 9am-6pm, Su 1-5pm.

Post Office: 715 NW Hoyt St. (☎800-275-8777). Open M-F 7am-6:30pm, Sa 8:30am-5pm. General delivery open M-F 8am-5:30pm, Sa 8:30am-noon. **Postal Code:** 97208.

⌐ ACCOMMODATIONS

Although Marriott-esque hotels dominate downtown and smaller motels are steadily raising their prices, Portland still welcomes the budget traveler. Two Hostelling International locations provide quality housing in happening areas. Prices tend to drop as you leave the city center, and inexpensive motels can be found on SE Powell Blvd. and the southern end of SW 4th Ave. Portland fills up during the summer months, especially during the Rose Festival, so make reservations early.

HOSTELS AND MOTELS

▧ **Portland Hawthorne Hostel (HI),** 3031 SE Hawthorne Blvd. (☎236-3380; www.portlandhostel.org), at 31st Ave. across from Artichoke Music. Take bus #14 to SE 30th Ave. Lively common space and a huge porch define this laid-back hostel. Kitchen, laundry. Free wireless Internet access; "conventional" Internet is $1 per 10min. The $1 all-you-can-eat pancakes are a big bonus. Fills early in summer. Reception daily 8am-10pm. Check-out 11am. 34 beds and a tent yard for overflow. Dorms $18, nonmembers $21; private rooms $41-46. ❷

Northwest Portland International Hostel (HI), 1818 NW Glisan St. (☎241-2783; www.2oregonhostels.com) at 18th Ave. Centrally located between Nob Hill and the Pearl District. Take bus #17 down Glisan to the corner of 19th Ave. This snug Victorian building has a kitchen, Internet access, lockers, laundry, and a small espresso bar. 34 dorm beds (co-ed available) and private doubles starting at $55. Reception 8am-11pm. $19 plus tax, with a $3 fee for nonmembers. Reservations at least 2 weeks in advance are recommended June-Sept. ❷

McMenamins Edgefield, 2126 SW Halsey St. (☎669-8610 or 800-669-8610; www.mcmenamins.com), in Troutdale. Take MAX east to the Gateway Station, then Tri-Met bus #24 (Halsey) east to the main entrance. This beautiful 38-acre former farm is a posh escape that keeps 2 hostel rooms. On-site brewery and vineyards, plus 18-hole golf course ($8-9, $1 club rental), and several restaurants and pubs. Offers many activities, including 2-day rafting trips ($140). Lockers included. Call ahead during summer (but no reservations for the hostel). Breakfast included with private rooms. Reception 24hr. 2 single-sex dorm-style rooms with 12 beds each ($20) are the budget option. Singles $50; 2 queen double $85-100. ❷

Clyde Hotel, 1022 SW Stark St. (☎517-5231; www.clydehotel.com), west of 10th Ave. Take MAX to SW 10th Ave., walk toward Burnside St. Built in 1912, the charming and historic Clyde has kept all its furniture in the original style, from Victorian tubs to bureau-sized radios. Internet available 24hr. in the lounge. Continental breakfast included. Reception 10am-9pm, front desk open 24hr. Reservations recommended. Rooms (double or queen) $80-115, 2-room suites $110-190 (for 2-4 people). Low-season rates about $10 less. ❺

⌐ FOOD

Finding good food in Portland isn't a problem, but finding it at the right price can be a little more tricky. Good food downtown and in the NW districts tends to be expensive. Restaurants and quirky cafes in the NE and SE quadrants offer great food at reasonable prices. Although it's hard to pinpoint specific establishments,

OREGON

the lunch trucks dispersed throughout the city tend to offer authentic food, cheap. For some reason (perhaps a cosmic one) depictions of The Last Supper seem to be a seal of approval for some of the best restaurants in Portland: be on the lookout for Christ and His apostles.

PEARL DISTRICT AND NOB HILL

Trendy eateries line NW 21st and 23rd St. **Food Front,** 2375 NW Thurman St., a small cooperative grocery, has a superb deli and a wonderland of natural foods, fruit, and baked goods. (☎222-5658. Open daily summer 8am-10pm; winter 9am-9pm.) Streets are in alphabetical order starting with Ankeny and Burnside, which border Old Town, and increase as you go north.

■ **Muu-Muu's Big World Diner,** 612 NW 21st Ave. (☎223-8169), at Hoyt St. Bus #17. Where high and low culture smash together. Artful goofiness—the name of the restaurant was drawn from a hat—amidst red velvet curtains and gold upholstery. Brutus salad, "the one that kills a caesar" $6, 'shroom-wich $7.50. Many vegetarian options. Open M-F 11:30am-1am, Sa-Su 10am-1am. ❷

■ **Garbonzos,** 922 NW 21st Ave. (☎227-4196), at Hoyt St. Bus #17. This quiet eatery offers delicious falafel and shish kebabs in a relaxed atmosphere. The falafel plate, 6 balls and 6 sides ($7), offers a taste of the menu's variety. Open daily 11am-11pm. ❷

Little Wing Cafe, 529 NW 13th Ave. (☎228-3101), off Glisan. Bus #17. The food is arranged nearly as well as the gallery of photos on the walls. Sandwiches include the eggplant supreme ($6). Full-sized dinner entrees run about $16-18; "small plates" are $8-9. Open M-Sa 11:30am-3:30pm; also Tu-Th 5:30-9pm, F-Sa 5:30-10pm. ❷

DOWNTOWN AND OLD TOWN

The center of town and tourism, Southwest Portland can get expensive. Street carts offer an array of portable food and bento boxes (lunches of meat or vegetables on a bed of rice), making it easy to grab a quick, healthful meal. A farmers' market offers fresh fruit, bread and sandwiches three times a week (W 10am-2pm, SW Park and Salmon; Th 4-8pm, NW 10th and Johnson; Sa 8:30am-2pm, SW Park at Portland State University). Ethnic restaurants also hawk cheap eats on Morrison St. between 10th and 11th Ave. A 24hr. **Safeway** (☎721-9150) supermarket is behind the PAM (see **Sights,** p. 87), 1030 SW Jefferson St.

Bleu, 921 SW Morrison St. (☎294-9770; www.westernculinary.com). The finest young chefs in the country come to the Western Culinary Institute to learn how to prepare and serve top quality meals. Someone's got to eat all that food, and for a reasonable price, it can be you. It's four-star food at a three-star price. When zatar crusted rack of lamb would really hit the spot, Bleu delivers. At lunch, a three-course meal is $10 and a five-course meal is $15. At dinner, a three-course meal is $19 and a five-course meal $25. Open Tu-F 11:30am-1pm and 6-8pm. ❸

The Roxy, 1121 SW Stark St. (☎223-9160). Giant crucified Jesus with neon halo, pierced wait staff, and quirky menu complement this quirky diner, open practically all the time. The owner's collection of signed celebrity photos graces the booths; Slash (from Guns N' Roses) and other celebs have been known to stop by. Visiting the Dysha Starr Imperial Toilet seems like an important thing to do, if only because of its name. Pancakes or omelets $3-8, burgers $5-7, Quentin Tarantuna Melt $6.25, coffees and chai $1-3. An ideal post-movie or after-bar stop. Open 24 hr. Tu-Su. ❷

O, Cielo! 911 SW 10th Ave. (☎222-5004; www.ocielo.qpg.com). Great Italian food, cheap. You can sit upstairs or down, inside or out in this friendly down-to-earth restaurant. The owner/chef/cashier/waiter will serve you bruschetta ($2-3), gnocchi, lasagna ($7-8), or nearly any other Italian food. Open M-Sa 10am-10pm. ❷

OREGON

Downtown Portland

Bus Route
Streetcar
MAX
Fareless Square

ACCOMMODATIONS
Clyde Hotel, **13**
Northwest Portland International Hostel (HI), **8**
Portland Hawthorne Hostel (HI), **23**

FOOD
Bleu, **16**
Coffee Time, **5**
Garbonzos, **1**
La Bonita, **3**
Little Wing Cafe, **7**
Montage, **22**
Muu-Muu's Big World Diner, **6**
Nicholas Restaurant, **17**
O, Cielo!, **18**
Rimsky Korsakoffee House, **20**
The Roxy, **11**
Vita Cafe, **4**

THEATERS
Artists' Repertory Theater, **12**
Newmark Theater, **21**
Oregon Ballet Theatre, **19**

NIGHTLIFE
Bridgeport Brewing Co., **2**
Brig, Fez, Panorama, Fish Grotto, Red Cap, Garage, Boxxes, **14**
Jimmy Mak's, **9**
Kells Irish Restaurant & Pub, **15**
Ohm, **10**

OREGON

Southeast Portland

▲ **ACCOMODATIONS**
Portland Hawthorne
  Hostel, **5**

🍴 **FOOD**
Jam on Hawthorne, **7**
Montage, **3**
Nicholas Restaurant, **2**

☕ **COFFEEHOUSES**
Palio Dessert and
  Espresso House, **8**
Pied Cow Coffeehouse, **6**
Produce Row Cafe, **1**
Rimsky Korsakoffee
  House, **4**

SOUTHEAST PORTLAND

Anchored at happening Hawthorne Blvd., Southeast Portland is a great place to
people-watch and tummy-fill. Eclectic eateries with exotic decor and economical
menus hide in residential and industrial neighborhoods. **Safeway** is at 2800 SE
Hawthorne, at 28th Ave. (☎232-5539; open daily 6am-1am). Bring cash to SE Portland restaurants, since many of the best do not accept credit cards.

▨ **Nicholas Restaurant,** 318 SE Grand Ave. (☎235-5123; www.nicholasrestaurant.com),
between Oak and Pine, opposite Miller Paint. Bus #6 to the Andy and Bax stop. Phenomenal Mediterranean food in an authentic and very relaxed atmosphere. The meat,
vegetarian, or vegan mezzas ($8) are fantastic deals for both quality and quantity
(might feed two). Sandwiches $5-6. Open M-Sa 10am-9pm, Su noon-9pm. ❶

▨ **Montage,** 301 SE Morrison St. (☎234-1324; www.montage.citysearch.com). Take bus
#15 to the east end of the Morrison Bridge and walk under it. Straight-laced, main-
stream Portlanders enter a surreal land of dining while seated Last-Supper style underneath a macaroni-framed mural of that famous meal. Try oyster shooters ($1.75) or
huge portions of jambalaya ($11 chicken, $15 gator). Vegetarian options like veggie
gumbo ($5.50). Open M-Th and Su 6pm-2am, F-Sa 6pm-4am. No credit cards. ❷

Delta Cafe, 4607 SE Woodstock Blvd. (☎771-3101). The decor is typical Portland: pas-
toral paintings in one room, voodoo dolls and a lone, framed Chewbacca portrait in the
other. 40 oz. Pabst Blue Ribbon comes in champagne bucket, $3. Tasty Southern com-
fort food, including Po' Boy "Samwiches," $4-7. Open daily 5pm-1:30am. ❶

Jam on Hawthorne, 2239 SE Hawthorne Blvd. (☎234-4790). Bus #14. Offers delicious
breakfast wraps ($7) and eggs ($4-7) with many vegetarian and vegan options. Marley
and Garcia decor makes the requisite Hawthorne appearance. Open Tu-F 7:30am-
2:30pm, Sa-Su 8am-3pm. ❷

NORTHEAST PORTLAND

The northeast is distant from any hostel, but the food is worth a short trip.
Places to eat line Broadway and Alberta (1½ mi. north of where Grand merges
with MLK) east of the river, and other pockets of commerce produce good eats
for Portland's most residential area.

OREGON

La Bonita, 2839 NE Alberta St. (☎281-3662). This is not your average taqueria. Fresh, authentic Mexican food awaits at this family restaurant. Burritos $3-4.50, enchiladas $1.50-2, combos $7.50-8.50. Delicious salsa. Open Tu-Su 11am-9pm. ❷

Vita Cafe, 3024 NE Alberta St. (☎335-8233). Huge portions of "comfort food," with an emphasis on vegetarian and vegan fare, but meat lovers will be soothed as well. American, Asian, Mediterranean, and "Mexican Fiesta" food. Lasagna $8.25, chicken-fried steak $7. Open M-Th 10am-10pm, F 10am-11pm, Sa 8am-11am, Su 8am-10pm. ❷

▛ CAFES

Although locals sometimes complain that cafes are overrun by trendy Portlanders trying excessively hard to be cool, the decor, delicious food, and caffeine of these establishments still make them great places to make an appearance.

▨ Palio Dessert and Espresso House, 1996 SE Ladd St. (☎232-9214), on Ladd Circle. Bus #10 stops right in front of the cafe, or walk south 3 blocks on SE 16th Ave. from Hawthorne. This tranquil cafe offers Mexican mochas ($2.50), espresso mousse ($4), and sandwiches (half $3.50-7). Open M-F 8am-11pm, Sa-Su 10am-11pm. ❶

Pied Cow Coffeehouse, 3244 SE Belmont St. (☎230-4866). Bus #15. Sink into velvety cushions in this friendly Victorian parlor, or puff a hookah in the spacious garden. Coffee $1-3, cakes $4. Open M-F 4pm-1am, Sa noon-1am, Su noon-midnight. ❶

Coffee Time, 712 NW 21st Ave. (☎497-1090). Sip a cup of chai ($2-3) while watching locals play chess. The intelligentsia mingle on the couches while bohemians chill to music in the parlor. Lattes $2-3. Incredible smoothies $3-4. Open daily 6am-3am. ❶

Rimsky Korsakoffee House, 707 SE 12th Ave. (☎232-2640), at Alder St. Bus #15 to 12th St., then walk 2 blocks north. Unmarked and low-key, this red Victorian house is a hidden gem with a frenzy of desserts. Ask for a "mystery table." A grand piano and nightly live music add ambiance. Open M-Th and Su 7pm-midnight, F-Sa 7pm-1am. ❶

◎ SIGHTS

Parks, gardens, open-air markets, museums, and galleries bedeck Portland. For $1.25, bus #63 stops at 13 attractions. Catch Portland's dizzying art scene on the first Thursday of each month, when the Portland Art Museum and small galleries in the Southwest and Northwest stay open until 8pm. For more info, con-

THE LOCAL STORY

WHEN IS A HOLE NOT A HOLE

In 1948, a hole was cut through the sidewalk at the corner of SW Taylor St. and SW Naito Pkwy. (Front St.). It was expected to accommodate a mere lamp post, but greatness was thrust upon it. The street lamp was never installed, and the 24-inch circle of earth was left empty until noticed by Dick Fagan, a columnist for the *Oregon Journal*, who grew tired of looking at the unsightly hole from his office window. Fagan used his column, "Mill Ends," to publicize the patch of dirt, pointing out that it would make an excellent park. Fagan planted flowers in the park and regularly chronicled the comings and goings of its resident leprechaun colony, with whom he frequently conversed. According to the explanatory plaque (which is bigger than the park itself), the park has hosted weddings and is presided over by an invisible leprechaun named Patrick O'Toole.

The park was added to the city's roster on St. Patrick's Day, 1976, seven years after Fagan's death. At 452.16 square inches, Mill Ends Park is officially the world's smallest. Locals have enthusiastically embraced it, planting flowers and hosting a hotly-contested annual snail race on St. Patrick's Day. The park also contains a swimming pool and diving board (for butterflies) as well as a miniature Ferris wheel.

tact the **Regional Arts and Culture Council,** 620 SW Main St. #420 (☎823-5111; www.racc.org), across from the Portland Center for the Performing Arts, or grab the *Art Gallery Guide* at the visitors center. For information on Portland's many city parks and gardens, including Washington Park and Crystal Springs Rhododendron Garden, contact **Portland Parks & Recreation,** 1120 SW 5th Ave., #1302 (☎832-PLAY/832-7529; www.parks.ci.portland.or.us/Gardens/Publicgardens.htm).

DOWNTOWN

Portland's downtown centers on the pedestrian and bus mall, which runs north-south on 5th and 6th Ave. between W Burnside Blvd. on the north end and SW Clay St. on the south. On the **South Park Blocks,** a cool and shaded park snakes down the middle of Park Ave., bordered on the west by **Portland State University (PSU).** The area is accessible by any bus from the Transit Mall; once there, set out on foot.

PORTLAND ART MUSEUM (PAM). PAM sets itself apart from the rest of Portland's burgeoning arts scene on the strength of its collections, especially in Asian and Native American art. The Northwest Film Center (see **Cinema,** p. 93) shares space with the museum and shows classics, documentaries, and off-beat flicks almost every day. The Bierstadt painting of Mt. Hood on the second floor is spectacular. Call to find out the current special exhibition. (*1219 SW Park, at Jefferson St. on the west side of the South Block Park. Bus #6, 58, 63. ☎ 226-2811. Dial ext. 4245 for info on new exhibits. Open Tu-W and Sa 10am-5pm, Su noon-5pm, Th-F 10am-8pm. Th-F close at 5pm during winter. $15, students and ages 55 and older $13, 6-19 $6, under 5 free.*)

PIONEER COURTHOUSE SQUARE. The still-operational **Pioneer Courthouse,** at 5th Ave. and Morrison St., is the centerpiece of the **Square.** Since opening in 1983 it has become "Portland's Living Room." Tourists and urbanites of every ilk hang out in the brick quadrangle. During late July and most of August, **High Noon Tunes** (p. 92) draws music lovers in droves. (*701 SW 6th Ave. Along the Vintage Trolley line and the MAX light rail. Events hotline ☎ 223-1613. Music W noon-1pm.*)

5TH AVENUE ARCHITECTURE. The most controversial structure downtown is Michael Graves's **Portland Building,** 1120 SW 5th Ave., on the mall. This assemblage of pastel tile and concrete, the first major work of postmodern architecture built in the US, has been both praised as PoMo genius and condemned for resembling an overgrown jukebox. Walking underneath, look out for the giant pitchfork-wielding woman, *Portlandia,* reaching down from above: she's the second largest hammered copper statue in the US. Nearby, the **Standard Insurance Center,** 900 SW 5th Ave., between Salmon and Taylor, strokes the libido with **The Quest,** a sensual white marble sculpture commonly known as "Five Groins in the Fountain."

OLD TOWN AND CHINATOWN

The section of downtown above SW Stark running along the Willamette River is known as **Old Town.** Although not the safest part of Portland, Old Town has been revitalized in recent years by storefront restoration, and new shops, restaurants, and nightclubs. On weekends, **Saturday Market** draws all of Portland for food, crafts, hackey-sack, and live entertainment. Just west of Old Town the arched **China Gates** at NW 4th Ave. and Burnside provide an entrance to a Chinatown that, apart from a few restaurants and shops, is now more about business than Asian culture. As in Old Town, travelers should take caution in Chinatown after dark.

SHANGHAI TUNNELS. Downtown's waterfront district is laced with a complex web of underground passages known as the **Shanghai tunnels.** Urban lore has it that seamen would get folks drunk, drag them down to the tunnels, and store them there until their ship sailed. Forced aboard and taken out to sea, these hapless

Portlanders would provide a free crew. Unfortunately, all entrances to the tunnels are in private businesses. **Portland Underground Tours** guides trips through the historic passageways. (☎ 622-4798; www.members.tripod.com/cgs-mthood/shanghai_tunnels.htm. $11, under 12 $6.)

CLASSICAL CHINESE GARDENS. The newest addition to Portland's long list of gardens, this city block makes up the largest Ming-style garden outside of China. The large pond, winding paths, and ornate decorations invite a relaxing, meditative stay. Ignore the skyscrapers and warehouses looming over the garden's walls, and you'll think you were back in a simpler time. A tea house also offers a chance to experience authentic Chinese tea $4-5. (NW 3rd and Everett. ☎ 228-8131; www.portlandchinesegarden.org. Open daily Apr.-Oct. 9am-6pm.; Nov.-Mar. 10am-5pm. $7; seniors, students, and ages 6-18 $6; under 6 free.)

PEARL DISTRICT

Opposite the North Park Blocks, between NW 8th and Park Ave., the Pearl District buzzes. Stretching north from Burnside to I-405 along the river, this former industrial zone is packed with galleries, loft apartments, and warehouses-turned-office buildings. Stores and cafes make the area welcoming despite its boxy architecture.

▧ POWELL'S CITY OF BOOKS. The largest independent bookstore in the world, Powell's is a must-see for anyone who gets excited about the written word. If you like to dawdle in bookshops, bring a sleeping bag and rations. Nine color-coded rooms house books on everything from criminology to cooking. The atmosphere is more like a department store than a bookstore, but the sheer volume of books, poetry and fiction readings, and an extensive travel section on the Pacific Northwest make Powell's a worthy stop. (1005 W Burnside St. on the edge of Northwest district. Bus #20. ☎ 228-4651 or 800-878-7323; www.powells.com. Open daily 9am-11pm.)

GALLERIES. *First Thursday* (free at PAM or www.firstthursdayportland.com) is a guide to local galleries and goings-on. For a nice selection, walk north on NW 9th Ave., turn left on NW Glisan and right on NW 12th Ave. On the way you'll pass some of the area's most engaging spaces, including the **Mark Woolley Gallery,** 120 NW 9th Ave. (☎ 224-5475; www.markwoolley.com; open Tu-Sa 11am-6pm, First Th 11am-9:30pm) and the visiting artists' exhibition space at the **Pacific Northwest College of Art,** 1241 NW Johnson (☎ 226-4391; www.pnca.edu; hours vary depending on exhibit). **Quintana Galleries,** 120 NW 9th St. (☎ 223-1729 or 800-321-1729; www.quintanagalleries.com; open Tu-Sa 10:30am-5:30pm, First W and Th 10:30am-8pm), displays work by contemporary Native American artists working in traditional styles. **Lawrence Gallery,** (☎ 228-1776; www.lawrencegallery.net; open M-Sa 10am-5:30pm, Su noon-5pm) at NW Davis and 9th, offers everything from spectacular landscapes to impressionistic portraits.

3D CENTER OF ART AND PHOTOGRAPHY. While it does have some spectacular images, the 3D Center is focused less on art than on the on the history and science behind 3D imagery. Images taken with cameras 30 yds. apart gives the viewer the perspective of a giant. Ask to see the 10-15min. slide show; it has some incredible images that pop out at you more than you ever thought possible with those red-and-blue glasses. (1928 NW Lovejoy St. ☎ 227-6667; www.3dcenter.us. Open F-Su 1-5pm, first Th of every month, 4-9pm. Suggested donation $4.)

NORTHEAST PORTLAND

Nicknamed "Munich on the Willamette," Portland is the uncontested **microbrewery** capital of the US, and residents are proud of their beer. The visitors center has a list of 26 metro area breweries, most of which happily give tours if you call ahead.

OREGON

Widmer Bros. Brewing Co., half a mile north of the Rose Garden, offers free tours that include a video, a viewing of the facilities, and complimentary samples. *(929 N Russell. ☎ 281-2437; www.widmer.com. Tours F 3pm, Sa 1pm and 2pm.)* Many beer factories are brew pubs, sometimes offering live music with their beers. Try the **Lucky Labrador Brew Pub,** where dogs rule the loading dock, for Miser Monday pints. *(915 SE Hawthorne Blvd. ☎ 236-3555; www.luckylab.com. Pints $3.50. Open M-Sa 11am-midnight, Su noon-10pm.)* Also try the **Bridgeport Brewing Co.** (see **Nightlife**). Visit the **Oregon Brewers Guild** to learn how these alchemists work magic on water and hops grain. *(510 NW 3rd Ave. ☎ 465-0013; www.oregonbeer.org. Open M-F 10am-4pm.)*

THE GROTTO. Minutes from downtown on Sandy Blvd., a 62-acre Catholic sanctuary houses magnificent religious sculptures and shrines, as well as running streams and gardens. At the heart of the grounds are "Our Lady's Grotto," a cave carved into a 110-foot cliff, and a replica of Michelangelo's *Pietà*. An elevator ($3, ages 65 and over and 6-11 $2.50) ascends from the Meditation Chapel for a serene view that takes in a life-size bronze statue of St. Francis of Assisi. *(Sandy Blvd. at NE 85th. ☎ 254-7371; www.thegrotto.org. Open daily Memorial Day-Labor Day 9am-7:30pm; Labor Day-Thanksgiving 9am-5pm; Thanksgiving-Memorial Day 9am-4pm. Exact closing time may vary.)*

SOUTHEAST PORTLAND

OREGON MUSEUM OF SCIENCE AND INDUSTRY (OMSI). Flocks of kids are mesmerized by the Paleontology Lab where staff work on real dinosaur bones. The Omnimax Theater provides an experience like no other, as viewers are completely surrounded by the domed screen. The Murdock Planetarium presents astronomy matinees and moonlights with rockin' laser shows—the Pink Floyd show is highly recommended. When you're done testing the earthquake resistance of Lego skyscrapers, visit the Navy's last diesel submarine, the U.S.S. Blueback. She never failed a mission, starred in the 1990 film *The Hunt for Red October*, and gets fantastic mileage. *(1945 SE Water Ave., 2 blocks south of Hawthorne Blvd. Right next to the river. Bus #63. ☎ 797-4000; www.omsi.edu. Open daily early June-Labor Day 9:30am-7pm; Labor Day-early June Tu-Su 9:30am-5:30pm. Museum and Omnimax admission each cost $8.50, ages 63 and older and 3-13 $6.50. Under 3 free. Omnimax ☎ 797-4640. Shows start on the hr. M-Tu and Su 11am-7pm and F-Sa 11am-9pm. Planetarium ☎ 797-4646. Shows every 30min. 11am-3:30pm. $5. U.S.S. Blueback ☎ 797-4624. Open Tu-Su 10am-5pm. 40min. tour $5-15. Min. age 3, min. height 3 ft. OMSI offers a package, as well: admission to the museum, an Omnimax film and either the planetarium or the sub, $18, ages 63 and older or 3-13 $14.)*

CRYSTAL SPRINGS RHODODENDRON GARDEN. Over 2500 rhododendrons of countless varieties and colors surround a lake and border an 18-hole public golf course. Take a mellow stroll through bloom-strewn paths, past cascading waterfalls and 90-year-old rhodies. The flowers are in full bloom from March to May. *(SE 28th Ave., near Woodstock. Just west of Reed College. Bus #63, or take #19 Woodstock to 28th and Woodstock and walk up 28th. Open daily Mar. 1 to Labor Day dawn-dusk; Oct.-Feb. 10am-6pm. Tu and W free all year, M and Th-Su $3, under 12 free.)*

WASHINGTON PARK

Ever wonder where Nike's craze for trail running shoes came from? Once you visit Washington Park, with its miles of beautiful trails, lofty trees, and serene gardens, you won't ask again. If possible, schedule in a day to enjoy the park to its fullest. Holding some of Portland's premier (and least expensive) attractions, the park is shaped like a large "V." Take the MAX to "Washington Park" and you will be rocketed via elevator to the base of the V, where the **Zoo** and **World Forestry Center** are found. The Washington Park Shuttle (10am-8pm), free with valid MAX ticket, stops in the Zoo parking lot, at the **Rose Garden** and **Japanese Garden,** runs through a posh neighborhood, then stops at the **Hoyt Arboretum's** visitors center. From there the bus completes its circuit with another 5min. ride back to the MAX and zoo. Though the tall trees and moss-covered paths seem to beckon camping, it's not allowed, and there are police horse patrols at night.

INTERNATIONAL ROSE TEST GARDEN. The pride of the city of roses, the Rose Garden is the most accessible and spectacular of Washington Park's attractions. The 4½ acres of crimson and pink and yellow flowers are more than just a beautiful garden for people to gawk at; they're a testing ground for new breeds of roses, which undergo rigorous two-year evaluations here and at other test gardens before they can be sold commercially. At any given time, there are over 550 varieties in the gardens. Look for the Gold Medal Gardens to see the most brilliant flowers. *(400 SW Kingston Ave. ☎823-3636. Open daily 5am-10pm. Free.)*

HOYT ARBORETUM. Forming the wooded backdrop for the rest of Washington Park's sights, Hoyt features 183 acres of trees and 12 mi. of trails with tree-themed names, including the charming, wheelchair-accessible Bristlecone Pine and Overlook Trails. All this in an area that 100 years ago was clear-cut. The 26 mi. Wildwood Trail winds through Washington and Forest Parks, connecting the Arboretum to the Zoo and Japanese Garden. Pick up a free map at the World Forestry Center, as trails are sometimes poorly marked. *(4000 SW Fairview Blvd. ☎823-8733. Visitors center open M-F 9am-4pm, Sa 9am-3:30pm. Free guided tours leave from the visitor's center Sa-Su 2pm.)*

 JUST DO IT. It's easy to get in on the trail running action. Park at the Hoyt Arboretum Visitors Center parking lot and pick up a map there. Follow the Overlook about 100 yards out of the parking lot to the wildwood trail. Follow that trail left and stay on it for about 20min.: you'll pass an archery range and cross 3 roads. When you get to the White Pine Trail junction, follow White Pine as it crosses the road and then becomes Hemlock and Fir and finally arrives back at the parking lot. This trail is a great intro to trail running: switchbacks mitigate the steepest hill and a wide smooth trail reduces the twisted ankle possibilities. Gorgeous views of Mt. Adams from the Overlook Trail are a nice bonus.

JAPANESE GARDENS. Just across from the Rose Garden, these more subtle grounds complete the one-two punch of what is one of Portland's best destinations. Planned and planted in the early 60s, the gardens shift gracefully between various styles of landscape design. The Dry Landscape Garden *(Karesansui)* is an amazing example of simplicity and beauty, and the mossy paths and rushing streams are sure to help you achieve that state. *(611 SW Kingston Ave. ☎223-1321; www.japanesegarden.com. Open Apr.-Sept. M noon-7pm, Tu-Su 10am-7pm; Oct.-Mar. M noon-4pm, Tu-Su 10am-4pm. Tours daily Apr. 15-Oct. 31. at 10:45am and 2:30pm. $6.50, age 62 and older $5, students $4, under 6 free.)*

FOREST PARK. This completely undeveloped tract of wilderness, stretching 5000 acres north of Washington Park, provides an idea of what the area was like before the arrival of Lewis and Clark. Horse and bike access is restricted, making this an idea place for walkers and hikers. A web of trails leads into lush forest, past scenic overlooks, and through idyllic picnic areas. The **Pittock Mansion,** *(3229 NW Pittock Dr. ☎823-3624; www.pittockmansion.com)* within Forest Park, was built by Henry L. Pittock, founder of the daily newspaper *The Oregonian.* Enjoy a striking panorama of the city from the lawn of this 85-year-old, 16,000 sq. ft. monument to the French Renaissance. To get there, take St. Helens Rd. (US 30) to Saltzman road or Germantown Road, which cut into the park, providing access. If you plan on doing anything serious in the park, pick up a copy of the *Hiking and Running Guide to Forest Park*, a booklet of maps provided by the **Friends of Forest Park** (☎ 223-5449; *www.friendsofforestpark.org*), also available at Powell's (p. 89).

OREGON ZOO. The zoo has gained fame for its successful efforts at elephant breeding. Exhibits include a Cascade Mountains-like goat habitat and a marine pool as part of the zoo's "Great Northwest: A Crest to Coast Adventure" program. The zoo also features weekend educational talks and a **children's petting zoo.** For over 22 years, from late June to August, nationally touring artists have performed at the **Rhythm and Zoo Concerts** on the concert lawn. (☎ 234-9694. W-Th 7pm; free with zoo admission.) **Zoobeat Concerts** feature artists in blues, bluegrass, pop, and world beat on selected summer weekend evenings. *(4001 SW Canyon Rd. ☎ 226-1561; www.oregonzoo.com. Open daily Apr.-Sept. 9am-7pm; Oct.-Mar. 9am-4pm. Entrance gates close one hour before park closes. $9, age 65 and older $7.50, 3-11 $6, under 3 free; 2nd Tu of each month free after 1pm.)*

🎵 ENTERTAINMENT

Prepare for culture. Upon request, the Visitors Association (see **Practical Information,** p. 82) will fork over a thick packet outlining the month's events. Outdoor festivals are a way of life in Portland; the city's major daily newspaper, *The Oregonian* (www.oregonian.com), lists upcoming events in its Friday edition. The city's favorite free cultural reader, the Wednesday *Willamette Week* (www.wweek.com), is a reliable guide to local music, plays, and art. Drop boxes are all over town, and the paper's office is right across from the library. The weekly, free *Portland Mercury* (www.portlandmercury.com) gives a salty, humorous take on Portland life and lists current events in a section titled "My, what a busy week!" Also call the *Oregonian's Inside Line* (☎ 225-5555) for up-to-date information on current happenings in the Portland area.

MUSIC

Most first-rate traveling shows hit Portland, and many have bargain tickets available; however, some of the best shows are free and outdoors. Live music venues are listed under **Nightlife,** p. 94.

Oregon Symphony Orchestra, 923 SW Washington St. (☎ 228-1353 or 800-228-7343; www.orsymphony.org). Box office open M-F 9am-5pm. Classical and pop Sept.-June starts at $23-30. Students and those ages 65 and older can purchase tickets half-price 1hr. before show time. "Symphony Sunday" afternoon concerts ($10-15); "Monday Madness" offers $5 student tickets 1 week before showtime. Call for park performance info. Wheelchair-accessible. Infrared listening devices available.

High Noon Tunes (☎ 223-1613), at Pioneer Courthouse Sq. Jammed concerts mid-July to Aug. W noon-1pm. A potpourri of rock, jazz, folk, and world music.

Sack Lunch Concerts, 1422 SW 11th Ave. (☎ 222-2031; www.oldchurch.org), at Clay St. and the Old Church. Classical and jazz music W at noon (usually 1hr).

THEATER

Anchored by the massive Portland Center for the Performing Arts, Portland has a bustling theater scene with many options for the student or budget traveler.

Portland Center for the Performing Arts (☎ 248-4335; www.pcpa.com) is the fourth-largest arts center in the US and is home to 21 companies. Free **backstage tours** begin in the lobby of the Newmark Theater, at SW Main and Broadway. Tours W at 11am and every 30min. Sa 11am-1pm. Any bus to the Transit Mall; walk from there.

Portland Center Stage (☎274-6588; www.pcs.org), in Newmark Theater of PCPA at SW Broadway and SW Main. Classics, modern adaptations, and world premieres run late Sept.-Apr. $27-55. $15 youth matinee seats sometimes available (age 30 and under). Half-price student rush tickets sometimes available 1hr. before curtain.

Artists' Repertory Theater, 1516 SW Alder St. (☎241-1278; www.artistsrep.org). Recruits local talent for top-notch, low-budget, and experimental productions. $24-32, seniors $21, students $15.

CINEMA

Portland is a haven for cinema lovers. With the help of *The Oregonian,* a full-price ticket to just about any screen can be scrupulously avoided, and McMenamins' theater-pubs are one of a kind.

Mission Theater and Pub, 1624 NW Glisan (☎225-5555 cat. 8832; www.mcmenamins.com) serves home-brewed ales and sandwiches ($6-7). Watch second-run flicks while lounging on couches or in the old-time balcony. Shows begin 5:30, 7:30, 9:30pm. $2-3. 21+.

Bagdad Theater and Pub, 3702 SE Hawthorne Blvd. (☎225-5555 cat. 8831; www.mcmenamins.com). Bus #14. This cine-pub is housed in a former vaudeville theater, with a separate pub in front. 21+. First show is at 5:30pm, and 2 others follow at approximately 2hr. intervals. Pub open M-Sa 11am-1am, Su noon-midnight. $2-3.

Northwest Film Center, 1219 SW Park Ave. (☎221-1156; www.nwfilm.org), screens documentary, foreign, classic, experimental, and independent films at the historic **Guild Theatre,** 829 SW 9th Ave., 2 blocks north of PAM, as well as in the museum's auditorium. Every Feb. the center also hosts the Portland International Film Festival, with 100 films from 30 nations. Screenings begin sometime between 7pm and 9pm. Box office opens 30min. before each show. $7, students and seniors $6.

SPORTS

When Bill Walton led the **Trailblazers** (☎321-3211; www.nba.com/blazers. Tickets $15-65) to the 1979 NBA Championship, Portland went berserk—landing an NBA team in the first place was a substantial accomplishment for a city of Portland's size. The Blazers came close to a title repeat in 2000, when they lost to the Los Angeles Lakers in the Western Conference Championships. The Blazers play November to May in the **Rose Garden Arena** (www.rosequarter.com) by the Steel Bridge in Northeast Portland, with its own stop on MAX. The **Winter Hawks** of the Western Hockey League (tickets ☎238-6366 or www.winterhawks.com; $12-20) play from September to March in the Rose Garden Arena and at the **Coliseum.** Take bus #9 or MAX. **PGE** (Portland General Electric) **Park,** 1844 SW Morrison St. (☎553-5555; www.pgepark.com) on the other side of town, is home to the **Beavers,** Portland's AAA-league baseball team, affiliated with the San Diego Padres. General admission is as little as $6.

FESTIVALS

Rose Festival, 5603 SW Hood Ave. (☎227-2681; www.rosefestival.org). Throughout June, but concentrated in the first couple weeks, Portland's premier summer event offers concerts, celebrities, auto racing, an air show, and the largest children's parade in the world. Larger events require tickets, but smaller ones are free.

Waterfront Blues Festival (☎282-0555 or 973-3378; www.waterfrontbluesfest.com), early July. High-quality entertainment featuring blues and folk artists on three stages with open air seating. Admission $5 and 2 cans of food to benefit the Oregon Food Bank.

OREGON

HAIR OF THE DOG

Hidden among factories and behind one of the least pretentious facades of any brewery around, ☕ *Hair of the Dog Brewing Company produces what might just be the best beer in a city known for its microbreweries. Let's Go took a tour of the small-scale brewery from co-owner Alan Sprints and got the skinny on the brewing process. These brews are superlative, and the experience is an essential notch on any microbrewery fan's belt.* (4509 SE 23rd Ave. ☎232-6585; www.hairofthedog.com. Tours by appointment weekdays only. 12 oz. bottles $3, 1.5L "magnums" $10.)

Q: Do your beers ferment in bottles?
A: They do ferment in the bottles, but it's a very small refermentation, just enough to get bubbles... if you do any more than that the bottles will explode.
Q: But they mature like wine?
A: Yeah.
Q: What's the reason for that?
A: Higher alcohol content, more hops, and also the bottle conditioning process...it's more like champagne, where the product is naturally fermented. That's a better environment for the product to age.
Q: Does that prevent contamination?
A: Refermentation scavenges oxygen out of the liquid, and that helps stop failing and off-flavors

Oregon Brewers Festival (☎778-5917; www.oregon-brewfest.com), the last weekend in July. The continent's largest gathering of independent brewers (72 breweries) parties at Waterfront Park. Sample the beer and talk to members of OSU's "Fermentation Science Program." $2 per taste, $3 per mug (required to taste). Under 21 must be with parent.

Mt. Hood Festival of Jazz (☎219-9833; www.mthood-jazz.com), on the 1st weekend in Aug. at Mt. Hood Community College in Gresham. Take I-84 to Wood Village-Gresham exit and follow the signs or ride MAX to the end of the line. The Pacific Northwest's premier jazz festival. Wynton Marsalis and the late Stan Getz have been regulars. Tickets from $28 per night, more deals through Ticketmaster. 3-day passes $70-130.

▣ NIGHTLIFE

Portland's nightclubs cater to everyone from the muscle-bound frat boy to the nipple-pierced neo-goth aesthete. Bigger, flashier clubs rule **Old Town** and central **Downtown,** where mainstream, punk, jazz, and gay joints all come alive on weekends. In the **Pearl District** and **Nob Hill,** yuppies and college kids kick back together in spacious bars. In the **Southeast,** cramped quarters make for instant friends over music and drinks. Hidden in the Northeastern suburb of **Laurelhurst,** locals gather in intimate clubs to listen to the city's best folk and rock. The plentiful neighborhood pubs often have the most character and the best music. Mischievous minors be warned: the drinking age is strictly enforced.

DOWNTOWN AND OLD TOWN

▣ **Ohm,** 31 NW 1st Ave. (☎796-0909; www.ohmnightclub.com), at Couch under the Burnside Bridge. A venue dedicated to electronic music and unclassifiable beats. Achieve oneness dancing in the cool brick interior or give your ears and feet a break and mingle outside. Tu brings Dhalia, W Breakbeat and Trance, Th spoken word, and weekends often bring big-name live DJs. 21+. Cover $3-15. Open M-W 9pm-2:30am, Th-F 9pm-3:30am, Sa 9pm-4am, Su 9pm-3am. After-hours for some shows and special events stretch past 6am. Kitchen service until 2am.

Brig, Fish Grotto, Fez, Red Cap Garage, Panorama and **Boxxes,** 341 SW 10th Ave. (☎221-7262; www.boxxes.com), form a network of clubs along Stark St. between 10th and 11th. On weekdays the clubs are connected, but on weekends they are often sealed off—check at the door to see what is happening where. The 23-screen video and karaoke bar is where magic happens. Brig (the dance floor extension of Red Cap) and Boxxes are gay clubs, while Panorama hosts the straight scene. Fez is a music venue catering to a diverse crowd, and Fish Grotto, more of a restaurant than a club, serves up seafood (entrees $15-18). Cover $2-5. Open M-Su 9pm-2:30am; Panorama stays open F-Sa until 4 or 4:30am.

Kells Irish Restaurant & Pub, 112 SW 2nd Ave. (☎227-4057; www.kellsirish.com). With a cigar bar and wood and brass interior, Kells caters to a more coiffed, upscale crowd, but a great space and live Irish music every night of the week make sure the scene is always buzzing. 21+. Happy hour M-F 4-7pm and 11pm-1am. Open M 11:30am-1am, Tu-Su 11:30am-2am.

SOUTHEAST AND HAWTHORNE

Produce Row Cafe, 204 SE Oak St. (☎232-8355). Bus #6 to SE Oak and SE Grand; walk west along Oak toward the river. A huge deck, hip staff, and enough beers to give a German a headache. 30 beers on tap and over 150 in bottles. Live music every night at 9 from a rotating line-up of bands (jazz, rock, bluegrass) and open-mic. Domestic bottles $2, pints $3. Open Mar. 15-Oct. 15 M-F 11am-1am; Oct. 16-Mar. 14 M-Th 11am-midnight, F 11am-1am, Sa noon-1am, Su noon-11pm.

Dots Cafe, 2521 SE Clinton St. (☎235-0203). Listen to Black Sabbath, electronica, jazz, and everything else in the company of Portland's young hipsters. The usual excellent microbrews, $6 pitchers of Pabst Blue Ribbon, and a regal assemblage of kitsch memorabilia accompany Victorian paintings. Rent a pool table for $0.25 per game. Cheese fries $3.50. Open daily noon-2am.

LAURELHURST

Laurelthirst Public House, 2958 NE Glisan St. (☎232-1504), at 30th Ave. Bus #19. Local talent makes a name for itself in 2 intimate rooms of groovin', boozin', and schmoozin'. Burgers and sandwiches $5-8. Free pool M-Th and Su before 7pm. Cover $3-6 after 8pm. Open daily 9am-1am.

Beulahland, 118 NE 28th Ave. (☎235-2794), at Couch opposite the Coca-Cola bottling plant. Bus #19. A small venue with local art on the walls and huge, inflatable toys hanging from the ceiling. DJs on F, often spinning Ska; live music Sa. Happy hour 4-7pm. Open M-Th and Su 7am-2am, F-Sa 9am-2am.

PEARL DISTRICT AND NOB HILL

Jimmy Mak's, 300 NW 10th Ave. (☎295-6542; www.jimmymaks.com), 3 blocks from Powell's Books at Flanders. Jam to Portland's renowned jazz artists. Shows 9:30pm-1am. Cover $3-6. Vegetarian-friendly Greek and Middle Eastern dinners ($8-17). Open M 11am-midnight, Tu-F 11am-2am, Sa 6pm-2am.

that might occur in beer if it ages.

Q: Are you more interested in product consistency, or do you prefer experimenting with different brews?

A: I enjoy when people like using our beer for celebrating special events and special occasions...it makes me feel good. If it wasn't for people that enjoyed drinking the beer, brewing it wouldn't be so much fun.

Q: What about the name of the brewery, Hair of the Dog?

A: Originally, the term literally referred to using the hair of a dog that bit you to help heal the bite. They'd chase a dog down, cut off some of its hair, [then] wrap it around the wound. And that helped chase away the evil spirit.

Q: And that's also for a hangover?

A: Yes, the term later became used in reference to curing a hangover—drinking some of the "hair of the dog" you had the night before (more beer).

Q: Do these beers, having a higher alcohol content, give drinkers a stronger hangover the next morning?

A: All I know is we've generated quite a few hangovers.

Q: Oh yeah...? [Feels forehead and eyes the empty glass warily.]

A: Whether the hangovers are worse or not, I don't know. It depends on what you are used to drinking. We only use quality ingredients, so you should have a quality hangover.

Bridgeport Brewing Co., 1313 NW Marshall (☎241-3612; www.bridgeportbrew.com), at 13th St. This old wood-beamed rope factory is the very best of beer and pizza joints, with sheltered outdoor eating and tables cut from old bowling alleys. The on-site micro-brewery produces a range of British-style ales. Open M-Th 11:30am-11pm, F-Sa 11:30am-midnight, Su 11:30-10pm. Also at 3632 SE Hawthorne (☎233-6540).

⚑ DAYTRIP FROM PORTLAND: SAUVIE

From I-405, Vaughn or Yeon Ave., take US 30 W (dir.: "Mt. St. Helens"). After about 20min. watch for Sauvie Island signs to the right; you can also take bus #17 (St. Helens Rd.) from SW 6th and Salmon (40-50min).

Peaceful Sauvie Island, found just northwest of downtown Portland at the confluence of the Columbia and Willamette Rivers, is part farming community and part nature preserve. A bridge connects Sauvie to the mainland at its southern tip, where produce-growing farms dominate, broken up only by pick-your-own berry stands and farmers markets. Most Portlanders head to Sauvie for its **beaches,** located on the northeast side of the island, which, along the rest of the northern half of the island, form the bird-laden **Sauvie Island State Wildlife Preserve** (www.sauvieisland.org). Parking in the preserve requires a permit and is efficiently enforced (daily permit $3.50, yearly $11). To get one, stop at **Sam's Cracker Barrel Grocery,** and grab a $0.10 map of the island while you're there. Sam's is located just over the bridge, about 50 yds. north on Sauvie Island Rd. (☎621-3960. Open daily 7am-8pm.) Plan ahead; Sam's is several miles from the beaches and is the most convenient place on the island to buy a permit. To get to the beaches head east and north from Sam's along Gillihan Loop Rd., and after 5 mi. bear right onto Reeder Road. Go another 4 mi. on Reeder and the beaches will be to your right. The local park office should know if there are any current advisories against dipping. The **Fish and Wildlife Office** (☎621-3488) is on the western side of the island, just north of where Reeder Rd. and Sauvie Island Rd. meet; the rangers will also be able to recommend nice routes for a short hike around the preserve (the preserve is closed to hikers from late Sept. to mid-Apr.) Sauvie is short on indoor accommodations, but camping is available at **Sauvie Cove RV Park ❷,** 31421 NW Reeder Rd., just south of the beaches. (☎621-9701. Sites with water and fire pits $17. RV sites available for short and long-term stays.)

MOUNT HOOD REGION

MOUNT HOOD   ☎503/541

You can't miss it—a magnet for the eyes, Mt. Hood is by far the most prominent feature on the northwest Oregon horizon. Fumaroles and steam vents near the top mark this as a (relatively) recently active volcano, but that's no deterrent for thousands of outdoors enthusiasts. Home to world-renowned ski resorts, the mountain satisfies Portland's skiing needs. The surrounding ridgelines and mountains are relatively mellow compared to the other mega-peaks to the north, Mt. Adams and Mt. Rainier, allowing for decent, non-technical hiking, albeit with less spectacular views. The mountain gets its fair share of climbers to a 11,235 ft. summit.

■✦ ⚑ ORIENTATION AND PRACTICAL INFORMATION

Mt. Hood stands just north of the junction of US 26 and Hwy. 35, 1½hr. east of Portland via US 26. For a scenic drive, take I-84 along the Columbia River Gorge to Exit 64 and approach the mountain from Hood River (p. 99) on Hwy. 35. **Government Camp,** 50 mi. east of Portland, has food, accommodations, and gear rental.

The nearest **hospitals** are in Portland and Hood River. The **post office** is at 88331 E Govt. Camp Loop Rd., in Government Camp. (☎800-275-8777. Open M-F 7:30am-noon, 1-4:30pm.) **Postal Code:** 97028. **Area code:** 503 to the west and south of Mt. Hood; 541 for Hood River and the northeast.

Hood River Ranger District Station, 6780 Hwy. 35, is 11 mi. south of Hood River and 25 mi. north of the US 26 and Hwy. 35 junction. It has more specialized info on the three ranger districts in the vicinity as well as a variety of trail maps ranging from free to $4. (☎541-352-6002. Open Memorial Day-Labor Day M-F 8am-4:30pm.) The **Mount Hood Information Center,** 65000 E US 26, 16 mi. west of the junction of US 26 and Hwy. 35 and 30 mi. east of Gresham at the entrance to the Mt. Hood village, has topo maps and info on ranger districts. Detailed hiking information is available on the website, and the friendly staff can direct you to the best trails. (☎503-622-7674 or 888-622-4822; www.mthood.info. Open M-Sa 8am-5pm, Su 8am-4pm.)

ACCOMMODATIONS AND CAMPING

Most campgrounds in **Mount Hood National Forest** cluster near the junction of US 26 and Hwy. 35, although they can be found along the length of both highways on the way to Portland or Hood River. To get to a **free camping** spot near the mountain, take the sign towards Trillium Lake (a few miles east of Government Camp on Hwy. 26), then take a dirt road to the right half a mile from the entrance with sign "2650 13," go 200 yd., and make a left towards "Old Airstrip." Campsites with fire rings line the abandoned runway. For a far more expensive, less outdoorsy experience, stay in a hotel in **Government Camp** or on the mountain itself.

Lost Lake Resort and Campground (☎541-386-6366; www.lostlakeresort.org). From Hwy. 35, turn east onto Woodworth Dr., right onto Dee Hwy., and then left on Lost Lake Rd. (Forest Service Rd. 13). A 3 mi. hike around the lake provides views of Mt. Hood. Rent a canoe ($8 per hr., $40 per day), or fish in the trout-stocked lake for free. 121 sites, $15; RV sites without electricity, $20-22; cabins, $50-100. $6 parking permit required for day use. Showers. ❶

Trillium Lake, 2 mi. east of the Timberline turn-off on US 26. Trails surround the crystal-clear lake. Lots of RVs. Paved, secluded sites, $12; lakeside, $14. ❶

Still Creek, 1 mi. west of Trillium Lake off US 26, offers sites that are unpaved and have a quieter, woodsy feel. Few RVs. $14-16. ❶

Sherwood, 14 mi. north of US 26 and just off Hwy. 35, beside a rambling creek, is several miles from Government Camp and, as a result, very quiet. Watch out for the easy-to-miss entrance. Sites $10. ❶

FOOD

Cafeteria food at the ski resorts is extraordinarily overpriced; bring a bag lunch. Food in Government Camp is more reasonable, but still pricey.

Mount Hood Brewing Co., 87304 E Govt. Camp Loop (☎503-622-0724; www.mthood-brewing.com). An angler-friendly interior with good, hearty burgers ($9.50) and plenty of on-site brewed beers. Open M-Th and Su noon-10pm, F-Sa noon-11pm. ❷

Huckleberry Inn, 88611 Hwy. 26 Business Loop (☎503-272-3325; www.huckleberry-inn.com), Government Camp. This diner-style restaurant serves up large portions in a friendly atmosphere. Omelettes $7.50. Open 24hr. ❷

The Taco Shoppe, 88786 Hwy. 26 Business Loop, across from the Huckleberry Inn in Government Camp. The closest thing you'll find to cheap food in the area, this tiny shop serves take-out burritos ($4-6), tacos, and other standard Mexican fare. Open M-W 2-8pm, Th-Sa noon-8pm, Su noon-7pm. ❶

OREGON

SIGHTS

Six miles up a road just east of Government Camp stands the historic **Timberline Lodge** (☎ 503-622-7979; www.timberlinelodge.com), built by hand in 1937 under the New Deal's Works Progress Administration. This is the building featured in the opening scene of the classic horror film *The Shining* (though you won't find Jack inside—the indoor scenes were shot elsewhere). On the Timberline grounds is the **Wy'East Day Lodge**, which offers complimentary ski storage in winter. Timberline's **Magic Mile** express lift carries passengers above the clouds for spectacular views of the mountains and ridges north, though if it's sunny extra elevation doesn't improve on the view from the Timberline Lodge road. (Lift open in summer 9am-4pm; call ☎ 503-222-2211 for spring and fall hours. $8, ages 7-12 $6, under 7 free.)

In the summer, Mt. Hood Ski Bowl opens **Action Park**, which features Indy Kart racing ($6 per 5min.), horseback riding ($25 per hr.), mini-golf ($5), bungee jumping ($25), and an alpine slide for $7. (☎ 222-2695; www.skibowl.com. Open M-Th 11am-6pm, F 11am-7pm, Sa-Su 10am-7pm.) The Ski Bowl maintains 40 mi. of bike trails ($5 trail permit), and **Hurricane Racing** rents mountain bikes from mid-June to October ($10 per hr.; half-day $25, full-day $32; trail permit included). The Mt. Hood Visitors Center also lists free mountain biking trails.

HIKING

Hiking trails encircle Mt. Hood; simple maps are posted around **Government Camp.** The free *Day Hikes* booklet, which describes 34 trails in the area, is available from the Mt. Hood Information Center (see **Orientation and Practical Information,** p. 96). A Northwest Forest parking pass, required for several trailheads, is also available at the info center. ($5 per day or $30 per year.) Mt. Hood is a respectable technical alpine climb. **Timberline Mountain Guides,** based out of Timberline Lodge, guides summit climbs for $375 per person. (☎ 541-312-9242; www.timberlinemt-guides.com.) **Mountain Tracks Ski and Snowboard Shop,** in the Huckleberry Inn, has details on more ski trails. (☎ 503-272-3380. Closed summer; call for winter hours.)

Mirror Lake Trail (6 mi. loop, several hr.) Trailhead at a parking lot off US 26, 1 mi. west of Government Camp. A very popular day hike, this trail winds its way to the beautiful Mirror Lake through the forest. Easy to moderate.

Trillium Lake Loop (4½ mi. loop, 1-2hr.) Trailhead in the day-use area of the Trillium Lake campground. A lakeside trail offering wildlife-viewing and alpine wetlands that becomes a challenging cross-country ski course in winter. Easy to moderate.

Old Salmon River Trail (5 mi. round-trip, 2-3hr.) Take Hwy. 26 to Welches. 1 mi. east of the signal, turn onto Salmon River Rd., and drive on for 2½ mi. Winds up gentle grades through the forests and meadows, and has creek-crossings in spring. Moderate.

Timberline Trail (41 mi., overnight). Trailhead at **Timberline Lodge** (see **Skiing,** below) was constructed by the New Deal Civilian Conservation Corps in the 1930s and circles the mountain, offering incomparable views of the Cascades. A total of 9000 ft. of elevation change and several serious stream crossings. Difficult.

SKIING

Two resorts on the mountain and one on nearby **Tom Dick Peak** rank as the best among the many ski areas around Mt. Hood. All offer **night skiing** and **terrain parks.** Mt. Hood Meadows is considered the best during the early winter for its breadth of terrain and decent snow, but when the temperature drops and the rain changes over to powder, Mt. Hood Ski Bowl has the biggest vertical drops and steepest terrain. Timberline isn't anything special by wintertime standards, but skiers and riders swarm to the slopes in summer, as do thousands of Monarch butterflies.

Mount Hood Meadows (☎503-337-2222, snow report 503-227-7669 or 541-386-7547; www.skihood.com). 9 mi. east of Government Camp on Hwy. 35. The volcanic terrain is a highlight, offering all kinds of interesting features from a natural half-pipe (it's off the Cascade Express lift, below the trail with the huge ridge/cornice) to the stark and steep Heather Canyon. Huge volumes of snow—not always the driest, but there's plenty of it. Mt. Hood Meadows has $25 lift tickets through participating hotels. Open daily Nov.-May 8am-4pm. Peak lift tickets $48, ages 65 and older and 7-12 $20, under 6 $6. Night skiing Dec.-Mar. F-Su 4-10pm, $17.

Mount Hood Ski Bowl, 87000 E US 26 (☎503-222-2695 or 800-754-2695; www.skibowl.com), in Government Camp 2 mi. west of Hwy. 35. Just a little guy, with a vertical drop of 1500 ft. The season is shorter (Nov.-Apr.) because of its lower elevation; however, the bowl boasts 34 lit trails, the most night skiing in the US, and a great terrain park. Open M-Tu 3:30-10pm, W-Th 9am-10pm, F 9am-11pm, Sa 8:30am-11pm, Su 8:30am-10pm. Lift tickets $28-30, under 12 $16-18; $20 per night.

Timberline (☎622-0750; snow report ☎503-222-2211 or 877-754-6734; www.timberlinelodge.com), off US 26 at Government Camp. Timberline becomes a hub for hucking, jibbing, and new-school craziness in the summer—besides Whistler, it's the only resort open. Though much of the resort is set aside for summer ski and riding camps, a snowfield lanes stay open. Wear goggles or sunglasses and sunscreen as well as long pants and long-sleeved tops, since sliding on the snow can be painful. Intermediate to advanced slopes. Open daily winter 9am-4pm; spring and fall 8:30am-2:30pm; summer 7am-1:30pm. Night skiing Jan.-Feb. W-F 4-9pm, Sa-Su 4-10pm. Lift tickets $39.

COLUMBIA RIVER GORGE   ☎541/509

Stretching 75 stunning miles east from Portland, the Columbia River Gorge carries the river to the Pacific Ocean through woodlands, waterfalls, and canyons. Heading inland along the Gorge, heavily forested peaks give way to broad, bronze cliffs and golden hills covered with tall pines. Mt. Hood and Mt. Adams loom nearby, and breathtaking waterfalls plunge over steep cliffs into the river. The river widens out and the wind picks up at the town of Hood River, providing some of the world's best windsurfing. Once fast and full of rapids, the Columbia is more placid now, as dams channel the water's fury into hydroelectric power.

▐ TRANSPORTATION

To follow the Gorge, which divides Oregon and Washington, take **I-84** east from Portland to Exit 22. Continue east uphill on the **Historic Columbia River Highway (US 30),** which follows the crest of the Gorge and affords unforgettable views. Or stay on I-84, which follows the Columbia River; **Highway 14** runs the length of the Washington side of the river. **Hood River,** at the junction of I-84 and **Highway 35,** is the hub of activity in the Gorge. It gives access to the larger city of **Dalles** to the east and **Mt. Hood** (p. 96) to the south. **Bingen, WA,** across the Hood River Bridge ($0.75 toll), provides access to the forests of **Mount Adams** (p. 271). **Maryhill, WA** is 33 mi. east of Bingen on Hwy. 14.

Trains: Amtrak (☎800-872-7245) disgorges passengers at foot of Walnut St. in **Bingen, WA,** across from Monterey Bay Fiberglass in the Burlington-Northern Santa Fe terminal. One train leaves per day for **Portland** (1¾hr., $9-20) and **Spokane** (5¾hr., $29-64).

Buses: Greyhound, 600 E Marina Way (☎541-386-1212), in the Hood River DMV building. Off I-84 at Exit 64, take a left at the intersection before the toll bridge and follow the signs to the DMV, the 2nd building on the right. Open M-F 8:30-11:30am and 1:30-4:30pm. To **Portland** (1¼hr., 5 per day, $13).

Public Transportation: Columbia Area Transit (CAT, ☎386-4202; http://community.gorge.net/hrctd) provides door-to-door service within the Hood River area during the week for $1.25; call well in advance for pick-up. Also provides weekend shuttle to Meadows during ski season ($3). Open daily 8am-4:30pm.

🔃 PRACTICAL INFORMATION

Visitor Information: Hood River County Chamber of Commerce, 405 Portway Ave. (☎541-386-2000 or 800-366-3530; www.hoodriver.org), in the Expo Center north off Exit 63. Helpful information on events in the region complements a plentiful collection of maps, including a massive relief map that stretches from Mt. Adams through the Gorge to Mt. Hood. Open Apr.-Oct. M-F 9am-5pm, Sa-Su 10am-5pm; Nov.-Mar. M-F 9am-5pm. Many other visitors centers also line the Gorge.

Outdoor Information: Columbia Gorge National Scenic Area Headquarters, Sprint's Waucoma Center Bldg., 902 Wasco St. ste. 200 (☎541-386-2333; www.fs.fed.us/r6/columbia), in Hood River. Forest Service camping map ($4). Open M-F 8am-4:30pm.

Internet Access: Hood River Library, 601 State St. (☎541-386-2535; www.co.hood-river.or.us), in Hood River. Six computers with 30-60min. of free Internet access. Open M-Th 8:30am-8:30pm, F-Sa 8:30am-5pm.

Weather: ☎541-386-3300.

Hood River Police: 211 2nd St. (☎541-386-3942).

Hospital: Hood River Memorial, 13th and May St., emergency entrance on 13th (☎541-386-3911). 24hr. emergency.

Post Office: 408 Cascade Ave. (☎800-275-8777), in Hood River. Open M-F 8:30am-5pm. **Postal Code:** 97031.

🏠🏠 ACCOMMODATIONS AND CAMPING

Hotel rooms in Hood River typically start around $50 and spiral upward from there. Cheaper motels line the west end of Westcliffe Dr., north off Exit 62 off I-84, although they're usually full on the weekends. Camping in state parks along the river is generally more affordable. **Ainsworth State Park** is also readily accessible (see **Portland,** p. 83). For a full list of camping facilities, contact the visitors center.

▩ **Bingen School Inn Hostel/Columbia Gorge Outdoor Center** (☎509-493-3363; www.bingenschool.com). 3rd left after the 141 turnoff onto Cedar St.; from there it's 1 block up the hill on Humbolt St. An outdoorsy converted schoolhouse with airy rooms that can accommodate over 70 people in both dorm-style and private rooms. The owner arranges water sports lessons and rentals in the Gorge. Kitchen, laundry, climbing wall, volleyball net, outdoor grill, TV/VCR, school lockers, and linen are available. Winter guests score $25 Hood Meadows lift tickets. Dorms $16; 5 large private rooms $35-45 for 2 people, $10 per additional person. 10 nights for $100. ❷

Beacon Rock State Park (☎509-427-8265), 7 mi. west of the Bridge of the Gods on Washington's Hwy. 14. Easy access to hiking, mountain biking, fishing, and rock climbing. 26 secluded, woodsy sites $16. Coin showers. ❷

Viento State Park (☎541-374-8811 or 800-452-5678). 8 mi. west of Hood River off I-84. Offers a noisy but pleasant experience and with access to river hiking. 13 tent sites $14, 61 RV sites $16. Showers. ❶

FOOD

Hood River's restaurant scene is best be described as "cool," marked by pleasant themed establishments run by upbeat 20-somethings. Portland's trademark micro-brews make an obligatory appearance at most pubs and bars. For groceries, head to **Safeway,** 2249 W Cascade St. (☎541-386-1841. Open 24hr.)

Andrew's Pizza & Bakery, 107 Oak St. (☎386-1448, theater 386-4888; www.sky-lighttheatre.com). Delicious pizza by the slice ($2.50) and salads ($5) in a chic, mini-malist setting. Free wireless Internet access and a movie theater upstairs. Open M-Sa 9am-10pm, Su 10am-10pm. Call for movie times. ❶

Sage's Cafe, 202 Cascade Ave. (☎541-386-9404). Hearty breakfasts ($3-6) and lunch-time options like quiche ($2.50), sandwiches ($4.50), and a veggie burrito ($5) in a relaxed environment. Open M-F 7:30am-5pm, Sa 8am-5pm, Su 9am-4pm. ❶

Full Sail Brewing Company and Pub, 506 Columbia Ave. (☎541-386-2247; www.full-sailbrewing.com). Take 5th St. 2 blocks toward the river from Oak St. Relax on the deck with the open grill and a view of the river. Entrees $6-8. Grill only open in the summer, daily noon-7pm. Pub open daily noon-9pm; winter noon-8pm. ❷

River City Saloon, 207 Cascade Ave. (☎541-387-2583; www.rivercitysaloon.com), hosts bluegrass and rock musicians. Chicken parmesan sandwich $9. Daily happy hour with $2.50 microbrews 4:30-6:30pm. 21+. Internet access $1 per 15min. Open daily 4:30pm-2am. ❷

⦿ SIGHTS

Well known for adventure sports and incredible scenic beauty, the Columbia River Gorge also harbors world-class sights between its walls. These have nothing to do with their location in the Gorge, but are world-class in their own right.

MARYHILL MUSEUM OF ART. This elegant museum sits high above the river on the Washington side. It was built in the 1920s by Sam Hill, a great benefactor of the area and instigator of the historic preservation of the Columbia Gorge. Hill was a friend of Queen Marie of Romania, whose coronation garb is displayed along with Rodin plasters. (*35 Maryhill Museum Dr. Hwy. 14 from Bingen or I-84 to Biggs, Exit 104; cross Sam Hill Bridge, then turn left onto Hwy. 14 for 3 mi. ☎509-773-3733; www.maryhillmuseum.org. Open daily mid-Mar. to mid-Nov. 9am-5pm. $7, seniors $6, ages 6-16 $2.*)

INTERNATIONAL MUSEUM OF CAROUSEL ART. 150 carousel mounts line the walls and vault of this old bank building. Each one has a detailed history and explanation of its significance, from the traditional upright horses to tigers and dragons. The highlight of this museum, however, is the 17 instrument player-band (think player-piano and then add drums, cymbals, and 14 other instruments), sal-vaged, believe it or not, from an old carousel. (*304 Oak St. ☎541-397-4622; www.car-ousemuseum.com. Open daily 10am-4pm. $5, ages 65 and older and 11-17 $4, 5-10 $2.*)

STONEHENGE. Sam Hill built this full-scale replica of the English monument out of concrete as a memorial to the men of Klickitat County killed in WWI. Thinking that the original monument was used in sacrificial rituals before its astronomical properties became known, Hill hoped to express that "humanity still is being sac-rificed to the god of war on fields of battle." People gather here for patriotic holi-days and pagan celebrations alike. (*3 mi. east from the Maryhill Museum along Hwy. 14.*)

OREGON

GO FOR THE GORGE

The rugged walls and high winds of the Columbia River Gorge make it a mecca for a multitude of adventure sports, including kayaking, windsurfing, and skateboarding. The best athletes in the world flock annually to the section of the gorge between Hood River, OR and Stevenson, WA.

Although extreme sports are not as popular with spectators as, say, baseball, the Games maximize enjoyment for spectators. Kiteboarding, for example, takes place just off a beach where hundreds watch the athletes soar 40 ft. into the air, dragged along by their powerful kites, somehow managing to land on their feet and continue racing across the water at 20-30mph.

You can even get in on the action for the mountain bike orienteering challenge's beginner, intermediate, or family divisions, where teams put their navigational abilities to the test. The trail run that kicks off the week is also open to anyone who wants to enjoy the scenery.

The fun doesn't end when the sun goes down. Nightclubs ensure happenings every night of the week. There's a contest featuring the best sports photographers around. If you're looking for sights that are a little bit hotter, check out the Bikini/Boardshorts Contest, or if you're feeling a little daring, enter it.

The competition runs for 9 days in mid-July. (☎386-7774; www.gorgegames.com.)

☒ OUTDOOR ACTIVITIES

WATERFALLS. A string of waterfalls adorns the Historic Columbia River Hwy. (US 30) east of Crown Point; pick up a waterfall map at the visitors center in Hood River. A short paved path leads to the base of **Latourell Falls**, 2½ mi. east of Crown Point. East another 5½ mi., **Wahkeena Falls**, beautiful and visible from the road, splashes 242 ft. down a narrow gorge. The base of the falls is less than half a mile farther east on the Historic Columbia River Hwy. From I-84 Exit 31, take the underpass to the **Multnomah Falls Lodge.** On a platform next to the lodge, you can watch the falls cascade 600 ft. into a tiny pool. For a more strenuous hike, follow the **Larch Mountain Trail** 1 mi. and 600 ft. in altitude to the top of the falls. The **Multnomah Falls visitors center** in the lodge has free trail maps. (☎504-695-2372. Open daily July-Aug. 9am-8pm; June and Sept. 9am-7pm; Oct.-May 9am-5pm.)

WINDSURFING. Frequent 30 mph winds make Hood River a windsurfing paradise. Considered one of the best sites in the world for freestyle sailboarding (the professional term for the sport), Hood River attracts some of the best windsurfers around, making watching as interesting as participating. The venerated **Rhonda Smith Windsurfing Center,** in the Port Marina Sailpark, Exit 64 off I-84, under the bridge and left after the blinking red light, offers classes. (☎541-386-9463. $140 for two 3hr. classes and 10hr. of equipment rental, or take one 3hr. lesson for $75.) **Big Winds,** 207 Front St., has cheap beginner kite board rentals, plenty of helpful advice, and a wealth of equipment. (☎541-386-6086; www.bigwinds.com. $55 per day.) Watch surfers in action at **The Hook,** a shallow, sandy cove off Exit 63 off I-84. Here, beginners learn the basic techniques of starting, handling, and jibing before moving out to the deep water of the river. **Spring Creek Fish Hatchery,** a.k.a. "The Hatch," is on Hwy. 14 west of Bingen. This is place to go to see the best in the windsurfing business; there is plenty of parking, and the shore offers a view of the most popular stretch of water.

▧ KITEBOARDING. Even more interesting than the windsurfers, at least to the layman observer, is kiteboarding, which can be watched from the **Event Site,** on the river across the street from the Chamber of Commerce. Kiteboarders have wakeboard-style boards on their feet and are tethered to enormous kites via 60 ft. lines. They rip through the water at incredible speeds, but even more impressive are the jumps, which can lift boarders 20 ft. off the water and take them 100 ft. Don't be surprised if you see people flipping and corkscrewing through the air. You also shouldn't be shocked to see some serious face-plants.

MOUNTAIN BIKING. The Gorge has excellent mountain biking, with a wide variety of trails for bikers of all levels. **Discover Bicycles,** 116 Oak St., rents mountain bikes (starting at $6 per hr., $35 per day), suggests routes, and sells maps for $5-9. (☎541-386-4820; www.discoverbicycles.com. Open daily summer 9am-6pm; winter 10am-6pm.)

Mosier Twin Tunnels (4½ mi., 1hr.) A segment of the Historic Columbia River Hwy. that is too narrow for cars, between Hood River and Mosier. Parking is available at both the east and west end of the tunnels for $3. Offers mainly an on-road ride, with views of the river and the tunnels. Easy to moderate.

Seven Streams Canyon Loop (8 mi. loop, 1-2hr.) To get to the trailhead, take Oak St. from Hood River past where it merges with W Cascade Ave., and turn left on Country Club Rd. After 1½ mi., take a right on Post Canyon Rd. and park on the right where the road becomes gravel. The trail offers great views as it winds through canyons. Moderate.

Surveyor's Ridge Trail (13mi. one-way, several hr.) To get to the trailhead, take Rte. 35 south from Hood River for 11 mi. to Pinemont Dr. (Rd. 17), and go east for 6 mi. Turn right onto the dirt road at the "Surveyors Ridge" sign and park in the area by the power lines. Trail mainly follows the ridgeline and offers spectacular views of the Hood River Valley, Mt. Hood, and Mt. Adams. Open June-Oct. Moderate to difficult.

HIKING. Hikes abound throughout the gorge, and the proximity of Mt. Hood and the Columbia River makes for rewarding views on nearly any path.

Catherine Creek Trail (1¼ mi. round-trip, less than 1hr.). From Bingen, go east on Hwy. 14 and turn left on County Rd. 1230 at Rowland Lake. After about 1½ mi., park at the Catherine Creek lot. Goes along a paved path on the Washington side through wildflowers with dramatic views of the Columbia River and Mt. Hood. Easy.

Mount Hamilton Trail (4½ mi. round-trip, several hr.) Follow the directions in **Accommodations** (p. 100) to **Beacon Rock State Park,** and park in the lot east of Beacon Rock, the 848 ft. neck of an old volcano. Climbing 2250 ft. up Mt. Hamilton on the Washington side of the river, the trail leads hikers up switchbacks to find the summit bursting with wildflowers in June and July. Moderate to difficult.

Mazama Trail (7½ mi., several hr.) Take Hwy. 35 for 13 mi. to Woodworth Rd., then go 3 mi. to Dee Hwy. (Hwy. 281). Turn right and go 5 mi. before turning and following the signs to Lost Lake for 7 mi. on Rd. 18, then turn left onto Rd. 1810. Take 1810 to 1811 and drive 3 mi. to the trailhead. This trail begins in the forest, with Mt. Hood as a magnificent backdrop, then climbs up a steep ridge and through a dense forest to flowered glades and amazing vistas. Open June-Oct. $3 permit required. Difficult.

THE COAST: US 101

If not for the renowned US 101, Oregon's sandy beaches and dramatic seaside vistas might be only a beautiful rumor to those on the interior. In addition to offering breathtaking views of the coast, US 101 goes through every major town from Brookings to Astoria. The easy access to beaches and state parks ensures that no outdoors activity is unavailable.

There are 17 major state parks along the coast, many of which offer **campgrounds** with electricity and showers. While most of the traffic seems to be tourists in RVs, some savvy travelers choose to experience the coast by **bicycle.** In summer, prevailing winds blow southward, keeping at the backs of cyclists and easing their journey. Cyclists can contact virtually any visitors center or Chamber of Commerce on the coast for a free copy of the *Oregon Coast Bike Route Map*, which provides invaluable info for the ride. **Buses** run up and down the coast, stopping in most sizable towns. Many local lines are affiliates of Greyhound and make connections to major urban centers like Seattle, Portland, and Eugene. The fastest way to experience the coast, however, is by car.

ASTORIA ☎ 503

Established in 1811 by John Jacob Astor's trading party, Astoria is the oldest US city west of the Rocky Mountains. Originally built as a fort to guard the mouth of the Columbia River, it quickly became a port city for ships heading to Portland and Longview, WA. Astoria's Victorian homes, bustling waterfront, rolling hills, and persistent fog suggest a smaller-scale San Francisco. Differentiating it from that metropolis is a microclimate with wicked storms; gale-force winds aren't uncommon, and many visitors come to watch storms roll into the Columbia river outlet.

▐ TRANSPORTATION

From Astoria, US 30 runs 95 mi. to Portland, a convenient link between Washington and the Oregon coast. Astoria can also be reached from Portland on US 26 and US 101 via **Seaside** (p. 108). Two bridges run from the city: the **Youngs Bay Bridge** leads southwest where Marine Dr. becomes US 101, and the **Astoria Bridge** spans the Columbia River into Washington.

> **Buses: Pierce Pacific Stages,** (☎692-4437). A Greyhound affiliate. Pickup at Video City, 95 W Marine Dr., opposite the Chamber of Commerce. To: **Portland** (3hr., $22). **Sunset Empire Transit,** 465 NE Skipanon Dr. (☎861-7433 or 800-766-6406; www.ridethebus.org), Warrenton. Pickup at Duane and 9th St. To: **Seaside** (7 per day; $2.25, ages 65 and older, disabled, students, and ages 6-12 $1.75).

> **Public Transportation: Astoria Transit System** (contact Sunset Empire for info, above). Local bus service M-Sa 7am-7pm. $0.75; ages 65 and older, disabled, students, and ages 6-12 $0.50.

> **Taxis: Old Gray Cab,** (☎338-6030). $1.80 per mi., 24 hr.

✳ ▐ ORIENTATION AND PRACTICAL INFORMATION

Astoria is a peninsula that extends into the Columbia River, approximately 7 mi. from the ocean beaches in both Fort Stevens and nearby Washington. All streets parallel to the water are named in ascending alphabetical order, with the first main street downtown being Commercial, then Duane, Exchange, etc. **Marine Drive** is an exception to this rule, hugging the water throughout Astoria.

> **Tourist Information:** 111 W Marine Dr. (☎325-6311), just east of Astoria Bridge. Loads of info on Astoria and its surrounding attractions. Open June-Sept. M-Sa 8am-6pm, Su 9am-5pm; daily Oct.-May 9am-5pm.

> **Equipment Rental: Bikes and Beyond,** 1089 Marine Dr. (☎325-2961; www.bikesandbeyond.com) rents bikes. $6 per hr. or $20 per day.

> **Laundromat: Maytag Self-Service Laundry,** 127 W Bond St. (☎325-7815), 1 block away from Marine Dr. Wash $1, dry $0.25 per 10min. or $0.50 per 40min. Open daily 8am-9pm, last wash load at 7:45pm.

> **Crisis Line:** ☎800-562-6025.

OREGON

Police: 555 30th St. (☎325-4411).

Hospital: Columbia Memorial, 2111 Exchange St. (☎325-4321). 24hr.

Internet Access: Astoria Library, 450 10th St. (☎325-7323). 1hr. of free Internet access (ID required as deposit). Open Tu-Th 10am-7pm, F-Sa 10am-5pm.

Post Office: 748 Commercial St. Open M-F 8:30am-5pm. **Postal Code:** 97103.

ACCOMMODATIONS AND CAMPING

Motel rooms can be expensive and elusive during summer. US 101, both north and south of Astoria, is littered with clean and scenic campgrounds.

Ft. Stevens State Park (☎861-1671, reservations 800-452-5687), over Youngs Bay Bridge on US 101 S, 10 mi. west of Astoria. Rugged, empty beaches, hiking paths, and bike trails surround the campground. Reservations ($6) recommended. Wheelchair-accessible. 600 sites, $18; hiker/biker sites $4.25 per person; full RV sites $21; yurts $29. Showers included. ❷

Grandview B&B, 1574 Grand Ave. (☎325-0000 or 325-5555; www.pacifier.com/~grndview). Cheery and luxurious rooms. Includes delicious breakfast. Rooms from $77. low-season 2nd night is $36 (Sept.-May). ❹

Lamplighter Motel, 131 W. Marine Dr. (☎325-4051 or 800-845-8847;), about ¼ mi. after going under the Astoria Bridge from the south. These well-lit rooms have cable TV, microwaves, and refrigerators as well as large bathrooms. Free coffee Is available in the lobby all day. Rooms $66-69, $38 in winter. ❸

FOOD

Safeway, 3250 Marine Dr., provides groceries. (☎325-4662. Open daily 6am-1am.) A **farmers market** convenes summer Sunday mornings at 12th St. and Commercial.

Columbian Cafe, 1114 Marine Dr. (☎325-2233; www.columbianvoodoo.com). A friendly, fun, local favorite with wines by the glass and fantastic pasta and seafood ($12-17, lunches $4-8). Try "Seafood" or "Vegetarian Mercy"—name the heat your mouth can stand and the chef will design a meal for you ($8-9). Open M-Tu 8am-2pm, W-Sa 8am-9pm, Su 9am-2pm. ❷

T. Paul's Urban Cafe, 1119 Commercial St. (☎338-5133; www.tpaulsurbancafe.com). No two square feet of the restaurant are alike, as part of a chaotic but endearing decoration scheme. Very satisfying dinner quesadillas $7; delicious pastas $8. Lunches around $7. Open M-Th 9am-9pm, F-Sa 9am-10pm, Su 11am-4pm. ❷

Home Spirit Bakery and Cafe, 1585 Exchange St. (☎325-6846; www.home-spirit.com). Tasty, inexpensive lunch ($4-9) in a restored Victorian home just a block away from the Shallon Winery. Call ahead. Open Tu-Th 11am-2pm, F-Sa 11am-2pm and 5:30-8pm. ❷

Shallon Winery, 1598 Duane St. (☎325-5978; www.shallon.com). Two blocks from the Maritime Museum, owner Paul van der Veldt presides over a kingdom of fantastic wines. A self-proclaimed connoisseur of fine food, he insists that visitors call him at any time of day or night before considering a meal at any restaurant within 50 mi. Samplers taste wines made from local berries and the world's only commercially produced whey wines (from the cheese factories in Tillamook). Sampling lemon meringue pie wine is likely to be the highlight, and Paul's chocolate orange wine ($29) is quite the decadent liqueur. Open virtually every afternoon noon-6pm-ish. Gratuities and purchases appreciated. ❺

OREGON

OREGON

SIGHTS

On the rare clear day, ◪**Astoria Column** (☎325-2963) grants its climbers a stupendous view of Astoria cradled between **Saddle Mountain** to the south and the **Columbia River Estuary** to the north. You can get there by following signs for about 5min. from 16th Ave. and Commercial St. Completed in 1926, the column on Coxcomb Hill Rd. encloses a dizzying 164 steps past newly repainted friezes depicting local history; picture something like an exceptionally well-decorated barber's pole jutting into the sky, albeit one that (luckily) doesn't spin. (Open dawn-dusk. Parking $1.) The cavernous, wave-shaped **Columbia River Maritime Museum,** 1792 Marine Dr. on the waterfront, is packed with marine lore, including displays on the salmon fisheries that once dominated Astoria and an exhibit on the thousands of ships that have sunk in the notorious waters just off the coast. Among the model boats is the 1792 vessel that Robert Grey first steered into the mouth of the Columbia River. (☎325-2323; www.crmm.org. Open daily 9:30am-5pm. $8, ages 65 and older $7, ages 6-17 $4, under 6 free.) The annual **Astoria-Warrenton Crab and Seafood Festival** is a misnomer for a large assembly of Oregon winemakers, brewers, and restaurants. ($5. Call the Chamber of Commerce ☎800-875-6807 for more info.)

NIGHTLIFE

◪**Voodoo Room,** (☎325-2233; www.columbianvoodoo.com) adjacent to the Columbian Cafe. The hot venue for live music, known by many as the artists' hang. Egyptian sarcophagi complete the scene. Drinks about $4. F-Sa funk, jazz, and every other kind of music; cover $3-5. Su bluegrass, no cover. Open daily 5-10pm or later.

Wet Dog Cafe & Pacific Rim Brewing Co., 144 11th St. (☎325-6975; www.pacificrimbrewing.com). Youthful crowds pack in every weekend for hip-hop and top-40 music. Burgers $5.50-8, microbrews $3.25. Occasional live music. Live comedy W 9:30pm ($3). Game room. DJ Th-F. 21+ after 9pm. Open M-Tu, Th, and Su 11am-9:30pm, W 11am-midnight and F-Sa 11am-1:30am. Dinner served until 9pm.

▶ DAYTRIPS FROM ASTORIA

FORT CLATSOP NATIONAL MEMORIAL. Reconstructs Lewis and Clark's winter headquarters from journal descriptions. The fort has been completely restored and contains exhibits about the explorers' quest for the Pacific Ocean. In summer, rangers in feathers and buckskin demonstrate quill writing, moccasin sewing, and musket firing. (5 mi. southwest of town on US 101, south from Astoria to Alt. Rte. US 101; follow signs 3 mi. to park. ☎861-2471. Open daily 9am-5pm. $3, under 17 free, families $5 per car.)

FORT STEVENS STATE PARK. Fort Stevens was constructed in 1863 to prevent attack by Confederate naval raiders and was significantly upgraded in 1897 with the addition of eight concrete artillery batteries. Several of these remaining batteries are the focus of a 2hr. self-guided walking tour that begins up the road from the campground area. (Off US 101 on a narrow peninsula 10 mi. west of Astoria. ☎861-2000. Day-use pass $3. Get a map and pass from the camp registration.)

SOUTH JETTY. The South Jetty, the northern tip of the peninsula in Fort Stevens State Park, offers great places ride the surf on both board and kayak. Waves get particularly big as they get in close to the jetty. Catching a wave in front of the **Wreck of the Peter Iredale** that sticks out of the sand is a novel experience, even though the breaks are nothing special. Both beaches are easy to find within Fort Stevens State Park. Look for parking lot A or B for the

OREGON

South Jetty; the main road goes straight to the Peter Iredale. No shop specializes in surfboards in Astoria, but **Pacific Wave** in Warrenton, immediately across the Youngs Bay Bridge in the mall on the right, embraces the growing kayak-surfing movement and offers lessons, as well as the latest wave forecasts and other surf info.

SEASIDE ☎ 503

In the winter of 1805-1806, explorers Lewis and Clark made their westernmost camp near Seaside. While the amenities were few and far between at the time, after the development of a resort in 1870 the situation improved and visitors began to pour in. The tourism industry, replete with indoor mini-golf and barrels of salt-water taffy, has transformed Seaside from a remote coastal outpost to a bustling beachfront. For those uninterested in video arcades, Seaside still has merit as a base for exploring the beautiful Oregon coast. Seaside is also less expensive than nearby Cannon Beach, and its hostel is one of the best in the Northwest.

▐▀ TRANSPORTATION. Pierce Pacific Stages, a Greyhound affiliate, runs buses from the Seaside International Hostel, 930 N Holladay Dr., at 3pm for **Portland** (2hr., $15) and **Seattle** (7hr., $44, via **Kelso, WA**). (☎692-4437; call Greyhound at 800-231-2222 for schedules and fares). **Sunset Empire Transit** runs between Astoria and Cannon Beach 7 times per day M-Sa, stopping at the hostel in addition to the bus stops. Tickets available from drivers. (☎861-7433 or 800-776-6406. Round-trip $4; ages 65 and older, disabled, students, and ages 6-12 $2; under 6 free.) **Yellow Cab** services the Seaside area 24hr. (☎738-5252. $1.75 base, $1.50 per mi.)

▐▐▀ ORIENTATION AND PRACTICAL INFORMATION. Seaside lies 17 mi. south of Astoria and 8 mi. north of Cannon Beach along **US 101.** The most direct route between Seaside and Portland is **US 26,** which intersects US 101 just south of Seaside near Saddle Mountain State Park. The Necanicum River runs north-south through Seaside, two blocks from the coastline. In town, US 101 becomes **Roosevelt Drive,** and another major road, **Holladay Drive,** splits off from it. **Broadway** runs perpendicular to the two, and is the town's main street and a black hole for tourist dollars. Streets north of Broadway are numbered, and those south of Broadway are lettered. The **Promenade** (or "Prom") is a paved foot-path that hugs the beach for the length of town.

The **Seaside Visitor Bureau** is on US 101 and Broadway. (☎738-3097 or 888-306-2326. Open daily June-Aug. 8am-5pm; Oct.-May M-F 9am-5pm, Sa-Su 10am-4pm.) **Prom Bike Shop,** 622 12th Ave. at 12th and Holladay, rents bikes ($8 per hr., $30 per day), in-line skates ($6 per hr.), beach tricycles ($9 per 1½ hr.), and surreys ($12-36 per hr.). Excellent repair work. Must be 18 or older to sign for rental. (☎738-8251. Open daily 10am-6pm.) Do **laundry** at **Clean Services,** 1223 S. Roosevelt Dr. (☎738-9513. Open daily 8am-10pm. Wash $1.25, dry $0.25 per 8min.) The **police** are at 1091 S Holladay Dr. (☎738-6311) and the **Coast Guard** is at 2185 SE Airport Rd. (☎861-6140), in Warrenton. For medical needs, head to **Providence Seaside Hospital,** 752 S Wahanna Rd. (☎717-7000.) Free 1hr. of **Internet** access is available at the **Seaside Library,** 60 N Roosevelt Dr. (☎738-6742. Open Tu-Th 9am-8pm, F-Sa 9am-5pm, Su 1-5pm.) The **post office** is at 300 Ave. A, off Columbia Ave. (☎800-275-8777. Open M-F 8:30am-5pm, Sa 8:30-10:30am.) **Postal Code:** 97138.

▐▀ ACCOMMODATIONS AND CAMPING. Seaside's expensive motels are hardly an issue for the budget traveler thanks to the large hostel on the south side of town. Motel prices are directly proportional to their proximity to the beach and start at $50 (less during the low season). The closest state parks are **Fort Stevens ❶** (☎861-1671; see p. 107), 21 mi. north and **Saddle Mountain ❶** (☎800-551-6949), 10 mi. east of town off US 26 after it splits with US 101. Drive 8 mi. northeast of Necanicum Junction, then another 7 mi. up a winding road to the parking lot. Ten beautiful, secluded sites are spread out 5-30 yards from the parking lot. (Drinking water. 10 sites. Oct.-Apr. $7; May-Sept. $10.) Sleeping on the beach in Seaside is illegal, as it is in all of Oregon. **Seaside International Hostel (HI) ❷**, 930 N Holladay Dr., has free nightly movies, a well-equipped kitchen, an espresso bar, and a grassy yard along the river. (☎738-7911; www.2oregonhostels.com. Office open 8am-11pm. Call well ahead on weekends. 34 large bunks. $19, nonmembers $22; private rooms with bath and cable from $46/$52. $2 off for touring cyclists.) The **Colonial Motor Inn ❸**, 1120 N Holladay Dr., is a standout for the price, with colonial furniture, free snacks, and small, clean rooms; free Internet in office and some rooms. (☎738-6295 or 800-221-3804. Singles $50; doubles $70. $15-20 less in winter.)

◻ FOOD. Prices on Broadway, especially toward the beach, are outrageous. **Safeway**, 401 S. Roosevelt Dr., stocks the basics. (☎738-7122. Open daily 6am-1am.) Opposite Safeway is the **Morning Star Cafe ❶**, 280 S. Roosevelt Dr. Comfy beat-up couches and aging board games may remind you of your old basement rec room, but the chicken quesadilla ($4.75) and quiche ($3.50) bear little resemblance to your old TV dinners. (☎717-8188. Open daily 7am-4pm.) **The Stand ❶**, 101 N. Holladay Dr., serves the cheapest Mexican meals around, fast-food style, to a local crowd. Burritos $2.25-4. (☎738-6592. Open daily 11am-8pm.) Seaside's famous beach bread and a font of frosted treats are made every day at low tide at **Harrison's Bakery ❶**, 608 Broadway. The plate-sized donuts are complemented by hosteling discounts. (☎738-5331. Open W-Su 7am-4pm.)

◙ ◻ SIGHTS AND ENTERTAINMENT. Seaside's tourist population (which often outnumbers that of true locals) swarms around **Broadway,** a garish strip of arcades and shops running the half mile from Roosevelt (US 101) to the beach. "The Arcade," as it is called, is the focal point of downtown and attracts a youthful crowd. Bumper cars, basketball games, and other methods of fleecing visitors abound. The turnaround at the end of Broadway signals the end of the **Lewis and Clark Trail.** Perhaps the US's premier recreational road race, the **Hood to Coast Relay** is the ultimate team running event. Held annually at the end of August, runners cover the 195 miles of trails between Mt. Hood and Seaside, relay-style, in over 750 12-person teams. For info, call ☎292-2626 or 800-444-6749.

◪ OUTDOOR ACTIVITIES. Seaside's beachfront is sometimes crowded despite bone-chilling water and strong undertows that preclude swimming. For a slightly quieter beach, head to **Gearhart,** 2 mi. north of downtown off US 101, where long stretches of dunes await exploration. The local surfers know that one of Northern Oregon's **finest breaks** is south of town in **The Cove**, but don't tell anyone that *Let's Go* told you. To get there, take Ave. U towards the beach of Hwy. 101 and then make a left on Edgewood. **Cleanline Surf**, 719 1st Ave., rents surfing gear and also has a location in Cannon Beach. (☎738-7888 or 888-546-6176; www.cleanline-surf.com. Open daily summer 10am-8pm; winter M-Sa 10am-6pm, Su 10am-5pm.)

CANNON BEACH ☎503

Cannon Beach has come a long way since a rusty cannon from a shipwrecked schooner washed ashore, giving it its name. Today, Cannon Beach is home to an impressive array of boutiques, bakeries, and galleries, making it a more refined alternative to Seaside's carnival-like atmosphere. Arguably the most worthwhile destination on the entire Oregon Coast because of its amazing ocean views and interesting shops, Cannon Beach is always crowded with Portlanders and other tourists. If you're just driving down US 101, it's well worth the small detour down Hemlock St. to take in the view.

⚡ ORIENTATION AND PRACTICAL INFORMATION. Cannon Beach lies 8 mi. south of Seaside, 42 mi. north of Tillamook on US 101, and 79 mi. from Portland via US 26. **Ecola** and **Oswald State Parks** lie just to the north and a few miles south of the town, respectively. The four exits into town from US 101 all lead to **Hemlock Street,** lined with galleries and restaurants. The **Sunset Transit System** serves **Seaside** ($1, students $0.50) and **Astoria** ($2, students $1). (☎800-776-6406; www.ridethebus.org.) **Cannon Beach Shuttle** traverses downtown; to board, just signal to the driver. (☎861-7433; www.cannon-beach.net/shuttle. Runs daily 9am-6pm.) Visitor info is at the **Cannon Beach Chamber of Commerce and Visitor Info,** 207 N. Spruce St., at 2nd St. (☎436-2623; www.cannonbeach.org. Open M-F 9:30am-5pm. Visitor info open M-Sa 10am-5pm, Su 11am-4pm.) **Mike's Bike Shop,** 248 N. Spruce St., rents bikes for $7 per hr.and $20 for 24hr.; beach tricycles are $10 per 1½hr. (☎436-1266 or 800-492-1266. Open daily 10am-6pm.) **Cleanline Surf,** 171 Sunset Blvd., has surf and boogie boards for $15 per day, wet-suits for $20 per day, and a complete package for $35 per day. (☎436-9726; www.clean-linesurf.com. Open daily summer 9am-7pm; winter 10am-5pm.) The **police** are at 163 Gower St. (☎436-2811); the nearest emergency care is in **Seaside** (☎717-7000; p. 108). **Internet** access is $6 per hr. at the **Cannon Beach Library,** 131 N. Hemlock St. (☎436-1391; open M-W and F 1-5pm, Th 1-7pm) and at $5 for 1st 30min., $5 for each additional hr. at **Copies and Fax,** 1235 S Hemlock St. (☎436-2000. Open M-F 10am-6pm.) The **post office** is at 163 N Hemlock St. (☎436-2822. Open M-F 9am-5pm.) **Postal Code:** 97110.

🏠 ACCOMMODATIONS AND CAMPING. During the low season, inquire about specials; many motels offer two-for-one deals. In the summer, however, it's a seller's market, so most motels have two- night minimum stays if you want a res-ervation. Real budget deals are a short drive away: the **Seaside International Hostel** (p. 108) is 7 mi. north, and **Oswald West State Park** (p. 111), 10 mi. south of town, has a stunning campground. **Nehalem Bay State Park,** only a few miles farther south than Oswald West outside of Nehalem, has plentiful camping options. **McBee Cottages ❸,** 888 S Hemlock St., offers bright and cheerful rooms a few blocks from the beach. The office is in the **Cannon Beach Hotel,** 3 blocks south on Hemlock; some kitchen units and cottages available as well. (☎436-2569; www.mcbeecot-tages.com. Queen beds start at $49; 2 twin beds start at $79. $30 less between Labor Day and June 15th.) Tree-shaded sites make family-owned **Wright's for Camp-ing ❷,** 334 Reservoir Rd., off US 101, a relaxing retreat from RV mini-cities. Wheel-chair-accessible; reservations advised in summer. (☎436-2347; www.wrightsforcamping.com. 19 sites, $17. Showers.)

🍴 FOOD. The deals are down Hemlock St. in mid-town. **Mariner Market,** 139 N. Hemlock St., provides an impressive variety of food in a corner-market like atmo-sphere. (☎436-2442. Open July-Sept. M-Th and Su 8am-10pm, F-Sa 8am-11pm; Oct.-June M-Th and Su 8am-9pm, F-Sa 8am-10pm.) **Lazy Susan's Cafe ❷,** 126 N Hemlock St., in Coaster Sq., has an intimate and woodsy interior and serves excellent home-made scones ($1.75) and daily waffle and omelette specials ($8-9). (☎436-2816. Open M-Sa 7:30am-10pm, Su 8am-4pm.) **Cafe Mango ❷,** 1235 S Hemlock St., in Hay-stack Sq., is an up-and-coming restaurant; the savory crepes ($5-7) are a highlight. (☎436-2393. Open summer M and Th-Su 7:30am-2:30pm. Also has a new restaurant at 123 S. Hemlock, open daily 7am-9pm.) **Bill's Tavern ❶,** 188 N Hemlock St., is a local spot for down-to-earth eatin'. Beer on tap (pints $3) is brewed upstairs and served with basic, tasty pub grub ($4-7). (☎436-2202. Open M-Tu and Th-Su 11:30am-midnight, W 4:30pm-midnight. Kitchen closes around 9:30pm.)

🔦🎨 **ENTERTAINMENT AND OUTDOOR ACTIVITIES.** The town of Cannon Beach has expensive, sporadically elegant galleries and gift shops. A stroll along the 7 mi. stretch of flat, bluff-framed beach may be a better way to experience Cannon Beach. **Coaster Theater,** 108 N. Hemlock St., is a small playhouse that stages theater productions, concerts, dance performances, comedy, and musical revues. Schedule varies, so call or check the website. (☎436-1242; www.coastertheatre.com. Box office open W-Sa 1-5pm. Tickets $12-15.)

The best place to enjoy the dramatic volcanic coastline of Cannon Beach is at **Ecola State Park,** ($3) at the north end of town, which attracts picnickers, hikers, and surfers alike. Ecola Point's views of hulking **Haystack Rock,** covered by seagulls, puffins, barnacles, anemones, and the occasional sea lion are stunning. **Indian Beach,** accessible off US 101 north of Cannon Beach, is a gorgeous surfing destination where you can catch waves between volcanic rock walls, with a freshwater stream running down the beach to rinse the salt off. Surfboards are available from **Cleanline Surf** (p. 110). There is also good hiking in the area. **Indian Beach Trail** (2 mi. round-trip, easy to moderate) leads to the Indian Beach tide pools, which teem with colorful sea life. Follow signs to "Ecola" to reach the trailhead. **Tillamook Head Trail** (12 mi. round-trip, moderate), leaves from Indian Beach and hugs the coast to the mini-cape that separates Seaside Beach from Cannon Beach. The trail passes the top of Tillamook Head (2 mi. up the trail), where five hiker sites await those willing to make the trek for free camping. **Saddle Mountain Trail** (5 mi. round-trip, difficult), 14 mi. east of Cannon Beach on US 26, climbs the highest peak in the Coast Range. The trail leads to the mountain's 3283 ft. summit and ends with astounding views of the Pacific Ocean, Nehalem Bay, and the Cascades.

CANNON BEACH TO TILLAMOOK ☎503

The coastal mountains south of Cannon Beach culminate in a scenic section of roadway that cuts into the ocean cliffside of Neahkahnie Mountain. Farther south is **Tillamook State Forest,** so named after the infamous Tillamook Burn (a series of fires in 1933) reduced 5 sq. mi. of coastal forest near Tillamook to charcoal. While nature has restored Tillamook State Forest to health, coastal towns to the west are still scarred. The coastline alongside these tiny towns is much less crowded than Seaside and Cannon Beaches. Tourist info for the area is available at the visitors center in Tillamook (p. 112) or the **Rockaway Beach Chamber of Commerce,** 103 S. 1st St., off US 101. (☎355-8108; www.rockawaybeach.net. Open M-F 10am-3pm.)

HUG POINT. The tidal caves, Hug Point's main claim to fame, are accessible only at low tide. A waterfall cascading right down onto the beach between two cliffs makes this spot even more breathtaking. The beach is framed by tall cliffs, and secluded picnic tables dot the headlands near the parking lot. This point is about 2 mi. south of Cannon Beach.

OSWALD WEST STATE PARK. Ten miles south of Cannon Beach, Oswald West State Park is a tiny headland rainforest of hefty spruce and cedars. Local surfers call the sheltered beach here **Short Sands Beach,** or Shorty's; with a first-rate break and camping so close by, the beach is a premier surf destination. The beach and woodsy campsites are only accessible by a ¼ mi. trail off US 101, but the park provides wheelbarrows for transporting gear from the parking lot to the 29 sites. (Open Mar.-Nov. $15.) The campground fills quickly; call ahead. From the south side of the park, a segment of the Oregon Coast Trail leads over the headland to 1661 ft. Neahkahnie Mountain.

NEHALEM. Eight miles south of Oswald State Park, a cluster of made-in-Oregon-type shops along US 101 make up Nehalem. The **Nehalem Bay Winery,** 34965 Hwy. 53, 3 mi. south of town, has free tastings of local cranberry and blackberry vin-

OREGON

tages. The backpacker-friendly winery sponsors performances in a small theater and an annual reggae festival in June and blues festival in August, providing a forum for general bacchanalian revelry. (☎368-9463; www.newhalembaywinery.com. Open daily summer 9am-6pm; winter 10am-5pm.)

TILLAMOOK   ☎503

Although the word Tillamook (TILL-uh-muk) translates to "land of many waters," in the Northwest it is synonymous with cheese. Tourists come by the hundreds to gaze at blocks of cheese being cut into smaller blocks on a conveyor belt at the **Tillamook Cheese Factory.** The dairy cows themselves give the town a rather bad odor; still, two good museums, hiking and biking in the nearby coastal mountains, and the Three Capes Loop redeem Tillamook for the adventurous traveler.

■■ **ORIENTATION AND PRACTICAL INFORMATION.** Tillamook lies 49 mi. south of Seaside and 44 mi. north of Lincoln City on **US 101.** It's also 74 mi. west of Portland on **Route 6** and **US 26.** Tillamook's main drag, US 101, splits into two one-way streets downtown: **Pacific Avenue** runs north and **Main Avenue** runs south. The east-west streets are labeled numerically. **Ride the Wave Bus Lines** (☎815-8283) runs locally (M-Sa; $1) as well as to Portland (2½hr., 5 per week, $10). You can also call **Dial-a-Ride** (☎800-815-8283) between 8am and 5pm M-F for $1. Find a list of campsites and hiking trails in Tillamook County at the **Tillamook Chamber of Commerce,** 3705 US 101 N, in the big red barn near the Tillamook Cheese Factory, 1½ mi. north of town. (☎842-7525; www.tillamookchamber.org. Open M-F 10am-5pm, Sa 11am-3pm.) **Equipment repair** is at **Trask Mountain Cycle,** 2011 3rd St., by Pacific Ave., where they also give advice and sell maps of mountain biking trails in the area. (☎842-9220. Open M-Th 9am-8pm, F-Sa 9am-9pm, Su 11am-7pm.) The **police,** 210 Laurel St. (☎842-2522) are in City Hall; the **Coast Guard** is ☎322-3531. The **post office** is at 2200 1st St. (☎800-275-8777. Open M-F 9am-5pm.) **Postal Code:** 97141.

■■ **ACCOMMODATIONS AND CAMPING.** Motel prices in Tillamook are steep (and aren't helped by the 7% city lodging tax), but the camping is some of the area's finest. The only reasonably priced motel in town is the **MarClair Inn ❹,** 11 Main Ave. at the center of town, which rents dark but clean rooms. Enjoy the outdoor pool, hot tub, and sauna. (☎800-331-6857. Singles $72; doubles $74. 10% AAA discount. Credit card required.) **Kilchis River Park ❶,** 6 mi. northeast of town at the end of Kilchis River Rd., which leaves US 101 1 mi. north of the factory, has 35 sites between a mossy forest and the Kilchis River. The campground itself is mostly geared towards families, with a baseball field, volleyball court, horseshoes, and swimming. Mountain bikers can find excellent trails within short rides of the campground on former logging roads. Hiking options abound in the mountains, and the campground offers access to one of the **best salmon-fishing** rivers in the lower 48. (☎842-6694. Open May-Oct. Walk-ins $3; tent sites $10.) To sleep on the sand, try the **campgrounds** on the Three Capes Loop.

■ **FOOD.** Tillamook may be a cheese-lover's paradise, but other food choices in town are lacking. Pick up some Velveeta at **Safeway,** 955 US 101, on the north side of downtown. (☎842-4831. Open daily 6am-1am.) The **Blue Heron French Cheese Company ❷,** 2001 Blue Heron Dr., north of town and 1 mi. south of the Tillamook Cheese factory, has tasty deli offerings. Although the sheer quantity and variety of jelly, wine and cheese is almost overwhelming, sandwiches stand out at $6.25. (☎842-8281; www.blueheronoregon.com. Open daily summer 8am-8pm; winter 9am-5pm. Deli open daily summer 11:30am-4:30pm; 11:30am-3:30pm in winter).

THREE CAPES LOOP ■ 113

⬛ SIGHTS. Plane buffs and all who celebrate mechanical marvels will appreciate the impressive **Tillamook Naval Air Station Museum,** 2 mi. south of town. This hulking seven-acre former blimp hangar is the largest wooden clear-span structure in the world. The airy cavern is home to over 34 fully functional war planes, including WWII beauties and an incredibly massive F-14 Tomcat. If you've never seen a fighter plane up close, it's truly a unique experience. (☎842-1130; www.tillamookair.com. Open daily 10am-5pm. $9.50, over 65 $8.50, ages 13-17 $5.50, 12 and under $2.) Downtown, the **Tillamook County Pioneer Museum,** 2106 2nd St., features exceptionally thorough collections of WWII medals, rifles, and collectibles. Also displays the head-turning work of taxidermist and big game hunter Alex Walker. (☎842-4553; www.tcpm.org. Open Tu-Sa 9am-5pm, Su 11am-5pm. $2, seniors $1.50, ages 12-17 $0.50, under 12 free.)

THREE CAPES LOOP ☎503/541

Between Tillamook and Lincoln City, US 101 wanders east into wooded land, losing contact with the coast. The Three Capes Loop is a 35 mi. circle that connects a trio of spectacular promontories—Cape Meares, Cape Lookout, and Cape Kiwanda State Parks—whose beauty will almost certainly make you linger; plan accordingly. The loop leaves US 101 at Tillamook and rejoins it about 10 mi. north of Lincoln City. Unless time is of the utmost importance, taking the loop is a far better choice than driving straight down US 101.

CAPE MEARES STATE PARK. Cape Meares State Park, at the tip of the promontory jutting out from Tillamook, protects one of the few remaining old-growth forests on the Oregon Coast. The **Octopus Tree,** a gnarled Sitka spruce with six candelabra trunks, looks like the imaginative doodlings of an eight-year-old. The **Cape Meares Lighthouse** functions as an illuminating on-site interpretive center. (Open daily Apr.-Oct. 11am-4pm. In Oct. call ☎503-842-2244 in case of bad weather. Free.) If you walk down to the lighthouse, you can bring binoculars or use the $0.25 viewer to look at the amazing seabird colony on the giant volcanic rock. As you drive south of Cape Meares, a break in the trees reveals a beach between two cliffs; this is a beautiful, quiet place to pull off the road and explore.

Oceanside and **Netarts** lie a couple miles south of the Cape, and offer overpriced gas, a market, and a few places to stay that tend to fill up fast. **The Terimore ❹,** 5105 Crab Ave., in Netarts, has the least expensive rooms in the two towns, some with ocean views. (☎503-842-4623 or 800-635-1821; www.oregoncoast.com/terimore. Rooms with views $65-75, without $56-66.) The **Whiskey Creek Cafe ❷,** 6060 Whiskey Creek Road in Netarts offers fresh seafood (particularly shellfish) in a bright and slightly hippyish atmosphere; halibut and chips $9.25. (☎503-842-5117. Open M-Th and Su 11am-9pm, F-Sa 11am-10pm.)

CAPE LOOKOUT STATE PARK. Another 12 mi. southwest of Cape Meares, Cape Lookout State Park offers a small, rocky beach with incredible views of the coast, as well as some fine camping near the dunes and the forests behind them. From the trailhead a few minutes south on US 101, the 2½ mi. (one-way) **Cape Trail** goes to the end of the lookout, where a spectacular 360-degree view featuring **Haystack Rock** awaits. If you're looking for something more challenging, try the South trail (same trailhead) which leads 1¾ mi. down to a secluded beach. **Cape Lookout Campground ❷** offers a pleasant camping option, although sites with better privacy go far in advance. 216 sites. Showers. (☎503-842-4981 or 800-551-6949, reservations 800-452-5687. Tent sites $16, non-camper showers $2. State park day-use fee $3.)

CAPE KIWANDA STATE PARK. Cape Kiwanda State Park (☎800-551-6949), 1 mi. north of Pacific City, is the jewel of the Three Capes Loop's triple crown. This sheltered cape draws beachcombers, kite-flyers, volleyball players, surfers, and wind-

OREGON

surfers, not to mention the odd snowboarder out to ride a giant sand hill. A 5min. walk up the sculptured sandstone on the north side (wear shoes with good grips) reveals a ■**hypnotic view** of swells rising over the rocks, forming crests, and smashing into the cliffs. If the surf is up, head to **South County Surf**, 33310 Cape Kiwanda Dr., a little way down the beach, where the walls are lined with shots of wipeouts and the Northwest's biggest surfing days. (☎503-965-7505. Surfboard rental $20; boogie board $10; wetsuit $15. Open Tu-F 10am-5pm, Sa 9am-5pm, Su 10am-5pm.)

PACIFIC CITY. The nearest town to Cape Kiwanda, Pacific City is a gem that most travelers on US 101 never even see. The **Anchorage Motel ❸**, 6585 Pacific Ave., offers homey rooms. (☎503-965-6773 or 800-941-6250; www.oregoncoast.com/anchorage. Rooms from $45, low-season $40.) Camping on beaches in Oregon is illegal, but local youth have been known to do it anyway, or on more secluded beaches north of Cape Kiwanda. The town hides some surprisingly good restaurants; the **Grateful Bread Bakery ❷**, 34805 Brooten (BRAW-ten) Rd., creates monuments to the art of dining. Get anything from a vegetarian stuffed focaccia ($7) to one of many excellent omelettes. On Th "cheap nights," entrees are $5. (☎503-965-7337; www.pacificcity.org/GratefulBread/home.html. Open summer M and F-Su 8am-8:30pm, Th 8am-3:30pm and 4:30-7:30pm; winter M and Th-Su 8am-8:30pm.)

LINCOLN CITY   ☎541

Lincoln City is actually five towns wrapped around a 7 mi. strip of ocean-front motels, gas stations, and souvenir shops along US 101. Most budget travelers—and this travel guide—will tell you that the Three Capes area is far superior as a destination. As one of the largest "cities" on the North Coast, Lincoln City is, however, a gateway to better points north and south.

■ � **ORIENTATION AND PRACTICAL INFORMATION.** Lincoln City lies between Devils Lake and the ocean, 42 mi. south of Tillamook, 22 mi. north of Newport, and 88 mi. southwest of Portland. The city proper is divided into quadrants: the D River ("the shortest river in the world") is the north-south divide; US 101 divides east from west. **Greyhound** buses, 3350 NW US 101 (☎800-454-2487) depart to Newport (¾hr., 1 per day, $9.50) and Portland (2½hr., 1 per day, $18). Tickets are available at the **visitors center**, 801 US 101 SW #1. (☎800-452-2151 or 996-1274. Open M-F 9am-5pm, Sa-Su 10am-4pm.) **Robben-Rent-A-Car**, 3244 US 101 NE, has rental cars starting at $30 per day or $180 per week. Must be 21 or over with credit card. (☎994-2454 or 800-305-5530. Open daily 8am-5pm.) The **Oregon Surf Shop**, 4933 US 101 SW, rents a wetsuit and surfboard for $30 per day or wetsuit and boogie board for $25; expert instructors offer lessons for $30 per hour. Sit-on-top kayaks are $25 per 4hr. (☎996-3957 or 877-339-5672. Open M-F 10am-5pm, Sa 9am-5pm, Su 10am-5pm.) Contact the **police** at 1503 East Devils Lake Rd. SE (☎994-3636). **Samaritan North Lincoln Hospital** is at 3043 NE 28th St. (☎994-3661). To get there, take either 22nd St. or Holmes Rd. to West Devils Lake Rd., and take that to 28th St. and the hospital. The **Driftwood Library**, 801 US 101 SW above the visitors center, provides 1hr. of free **Internet** access. (☎996-2277; www.driftwoodlib.org. Open M-W 9am-9pm, Th-Sa 9am-5pm.) The **post office** is at 1501 East Devils Lake Rd. SE. (☎800-275-8777 or 994-2148. Open M-F 9am-5pm.) **Postal Code:** 97367.

■☐ **ACCOMMODATIONS AND FOOD.** Beautiful, new looking rooms await at the **Captain Cook Inn ❸**, 2626 US 101 NE. (☎994-2522 or 800-994-2522; www.captaincookinn.com. Singles $48; doubles $52.) **Dory Cove ❸**, 5819 Logan Rd., at the north end of town, is a popular choice for affordable seafood. Dinners start at $12 a plate. (☎994-5180; www.dorycove.com. Open summer M-Sa 11:30am-8pm, Su noon-8pm; winter M-Th 11:30am-8pm, F-Sa 11:30am-9pm, Su noon-8pm.) The supermarket **Price n' Pride,** 801 US 101 SW, is handily located in the same parking lot as the library and visitors center. (☎994-4354. Open daily 6am-midnight.)

DEPOE BAY AND OTTER CREST   ☎541

Rest stops and beach-access parking lots litter the 30 mi. of US 101 between Lincoln City and Newport. In addition to claiming the title of "smallest harbor in the world", diminutive Depoe Bay boasts gray whale viewing along the town's low seawall, at the **Depoe Bay State Park Wayside** and the **Observatory Lookout,** 4½ mi. to the south. Go early in the morning on a cloudy day during the annual migration (Dec.-May) for your best chance of spotting the giants. **Tradewinds Charters,** on US 101 just north of the bridge (☎765-2345 or 800-445-8730) has 5hr. ($60) bottom fishing, and 1hr. ($15) and 2hr. ($20) whale watching trips. **Dockside Charters** offers similar trips; turn east at the only traffic light in Depoe Bay. They're next to the Coast Guard. (☎765-2545 or 800-733-8915. 5hr. bottom fishing $60; 1hr. whale watching $15, ages 13-17 $11, 4-12 $7.) Just south of Depoe Bay, detour east from US 101 on the renowned **Otter Crest Loop,** a twisting 4 mi. excursion high above the shore that affords spectacular vistas at every bend and includes views of **Otter Rock** and the **Marine Gardens.** A lookout over the aptly named **Cape Foulweather** has telescopes ($0.25) for spotting sea lions lazing on the rocks. **The Devil's Punch Bowl,** formed when the roof of a seaside cave collapsed, is also accessible off the loop. It becomes a frothing cauldron during high tide when ocean water crashes through an opening in the side of the bowl. **Otter Rocks** beach is known as a great place to learn to surf; beginners can have a blast in the smaller breaks close to shore. **Otter Rock Surf Shop,** 488 N. Hwy. 101, (☎765-2776) rents surfing equipment ($20-25 for just the board, $35-40 for board, wet suit and boots). If you've never surfed before, you might want to take one of their lessons ($85 including all rental equipment, W and Sa 10am-noon, or by appointment. Call 24hr. in advance.)

NEWPORT   ☎541

After the miles of malls along US 101, Newport's renovated waterfront area of pleasantly kitschy restaurants and shops is a delight. Newport's claim to fame, however, is the world-class **Oregon Coast Aquarium.** Best known as former home to Keiko the orca whale of *Free Willy,* the aquarium offers several interesting exhibits. This, in addition to the **Mark Hatfield Marine Science Center** and loads of inexpensive seafood, makes Newport a marine lover's starred attraction.

✴ ? ORIENTATION AND PRACTICAL INFORMATION

Corvallis lies 55 mi. east of Newport on **US 20,** Lincoln City is 22 mi. north of town on **US 101,** and **Florence** sits 50 mi. south. Newport is bordered on the west by the foggy Pacific Ocean and on the south by Yaquina Bay. US 101, known in town as the **Coast Highway,** divides east and west Newport. US 20, known as **Olive Street** in town, bisects the north and south sides of town. The compass letters at the end of most street addresses designate the quadrant of town. Just north of the bridge, **Bay Boulevard** (accessible via Herbert St., on the north side of the bay bridge) circles the bay and runs through the heart of the port. Historic **Nye Beach,** bustling with tiny shops, is on the northwest side of town between 3rd St. and 6th St.

Buses: Greyhound, 956 10th St. SW (☎265-2253 or 800-454-2487), at Bailey St. Open M-F 8-10am and 1-4:15pm, Sa 8am-1pm. To: **Portland** (4hr., 4 per day, $21); **San Francisco** (16½-21hr., 2 per day, $100); and **Seattle** (11hr., 32 per day, $55).

Taxis: Yaquina Cab Company (☎265-9552). $2.75 base, $3 per mile. 24hr.

OREGON

A WRITERS RETREAT

The **Sylvia Beach Hotel ❺** sits right on the edge of a bluff overlooking historic Nye Beach. While not all rooms have oceanfront views, all guests have access to the common room/ library, where three walls of plate glass windows and a small balcony provide a stunning view up and down the coast. Inside, the room is packed with almost 20 comfy armchairs. A recliner next to a large north-facing window is probably the nicest perch on the whole Oregon coast.

The theme of the establishment is books, with each of the 20 rooms named after a famous author (the Edgar Allen Poe room is not for the faint of heart: a swinging blade hangs above the bed). Each room is decorated to match the tone of the writer—from the whimsical Dr. Seuss room to the Agatha Christie room, which contains clues from all her classic mysteries hidden throughout.

Packed with books and littered with board games and half-finished puzzles, the B&B's communal feel is matched at meals, served family style at the restaurant *Tables of Content*. Breakfast is included for all guests; dinner is a four-course affair and offers a choice of several entrees ($19).

Dorm-style rooms, popular among Oregon Coast bikers, are available for $28.

267 NW Cliff St. ☎ 265-5428; www.sylviabeachhotel.com. Singles $88-123; low-season $68-94.

Visitor Information: Chamber of Commerce, 555 Coast Hwy. SW (☎ 265-8801 or 800-262-7844; www.discovernewport.com). 24hr. info board outside. Open M-F 8:30am-5pm; summer also Sa-Su 10am-4pm.

Laundry: Eileen's Coin Laundry, 1078 Coast Hwy. N (☎ 265-5474). Wash $1.25, dry $0.25 per 8min. Open daily 6am-11pm.

Weather and Sea Conditions: ☎ 265-5511.

Police: 169 SW Coast Hwy. (☎ 265-5331). **Coast Guard:** ☎ 265-5381.

Hospital: Samaritan Pacific Community Hospital, 930 Abbey St. SW (☎ 265-2244).

Internet Access: Newport Public Library, 35 Nye St. NW (☎ 265-2153; www.newportlibrary.org), at Olive St. Four computers on the main level offer 30min. free per day, but the better deal is the basement, which has 6 computers available for up to 1hr. per day. Open M-Th 10am-9pm, F-Sa 10am-6pm, Su 1-4pm.

Post Office: 310 2nd St. SW (☎ 800-275-8777). Open M-F 8:30am-5pm, Sa 10am-noon. **Postal Code:** 97365.

ACCOMMODATIONS AND CAMPING

Motel-studded US 101 provides affordable but sometimes noisy rooms. Nearby camping facilities often fill on summer weekends, despite being enormous.

Beverly Beach State Park, 198 123rd St. NE (☎ 265-9278; reservations 800-452-5687), 7 mi. north of Newport and just south of Devil's Punch Bowl. A year-round campground of gargantuan proportions set in a mossy forest next to a small creek. Many non-RV areas. 129 tent sites, $17; 76 electrical, $21; 53 full RV sites, $21; 21 yurts, $29; hiker/ biker sites $4; non-camper showers $2. ❷

Money Saver Motel, 861 SW Coast Hwy. (☎ 888-461-4033; www.newportnet.com/moneysaver). Basic, well-equipped clean rooms with friendly management. Summer singles $49-53; doubles $53-61. Winter singles $38/$40. ❸

South Beach State Park, 5580 Coast Hwy. S (☎ 867-4715, reservations 800-452-5687), 1 mi. south of town. ¼ mile from the quiet South Beach, the campground has sparse conifers which offer little shelter and no privacy. Offers 2hr. kayak tours on nearby Beaver Creek, May-Sept., for $10 per person. 227 electric RV sites, $21; 27 yurts, $29; hiker/ biker sites $4. Showers $2 for non-campers. ❷

Inn at Yaquina Bay, 2633 S Pacific Way. (☎ 888-867-3100) just south of the bridge, has large rooms with views of the bay and marina. The aquarium is just across the street. Continental breakfast. Jacuzzi, small exercise room. Call for rates. ❸

FOOD

Food in Newport is surprisingly varied, but seafood is the dining option of choice. **Oceana Natural Foods Coop,** 159 2nd St. SE, has a small selection of reasonably priced health foods and produce. (☎265-8285. Open M-F 8am-7pm, Sa 8am-6pm, Su 10am-6pm.) **J.C. Sentry,** 107 Coast Hwy. N, sells standard supermarket stock. (☎265-6641. Open 24hr.)

Mo's Restaurant, 657 Bay Blvd. SW (☎265-2979; www.moschowder.com). A local favorite now with locations up and down the coast, the original Mo's is just about always filled to the gills. You can get anything from a tasty burger ($6) to a salad ($7) to their specialty, seafood ($9-11). Open daily 11am-10pm. ❷

April's, 749 3rd St. NW (☎265-6855), down by Nye Beach, is the pinnacle of local dining. The serene ocean view and good Italian and Mediterranean fare are worth every penny. Tables fill early, especially on weekends. Dinners $13-21; daily specials are pricier. Towering chocolate eclairs $4. Reservations suggested. Open Tu-Su for dinner from 5pm. ❹

Canyon Way Restaurant & Bookstore, 1216 SW Canyon Way (☎265-8319). Browse through the quirky bookstore before or after your meal. Deli sandwiches hover around $6-8. Dinner entrees in the restaurant are pricier ($16-21). Restaurant open M 12pm-8:30pm, Tu-Th 11am-8:30pm, F-Sa 11am-9pm. Bookstore open M-Th 10am-8:30pm, F-Sa 10am-9pm. Deli open Tu-Sa 10am-4pm. ❸

Rogue Ale and Public House, 748 Bay Blvd. SW (☎265-3188; www.rogue.com). They "brew for the rogue in all of us," and bless 'em for it. Plenty of brew on tap ($3.50-4 per glass)—including "extreme ales" for the expert drinker and garlic ale bread ($2.25). Most lunch items $10-13 (10-inch pizzas are $11-15). Fish and chips with Rogue Ale batter $10. Locals pack it in for F and Sa night trivia. Open M-Th and Su 11am-midnight, F-Sa 11am-1am. ❸

SIGHTS

MARK O. HATFIELD MARINE SCIENCE CENTER. This is the hub of Oregon State University's coastal research. The 300 scientists working here ensure rigorous intellectual standards for the exhibits, which are on fascinating topics that range from chaos—demonstrated by a paddle wheel/waterclock—to local issues, such as the mysterious disappearance of the Cascade frogs and the potential impacts of a tsunami on Newport. While the live octopus is off-limits, sea anemones, slugs, and bottom-dwelling fish await

THE LOCAL STORY

FREE KEIKO

From 1996-98, the small town of Newport was home to one of the biggest movie stars ever. Literally. Keiko, the 9000 lb. star of the *Free Willy* movies, went through a 32-month rehabilitation program at Newport's Oregon Coast Aquarium.

Keiko was not in rehab for a traditional Hollywood reason. He came to regain his strength after spending years at a Mexico amusement park; a cruel irony, as his character Willy is last seen escaping from just such a park in *Free Willy* (1993).

In 1994, the Free Willy Foundation was formed and Keiko's journey to the wild began. A large donation from Warner Bros. and UPS's expertise in shipping led to Keiko's safe arrival at a new facility at the Aquarium in Dec. 1995. Keiko made rapid progress, quickly getting over his ailments and gaining muscle mass (putting him in top shape for *Free Willy 2* (1995) and *Free Willy 3* (1997)). He was also taught the skills to survive in the wild; when he was first introduced to live fish, he would catch them only to return them to his trainer.

In 1998, Keiko was moved to Klettsvik Bay, Iceland, to complete his reintroduction into the wild. When he was released in 2002, Keiko seemed reluctant to stray far from humans, and he headed for populated coastal areas in Norway. Keiko maintained this pattern until his death from pneumonia in Dec. 2003.

your curiosity in the touch tanks. There is a strong focus on indigenous ecosystems that might make you think twice about going for a swim. *(At the south end of the bridge on Marine Science Dr. ☎867-0100; http://hmsc.oregonstate.edu. Open daily Memorial Day to Sept. 10am-5pm and Oct. to Memorial Day M and Th-Su 10am-4pm. Donations of $4 per person or $10 per family accepted.)*

OREGON COAST AQUARIUM. More famous, less serious, and much more expensive than the Science Center is the Oregon Coast Aquarium. This world-class aquarium housed Keiko, the much-loved *Free Willy* orca during his rehabilitation before he returned to his childhood waters near Iceland. A zoo-like atmosphere surrounds the larger animals (sea otters, sharks), while the exhibits on local ecosystems are treated much more scientifically. *(2820 Ferry Slip Rd. SE, at the south end of the bridge. ☎867-3474; www.aquarium.org. Open daily June-Sept. 9am-6pm; Sept.-June 10am-5pm. $11, ages 65 and older $9.25, 4-13 $6.25.)*

ROGUE ALE BREWERY. The Brewery has won more awards than you can shake a pint at. Cross the bay bridge, follow the signs to the aquarium, and you'll see it. Twenty brews, including Oregon Golden, Shakespeare Stout, and Dead Guy Ale, are available at the pub in town (see **Food,** above) or upstairs at **Brewers by the Bay.** Follow the signs though the warehouse among the 20-foot vats, hundreds of kegs and overwhelming smell of hops (watch out for forklifts), to get to Brewers by the Bay, where taster trays of four beers cost $4.50. *(2320 Oregon State University Dr. SE. Brewers by the Bay ☎867-3664. Brewery 867-3660; www.rogue.com. Open M-Th and Su 11am-9pm, F-Sa 11am-10pm. Free tours of the brewery leave daily at 4pm, depending on demand.)*

NEWPORT TO REEDSPORT   ☎541

From Newport to Reedsport, US 101 slides through a string of small towns, beautiful campgrounds, and spectacular stretches of beach. The **Waldport Ranger Station,** 1049 Pacific Hwy. SW, is located 16 mi. south of Newport in Waldport. The office describes hiking in **Siuslaw National Forest,** a patchwork of three wilderness areas along the Oregon Coast. Furnishes detailed maps ($4-6) and advice on the area's campgrounds. For detailed hiking information, visit www.fs.fed.us/r6/siuslaw. (☎563-3211. Open M-F 8am-4pm.)

CAPE PERPETUA. Cape Perpetua, 11 mi. south of Waldport and 40 mi. north of Reedsport, is the highest point on the coast (803 ft.) and a must-see for its scenic beauty. Even if you're only passing through, it's still worth driving to the top of the Cape Perpetua **viewpoint** (2 mi.) and walking the quarter-mile loop to gaze out at the ocean and headlands to the north and south. Those looking for a more challenging hike can take the difficult 1¼ mi. **Saint Perpetua Trail** from the visitors center up to the same viewpoint. The **Cape Perpetua Interpretive Center,** 2400 US 101 just south of the viewpoint turn-off, has hilarious rangers and informative exhibits about the surrounding area. (☎547-3289. Open daily May-Nov. 9am-5pm; also open for Whale Week, the peak of the Gray Whale migration, from Christmas to New Year's.) At high tide, a 30-ft. jet of air and water erupts out of a gap in the rock with the crash of each wave at the **Devil's Churn** (¼ mi. north of the visitors center down Restless Water Trail) and **Spouting Horn** (on the Captain Cook Trail, across the street from the interpretive center turnoff). The two sites, as well as the **tidal pools,** are connected; the tidal pools can also be reached from the visitors center. The **Cape Perpetua campground ❷** is an excellent place to sleep. Located at the viewpoint turn-off, it has 39 sites alongside a tiny, fern-banked creek, some of which offer privacy. (☎877-444-6777 for reservations. Sites $17. Firewood $5.) The **Rock Creek Campground ❶**, 8 mi. farther south, has 15 very secluded sites in a near-rainforest environment a half-mile from the sea. ($15.)

ALPHA FARM. A communal alternative to the coast's bourgeois tourism. Members farm and produce gift shop-type items to support the communal purse. Drive 14 mi. east of **Florence,** a long strip of fast-food joints and expensive motels, to the tiny community of **Mapleton;** press on 30min. along Rte. 36 and then 7 mi. up Deadwood Creek Rd. Anyone willing to lend a hand with the chores is welcome to camp out or stay in the beautiful, simple bedrooms. Visitors can stay up to 3 days; afterward, a long-term commitment (at least 3 months) to the farm is required. The **Alpha Bit Cafe ❶,** in Mapleton on Rte. 126, is owned and staffed by the very chill and very dreadlocked members of Alpha Farm. (Farm ☎964-5102, cafe 268-4311; www.pioneer.net/~alpha. Cafe open M-Th and Sa 10am-6pm, F 10am-9pm.)

OREGON DUNES AND REEDSPORT ☎541

Nature's ever-changing sculpture, the **Oregon Dunes National Recreation Area,** presents sand in shapes and sizes unequaled in the Pacific Northwest. Formed by millennia of wind and wave action, the dunes shift constantly and the sand sweeps over footprints, tire marks, and—in years past—entire forests. Perhaps the only hotbed of "reverse conservation," the dunes are actually greening rapidly as European beachgrass, planted in the 1920s, spreads its tenacious roots and sparks concerns that the dunes may disappear in as few as 100 years. The dunes have something for everyone, from the hard-partying buggy or ATV rider to the hiker seeking solitude in the endless expanses of windblown sand.

▌▊ ORIENTATION AND PRACTICAL INFORMATION

The dunes stretch from Florence to Coos Bay, broken only where the Umpqua and Smith Rivers empty into Winchester Bay. On the south side of the bay is the town of **Winchester** and to the north is **Reedsport.** At the junction of **Route 38** and **US 101,** Reedsport is 185 mi. southwest of Portland, 89 mi. southwest of Eugene, and 71 mi. south of Newport.

> **Tourist Information: Oregon Dunes National Recreation Area Visitor Center,** 855 US 101 (☎271-3611), at Rte. 38 in Reedsport, just south of the Umpqua River Bridge. Has displays, a 10min. video on dune ecology, and essential info on fees, hiking, and camping. Maps $4-6. Open daily June-Oct. 8am-4:30pm; Nov.-May M-F 8am-4:30pm.
>
> **Passes and Permits:** Most parking areas in the NRA now require day-use passes, which are $5 per day or $30 per year. The **Northwest Forest Pass** can be purchased at most places where it is required. Those staying at a campground and already paying a $15 fee are exempt from day-use fees.
>
> **Laundromat: Coin Laundry,** 420 N 14th St. (☎271-3587), next to McDonald's in Reedsport. Wash $1.25, dry $0.25 per 7½min. Open daily 8am-9:30pm.
>
> **Police:** 146 N 4th St. (☎271-2100). **Coast Guard:** ☎271-2138.
>
> **Internet Access: Reedsport Public Library,** 395 Winchester Ave. (☎271-3500). 1hr. of free access. Open M 2-8:30pm, Tu-W and F 10am-6pm, Th 2-6pm, Sa 10am-1:30pm.
>
> **Post Office:** 301 Fir Ave. (☎800-275-8777), off Rte. 38. Open M-F 8:30am-5pm. **Postal Code:** 97467.

▐ ▐ ACCOMMODATIONS AND CAMPING

Although they often fill during summer, motels with singles from $40 abound on US 101. Sixteen campgrounds, many of which are very near the dunes, also dot the coast. During the summer, RVs and ATVers dominate local campsites. Permits for

RIDING THE DUNES

I had just crested the highest point of the "Coliseum" dune, a short walk from Umpqua Beach parking lot #3 in the Oregon Dunes, and the wind was pulling a smoky plume of sand up into my face. I grabbed my sandboard (essentially a snowboard made to ride on sand), slid my bare feet into the bindings, and attempted to descend. 25 ft. down the 33° dune, I caught an edge and started tumbling down the hill. When I slid to a halt, I spat out the sand in my mouth, attempted to pry sand out of my ear, jumped up, and ran to the next hill.

As the day wore on, I realized that waxing the board before each run was essential for a smooth ride. Furthermore, I learned that the drier the sand was, the faster the ride was; I sought out the driest terrain possible. Most of all, however, I learned that I needed a pair of goggles to guard my eyes from the relentless sand.

What does sand have over snow? For starters, you have to earn your rides by hiking up the hill. The dunes are beautiful, and the sun on your shoulders only heightens the experience. Gliding down the hill and sending up billows of sand with the sun beating down is, some would say, the only way to see the dunes. Riding the dunes is worth a shot for intermediate or better snowboarders with humility and a love for the beach...or at least for sand.

–Carleton Goold

dispersed camping (allowed on public lands 200 ft. from any road or trail) are required year-round and available at the **Dunes Information Center.**

Harbor View Motel, 540 Beach Blvd. (☎271-3352), off US 101 in Winchester Bay, is so close to the marina that there are boats in the parking lot. Many of the wood panelled rooms come with a La-Z-Boy recliner, and for an extra $3 you can get a kitchen unit (stove, oven, fridge, microwave). Striking color schemes. Queen $42, double occupancy $44. $5 cheaper in winter. ❸

Eel Creek Campground, 9½ mi. south of Reedsport. Sandy, spacious sites very well hidden from the road and each other by tall brush. Lack of RV and ATV traffic keeps this campground quiet. Trailhead for the 2½ mi. John Dellenbeck Dunes Trail, one of the best dune walks. No RV sites or ATVs. 53 sites, $17. ❷

William M. Tugman State Park, (☎759-3604; reservations 800-452-5687), 8½ mi. south of Reedsport on US 101. Close to gorgeous Eel Lake. Less private than Eel Creek, but still pleasantly free of ATVs. Wheelchair-accessible. 115 sites, $16; hiker/biker sites (the most private option) $4; yurts $27. Electricity. Non-camper showers $2. ❷

Carter Lake Campground, 13 mi. north of Reedsport on US 101. Boat access to the lake; some sites are lakeside. The well-screened, private spots are as quiet as it gets out here. No ATVs. Open May-Sept. 23 sites, $17. ❷

🍴 FOOD

Cheap, tasty food prevails in Winchester Bay and Reedsport. Grab a shrink-wrapped T-bone and a box of fudgesicles at **Safeway,** right off US 101 in Reedsport. (Open daily 7am-11pm.) **Griff's on the Bay ❸,** 142 Bay Front Loop in Winchester Bay. offers a great view of the harbor and seafood fresh off the boat to match. Diners can sit inside or out to enjoy a hearty meal of salmon, halibut or ahi. (☎271-2512, Open M-F 9am-8:30pm, Sa-Su 9am-9pm.) **Back to the Best ❷,** on US 101 at 10th St., may look dated, but the food is fresh, specializing in smoked meats and cheeses. (☎271-2619. Open M-Sa 6:30am-2pm, Su 9am-2pm.)

🏔 OUTDOOR ACTIVITIES

Depending on where you see them, the dunes will leave widely varying impressions. Regions that allow off-road vehicles will probably seem like ear-splitting mazes of madcap buggy riders, but other hiker-only areas offer timeless dreamscapes with nothing but sand, shrubs, and footprints vanishing in the wind.

⚙ OFF-ROAD RIDING. For an unmuffled and undeniably thrilling dune experience, venture out on wheels. While there are no accurately defined buggy trails through the dunes, simply following other riders can yield the best action in the sand. Plenty of shops on Hwy. 101 between Florence and Coos Bay rent and offer tours, and most either transport ATVs to the dunes or are located on them; the **Oregon Dunes National Recreation Area Visitors Center** (☎271-3611) also offers a list of places that rent. **Dune Buggy Adventures**, off Hwy. 101 in the Pelican Plaza in Winchester Bay, rents 250 Trailblazer ATVs for $45 per hr. as well as sandboards for $7 per hour. Free transport of ATV to the dunes. $150 deposit required. (☎271-6972; www.dunebuggyadventure.com. Open daily summer 8:30am-dusk, winter same hours F-Su, weather permitting.)

🥾 HIKING. Simply put, the dunes are beautiful and require a hiker's slow pace to be fully appreciated. Multiple ecosystems separated by the sands harbor birds, insects, and occasional larger animals such as foxes. The vast stretches of sand south of Winchester Bay and around Eel Creek represent dunes at their most primal. The experience of any day hike is heightened by solitude: going towards sunrise or sunset offers the best opportunity to avoid tourists and assures you of an unforgettable view.

⚙ John Dellenbeck Dunes Trail. With little to guide you besides an occasional marking pole, the "trail" wanders through unparalleled beauty in the sand slopes, wind cornices and rippled surfaces of the dunes. The area is ATV-free, and leaving you to wander along the ridgetops of the dunes in peace. The views are best when the sun is low in the sky and the shadows highlight the precise transitions between slopes and other wind-sculptured features. Walk as long as you like; the trail goes 2 mi. to the ocean over progressively softer (and, from a hikers perspective, more difficult) sand, requiring several hours of hiking. Access the trailhead off US 101, ¼ mi. south of Eel Creek campground.

Oregon Dunes Overlook (Tahkenitch Creek Trail). Most tourists content themselves with stopping at the Oregon Dunes overlook (10 mi. north of Reedsport). Here, they peer out at a smallish stretch of oblique dunes whose lines of shrub stretch to the ocean. 1½-3hr. walks (1½ mi., 2½ mi., and 3½ mi. trails) off the overlook are far more satisfying, though, and feature a wider variety of dunes to explore. Wildlife lovers will enjoy this hike the most—you'll experience a constant barrage of bird calls from the cover of the shrubs.

🏂 SANDBOARDING. Sandboarding fills the gap between the earsplitting adrenaline rush of an ATV and the slow paced serenity of a hike. A day of zipping down the dunes on slightly-modified snowboards requires equal parts patience (you have to hike up every dune you ski down) and daring (you have to ski down every dune you hike up), and is very satisfying. Sandboards can be rented in Winchester Bay at Dune Buggy Adventures, $7 per hr. or $30 per day (see Outdoor Activities, above) or, further north, in Florence at Central Coast Watersports, Hwy 101 and 19th St., for $15 per day. (☎997-1812 or 800-789-3483. Open M-Tu and Su and Th-F 10am-5pm, Sa 9:30am-5:30pm.)

OTHER ACTIVITIES. Bird-watching is popular around Reedsport; lists of species and their seasons are available at the **visitors center.** Throughout August, the **Crab Bounty Hunt** offers a whopping $10,000 reward for catching a particular tagged crustacean. Traps can be rented in Winchester Bay; rumor has it that the crab is most often caught in Salmon Harbor.

COOS BAY, NORTH BEND, AND CHARLESTON ☎541

A string of state parks along the coastline and a pristine estuary near Charleston Bay make Charleston the most interesting of the three towns. While Coos Bay and North Bend provide many of the necessities and amenities of life, it is

OREGON

the parks north of town and past Charleston that are really worth visiting. The largest city on the Oregon Coast, Coos Bay also claims fame as the birthplace of Steve Prefontaine, the US Olympian and distance running legend who died in a tragic car accident in his early 20s.

■✈ 🛈 ORIENTATION AND PRACTICAL INFORMATION

US 101 jogs inland south of Coos Bay, rejoining the coast at Bandon-by-the-Sea. From Coos Bay, **Route 42** heads east 85 mi. to **I-5**, and US 101 continues north over the bridge into dune territory. **Coos Bay** and **North Bend** are so close together that one town merges seamlessly into the next, but street numbers start over again at the boundary; for instance, there are two Broadways, one for each city. US 101 runs along the east side of town (as Coos Bay's Broadway), and **Cape Arago Highway** runs along the west side, connecting Coos Bay to **Charleston** and the coast.

> **Buses: Greyhound,** 275 N Broadway (☎267-4436), Coos Bay. Open M-F 6:30am-4pm, Sa 6:30am-noon. To: **Portland** (6½hr., 3per day, $35) and **San Francisco** (14hr., 2 per day, $79).
>
> **Taxis: Yellow Cab** (☎267-3111). $5 anywhere within town, and $1 per mi. outside. 24hr.
>
> **Car Rental: Verger,** 1400 Ocean Blvd. (☎888-5594), Coos Bay. Must be 23+ with credit card. Open M-F 8am-5:30pm, Sa 8am-5pm Su 9am-5pm. Cars from $30, 150 mi. per day free, $0.25 per mi. thereafter.
>
> **Tourist Information:** All the following cover the whole area.
>
> > **Bay Area Chamber of Commerce,** 50 E Central Ave. (☎269-0215 or 800-824-8486; www.oregons-bayareachamber.com), off Commercial Ave., Coos Bay. Open M-F 9am-5pm, Sa noon-4pm.
> >
> > **North Bend Visitor Center,** 1380 Sherman Ave. (☎756-4613), on US 101, south of North Bend bridge. Open summer M-F 8am-5pm, Sa 10am-5pm, Su 12:30-5pm; winter M-F 8am-5pm.
> >
> > **Charleston Visitor Center** (☎888-2311), at Boat Basin Dr. and Cape Arago Hwy., has brochures. Open daily May-Sept. 9am-5pm.
>
> **Outdoor Information: Oregon State Parks Information,** 89814 Cape Arago Hwy. (☎888-8867), Charleston. Open M-F 8am-noon and 1-4:30pm.
>
> **Equipment Rental: Sunset Sports,** 1611 Virginia Ave. #59 (☎756-3483), in North Bend rents kayaks for $30 per day. M-F 10am-8pm, Sa 10am-6pm, Su 11am-6pm.
>
> **Laundromat: Wash-A-Lot,** 1921 Virginia Ave., North Bend. Wash $1.75; dry $0.25 per 6min. Open 24hr.
>
> **Police:** 500 Central Ave. (☎269-8911), Coos Bay. **Coast Guard:** 63450 Kingfisher Dr. (☎888-3266 emergency, 888-3267 non-emergency), Charleston.
>
> **Hospital: Bay Area Hospital,** 1775 Thompson Rd. (☎269-8111), Coos Bay.
>
> **Internet Access: Coos Bay Library,** 525 W Anderson Ave. (☎269-1101; http://bay.cooslibraries.org), Coos Bay. Free 30min. of Internet access. Open M-W 10am-8pm, Th-F 11am-5:30pm, Sa 11am-5pm.
>
> **Post Office:** 470 Golden Ave. (☎800-275-8777) at 4th St., Coos Bay. Open M-F 8:30am-5pm. **Postal Code:** 97420.

🏠 🏕 ACCOMMODATIONS AND CAMPING

Cheap, noisy motels line Hwy. 101 for those just passing through; quieter rooms with a roof lie close to the outdoor attractions in Charleston. Campers, rejoice: the nearby state-run and private sites allow full access to the breathtaking coast.

Bluebill Campground, (☎271-3611), off US 101, 3 mi. north of North Bend. Camping among sandy scrub; some sites with good privacy. To get there, take the first turn north of the bridge north of town. Follow the road 2¾mi. past Horsefall Campground to this relaxed campground, just ½ mi. from the ocean and dunes. No off-road vehicles allowed. Closed in winter. 18 sites, $15. ❶

Sunset Bay State Park, 89814 Cape Arago Hwy. (☎888-4902; reservations 800-452-5687), 12 mi. south of Coos Bay and 3½ mi. west of Charleston. Akin to camping in a well-landscaped parking lot; **Loop B** sites

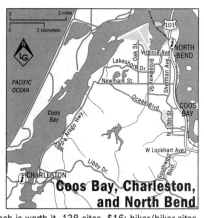

Coos Bay, Charleston, and North Bend

have a bit more seclusion. Sunset Beach is worth it. 138 sites, $16; hiker/biker sites $4; full RV sites $19; yurts $27. ❶

Captain John's Motel, 63360 Kingfisher Dr. (☎888-4041; www.captainjohnsmotel.com), in Charleston, escapes the highway noise and attracts anglers; this is the closest good place to the state parks and the estuary. Queen-sized beds from $65, 2 double beds from $69; $10-15 cheaper in winter. ❹

Bay Bridge Motel, 66304 Hwy. 101 (☎756-3151), just north of the bridge, offers spacious, quiet and very clean rooms. A clientele of tourists and retirees helps to make it a relaxing place. Half the rooms have a stunning view of the bay. Queen bed is $40 and 2 twins are $60; slightly cheaper in winter. ❸

▐ FOOD

There are **Safeways** at 230 E Johnson Ave. (☎267-1700) off US 101 north, at the southern end of town and at 1735 Virginia Ave (☎751-7000) at the northern end of town. (Both open daily 6am-1am.)

City Subs, 149 N 4th St., Between Commercial and Central (☎269-9000), offers great toasted subs at an unbeatable price ($3.50-4.50). Very friendly service. If you're feeling clever, try your hand at solving the puzzles on each table for a chance to win a free drink and the right to buy an "I'm A Smarty" hat. Open M-F 8am-7pm, Sa 10am-4pm. ❶

Davey Jones Locker, 91139 Cape Arago Hwy., Charleston, (☎888-3941) provides everything from a small deli to a pair of rubber boots to use to wade in the tidal flats. The deli offers corn dogs and pizza ($2-5), and the rest of the store matches anything you'd find in a Rite Aid. Open daily 6am-10pm. ❶

Cranberry Sweets, 1005 Newmark St. (☎888-9824 or 800-527-2748, www.cranberrysweets.com), Coos Bay, near junction of Ocean Blvd. and Newmark St. This far-from-average candy factory serves up enough ambitious ventures (think beer squares and cheddar cheese fudge) to make lunch moot. $2-5 per lb. Cheapskates may exploit the free samples. Open M-Sa 9am-6pm, Su 11am-4pm. ❶

Fisherman's Grotto, 91149 Cape Arago Hwy., Charleston, (☎888-3251), offers fresh seafood ($10-15) in an unpretentious setting. Meals include a salad and a starch. Open daily 11am-8pm. ❸

OREGON

👁 ⚲ SIGHTS AND EVENTS

Four miles south of Charleston up Seven Devils Rd., the ◪**South Slough National Estuarine Research Reserve** ("Slough" is pronounced "Slew") is one of the most fascinating and under-appreciated venues on the central coast. Spreading out from a small interpretive visitors center, almost 7 sq. mi. of salt- and freshwater estuaries nurture all kinds of wildlife, from sand shrimp to blue herons to deer. Check the interpretive center first to see if there are any guided hikes or paddles going out (free) or to start on some of the short trails leading from the center. A great way to observe wildlife close-up by canoe or kayak is to start from the Charleston marina (near the Charleston Bridge) at low tide and paddle into the estuary with the tide and out as it subsides; much of the interior is miserable mud flats at low tide. (☎ 888-5558; www.southsloughestuary.org. Open daily June-Aug. 8:30am-4:30pm; closed Sa-Su Sept.-May. Trails open year-round dawn-dusk.)

Inland 24½ mi. from Coos Bay, at **Golden and Silver Falls State Park,** three trails lead to the awesome Golden Falls, a 210 ft. drop into the abyss, and the beautiful Silver Falls, thin sheets of water cascading down a rock face. From Coos Bay, take the Eastside-Allegany exit off US 101 and follow it along a narrow gravel road.

For two weeks in mid-July, Coos Bay plays host to the **Oregon Coast Music Festival,** the most popular summer music event on the coast. (☎ 267-0938; www.oregoncoastmusic.com. Festival concerts $6-10, orchestra concerts $12-20.) Art exhibits and a free classical concert in Mingus Park spice up the festival for the ticketless.

🏔 OUTDOOR ACTIVITIES

Sunset Bay, 11½ mi. from Coos Bay along Cape Arago State Hwy. (follow Central Ave off of US 101, which turns into Cape Arago State Hwy), has been rated one of the top-10 American beaches. Sheltered from the waves by two parallel cliffs, the warm, shallow bay is perfect for **swimming.** The magnificent and manicured **Shore Acres State Park** rests a mile beyond Sunset Bay on the Cape Arago Hwy. (☎ 888-3732. Open daily summer 8am-9pm, winter 8am-dusk. Wheelchair-accessible. $4 per car.) Once the estate of local lumber lord Louis J. Simpson, the park contains elaborate botanical gardens that outlasted the mansion and a short trail to peaceful Simpson Beach. Displays rose gardens and several rare trees. At the south end of the highway is breezy **Cape Arago,** notable for the rich life of its tide pools. Paved paths lead out toward the tip of the cape and provide an excellent view of Shell Island, a quarter-mile offshore, which is a protected elephant and harbor seal rookery. Fishing enthusiasts can hop on board with **Bob's Sportfishing,** operating out of a small building at the west end of the Charleston Boat Basin, where they can buy one-day fishing licenses for $8. (☎ 888-4241 or 800-628-9633; www.bobssportfishing.com. 5hr. bottom-fishing trip mid-May to Sept., $60 5hr. salmon-fishing trip mid-June to mid-July, $70.)

BANDON-BY-THE-SEA   ☎ 541

Despite a steady flow of summer tourists, the fishing town of Bandon-by-the-Sea (designated as simply "Bandon" on most maps) has refrained from breaking out the pastels and making itself up like an amusement park. Walking though Old Town, you feel like you have stumbled onto the set of *Jaws*. A few outdoor activities make Bandon-by-the-Sea worth a stop on a coastal tour.

🛈 **PRACTICAL INFORMATION.** Bandon-by-the-Sea is 24 mi. south of Coos Bay and 27 mi. north of Port Orford on US 101. The **visitors center** is at 300 SE 2nd St. immediately on your right after you go under the "Welcome to Old Town" sign, from the south (☎347-9616. Open daily Memorial Day to Labor Day 10am-5pm; winter 10am-4pm.) Wash your clothes at the **Laundromat** in the shopping center just north of the junction of Rte. 42 and US 101. (Open daily 7:30am-9:30pm; wash $1.50, dry 9min. per $0.25.) The **post office** is at 105 12th St. SE (☎800-275-8777. Open M-F 8:30am-4:30pm.) **Postal Code:** 97411.

▞▚ ACCOMMODATIONS AND FOOD. The **Bandon Wayside Motel and RV Park ❸**, 1175 2nd St. SE, just after US 101 splits off from 2nd St., offers 10 immaculate rooms with tile floors, nice beds, and cable TV. The motel has recently undergone serious improvements under new management. (☎347-3421; www.bandonwayside.com. June-Oct. $45-60. Nov.-May $35-40.) The quaint **Sea Star Guest House ❷**, 270 1st St., offers several elegant guest house rooms overlooking the marina. (☎347-9632; www.seastarbandon.com. May-Sept. 2-person dorm rooms $19, private rooms $75; Oct.-Apr. 2-person dorms $16, private rooms $50; the penthouse, complete with full kitchen and room for six, is $135.) Two miles north of town and across the bridge, **Bullard's Beach State Park** houses the **Coquille River Lighthouse ❷**, built in 1896. The 185 sites have little privacy. (☎347-2209. Hiker/biker sites $4 per person; sites $20; yurts $27. Showers $2 for non-campers.)

For a tasty and healthy morsel, step into **Mother's Natural Grocery and Deli ❶**, 975 US 101, south of the junction with Rte. 42 south. If you've been searching the Northwest for things like crushed dandelion root (or delicious fruit), your search is over. Sandwiches cost about $3.75-4.25. (☎347-4086. Open M-Sa 9am-6pm.) **Rayjen Coffee Company ❶**, 373 2nd St., offers more than just a wide variety of coffee. For a light meal, a bagel ($2) or pita ($5) is cheap and filling. (☎347-1144. Open daily 6:30am-5pm.) The name says it all for the **High Dock Bistro ❸**, 315 3rd St., perched on the second floor of a harborside building right in the middle of Old Town. The fresh menu changes daily, and the great view and friendly atmosphere make this a worthwhile stop. (☎347-5432. Lunch $7-12, Dinner $12-20. Open daily July 4-Sept. 11am-3pm and 5-9pm; Oct.-July 4 W-Su 11am-3pm and 5-9pm.)

◪◩ SIGHTS AND EVENTS. A stroll around **Old Town** is pleasant, offering unspoiled fishing village charm, as is exploring the beach on a horse from **Bandon Beach Riding Stables.** (☎347-3423. $30 for 1hr.) The well-marked beach loop road that leaves from Old Town and joins US 101 5 mi. south passes **Table Rock, Elephant Rock,** and **Face Rock,** three of the coast's most striking offshore outcroppings.

BANDON-BY-THE-SEA TO BROOKINGS
Whether it's because of the general lack of development in this area or the proliferation of offshore volcanic rocks and vertiginous shorelines, this stretch of the coast is the most beautiful segment of the Oregon Coast. Although this area tends to be socked in with morning cloud and fog, when it burns off in the afternoon the views of cliff-lined coves and grassy hills are incredible.

Cape Blanco State Park, north of Port Orford, offers a long stretch of empty beach; it is the farthest point west on the Oregon Coast and its **lighthouse,** the Coast's oldest, offers incredible views up and down the coast. You can see this view for yourself by taking a tour of the lighthouse, located at the end of the six-mile road off US 101 (Open Apr.-Oct. M and Th-Su 10am-3:30pm.) The **campground ❶** just before the lighthouse, offers exceptional seclusion between hedges plus access to a beautiful but isolated beach. (Hiker/biker sites $4; RV sites $18. Showers.) Six miles south of Port Orford, a moderate trail (3 mi) ascends to the 1700 ft. peak of Humbug Mountain providing amazing views of surrounding **Humbug Mountain State Park,** as well as the beaches up and down the coast. The trail is accessible from **Humbug Mountain State Park Campground ❶** at the foot of the mountain, which has 101 tightly packed sites. (☎332-6774. Hiker/biker sites $4, tents $14. Showers $2 for non-campers.)

OREGON

Boardman State Park is the best example of Oregon Coast preservation, stretching across 15 mi. of the finest and most rugged coastal terrain in Oregon. The park has frequent overlooks and trailheads along US 101. With a little bit of walking, you could easily obtain an entire pristine cove for yourself. If you're not looking for seclusion as much as majesty, pull off at the **Whalehead Trailhead** (mi. 349.3). A steep cliff abuts the beach to the north, two massive sea stacks tower just offshore, and the wide (100-200 yds.) beach stretches for almost a mile to the south. The undertouristed park begins about 8 mi. north of Brookings. A complete list of the different trail segments is available, free, at the ranger station in Brookings.

Thirty miles north of Brookings, in **Gold Beach,** you can ride a jet boat up the **Rogue River. Mail Boat Hydro-Jets,** 94294 Rogue River Rd. (just north of the Rogue River on 101), offers 64, 80, and 104 mi., 6-7hr. whitewater daytrips. (☎247-7033 or 800-458-3511. May-Oct. $30-75.) Longer trips get more whitewater; all trips offer opportunities to see eagles, bears, and deer.

BROOKINGS   ☎541

Brookings is the southernmost stop on US 101 before California and one of the few coastal towns that remain relatively tourist-free. Here, hardware stores are easier to find than trinket shops, and the beaches are among Oregon's least spoiled and most striking. The city also sits in Oregon's "banana belt" (a.k.a. California's "Arctic Circle"): warm weather is not rare in January, and some Brookings backyards even boast scraggly palm trees. For exhaustive coverage of all that is hot and cool down south, consult *Let's Go: California.*

🛈 **PRACTICAL INFORMATION.** US 101 is called Chetco Ave. in town. Strictly speaking, there are two towns here, separated by the **Chetco River**—Brookings to the north and **Harbor** to the south—which share everything and are referred to as Brookings Harbor. The **Greyhound** station is at 601 Railroad Ave., at the corner with Tanbark, behind Fiji Island Tan. (☎469-3326. Open M-F 9am-noon and 4-6pm, Sa 9am-noon.) Daily buses leave for Portland (9hr, $51) and San Francisco (11hr, $63). The **Brookings Welcome Center,** 1650 US 101, is just across the street from Harris Beach State Park. (☎469-4117. Open M-Sa 8am-6pm, Su 9am-5pm.) The **Chamber of Commerce,** 16330 Lower Harbor Rd., is just south of the river and can be reached by taking the first turn towards the ocean south of the bridge. (☎469-3181 or 800-535-9469; www.brookingsor.com. Open M-F 8am-5pm.) The **Chetco Ranger Station,** 539 Chetco Ave., distributes info on the **Siskiyou National Forest.** (☎412-6000. Open M-F 8:30am-12:30pm and 1:30-4:30pm.) Clean up at **Econ-o-Wash,** next door to the Westward motel on Chetco Ave. (Wash $1.75, dry $0.25 per 7min. Open daily 7:30am-10pm, last wash 9pm.) Kayaks ($25) and bikes ($20) are available for rent at **Escape Hatch,** 642 Railroad Ave. (☎469-2914. Open M-F 10am-5:30pm, Sa 10am-5pm.) If you pick it up on Saturday, you can keep it through Sunday for free. Get the lowdown on local surf-spots (South Jetty in town, plus Harrison Sponge beach 1 mi. north of town) at **Sessions Surf Co.,** 800 Chetco Ave. (☎412-0810. Open M-Sa 11am-5:30pm, Su 11am-4pm.) Try not to think about what might be responsible for that semi-circular set of dents in the shop's prized board, especially if you plan on going into the water anytime soon. Rents combination body board and wetsuit for $10. Get a free 1hr. of **Internet** access at the **library,** 405 Alder St. (☎469-7738. Open M and F 10am-6pm, Tu and Th 10am-7pm, W 10am-8pm, Sa 10am-5pm.) **The Internet Cafe,** 632 Hemlock St. (☎469-7864; open M-Sa 8:30am-5pm) also provides an Internet connection for $0.10 per min. (15 min. minimum). The **post office** is at 711 Spruce St. (☎412-0117. Open M-F 9am-4:30pm.) **Postal Code:** 97415.

ACCOMMODATIONS AND FOOD. ⚑Harris Beach State Park Campground ❶, at the north edge of Brookings, has 63 good tent sites set back in the trees and easy access to an unspoiled beach. (☎469-2021 or 800-452-5687. Hiker/biker sites $4; sites $17; full RV sites $20; yurts $28. Free showers.) For campsites off the beaten path, travel east of Brookings on North Bank Rd. Go 10½ mi. to Miller Bar Campground, 12 mi. to the Nook Bar Campground or 13 mi. to the charming **Little Redwood Campground** ❶, alongside a salamander-filled creek. (12 sites, $10.) **Redwood Bar** ❶, ¼ mi. further, charges $5. Contact the Chetco Ranger Station for info on these sites (☎412-6000). **The Bonn Motel** ❸, 1216 US 101, has a heated indoor pool and cable. (☎469-2161. Singles $40; doubles $45; $10 less in winter.)

The **Homeport Bagel Shop** ❶, 1011 Chetco Ave. serves up a wide range of delicious fresh bagels ($0.65); a half-sandwich and a cup of soup or chili goes for $4.50 (☎469-6611. Open M-F 7am-3pm.) **La Flor de Mexico** ❷, 541 Chetco Ave., (☎469-4102; open daily 11am-9:30pm) offers a simple but filling all-you-can-eat buffet ($6.25) between 11am and 2pm. A number of seafood spots can be found near the harbor. The locals' favorite is **Oceanside Diner** ❷, 16403 Lower Harbor Rd. (☎469-7971. Open daily 4am-1:30pm.)

SIGHTS AND OUTDOOR ACTIVITIES. Brookings is known statewide for its flowers. To view the flora, head to downtown's **Azalea Park** (take the first inland turn north of the bridge, go left at the immediate fork onto Old County Rd. Azalea Park will be the next thing on the right). The park provides a visual sensory overload, particularly from April to June when the flowers bloom at intervals. Visitors can check what's blooming by calling the Chamber of Commerce (☎469-3181). Each Memorial Day weekend Brookings celebrates the Azalea Festival (☎469-3181), held in Azalea Park. For an incredible view of the coast, visit **Harris Beach State Park,** just north of town. Visitors can also stop at the first pullout in the park and follow the South Beach Trail down to the beach. A sea stack several hundred yards to the north provides a great place to watch the sunset, but be careful, the path to the sea stack goes underwater when the tide comes in.

INLAND VALLEYS

While jagged cliffs and gleaming surf draw tourists to the coast, many Oregonians opt for the inland Willamette and Rogue River Valleys for their vacations. Vast tracts of fertile land support agriculture and a burgeoning wine industry, while the immense forests have maintained a healthy timber business for decades. Since the fortunes of logging are becoming more uncertain, however, tourism has become the industry of choice in small-town Oregon. With festivals galore, Ashland, Eugene, Corvallis, and Salem are all worthy destinations for the traveler.

SALEM ☎503

The home of Willamette University and the third-largest urban center in Oregon, Salem gives off the vibes of a much smaller city. Although it's hardly a hopping tourist destination, Salem's fine museums, renowned wineries, and attractions like the Oregon State Fair draw throngs of visitors.

TRANSPORTATION

Salem is 47 mi. south of **Portland** and 64 mi. north of **Eugene** on **I-5. Willamette University** and the **capitol building** dominate the center of the city, and the nearby shops make up the heart of downtown. To reach downtown, take Exit 253 off I-5. Street addresses are divided into quadrants: the **Willamette River** divides east from west, while **State Street** divides SE from NE.

OREGON

Trains: Amtrak, 500 13th St. SE (☎588-1551 or 800-872-7245), across from the visitors center. Open daily 6:15am-7pm. To: **Portland** (1½hr., 3 per day, $8-13); **Seattle** (5-7hr., 2 per day, $27-46); and **San Francisco** (17hr., 1 per day, $76-120).

Buses: Greyhound, 450 Church St. NE (☎362-2428). Open M-F 5:30am-8:30pm, Sa 5:30am-8:30pm. To: **Portland** (1½hr., 9 per day, $10); **Eugene** (1½-2hr., 10 per day, $14); and **Seattle** (6hr., 7 per day, $31).

Local Transportation: Cherriots Customer Service Office, 220 High St. NE (☎588-2877; www.cherriots.org), provides free bus maps and monthly passes ($20). Routes leave from High St. in front of the courthouse every hr. M-F 6:15am-9:30pm, Sa 7:45am-9:30pm. All buses have bike racks. $0.75; ages 60 and older or disabled $0.35; under 19 $0.50.

Taxis: Salem Yellow Cab Co. (☎362-2411). $2.50 base, $1.90 per mi. 24hr.

AAA: 2909 Ryan Dr. SE (☎581-1608 or 800-962-5855). Open M-F 8am-5:30pm.

🛈 PRACTICAL INFORMATION

Tourist Information: 1313 Mill St. SE (☎581-4325 or 800-874-7012; www.scva.org), in the Mission Mill Museum complex; take I-5 Exit 253 and follow signs. Open M-F 8:30am-5pm, Sa 10am-5pm.

Equipment Rental: South Salem Cycle Works, 4071 S Liberty Rd. (☎399-9848). Rents road bikes and hybrids for $15 per day (helmets $2 per day). No shop in Salem rents mountain bikes. Open M-Sa 10am-6pm.

Laundromat: Suds City Depoe, 1785 Lancaster Dr. NE (☎362-9845). Snack bar and big-screen TV. Wash $1.50, dry $0.25 per 15min. Open daily 7:30am, last load 9:30pm. **Lancaster Self-Service Laundry,** 2195 Lancaster Dr. NE, next to Bi-Mart. Wash 18 lb. for $2 or 50 lb. for $4.50, dry $0.25 per 10min. Open daily 8am-10pm, last load 9pm.

Police: 555 Liberty St. SE (☎588-6123), in City Hall room 130.

24hr. Crisis Line: ☎581-5535.

Hospital: Salem Hospital, 665 Winter St. SE (☎561-5200).

Internet Access: Salem Public Library, 585 Liberty St. SE (☎588-6315; www.open.org/~library). Free 1hr. of Internet access on 25 computers. Metered parking in the adjacent garage. Open June-Aug. Tu-Th 10am-9pm, F-Sa 10am-6pm; Sept.-May also open Su 1-5pm.

Post Office: 1050 25th St. SE (☎800-275-8777). Open M-F 8:30am-5pm. **Postal Code:** 97301.

🏠📷 ACCOMMODATIONS AND CAMPING

The visitors center has a list of **B&Bs,** which provide a comfortable and often classy setting (from $45). A number of cheaper hotels line Lancaster Dr. along the length of I-5, and camping options are also available.

Silver Falls State Park, 20024 Silver Falls Hwy. (☎873-8681, reservations 800-452-5687; www.open.org/slvrfall). See **Sights,** below, for directions. Campsites are in a beautiful setting with access to the waterfalls; however, there is little privacy. Wheelchair-accessible. 60 tent sites, $16; 44 RV sites, $20; 14 cabins, $35. Showers. ❷

Alden House Bed and Breakfast, 760 NE Church St. (☎363-9574 or 877-363-9573). Conveniently located just a few blocks from downtown, Alden House offers six themed rooms (romantic, cowboy, etc.), all of which have private baths. Breakfast in the elegant dining room at 9am. Reservations recommended. Rooms $45-65. ❸

OREGON

Cozzzy Inn, 1875 Fisher Rd. NE (☎588-5423). From I-5 Exit 256 to Lancaster Dr., take Sunnyview Rd. west to Fisher Rd. and make a left. Comfortable, very clean rooms at bargain prices. Singles from $40, doubles from $45. ❸

▐ FOOD

Salem is no city for the budget gourmet, and many restaurants are somewhat bland. Groceries await at **Roth's,** 702 Lancaster Dr. NE. (☎585-5770. Open daily 6am-11pm.) Hit the **Farmers Market,** at the corner of Marion and Summer St., for local produce and crafts. (☎585-8264; www.salemsaturdaymarket.com. Open May-Oct. Sa 9am-3pm.)

Off-Center Cafe, 1741 Center St. NE (☎363-9245). Mismatched furniture and local banter fill this quirky diner tucked away just off Center St. Offers a good selection of reasonably-priced burgers, soups, and scrambles ($3-7). Open Tu-F 7am-2:30pm, W-Sa 6-9pm for dinner, Sa-Su 8am-2pm for brunch. ❷

Fuji Rice Time, 159 High St. SE (☎364-5512), serves traditional Japanese food in a calm atmosphere to the local lunch crowd. Grab a seat at the counter to watch the chef at work while you nibble on sushi ($4-6). Also open for dinner. Open M-F 11am-2:30pm and 5-9pm, Sa 5-9pm. ❷

Arbor Cafe, 380 High St. NE (☎588-2353), serves coffee and tea ($2-3) as well as delicious pastries ($1-2) for breakfast; panini and sandwiches for lunch and dinner ($6.75-7.50). Open M-F 7:30am-5pm. ❷

◉ ♫ SIGHTS AND ENTERTAINMENT

STATE CAPITOL. This gigantic marble building, topped by a 23 ft. gilt-gold statue of the "Oregon Pioneer," is located in the heart of Salem. *(900 Court St. NE. Bounded by Court St. to the north, Waverly St. to the east, State St. to the south, and Cottage St. to the west. ☎986-1388. Open M-F 10am-6pm. In summer, a free tour to the top of the rotunda and a tour of the various chambers leave every hour; call for low-season tours.)*

SILVER FALLS STATE PARK. A long (12 mi.) loop trail passes by 10 waterfalls, but for those with less time on their hands, the 106 ft. Middle North Falls is an easy 1 mi. round-trip hike away. The views are spectacular, with a trail actually going behind South Falls. *(Take Rte. 22 east for 5 mi., then take the exit for Rte. 214 N and follow it for about 18 mi. $3 day use fee.)*

OREGON STATE FAIR. Salem celebrates the end of summer in the 12 days leading up to Labor Day with the annual Oregon State Fair. With a whirl of rides, baking contests and performances, Salem is invaded and transformed from a picture of complacent suburbia to a barnyard celebration. *(2330 17th St. NE. At the Expo Center. ☎947-3247 or 800-833-0011; www.fun-oregon.com. Open M-Th and Su 10am-10pm, F-Sa 10am-11pm. $8, ages 65 and older $5, ages 6-12 $4.)*

SALEM ART FAIR AND FESTIVAL. During the third weekend of July, the Salem Art Association hosts the free **Salem Art Fair and Festival** in Bush's Pasture Park. While the food booths do brisk business and the local wineries pour from their most recent vintage, the artsy and crafty display their wares as bands strum away the afternoon. The visitors center has info on the fair and on local **wineries.** *(600 Mission St. SE. ☎581-2228; www.salemart.org/fair.)*

CORVALLIS   ☎541

Unlike so many Oregon towns, this peaceful residential community in the central Willamette Valley has no historic pretensions. Covered in black and orange—the colors of Oregon State University (OSU)—for nine months, Corvallis is at heart a

OREGON

college town. Life bustles downtown all year, but Corvallis mellows in the summer, hosting a few choice festivals and offering some outdoor exploration in the nearby Willamette and Deschutes National Forests. Corvallis makes for a nice stop on the way to bigger, better places.

⬛🔢 ORIENTATION AND PRACTICAL INFORMATION. Corvallis is laid out in a checkerboard fashion that quickly degenerates outside the downtown area. Numbered streets run north-south; east-west streets are a test of US historical knowledge, as they are named after presidents. More recent presidents are to the north, older to the south. Monroe divides the north half of town from south. **Route 99 West** splits in town and becomes two one-way streets: northbound **3rd Street** and southbound **4th Street. 2nd Street** becomes US 20 north of town and leads to Albany and I-5.

Greyhound, 153 4th St. NW, runs buses to: Portland (2¼hr., 4 per day, $14-15); Seattle, WA (7½hr., 4 per day, $25-27); Newport (1¼hr., 3 per day, $12); and Eugene (1hr., 4 per day, $8-9). Lockers $1 per day. (☎ 757-1797 or 800-231-2222. Open M-F 6am-6:15pm, Sa 7am-1:30pm, Su 11am-1:30pm.) **Corvallis Transit System,** 501 SW Madison Ave., runs public transit. (☎766-6998; www.ci.corvallis.or.us/pw/cts. $0.60, ages 60 and older and 6-18 $0.30. Service M-F 6:25am-6:25pm, Sa 9:30am-4:45pm.) The **Visitors Information Center,** 553 NW Harrison Ave., provides detailed maps of Corvallis and Albany as well as free bike trail maps and general information about Corvallis (☎757-1444 or 800-334-8118; www.visitcorvallis.com. Open M-F 9am-5pm). The **Chamber of Commerce,** 420 2nd St. NW, the first right past the bridge if you're coming from the east, provides maps of town and limited information. (☎757-1505; www.corvallischamber.com. Open M-F 8am-5pm.) **Oregon State University** has an info booth on Jefferson Ave., between 11th St. and 15th St. (☎737-0123, events info 737-6445; www.oregonstate.edu. Open M-F 8am-5pm.) **🅂Peak Sports,** 129 2nd St. NW., is an incredible outdoors shop covering almost all forms of outdoors recreation in three separate, adjacent locations. Sells trail maps ($2-10) and rents mountain bikes ($25 for first day, $15 each day after) and all kinds of kayaks ($30 per day) with gear included. (☎754-6444; www.proaxis.com/~peak. Open M-Th and Sa 9am-6pm, F 9am-8pm, Su noon-5pm. Adjacent locations at 135 NW 2nd St. and 207 NW 2nd St.) **Campbell's Laundry,** 1120 9th St. NW, has wash for $1.35, dry $0.25 per 10min. (☎752-3794. Open daily 6am-10:30pm.) Contact the **police** at 180 5th St. NW (☎757-6924). The **Corvallis Clinic,** 3680 Samaritan Dr. NW., has **medical services.** Take 9th St. north from downtown. (☎754-1150, walk-ins 754-1282. Open M-F 8am-8pm, Sa-Su 10am-5pm.) For after-hours medical attention, go to the **Good Samaritan Hospital Emergency Room,** 3600 NW Samaritan Dr. (☎768-5111 or 888-872-0760. Open 24hr.) **Corvallis Public Library,** 645 Monroe St. NW, offers free 1hr. of **Internet** access on 15 computers. (☎766-6926; http://library.ci.corvallis.or.us. Open M-Th 10am-9pm, F-Sa 10am-6pm, Su 2-6pm.) The **post office** is at 311 2nd St. SW. (Open M-F 8am-5:30pm, Sa 9am-4pm.) **Postal Code:** 97333.

▌ ACCOMMODATIONS. The few campgrounds in and around Corvallis are less RV-infested than their counterparts up and down Western Oregon. The few motels are reasonably priced but occasionally fill during conventions or important college weekends. The **Budget Inn Motel ❸,** 1480 SW 3rd St., has clean, decently sized rooms for undersized prices. (☎752-8756. Fridges, A/C, cable TV. Singles $35; doubles $45. Kitchenettes $5 extra.) **Salbasgeon Suites ❺,** 1730 NW 9th St., pampers guests with a pool and private spa. The hotel offers free Internet browsers in every room and included continental breakfast. (☎800-965-8808; www.salbasgeon.com. Singles from $88; doubles from $93.)

FOOD AND NIGHTLIFE. Corvallis has a smattering of collegiate pizza parlors, noodle shops, and Mexican food. OSU students prowl Monroe Ave. for cheap, filling grub. **First Alternative Inc.,** 1007 3rd St. SE, is a co-op stocked with a range of inexpensive, natural products. (☎753-3115; www.firstalt.com. Open daily 9am-9pm.) The **Safeway** grocery store and pharmacy is at 450 3rd St. SW. (☎753-0160. Open daily 6am-1am. Pharmacy open M-F 9am-8pm, Sa 9am-6pm, Su 11am-4pm.) **Nearly Normal's Gonzo Cuisine ❶,** 109 15th St. NW, a purple cottage turned veggie-haven, has masses of flowers and hanging plants. The decor whets the appetite for low-price, large portion vegetarian options ($4-8). Sunburgers are $7. (☎753-0791. Open M-F 8am-9pm, Sa 9am-9pm.) **Bombs Away Cafe ❶,** 2527 Monroe St. NW is a mainstay of the college crowd. The adobe facade hides great burritos ($6-7) and live music every Wednesday and Thursday. This spot's thriving bar scene explodes on Tuesday with $2 beers; don't neglect Monday $2 margaritas, either. Happy hour with $2.50 pints M-F 3-5pm, 10pm-midnight, Sa 10pm-midnight. (☎757-7221; www.bombsawaycafe.com. Open M-F 11am-midnight, Sa 5pm-midnight, Su 5-9pm. 21+ after 10pm.) The Oregon-based pub chain **McMenamins ❶,** 420 3rd St. NW, has the best beer-and-burger fare in town. Have a sandwich ($5-7) or try a taster of six hand-brewed ales. Cheap burgers and sides are $2-4 10pm to close M-Th and Su. (☎758-6044. Open M-Sa 11am-1am, Su noon-midnight.)

ENTERTAINMENT. Ten miles east in **Albany** (off US 20 before I-5), the **River Rhythms** concert series attracts thousands every Monday and Thursday night at 7pm July through August for free music in the picturesque Monteith River Park. Musical acts vary from bluegrass to candy-coated pop. Call the **Albany Visitor Center** for more info. (☎800-526-2256. Open M-F 9am-5pm, Sa 9am-3pm, Su 10am-2pm.) The musically oriented can always check the **KBBR concert line** (☎737-3737).

MOUNTAIN BIKING. Mountain biking is a way of life in Corvallis, and all roads seem to lead to one bike trail or another. A map of the trails around Corvallis can be found at the visitors center (see **Practical Information,** above). Those searching for a hardcore mountain biking experience can head to the western part of OSU's **McDonald Forest,** or to the Willamette or Deschutes National Forests near **Sisters.** Local trails remain popular even in their soupy winter conditions. Maps for biking are available at **Peak Sports** ($6; see **Practical Information,** above). To get to the MacDonald forest, go west out of town on Harrison Blvd. for 4½ mi., then turn right on Oak Creek Dr. until the pavement dead-ends at OSU's lab.

KAYAKING. The Class IV "Concussion Run," on the **Middle Santiam,** is a summertime classic. The run is short but sweet and has three rapids that get successively more difficult, culminating with Concussion itself (which must be scouted before the run is attempted). Only runs when there's a dam release; call ☎367-5132 to get the schedule. The run begins at **Green Peter Reservoir** and ends at **Foster Reservoir,** off of Hwy. 20. Another popular run is on the **North Santiam,** which is mellower (class II and III) but still a classic. Put in at Pack Saddle on Rte. 22, east of Salem. Run ends at Mill City; ask the folks at Peak Sports for directions.

EUGENE
☎541

Epicenter of the organic foods movement and a haven for hippies, Eugene has a well-deserved liberal reputation. Any questions about Eugene's liberal bent can be resolved during the Oregon Country Fair. Home to the University of Oregon, the city is packed with college kids during the school year but mellows out considerably in summer. Eugene's Saturday market, nearby outdoor activities, and overall sunny disposition make Oregon's second-largest city one of its most attractive.

OREGON

OREGON

Eugene

▲ ACCOMMODATIONS
Campus Inn, **11**
Downtown Motel, **5**
The Eugene Hummingbird
Hostel, **13**

🍴 FOOD
Bene Gourmet Pizza, **8**
Cozmic Pizza, **6**
The Glenwood, **12**
Keystone Cafe, **2**
Morning Glory Cafe
and Bakery, **3**
New Frontier Market, **9**

🎷 NIGHTLIFE
The Downtown Lounge/
Diablo's, **10**
Jo Federigo's Jazz Club
and Restaurant, **4**
John Henry's, **7**
Sam Bond's Garage, **1**

TRANSPORTATION

Eugene is 110 mi. south of Portland on I-5. The main north-south arteries are, from west to east, **Willamette Street, Oak Street, Pearl Street,** and **High Street. Highway 99** runs east-west and splits in town—**Sixth Avenue** runs west, and **Seventh Avenue** goes east. Willamette St. divides the numbered avenues into eastern and western halves, with street numbers ascending as they get farther from Willamette. The **pedestrian mall** is downtown on Broadway between Charnelton and Oak St. The numbered avenues run east-west and increase toward the south. Eugene's main student drag, **Thirteenth Avenue,** leads to the **University of Oregon (U of O)** in the southeast part of town. Walking the city can be time-consuming—the best way to get around is by bike. Every street has at least one bike lane, and the city is quite flat. The **Whitaker** area, around Blair Blvd. near 6th Ave., can be unsafe at night.

Trains: Amtrak, 433 Willamette St. (☎687-1383), at 4th Ave. To: **Seattle** (6-8hr., 3 per day, $37-62) and **Portland** (2½-3hr., 3 per day, $17-29). Don't count on taking the third train at 12:44pm—it is regularly 5-10 hours late. Open daily 5:15am-9pm.

Buses: Greyhound, 987 Pearl St. (☎344-6265), at 10th Ave., runs to **Seattle** (6½-9hr., 4 per day, $35) and **Portland** (2½-3hr., 9 per day, $18). Open M-Sa 6:15am-9:30pm, Su 6:15-10:45am, 12:30-9:30pm.

Public Transportation: Lane Transit District (LTD; ☎687-5555; www.ltd.org) handles public transportation. Map and timetables available at the LTD Service Center, at 11th Ave. and Willamette St. $1.25, ages 62-79 and 6-18 $0.60, ages 80 and older and 6 and under free. Runs M-F 6am-10:40pm, Sa 7:30am-10:40pm, Su 8:30am-7:30pm. Wheelchair-accessible.

Taxis: E-Z Taxi (☎341-1550). $2 base rate, $2 per mile. 24hr.

Car Rental: Enterprise Rent-a-Car, 810 W 6th Ave. (☎344-2020; www.enterprise.com). $45 per day; unlimited mileage within OR. Will beat any competitor's price. 10% county tax. 18 and older with a credit card and full insurance coverage. Open M-F 7:30am-6pm, Sa 9am-noon.

AAA: 983 Willagillespie Rd. (☎484-0661), near Valley River Center Mall, 2 mi. north of the U of O campus. Open M-F 8am-5:30pm.

PRACTICAL INFORMATION

Tourist Information: 754 Olive St. (☎484-5307 or 800-547-5445; www.visit-lanecounty.org), Courtesy phone. Free maps. Open Memorial Day-Labor Day M-F 8am-5pm, Sa-Su 10am-4pm; Labor Day-Memorial Day M-F 8am-5pm, Sa 10am-4pm. **University of Oregon Switchboard,** 1244 Walnut St. (☎346-3111), in the Rainier Bldg., is a referral service for everything from rides to housing. Open M-F 7am-6pm.

Outdoors Information: Ranger Station (☎822-3381), about 60 mi. east of Eugene on Rte. 126, sells maps and $5 per day parking passes for the National Forest. Open daily 8am-4:30pm Memorial Day-Columbus Day; closed weekends in winter.

Outdoor Equipment: Mckenzie Outfitters, 566 Olive St. (☎343-2300), has very knowledgeable staff, a great collection of local guide books, and quality climbing and camping gear. Open M-Sa 10am-6pm, Su noon-5pm. **REI,** 306 Lawrence St. (☎465-1800), offers its usual large selection of outdoor gear, from climbing to biking to paddling. Open M-F 10am-9pm, Sa 10am-6pm, Su 11am-6pm.

Equipment Rental: Paul's Bicycle Way of Life, 152 W 5th Ave. (☎344-4105; www.bicycleway.com). Friendly, knowledgeable staff and a wide selection. City bikes $18 per day, $60 per week. Open M-F 9am-7pm, Sa-Su 10am-5pm. Also at 2480 Alder St. (☎342-6155) and 2580 Willakenzie (☎344-4150). **Oregon Riversports,** 3400 Franklin Blvd. (☎334-0696 or 888-790-7235; www.oregonriversports.com) rents whitewater gear and offers kayak and rafting trips to the Upper and Lower Mckenzie. Whitewater kayak rentals, all accessory gear included, $25 per day, inflatable kayaks $30 per day, rafts $55-75 per day. Credit card required. Open summer M-F 9am-6pm, Sa-Su 8am-6pm; winter M-F 10am-6pm, Sa 9am-6pm.

Laundromat: Holiday Coin Laundromat, 381 W 11th Ave., (☎726-1751; http://laundrymatters.com). Wash $1, dry $0.25 for 10min. Open daily 6am-11pm.

Police: 777 Pearl St. #107 (☎682-5111), at City Hall.

Hospital: White Bird Clinic Medical Center, 1400 Mill St. (☎800-422-7558; www.whitebirdclinic.org), provides low-cost medical care. Open M, W, F 9am-noon, 1-5pm, Tu 1-5pm, Th 9am-noon, 2-5pm. Call 342-8255 for appointments at clinic.

Internet Access: The brand new **library,** 100 W 10th Ave., (☎682-5450; www.ci.eugene.or.us/library) offers 15min. of usage on two computers. Open M-Th 10am-8pm, F-Sa 10am-6pm. **Oregon Public Networking,** 43 W Broadway (☎484-9637; www.opn.org), offers 30min. of free Internet access, or a full day of access for $1. Open M-F 11am-5pm, Sa noon-4pm. **CS Internet Cafe,** 747 Willamette Ave. (☎345-0408). First 15min. $2, then $7.20 per hr. Open M-F 7am-5pm.

Post Office: 520 Willamette St. (☎800-275-8777), at 5th Ave. Open M-F 8:30am-5:30pm, Sa 10am-2pm. **Postal Code:** 97401.

▚ ▞ CAMPING AND ACCOMMODATIONS

A choice hostel and inexpensive hotels make Eugene particularly budget-friendly. Ask at the visitors center for directions to the cheap hotel chains scattered about the town—the cheapest are on E Broadway and W 7th Ave. and tend toward seediness. Tenters have been known to camp by the river, especially in the wild and woolly northeast side near Springfield. Farther east on Rte. 58 and 126, the immense **Willamette National Forest ❶** is full of campsites ($6-16). Superb campgrounds cluster around the town of McKenzie Bridge and along the river. **Paradise Campground ❶,** east of McKenzie Bridge, is surrounded by greenery and great fishing. **McKenzie Bridge Campground ❶,** west of the town, has secluded sites under old-growth trees; loop B is best. (Reservations for both ☎877-444-6777. Sites $12.)

▨ **The Eugene Hummingbird Hostel,** 2352 Willamette St. (☎349-0589). Take bus #24 or 25 south from downtown to 24th Ave. and Willamette, or park in back on Portland St. A graceful neighborhood home and a wonderful escape from the city, offering a back porch, book-lined living room, (vegetarian) kitchen, and mellow atmosphere. Check-in 5-10pm. Lockout 11am-5pm. Dorms $16 with any hosteling membership, otherwise $19; private rooms from $30. You can also pitch a tent in the fenced-in yard for $10 per person. Cash or travelers checks only. ❶

Pine Meadows, (☎942-8657 or reservations 877-444-6777). Take I-5 S. to Exit 172, then head 3½ mi. south, turn left on Cottage Grove Reservoir Rd., and go another 2½ mi. Alongside a reservoir with plenty of RV and jet ski traffic. Open May 20-Sept. 11 2005, May 19-Oct. 10 2006. 93 sites, $14. Another 15 sites ¼ mi. down the road, $8. Free showers. ❶

Schwarz Park, (☎942-1418, reservations 877-444-6777), off I-5 S. Exit 174, about 15-20min. south of Eugene. Bear left at the fork in the off-ramp and turn left at the first traffic light, then go about 4¾ mi. The camp lies below beautiful and swimmable Dorena Lake. Flat and quiet enough that the lack of privacy is unimportant. Toilets and water. 82 sites, $12. ❶

Downtown Motel, 361 W 7th Ave. (☎345-8739 or 800-648-4366; www.downtownmotel.com), located near downtown and the highway, but still quiet and peaceful. Fridges and free sweets. Strong coffee in the morning. Singles $35; doubles $40. ❸

Campus Inn, 390 E Broadway (☎343-3376; www.campus-inn.com), has plenty of amenities like wireless Internet access and Starbucks coffee in the spotless rooms, cable TV with HBO, and tea in the lobby. Included continental breakfast. Singles from $60; doubles from $74. AAA and AARP discounts. ❹

◘ FOOD

Eugene's downtown area specializes in gourmet food; the university hangout zone at 13th Ave. and Kincaid St. has more grab-and-go options, and natural food stores are everywhere. *Everything* is organic. The **New Frontier Market,** with the **Broadway Bistro and Wine Bar,** at 200 W Broadway and Charnelton, is an organic store that also features an amazing wine bar and take-out lunch counter. (☎685-0790. Open M-Th 7am-9pm, F 7am-10pm, Sa-Su 8am-8pm.) For groceries, head to **Safeway,** 145 E 18th Ave. at Oak. (☎485-5051. Open daily 6am-2am.)

ORGANIC DINING

Perhaps most noteworthy of Eugene dining is the craze for "organically grown" products. Avoiding antibiotics, hormones, and nasty chemicals, these restaurants serve only food that undergoes organic certification.

▧ **Cozmic Pizza,** 199 W 8th Ave. (☎338-9333; www.cozmicpizza.com), has piping hot vegetarian, organic pizzas served with gourmet toppings and crust. It shares space with a coffee bar, Internet cafe, and nightclub. Enormous seating area with chess boards, huge plush chairs, and free wireless access. Pizza by the slice is $2.50, small one-person pizzas are $5 and 12 in. pizzas are $10, each of which take about 15min. to make. Open M-F 11am-11pm, Sa-Su 4-11pm. ❷

▧ **Keystone Cafe,** 395 W 5th Ave. (☎342-2075), serves creative dinners with entirely organic ingredients and many vegetarian options. Famous pancakes $3.25. M, F-Su 7am-3pm, Open Tu-Th 7am-2pm. ❶

Morning Glory Cafe and Bakery, 450 Willamette St. (☎687-0709), is a local favorite, particularly among the uber-liberal, with spoken word on the stereo and collages celebrating the beauty of the natural world adorning the walls. Though the food is a bit pricey ($7-8.50), it gets local raves. Even a caffeine habit can be satisfied organically here, since Morning Glory shares space with **Out of the Fog Organic Coffee House.** Breakfast dishes and sandwiches $6-7.50. Both open Tu-Su 7:30am-3:30pm. ❷

OTHER RESTAURANTS

The Glenwood, 1340 Alder St. (☎687-0355), on 13th Ave., has delicious, cheaper-than-usual sandwiches ($5-7) and a sunny deck—just expect to compete with crowds of students during the school year. Breakfast features scrambles and breakfast burritos ($5-7). Open daily 7am-10pm. ❷

Bene Gourmet Pizza, 225 W Broadway (☎284-2700), serves huge salads and delicious pizza by the slice ($2.50). 14 in. pies $13-15. Open M-F 11am-9pm, Sa 4-9pm. Also has locations at 4 Oakway Center (☎284-2701) and 2566 Willamette St. (☎284-2702), both of which are open the above hours and Su noon-9pm. ❷

◢ OUTDOOR ACTIVITIES

To escape the city, Eugene residents flock to the **McKenzie River Corridor,** which harbors the clear and continuous rapids of the McKenzie River and a gentle trail along its banks. For rafting, the Upper McKenzie is a wild and scenic stretch, much preferred to the sometimes clear-cut lower section.

◢ **KAYAKING AND RAFTING.** Within an 1½hr. drive from Eugene, the McKenzie River has several stretches of class II-III whitewater. The river can be run all year, but pleasant summer weather and high water make June through August the best time to run it. The Upper McKenzie is continuous for 14 mi. and can easily be paddled within 2-2½hr. One class III, 9 mi. trip begins at Olallie Campground and ends at Paradise Campground. Both access points are on Rte. 126; Olallie is about 12 mi. east of McKenzie Bridge. A class II+ stretch begins at the Paradise Campground and continues downstream. These are not the only options, as many campgrounds along the river offer access; put-ins upstream of Olallie Campground are feasible except during late-summer low water.

High Country Expeditions, on Belknap Springs Road about 5 mi. east of McKenzie Bridge, is one of the few rafting companies that floats the Upper McKenzie. (☎ 888-461-7233. Half-day, 14 mi. trips $50; full-day, 18-19 mi. trips $75. Student and senior discounts.) **Oregon Riversports** (p. 133) also offers trips.

🔌 **HIKING.** The 26 mi. **McKenzie River Trail** starts 1½ mi. west of the ranger station (trail map $1) and ends north at Old Santiam Rd. near Fish Lake's old-growth grove. Parallel to Rte. 126, the trail winds through mossy forests, and leads to two of Oregon's most spectacular waterfalls—**Koosah Falls** and **Sahalie Falls.** They flank **Clear Lake,** a volcanic crater now filled with crystal clear waters. The entire trail is also open to mountain bikers and considered fairly difficult because of the volcanic rocks. A number of Forest Service campgrounds cluster along this stretch of Rte. 126 (see **Camping and Accommodations,** above). More ambitious hikers can sign up for overnight permits at the ranger station and head for the high country, where the hiking opportunities are endless.

DRIVING. To see the country as 19th-century settlers saw it, take Rte. 126 east from Eugene. On a clear day, the mighty and perpetually snow-capped **Three Sisters** are visible. Just east of **McKenzie Bridge,** the road splits into a scenic byway loop. Rte. 242 climbs east to the vast lava fields of **McKenzie Pass,** while Rte. 126 turns north over Santiam Pass and meets back with Rte. 242 in Sisters (p. 153). Rte. 242 is often blocked by snow until the end of June. Call the McKenzie Ranger Station for information, below. The exquisite drive winds its narrow way between **Mt. Washington,** which looks like it got lost on its way to the Swiss Alps, and the **Three Sisters Wilderness** before rising to the high plateau of McKenzie Pass. Here, lava outcroppings once served as a training site for astronauts preparing for lunar landings. The Civilian Conservation Corps-built **Dee Wright Observatory** has incredible views on clear days. The **McKenzie Ranger Station,** 3 mi. east of McKenzie Bridge on Rte. 126, has more info. (☎ 822-3381. Open daily summer 8am-4:30pm; winter M-F 8am-4:30pm.) Check with rangers about hiking permits (usually free) before going to the trailheads. The **Willamette National Forest** (see **Practical Information,** p. 133) has information on the McKenzie Pass.

HOT SPRINGS. The large and popular Cougar Lake features the Terwilliger Hot Springs a network of six cascading pools known by all as **Cougar Hot Springs.** Drive through the town of Blue River, 60 mi. east of Eugene on Rte. 126, and then turn right onto Aufderheide Dr. (Forest Service Rd. 19) and follow the road 7¼ mi. as it winds on the right side of Cougar Reservoir. (Open dawn-dusk. $3 per person. Clothing optional.)

👁 **SIGHTS**

Every Saturday the area around 8th Ave. and Willamette St. fills up for the **Saturday Market,** featuring live music and stalls hawking everything from hemp shopping bags to tarot readings. The food stalls serve up delicious, cheap local fare. Right next to the shopping stalls is the **farmers market,** where you can buy (you guessed it) organic, locally-grown produce. (June-Oct. Tu 10am-3pm; Apr. to mid-Nov. Sa 9am-5pm.) Take time to pay homage to the ivy-covered halls that set the scene for National Lampoon's *Animal House* at Eugene's centerpiece, the **University of Ore-**

gon. The visitor parking and info booth are on 13th Ave., the first right after the entrance off Franklin. Tours begin from the reception desk at **Oregon Hall.** (At E 13th Ave. and Agate St. ☎346-3014; www.uoregon.edu. Tours M-F 10am and 2pm, Sa 10am. Reception desk open M-F 8am-5pm.) A few blocks away, the **Museum of Natural History,** 1680 E 15th Ave., at Agate St., shows a collection of relics from native cultures, including the world's oldest pair of shoes. (☎346-3024; http://natural-history.uoregon.edu. Open W-Su noon-5pm. Suggested donation $2.)

🎵 ENTERTAINMENT

The **Eugene Emeralds** are the local Triple-A minor league baseball team; they play in **Civic Stadium,** at 20th Ave. and Pearl St., throughout the summer. (For tickets call ☎342-5376; www.go-ems.com. The season lasts from mid-June to mid-Sept. $5-8, seniors and children $4-7.) The *Eugene Weekly* (www.eugeneweekly.com), a free magazine available all over town, has a list of concerts and local events as well as features on the greater Eugene community. The *Sentient Times* (www.sentienttimes.com) is worth a read to see what Eugene's liberal bent is all about. The **Community Center for the Performing Arts** operates the **WOW Hall,** 291 W 8th Ave., a historic dance venue on the National Register of Historic Places. All kinds of public speaking, dance, and theater events, as well as workshops and classes, are hosted here. Tickets are available at the Hall and at local ticket outlets. (☎687-2746; www.wowhall.org. Open M-F 3-6pm. Tickets up to $18.) High-brow culture finds a home at the extravagant **Hult Center for the Performing Arts,** 1 Eugene Center, at 7th Ave. and Willamette St. The two theater halls host a variety of music from Tool to Tchaikovsky and from blues to Bartók, as well as theater and opera. (Info ☎682-5087, ticket office 682-5000, 24hr. event info 682-5746; www.hultcenter.org. Free tours Th and Sa at 1pm. Tickets $8-55. Box office open Tu-F noon-5pm, Sa 11am-3pm, and 1hr. before curtain.) The **Bijou Art Cinema,** 492 E 13th Ave. at Ferry St., is a local favorite where indie and art films are screened in the sanctuary of an old Spanish church. (☎686-2458; ww.bijou-cinemas.com. Box office open 20min. before the first screening. M-W and Su $5, Th-Sa $7, seniors $4.50, 12 and under $3.50. Before 6pm $4, after 11pm F-Sa $4, Su $3.)

📷 **OREGON COUNTRY FAIR.** The fair takes place in **Veneta,** 13 mi. west of town on Rte. 126, and is by far the most exciting event of the summer. Started in 1969 as a fundraiser for a local Waldorf school, the fair has become a magical annual gathering of hippies, artists, musicians, misfits, and activists. Every July 50,000 people, many still living in 1960s bliss, flock from across the nation to experience this festival unlike any other. Hundreds of performers crowd onto 12 different stages, and 700 booths fill with art, clothing, crafts, herbal remedies, exhibits on alternative energy sources, and food. Lofty treehouses, parades of painted bodies, dancing 12 ft. dolls, and thousands of revelers transport travelers into an enchanted forest of frenzy. Parking is extremely limited ($5) and the fair requires advance tickets. Most people park for free at Civic Stadium, at 19th and Willamette in Eugene. From there, free, wheelchair-accessible buses run every 10-15min. from 10am until the fairgrounds close at 7pm. (☎343-4298; www.oregoncountryfair.org. Every year on the weekend after the Fourth of July. Advance tickets F and Su $13, Sa $16, $2 extra if bought day of event; 3-day pass $40; under 6 free. Tickets are available only through Ticketswest, ☎800-325-7328; www.tickestwest.com. Ticketswest also sells tickets for nearby camping for the weekend, $30-36 per person.)

OREGON BACH FESTIVAL. For 16 days in June and July (June 24-July 10 2005, June 23-July 9 2006), Baroque authority Helmut Rilling conducts performances of Bach's concerti and other works by Bach's contemporaries. (☎346-5666; www.oregonbachfestival.com. Concert/lecture series $16; main events $23-55.)

◢ NIGHTLIFE

According to some, Eugene's nightlife is the best in Oregon, outside of Portland. Not surprisingly, the string of establishments by the university along 13th St. are dominated by the college crowd. Come nightfall, bearded hippies mingle with pierced anarchists and muscle-bound fratboys in Eugene's eclectic nightlife scene. In the *Animal House* tradition, the row by the university along 13th Ave. is often dominated by fraternity-style beer bashes. Refugees from this scene will find a diverse selection throughout town. Cozmic Pizza at 8th and Charnelton, see p. 135, offers a laid back scene. Check out *Eugene Weekly* (p. 137) for club listings.

■ **Sam Bond's Garage,** 407 Blair Blvd. (☎431-6603; www.sambonds.com). Take bus #50 or 52 or a cab at night. A laid-back gem in the Whitaker neighborhood. Live entertainment every night complements an evolving selection of local microbrews ($3 per pint). 21+ after 8:30pm. Happy hour daily 4-7pm, $2.50 pints. Open daily 3pm-1am.

The Downtown Lounge/Diablo's, 959 Pearl St. (☎343-2346; www.diablosdowntown.com), offers a casual scene with pool tables upstairs and Eugene's most beautiful people shaking their thangs amid flame-covered walls downstairs. Cover $2-3. Open M-F 11am-2:30pm, Sa-Su 4pm-2:30am.

John Henry's, 77 W Broadway (☎342-3358; www.johnhenrysclub.com), is Eugene's prime site for punk, reggae, and virtually any other kind of live music you'd like to hear. Call or check the website for schedule and covers. 21+. Open daily 5pm-2:30am.

Jo Federigo's Jazz Club and Restaurant, 259 E 5th Ave. (☎343-8488; http://users.rio.com/jofeds), across from 5th St. Public Market, swings with live jazz nightly. Shows start M-Th 8:30pm or 9pm, F-Sa at 9pm. Open Tu-Th 11:30am-2pm and 5-10pm, Sa-Su 5-10pm. Bar open M-F 3:30pm-close, Sa-Su 5pm-close.

GRANTS PASS   ☎541

Workers building a road through the Oregon mountains in 1863 were so overjoyed by the news of General Ulysses S. Grant's Civil War victory at Vicksburg that they named the town Grants Pass after the burly President-to-be. Today, the city colonizes the hot, flat valley with espresso stands and fast-food joints. It's a fine place to sleep, but real adventure lies in the nearby Rogue River and Illinois Valleys.

■◪ **ORIENTATION AND PRACTICAL INFORMATION.** The town lies within the triangle formed by **I-5** in the northeast, **Route 99** in the west, and the **Rogue River** to the south. In town, Rte. 99 splits into one-way **6th** and **7th Streets,** which run through the heart of downtown and separate east from west. The railroad tracks (between G and F St.) divide north and south addresses. Within historic downtown, north-south streets are numbered increasing heading east, and east-west streets are lettered heading south. **Greyhound,** 460 NE Agness Ave. (☎476-4513; open M-Sa 6am-6:30pm), at the east end of town, runs to **Portland** (5½hr., 2 per day, $34) and **San Francisco** (12hr., 4 per day, $60). **Enterprise,** 1325 NE 7th St., rents cars from $30 plus $0.25 per mi. after 150 mi.; they'll also match any major rental company's price. (☎471-7800. Must be over 21 with a credit card. Open M-F 7:30am-6pm, Sa 9am-noon.)

The **Chamber of Commerce,** 1995 NW Vine St., off 6th St., provides info beneath an immense plaster caveman. (☎476-7717 or 800-547-5927; www.visitgrantspass.org. Open M-F 8am-5pm, Sa 9am-5pm, Su 10am-4pm; winter closed Sa-Su.) **MayBelle's Washtub** is at 306 SE I St. at 8th St. (☎471-1317. Wash $1.25, dry $0.25 per 8min. Open daily 7am-10pm; last wash 8:30pm.) Contact the **police** at 500 NW 6th St. (☎955-1945). The **Three Rivers Community Hospital** is at

500 Ramsey Ave. (☎472-7000), just south of town. Get **Internet** access at the **Josephine County Library,** 200 NW C St., where it's free for 1hr. on one of 10 computers. (☎474-5480; www.co.josephine.or.us/library/index.html. Open M-Tu noon-7pm, W-Th 10am-5pm, Sa 10am-1pm.) The **post office** can be found at 132 NW 6th Ave. at F St. (☎800-275-8777. Open M-F 9am-5pm.) **Postal Code:** 97526.

☀☀ ACCOMMODATIONS AND CAMPING.

Grants Pass supports one of every franchise motel on earth, from Motel 6 to the Holiday Inn Express. The one-of-a-kind cheapo motels are farther back from the interstate on 6th St. and cost $25-35. The **Buena Sera Inn ❹,** 1001 NE 6th St., offers spotless rooms and hardwood floors right in the heart of town. (☎476-4260; www.buenaserainn.com. Singles from $48; doubles $59; $10 cheaper in winter). Of the camping options, **Valley of the Rogue State Park ❷** is your best choice, 12 mi. east of town off I-5 Exit 45B. The valley is just wide enough for the river, a row of tents, RVs interspersed with a few trees, and the noise of the interstate. (☎582-1118, reservations 800-452-5687. $16, with electricity $20; RV sites $20; yurts $30.)

☐ FOOD.

For spatulas and spaghetti noodles, try **Safeway,** 115 NE 7th St. (☎479-4276. Open daily 6am-1am.) The **Growers' Market,** held in the parking lot between 4th and F St., is the state's largest open-air market and has arts and crafts, produce, food, and music everywhere. (☎476-5375; www.growersmarket.org. Sa 9am and 1pm.) ▨**Wild River Brewing and Pizza Co. ❸,** 595 NE E St., is a local favorite offering gourmet pizza and a signature microbrew ($3.25 per pint). Offerings like the woodfired artichoke, avocado, and alfredo sauce pizza ($15, feeds 2) overshadow the more pedestrian salads, burgers, pastas and sandwiches. (☎471-7487, pub 472-9766; www.wildriverbrewing.com. Open M-F 10:30am-10:30pm, Sa-Su 11am-11pm.) **Thai BBQ ❷,** 428 SW 6th St. at J St., is decorated like an English teahouse but serves authentic Thai. Fancier than the name suggests but just as cheap: most lunch dishes are $5-7, and many dinner entrees are only a few dollars more. (☎476-4304. Open M-Sa 11am-9pm.) **Matsukaze Japanese Restaurant ❷,** 1675 NE 7th St. at Hillcrest, is the best Japanese food in town. At what has become a youth hangout, sushi goes for $3-5, while most dinners are $10-13. Traditional entrees run $4-15. (☎479-2961. Open M-Th 11am-2pm and 5-9pm, F 11am-2pm and 5-9:30pm, Sa 5-9:30pm; closes 30min. earlier in winter.)

THE LOCAL STORY

HOUSE OF MYSTERY

In the Gold Hills off I-5 Exit 40 is an area 167 ft., 5¼ in. in diameter where all hell has broken loose. Balls roll uphill, birds fly into trees, and your height fluctuates based on where you stand. This circle of chaos is known as the Oregon Vortex.

The Vortex has baffled scientists for 70 years. Great minds like Albert Einstein have pondered the question, and, in spite of many theories (such as a spaceship circling a black hole at light speed), there are no solutions.

In fact, it's not even completely clear what's wrong. Two people of the same height stand on a level board. When a board is placed on top of their heads it, too, is level. Everything works...or does it? The person nearer the center looks dramatically shorter and the board appears to slope. As they switch places, the person walking away from the center becomes taller while the person nearing it looks shorter.

Pictures don't do this justice. It's not that they're unbelievable, it's just that they're unimpressive compared to actually seeing a person's height change or watching a golf ball roll uphill (an optical illusion, but an incredible one). Bring your cynicism, but with the help of a bunch of boards and a level, you will be convinced that there is something significantly wrong with this bit of forest.

The Oregon Vortex ☎855-1543; www.oregonvortex.com. Located about 8 mi. off Exit 40. $6-8.

◢ RAFTING AND KAYAKING. The **Rogue River** is the greatest draw in the town of Grants Pass. A federally protected "Wild and Scenic River," the Rogue can be enjoyed by raft, jet boat, mail boat, or hiking on foot. Anglers are in good company—Zane Grey and Clark Gable used to roam the Rogue River with tackle and bait. For more information on fishing licenses and the best places to go, head to the **ranger station,** 200 NE Greenfield Rd., (☎471-6500) northeast of I-5 at Exit 58. Prime rafting and kayaking can be found on an impressive 35 mi. stretch of Class III and IV rapids starting just north of Galice. Paddling this restricted area requires a permit ($10) or guide (try **Orange Torpedo Trips,** below). Permits run out with remarkable swiftness—to secure one, call ☎479-3735 at 8am exactly nine days before your trip; see www.or.blm.gov/rand for more info. Although the rest of the river near Grants Pass is very popular, it is not nearly as scenic, and can be downright residential; still, the whitewater gives plenty of thrills, especially for the uninitiated. The river can be found just outside of **Merlin,** where the necessary equipment can be procured as well. To get there, head west off I-5 Exit 61. **White Water Cowboys,** 210 Merlin Rd., rents rafts, and offers shuttle services. (☎479-0132. Discounts for multi-day rentals. Inflatable kayaks $20 per day, rafts $65-95 per day.) **Orange Torpedo Trips,** in the same building, runs tours down every section of the Rogue River in orange inflatable kayaks. OTT was the first to use these interesting contraptions all the way back in 1969. (☎479-5061 or 800-635-2925; www.orangetorpedo.com. Half-day "dinner trip" $55; full-day $75.)

◣ CAVING. To reach **Oregon Caves National Monument,** 30 mi. south of Grants Pass via US 199, drive through plush, green wilderness to Cave Junction, and then 20 mi. east along Rte. 46. Here, in the belly of the ancient Siskiyous, enormous pressure and acidic waters created some of the only caves with walls of glistening marble in North America. A guided cave tour runs 1½hr. The temperature inside is 42°F and the walk can be rather strenuous, so bring layers and comfortable shoes. Reservations are not available; to avoid crowds, arrive before 11am or after 5pm. (☎592-2100; www.nps.gov/orca. $7.50, ages 16 and under $5; free with National Parks pass (p. 64). Tours leave every 30min. in the summer, every 1hr. Sept.-Nov. and mid-March to mid-June, and every 2hr. late Oct.-late Nov. Open mid-Mar. to late May 10am-4pm; late May to mid-June 9am-5pm; mid-June to early Sept. 9am-7pm; early Sept.-early Oct. 9am-5pm; mid-Oct. to late Nov. 10am-4pm.)

ASHLAND ☎541

Set near the California border, Ashland mixes hip youth and British literary history, setting an unlikely but intriguing stage for the world-famous ▧**Oregon Shakespeare Festival.** From mid-February to October, drama devotees can choose among 11 Shakespearean and newer works performed in Ashland's three elegant theaters. But to locals and the outdoorsy, Ashland is far more than a town crazy for an old, dead bard. Unexpected in every way, it's a small (pop. about 20,000, not including students) town crammed between mountains to the west and east and culturally smeared somewhere between liberal Portland and new-age Northern California. To add to the fun, Ashland and the surrounding area are packed with all the biking, boating, hiking, and beautiful people you could ever hope for. Ashland is a great place to linger a few more days than planned.

▣ ✦ JOURNEY'S END

Ashland is in the foothills of the Siskiyou and Cascade Ranges, 285 mi. south of Portland and 15 mi. north of the California border, near the junction of **I-5** and **Route 66. Route 99** cuts through the middle of town on a northwest-southeast axis.

It becomes **North Main Street** as it enters town from the west, and then splits briefly into **East Main Street** and **Lithia Way** as it runs through the highly walkable downtown. Farther south, Main St. changes its name again to **Siskiyou Boulevard,** where Southern Oregon University (SOU) is flanked by affordable motels.

Buses: Greyhound (☎482-8803) runs from Mr. C's Market, where I-5 meets Rte. 99 north of town. 3 buses per day to: **Portland** (6¾hr., $54); **Eugene** (4½hr., $24); **Sacramento** (6¼hr., $54); and **San Francisco** (10½hr., $64). Weekday rates $4 cheaper, to Eugene $2 cheaper.

Public Transportation: Rogue Valley Transportation District (RVTD; ☎779-2877; www.rvtd.org), in Medford. Bus schedules available at the Chamber of Commerce. The #10 bus runs between the transfer station at 200 S Front St. in **Medford** and the plaza in Ashland (35min.) then makes several stops on a loop through downtown. In-town rides are free. #10 runs through Ashland every 30min. daily 5am-7pm.

Taxis: Yellow Cab (☎482-3065 or 800-527-0700), $3 base, $2.20 per mi. 24hr.

Car Rental: Budget, 3038 Biddle Rd. (☎779-0488), at the airport in Medford. $29 per day, $0.30 per mi. after 200 mi. Must have credit card. Ages 21-24 $10 extra per day.

❓ HERE CEASE MORE QUESTIONS

Tourist Office: Chamber of Commerce, 110 E. Main St. (☎482-3486; www.ashland-chamber.com). Open M-F 9am-5pm. The Chamber of Commerce runs a smaller **info booth** in a plaza at Windbum and E Main. Open M-Sa 10am-6pm, Su 11am-4pm.

Outdoor Information: Ashland District Ranger Station, 645 Washington St., off Rte. 66 (☎552-2900 or 482-3333; www.fs.fed.us/r6/rogue), by Exit 14 on I-5, provides info on hiking, biking, and the Pacific Crest Trail. Open M-F 8am-1pm and 2-4:30pm. For the inside scoop on outdoor sports and activities, it's better to talk to the people at Ashland Mountain Supply.

Equipment Rental: ■**Ashland Mountain Supply,** 31 N Main St. (☎488-2749; www.hikinggearnw.com). Rents internal frame backpacks and many other "accessories" (ice axes, crampons, helmets, etc.) for $5 per day. Tents $15 per day. Mountain bikes $13 for 2hr., $30 per day. Cash deposit or credit card required. Copious and multidisciplinary (climbing, fishing, skiing, biking) outdoors advice is free; the staff can refer you to fishing guides for almost every local river. Open daily 10am-6pm.

Laundromat: Main Street Laundromat, 370 E Main St. (☎482-8042). Wash $1.50, dry $0.25 per 8min. Open daily 24hr.

Pharmacy: Rite Aid, 2341 Ashland St. (☎482-7409). Store open M-Sa 8am-9pm, Su 9am-9pm. Pharmacy open M-F 9am-9pm, Sa 9am-7pm, Su 10am-6pm.

Police: 20 E Main St. (☎488-2211).

Crisis Line: ☎779-4357 or 888-609-4357. 24hr.

Hospital: Ashland Community Hospital, 280 Maple St. (☎482-2441). Open 24hr.

Internet Access: The newly expanded **Ashland Library,** 410 Siskiyou Blvd. (☎482-1151; www.jcls.org), at Gresham St. Free 18min. of Internet access on three computers. Free wireless Internet access. Open M-Tu noon-7pm, W-Th 10am-6pm, F-Sa noon-5pm. **Evo's Java House,** 376 E Main St. (☎482-2261), also offers free access on one computer or via their wireless network; see **Food of Love,** below.

Post Office: 120 N 1st St. (☎800-275-8777), at Lithia Way. Open M-F 9am-5pm. **Postal Code:** 97520.

OREGON

OREGON

Ashland

▲ ACCOMMODATIONS
Ashland Hostel, 2
Columbia Hotel, 5
Mt. Ashland
Campground, 12
Relax Inn, 11
Wellsprings Healing
Community, 1

◆ FOOD
Bento Express, 3
Evo's Java House, 8
Morning Glory, 9
Munchies, 4
Pangea, 6
Pasta Piatti, 7
Three Rivers, 10

Ashland Municipal Airport

Clover Ln.

Oak Knoll Dr.

Washington St.

Ashland District Ranger Station ■

Mistletoe

Mill Rd.

Tolman Creek Rd.

Rite Aid ■

Hamilton Creek

Clay St.

Clay St.

Glendale Ave.

TO MT. ASHLAND (35mi.)

Faith Ave.

Park Ave.

Park St.

Beswick Way

Normal Ave.

Ray Ln.

Hillview Dr.

Harmony Ln.

Garden Ave.

Frances Ln.

Windsor St.

Woodland Dr.

Indiana St.

Palmer Rd.

Leonard St.

Roca St.

Elkader St.

Prospect St.

Holmes Ave.

Parker St.

Ashland St.

Walker Ave.

Southern Oregon University

Webster St.

Wightman St.

Bridge St.

Avery St.

Southern Oregon State College

Garfield St.

Iowa St.

Palm Ave.

Mountain Ave.

Emerick St.

Mallard St.

N Wightman St.

Fordyce St.

Beach St.

Liberty St.

Morton St.

Harrison St.

Kearney St.

Idaho St.

Taylor St.

Euclid Ave.

Pracht St.

Siskiyou Blvd.

E Main St.

8th St.

7th St.

6th St.

A St.

B St.

C St.

Union St.

Gresham St.

Meade St.

Hillcrest St.

Courtney St.

Terrace St.

Ridge Rd.

Glenview Dr.

Pioneer St.

Windburn Way

Granite St.

Ashland Ck.

Lithia Park

Black Swan Lake

Patterson St.

Hersey St.

SEE INSET

TO MEDFORD (12mi.)

Central Ave.

Helman St.

Water St.

Oak St.

Pioneer St.

1st St.

2nd St.

3rd St.

4th St.

A St.

B St.

C St.

E Main St.

Siskiyou Blvd.

Safeway

Gresham St.

Alison St.

Main St.
Laundromat

Lithia Way

Will Dodge Way

Chamber of Commerce

Enders Alley

Oregon Cabaret Theatre

Hargadine St.

Black Swan

Vista Pl.

West Fork St.

Terrace Ave.

Glenview Dr.

Box Office

New Theatre

Elizabethan Theatre

Angus Bowmer Theatre

Ashland Mtn. Supply

Adventure Center

Co-op

N Main St.

Bush St.

Church St.

High St.

Baum St.

Pine St.

Granite St.

Pioneer Ave.

Windburn Way

TO MEDFORD (12mi.)

N Main St.

400 yards

400 meters

0

0

TO (500yd.);
(2mi.)

(1mi.)

⌂ ⌂ TO SLEEP, PERCHANCE TO DREAM

In the winter, Ashland is a budget traveler's paradise of motel vacancy and low rates; in summer, every room in town fills in the blink of an eye and rates rise sky high. Only rogues and peasant slaves arrive without reservations. The nearest state park offering a decent-sized campground is the **Valley of the Rogue State Park** (p. 139), about 30 mi. north on I-5.

Ashland Hostel, 150 N Main St. (☎482-9217; www.ashlandhostel.com). The Victorian parlor and sturdy bunks play host to Pacific Coast Trail hikers, theater-goers, and other Ashland visitors in search of entertainment, outdoors or in. It's very well-positioned for living the nightlife to its fullest. Linens $2. Laundry, kitchen. No A/C. Check-in 5-10pm. Lockout 10am-5pm. Dorms $21; private rooms $50. Cash only. ❷

Mount Ashland Campground, 20min. south of Ashland off I-5 at Exit 6. Follow signs for Mt. Ashland Ski Area through the parking lot. 9 sites in the forest overlook the valley and Mt. Shasta. Can be snowy in June. No drinking water. Free. ❶

Columbia Hotel, 262½ E Main St. (☎482-3726 or 800-718-2530; www.columbiahotel.com). Oozes with charm; each room is different, with antique style furniture. A reading alcove and morning tea round out this historic home turned Euro-style hotel. Wireless Internet access throughout the hotel. Only 1½ blocks from theaters. June-Oct. rooms $69; private baths begin at $105. Mar.-June $49-89. 10% HI discount in low season. ❹

Wellsprings Healing Community, 2253 N Rte. 99 (☎482-3776), 200 yd. northwest of where I-5 meets 99, is built around a spa fed by springs believed to have healing powers. The complex includes a large field where you can pitch your tent. Massages go for $50-60; clothing-optional adult swim at 7:45pm. Sites $14, with electricity $17, each additional person $6.50. ❶

Relax Inn, 535 Clover Ln. (☎482-4423 or 888-672-5290), just off I-5 at Exit 14 behind a 76 gas station. The small building conceals recently remodeled rooms with cable TV and A/C. Singles $38; doubles $52. ❸

◖ FOOD OF LOVE

The incredible food selection on N and E Main St. has earned the plaza a culinary reputation independent of the festival, though the food tends to be pricey. **The Ashland Food Cooperative,** 237 N 1st St., stocks cheap and organic groceries in bulk. (☎482-2237; www.asfs.org. Open M-Sa 8am-9pm, Su 9am-9pm.) Cheaper groceries are available at **Safeway,** 585 Siskiyou Blvd. (☎482-4495. Open daily 6am-midnight.)

Evo's Java House and Revolutionary Cafe, 376 E. Main St. (☎774-6980). If you're hungry and sick of the Man keeping you down, fight back at Evo's, where the politics are as radical as the vegetarian burritos and sandwiches ($3.50-5) are tasty. Once or twice a week you can listen to live folk, punk, metal, or a duet. There may be a cover charge for music. Free wireless Internet access. Open M-Sa 7am-5pm, Su 7am-2pm. ❶

Munchies, 59 N Main St. (☎488-2967), below the Ashland Chocolate Factory, offers everything from burgers and sandwiches to Mexican food ($7-9). Fast service, great food, and prime location on the plaza make Munchies very popular. Open M-F 9am-8pm, Sa-Su 8am-9pm. ❷

Morning Glory, 1149 Siskiyou Blvd. (☎488-8636; www.morninggloryrestaurant.com), deserves a medal for "most pleasant dining environment," earned either inside by the fireplace and bookcases or outside by the rose-entwined wooden porticos. Sandwiches, scrambles, and waffles all around $9. Open daily 7am-2pm. ❸

OREGON

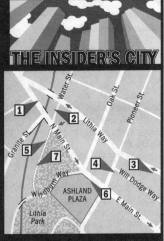

THE INSIDER'S CITY

[map locations] 1, 2, 5, 7, 4, 3, 6

Water St., Oak St., Pioneer St., Lithia Way, Granite St., N Main St., Winburn Way, ASHLAND PLAZA, Will Dodge Way, E Main St., Lithia Park

DRINK DEEP ERE YOU DEPART

Ashland's nightlife scene is denser than dark microbrewed stout—you could easily enjoy a week of partying in the clubs and bars on E Main St. between 2nd and Water St. All pubs are 21+ unless otherwise noted.

1 Mellow out on the huge outdoor deck at the Ashland Creek Bar & Grill, 92 N Main St. (☎482-4131). W DJ, F-Sa blues, ska and reggae. Cover $1-3. Open daily 11am-2am.

2 Head next to the **Siskiyou Brew Pub**, 31 Water St. (☎482-7718), the most laid-back bar in town. Live music once or twice a week. Cover $5-10. Opens M-Th 4pm, F-Su 3pm. No minors after 9pm.

3 If you shoot pool, the place to be is **Q's Bar & Grill**, 140 Lithia Way (☎488-4880; http://medford.unclewebster.com/lc/bus/536.) W live music, Th college night with well drinks $1-3, Sa shot night. No cover. Open Th-Sa 11am-2:30am, Su-W 11am-1am.

Three Rivers, 1640 Ashland St. (☎482-0776). If you like Indian, load up at the tasty buffet for the weeks ahead. All-you-can-eat lunch buffet $7.95, dinner buffet $8.95. Open M-Su 11:30am-2:30pm and 5-9pm. ❷

Pangea, 272 E Main St. (☎552-1630), has a menu of creative wraps and grilled panini sandwiches ($8). The Wrap of Khan is a meal in itself ($7.45). Almost anything on the menu can be made without meat. Open M-Th and Su 11am-9pm, F-Sa 11am-10pm. ❷

Pasta Piatti, 358 E Main St. (☎488-5493), has gourmet Italian food for a very good price. Whether you're craving crab ravioli and fettuccine alfredo ($8-10), or pizza and panini ($8-9), Pasta Piatti is the place to go. Eat in the elegant dining room or out on the deck overlooking bustling Main St. Open daily 11:30am-9pm. ❷

Bento Express, 3 Granite St. (☎488-3582) is a tiny restaurant offering large portions of rice and cheap bento lunches (boxes of rice with a few side dishes). Eat on the covered porch outside or take your food to go. Bao and potstickers are $1.95, bento meals are $4.75. Open M-Sa 11am-5pm, Su noon-4pm. ❶

♫ ♩ HEAVENLY MUSIC

Ashland's renowned nightlife, which befits a town 10 times its size, is concentrated around N and E Main St. The bar scene tends toward either the raucous and collegiate or the mellow and laid-back.

Ashland remains a cultural center even after the festival ends. Local and touring artists alike play throughout the year to the town's enthused audiences. The **Oregon Cabaret Theater,** at 1st and Hagardine St., stages light musicals in a cozy former church with drinks, dinners, and Sunday brunch. (☎488-2902; www.oregoncabaret.com. Box office open M and W-Sa 11am-2pm and 3-6pm, Th 11am-2pm; open Th 4-6pm and Su 4-8pm when there is a performance. Tickets $19-26, food not included; reservations required 48hr. in advance.) Small groups, such as **Camelot** (☎535-5250; www.camelottheatre.org; $15, seniors and students $13), **Ashland Community Theatre** (☎482-7532), and **Southern Oregon University**'s theater department (☎552-6346; www.sou.edu/thtr; $15, seniors $13, students $8) also sporadically raise the curtains year-round. Ashland also finds space for great music. When in town, the traveling **Rogue Valley Symphony** performs in the Music Recital Hall at SOU and at Lithia Park. (☎552-6398; www.rusymphony.org. $31, students $10.) In July and August, the **Oregon Ballet Theatre** (☎535-4112; www.obt.org) graces the stage in a variety of venues Monday nights for free performances.

🔅 MIDSUMMER MADNESS

The 🔖**Oregon Shakespeare Festival,** (☎482-4331; www.osfashland.org) was begun in 1935 by local college teacher Angus Bowmer as a nighttime complement to the daytime boxing matches in the old **Chautauqua Dome.** Today, the former site of the dome is the festival's featured theater, the **Elizabethan Stage;** instead of local college students, professional actors perform 11 plays in repertory, five or six of which are contemporary and classical works. Performances run on the three Ashland stages from mid-February through October and the only boxing that takes place is over scarce tickets. The 1200-seat Elizabethan Stage, an outdoor theater modeled after an 18th-century London design, is open from mid-June to mid-October and hosts three Shakespeare plays per season. The **Angus Bowmer Theater** is a 600-hundred seat indoor stage that shows one Shakespearean play and a variety of dramas. The **New Theater,** still awaiting a $7 million donor for a name, seats 250-350 and serves as a modern replacement for the aging **Black Swan** theater, which is now used for festival lectures and rehearsals. The 2005 schedule includes *Twelfth Night, Richard III, Love's Labours Lost,* and *The Tragical History of Doctor Faustus,* as well as several contemporary plays.

In mid-June, the **Feast of Will** celebrates the annual opening of the Elizabethan Theater with dinner and merry madness in Lithia Park. ($12. Call the box office at ☎482-4331 for details.) **Festival Noons,** a mix of lectures and concerts held outside the Elizabethan Theatre, occur almost every day at noon beginning in mid-June. Most are free, but some require tickets ($7-9), available at the box office.

TICKETS. Ticket purchases are recommended six months in advance. The **Box Office,** 15 S. Pioneer St., is next to the Elizabethan and Bowmer Theaters, across the street from the New Theater. (☎482-4331; www.osfashland.org. Open Tu-Su 9:30am-performance, M and non-performance days 9:30am-5pm. General mail-order and phone ticket sales begin in January, and many weekend shows sell out within the first week. Tickets cost $23-44 for spring previews and fall shows, summer shows $29-55, plus a $5 handling fee per order for phone, fax, or mail orders. Children under 6 are not admitted. Those under 18 receive 25% discounts in the summer and 50% in the spring and fall. For complete ticket info, visit the website.)

Last-minute theatergoers should not abandon hope. At 9:30am, the box office releases **unsold tickets** for the day's performances. Prudence demands arriving early;

4 Once you've cleaned out your friends playing 9-ball, let the dancing begin at **Tabú,** 79 N Pioneer St. (☎482-3900; www.taburestaurant.com). Choice acoustics and a great bar area give this place a classy feel. Th and Sa salsa, F DJ. Cover $3. Gay-friendly. Afterwards, relax downstairs at the gay-friendly bar **Abajo.** W ladies night and F/Sa martini bar. Restaurant open W-Su 11:30am-3pm, daily 5-10pm. Club open Th-Sa 10pm-2:30am. Lounge open W-Th 7:30pm-1am, F-Sa 5am-1am.

5 After dancing, regain your saucy edge with an ale from **Black Sheep,** 51 N Main St. (☎482-6414; www.theblacksheep.com), one of the only authentic English pubs in Oregon. No cover. Open daily 11:30am-1:30am. No minors after 11pm.

6 If drinking ballads aren't your thing, go techno at **Kat Wok,** 62 E Main St. (☎482-0787; www.katwok.com). By day a restaurant/sushi bar, by night a club with laser lights and a glow-in-the-dark pool table. Th hip-hop/R&B, F alternative. Sa dance mix. Cover $3-5. Open daily at 5pm.

7 Finally, to sample a slice of student life, visit **Louie's,** 41 N Main St. (☎482-9701), a sports bar with cheap beer that is packed during the school year. Bar open Th-Sa until 1:30am.

local patrons have been known to leave their shoes in line to hold their places. When no tickets are available, limited priority numbers are given out. These entitle their holders to a designated place in line when the precious few returned tickets are released (noon for matinees, 6pm for evening shows). For those truly desperate for their Shakespeare fix, the box office also sells 20 clear-view **standing room tickets** for sold-out shows on the Elizabethan Stage ($13, available on the day of the show). Half-price **rush tickets** are occasionally available 1hr. before performances not already sold out. All three theaters hold full-performance **previews** in the spring and summer at considerable discounts. Unofficial ticket transactions take place all the time just outside the box office, but those who decide to "buy on the bricks" should check the date and time on the ticket carefully and pay no more than the face value.

BACKSTAGE TOURS. Backstage tours provide a wonderful glimpse of the festival from behind the curtain. Tour guides (usually actors or technicians) divulge all kinds of anecdotes—from the story of the bird songs during an outdoor staging of *Hamlet* to the time when a door on the set used for almost every stage entrance and exit locked itself midway through the show, provoking over 30min. of hilarious improvisation before it was fixed during intermission. (2hr. tours leave from the Black Swan Tu-Su at 10am. Call box office in case of changes. $11, ages 6-17 $8.25; no children under 6.)

🕐 🏛 THE GILDED MONUMENTS

LITHIA PARK. Before it imported Shakespeare, Ashland was naturally blessed with supposedly-healing **lithia water.** Besides aquatic phenomena, Lithia Park features free concerts, readings, nature walks around hiking trails, a Japanese garden, and swan ponds. There is an artisans' market on summer weekends.

EMIGRANT LAKE PARK. Scads of kids and kids-at-heart flock to the 280 ft. **waterslide** at **Emigrant Lake Park,** 6 mi. east of town on Rte. 66. Popular for boating, hiking, swimming, and fishing, the park offers fantastic views of the valley. ($3 entry fee. Ten slides for $5 or unlimited slides for 3hr. $10-12. Sites $16, RV sites $20. Park open daily 8am-sunset, waterslide May-Sept. noon-6:30pm.)

🏔 🚴 **MOUNT ASHLAND.** If your muscles demand a little abuse after all this theater-seat lollygagging, head out to Mt. Ashland for some serious **hiking** and **biking.** One of the best options for those looking for a long day's worth of downhill is a shuttle to the Mt. Ashland Ski Lodge (6200 ft.) that allows a 15-25 mi. (1½-2½hr.) ride down to Ashland. (1800 ft.) **Bear Creek Bicycles,** 1988 Hwy. 99 N, offers this service ($5-10, 3 per day on the weekend plus additional times during the week; call about specific days) and $10 waterproof Jackson County bicycle maps; mountain bike rentals are $15 per hr. or $45 per day. (☎488-4270; www.bearcreekbicycle.com.) Both hiking and biking on and around Mt. Ashland require a Northwest Forest pass, available at the ranger station for $5 per day. The ranger station can also provide an excellent guide to hiking and biking in the area for free. The folks at the **Adventure Center** (see **Rafting,** p. 147) can give tips on biking trails.

Pacific Crest Trail (3½ mi. one-way, 2hr.) Forest boundary to Grouse Gap. Take Exit 6 off I-5 and follow the signs along the Mt. Ashland Access Rd. for 7¼ mi. to the sign denoting the Rogue River National Forest Boundary. This section of the Pacific Crest Trail begins to climb Mt. Ashland, passing through forests and meadows covered with wildflowers, and ends at the Grouse Gap shelter. Moderate.

Horn Gap Mountain Bike Trail (3 mi. one-way or 9 mi. loop, 1-3hr.) To reach the trailhead from Lithia Park, take Granite St. along Ashland creek 1 mi. to Glenview, and park along the road. This is the upper trailhead; the lower trailhead is 4 mi. down the road. This ride offers both incredible views of Mt. Ashland and technical fun in steep slopes and several slalom courses. It can be linked with Forest Rd. 2060 to create the 9 mi. loop. Moderate.

Mount McLoughlin (11 mi. one-way, 6hr.) As you drive south on I-5 towards Ashland, Mt. McLoughlin towers above all of the surrounding peaks, dominating the skyline with its symmetrical cone. This trail starts out on easy grade though a forest before gaining the final steep section to the summit. Moderate.

Wagner Butte Trail (5¼ mi. one-way, several hours). From Ashland, take Rte. 99 north of town to Rapp Rd. in Talent. Turn left and drive 1 mi. to the junction with Wagner Creek Rd. and then 8 mi. to Forest Rd. #22. Turn left and drive 2 mi. to the trailhead across from a parking area. This trail climbs 3000 ft. through a landslide area and tufts of old-growth fir to the top of Warner Butte. Breathtaking views on sunny days. Difficult.

🎿 **SKIING.** At the top of the 8 mi. road leading from I-5 Exit 6 is **Mount Ashland,** a small ski area with 23 runs, a vertical drop of 1150 ft., a new half-pipe, and over 100 mi. of free **cross-country** trails. (☎482-2897, snow report 482-2754; www.mtashland.com. Lift tickets $34, seniors and ages 9-17 $27, 70 and older and 8 and under free. Ski rentals $19 per day, snowboards $28. Open daily late Nov. to mid-Apr. 9am-4pm. Night skiing mid-Dec. to mid-Mar. Th-Sa 3-9pm.)

🛶 **RAFTING.** The wild and scenic Upper Klamath offers hardcore Class IV-V action all summer. Depending on water level, the run can be a technical rockbash or a continuous wave-train ride. This is more of a rafter-friendly run, as the sharp rocks have ruined many an upside-down kayaker's day (and dental work). If water color is your only criterion for a river, don't paddle here; it's brown. **The Adventure Center,** 40 N Main St. (☎488-2819 or 800-444-2819; www.rafting-tours.com), guides rafting trips. (Half-day $69; full-day $125-139; bike tours around Mt. Ashland $69 for 3hr., $119 per day. A water release schedule is available at ☎800-547-1501, or www.pacificorp.com/applications/hydro/waterrelease.cfm.)

CENTRAL AND EASTERN OREGON

Central Oregon is made up of the area surrounding the snow-capped peaks of the Cascades, while eastern Oregon spans gorges, desert mountain ranges, and alkali flats to the east. Tourists come to eastern Oregon for the rodeos and festivals, to follow in

THE HIDDEN DEAL

PLUG AND CHUG

Ashland is known for its Shakespeare Festival, and visitors are impressed by its quaint downtown and access to plentiful wilderness options, but it is the Lithia water, piped into the plaza, that's really special. If "special water" gets you thinking along the lines of Evian's cool, cascading glacial runoff, head back to the specialty grocery store—rotten eggs is closer to the truth. While the foamy liquid bubbling out of the fountain looks like sweet cream soda, a high sulfur content gives the Lithia Water a distinct eggy smell and a pungent metallic taste, in addition to some other exciting properties.

The high mineral content (6.15 grams/liter) of the water is reputed to have curative powers. For over a hundred years, visitors have flocked to Ashland seeking a cure for their asthma or rheumatism. Even earlier, Native Americans were known to travel great distances when chiefs developed ailments that traditional medicine could not cure. The Native American treatment program involved laying the patient in a pit filled with CO_2 until he passed out, then alternating between religious chants, chugging the water, and inhaling the fumes.

More recent visitors seeking the water's legendary healing powers would merely drink it. If the power of suggestion is worth anything, they would at least feel a bit more spring in their step.

Lewis and Clark's footsteps along the Oregon Trail, or to gape at the stunningly blue water of Crater Lake. Backcountry hikers hit majestic Mt. Hood, Hells Canyon—the deepest gorge in the US—and the isolated volcanic features and wildlife preserves of the southeast. The severe landscape has changed little but never ceased to test the resolve of its inhabitants. Today, those in search of extreme adventure can hike across sagebrush-covered desert in the state's southeastern corner, ski Mt. Bachelor or Mt. Hood's challenging slopes in any month of the year, or test the raging waters of the Rogue River.

THE CASCADES

The Cascade Range connects California's Mt. Shasta with Washington's Mt. Baker. Once highly volcanic, the Cascades have settled down enough for wind and water to have their way. Slicing Oregon almost completely from north to south, the Cascades create a natural barrier for moisture and lush vegetation. Central Oregon's towns are dotted throughout the mountains and receive most of the precipitation from the Pacific Ocean. The bases of Bend, Klamath Falls, and Sisters are perfect jumping-off points to conquer the wilderness.

BEND   ☎541

Surrounded by a dramatic landscape, with volcanic remnants to the south, the Cascades to the west, and the Deschutes River running through its heart, Bend attracts outdoors enthusiasts from all over the Pacific Northwest. Its proximity to wilderness areas makes Bend an unbeatable base for hiking, rafting, and skiing, while the charming downtown is packed with restaurants, pubs, and shops. Settled in the early 1800s as "Farewell Bend," a pioneer trail waystation along the Deschutes, Bend is now a secret that everyone knows. SUVs with bikes, boards, or boats (or all three) on top have replaced covered wagons, and the Three Sisters to the west are viewed as insurance against boredom, not a daunting obstacle.

■ ■ ORIENTATION AND PRACTICAL INFORMATION

Bend is 160 mi. southeast of Portland and 144 mi. north of Klamath Falls on **US 97,** and 100 mi. southeast of Mt. Hood via **US 26. US 97 (Bend Parkway)** bisects the town. West along the Deschutes River is downtown; **Wall Street** and **Bond Street** are the two main arteries. Avenues run east-west and are labeled alphabetically starting in the south. Streets run north-south and are numbered increasing toward the west. From east to west, Franklin Ave. becomes Riverside Blvd.; at the edge of Drake Park, Tumalo Ave. becomes Galveston Ave.; Greenwood Ave. becomes Newport Ave.; 14th St. becomes Century Dr. and is the first leg of the **Cascade Lakes Highway.** Grab a handy map ($4) at the **visitors center.**

Buses: Greyhound, 1315 NE 3rd St. (☎382-2151). Open M-F 8am-4:30pm and 8:30-10pm, Sa-Su 8:30am-2pm and 8-10pm. Call for info on other bus and van lines. To **Portland** (6¼hr.; 1 per day; $28).

Taxi: Owl Taxi, 1919 NE 2nd St. (☎382-3311). $2 base, $2.20 per mi. 24hr.

Tourist Information: Bend Visitors and Convention Bureau, 63085 Business Rte. 97N (☎382-3221; www.visitbend.org). Full-time ranger on duty. Offers a mother lode of brochures in addition to an "Attractions and Activities Guide" and a map of the area. Open M-Sa 9am-5pm.

Outdoor Information: The forest headquarters maintains an info desk at the visitors center. A "Recreation Opportunity Guide" covers each of the 4 ranger districts. **Deschutes National Forest Headquarters,** 1645 20E (☎383-5300) and **Bend/Fort Rock District Ranger Station,**

1230 NE 3rd St. #A262 (☎383-4000; www.fs.fed.us/r6/deschutes), have additional info on Deschutes National Forest. Both open M-F 7:45am-4:30pm. **Oregon Department of Fish and Wildlife,** 61374 Parrell Rd. (☎388-6363; www.dfw.state.or.us), sells fishing licenses for $8 per day; inquire about hunting permits. Open M-F 8am-5pm.

Equipment Rental:

Redpoint Climbers Supply, 639 NW Franklin Ave. (☎382-6872; www.goclimbing.com). They'll have what you need to replace the #2 cam that you just couldn't get out of the crack. Also has clothing as well as info on local routes. Open M-Tu noon-7pm, W-Sa 9am-7pm, Su 9am-5pm. Redpoint operates a second, smaller store, closer to Smith Rock, just off US 97 in **Terrebonne** at 975 Smith Rock Way (☎923-6207). Open M-Tu 8am-noon and 3-8pm, W-Th and Sa 8am-8pm, F 8am-9pm, Su 8am-6pm.

Sunnyside Sports, 930 NW Newport Ave. (☎382-8018; www.sunnysidesports.com), has front suspension bikes for $20 per day; each additional day $10; full suspension bikes $40 for the first day, then $20 per day; cross-country skis $10-20 per day; each additional day $5; snow shoes $10 per day. Open summer M-Th and Sa-Su 9am-7pm, F 9am-8pm; winter M-Th 9am-7pm, F 9am-8pm, Sa-Su 8am-6pm.

Pine Mountain Sports, 255 SW Century Dr. (☎385-8080; www.pinemountainsports.com), has mountain bikes for $20 per day. Also rents skis ($25) and snowshoes ($10) and sells high quality camping gear. Full suspension models $45 per day. Open M-Sa 9am-6pm, Su 9am-5pm.

Kayak and Canoe Rental: Alder Creek, 805 SW Industrial Way (☎317-9407; www.aldercreek.com), on the river next to the Colorado Ave. bridge. An excellent source of river level info and advice on boating in the area. Whitewater kayak rental $30 per day. Canoe and tandem kayak $40. Open M-F 10am-6pm, Sa 9am-6pm, Su 9am-5pm.

Laundromat: Westside Laundry and Dry Cleaners, 738 NW Columbia Ave. (☎382-7087). Wash $1.25, dry $0.25 per 7min. Open daily 6:30am-9:30pm.

Police: 555 NE 15th St. (☎388-0170).

Hospital: St. Charles Medical Center, 2500 NE Neff Rd. (☎382-4321).

Internet Access: At the **Bend Public Library,** 601 NW Wall Ave. (☎388-6679; www.dpls.lib.or.us). Free, no hassle Internet access on the 2nd floor next to the reference desk. Open M-Th 10am-8pm, F 10am-6pm, Sa 10am-5pm, Su 1-5pm.

Post Office: 2300 NE 4th St. (☎318-5068). Open M-F 8:30am-5:30pm, Sa 10am-1pm. **Postal Code:** 97701.

🏠🏕 ACCOMMODATIONS AND CAMPING

Most of the cheapest motels line 3rd St. just outside of town, and rates are surprisingly low. Camping in the national forest is cheap and relatively pleasant.

Deschutes National Forest, along the Cascade Lakes Hwy., west of town, maintains a huge number of lakeside campgrounds. Backcountry camping in the national forest area is free, though parking permits may be required. Contact the Bend/Ft. Rock Ranger District Office (above) for more info. Tents $12-18; RVs $15-21. ❶

Tumalo State Park, 62976 OB Riley Rd. (☎388-6055 or 800-452-5687), 4 mi. north of Bend off US 20W. Popular riverside campsites in loop A go early, despite road noise. Though the campground is crowded with people, curious chipmunks vastly outnumber humans. Lots of tubing nearby. 65 sites $17; 22 full RV sites $21; 4 yurts $29; hiker/biker sites $4. Solar showers $2. ❶

Rainbow Motel, 154 NE Franklin Ave. (☎382-1821 or 877-529-2877). Large, clean rooms surround a central mini-park lined with roses. TV, microwave, fridge. Included continental breakfast. Single $35; double $45. ❸

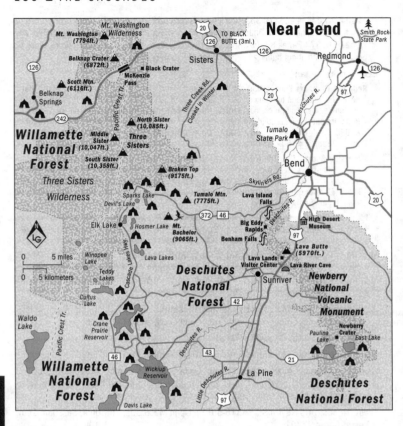

Near Bend

OREGON

FOOD

Bend has a huge number of restaurants. Four mega-markets line S 3rd St. For good coffee, pastries, and smoothies ($3.25), try **Tuffy's Coffee & Tea ❶,** 961 NW Brooks St., right off the intersection of Wall St. and Greenwood Ave. (☎389-6464. Open M-Sa 7:30am-5pm, Su 9am-2pm.)

■ **Taqueria Los Jalapeños,** 601 NE Greenwood Ave. (☎382-1402), fills a simple space with locals hungry for good, cheap food. Burritos $2.25. Open summer M-Sa 10:30am-8pm; winter M-Sa 11am-7pm. ❶

■ **Mother's Juice Cafe,** 1255 NW Galveston Ave. (☎318-0989). Friendly staff blends exquisite smoothies ($4.25), with ginkgo biloba or ginseng for another $0.50. Food menu standouts include the Mt. Everest sandwich ($6.25, $4.25 for half). Open summer M-F 7am-7pm, Sa 8am-7pm, Su 8am-6pm; closes daily at 5pm in winter. ❷

Pizza Mondo, 811 NW Wall St. (☎330-9093). Once the sun goes down, you'll have to fight through the crowds to get a slice of New York style pizza ($2) or a 15 in. creative pie ($14), but it's worth it. Open M-Th and Su 11am-9:30pm, F-Sa 11am-10pm. ❸

West Side Bakery & Cafe, 1005 NW Galveston Ave. (☎382-3426). You won't be able to peel your eyes away from the tempting case of sugary desserts (under $3) on your way to the table. Burgers and heaping sandwiches $5.75-8.50; stop in at 1pm for $1 pastries. Open daily 6:30am-2:30pm. ❷

👁 🎇 SIGHTS AND FESTIVALS

HIGH DESERT MUSEUM. The museum is one of the premier natural and cultural history museums in the Pacific Northwest. Fantastic life-size dioramas recreate rickety cabins, cramped immigrant workshops, and Paiute teepees. While the desertarium doesn't taste as good as it sounds, it does provide a peek at shy desert creatures. Catch one of the hourly talks on various desert subjects, and don't miss the 7000 sq. ft. wing featuring birds of prey in their natural habitats, including the endangered spotted owl. *(59800 Hwy. 97 S, 3½ mi. south of Bend on US 97. ☎382-4754; www.highdesertmuseum.org. Open daily 9am-5pm. $12, ages 66 and older $11, 5-12 $7.)*

DRAKE PARK AND THE CASCADE FESTIVAL OF MUSIC. Picnic by the river or float down it on a raft at beautiful Drake Park. The park hosts many events and festivals, most notably the Cascade Festival of Music, a week-long series of classical and pop concerts during the week before Labor Day. *(Between Mirror Pond and Franklin St., 1 block from downtown. ☎382-8381; www.cascademusic.org. Tickets $16-25; rush tickets, students, and under 12 half-price.)*

🏔 OUTDOOR ACTIVITIES

The outdoors opportunities near Bend are limitless and without peer in Oregon. From skiing, snowboarding, and snowshoeing in the winter to hiking, biking, climbing, and whitewater in the summer, Bend can be an inexpensive outdoor adventure waiting to happen. The **Three Sisters Wilderness Area,** north and west of the Cascade Lakes Hwy., is one of Oregon's largest and most popular wilderness areas. Pick up a parking permit at a ranger station or the visitors center ($5). Within the wilderness, the 🗻**South Sister** makes for the best trek as well as the most accessible peak, making for a simple, if long (11 mi., 5000 ft. vertical), hike in late summer that threads between glaciers. The other Sisters provide more difficult technical climbs, with opportunities for multi-pitch ice or rock climbs.

🎿 **SKIING.** Those who ski the 9065 ft. **Mount Bachelor,** with its 3365 ft. vertical drop, are in good company—the mountain has been home to the US Ski Team and the US Cross-Country Ski Team, and hosts many of the largest snowboarding competitions in the country. Just 22 mi. southwest of Bend on the Cascade Lakes Hwy., it's considered by many to be the best ski resort in Oregon, with snow that's unusually dry in comparison to the soppy stuff farther west in the Cascades. The ski season runs September to June. (☎800-829-2442, snow report 382-7888; www.mtbachelor.com. Alpine day tickets $44, ages 7-12 $22.) A shuttle bus service runs between the parking lot at the corner of Simpson and Columbia in Bend and the mountain (Nov.-May; $2). Many nearby lodges offer **ski packages** (contact Central Oregon Visitors Association at ☎800-800-8334; www.covisitors.com for info). **Chairlifts** run for sightseers in summer. (Open daily 10am-4pm. $11, seniors $10, ages 7-12 $7. A parking permit is necessary on the mountain; $5 per day from the ranger. See **Orientation and Practical Information,** p. 148, for equipment rental info.)

🚵 **MOUNTAIN BIKING.** Mountain biking is forbidden in the wilderness area, but Benders have plenty of other places to spin their wheels. Be forewarned: the loose "pummy dust"—ground-up pumice—makes riding slow and corners

OREGON

sketchy. The most renowned area for biking is **Phil's Trail** (9 mi.) which fills the space between Skyliners Rd. and the Cascade Lakes Hwy. west of Bend. A map is necessary, as is a compass. Go west on Skyliners Road out of Bend 2½ mi., then make a left (south) on Forest Rd. 220. Try **Deschutes River Trail** (6 mi.) for a fairly flat, forested trail ending at **Deschutes River.** To reach the trailhead, go 7½ mi. west of Bend on S. Century Dr. (Cascade Lakes Hwy.) until Forest Rd. 41, then turn left and follow the signs to Lava Island Falls. For a technical ride, hit **Waldo Lake Loop,** a grueling 22 mi. around the lake (4-4½hr.). Take Cascade Lakes Hwy. to Forest Rd. 4290. A guide to mountain bike trails around Bend ($9) and a Mountain Biking Route Guide (free) are available at the **Bend/Fort Rock District Ranger Station.** For rental information, consult **Orientation and Practical Information,** p. 148.

◪ RAFTING AND KAYAKING. Bend has a large kayaking and rafting community. The powerful Deschutes River has year-round flows thanks to dam releases for irrigation, and its rapids—formed by lava flows—are unusual and range from Class II to unrunnable gnar-gnar. **Big Eddy** is the other big playspot, although the recovery pools are brief at summertime high flows, necessitating either a quick roll or a facemask. The class III-IV or IV stretch, depending on flow, is accessed by taking 14th St. south 6½ mi. from Bend, and then making the next left after passing the Inn of the Seventh Mountain. Take the road marked by "Big Eddy/Aspen." A common run is to put in at Aspen and take out above Lava Island Falls. Along the same road, several of the Deschutes' falls (really huge rapids, not waterfalls), including Lava Island Falls, have extreme descents.

Rafting companies take 3hr. trips on the Upper Deschutes' tame waters from Aspen to above Lava Island Falls. Full-day trips require a 1hr. drive to Maupin to run the Class III+ rapids of the Lower Deschutes. **Sun Country Tours** runs half-day and full-day trips out of the Sun River Resort, 17 mi. south of Bend off US 97, and at 531 SW 13th St. in Bend. (☎800-770-2161; www.suncountrytours.com. Half-day $40; full-day $95-105, ages 6-12 $80-105.) **River Drifters** offers trips on the Deschutes as well, but also has trips to other rivers close by. (☎800-972-0430; www.riverdrifters.net. Trips on the Deschutes are $65-75 per day for adults, $55-65 for kids. Trips to other rivers such as the Klickitat and the Sandy Gorge cost $75.)

◪ ROCK CLIMBING. Smith Rock State Park (☎541-548-7501 or 800-551-6949; www.smithrock.com), 4 mi. east of Hwy. 97 at Terrebonne, is home to the best rock climbing north of Yosemite. Sheer, jagged rock formations rise abruptly for hundreds of feet, towering over the Crooked River and the several miles of trail that wind their way through the park. A popular loop starts at the bridge below the main parking area and tours the most spectacular areas of the park in 3½ mi. before returning to the bridge. (If you're feeling adventuresome, cut some distance off this trail by going left at the bridge and then scrambling over Asterisk Pass ½ mi. into the hike). Even those with a fear of heights can enjoy watching the climbers make their way up the impossibly minute holds on the walls. From the loop trail you can call across a 300 ft. deep void to climbers just 20 ft. away on the Monkey Face formation (you'll see immediately how it got its name). Budding ornithologists might be interested to know that the park is also home to several birds of prey, most notably bald eagles. **First Ascent** has lessons for first-timers. (☎800-325-5462; www.goclimbing.com. $230 per day; groups of 2-4 $140 per person per day.)

There are no motels in the park, but camping is permitted at the **Smith Rock Bivouac Area ❶,** 100 yd. before the sign marking the official entrance to the park. A 200 yd. trail leads from the parking area to a somewhat rocky field where you can throw down for the night. ($4 per person.)

■ DAYTRIP FROM BEND: NEWBERRY NATIONAL MONUMENT

The Newberry National Volcanic Monument was established in 1990 to link and preserve the volcanic features in south Bend. Featuring such volcanic wonders as **Lava Butte, Lava River Cave, Newberry Crater,** and the **Paulina Lakes,** the Newberry National Monument offers visitors plenty of sights and a wealth of hiking. Immediately behind the **Lava Lands Visitor Center** is **Lava Butte,** a 500 ft. cinder cone from which lava once flowed. Between Memorial Day and Labor Day, you can drive 2 mi. up the narrow road (no RVs) that leads to the butte. (11 mi. south of Bend on US 97. ☎593-2421. Open daily mid-May to Labor Day 9am-5pm.) The monument's centerpiece is **Newberry Crater,** the remains of what was once the Newberry Volcano, one of three volcanoes in Oregon likely to erupt again "soon." The 500 sq. mi. caldera contains Paulina Lake and East Lake. (13 mi. south of Lava Lands Visitor Center on US 97, then 13 mi. east on Rte. 21.) Another popular attraction is the ▨**Lava River Cave,** a mile-long lava tube that goes under US 97. Huge lanterns can be rented for $3 at the visitors center or at the cave mouth (it's pitch black inside). Bring a jacket—the cave has cooled down a lot since it was filled with lava and now stands at a chill 40°F. (12 mi. south of Bend on US 97. Parking anywhere in the monument requires a Northwest Forest pass or a $5 permit, available at the visitors center or from the ranger.)

Obsidian Flow Trail (½ mi.) This trail is the result of one of the most recent geological events in the Cascades, the Big Obsidian Flow. Formed only 1300 years ago when the Newberry volcano erupted, the hike crosses 170 million cubic yd. of obsidian. Easy.

Paulina Lake Trail (7 mi.) Beginning at the visitors center and circumnavigating the gorgeous Paulina Lake, this trail provides views of the wildlife surrounding the water. Paulina Lake also offers excellent fishing. Easy to moderate.

Crater Rim Trail (21 mi.) Encircling the entire Newberry Caldera, the trail offers vistas of the entire Bend area as well as the surrounding mountains. While hikers share this trail with bikers and horseback riders, there are plenty of sights to go around. Difficult.

SISTERS ☎541

A gateway to the nearby **Deschutes National Forest** and **Cascade Lakes,** Sisters offers those in town and those just passing through the same warm welcome—although it sometimes seems like *everyone* is just passing through. Authentic or not, Sisters features a refined Old West look, which is bolstered by the annual Sisters Rodeo. Sisters also provides access to world-class climbing in nearby Smith Rock State Park as well as the sights of the Warm Springs Indian Reservation.

■ ⏿ ORIENTATION AND PRACTICAL INFORMATION. From Sisters, **Route 126** heads east to **Redmond** (20 mi.) and **Prineville** (39 mi.). To the west, Rte. 126 joins **US 20** to cross the Cascades and continues towards **Eugene** and **Albany. Route 242** heads southwest over McKenzie Pass to rejoin Rte. 126. In town, avenues run east-west and are named after mountains (except for Main Ave.), including Rte. 242 which turns into **Cascade Avenue** in Sisters. North-south streets are named for trees. The **visitors center,** 164 N Elm St., is one block from Cascade Ave. (☎549-0251; www.sisters-chamber.com. Open M-F 9am-5pm; Sa-Su hours vary, call ahead.) Sisters' **Deschutes National Forest Ranger District Station,** on the corner of Cascade Ave. and Pine St., has detailed info on nearby campgrounds, local day hikes, and biking trails, and sells the required $5 parking permit for the national forest. (☎549-7700. Open summer M-F 7:45am-4:30pm, Sa 8am-4pm; winter M-F 7:45am-4:30pm.) **Eurosports,** 182 E Hood Ave., **rents** mountain bikes, snowshoes, snowboards, and skis. (☎549-2471. Front suspension bikes $20 per day, $100 per week; snowshoes, skis, and snow-boards $12-25 per day. Open daily summer 9am-5:30pm; winter M-F 9am-5:30pm, Sa-Su 8am-6pm.)

◪◨ CAMPING AND FOOD. Budget travelers generally pass up expensive Sisters for Bend's cheap lodging. Camping, however, is as good as it gets in the Deschutes National Forest. The Ranger District maintains many spectacular **campgrounds** near Sisters; most of them cluster around **Camp Sherman,** a small community on the Metolius River 16 mi. northwest of Sisters. Two noteworthy sites are **Riverside ❶,** 10 mi. west on Rte. 20 and 4½ mi. northeast on Forest Rd. 14, which consists entirely of walk-in sites (16 sites, $10), and **Allingham ❶,** 1 mi. north of the Camp Sherman store on Rd. 14 (10 sites, $12) right on the river with ample fishing opportunities (license required, $8). Both are maintained by **Hoodoo Recreation Services** through the ranger. (☎822-3799; www.hoodoo.com.)

Plan on exploring Sisters during daylight; things are slow at 6pm and dead by dark. Overpriced food is available anytime at the faux-western tourist joints, but delis that close by 5pm or even 3pm are better for purse and palate. **Sisters Bakery ❶,** 251 E Cascade Ave., has all kinds of baked goods, including marionberry cobbler ($2.25), loaves of top-notch bread ($3), and enormous maple bars ($0.85). (☎549-0361. Open M-F 5am-6pm, Sa-Su 6am-6pm.) **The Harvest Basket ❷,** 110 S Spruce St., features organic groceries and $3 fresh fruit smoothies. (☎549-0598. Open summer M-F 8am-7pm, Sa 9am-7pm, Su 10am-5pm; winter M-F 9am-6pm, Sa 9am-5pm, Su 10am-5pm.) **Ski Inn ❷,** 310 E Cascade Ave., is perfect if you're looking for fast, filling food. This tiny diner serves up burgers ($4) and burritos ($2) with no pretensions about appearance. (☎549-3491. Open M-Sa 6am-9pm, Su 7am-9pm.)

◩▧ SIGHTS AND FESTIVALS. The annual **Sisters Rodeo,** sanctioned by the prestigious Professional Rodeo Cowboy Association, takes place during the 2nd weekend in June, drawing big-time wranglers to this tiny town for three days and nights of bronco-riding, calf-roping, and steer-wrestling, all in pursuit of the $100,000 purse. Have a rip-roaring time at the Rodeo Parade and the Buckaroo Breakfast. (☎549-0121 or 800-827-7522; www.sistersrodeo.com. $10-15. Shows often sell out.) If music's more your thing, check out the **Sisters Jazz Festival,** usually around the 3rd weekend in September. This growing concert features a mix of high profile shows and impromptu performances. (☎549-1332 or 800-549-1332; www.sistersjazzfestival.com. 3-day pass $50-60, cheaper if purchased well in advance. Ages 12-18 $10, under 12 free. Day passes $15-30.) **The Museum at Warm Springs** is located off Hwy. 26 north of Sisters and Bend (look for the signs), on the **Warm Springs Indian Reservation.** A stunning piece of architecture, documenting the tribal history of the Wasco, Paiute, and Warm Springs Indians via interactive exhibits. (☎553-3331; www.warmsprings.biz/museum. Open daily 10am-5pm. $6, ages 60 and older $5, 13-18 $4.50, 5-12 $3.)

◪ OUTDOOR ACTIVITIES. A 45 mi. segment of the Pacific Crest Trail runs from Lava Lakes through the Three Sisters Wilderness, with plentiful opportunities for side-hikes. A permit ($5 per day), available at the trailheads or from the ranger in Sisters, is required for most activities. The ranger station in Sisters offers free guides to local hiking and biking trails. The **Metolius River Trail** (10 mi., easy), is also open to mountain biking, a trickier endeavor than the hiking option. To get there, go west on Rte. 20 from Sisters, then make a right at the sign for Camp Sherman (Rd. 14). Proceed 7 mi. on Rd. 14 past the "Head of the Metolius" and park at the **Wizard Falls Fish Hatchery** (☎595-6611; open daily 8am-5pm), right on the Metolius River. The **Black Butte Trail** (2 mi. one-way, 1½hr. up, moderate) is a short hike with a spectacular view at the top. Alongside an active fire lookout, survey 180 degrees of the Cascade Range from Mt. Adams to the north (on a very clear day) to Broken Top to the south. Bring binoculars if you want to see glaciers. About 11 mi. west of Sisters off the left side of Rte. 242 is the hike up **Black Crater** (8 mi. round-trip, difficult). Deeper in the mountains, the hike offers unsurpassed views of snow-capped peaks as well as lava flows on McKenzie Pass, and intimate encounters with volcanic debris. Access is often limited due to snow. **McKenzie Pass** (15 mi., difficult) is the site of a relatively recent lava flow that created barren fields of rough, black a'a (AH-ah) lava. The ½ mi. trail from the Dee Wright Observatory winds among basalt boulders, cracks, and crevices. Snow closes the trail in winter.

Opportunities for both novice and hardcore **mountain biking** abound. No bikes or motor vehicles are allowed in wilderness areas, but most other trails and little-used dirt roads are open to bikes. The ranger station offers a packet detailing some moderate trails; the folks at Eurosports also know about the best trails (p. 153).

CRATER LAKE AND KLAMATH FALLS ☎541

The deepest lake in the US, the seventh deepest in the world, and one of the most beautiful anywhere, Crater Lake National Park is one of Oregon's signature attractions. Formed about 7700 years ago in a cataclysmic eruption of Mt. Mazama, the lake began as a deep caldera and gradually filled with centuries worth of snowmelt. The circular lake plunges from its shores to a depth of 1936 ft. Though it remains iceless in the winter, its banks, which loom as high as 2000 ft. above the 6176 ft. lake surface, are snow-covered until July. Visitors circle the 33 mi. Rim Dr., gripping the wheel as the ▓impossibly blue water enchants them. Klamath Falls, one of the nearest cities, makes a convenient stop on the way to the park and contains most of the services, motels, and restaurants listed below.

▐ TRANSPORTATION

Route 62 skirts the park's southwestern edge as it arcs 130 mi. between Medford in the southwest and Klamath Falls, 56 mi. southeast of the park. West of the park, Rte. 62 follows the Upper Rogue River. To reach Crater Lake from Portland, take **I-5** to Eugene, and then **Route 58** east to **US 97** south. From US 97, **Route 138** leads west to the park's north entrance, but Crater Lake averages over 44 ft. of snow per year, which usually keeps the northern entrance closed as late as July; the roads to **Rim Village** stay open year-round. Before July, enter the park from the south. **Route 62** runs west from US 97 about 40 mi. south of the park, through **Fort Klamath,** and on to the south access road that leads to the caldera's rim. Driving 20mi. south from the intersection of Rte. 62 and US 97 brings you to Klamath Falls.

Trains: Amtrak, 1600 Oak Ave. (☎884-2822 or 800-872-7245). Follow Klamath Ave. until you see signs for the station. Open daily 7:30-11am and 8:30-10pm. To **Portland** (7¼hr., $46).

Buses: The Shuttle, 445 Spring St. (☎883-2609 or 866-242-1990), between S 6th St. and Oak Ave. Runs M-F 5am-3pm. One bus per day to **Ashland** (2½ hr., $16, students $13) with continuing service to Medford.

Public Transportation: Basin Transit Service (☎883-2877; www.basintransit.com) runs 6 routes. Runs M-F 6am-7:30pm, Sa 10am-5pm. $1, ages 60 and older $0.50.

Taxis: Classic Taxi (☎885-8294). $2 base, $2 per mi. 24hr.

Car Rental: Budget (☎885-5421), at Klamath Falls airport. From S 6th St., go south on Washburn Dr. and follow the signs. $39 per day plus 200 free mi. per day, then $0.25 per mi. Open M-F 8am-9pm, Sa-Su 8:30am-6pm.

OREGON

🛈 PRACTICAL INFORMATION

Tourist Information: Great Basin Visitor Association, 507 Main St. (☎882-1501 or 800-445-6728; www.greatbasinvisitor.info). If for no other reason, stop by for the free coffee and homemade cookies. Open May-Oct. M-Sa 8am-5pm; Nov.-Apr. M-F 9am-5pm.

Outdoor Information: William G. Steel Center (☎594-2211, ext. 402; www.nps.gov/crla), 1 mi. from the south entrance. Free backcountry camping permits. Also shows a 15min. video on the history of the lake twice each hour. Open daily 9am-5pm. **Crater Lake National Park Visitors Center** (☎594-3100), on the lake shore at Rim Village. Open daily June-Sept. 9:30am-5pm. Park main phone ☎594-3000.

Park Entrance Fee: Cars $10, $5 if you hike or bike in.

Laundromat: Main Street Laundromat, 1711 Main St. (☎883-1784). Wash $1.25, dry $0.25 per 10min. Open M-Sa 8am-7pm; last wash 5:30pm.

Police: 425 Walnut St. (☎883-5336).

Crisis and Rape Crisis Line: ☎884-0390. 24hr.

Hospital: Merle West Medical Center, 2865 Daggett Ave. (☎882-6311). From US 97 N, turn right on Campus Dr., then right onto Daggett.

Internet Access: Klamath County Library, 126 S 3rd St. (☎882-8894; www.lib.co.klamath.or.us). Four computers with 1hr. free Internet access and 3 computers with free 15min. Open M, F, and Sa 10am-5pm, Tu and Th 10am-8pm, W 1-8pm, Su 1-5pm.

Post Office: Klamath Falls, 317 S 7th St. (☎800-275-8777). Open M-F 7:30am-5:30pm, Sa 9am-noon. **Crater Lake,** (☎594-2211) in the Steel Center. Open M-Sa 9am-noon and 1-3pm. **Postal Code:** 97604.

🏠 🏕 ACCOMMODATIONS AND CAMPING

Klamath Falls has plenty of affordable hotels (mostly on US 97 north of town and on S 6th St. south of town) that make easy bases for Crater Lake. If you prefer to live in the trees, **Forest Service campgrounds ❶** ($4-8) line **Route 62** through Rogue River National Forest west of the park. The park itself contains two campgrounds, both of which are closed until roads are passable. **Backcountry camping** is allowed in the park; get a free backcountry permit from the Steel Center (see above).

Townhouse Motel, 5323 S 6th St. (☎882-0924). 3 mi. south of Main, on the edge of Klamath Falls' strip-mall land, offers large, clean, and comfy rooms, many with La-Z-Boy recliners, at a great price. Cable, no phones. Singles $32; doubles $38. Kitchen units available in the singles for $6-8. ❸

Williamson River Campground, 30 mi. north of Klamath Falls on 97N and 1½ mi. down a gravel road, is the best of the many camps in the area, run by the National Forest Service. Situated on the winding river, it offers secluded sites. Tents $6. ❶

Mazama Campground (☎594-2255, ext. 3703), near the park's south entrance off Hwy. 62. Tenters and RVs swarm this monster facility when it opens in mid-June, and some don't leave until it closes in Oct. Mostly tent sites. **Loop G** is more secluded and spacious, but opens later in the year. Sites in the backs of the loops tend to be the quietest. Laundry, telephone. General store and gas station open daily 7am-10pm. Wheelchair-accessible. No reservations. 213 sites, tents $16, RVs $21. ❷

Lost Creek Campground (☎594-2255), in the southeast corner of the park, 3 mi. on a paved road off Rim Dr. 16 mid-sized sites set amid pines. No reservations. Usually open mid-July to mid-Sept.; check at the Steel Center. Tent sites $10. ❶

Rivers Inn, 11 Main St. (☎882-4494; www.klamathfallsoregonmotels.com). If you're looking for a place to crash for the night, this is just right. Mere blocks away from downtown bars and restaurants, this hotel provides the necessities at a great price. $40. ❸

Collier Memorial State Park and Campground (☎783-2471), 30 mi. north of Klamath Falls on US 97, at the same turn off as the Williamson River Campground, offers tent and RV sites that are both less rugged and less private than the tent sites at the Williamson River Campground. The brilliant green lichen hanging off the timber is a highlight. Laundry. Sites $15; full RV sites $18. Showers. ❶

🖸 FOOD

Eating cheap ain't easy in Crater Lake, with dining limited to a cafeteria, restaurant, and cafe in Rim Village. **Klamath Falls** has some affordable dining and a **Safeway** at Pine and 8th St., one block north of Main St. (☎273-5500. Open daily 6am–11pm.) A lot of eats in Klamath Falls go hand in hand with billiards; if you're a pool shark, Main St. between 5th and 7th St. is the place to go. The **Fort Klamath General Store,** 52608 Hwy. 62, offers a limited supply of groceries, sells gas, and houses a cafe. (☎381-2263. Open daily summer 6:30am-9pm; winter 7am-8pm.)

Where's **Waldo's Mongolian Grill and Tavern?** 610 Main St. (☎884-6863). This large restaurant and lounge, remodeled for 2005, might play techno or reggae even if most patrons are wearing Stetsons. The food is standard Mongolian BBQ (you choose the ingredients, they cook them); the lounge has just about every equipment-intensive bar game known to man. Youthful bar scene weekends. Medium bowl $8.50, all-you-can-eat $10. Open M-Th 11am-11:30pm, F-Sa 11am-1am. ❷

Klamath Grill, 715 Main St. (☎882-8573). This local breakfast favorite serves up huge omelettes ($5-7) and hearty pancakes ($5-6). Burgers any way you like 'em $4-6. Open M-F 6am-2:30pm, Sa-Su 7am-2pm. ❷

Beckie's Cafe (☎866-560-3563), in the tiny town of Union Creek just south of the Rogue River Gorge, is a decent place to fuel up en route to or from the lake on Rte. 62, west of the lake. Highlights are specialty burgers ($6.25) and homemade huckleberry pie ($3.50). Open daily summer 8am-9pm; winter M-F 11am-3pm, Sa-Su 9am-5pm. ❷

🏔 OUTDOOR ACTIVITIES

Crater Lake averages over 44 ft. of snow per year. Snowbound roads keep the rim road closed for much of the spring and fall and can keep the northern entrance closed as late as July. Before July, enter the park from the south. The park entrance fee is $10 for cars, $5 for hikers and cyclists. The area around Crater Lake is filled with all sorts of outdoor adventures. With ample options for hiking and biking, as well as easy access to the backcountry regions outside the park, you may feel overwhelmed with options. The best jumping-off point is the Steel Center (see **Outdoor Information,** p. 156), although the Rim Village, where the information center and the Crater Lake Lodge are located, can also offer some help. **Crater Lake Lodges** (☎594-2255; www.craterlakelodges.com) is a few hundred yards east of Sinnott Memorial Overlook in the Rim Village. Rooms will break your budget, but fun in the lodge can be had for free: make a quick visit to the rustic "great hall," rebuilt from its original materials, and warm yourself by the fire or relax in a rocking chair on the observation deck. The friendly staff will be happy to help you find any info on the lake that you need. In addition to trails around the lake, the park contains over 140 mi. of wilderness trails for hiking and cross-country skiing. Picnics, fishing, and swimming are allowed, but surface water temperatures reach a maximum

OREGON

of only 50°F. Park rangers lead free tours daily in the summer and periodically in the winter (on snowshoes). These tours are based on ranger availability; call the Steel Center to check on specific times.

DRIVING. Rim Drive, usually not open until mid-July, loops 33 mi. around the rim of the caldera, high above the lake. The shorter western half of the loop tends to be more crowded, but its views of **Wizard Island** are not to be missed. Pull-outs are strategically placed along the road wherever the view might cause an awestruck tourist to drive off the cliff. Don't despair when the caldera walls block the lake: the views of Cascade volcanoes as distant as Mt. Shasta, 100 mi. south, will console your eyes.

🏔 **HIKING.** Most visitors never stray far from their vehicles as they tour the lake, so hiking provides a great way to get away from the crowds. Trailheads are scattered along the rim, so just park and hike away from the road. The Steel Center has a trail map and info about which trails are closed due to weather.

> **Watchman Peak** (¾ mi. one-way, 1hr.) Begins on the lake's west side. Short, but yields a great view of Wizard Island, one of the lake's 2 active cinder cones. This is the last trail in the park to open and is often closed until mid-Aug. Moderate.
>
> **Mount Scott** (5 mi. round-trip, 2-3hr.) The trailhead is 17 mi. clockwise from Rim Village. Although steep, the ascent to the top of 9000 ft. Mt. Scott and the historic fire tower on top afford a beautiful panoramic view of the lake. Moderate to difficult.
>
> **Cleetwood Cove Trail** (2¼ mi. round-trip, 2hr.), leaves from the north edge of the lake and is the only route down to the water and the park's most traveled trail. It drops 700 ft. in 1 mi. to get to the shore. Moderate to difficult.

ON THE LAKE. From July to mid-September, park rangers lead 1¾hr. boat tours from the base of the Cleetwood Cove trail. Aside from giving a comprehensive history of the lake and its formation, the tours provide breathtaking views of both **Wizard Island,** a cinder cone rising 760 ft. above the western portion of the lake, and **Phantom Ship Rock,** a spooky rock formation in the southeast area of the lake. (Tours run 7 times daily 10am-4pm on the hour. $21, under 11 $13.) The 10am, 11am, and noon boat tours provide foot access to the island, weather permitting, hikeable for a view into its crater (1 mi., 700 ft. of elevation gain). Land-lubbers may prefer picnics and fishing (artificial lures only) at the bottom of the trail. Though the lake (supposedly without outlet, though many contend the Rogue River drains out the bottom) was virtually sterile when modern man found it, it has since been stocked with rainbow trout and kokanee. Those who walk down to the lake at Cleetwood Cove can take a dip, but the water reaches a maximum temperature of only 50°F (10°C).

🥾 **BACKCOUNTRY EXPLORATION.** A hiking trip into the park's vast **backcountry** leaves all the tourists behind. Hiking or climbing in the caldera is prohibited. Other than near water sources, dispersed camping is allowed anywhere in the area but is complicated by the absence of water and the presence of bears. Get info and required backcountry permits for free at either visitors center. The **Pacific Crest Trail** begins from the trailhead ¾ mi. west of the south entrance. The ultimate backcountry trail passes through the park and three backcountry campsites, giving great views of mountain meadows, old-growth timber, and, of course, the lake. The **Red Cone trailhead,** an excellent loop on the north access road, passes the less-traveled **Crater Springs, Oasis Butte,** and **Boundary Springs** trails. Another shorter loop follows the **Lightning Spring Trail** from Rim Dr. west of Rim Village to the Pacific Crest Trail (4 mi.). It follows the PCT south to Dutton Creek (3¼ mi.), which it then follows to Rim Village (2½ mi.). Once again, many of these trails are blocked by snow until July and open only at the discretion of the ranger. Contact the Steel Center for more information.

UPPER ROGUE RIVER. If you prefer your water more vertical than anything the lake can offer, try the Upper Rogue, easily accessible from Rte. 62 southwest of Crater Lake. Emerging from a spring on the northern slope of Mt. Mazama, the river contends with the area's lava flows by raging through scenic gorges, passing through huge waterfalls and cataracts, and even going underground for a stretch. The fish are seemingly unfazed by the river's commotion, especially in places like **Casey State Park,** 46 mi. SW of the park; here, the angling is good but crowded.

Mill Creek Falls drops 174 ft. into a deep canyon downstream of the Avenue of Giant Boulders, where a huge jumble of rocks offers navigational puzzles for the feet and sublime **sunning** for your back. The pools formed between cascades also make for equally great **splashing around.** From Rte. 62, easy, short trails to both sites are accessed from a trailhead; follow signs to "Mill Creek Falls/Prospect Access Road," about 32 mi. southwest of Crater Lake on Rte. 62.

Things get steamier for the Rogue as it approaches Mt. Mazama: lava flows are clearly at work in both the **Natural Bridge** and the **Rogue River Gorge.** The river performs a natural, but still frightening, disappearing act under the bridge, where it descends into a lava tube and reappears 200 ft. downstream. In the Gorge, the river is forced through a lava flow and gets angry about it, smashing through in a series of short but raging waterfalls. Amazingly, the gorge has been kayaked, starting below the Natural Bridge, by very experienced paddlers. The Gorge and Natural Bridge are about 20 and 23 mi. southwest of Crater Lake on Rte. 62, respectively.

EASTERN OREGON

HELLS CANYON AND WALLOWA MTS. ☎ 541

The northeast corner of Oregon is the state's most rugged, remote, and arresting country, with jagged granite peaks, glacier-gouged valleys, and azure lakes. East of La Grande, the Wallowa Mountains (wa-LAH-wah) rise abruptly, looming over the plains from elevations of more than 9000 ft. Thirty miles east, North America's deepest gorge plunges to the Snake River. It may take a four-wheel-drive vehicle to get off the beaten path, but those with the initiative and the horsepower will find stunning vistas and heavenly solitude in the backcountry.

▐ TRANSPORTATION

There are three ways to get to the **Wallowa Valley,** which lies between the **Hells Canyon National Recreation Area** and the **Eagle Cap Wilderness.** From **Baker City,** Rte. 86 heads east through **Halfway** (also known as **Half.com,** the world's first dot-com city; in 2000, the struggling town decided to adopt the Internet company's name to provide an economic and tourist boost) to connect with Forest Rd. 39, which winds north over the southern end of the Wallowas, meeting Rte. 350 (also known as Little Sheep Creek Hwy.) 8 mi. east of **Joseph.** From **La Grande,** Rte. 82 arcs around the north end of the Wallowas, through the small towns of Elgin, Minam, Wallowa, and Lostine, continuing through **Enterprise** and **Joseph,** and terminating at **Wallowa Lake.** From **Lewiston, ID,** Rte. 129 heads south into Washington, then over Rattlesnake Pass, becoming Rte. 3 in Oregon and joining Rte. 82 in Enterprise.

⊕ ？ ORIENTATION AND PRACTICAL INFORMATION

Three main towns offer services within the area: Enterprise, Joseph, and Halfway. Joseph lies 6 mi. east of Enterprise on Rte. 82. In **Enterprise**, Rte. 82 is called North St., and in Joseph it goes by Main St. **Halfway** is about 65 mi. south of Joseph. To get there, take E Wallowa Rd., off Main St. in Joseph, and follow the signs to Halfway (the drive takes 2hr., the majority of which is on **Forest Road 39,** a paved but brutally curvy route). Other major roads in the area are **Route 350,** a paved route from Joseph 30 mi. northeast to the tiny town of **Imnaha,** and the **Imnaha River Road** (a.k.a. Country Rd. 727 and Forest Rd. 3955), a good gravel road that runs south from Imnaha to reconnect with Forest Rd. 39 about 50 mi. southeast of Joseph. The invaluable and free *Wallowa County Visitor Map* is available in visitors centers and ranger stations, as are current road conditions information.

Buses: Moffit Brothers Transportation (☎ 569-2284; www.moffitbros.com) runs the **Wallowa Valley Stage Line,** which makes 1 round-trip M-F between **Joseph** and **La Grande.** Pickup at the **Chevron** on Rte. 82 in Joseph (6:30am), the **Amoco** on Rte. 82 in Enterprise (7am), and the **Greyhound terminal** in La Grande. Will stop and pick up at Wallowa Lake with advance notice. One-way from **La Grande** to: **Enterprise** ($13); **Joseph** ($14); and **Wallowa Lake** ($18).

Visitor Information: Wallowa County Chamber of Commerce, 115 Tejaka Ln., across from the visitors center. (☎ 426-4622 or 800-585-4121; www.wallowacountychamber.com), in Enterprise. General tourist info as well as the comprehensive and free *Wallowa County Visitor Guide.* Open M-F 8am-5pm. **Hells Canyon Chamber of Commerce** (☎ 742-4222; www.halfwayor.com/chamberofcommerce), in the office of Halfway Motels (see **Accommodations,** below), provides info on accommodations and guides.

Outdoor Information: Wallowa Mountains Visitor Center, 88401 Rte. 82 (☎ 426-5546; www.fs.fed.us/r6/w-w), at the west end of Enterprise. $6 map a necessity for navigating area roads. Open Memorial Day to Labor Day M-Sa 8am-5pm; Labor Day to Memorial Day M-F 8am-5pm. **Hells Canyon National Recreation Area Office,** 2 mi. south of Clarkston, WA on Rte. 129 (☎ 509-758-0616), carries all sorts of information on Hells Canyon. Open M-F 7:30-11:30am and 12:30-4:30pm. Memorial Day to Labor Day also open same hours Sa-Su.

Laundromat: Joseph Laundromat and Car Wash, on Rte. 82 in Joseph, across from the Indian Lodge Motel. Wash $2, dry $0.25 per 8min. Open daily 6am-10pm.

Police: State police ☎ 426-3036. In Enterprise, 108 NE 1st St. (☎ 426-3136), at the corner of North St.

Hospital: Wallowa Memorial, 401 NE 1st St. (☎ 426-3111; www.wchcd.org), Enterprise.

Internet Access: The **Enterprise Public Library,** 101 NE 1st St. (☎ 426-3906), at Main St., offers a free 1hr. of Internet access on 1 of 3 computers. Open M and F noon-6pm, Tu-Th 10am-6pm, Sa 10am-2pm.

Post Office: 201 W North St. (☎ 426-5980), on Rte. 82 in Enterprise. Open M-F 9am-4:30pm. **Postal Code:** 97828.

⌂ ⌂ ACCOMMODATIONS AND CAMPING

Most of the towns along Rte. 82 have motels with plenty of vacancies during the week. On weekends rooms are more scarce. Campgrounds here are plentiful, inexpensive, and sublime. Pick up the free *Campground Information* pamphlet at the Wallowa Mountains Visitor Center (p. 160) for a complete listing of sites in the area. Many **free campgrounds** are not fully serviced, and even some of the very rugged campgrounds may have fees ($6-8).

Indian Lodge Motel, 201 S Main St. (☎432-2651 or 888-286-5484; www.eoni.com/
~gingerdaggett), on Rte. 82 in Joseph. Elegant rooms with dark wood furniture and
plush blue carpet. A/C, cable, coffee makers, and fridges. Singles $46; doubles $49.
Winter $37/$40. ❸

Country Inn Motel, 402 W North St. (☎426-4986 or 877-426-4986), in Enterprise.
Reminiscent of a country farmhouse. Rooms stay remarkably cool without A/C. Cable,
coffee makers, and fridges. Singles $50; doubles $54. Rates lower in winter. ❸

Wallowa Lake State Park Campground (☎432-4185; reservations 800-452-5687), at
the eastern end of Rte. 82. The campground population rivals that of Joseph itself. Sites
can be reserved up to nine months in advance. In the summer, weekends are always
booked in advance. Walk-ins can sometimes be accommodated during the week. D
loop (only tents) is by far the quietest. Sites $17, full RV sites $21. Showers. ❷

Snake River Campgrounds (☎785-3323). Only three are open year-round: **Copperfield,**
at the northern end of Hwy. 86; **McCormick,** 12 mi. south of Copperfield off Hwy. 71;
and **Woodhead,** 4 mi. south of McCormick on Hwy. 71. No reservations. Sites $8, RV
sites $12. Hot showers. ❶

Saddle Creek Campground. From Rte. 82, turn on E Wallowa Rd. (a.k.a. Rte. 350) in
Joseph. Drive 19 mi. on the unpaved and steep Hat Point Rd. Seven sites perched on the lip
of Hells Canyon featuring unbelievable views. No water. Wheelchair-accessible. Sites $6. ❶

FOOD

If you're heading out onto the roads of Hells Canyon, bring some provisions—a
flat or breakdown could require a roadside meal or two. Find groceries at **Safeway,**
601 W North St., on Rte. 82 in Enterprise. (☎426-3722. Open daily 6am-11pm.)

 Wildflour Bakery, 600 N Main St. (☎432-7225), in Joseph, offers an amazing selection
of scrumptious baked goods, as well as giant sourdough and cornmeal pancakes ($2
per cake). Sit on the patio and enjoy the day with a chicken sausage sandwich or giant
burrito ($5.75). Open M and W-Sa 7am-3pm, Su 7am-noon. Breakfast until 11am. ❶

Old Town Cafe, 8 S Main St. (☎432-9898), in Joseph. Sit in the outdoor grotto and dig
into a bottomless bowl of homemade soup ($3) or a giant fresh baked cinnamon roll
($1.75). Sandwiches $5-7. Breakfast all day. Open M-W and F-Su 7am-2pm. ❶

Embers Brew House, 207 N Main St. (☎432-2739), in Joseph. On summer evenings,
the patio is packed outside this popular dinner spot. Sample 5 of 17 microbrews ($5).
Fries $5. Open daily June-Sept. 11am-11pm; in winter M-Th and Su 11am-8pm, F-Sa
11am-11pm. ❷

Vali's Alpine Delicatessen Restaurant, 59811 Wallowa Lake Hwy. (☎432-5691), in
Wallowa Lake. For 30 years in this small, alpine-esque cottage, Mr. Vali has cooked one
authentic European dish and Mrs. Vali has served it. Hungarian Kettle Goulash $9.50,
schnitzel $12. Reservations required for dinner. Breakfast W-Su 9-11am, dinner seat-
ings W-Su at 5 and 7pm. Labor Day to Memorial day open Sa and Su only. ❸

♞ OUTDOOR ACTIVITIES

HELLS CANYON

The deepest canyon in the US, Hells Canyon has staggering proportions: 8000 ft.
deep and 10 mi. wide. The enormous range in altitudes allows an impressive array
of climatic zones, from the snow capped alpine peaks, to lush forests to the
scorching heat along the Snake River.

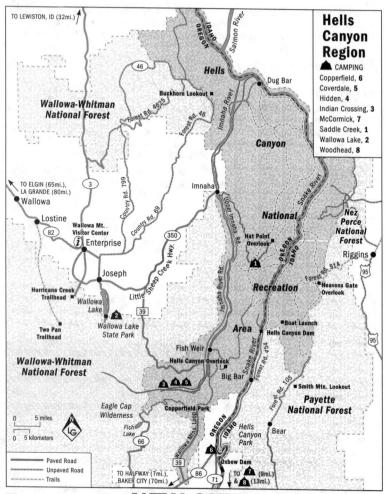

Hells Canyon Region

▲ CAMPING

Copperfield, **6**
Coverdale, **5**
Hidden, **4**
Indian Crossing, **3**
McCormick, **7**
Saddle Creek, **1**
Wallowa Lake, **2**
Woodhead, **8**

█**LOOKOUTS. Hells Canyon Overlook,** the most accessible of the lookout points, is up Forest Rd. 3965. The road departs Forest Rd. 39 about 5 mi. south of the Imnaha River crossing. If you've got 2hr. to spare, the **Hat Point Lookout Overlook** offers frighteningly huge views all the way down to the Snake River from a 90 ft. wooden fire lookout. To get there, go 24 mi. up a steep but well-maintained gravel road (not recommended for trailers) from Imnaha (Forest Rd. 4240, a.k.a. Hat Point Rd.), and follow the signs. There are pit toilets at the overlook and several picnic sites for day use as well as one campsite, **Saddle Creek ❶,** a couple miles before the lookout. The **Buckhorn Lookout** lies far off the beaten path, 42 mi. northeast of Joseph, and offers lofty views of the Imnaha River Valley. Take Rte. 82 north 3 mi. out of Joseph or 3 mi. south out of Enterprise and look for the green sign for Buckhorn. Turn off and follow Zumwalt Rd. (a.k.a. Country Rd. 697, which turns into Forest Rd. 46) for 40 bumpy miles to Buckhorn—about a half-day round trip. At that end of the canyon, the immense **Hells Canyon Dam** lies 23 mi. north of Oxbow on Rte. 86, which turns into Forest Rd. 454. This drive is one of only three ways to get near the bottom of the canyon by car, and the dam is the only place to cross.

🄺 **HIKING.** There are over 1000 mi. of trails in the canyon, only a fraction of which are maintained. Most don't open until April. The dramatic 56 mi. **Snake River Trail** runs by the river for the length of the canyon. At times, the trail is cut into the side of the rock with just enough clearance for a horse's head. This trail can be followed from **Dug Bar** in the north down to the Hells Canyon Dam or accessed by steep trails along the way. From north to south, **Hat Point, Freezeout,** and **P.O. Saddle** are access points. To reach Dug Bar, get a high-clearance 4WD vehicle and hit the steep, slippery Forest Rd. 4260 for 27 mi. northeast from **Imnaha.** Bring snakebite kits, boots, and water. Rangers patrol the river by boat at least once a day.

🄖 **WATER.** The easiest way to see a large portion of the canyon is on the Snake River by jet boat or raft; both pursuits are guaranteed to drench. Numerous outfitters operate out of Oxbow and the dam area; the Wallowa Mountains Visitor Center (p. 160) and all local chambers of commerce have a list of the permittees. **Hells Canyon Adventures,** 4200 Hells Canyon Dam Rd., 1½ mi. from the Hells Canyon Dam in Oxbow, runs a wide range of jet boat and raft trips. (☎ 785-3352 or 800-422-3568; www.hellscanyonadventures.com. Jet boats 2hr. $32, 3hr. $42, full-day $108. Whitewater rafting $160 for a day trip.)

WALLOWA MOUNTAINS

Without a catchy, federally approved name like "Hells Canyon National Recreation Area," the Wallowas often take second place to the canyon. They are equally magnificent, however, as their canyons echo with the rush of rapids and their jagged peaks cover with wildflowers in spring.

🄺 **HIKING.** Over 600 mi. of **hiking trails** cross the **Eagle Cap Wilderness** and are usually free of snow from mid-July to October. Deep glacial valleys and high granite passes make hiking this wilderness difficult. It often takes more than a day to get into the most beautiful areas, so carry adequate supplies and prepare for sudden weather changes. The 5 mi. hike to **Chimney Lake** from the **Bowman** trailhead on the Lostine River Rd. (Forest Rd. 8210) traverses fields of granite boulders sprinkled with a few small meadows. A little farther on lie the serene **Hobo** (5½mi.) and **Wood Lakes** (7½ mi.), where the road is less traveled. The **Two Pan** trailhead at the end of the Lostine River Rd. starts a forested 6 mi. hike to popular **Minam Lake,** just below Eagle Cap, which makes a good jump-off point for other backcountry spots.

By far the most popular area in the Eagle Cap Wilderness is the **Lakes Basin** (a 7-9 mi. hike from the Two Pan trailhead), where explorers can find unsurpassed scenery, good fishing, and hikes to Eagle Cap Peak. While it is possible to escape the crowds in the basin during the week, the lake is packed on weekends. **Steamboat, Long,** and **Swamp Lakes** (also accessible from the Two Pan trailhead) are as magnificent as the Lakes Basin but receive only half as many visitors. Rangers at the visitors center can also recommend more secluded routes. Many excellent day hikes to **Lookingglass, Culver, Bear, Eagle, Cached, Arrow,** and **Heart Lakes** start from the Boulder Park trailhead, on Forest Rd. 7755, on the southern side of the Eagle Cap Wilderness (accessible from Baker City and Halfway).

Lost between the massive canyon to the east and the snowcapped peaks to the west, the Imnaha River cuts an impressive canyon through the heart of the Wallowa-Whitman National Forest. Forest Rds. 3955 and 3960 follow the canyon floor. At the west end, where Forest Rd. 3960 ends, a hiking trail continues up the river amid stunning scenery. There are three campgrounds: **Coverdale, Hidden,** and **Indian Crossing** ($6, only Indian Crossing has potable water) along Forest Rd. 3960, and one, Olokott ($8, pumped water) where Forest Rd. 39 enters this canyon.

FISHING. Trout fishing in the Eagle Cap Wilderness is incredible, but it's illegal even to catch and release without a permit. Some fish, such as bull trout, are entirely protected. Get permits ($12 per day, $62 per year) at **The Joseph Fly Shop,** 203 N. Main St. (☎432-4343; www.josephflyshop.com) and the Oregon Sport Fishing Regulations booklet at any local sporting store.

⏏ SKIING. The town of Joseph looks like Jackson Hole before it was built up and the same holds true for the skiing: impressive, undeveloped potential. The mountains that rise up just south of town offer backcountry powder opportunities for those skiers willing to work for their turns. If you're more of a scenery junkie, you can take advantage of the alpine hut system and multi-day tours offered by **Wallowa Alpine Huts** (☎432-4887 or 800-545-5537; www.wallowahuts.com).

PENDLETON   ☎541

This agricultural town is best known for its locally processed wool and for the bustling **Pendleton Round-Up.** In mid-September, the population of this small northeastern Oregon town triples to 50,000 as cowfolk and horsedudes gather for the rodeo of a lifetime, Pendleton's annual celebration of machismo. Other than Round-Up weekend, Pendleton proves to be a worthwhile stop-over in a trip to the beautiful national forests that surround it, or on the way to better things.

■ ⏏ ORIENTATION AND PRACTICAL INFORMATION. Pendleton is at the junction of I-84, Rte. 11, and US 395, just south of the Washington border, roughly equidistant (200-230 mi.) from **Portland, Spokane,** and **Boise.** Pendleton is divided into quadrants: east-west by Main St. and north-south by the Umatilla River. Streets parallel to the river are named alphabetically. The main thoroughfares are Court Ave., Dorian Ave., and Emigrant Ave.; streets parallel to Main St. are numbered. **Greyhound,** 320 SW Court Ave., runs to **Portland** (3-4hr., 4 per day, $40) and **Seattle** (6hr., 2 per day, $70). (☎276-1551 or 800-231-2222. Open daily 10am-1pm, 4-9pm, and midnight-3am.) **Enterprise Rent-A-Car,** at 1520 Southgate, has rentals from $32 per day. (☎966-4150. Unlimited mileage in OR; must be 25 with credit card. Open M-F 8am-5pm.) The **Pendleton Chamber of Commerce,** 201 S Main St., offers cheerful help with housing, directions, and Round-Up tickets. (☎276-7411 or 800-547-8911; www.pendleton-oregon.org. Open M-Th 8:30am-5pm, F 10am-5pm. Also open Sa 9am-4pm Memorial Day-Labor Day.) For **outdoor information,** the **Umatilla Forest Headquarters,** 2517 SW Hailey Ave., up the hill from I-84 Exit 209, answers questions about Umatilla National Forest. (☎278-3716; www.fs.fed.us/r6/uma. Open M-F 7:45am-4:30pm.) The **police** are at 109 SW Court Ave. (☎276-4411), and the **Saint Anthony's Hospital** is at 1601 SE Court Ave. (☎276-5121). **Internet** access is available at the **library,** 502 SW Dorian Ave. in the City Hall Complex, with free 1hr. Internet access on 10 computers. (☎966-0380. Open M-Th 10am-8pm, F-Sa 10am-5pm.) Mail letters at the **post office,** 104 SW Dorian Ave., in the Federal Building at SW 1st St. (☎800-275-8777. Open M-F 9am-5pm, Sa 10am-1pm.) **Postal Code:** 97801.

⌂ ⏏ ACCOMMODATIONS AND CAMPING. For most of the year, lodging in Pendleton is inexpensive. During the Round-Up, rates double, and rooms are booked up to two years in advance. The nearest decent camping is 25 mi. away at Emigrant Springs State Park, or in the **Mountain View RV Park ❷,** 1375 SE 3rd St. (☎276-1041), which has six tent sites where they couldn't quite fit RVs ($18). Fortunately, the Round-Up provides an additional 1500 spots at schools around town (tents $10, RVs $15). Call the Chamber of Commerce after April 1 to lasso a spot. **Travelodge ❸**, 411 SW Dorian Ave. is just a couple blocks from downtown to the east and Big John's Pizza to the west, and offers clean, hotel-quality rooms with fridges and Ethernet access. (☎276-7531. Singles $45; doubles $60.) **Relax Inn ❸**, 205 SE Dorian Ave., just 2 blocks east of Main St., has dimly lit rooms at unbeatable prices. (☎276-3293. Singles $35; doubles $45.) **Emigrant Springs State Park ❶** is 26 mi. southeast of Pendleton off I-84 Exit 234. Get away from the Round-Up in this shady grove of evergreens at a historic Oregon Trail camp; there's some highway noise, but the park is wheelchair-accessible and has hot showers. (☎983-2277; reservations 800-452-5687. 32 tent sites $14.)

█ **FOOD.** It should come as no surprise that a town that lives for its rodeo would have dining focused on beef. **Cimmiyottis ❷**, 137 S Main St. (☎276-4314; open M-Sa 4-10:30pm) and **Circle S Barbecue ❷**, 210 SE 5th St. (☎276-9637; open Tu-Sa 7am-9pm, Su 7am-2 pm) are the cream of the red meat crop. For your grocery needs go to **Safeway**, 201 SW 20th St. (☎278-4280. Open daily 6am-1am.) █**Big John's Hometown Pizza ❷**, 225 SW 9th St. has some of the best pizza in Oregon. The thin crust pizza ($6.50 for a 10 in. pie) arrives quick and hot. (☎276-0550. Open M and Su 11am-9pm, Tu-Th 11am-10pm, F-Sa 11am-10:30pm.) The **Great Pacific Cafe ❷**, 403 S Main St., provides light fare every day of the week and hosts wine tastings every other F at 4:30pm ($1.50 per half-glass) and bluegrass every Sa afternoon. The coffee and sandwiches ($4-7) draw in locals. (☎276-1350. Open daily 8:30am-8pm.) **The Main Street Diner ❷**, 349 S Main St., has a friendly staff and everything from omelettes to a parmesan taco sandwich. If it's cool out, take advantage of the outdoor seating. (☎278-1952. Open M-F 7am-3pm, Sa-Su 6am-3pm.)

█ **SIGHTS AND EVENTS.** The █**Tamastslikt Cultural Institute,** at the Wildhorse Resort, 4 mi. east of Pendleton off I-84 Exit 216, is a huge and carefully designed tribute to the Confederated Tribes of the Umatilla Reservation. It tells the story of the Oregon Trail from the perspective of indigenous peoples. The museum features hours of taped and filmed interviews with tribal elders and activists, as well as a real tule mat winter lodge and a 12,000 year-old mammoth tooth. Check out the beautiful beadwork in the gift shop afterward. (☎966-9748; www.tamastslikt.com. Open daily 9am-5pm. $6; students, children, and ages 55 and older $4; under 5 free.)

The **Pendleton Underground Tours,** 37 SW Emigrant Ave., are a great year-round attraction, retelling Pendleton's wild history from its pinnacle (when the town claimed 32 bars and 18 brothels within 4 blocks) to the unscrewing of the last red lightbulb (well into the 1950s). The 1½hr. tour meanders through former speakeasies, inhuman living quarters for Chinese laborers, a high-stakes poker room, a brothel, and an opium den, mostly below the town's sidewalks. (☎276-0730 or 800-226-6398; www.pendletonundergroundtours.org. Reservations recommended in summer. Call for tour times and reservations. $10, ages 12 and under $5. AAA discount $1.) The **Pendleton Woolen Mills,** 1307 SE Court Pl., have manufactured the wool blankets and clothing bearing their name since 1909. The mills now draws devotees and tourists eager to own a Native American patterned blanket or a thick wool shirt. (☎276-6911; www.pendleton-usa.com. Open May-Dec. M-Sa 8am-5pm, Su 11am-3pm. Free 20min. tour M-F 9am, 11am, 1:30pm, and 3pm. Blanket seconds go for $30-89, perfect patches $140-200, shirts $45.)

At its heart, Pendleton remains a fervent, frothing rodeo town, a fact which is fully revealed during the second weekend in September at the **Pendleton Round-Up.** this has been one of the premier events in the national circuit since 1910 and is known as the "fastest moving rodeo in America." Ranchers from all over the US flock to Pendleton for steer-roping, bulldogging, bareback competitions, buffalo

O R E G O N

chip tosses, wild-cow milking, and greased-pig chases. Tickets go on sale 22 months in advance (mid-Nov.) and often sell out. Get yours today (for next year, of course) through the Chamber of Commerce. Lucky callers may even snag a resell to this year's event. If all else fails, try the ever-present scalpers. (☎276-2553 or 800-457-6336; www.pendletonroundup.com. Tickets $11-18 per day.)

♫ OUTDOOR ACTIVITIES. Pendleton makes a good stop-off on the way to the **Blue Mountains** in the **Umatilla National Forest** (yoo-ma-TILL-uh). The abundance of hiking, fishing, boating, and other recreational activities makes the Umatillas a popular yet still pristine place to explore. To get there, take Rte. 11 north for 20 mi. to Rte. 204 E. After 41 mi., Rte. 204 meets Rte. 82 on the east side of the mountains at **Elgin**. There are five main **campgrounds ❶** along this route, all with picnic tables and drinking water (except Woodland). All five offer great hiking trails; check with the ranger station for maps and suggestions. The most convenient are **Woodward** (18 sites; $10) and **Woodland** (7 sites; free), just before and just after the town of **Tollgate** off Rte. 204. **Target Meadows** (20 sites; $10) is an isolated spot only 2 mi. off the highway; take Forest Rd. 6401 north from Tollgate off Rte. 204. **Jubilee Lake** (51 sites; $14), 12 mi. northeast of Tollgate, is popular for swimming, boating, and fishing. Turn north onto Forest Rd. 64 at Tollgate, 22 mi. east of the junction of Rte. 204 and Rte. 11, and follow the signs. (Wheelchair-accessible. 50 sites; $14.) This portion of Rte. 204, between Rte. 11 and Elgin, winds through dense timber and creeks, near two wilderness areas: the small **North Fork Umatilla** (20,144 acres) to the south, and the large **Wenaha-Tucannon Wilderness** (177,465 acres) to the north. Both are little-used and offer 200 mi. of challenging hiking trails, as well as solitude for hunters, fishermen, and horseback riders.

In April and May you can raft Class III **rapids** on the north fork of the **John Day River.** The 40 mi. journey begins at Dale, south of Pendleton on I-395, and ends at the town of Monument; call the ranger station (☎278-3716) for details.

In the winter, **snowmobiling** is a popular pastime; the north half of the Umatilla National Forest is crisscrossed with over 200 mi. of groomed trails. Ask for the *Winter Sports on the Umatilla National Forest* brochure at the Chamber of Commerce for information on specific trails. **Cross-country skiers** will find marked trails at Horseshoe Prairie, 7 mi. south of Tollgate on the west side of Rte. 204, and are welcome (along with snowmobiles), on forest roads in winter. Contact the ranger for trailhead **parking permits.** Further info on the Umatilla National Forest is available at the Umatilla Forest Headquarters in Pendleton.

BURNS   ☎541

Tiny Burns and its even tinier neighbor Hines serve as traveler waystations and supply centers. Packed with cheap motels and fast food joints, Burns offers sustenance, shelter, and a wealth of information on the surrounding country. And what great outdoor country it is: ideally situated between the Ochoco and Malheur National Forests, Steens Mountain, the Alvord Desert, and the Malheur National Wildlife Refuge, Burns is the center for outdoor activities in the otherwise uninhabited wilderness of southeastern Oregon.

◨◪ ORIENTATION AND PRACTICAL INFORMATION. US 20 from Ontario and **US 395** from John Day converge 2 mi. north of Burns, continue through Burns and Hines as one, and diverge about 30 mi. west of town. US 20 continues west to Bend and the Cascade Range; US 395 runs south to Lakeview, OR and California; Rte. 205 runs south to Frenchglen and Fields. Although buses and vans run to and from some of the nearby towns, you're better off making like Moses and heading for the desert than waiting for public transportation there. **Harney County Chamber of Commerce**, 76 E Washington St., has excellent maps and info on both towns. (☎573-2636; www.harneycounty.com. Open M-F 9am-5pm.) Even more useful is the **Emigrant Creek Ranger District** on the main drag about 4½ mi. south of Burns, which provides information on camping, hiking, and every other wilderness activity imaginable in the Malheur and Ochoco National Forests. (☎573-4300. Open M-F 8am-4:30pm.) For information on the Steens Mountain area, as well as the Alvord Desert, head to the **Burns Bureau of Land Management (BLM)**, on US 20 a few miles west of Hines. The BLM office and website provide essential information on road closings, fires and other things that can ruin your fun if you don't know about them before heading out. The office also has a nifty relief map to help you get acclimated to the area, and sells recreation maps for $4. (☎573-4400; www.or.blm.gov/burns. Open M-F 7:45am-4:30pm.) Contact the **police** at 242 S Broadway, (☎573-6028) behind City Hall. The **hospital**, at 557 W Washington St. (☎573-7281), has 24hr. emergency care. The **post office** can be found at 100 S Broadway. (☎800-275-8777. Open M-F 8:30am-5pm.) **Postal Code:** 97720.

⚏◨ ACCOMMODATIONS AND FOOD. Don't let the rustic outside fool you, the **Bontemps Motel ❷**, 74 W Monroe St., provides clean comfortable rooms with firm beds. Cable TV and A/C; kitchenettes are about $5 more. (☎573-2037 or 877-229-1394. Singles $29; doubles $33; pets $5.) There's a **Days Inn ❸** at 577 W Monroe St. (☎573-2047. Singles $50; doubles $60.) **Joaquin Miller ❶** campground, just off of US 395 19 mi. north of town, has sites surrounded by Ponderosa pines ($5, $2.50 for each additional night or car). No water. **Safeway** is at 246 W Monroe St. (☎573-6767. Open daily 6am-11pm.) **Broadway Deli ❶**, 528 N Broadway, is a great alternative to fast food fare, selling cheap but good and filling sandwiches ($5.50) and homemade soups. (Open M-F 8am-4pm, Sa 11am-3pm.) **Elkhorn Club & Linda's Thai Room ❷**, 457 N Broadway, juxtaposes Thai cuisine and greasy spoon fare, ornate chandeliers and Thai spiritual figures against elk wallpaper. Decent Thai or Chinese dinners $8-12. (☎573-3201. Open daily 8am-2pm, 5-9pm.)

MALHEUR REFUGE AND DIAMOND CRATERS ☎ 451

About 40 mi. south of Burns, miles of sagebrush give way to the grasslands and marshes of **Harney** and **Malheur Lakes,** where thousands of birds end their migratory flight paths each year at **Malheur National Wildlife Refuge.** Stretching 35 mi. south along Rte. 205, the refuge covers 185,000 acres and is home to 58 mammal species and over 320 species of birds, including grebes, ibis, plovers, shrikes, owls, wigeons, and waxwings. Starting in June another species makes its presence felt: the mosquito. Bring lots of bug spray, lots of patience, and maybe something to scrape them off your windshield (keep in mind that a baggie full of dead mosquitoes kept as a memento will put any postcard to shame). The best time to see the birds is in April; bald eagles are best seen in the coldest months. The refuge takes 2hr. to traverse, and some areas require a 4WD vehicle.

The refuge headquarters, 36391 Sodhouse Ln., is 6 mi. east of Rte. 205 on a well-marked turn-off at the Narrows—a convenience store, restaurant and, most importantly, the last place to get gas for 70 mi. (☎495-2006. Open daily 8am-8pm.) The headquarters also houses a useful **visitors center** that provides trail directions and area info. (☎493-2612. Open M-Th 8am-4pm, F 8am-3pm.) No camping is allowed within the refuge, but **accommodations** are available at the **Malheur Field Station ❷**, 34848 Sodhouse Ln., an old government training camp 3 mi. west of headquarters. Make reservations well in advance, especially for spring, fall, and holiday weekends. Meals are available when large

OREGON

groups are eating; call to see if any groups will be there during your stay. Bring your own sheets or a sleeping bag to throw down on top of the mattress covers. (☎493-2629; www.malheurfieldstation.org. Spartan bunks $20; available for large groups. Kitchenette singles $22, $18 if shared. Singles in a trailer $40; doubles $60; RV sites $16.) The Field Station occasionally hosts professors who conduct classes (3-7 days) on subjects like botany, birding and natural history in the refuge. Check the website in the spring for the summer's courses, and call ahead to make sure space is available.

🏞 **HIKING.** Hiking is generally allowed only along roads. Two short trails depart from the visitors center. The largely unmarked and primitive **Loop Trail** (11 mi. loop, several hr.) departs from the P Ranch just before Frenchglen. This moderately difficult trail offers great opportunities to see migratory birds.

DIAMOND CRATERS. A well-marked turn-off 50 mi. south of Burns on Hwy. 205 leads to the **Diamond Craters,** located just east of the Malheur Refuge. This outstanding national area has more than meets the eye and is a geologist's playground of craters, lava flows, and cinder bomb piles. For laypeople, the BLM's self-guided tour (available at any visitors center, ranger station, or at the hotel or mercantile in Frenchglen) and a fair bit of patience are essential to make any sense of the volcanic history here. The **Lava Pit Crater** is most worthy of a stop. Bring water and be conscious of rattlesnakes; the nearest medical facilities are in Burns, 55 mi. to the northwest. For information on rattlesnake safety, ask a park ranger or see **The Great Outdoors,** p. 62.

FRENCHGLEN   ☎541

An hour south of Burns along Rte. 205 (Catlow Valley Rd.), Frenchglen provides access to wildlife refuges and the western side of Steens Mtn. via the Steens Mtn. Loop. **Fields,** 55min. farther south of Frenchglen on Rte. 205 at the southern tip of the mountain, provides access to the eastern face and the Alvord Desert. Both towns are little more than a few buildings along the highway, but they can provide food, shelter, and sound advice. The **Steens Mountain Resort ❸,** on North Steens Mtn. Loop Rd. just 3 mi. outside of town, has a small general store with canned goods, ice cream, and laundry facilities. Also offers tent sites ($12) and cabins. (☎493-2415, reservations 800-542-3765; www.steensmountainresort.com. Laundry $0.75 per load, dry $0.50 for 20min. Showers $5. Store open daily 8:30am-6pm. Cabins $50 for up to two people; $10 per additional person.) The **Frenchglen Hotel ❹,** 39184 Hwy. 205, at the southern end of town, is also a state heritage site. Built in the 1920s, this quaint white hotel offers meals on a screened-in porch. (☎493-2825. Rooms start at $65. Open Mar. 15-Nov. 15.)

FIELDS   ☎541

About 5 mi. northwest of Fields, Rte. 205 squeezes through a small pass and the scenery rapidly evolves from rugged to lunar, with hulking fault-block mountains all around. Consisting of only a few buildings, the rambling **Fields Station** provides food, gas, a place to sleep, and not much else. The general store and gas station are the last of each for about 100 mi. on the east side (55 mi. on the west side of the mountain). The **General Store** and gas station are open M-Sa 8am-6pm, Su 9am-5pm. The **cafe ❶** serves remarkably large burgers

($5.25), scrumptious onion rings ($3), and 6000 milkshakes a year ($3). The **hotel ❸** and **campground ❶** next door to the cafe rent pleasant rooms and sites. (☎495-2275. Singles $45; doubles $60; RV sites $10; tenting areas $2.)

STEENS MOUNTAIN   ☎541

Oregon's most unearthly landscape lies in the southeast, where **Steens Mountain** rises to an elevation of nearly 10,000 ft. and reaches a vertical mile above an uninhabited, bone-dry alkali flat to the east. Although its fault block geology might seem a letdown from the western view—the sloped road ascends very gradually—on the substantially more remote east side, the incredible 30 mi. north-south stretch of mountain presents huge cliffs and deep canyons. Contact the Burns District BLM for road info and get **maps** of the area at the **Frenchglen Hotel** and the **Steens Mountain Resort** (see above). There are four campgrounds on the west side, all with pit toilets and drinking water; they charge $6-8 per night. Each is just off the Steens Mtn. Rd., which leaves from Frenchglen. **Page Springs ❶,** only 4 mi. from Frenchglen, is accessible year-round and has 31 grassy sites surrounded by cliffs; **Fish Lake ❶,** 19 mi. in and 1½ mi. up toward the mountain, has 23 sites and a boat ramp with access to the best fishing in the area; **Jackman Park ❶,** 3 mi. farther in, has six mountainside sites; and **South Steens ❶,** several miles farther in, features 21 sites and 15 equestrian sites. Additionally, you can camp for free anywhere along the road. There is **❶one site** with a protective rock wall just a half mile below the rim. This site offers incredible views of sunset and easy access to the rim. The campgrounds on the east side are free and offer plenty of solitude; as a major plus, the stargazing doesn't get any better. **Pike Creek ❶** has a pit toilet and a creek nearby. It's 1½ mi. north of the **Alvord Hot Springs** (see below). Make a left after the second creek north of the desert (marked by a line of trees), and drive up the very rough road. Keep your eyes peeled; it's easy to miss.

DRIVING. Don't think that driving is a cop-out—the 56 mi. dirty track **Steens Mountain Loop Road** (open July-Oct.) is rutted and washboardy. The route up to the rim from Frenchglen should not pose a problem, but if you're in a 2WD vehicle, don't plan on doing the whole loop. Check with BLM for the status of the road. The route climbs the west slope of the mountain from Rte. 205 near Frenchglen, and rejoins the highway only 8 mi. farther south.

OTHER EXPLORATION. Though hot, dusty, and chock full of rattlesnakes, the canyons of the mountain, gouged deep into the rock by glacial activity, are beautiful and difficult hikes. **Pike Creek** trail (see above for directions; the trail and road are unmarked) begins as an old mining road, goes past an abandoned mining shack and under towering rock spires, and then gradually fades about 1½ mi. in as it switchbacks and continues to the mouth of Pike Creek's canyon. To find the trail, just walk up the creek and follow the cairns in the canyon. The trail ends at the mouth, but the summit can be attained by a very difficult scree scramble to the top. (Hiking to the mouth is moderate to strenuous; to the summit is very strenuous and takes 1-1½ days. Consider having a car meet you at the top.)

For something a little more mellow with spectacular views, check out **Wildhorse Lake,** a beautiful lake set in a hanging valley just below the summit. To access the hike, park at the east rim parking lot and walk along the road towards the summit (or park at the Wildhorse parking lot, near the summit, if it's open). Signs will indicate the turnoff for the lake. This route is usually not open until July, when the notoriously treacherous snow hollows melt.

OREGON

For more intense explorations, a four-day trip ascends the **Big Indian Creek Gorge** on the west side to the summit and descends via the **Little Blitzen River Gorge,** also on the west side, going cross country most of the way. Water is not available between Big Indian Creek and Little Blitzen River. The canyons are also good for shorter day hikes, returning via the ascent route. A popular and moderately difficult hike goes along the **Blitzen River Trail** (4 mi. one-way, several hr.) which follows along the river, crossing in certain places to avoid steep cliffs, to some great places for **fishing.** The river passes through the Steens Mtn. Resort. Fishing licenses are available at **B & B Sporting Goods,** Hwy. 20 and Conley Ave. (☎573-6200. Licenses $12 per day, $23 for two days, $33 for three days or $60 annually.)

ALVORD DESERT

The utterly flat and barren Alvord Desert supports no terrestrial life. On the other hand, if a giant metal craft lands bearing beings from outer space, don't worry: the Alvord Desert is reportedly the US space shuttle's 4th-choice landing spot. It's also a favored place for sand yachting, where the wheeled sailcraft can achieve speeds up to 100 mph during the occasional regattas. To get in on the action, get out on the flat about 25 mi. north of Fields on E. Steens Rd. a dirt road that goes from Rte. 78 to a mile north of Fields, at 35145 E. Steens Rd. Once you're out there you're free to be Mario Andretti or James Bond. Regardless of your intentions, a gaze over this bona fide wasteland is worth the long trip—although enjoying the desert requires a sense of humor. Make sure to bring lots of water and plenty of gas.

The borate-rich **Alvord Hot Springs** emerges next to the desert; a couple of enterprising, and probably reclusive, miners once extracted cinnabar up a dirt road opposite the springs. A tin shack houses a small pool for bathing, kept much cooler than the 174°F of the spring. It's on the right side of the road, about 200 ft. north of a cattleguard. About 20 mi. farther north, **Mann Lake** is open to excellent fishing and **free camping ❶** with pit toilets but no piped water. For those in search of a rough, multi-day desert adventure well beyond anything a car could give, the Desert Trail runs through the area. **Trail guides** and info are available from the Desert Trail Association in Madras (www.thedeserttrail.org).

JOHN DAY FOSSIL BEDS   ☎541

The John Day Fossil Beds National Monument (www.nps.gov/joda) is one of eastern Oregon's most interesting sites. A place where paleontological reputations are made, the beds hold the bones of ancient monsters from sabertooths and "bear dogs" to ever-elusive gomphotheres. Though no original fossils are on display outdoors because of the incredible amount of information they can provide in a lab, the beds themselves are topographically remarkable. The monument is split up into three units, 50-80 mi. away from each other; the **Sheep Rock, Painted Hills,** and **Clarno** units each depict one facet of a 40-million-year geological history. The nearby town John Day is at best a stopover.

☗☗ ACCOMMODATIONS AND CAMPING. Clyde Holiday State Park ❶, 7 mi. west of town on US 26, has grassy sites and a less-than-primitive aura. It offers electricity, carpeting, and foam mattresses. (☎932-4453, reservations 800-452-5687. Hiker/biker sites $4; 30 sites with RV sites, $16; 2 tepees are available, $28 each. Showers for non-campers $2.) For those who prefer bed and a roof, **Dreamer's Lodge ❸,** 144 N Canyon Blvd., has large rooms with fridges, microwaves, and cable. (☎575-0526. Singles $56; doubles $60; $7-9 more for a kitchenette.) **Little Pine Inn ❸,** 250 E Main St., has recently remodeled rooms and free breakfast at a local restaurant. (☎575-2100. Singles $43; doubles $49.)

🖸 **FOOD.** Pick up groceries at **Chester's Thriftway,** 631 W Main St., in John Day Plaza. (☎575-1899. Open daily 7am-9pm.) The **Dirty Shame Tavern and Pizzeria ❶,** 145 E. Main St., next to the Grubsteak Mining Co., has very cheesy and very cheap pizza. (☎575-1935. 16 in. pizza $9.50. Open Tu-Th 3pm-11pm, F-Sa 3pm-1am.) Have a burger or a steak at the **Grubsteak Mining Co. ❶,** 149 E Main St. Pool and beer ($2 bottles) are available at the saloon in the back. (☎575-1970. Open M-Th 7am-9pm, F-Sa 7am-10pm, Su 7am-8pm. Lounge open M-Sa 11am-2am, Su 1am-9pm.) Enjoy a sit-down meal at **Dayville Cafe ❷,** 212 W Franklin St. (Rte. 26) in Dayville. Big breakfasts, grilled sandwiches ($5-6) and steaks ($15) are served in a calico country atmosphere. Everything is fresh and homemade by mom and pop. (☎987-2132. Open W-Sa 7am-8pm, M and Su 8am-5pm. No credit cards.)

🏃 **OUTDOOR ACTIVITIES.** The **Sheep Rock Unit** has some of the best hiking in the area, with trails that show off prehistoric fossils. It also contains the **visitors center** on Rte. 19, 2 mi. north of US 26. The center has displays and interactive exhibits that help make sense of the area. (☎987-2333. Open daily 8:30am-4:30pm.)

The **Blue Basin** area (3 mi. up the road from the visitors center) provides two distinct hiking opportunities from the same trailhead: the **Island in Time Trail,** an easy 1 mi., 45min. round-trip into the canyon that passes by a blue-green rock formation, and the **Blue Basin Overlook Trail,** a more challenging 3 mi., 2½hr. loop up to the basin's rim and a view of the John Day River Valley. The former's fossil replicas of sea turtles and saber-toothed carnivores are intriguing, but are surpassed by the latter's views of bright red and white badland spires.

Six miles north of US 26 from the turn-off, 3 mi. west of Mitchell, the **Painted Hills Unit** offers several short hikes that present a better way to examine the incredibly colored mounds, once tropical rainforests. It focuses on an epoch thirty million years ago, when the land was in geologic transition. Smooth mounds of brilliant red, yellow, white and black sediment are most vivid at sunset and dawn, or after rain when the whole gorge glistens with brilliantly colored layers of claystone.

The **Clarno Unit,** on Rte. 218, is accessible by US 97 to the west or Rte. 19 to the east. If you're coming from the south, the 207 route offers spectacular high country scenery. Short trails wind through ancient ash-laden mudflows from volcanic eruptions. Many of the hikes are more scenic than strenuous, offering ample opportunities to witness the stark beauty of this national monument.

STRAWBERRY MOUNTAIN WILDERNESS

Tall, rocky peaks make the Strawberry Mountains a great cure for any case of desert blues. Needle-sharp summit ridges, snow-lined cliffs, and forested lakes make it a justly popular destination for Oregon city-folk. Though it can get slightly crowded (by wilderness standards) with vacationers and their angry dogs, a weekday trip will offer refreshing views and clean (but thin) air. To squeeze in the best views in the least time, try day hikes and overnight camping in the lakes basin, around **Strawberry Lake.** Backpackers enjoy more solitude in the west side of the wilderness, accessible from forest roads south of John Day. Ask at the ranger station for details; in any case, wilderness maps are essential as trail signs are perplexing. Get one at the Prairie City **ranger station,** 327 Rte. 26 at the west end of Prairie City (☎820-3311; open M-F 7:45am-4:30pm), for $6. In case of emergency, **Blue Mountain Hospital** is in John Day, 170 Ford Rd. (☎575-1311).

To get to Strawberry Campground and the trailhead for the lakes basin, head south on Main St. in Prairie City, 13 mi. east of John Day. Take the next left, and then drive straight at the mountains on Forest Rd. 60, which becomes Forest Rd.

6001; follow it until the end. The **campground** ❶ itself is a decent campsite (sites $6). A better, cheaper option is to hike up into the high country. Free **camping** ❶ is allowed anywhere in the wilderness; many people camp around Strawberry Lake, fewer at the more rugged Little Strawberry Lake and its surrounding streams.

Strawberry Lake, a moderate 1½ mi. hike from Strawberry Campground, is the base of most of the popular trails. A strenuous 6 mi. (4hr. up) trail through the lake to the top of Strawberry Mtn. passes through ghostly-white burns and sub-alpine meadows peppered with wildflowers. The windy and razor-sharp 9000 ft. summit ridge has a view across the rest of the Strawberry wilderness and the Monument Rock wilderness. To get there, head up the trail to Little Strawberry Lake from the south side of Strawberry Lake.

WASHINGTON

> **WASHINGTON FACTS AND FIGURES**
> **Capital:** Olympia. **Area:** 66,582 sq. mi. **Population:** 6,131,445.
> **Motto:** *"Alki"* ("by and by" in Salish). **Nickname:** Evergreen State.
> **State Bird:** Goldfinch. **State Fruit:** Apple. **State Dance:** Square Dance.
> **State Tree:** Western Hemlock. **State Fossil:** Columbian Mammoth.

What is now Washington was home to only 400 settlers when Oregonians rallied for territorial recognition in the 1840s. The indigenous nations of the coast and plains still outnumbered the newcomers when Washington became a territory in 1853 (encompassing much of present-day Idaho and Montana). By 1863, 4000 settlers had journeyed along the Oregon Trail and the state had attained roughly its present shape. Over the course of the 1900s, the development of towns depended on the railroads linking west with east. During World War II, Seattle's resource-driven economy was transformed by the nation's need for ships and aircraft.

On Washington's western shore, concert halls and art galleries offer cosmopolitan entertainment within easy reach of Puget Sound, its gorgeous islands, and the temperate rainforests of the Olympic Peninsula. Seattle is the home of coffee, grunge, Microsoft, scattered hilly neighborhoods, fantastic parks, and miles of waterfront. The lush San Juan Islands boast puffins, sea otters, and sea lions. Pods of orcas circle the islands, followed by pods of tourists in yachts and kayaks. East of Puget Sound, the North Cascades rise up with fury and the Columbia River flows from the Canadian border to the Pacific Ocean, interrupted by dams providing the state with water and electricity. The drier, less populous eastern half of the state is home to miles of rich farmland and dotted with unassuming small towns.

HIGHLIGHTS OF WASHINGTON

ROCK out at the architectural wonder of Experience Music Project in Seattle (p. 191).

EXPLORE the micro-environments of Olympic National Park (p. 231).

FLOAT along Lake Chelan to Stehekin, accessible only by ferry, foot, or plane (p. 260).

CONQUER spectacular Mt. Rainier, Washington's highest peak (p. 273).

ADMIRE the work of Tacoman glass artists at the Tacoma Museum of Glass (p. 205).

TREK the isolated wilderness trails of North Cascades National Park (p. 252).

SEATTLE ☎ 206

While Seattle's mix of mountain views, clean streets, espresso stands, and rainy weather has long pleased its residents, the 1990s saw the city gain national attention for two sides of its personality: its grunge rock underbelly and its computer whiz crowd. Although a slowdown in the tech sector has turned some computer magnates' smiles into frowns, the culture continues on in Seattle without missing a beat. The city is one of the youngest and most vibrant in the nation, with a flourishing educated, artistic, and outdoorsy population. The droves of newcomers provide an obvious but amicable contrast to the older residents who remember Seattle as a city-town, not a thriving metropolis bubbling over with young million-

WASHINGTON

Washington

IDAHO

CANADA
USA

OREGON

PACIFIC OCEAN

Vancouver Island

Strait of Georgia

Strait of Juan De Fuca

Puget Sound

Grays Harbor

Colville Nat'l Forest

Okanogan Nat'l Forest

Pasayten Wilderness

North Cascades Nat'l Park

Mt. Baker Nat'l Forest

Mt. Baker (10,778ft.)

Mt. Baker-Snoqualmie Nat'l Forest

Okanogan Nat'l Forest

Lake Chelan

Wenatchee Nat'l Forest

Stevens Pass

Alpine Lakes Wilderness

Snoqualmie Pass

CASCADE MOUNTAINS

Mt. Rainier Nat'l Park

Mt. Rainier (14,411ft.)

Mt. St. Helens Nat'l Volcanic Monument

Mt. St. Helens (8,366ft.)

Gifford Pinchot Nat'l Forest

Mt. Adams

Olympic National Forest

OLYMPIC MOUNTAINS

Olympic Nat'l Park

Umatilla Nat'l Forest

Columbia River

Snake River

Cape Flattery

Towns: Newport, Coeur d'Alene, Moscow, Lewiston, Spokane, Colville, Chewelah, Colfax, Pullman, Pomeroy, Davenport, Sprague, Dayton, Walla Walla, Wilbur, Ritzville, Washtucna, Kennewick, Pasco, Pendleton, Republic, Grand Coulee, Moses Lake, Othello, Richland, Prosser, Tonasket, Brewster, Ephrata, Chelan, Leavenworth, Ellensburg, Yakima, Toppenish, Goldendale, Trout Lake, Stehekin, Winthrop, Twisp, Bellingham, Sedro-Woolley, Mt. Vernon, Everett, Bellevue, Snoqualmie, Seattle, Tacoma, Olympia, Elbe, Randle, Morton, Centralia, Chehalis, Kelso, Longview, Cathlamet, Astoria, Vancouver, Portland, Anacortes, Oak Harbor, Port Townsend, Port Angeles, Bremerton, Shelton, Montesano, Aberdeen, Willapa, Long Beach, Quinault, Forks, La Push, Neah Bay, Sidney, Victoria

Whidbey Island, Vashon Island, San Juan Islands

30 miles
30 kilometers

N

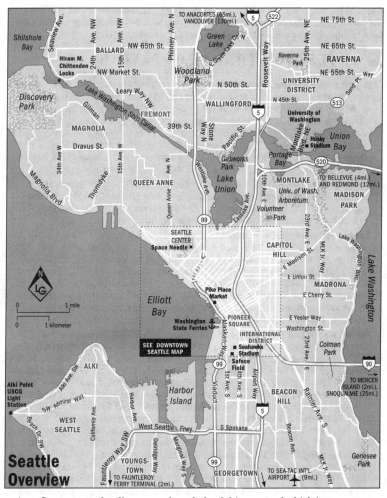

Shilshole
Bay

Discovery
Park

Seaview Ave.

24th Ave. NW

15th Ave. NW

Ave. NW

Hiram M.
Chittenden
Locks

BALLARD

NW 65th St.

NW Market St.

Phinney Ave. N

Green
Lake

TO ANACORTES (65mi.),
VANCOUVER (130mi.)

5

522

Roosevelt Way

NE 75th St.

25th Ave. NE

Ravenna
Park

25th

NE 65th St.

RAVENNA

NE 55th St.

Sand Pt. Way

Woodland
Park

N 50th St.

UNIVERSITY
DISTRICT

N Green Lake Dr. N

Leary Way NW

Lake Washington Ship Canal

Gilman

Fremont

39th St.

WALLINGFORD

N 45th St.

5

University of
Washington

513

MAGNOLIA

Dravus St.

34th Ave W

Thorndyke

15th Ave. W

Stone Way N

N 39th St.

Pacific St.

Gasworks
Park

Lake
Union

Montlake Blvd. NE

Husky
Stadium

Union
Bay

Magnolia Blvd.

QUEEN ANNE

Queen Anne Ave. N

Nickerson Ave.

Westlake Ave.

N Ave. E

Eastlake Ave.

Portage
Bay

520

TO BELLEVUE (4mi.)
AND REDMOND (12mi.)

Lake Washington

10th Ave. E

MONTLAKE

Univ. of Wash.
Arboretum

Volunteer
Park

MADISON
PARK

99

SEATTLE
CENTER

Space Needle ■

CAPITOL
HILL

23rd Ave. E

E Madison St.

MLK Jr. Way

Lake Washington Blvd.

E Union St.

MADRONA

N
LG

0   1 mile

0   1 kilometer

Elliott
Bay

Pike Place
Market

Washington
State Ferries

PIONEER
SQUARE

INTERNATIONAL
DISTRICT

Alaskan Way

Washington St.

E Madison St.

E Cherry St.

E Yesler Way

Washington St.

23rd Ave. S

Colman
Park

E

SEE DOWNTOWN
SEATTLE MAP

99

■ Seahawks
■ Stadium

Safeco
Field

1st Ave. S

4th Ave. S

Airport Way

90

TO MERCER
ISLAND (2mi.),
SNOQUALMIE (25mi.)

Alki Point
USCG
Light
Station

ALKI

Alki Ave. SW

SW Admiral Way

WEST
SEATTLE

California Ave.

Beach Dr. SW

Harbor Ave.

Harbor
Island

Delridge Way

Marginal Way S

West Seattle Frwy.

West Seattle Frwy.

S Spokane

BEACON
HILL

5

Rainier Ave. S

Beacon Ave.

MLK Jr. Way

Genesee
Park

Seattle
Overview

Fauntleroy Way SW

YOUNGS-
TOWN

TO FAUNTLEROY
FERRY TERMINAL (2mi.)

99

GEORGETOWN

TO SEA-TAC INT'L
AIRPORT (9mi.)

WASHINGTON

aires. Computer and coffee money have helped drive rents sky high in some areas,
but the grungy, punk-loving street culture prevails in others. In the end, there is a
nook or cranny for almost anyone in Seattle.

The Emerald City sits on an isthmus, with mountain ranges to the east and west.
Every hilltop in Seattle offers an impressive view of Mt. Olympus, Mt. Baker, and
Mt. Rainier. To the west, the waters of Puget Sound glint against downtown skyscrapers and nearly spotless streets. The city's artistic landscape is as varied and
exciting as its physical terrain. The monthly Gallery Walk floods the spaces with
eager onlookers and the theater community is one of the largest and most prestigious in the country. When Nirvana introduced the world to their discordant sensi-
bility, the term "grunge" and Seattle became temporarily inseparable, and the city
that produced Jimi Hendrix again revitalized rock 'n' roll. Good bands thrive in
grunge's wake, keeping the Seattle scene a mecca for edgy entertainment. Bill

Gates of Microsoft and Howard Shultz of Starbucks have achieved vast success on the backs of software and coffee beans, allowing Seattle's residents go about their lives technologically connected and in a state of caffeinated bliss.

■ INTERCITY TRANSPORTATION

Flights: Seattle-Tacoma International (Sea-Tac; ☎433-5388; www.portseattle.org), on Federal Way, 15 mi. south of Seattle, exit right off I-5 to Rte. 518 (signs are clear). Bus #194 departs the underground tunnel at University St. Station and 3rd Ave. and Union St. (30min., every 30min. 5:25am-8:45pm, alternating from the two spots. $1.25 one-way, $2 round-trip, ages 6-17 $0.50) and #174 departs from Union St. and 2nd Ave. (45min., every 30min. 5:25am-3:30am, $1.25 one-way, $2 round-trip) for the airport. These routes leave from the airport for Seattle from outside the baggage claim (every 15min. 4:45am-2:45am, $1.25 one-way, $2 round-trip). Airport code: SEA.

Trains: Amtrak (☎382-4125, reservations ☎800-872-7245), King St. Station, at 303 S. Jackson St., 1 block east of Pioneer Square. Open daily 6:15am-10pm. To: **Portland** (4 per day, $26-37); **Tacoma** (4 per day, $9-15); **Spokane** (4 per day, $41-85); **San Francisco** (1 per day, $100-167); and **Vancouver, BC** (1 per day, $23-36).

Buses: Greyhound (☎628-5526 or 800-231-2222), at 8th Ave. and Stewart St. Try to avoid night buses, since the station can get seedy after dark. Ticket office open daily 6:30am-2:30am, station open 24hr. To: **Portland** (11 per day, $25); **Spokane** (3 per day, $28); **Tacoma** (8 per day, $6); and **Vancouver, BC** (8 per day, $24). **Quick Shuttle** (☎604-940-4428 or 800-665-2122; www.quickcoach.com) makes 5-8 cross-border trips daily from Seattle (Travelodge hotel at 8th and Bell St.) and the Sea-Tac airport to the **Vancouver, BC** airport and the Holiday Inn on Howe St. in downtown Vancouver (4-4½hr.; $33 from downtown, $41 from Sea-Tac).

Ferries: Washington State Ferries (☎464-6400 or 888-808-7977; www.wsdot.wa.gov/ferries) has 2 terminals in Seattle. The main terminal is downtown, at Colman Dock, Pier 52. From here, service departs to **Bainbridge Island** (35min.; $5.70, with car $13), **Bremerton** on the Kitsap Peninsula (1hr.; 40min; $5.70, with car $13), and **Vashon Island** (25min., passengers only, $7.70). From the waterfront, passenger-only ferries leave from Pier 50. The other terminal is in **Fauntleroy**, West Seattle: to reach the terminal, drive south on I-5 and take Exit 163A (West Seattle) down Fauntleroy Way. Sailings from Fauntleroy to **Southworth** on the Kitsap Peninsula (35min.; $4.40, with car $9.75); **Vashon Island** (15min; $3.70, with car $17.) If ferry travel is in your plans, pick up both the sailing schedule and the fares pamphlet. Schedules are tricky, so it's worth spending a few minutes perusing the schedule or calling the toll-free info line. Ferries leave frequently from 6am-2am. The **Victoria Clipper** (☎800-888-2535, reservations 448-5000; www.victoriaclipper.com) takes passengers from Seattle to **Victoria** only. Departs from Pier 69. (3hr.; 2 per day mid-Sept. to Apr.; 4 per day May to mid-Sept.; one-way $60-79, round-trip $106-129, under 12 half-price; bikes $10, no cars.)

■ ORIENTATION

Seattle stretches from north to south on an isthmus between **Puget Sound** to the west and **Lake Washington** to the east. The city is easily accessible by car via **I-5**, which runs north-south through the city, and by **I-90** from the east, which ends at I-5 southeast of downtown. Get to **downtown** (including **Pioneer Square, Pike Place Market**, and the **waterfront**) from I-5 by taking any of the exits from James St. to Stewart St. Take the Mercer St./Fairview Ave. exit to the **Seattle Center;** follow signs from there. The Denny Way exit leads to **Capitol Hill,** and, farther north, the 45th St. exit heads toward the **University District**. The less crowded **Route 99**, also called Aurora Ave. or the Aurora Hwy., runs parallel to I-5 and skirts the western side of downtown, with great views from the Alaskan Way Viaduct. Rte. 99 is often the better choice when driving downtown or to **Queen Anne, Fremont, Green Lake, Ballard,** and the northwestern part of the city. For more detailed directions to these and other districts, see the individualized neighborhood listings under **Food** (p. 180), **Nightlife** (p. 198), and **Sights** (p. 188).

⊑ LOCAL TRANSPORTATION

Even the most road-weary drivers can learn their way around the Emerald City, but street parking and excessive numbers of parking garages creates many blind pull-outs in Seattle, so be extra careful when turning onto cross roads. Downtown, **avenues** run northwest to southeast and **streets** run southwest to northeast. Outside downtown, everything is simplified: with few exceptions, avenues run north-south and streets east-west. The city is in **quadrants:** 1000 1st Ave. NW is a long walk from 1000 1st Ave. SE. Do not be confused if the street you are on changes its name as you round a corner; the numbered roads lie along predecided lines, meaning the name changes if they depart from that course.

When driving in Seattle, **yield to pedestrians.** They will not look, so make sure you do. But those pedestrians who do wait at the crosswalk aren't just polite: jaywalking is illegal in Seattle, and police are known to ticket unsuspecting out-of-towners. The police are also active on the roads, leading locals to drive slowly, calmly, and politely. Downtown driving can be nightmarish: parking is expensive, hills are steep, and one-way streets are ubiquitous. Read the street signs carefully, as many areas have time and hour restrictions; ticketers know them by heart. **Parking** is reasonable, plentiful, and well lit at **Pacific Place Parking** between 6th and 7th Ave. and Olive and Pine St., or at the **Pike Street Garage,** between 7th and 8th Ave. between Pike and Pine St., both with hourly rates comparable to the meters. Parking is also available at **Seattle Center,** near the Space Needle. (☎652-0416; www.seattlecenter.com. 24hr. $2 per hr.; $19 per day.) From parking at the Needle, the monorail can take you to the convenient **Westlake Center** at the heart of downtown, with access to many nearby attractions. If you are driving in Seattle, prepare yourself for at least moderate traffic, especially on I-5, at almost any hour of the day. Public transportation on the whole in Seattle is not stellar. Although buses are large and schedules are flexible, the transit is slow and infrequent.

The **Metro ride free zone** includes most of downtown Seattle (see **Public Transportation,** below). The **Metro** buses cover King County east to North Bend and Carnation, south to Enumclaw, and north to Snohomish County, where bus #6 hooks up with **Community Transit.** This line runs to Everett, Stanwood, and into the Cascades. Bus #174 connects to Tacoma's Pierce County System at Federal Way.

Seattle is a **bicycle-friendly** city. All buses have free, easy-to-use bike racks (bike shops have sample racks on which to practice). From 6am-7pm, bikes may only be loaded or unloaded at stops outside the ride free zone. Check out Metro's *Bike & Ride,* available at the visitors center. For a bike map, call **City of Seattle Bicycle Program** (☎684-7583; www.ci.seattle.wa.us/transportation/bikeprogram.htm. 700 5th Ave., ste. 3900) or pick one up from the visitors center or the website.

Public Transportation: Metro Transit, Customer Service Offices, King Street Center, 2nd Ave S and S Jackson St. and Westlake Station in Downtown Metro Bus Tunnel. (☎553-3000 or 24hr. 800-542-7876; http://transit.metrokc.gov). King Street Center open M-F 8am-5pm; Westlake Station open M-F 9am-5pm. The bus tunnel under Pine St. and 3rd Ave. is the heart of the downtown bus system. Fares are based on a 2-zone system. **Zone 1** includes everything within the city limits (peak hours $1.50, off-peak $1.25). **Zone 2** includes everything else (peak $2, off-peak $1.25). Ages 5-17 always $0.50.

Peak hours in both zones are M-F 6-9am and 3-6pm. Weekend day passes $2.50. Ride free daily 6am-7pm in the downtown **ride free area,** bordered by S Jackson St. on the south, 6th Ave. and I-5 on the east, Blanchard St. on the north, and the waterfront on the west. Free **transfers** can be used on any bus, including a round-trip on the same bus within 2hr. Most buses are **wheelchair-accessible** (info ☎684-2046). The **Monorail** runs from the Space Needle to Westlake Center every 10min. 7:30am-11pm. ($1.50, ages 65 and older $0.75, 5-12 $0.50.) The center of years of heated debate and legislation, the Monorail may be undergoing renovation and expansion over the next few years. Call ahead to check hours.

Taxi: Farwest Taxi (☎622-1717) or **Orange Cab Co.** (☎522-8800), $1.80 base, $1.80 per mi. Both 24hr.

Car Rental: U Save Auto Rental, 16223 Pacific Hwy. S (☎242-9778; www.rentusave.com). $37 per day for compacts, plus $0.22 per mi. over 100 mi. Unlimited mileage in WA and BC. Must be 21 with a major credit card. **Enterprise,** 11342 Lake City Way NE (☎364-3127). $38 per day for compacts, plus $0.20 per mi. over 150 mi. Must be over 21 with a major credit card. Their **airport location,** 15667 Pacific Hwy. S (☎246-1953), charges an additional 10%.

🛈 PRACTICAL INFORMATION

TOURIST AND FINANCIAL SERVICES

Tourist Information: Seattle's Convention and Visitors Bureau (☎461-5840; www.seeseattle.org), at 7th and Pike St., on the 1st floor of the convention center, look for the signs to the "City Concierge." Helpful staff doles out maps, brochures, newspapers, and Metro schedules. Open Memorial Day-Labor Day M-F 9am-6pm, Sa-Su 10am-4pm; Labor Day-Memorial Day M-F 9am-5pm.

Outdoor Information: Seattle Parks and Recreation Department, 100 Dexter Ave. N (☎684-4075; www.co.seattle.wa.us/parks). Open M-F 8am-5pm for info and pamphlets on city parks. **Outdoor Recreation Information Center,** 222 Yale Ave. (☎470-4060; www.nps.gov/ccso/oric.htm), in REI (see **Equipment Rental,** below). A joint operation between the Park and Forest services. Able to answer any questions that might arise as you browse REI's huge collection of maps and guides. Unfortunately, the desk does not sell permits. Free brochures on hiking trails. Open M-F and Su 10:30am-8pm, Sa 10am-8pm. Closed M late Sept. to late spring.

Equipment Rental:

REI, 222 Yale Ave. (☎223-1944 or 888-873-1938; www.rei.com), near Capitol Hill. The mothership of camping supply stores rents everything from camping gear to technical mountaineering equipment plus boasts the unique features that make this flagship store its own tourist attraction: a mountain bike test trail, gear-testing stations, and its 65 ft. climbing wall, the world's tallest indoor free-standing climbing structure. Open M-F 10am-9pm, Sa-Su 10am-7pm.

Gregg's Greenlake Cycle, 7007 Woodlawn Ave. NE (☎523-1822; www.greggscycles.com). Wide range of bikes conveniently close to the Green Lake and Burke-Gilman bike trails ($5 per hr., $25 per day, $120 per week). Photo ID and cash or credit card deposit required. Also rents in-line skates ($5 per hr., $20 per day, $25 per 24hr.). Hourly rentals are weather-dependent; they do not rent skates when the Green Lake path is wet. Last hourly rentals at 6:30pm on weekdays, 4:30pm on weekends. Overnight rentals require deposit. Winter rentals include snowboards and snowshoes. Open M-F 10am-9pm, Sa-Su 10am-6pm.

Currency Exchange: Thomas Cook Foreign Exchange, 400 Pine St. (☎682-4525), on the 3rd floor of the Westlake Shopping Center. Open M-Sa 9:30am-6pm, Su 11am-5pm. Also behind the Delta Airlines ticket counter and at other airport locations.

LOCAL SERVICES

Library: The (literally) shiny new **Seattle Public Library,** 1000 4th Ave. (☎386-4636; www.spl.org.) at Madison, reopened at its original site in the spring of 2004. Worth a visit for a book or just a look around. A visitor's library card (must have local address) lasts 3 months ($10). Internet free with photo ID for 15min.; free unlimited wireless Internet. Open M-Tu 1-8pm, W 10am-8pm, Th-Sa 10am-6pm, Su 1-5pm.

Ticket Agencies: Ticketmaster (☎628-0888; www.ticketmaster.com) in Westlake Center and every Tower Records store. **Ticket/Ticket,** 401 Broadway E (☎324-2744), on the 2nd floor of Broadway Market, sells discounted day-of-show tickets for theatres, music, tours, and more. Cash only. Sales only done in person. Open Tu-Sa noon-7pm, Su noon-6pm. Also in **Pike Place Market Information Booth** at 1st Ave. and Pike St. 30min. free parking in garage under Harrison St. with ticket purchase. Open Tu-Su noon-6pm.

Laundromat: Sit and Spin, 2219 4th Ave. (☎441-9484). A laundromat and local hot spot (see **Nightlife,** p. 198). Wash $1.25, dry $0.25 per 10min. Open M-Th and Su 11am-midnight, F-Sa 11am-2am.

EMERGENCY AND COMMUNICATIONS

Police: 810 Virginia St. (☎625-5011).

Crisis Line: ☎461-3222.

Rape Crisis: King County Sexual Assault Center (☎800-825-7273). Crisis counseling and advocacy. **Harborview Medical** (☎731-3000), **Harborview Center for Sexual and Traumatic Stress** (☎521-1800). All 24hr.

Medical Services: International District Emergency Center, 720 8th Ave. S, Ste. 100 (☎461-3235). Medics with multilingual assistance available. Clinic M-F 9am-6pm, Sa 9am-5pm; phone 24hr. **Swedish Medical Center, Providence Campus,** 500 17th Ave. (☎320-2111), for urgent care and cardiac. 24hr.

Internet Access: Available at the **Seattle Public Library** (see **Local Services,** above). Both Starbucks and Tully's allow you to purchase membership to their wireless networks, while a few other coffeeshops provide the service for free. **Internet cafes,** like their computer-free cousins, cover the city, and are especially common on Capitol Hill:

Aurafice Internet and Coffee Bar, 616 E. Pine St. (☎860-9977; www.aurafice.com). Even without its Internet services ($6 per hr., $20 per 4hr.) this bustling hotspot is great place to rest your feet, hosting gallery presentations, spoken-word, and DJed events. The food and beverage options are almost entirely locally-produced. Open M-Th 8am-midnight, F-Sa 8am-2am, Su 8am-midnight.

Capitol Hill Net, 216 Broadway Ave E (☎860-6858; www.capitolhill.net), is a large and very open space, surprisingly tranquil for its location. $6 per hr., 15min. free with food purchase of $1.50. Let's Go readers and all hostelers get 15min. free. Open M-Su 8am-midnight.

Cyber Dogs, 909 Pike St. (☎405-3647; www.cyber-dogs.com). Surely the only combination vegetarian/vegan hot-dog vendor and Internet cafe around. The intimate venue charges $0.10 per min., first 20min. free with a purchase over $2. Open daily 9am-midnight.

Post Office: 301 Union St. (☎748-5417 or 800-275-8777) at 3rd Ave. downtown. Open M-F 8am-5:30pm, Sa 8am-noon. General delivery window open M-F 9-11:20am and noon-3pm. **Postal Code:** 98101.

PUBLICATIONS

The city's major daily, the *Seattle Times* (☎464-2111; www.seattletimes.com), lists upcoming events in its Thursday "Datebook" section. Its major "competitor" (actually its partner), the *Seattle Post-Intelligencer* (☎448-8000; www.seattlepi.com), has an award-winning sports section and great news coverage. The two papers publish jointly on Sundays. The *Seattle Weekly* (www.seattleweekly.com) is free and left-of-center. Even farther left is *The Stranger* (www.thestranger.com), a free weekly which covers music and culture and is omnipresent at music, coffee, and thrift shops. The weekly *Seattle Gay News* (www.sgn.org) sells at newsstands and bookstores. The independent monthly magazine *Tablet* (www.tabletmag.com) focuses on Pacific Northwest music, arts, and culture.

■ ACCOMMODATIONS

Seattle's hostel scene is not amazing, but there are plenty of choices and establishments to fit all types of personalities. The **Vashon Island Hostel** is probably the best bet for beds in the area and most certainly the most relaxing (see **Accommodations**, p. 210). **Pacific Reservation Service** arranges B&B singles in the $50-65 range. (2520 Westlake Ave. North. ☎439-7677 or 800-684-2932; www.seattlebedandbreakfast.com. Open M-F 8am-5pm.) For inexpensive motels farther from downtown, drive north on Hwy. 99 (Aurora Ave.) or take bus #26 from the Fremont neighborhood. Budget chain motels line the highway north of the Aurora Bridge.

Seattle International Hostel (HI), 84 Union St. (☎622-5443 or 888-622-5443; www.hiseattle.org), at Western Ave. by the waterfront. Take Union St. from downtown; follow signs down the stairs under the "Pike Pub & Brewery." Great location on the water, but the space itself can feel like a cramped dorm on full nights. Coin laundry; included continental breakfast. Internet access $0.15 per min. 7-night max. stay in summer. Reception 24hr. Check-out 11am. Reservations recommended. $21, nonmembers $24. $2 extra for private bathroom. Private rooms sleep 2-4; $54/$60. ❷

Green Tortoise Backpacker's Hostel, 1525 2nd Ave. (☎340-1222; www.greentortoise.net), between Pike and Pine St. on the #174 or 194 bus route. A young party hostel downtown; lots of people, lots of activities. Free is the name of the game: beer on F, dinner on M, daily breakfast (7-9:30am), and Internet access. Kitchen, library, patio with a water view, and laundry. Bring your own bedding; blanket $1. $20 cash key deposit required. Reception 24hr. Dorm beds $22; private rooms $50. ❷

Moore Hotel, 1926 2nd Ave. (☎448-4851 or 800-421-5508; www.moorehotel.com), at Virginia, 1 block east from Pike Place Market, next to the historic Moore Theater. Built in 1905, the Moore beckons visitors with an swanky marble-covered lobby, cavernous halls, and attentive service. "European-style" rooms—smaller beds and shared bathrooms—from one-person $39, two-person $49. Standard rooms: singles $59; doubles $68. Large suites, some with kitchen, $150. ❸

Commodore Hotel, 2013 2nd Ave. (☎448-8868 or 800-714-8868; www.commodorehotel.com), at Virginia. Pleasant decor a few blocks from the waterfront. Front desk open 24hr. Coin laundry. European-style rooms with shared bathroom on each floor, one-person $49, two-person $55. Singles $59, with bath $69; 2 beds and bath $79. ❸

The College Inn, 4000 University Way NE (☎633-4441; www.collegeinnseattle.com), at 40th St. NE. This European-style inn offers charming rooms with classy brass fixtures and attractive views of the street. All rooms share bathrooms. Included continental breakfast, free Internet access. Reservations recommended, especially around graduation time. Singles from $45; doubles from $50. Credit card required. ❸

■ FOOD

Although Seattleites may appear to subsist solely on espresso and steamed milk, the city supports a burgeoning gastronomic culture, thanks in large part to an abundance of local seafood, produce, wine, and microbrews. The freshest fish, produce, and baked goods are at **Pike Place Market.** The **University District** supports a wide variety of inexpensive and international cuisine. The **Chinatown/International District** offers tons of rice, pounds of fresh fish, and enough veggies to keep your mother happy, all at ridiculously low prices. **Puget Sound Consumer Co-ops** (**PCCs;** www.pccnaturalmarkets.com) are local health food markets at 7504 Aurora Ave. N (☎525-3586), in Green Lake, and at 6514 40th NE (☎526-7661), in the Ravenna District north of the university, as well as five other locations. The U District, West Seattle, Columbia City, and two other neighborhoods close main thoroughfares in summer for **farmers markets,** open 9am to either noon or 2pm. (☎632-5234; www.seattlefarmersmarkets.org.)

PIKE PLACE MARKET AND DOWNTOWN

In 1907, angry citizens demanded the elimination of the middle-man and local farmers began selling produce by the waterfront, creating the Pike Place Market. Business thrived until an enormous fire burned down the building in 1941. The early 1980s heralded a Pike Place renaissance, and today thousands of tourists mob the market daily, particularly in the summer. (☎624-4029; www.pikeplacemaket.org. Open M-Sa 9am-6pm, Su 11am-5pm. Produce and fish open as early as 5 am; restaurants and lounges close as late as 9pm on weekends.) In the **Main Arcade** on the west side of Pike St., fishmongers compete for audiences as they hurl fish from shelves to scales. The market's restaurants boast stellar views of the Sound.

The array of establishments in the downtown and market area can be daunting; an **Information booth,** facing the bike rack by the Main Arcade at 1st Ave. and Pike St., can give you advice one restaurants as well as other sights and activities. (☎461-5800. Open Tu-Su 10am-noon.) The more expensive restaurants south of Pike Place cater mostly to suits on power lunches and tourists, but there are many sandwich and pastry shops with more character and lower prices scattered throughout downtown.

Piroshky, Piroshky, 1908 Pike St. (☎441-6068), across the street from the front entrance of the market building. The Russian piroshky is a croissant-like dough baked around sausages, mushrooms, cheeses, salmon, or apples doused in cinnamon, running $3-4. The $5.50 soup and piroshki combo is a steal. Muscle your way into a spot to watch the piroshky process in progress while you wait. Open daily 6am-6:30pm. ❶

Emmett Watson's Oyster Bar, 1916 Pike Pl. (☎448-7721). Intimate booths with an intentionally kitschy blue checkered pattern and trinkets from the sea are the background for the highlight, the Oyster Bar Special—2 oysters, 3 shrimp, bread, and a heaping bowl of chowder, all for $7.25. Shelves of bottles show off the selection of brews. Open M-Th 11:30am-7pm, F-Sa 11:30am-8pm, Su 11:30am-6pm. ❷

Ayutthaya, 727 E Pike St. (☎324-8833), on a side alley a block up from the main market building. Thai infused with Caribbean spices in a quiet mint-green nook. All lunch entrees are $5.95 and well-sized; go for those with spice if you can handle the kick. The deep-fried banana dessert ($2.50) is worth saving room for. Open M-Sa 11am-7pm. ❷

Garlic Tree, 94 Stewart St. (☎441-5681), 1 block up from Pike Place Market, boasts intimate knowledge of the healing powers of garlic. Loads of fabulous stir-fry ($7-9). Saturday specials include $3.50 soups, $5.95 vegetable tofu stir-fry, and $4.50 seasonal salad with sweet and sour vinaigrette. Open M-Sa 11am-8pm. ❷

PIONEER SQUARE

Pioneer Square is worthy of only the truly passionate budget eaters; quality food lurks in nearly every cranny, but requires some effort find the cheap. An even better option is to take a picnic to ▨**Waterfall Garden,** on the corner of S Main St. and 2nd Ave. S. The garden sports tables and chairs and a rushing, 20 ft. high manmade waterfall that masks the sound of traffic outside. (Open daily 8am-6pm.)

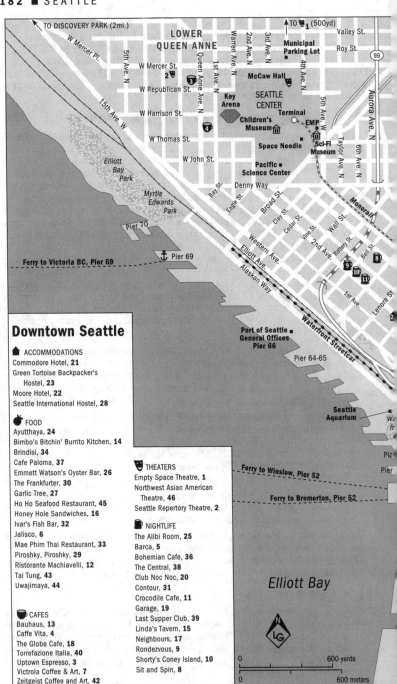

Downtown Seattle

🏠 ACCOMMODATIONS
Commodore Hotel, **21**
Green Tortoise Backpacker's
    Hostel, **23**
Moore Hotel, **22**
Seattle International Hostel, **28**

🍴 FOOD
Ayutthaya, **24**
Bimbo's Bitchin' Burrito Kitchen, **14**
Brindisi, **34**
Cafe Paloma, **37**
Emmett Watson's Oyster Bar, **26**
The Frankfurter, **30**
Garlic Tree, **27**
Ho Ho Seafood Restaurant, **45**
Honey Hole Sandwiches, **16**
Ivar's Fish Bar, **32**
Jalisco, **6**
Mae Phim Thai Restaurant, **33**
Piroshky, Piroshky, **29**
Ristorante Machiavelli, **12**
Tai Tung, **43**
Uwajimaya, **44**

☕ CAFES
Bauhaus, **13**
Caffe Vita, **4**
The Globe Cafe, **18**
Torrefazione Italia, **40**
Uptown Espresso, **3**
Victrola Coffee & Art, **7**
Zeitgeist Coffee and Art, **42**

🎭 THEATERS
Empty Space Theatre, **1**
Northwest Asian American
    Theatre, **46**
Seattle Repertory Theatre, **2**

🍸 NIGHTLIFE
The Alibi Room, **25**
Barca, **5**
Bohemian Cafe, **36**
The Central, **38**
Club Noc Noc, **20**
Contour, **31**
Crocodile Cafe, **11**
Garage, **19**
Last Supper Club, **39**
Linda's Tavern, **15**
Neighbours, **17**
Rondezvous, **9**
Shorty's Coney Island, **10**
Sit and Spin, **8**

WASHINGTON

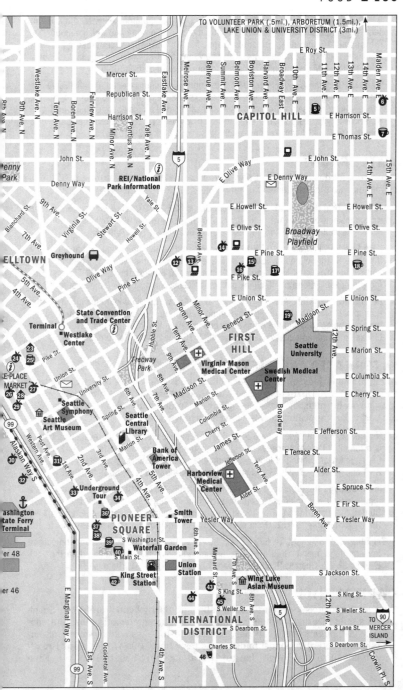

Cafe Paloma, 93 Yesler Way, (☎405-1920; www.cafepaloma.com). Mediterranean served either outside along the bustling street or inside in warm and welcoming booths. The panini ($6) are rich, served on warm, fresh bread; appetizers make great light meals, especially the meze plate, with everything from hummus to eggplant ($7.50). Open for lunch M-Sa 9:30am-5:30pm and for dinner Th-Sa 6-9:30pm. ❷

Brindisi, 106 James St., (☎223-0042). New and as yet undiscovered, Brindisi serves up authentic regional Italian cuisine between exposed brick walls. Rich sauces, meats, beans, and of course a variety of pastas and salads make up a gourmet lunch buffet for $7.95. Budget diners should stick to lunch; dinner prices veer into the realm of a splurge. Open M-F 11am-2pm for lunch, W-Sa for dinner 4:30-10pm. ❸

WATERFRONT

Waterfront food is for the most part as touristy as it comes, featuring fried foods on menus with pictures instead of words.

Mae Phim Thai Restaurant, 94 Columbia St. (☎624-2979), a few blocks north of the waterfront between 1st Ave. and Alaskan Way. Slews of pad thai junkies crowd in for cheap, delicious Thai cuisine. All dishes $6. Open M-Sa 11am-7pm. ❷

Ivar's Fish Bar, Pier 54 (☎467-8063; www.ivars.net). A fast-food window that serves the definitive Seattle clam chowder ($2). Brave flocks of aggressive seagulls for the clam and chips ($5). Open M-Th and Su 10am-midnight, F-Sa 10am-2am. ❶ For a slightly more upscale seafood meal, check out Ivar's Restaurant next door (same hours). ❸

The Frankfurter, 1023 Alaskan Way (☎622-1748; www.thefrankfurter.com), a Seattle area mini-chain with a stand right along the waterfront. This is the place if you want the best classic hot dog around or if you're craving a frank with a bit more flavor, like Thai chicken or sundried tomato ($2-5). Open M-F 10:30am-6pm, Sa-Su noon-7pm. ❶

INTERNATIONAL DISTRICT

Along King and Jackson St., between 5th and 8th Ave. east of Qwest Field, Seattle's International District is packed with great eateries. Competition keeps prices low and quality high, and unassuming facades front fabulous food. Lunch specials are particularly appealing, and the long lines move quickly.

▨ **Uwajimaya,** 600 5th Ave. S (☎624-6248; www.uwajimaya.com). The Uwajimaya Center is a full city block of groceries and gifts; it's the largest Japanese department store in the region. Don't miss the food court's panorama of delicacies, particularly the Korean BBQ and Taiwanese-style baked goods. Open M-Sa 9am-11pm, Su 9am-10pm. ❷

Ho Ho Seafood Restaurant, 653 S Weller St. (☎382-9671). Generous portions of Cantonese prepared tank-fresh seafood, including specialty steamed rock cod ($8.25). Stuffed fish hang from the ceiling in an otherwise spare but clean locale. Lunch $5-7 (until 4pm), dinner $7-12. Open M-Th and Su 11am-1am, F-Sa 11am-3am. ❷

Tai Tung, 655 S King St. (☎622-7372). Select authentic Chinese and Mandarin cuisine from the large menu. Grab a bite at the bar, where menus are plastered on the wall. Entrees $5-12. Open M-Th and Su 10am-11pm, F-Sa 10am-1:30am. ❷

CAPITOL HILL

With bronze dance-steps on the sidewalks and flashy neon storefronts, **Broadway** is a land of espresso houses, imaginative shops, elegant clubs, and eats aplenty. Although not the cheapest place to nosh, it has a great variety of cuisine options catering to most budgets and taste buds. Bus #7 runs along Broadway; bus #10 runs through Capitol Hill along more sedate 15th Ave. Free parking is behind the reservoir at Broadway Field, on 11th Ave. Don't test the parking enforcement at the establishment-specific lots right on Broadway; they will ticket and tow an illicitly parked car within minutes.

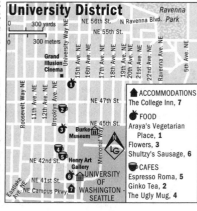

University District

ACCOMMODATIONS
The College Inn, 7

FOOD
Araya's Vegetarian Place, 1
Flowers, 3
Shultzy's Sausage, 6

CAFES
Espresso Roma, 5
Ginko Tea, 2
The Ugly Mug, 4

■ **Bimbo's Bitchin' Burrito Kitchen,** 506 E Pine St. (☎329-9978). The name explains it, and the decorations (fake palm trees and lots of plastic) prove it. Walk right on through the door to the **Cha Cha,** a similarly-decorated bar (tequila shots $3.50). Spicy Bimbo's burrito $4.25, with lots of options for extra fixins; tacos $2.50. Open M-Th noon-11pm, F-Sa noon-2am, Su 2-10pm. Happy hour daily 4-7pm; bar open nightly until 2am. ❶

Ristorante Machiavelli, 1215 Pine St. (☎621-7941), right across the street from Bauhaus (see **Cafes,** below). A small Italian place with deep Seattle roots whose simplicity in decor and food proves they have nothing to prove; get a table if you can. The gnocchi are widely considered the best in town ($8.25). Pasta $7-10. Open M-Sa 5-11pm, bar open until 2am. ❸

Honey Hole Sandwiches, 703 E Pike St. (☎709-1399). The deep red walls, abundant art, and skeleton hanging from a swing in this funky sandwich joint are only side perks to the tasty lunch menu. Abundant vegetarian, cold, and hot options—like the Texas Tease shredded BBQ chicken ($5.95)—are all served on fluffy fresh bread. Open daily 10am-2am. ❷

Jalisco Mexican Restaurant, 1467 E Republican St. (☎325-9005) on a side street off 15th St. Colorful theme decorations are the backdrop to this authentic, spicy taqueria. The Avocado Tostada ($6.75) blends smooth and spicy flavors and the three heaping tacos for $7.25 will fill you up. Open daily 11am-7:30pm. ❷

UNIVERSITY DISTRICT

The neighborhood around the immense **University of Washington** ("U-Dub"), north of downtown between Union Bay and Portage Bay, supports funky shops, scores of restaurants, and yes, coffeehouses. The best lattes and international food lie within a few blocks of University Way, known as "The Ave." Think student budget: this is probably the cheapest place to eat in the city. On Saturdays (June-Oct.) a **farmers market** at NE 50th St. and University Way NE sells fresh fruit and veggies to eager students. To get there, take Exit 169 off I-5 N, or take one of buses #70-74 from downtown, or #7 or 9 from Capitol Hill. (Open 9am-2pm.)

■ **Araya's Vegetarian Place,** 4732 University Way NE (☎524-4332). Consistently rated among the top vegan restaurants in Seattle, Araya's will satisfy any appetite, vegan or not. Lunch buffet has all the classics—pad thai and curries—as well as some more unconventional offerings ($6.50). Be sure to try the rice pudding. Buffet 11:30am-3:30pm. Open M-Th 11:30am-9pm, F-Sa 11:30am-9:30pm, Su 5-9pm. ❷

Flowers Bar & Restaurant, 4247 University Way NE (☎633-1903). This 1920s landmark was a flower shop; now, the mirrored ceiling reflects an all-you-can-eat vegetarian Mediterranean buffet ($7.50) plus sandwiches filled with everything from steak to falafel to Thai chicken ($4.95). Daily drink specials like $2 tequila shots W and $3 margaritas Sa. Open M-Sa 11am-2am, Su 11am-midnight. Bar open Th-Sa 6pm-2am. ❷

Shultzy's Sausage, 4114 University Way NE (☎548-9461). Once a crowded storefront, Shultzy's has been reincarnated as a spacious restaurant. The friendly sausage-loving owners have kept the rest of the formula—sausages and more sausages—with all the bases covered: kosher, Italian, and toppings too ($3-7). Lemonade makes a great summer accompaniment. Open M-Sa 11:30am-9pm, Su 1-7pm. ❶

FREMONT

This arts community wears its zany personality on its sleeve as well as in its food offerings. Restaurants abound in Fremont Center and along Fremont Ave and N 36th St.; not all are cheap, but most have some version of Fremont's trademark bohemian eccentricity. On Sundays a **street market** takes over N 34th St. (☎781-6776; www.fremontmarket.com. Apr.-Oct. 10am-5pm; Nov.-Mar. 10am-4pm.)

▨ **Paseo,** 4225 Fremont Ave. N (☎545-7440), up the hill from the town center, Caribbean spice oozes everywhere in this small local favorite. There is no sign, so park in the vicinity and follow your nose. For the Midnight Cuban, pick your meat (go for the pork), and watch it be piled on a bulky roll with cilantro, seasoned mayo, and sauteed onions ($5.95). Jerk chicken ($6.50) is less messy, but still tasty. Open M-Sa 11am-9 pm. ❷

Longshoreman's Daughter, 3510 Fremont Pl. N (☎633-5169). A diner with creative twists and an unbeatable day-long breakfast menu. With fluffy eggs, moist french toast, and crispy bacon, they've covered their bases ($3-9). Open daily 7:30am-4pm. ❷

Kwanjai Thai, 469 N 36th St. (☎632-3656). Thai and other Asian cuisines lurk around every corner in Fremont, and locals say this is the best; the lunch lines at the small, casual place second the praise. Elaborate curries include the Panang curry with beef, a fusion of flavors ($7.50); Pad Kee Mao rice noodles ($6.95) are lighter but just as zesty. Open M-Th 11am-9:30pm, F 11am-10pm, Sa noon-10pm, Su noon-9:30pm. ❷

BALLARD

Once a primarily Scandinavian community, Ballard's elderly population is now being replaced by hipsters and the occasional yuppie. With its identity and livelihood deeply imbedded in the fishing industry, Ballard's marine friends make it onto many menus. The best place to start in Ballard is **Market Street,** where bus routes 15, 17, and 18 all run.

Than Brothers Restaurant, 2021 NW Market St. (☎782-5715). Than Brothers is one of the originators of the pho trend that has spread throughout the city. With speedy, unbelievably cheap service, they remain one of the best. Soups served with fragrant broth, fresh noodles, thin meats, and a whole plate of garnishings. Don't pass up the complimentary melt-in-your-mouth cream puff. Soup $2.25-4.75. Open daily 11am-9pm. ❶

La Carta de Oaxaca, 5431 Ballard Ave. NW (☎782-8722). This coastal Mexican restaurant and its beautifully crafted dishes are small, but make up for size with flavor. Some of the tastiest include the albondigas (spicy meatball) soup ($4.75) and the tacos al pastor (BBQ pork with cilantro and onion, $5.25); be warned that you may find yourself ordering multiple items. Open Tu-Su 5 pm-midnight. ❷

Lockspot Cafe, 3005 NW 54th St. (☎789-4865). Charmingly uncool, with its share of local retirees and those looking for an uncluttered corner. Serves up great fish and chips ($6.50) with pitchers of beer, mostly unoccupied pool tables and a classic-filled jukebox. Open M-F 11am-2am, Sa-Su 8am-2am. ❷

GEORGETOWN

Seattle's oldest neighborhood, established with the arrival of early farming settlers in 1851, was sliced up by the introduction of I-5 in 1962. Georgetown is now experiencing a slow but steady resurgence, fueled by an influx of artists from neighborhoods become too expensive for their incomes. The constant rumble of airplanes and passing trains, however, will probably allow this neighborhood to continue to fly beneath the radar for a few more years. The food options are new, young, and eager for customers, despite a universal camouflage of bland exteriors.

- **Pig Iron Bar-BQ,** 5602 1st Ave. S (☎768-1009). This is BBQ at its best; tender meats in the sandwiches ($6.75) and entrees complimented by outstanding sides—crispy sweet potato fries, savory potato salad, and light cole slaw, to name a few; 4 sides dinner $8.75. The food comes on aluminum plates and iron skillets, while the fresh lemonade ($1.25) is served in mason jars. Open Tu-F 11am-6pm, Sa 2-9pm. ❷

- **Smarty Pants,** 6017 Airport Way S (☎762-4777). Don't let the sparse menu, exposed brick walls, and plastic baskets trick you; this place serves up sandwiches piled high with creative combinations of fresh ingredients sure to satisfy. All the classics are here, from grilled cheese and BLT to their own version of a cheesesteak. The "Gringa" takes the award: pulled pork doused with lime juice, served with mayo, lettuce, and tomato on a grilled French roll ($7.25). Open M-Sa 11am-midnight. ❷

- **Stellar Pizza,** 5513 Airport Way S (☎763-1660; www.stellarpizza.com). Spacious, with a pool table and a schizophrenic jukebox playlist, the atmosphere almost overshadows the food—but not quite. Unique toppings include Gorgonzola cheese and Yukon potatoes as well as red sauce with a real kick. 16 in. is the only size pie, ordered whole ($19-21) or half ($11-12). Open M-F 11am-midnight, Sa 3pm-midnight, Su 3-11pm. ❸

▐ CAFES

The coffee bean is Seattle's first love. One cannot walk a single block without passing a Starbucks, Tully's, or Seattle's Best Coffee (SBC). But if you're looking for a less homogenized experience, funky cafes can be found in every neighborhood, and are especially abundant on Capitol Hill and in the University District. See also **Internet Access,** p. 179, for even more places to get your coffee culture fix.

PIONEER SQUARE

- **Zeitgeist Coffee and Art,** 171 S Jackson St. (☎583-0497; www.zeitgeistcoffee.com). An artist's haven, screening films and avidly participating in the monthly gallery walk. This is truly an urban cafe, with a chill atmosphere and some of the city's best coffee to boot ($2.25). Free wireless Internet access. Open M-F 6am-7pm, Sa-Su 8am-7pm.

- **Torrefazione Italia,** 320 Occidental Ave. S (☎624-5847; www.titalia.com). The original location of what has now become a small chain still plays host to a serene front patio areas among the trees of Occidental Place. Authentic Italian coffee ($1.40-3.20) goes well with the gelato. Open M-F 6am-6pm, Sa 7am-6pm, Su 7am-5pm.

CAPITOL HILL

- **Victrola Coffee & Art,** 411 15th Ave. E (☎325-6520; www.victrolacoffee.com). On the mellow 15th Ave., this cafe possesses atmosphere in abundance; avoiding the table clutter that plagues other cafes, they balance private sitting space with an inviting, conversational sofa area. Their own espresso roasts ($2.15) are complimented by sandwiches and top-notch pastries. It's not uncommon to hear live music every night of the week. Open M-Th 5:30am-11pm, F 5:30am-midnight, Sa 6am-midnight, Su 6am-11pm.

- **Bauhaus,** 301 E Pine St. (☎625-1600). The stark, industrial architecture, adorned only with shelves of books and local art, make this a serene hangout for the artsy. Chai tea is the best non-coffee option on the menu ($1.60), although they also offer Kool-Aid ($1). Open M-F 6am-1am, Sa-Su 8am-1am.

- **The Globe Cafe,** 1531 14th Ave. (☎324-8815). Seattle's next literary renaissance is brewing here. Quotes overheard at the Globe are plastered on the tables. Fabulous all-vegan menu with fresh pastries and biscuits and gravy ($4-6). Open Tu-Su 7am-3pm.

QUEEN ANNE

Caffe Vita Coffee Roasting Company, 1005 E Pike St. (☎709-4440; www.caffe-vita.com). The source of much of the city's coffee; what they lack in decor they make up in superb blends like the cappucino ($1.85). Open M-F 6am-11pm, Sa-Su 7am-11pm.

Uptown Espresso, 525 Queen Anne Ave. N (☎285-3757; www.uptownespresso.net) The self-proclaimed "Home of the Velvet Foam," the store's first location hosts neighborhood art and opens its windows to the sky on sunny days. Fresh pastries and cheap lattes ($1.95). Open M-Th 5am-10pm, F 5am-11pm, Sa 6am-11pm, Su 6am-10pm.

UNIVERSITY DISTRICT

Ugly Mug Cafe, 1309 NE 43rd St. (☎547-3219), off University Way. A cozy nook off the main drag where the comfortable chair collection and antique lamps and tables create the atmosphere of a retro thrift store. Wide sandwich selection (turkey foccaccia $4) and homemade soups ($2.25-3.50). Open daily 7:30am-6pm.

Espresso Roma, 4201 University Way NE (☎632-6001). A pleasant patio, and quasi-former-warehouse interior result in spacious tables with an open air feel. Mocha $2. Internet access $0.15 per min, first 20min. free with a purchase. After 7pm, you get a grande for the price of a tall. Open M-F 7am-10pm, Sa-Su 8am-10pm.

Gingko Tea, 4343 University Way NE (☎632-7298). If you dig tea over coffee, you'll find a niche at Gingko. Classical music supplies the background; wood furniture and floral cushions provide the foreground. 5 types of chai ($2.55) and plentiful bubble tea ($2.45). Open M-Th 10:30am-11pm, F-Sa 10:30am-midnight, Su 11am-10pm.

FREMONT AND BALLARD

▨ Still Life, 705 N 35th St. (☎547-9850). Neighborhood classic Still Life remains bustling at the Center of the Universe. Avidly displaying local art and offering quality coffee, homemade soups ($2.75-4) and irresistible deserts to locals and tourists alike, Still Life proves there is still energy in the funky community. Open daily 7:30am-5pm.

▨ Cafe Besalu, 5909 24th Ave. NW (☎789-1463). The coffee is nice, but the real draw is Cafe Besalu's delectable pastries—from artisan bread to croissants and brioches ($0.95-3.25)—being made in the open kitchen. Open W-Su 7am-3pm.

Postmark Gelato, 3526 Fremont Pl. N (☎545-7560). Just behind Lenin's statue, the average coffee ($1.20 for drip) is overshadowed by over 20 flavors of gelato and the innumerable postcards, ranging from skyline to artsy to inexplicably zany, that are the heart of this business. Open Th-Sa 11:30am-11pm.

Fast Eddie's Lowbrow Lounge, 2311 NW Market St. (☎789-3251). Intentionally underwhelming with black paint and signs reading "koffee", the motto here is "Relax Daily." Serving Espresso Vivace coffee ($1.25-3.75), fresh bagels, and tasty pastries. Free wireless Internet. Open daily 6am-midnight.

◑ SIGHTS AND FESTIVALS

It takes only three frenetic days to get a decent look at most of the city's major sights; most are within walking distance of one another or the Metro's ride free zone (see p. 177). Seattle has unparalleled public art installations throughout the city (self-guided tours begin at the visitors center), and plentiful galleries. While dot-com success drove Seattle's collective worth up and some of the art out, the money has begun to pay off; the investments of Seattle-based millionaires have brought new architecture in EMP, the new Seattle Central Library, and the upcoming Olympic Sculpture Park. Outside cosmopolitan downtown, Seattle boasts over 300 areas of well-watered greenery (see **Waterways and Parks,** p. 200).

DOWNTOWN

■ **SEATTLE CENTRAL LIBRARY.** Opened in May 2004, the transparent new library by Rem Koolhaus, with its jagged angles and floating floors, hovers high above the downtown streets. The Book Spiral allows for four floors of constant walking through shelves, while the living room and 10th floor reading room provide comfortable, bright, and open spaces to relax. *(1000 4th Ave. at Madison St.* ☎ *386-4636; www.spl.org. 1hr. free general tours M-W 12:30pm, 2:30pm, and 4:30pm; Th-Sa 10:30am, 12:30pm, 2:30pm, and 4:30pm; Su 2pm and 4pm. 1hr. free architectural tours M-W 5:30pm and 6:45pm; Sa-Su 1:30pm and 3:30pm. Open M-W 10am-8pm, Th-Sa 10am-6pm, Su 1-5pm.)*

SEATTLE ART MUSEUM. Housed in a grandiose building designed by Philadelphia architect and father of Postmodernism Robert Venturi, the SAM balances special exhibits with the region's largest collection of African, Native American, and Asian art, and contemporary western painting and sculpture. Call for info on special musical shows, films, and lectures. Just up the hill is the museum's **Rental/ Sales Gallery,** displaying local art for perusal or purchase. The **Seattle Asian Art Museum (SAAM),** in Volunteer Park (p. 192) is home to the SAM's surplus but by no means sub-par Asian art collections; admission is free with a SAM ticket from the previous 7 days. *(100 University St., near 1st Ave.* ☎ *654-3100; www.seattleartmuseum.org. Open Tu-W and F-Su 10am-5pm, Th 10am-9pm. $15, students and ages 62 and older and 7-17 $12, under 6 free; first Th of the month free. Special exhibits $5-15. Rental/Sales Gallery: 1220 3rd Ave.* ☎ *343-1101; www.seattleartmuseum.org/artrentals. Open M-Sa 11am-5pm.)*

WATERFRONT

■ **PIKE PLACE MARKET.** The Market is worth a tour, even if food is not on your mind (In case it is, see **Food,** p. 181.) Guided tours start at the Market Heritage Center and fuse history with current anecdotes. *(1531 Western Ave.* ☎ *682-7453; www.pikeplacemarket.com. $7, ages 60 and older and under 18 $5. W-Sa 11am and 2pm, Su 2pm.)* The **Pike Place Hillclimb** descends from the south end of Pike Place Market past chic shops and ethnic restaurants to the Alaskan Way and waterfront. (Wheelchair-accessible.) The waterfront is lined with vendors and people, and if you're blessed with sun in Seattle, delivers a spectacular view of Puget Sound.

SEATTLE AQUARIUM. The aquarium's star attraction is a huge underwater dome, but harbor seals, fur seals, otters, and plenty of fish don't disappoint, either. Touch tanks and costumes delight kids. A million-dollar salmon exhibit and ladder teaches about the state's favorite fish. Feedings and interactive lectures occur throughout the day and shouldn't be missed. Next door, the **IMAX Dome** cranks out IMAX films, many of them focusing on natural events or habitats. *(1483 Alaskan Way, Pier 59.* ☎ *386-4300; www.seattleaquarium.org. Open daily Memorial Day-Labor Day 9:30am-7pm; Sept.-Mar. 10am-5pm; Apr.-May 9:30am-5pm; last admission 1hr. before closing. $12, ages 6-12 $7.50, ages 3-5 $5.25. IMAX Dome* ☎ *622-1868. Films daily 10am-10pm. $7, ages 6-12 $6. Aquarium and IMAX Dome combo ticket $17, ages 6-12 $13, 3-5 $5.25.)*

SEATTLE CENTER

The 1962 World's Fair demanded a Seattle Center to herald the city of the future. Now the Center houses everything from carnival rides to ballet; Seattle residents generally leave the Center to tourists and suburbanites, visiting only for the many festivals that take up residence on the Center's lawns, plazas, and stages. The Center is bordered by Denny Way, W Mercer St., 1st Ave., and 5th Ave., and has eight gates, each with a map of its facilities; it's also accessible via a short **monorail** which departs from the 3rd floor of downtown's **Westlake Center** (400 Pine St. ☎ 625-0280; www.seattlemonorail.com). The Center's anchor point is the **Center House,**

WASHINGTON

The Absolute Meaning of Seattle's New Downtown Library

In many of the articles and essays about Seattle's new Downtown Library it is stated or implied that as a work of architecture the new building is "refreshingly urban." Some writers go as far as to say it is more urban than the city in which it was built. As a thesis this is absolutely correct: the building's urbanity far exceeds that of the actual city, which until May 23, 2004 (the opening of the library) had "no real consciousness of its own urbanity."

Seattle is a big city. It has many tall buildings, a massive highway, and covers a wider area than Vancouver BC, also a big city with many tall buildings. But size doesn't make a difference when it comes to the matter of being urban. A small neighborhood of Vancouver BC—for example Yorktown (defined by a gleaming crop of aqua-blue and sea-green residential towers)—is more urban than all of Seattle put together (Everett-Seattle-Bellevue-Tacoma, population 3 million). Though being urban is dependent upon being in a city, a city can exist without being urban. This is exactly how some writers see Seattle: it is a city but it is not quite urban, or at least not yet conscious of its own urbanity.

What the Downtown Library did on the day its doors were opened was activate Seattle's latent urbanity. Seattle could have grown and grown, added more and more buildings here and there, but without the right building it would have never been able to become "conscious of its own urbanity." There had been several big and very expensive attempts to awaken the urban in our city, but all (Benaroya Hall, Seattle Art Museum, EMP) failed (often miserably) to shock it out of slumber and into a state of recognition.

To walk into the library is to finally see the city of Seattle. The awakening is occasioned by a series of shocks. The initial shock is caused by the sudden appearance of a fabulous (in both senses of that word) city through the blue glass and metal skin of the library. From outside, by car or on foot, downtown seems small and easily negotiated; inside, it is huge and dreamy. What was once fixed is all at once liberated and soars up to what is now a crowded sky. The effect simply astounds you. Most buildings in Seattle do not look out at Seattle, but by what we can now recognize as a provincial and unconscious preference, they look out at the mountains, the water, the natural wonders. The library doesn't attempt to do this at all. It practically ignores nature. You can barely see the waters of the Sound, only six blocks away.

The building, designed by famed Dutch architect Rem Koolhaas, fuses glass and steel in an erratic but flowing structure characterized by diamond-shaped glass panels that compose the entirety of the exterior. Simply by the numbers, it is a project of impressive proportions: with a total area of 362,987 sq. ft., the new space is able to house 1.45 million books and materials. The $165.5 million it cost purchased 18,400 cubic yards of concrete, 4644 tons of steel (or the equivalent of over 20 new Statues of Liberty), and hundreds of thousands of panes of glass, including almost 10,000 for the exterior work.

The clear, angled walls and floating platform floors allow for pedestrians and passersby to witness the activity occurring inside, completing Seattle's fusion of indoors and out. Those inside experience the Book Spiral, the only feature that has garnered more attention than the surprising design. For four floors, patrons wind their way up a gentle ramp that creates one continuous shelving space for the collection, revolutionizing book access and allowing for expansion of the collection without reorganization. Other user-friendly elements include the third floor "Living Room," filled with vibrant carpets, and the building's distinctive Nerf-like furniture for patrons to gather and read; the "Mixing Chamber," a unique interdisciplinary reference area; and the 10th floor's spacious, light-filled Reading Room, with views of Elliott Bay and nearly 40 ft. high ceilings featuring swollen white fabric squares intended to muffle noise and replicate clouds.

From top to bottom, the building forces you to look at the city—the new and old downtown buildings that surround it, the seemingly constant traffic that circulates around it. At each point within the library you discover a part or aspect of the city. For example, First Hill (the medical district), which can be viewed from the upper floors on the east of the building, seems more dense than usual. From Madison St. this part of the city may seem sparse and calm, but now you see a busy horde of buildings rushing out and up to a point in the sky. As for the usually omnipresent Mt. Rainier, the volcano may as well be in Florida; once you are in this building it is the last thing on your mind.

Upon entering Seattle's Downtown Library, one leaves behind the serene order of the city and enters the seeming disorder of the interior and its inescapable visual noise. The floating platforms, the neon-bold escalators, the tummy-twisting hallways, the gulfs of sudden space, the hanging office on the 11th floor, the brutal fences, the sloping floors—all of this and much more stimulates the senses in way that the first cast iron-framed mega-structures of the mid 19th century must have shocked Parisians and Londoners.

Here at last is a place for the ultimate urbanite.

Charles Mudede is an associate editor of the Seattle weekly The Stranger, where he has written extensively on everything from crime to theater to music to current events. He is also an adjunct professor of English at Pacific Lutheran University.

which holds a food court, stage, and information desk. The **International Fountain** squirts water 20 ft. in the air from all angles off its silver, semispherical base. The grass around it is a wonderful place to sit and relax. *(Info Desk: open daily 11am-6pm. For info about special events and permanent attractions, call ☎ 684-8582 for recorded info or 684-7200 for a live person; www.seattlecenter.com. Monorail: every 15min. M-F 7:30am-11pm, Sa-Su 9am-11pm. $1.50, ages 65 and over $0.75, 5-12 $0.50.)*

■ **EXPERIENCE MUSIC PROJECT (EMP).** Undoubtedly the biggest and best attraction at the Seattle Center is the architecturally abstract and technologically brilliant Experience Music Project. The museum is the brainchild of Seattle billionaire Paul Allen, whose pet project of a shrine to his music idol Jimi Hendrix ballooned to include the technological sophistication and foresight of Microsoft, dozens of ethnomusicologists and multimedia specialists, a collection of over 80,000 musical artifacts, the world-renowned architect Frank Gehry, and a cool $350 million. The result? The rock 'n' roll museum of the future. The building alone—consisting of sheet metal molded into abstract curves and then acid-dyed gold, silver, purple, light-blue, and red—is enough to make you gasp for breath. But it's what's inside that makes the true rock geek's heart pound; an incredible spread of interactive exhibits bring you inside influential tunes and the minds that created them. The whole thing's a treat, as well as a trip, but highlights include remnants of the guitar Hendrix smashed on a London stage; the Sound Lab's state-of-the art computer teaching devices that let you try your own hand at music making; and On Stage, a first-class karaoke stage gone haywire. Expect to spend several hours testing your creativity, jamming, and meandering in awe; you can also make a day of it, using readmission to go in and out. *(325 5th Ave. at Seattle Center. From I-5, take Exit 167 and follow signs to Seattle Center. Bus #3, 4, or 15. ☎ 367-5483 or 877-367-5483; ticket office 770-2702; www.emplive.com. Open Memorial Day-Labor Day M-Th and Su 9am-6pm, F-Sa 9am-9pm; Labor Day-Memorial Day M-Th and Su 10am-5pm, F-Sa 10am-9pm. $20; military with ID and ages 65 and older and 13-17 $16; 7-12 $15. Free live music Tu-Sa in the lounge; national acts perform almost every F and Sa in the Sky Church.)*

SPACE NEEDLE. The Space Needle was built in 1962 for the Seattle World's Fair. When this 607 ft. rotating building was constructed it was hailed as futuristic and daring. Today, the Space Needle is still internationally recognized as a symbol of Seattle. On a clear day, the Needle provides a great view and is an invaluable landmark for the disoriented. The elevator ride itself is a show—goofy operators spew Seattle trivia. The needle houses an observation tower and a high-end rotating restaurant. The Needle's top changes colors and accessories to celebrate local events. *(400 Broad St. ☎ 905-2100; www.spaceneedle.com. $13, ages 65 and older $11, 4-13 $6.)*

SCIENCE FICTION MUSEUM AND HALL OF FAME. The newest addition to Seattle Center, opened in June 2004, operates out of the EMP building. The space is as futuristic as its content, with funky lighting and dark display cases; push through the crowds of wide-eyed Trekkies for a glimpse at Darth Vader's helmet and the original alien used in the *Alien* films. *(325 5th Ave. at Seattle Center. From I-5, take Exit 167 and follow signs to Seattle Center. Bus #3, 4, or 15. ☎ 724-3428; www.sciencefictionexperience.com. $13; ages 65 and older and 7-17 $9; military with ID $11. Open daily May-Sept. 10am-8pm; Oct.-Apr. Tu-Th 10am-5pm, F-Sa 10am-9pm, Su 10am-6pm.)*

PACIFIC SCIENCE CENTER. The get-down-and-dirty approach of this museum ropes kids into loving to learn. Ride a high-rail bike, run in a giant hamster wheel, or play virtual basketball. The tropical butterfly garden is amazing and the Center also houses a **laserium,** popular among the teenage set, as well as two **IMAX theaters** that show both educational and mainstream films. *(200 2nd Ave. N, under the five white arches near the Space Needle. Monorail or bus #1, 2, 3, 4, 6, 8, 19, 24. ☎ 443-2001; www.pacsci.org. Exhibits open summer daily 10am-6pm; winter Tu-F 10am-5pm, Sa-Su 10am-*

WASHINGTON

6pm. $10, ages 65 and older $9, 3-13 $8, under 3 free. Laserium: ☎443-2850. Laser shows every 1¼hr. starting at 8pm. 2 shows Th $5; 4 shows F-Sa $7.50; 2 shows Su $7.50. IMAX: ☎443-4629. Shows daily from 10am-7pm. $7.50, ages 65 and older and 3-13 $6.50. Various combo tickets range from $13-25 for adults.)

PIONEER SQUARE

From the waterfront or downtown, it's just a few blocks south to historic **Pioneer Square,** centered around Yesler Way and 2nd Ave., home of the first Seattleites. The 19th-century buildings were restored in the 1970s as the neighborhood became the center of the city's arts community. Now home to chic shops and trendy pubs, the buildings still retain their historical intrigue. Pioneer Square is especially busy on game days as baseball moms and dads walk their children to Safeco Field to see the Mariners in action, or on fall Saturdays when the neighboring Qwest Field draws the Seahawks football crowd.

UNDERGROUND TOUR. Originally, downtown stood 12 ft. lower than it does today. This tour winds through the subterranean city of old. Be prepared for lots of company, comedy, and toilet jokes; this is the kind of classic tourist must that is corny, informative, and utterly ignored by locals. Tours depart from Doc Maynard's Pub, 608 1st Ave. "Doc" Maynard, a charismatic early resident, gave a plot of land here to one Henry Yesler to build a steam-powered lumber mill. The logs dragged to the mill's front door earned the street its nickname at the time, **Skid Row,** and the smell of the oil used to lubricate the slide was so overwhelming that the self-respecting Seattleites of the day left the neighborhood to gamblers and prostitutes. *(☎682-4646; www.undergroundtour.com. 1½hr. tours daily, roughly hourly 10am-6pm, with a changing schedule depending on the month. $10, ages 60 and older and 13-17 $8, children $5. Cash only, AAA and HI 10% discount. No reservations—arrive early on weekends.)*

INTERNATIONAL DISTRICT

▧ **WING LUKE ASIAN MUSEUM.** This prize of the International District gives a thorough description of life in an Asian-American community, investigates different Asian nationalities in Seattle, and shows work by local Asian artists. Special exhibits add even more to the tight space. One permanent exhibit is Camp Harmony, a replica of a barrack from a Japanese internment camp in WWII. The museum also hands out the helpful "Walking Tour of the International District." *(407 7th Ave. S. ☎623-5124; www.wingluke.org. Open Tu-F 11am-4:30pm, Sa-Su noon-4pm. $4, students and seniors $3, ages 5-12 $2. Free 1st Th of every month.)*

CAPITOL HILL

▧ **SEATTLE ASIAN ART MUSEUM.** What do you do when you have too much good art to exhibit all at once? Open a second museum; which is just what SAM did, creating a wonderful stand-on-its-own attraction. The collection is particularly strong in Chinese art, but most of East Asia is well represented, with exhibits on Buddhist art and daily life in Japan. *(1400 E Prospect St., in Volunteer Park, just beyond the water tower. ☎654-3100; www.seattleartmuseum.org. Open Tu-Su 10am-5pm, Th 10am-9pm. Suggested donation $3, under 12 free; free with SAM ticket from the previous 7 days; SAAM ticket good for $3 discount at SAM. First Th and Sa of every month free.)*

▧ **UNIVERSITY OF WASHINGTON ARBORETUM.** The Arboretum nurtures over 4000 species of trees, shrubs, and flowers, and maintains superb trails. There's ample space to wander wooded areas, stroll along a waterfront pathway, or explore the carefully crafted and tenderly cared-for gardens, including a serene Japanese Garden, Rhododendron Glen, and Azalea Way. Tours depart the **Graham**

Visitor Center, at the southern end of the arboretum on Lake Washington Blvd. *(10 blocks east of Volunteer Park. Bus #11, 43, or 48 from downtown. ☎ 543-8800; http:// depts.washington.edu/wpa. Open daily dawn-dusk, visitors center 10am-4pm. Japanese Garden: $2.50, students, ages 60 and older and 15 and under $1.50. Open Apr.-Nov. 10am-dusk. Free tours 1st Su of the month and by appointment.)*

VOLUNTEER PARK. Although it is unsafe (and closed) at night, the park is a popular afternoon destination. The **outdoor stage** often hosts free performances on summer Sundays. Scale the **water tower** at the 14th Ave. entrance for a stunning 360° panorama of the city and the Olympic Range, or just gaze upon the view from the fountain in front of the SAAM. The **glass conservatory** houses dazzling orchids. *(Between 11th and 15th Ave. at E Ward St., north of Broadway. Open daily Memorial Day-Labor Day 10am-7pm; Labor Day-Memorial Day 10am-4pm. Free. Conservatory: ☎ 684-4743.)*

UNIVERSITY DISTRICT

▨HENRY ART GALLERY. Specializing in modern and contemporary art, the Henry reflects its innovative curators' enthusiasm with unconventional installations and works by obscure artists. Lecture series and controversial films are featured frequently. Coming in early 2005 is an exhibit of new work by Axel Lieber, a German artist who uses sculpture to explore domestic environments. *(At the intersection of NE 41st St. and 15th Ave. NE ☎ 616-9894; www.henryart.org. Open Tu-Su 11am-5pm, Th 11am-8pm. $8, ages 62 and older $6, students free. Free Th after 5pm.)*

THOMAS BURKE MUSEUM OF NATURAL HISTORY AND CULTURE. Home to the only dinosaur bones on display in Washington and a superb collection on Pacific Rim cultures. Kid-friendly explanations of the natural history of Washington's formation make for a casual environment. Across the street, the astronomy department's old stone **observatory** is open to the public. *(NE 45th St. and 17th Ave. NE, in the northwest corner of the UW campus. ☎ 543-5590; observatory 543-0126; www.washington.edu/ burkemuseum. Open daily 10am-5pm and until 8pm on Th $8, ages 60 and over $6.50, students $5, under 5 free. First Th of the month free.)*

MUSEUM OF HISTORY AND INDUSTRY. Declaring that they "believe in the power of history to enrich the present and enlighten the future," MOHAI brings a range of exhibits focusing on Seattle's history from geographical, ecological, and cultural angles. Permanent exhibits include Seattle's Great Fire of 1889, "Salmon Stakes," on the controversial history and decline of the species, and Boeing's first floatplane, which dangles from the ceiling of the exhibit. *(2700 24th Ave. by the Arboretum. ☎ 324-1126; www.seattlehistory.org. Open daily 10am-5pm and 10am-8pm the first Th of each month. $7, ages 62 and older and 6-17 $5. First Th of month free.)*

FREMONT

Fremont is home to residents who pride themselves on their love of art, antiques, and the liberal atmosphere of their self-declared "center of the world" under Rte. 99. Although perhaps not the same counter-culture center of decades past, it remains deliberately against the grain; twice in the past 10 years Fremont has applied (unsuccessfully) to secede from the city of Seattle. Evidence of the neighborhood's communal oddity abounds in the sights around town: A statue entitled **"Waiting for the Interurban"** laments the loss of the neighborhood's public transportation to downtown. The immense **troll** beneath the Aurora Bridge on N 35th St. grasps a Volkswagen Bug with a confounded expression. Some say kicking the bug's tire brings good luck; others say it hurts the foot. **Vladimir Lenin** resides in statue form at the corner of N 36th St. and N Fremont Pl.; this work from the former Soviet Union will be around until it's bought by a permanent collection, presumably of Soviet artwork.

DE LIBERTAS QUIRKAS

Of all the corners of Seattle, Fremont has undeniably set itself furthest apart; its motto is "De Libertas Quirkas," or "freedom to be peculiar." Fremont proudly flaunts its individuality. Here are the top 10 things that make Fremont, well, Fremont:

10 History House. This house preserves the stories of Fremont and its surrounding neighborhoods. Displays are mostly handmade and occasionally constructed by high school students. They are, nonetheless, very informative. (790 N 34th St. ☎ 675-8875; www.historyhouse.org. $5 suggested donation. Open W-Su noon-5pm.)

9 Fremont Drawbridge. Fremonters consider this bright blue and red contraption the only proper way to enter town.

8 Rocket Monument. For unknown reasons, Fremonters believe the 53 ft. rocket perched at N 34th St. and Evanston Ave. marks the Center of the Universe.

7 Fremont Fair. For over 30 years, Fremont has celebrated the summer Solstice with gusto. This festival features a costume and float parade of epic proportions, topped by a nude bicycle ride. The event is for charity; all attendees are asked to donate to the Fremont Public Association. (☎ 694-6706; www.fremontfair.com.)

BALLARD

Despite having incorporated into Seattle almost a hundred years ago, Ballard remains proud of its particular roots, grounded in the fishing and Scandinavian communities; the most decadent annual gala is the **Syttende Mai** (May 17th) festival in honor of Norway's Constitution Day. The day features a parade with floats and clowns as well as traditional food and dance. The neighborhood has recently begin to see a surge in its young population, bringing a new hipster energy to the area. Ballard is bordered by Shilshole Bay to its west and Salmon Bay to its south; to get there follow Rte. 99 to N 46th St. which becomes NW Market St. or use bus routes 15, 17, or 18 that also arrive at NW Market St.

▧ HIRAM M. CHITTENDEN LOCKS. Lying across the Lake Washington Ship Canal, the system of locks is the mediator between the freshwater lake and Puget Sound. A birds-eye view of the whole contraption—consisting of two navigational locks, a dam, a spillway, and a fish ladder—allows for easy understanding. The **Fish Ladder,** an innovation in 1916, still helps the salmon and steelhead gradually travel upstream via 21 steps, or weirs. Adjacent to the locks is the **Carl S. English, Jr. Botanical Garden,** which flourishes in the spring and summer with more than 500 species of plants and flowers. (3015 NW 54th St. off Market St. ☎ 783-7059. Open daily 7am-9pm. Free tours M-F 1 and 3pm, Sa 11am or by request.)

NORDIC HERITAGE MUSEUM. Ballard's Scandinavian heritage is still evident in the wide variety of Scandinavian eateries and shops along Market St. The museum presents realistic exhibits on the history of Nordic immigration and influence in the US. Stumble over cobblestones in old Copenhagen or visit the slums of New York City that turned photographer and Danish immigrant Jacob Riis into an important social reformer. The museum hosts numerous **Nordic concerts** by national and international musicians throughout the year and a handful of Scandinavian festivals; **Tivoli Days** in July feature beer gardens, folk music, and a salmon BBQ. (3014 NW 67th St. ☎ 789-5707; www.nordicmuseum.com. Open Tu-Sa 10am-4pm, Su noon-4pm. $4, students and ages 65 and older $3, 6-18 $2.)

ANNUAL EVENTS

Pick up a copy of the visitors center's *Calendar of Events* (www.seeseattle.org/events), published every season, for event coupons and an exact listing of innumerable area happenings. The first Thursday evening of each month, the art community sponsors **First Thursday,** a free and well-attended gallery walk where galleries and art-sporting cafes open their doors to the city. Watch for **street fairs** in the University District during mid- to late May and at Pike Place Market over Memorial Day weekend, and also the **Fremont Fair** (☎ 694-6706; www.fremontfair.com) in mid-June, held in honor of the summer solstice. Don't miss its accompanying **Fremont Solstice Parade**, led by dozens of bicyclists wearing nothing but brightly-colored body paint. The International District holds its annual two-day bash in mid-July, featuring arts and crafts booths, East Asian and Pacific food booths, and presentations by a range of groups from the Radical Women/Freedom Socialist Party to numerous cultural dance groups. For more info, call **Chinatown Discovery** (☎ 382-1197; www.seattlechinatowntour.com). Capitol Hill bursts into rainbows at the end of June during **Seattle Pride** (☎ 324-0405; www.seattlepride.org), when the GLBT community anchors a weekend of marches and events.

Puget Sound's yachting season begins in May. **Maritime Week**, during the third week of May, and the **Shilshole Boats Afloat Show** (☎ 634-0911; www.boatsafloatshow.com), in August, give area boaters a chance to show off their crafts. Over the 4th of July weekend, the Center for Wooden Boats sponsors the free **Wooden Boat Festival** (☎ 382-2628; www.cwb.org) on Lake Union. Blue blazers and deck shoes are *de rigueur.* Size up the entrants (over 100 wooden boats), then watch a demonstration of boat-building skills. The big finale is the **Quick and Daring Boatbuilding Contest,** when nautical hopefuls build and sail wooden boats of their own design using a limited kit of tools and materials. Plenty of music, food, and alcohol keep the sailing smooth. Listed below are other noteworthy festivals in the Seattle area.

Northwest Folklife Festival (☎ 684-7300; www.nwfolklife.org), over Memorial Day weekend, 11am-11pm. One of Seattle's most notable events, held at the Seattle Center. Dozens of booths, artists, and musicians celebrate the area's heritage. $5 donation.

Bite of Seattle (☎ 425-283-5050; www.biteofseattle.com), in mid-July at the Seattle Center. Seattle wants you to "Get your Bite on": snacks to full meals from free to $5. Decide the best for yourself while listening to music on over a half dozen stages. Free.

Seattle Seafair (☎ 728-0123; www.seafair.com), spread over 4 weeks beginning in early July. The biggest, baddest festival of them all. Each neighborhood contributes with street fairs, parades, balloon races, musical entertainment, and a seafood orgy, capped by a city-wide torch run at the end of July. Bring your earplugs for the hydroplane races on Lake Washington and thunderous airshows by the US Navy Blue Angels in early Aug.

6 **Outdoor movies.** Fremont boasts two outdoor movie locations. F, **Cinema Dali,** at N 34th St. and Stone Way N, shows cult films accompanied by costumes and contests. Sa, the party moves to N 35th St. and Phinney Ave. N, where it's BYOC (bring your own couch). The theater shows "Pop Classics" with local improv on the side. (☎ 781-4230; www.outdoorcinema.net/seattle.com.)

5 **Oktoberfest.** Street fair. Beer. Lederhosen. Toto, I don't think we're in Germany anymore. (☎ 633-0422; www.fremontoktoberfest.com. 3rd weekend in Sept.)

4 **Dinosaur topiary.** Maintained by a local artist, Dino's Dinos, as they're fondly called, pose for portraits on the corner of Canal St. and N 34th St.

3 **Waiting for the Interurban.** At the neighborhood center, five people, a baby, and a dog forever wait for the public transportation that will never come.

2 **State of Lenin.** If there are any doubts about Fremont's political leanings, this 7-ton Soviet leader looming over the corner of N 36th and N Fremont Pl. should clear things up.

1 **Fremont Troll.** Underneath the Aurora Bridge lives Fremont's most famous resident: the enormous car-munching troll. The result of a public art competition, he has his own holiday: Trolloween, on Oct. 31.

Bumbershoot (☎281-7788; www.bumbershoot.org), over Labor Day weekend. A massive 4-day arts festival that caps off the summer, held at the Seattle Center. Attracts big-name rock bands, street musicians, and a young, exuberant crowd. An amazing chance—and deal—to hear an almost inconceivable amount of music. 4 days $48-55; 2 days $26-28; 1 day $15-25. Tickets are cheaper if bought in advance. Additional tickets needed for certain big-name concerts or events.

🎵 ENTERTAINMENT

Seattle has one of the world's most famous underground music scenes and a bustling theater community to boot (said to be second only to New York and Chicago), and supports performance in all sorts of venues, from bars to bakeries. The half-price tickets of big performance houses and abundance of alternative theaters means high-quality drama at downright low prices is yours to enjoy. The free **Out to Lunch** series (☎623-0340; schedules at www.downtownseattle.com) brings everything from reggae to folk dancing to downtown parks, squares, and office buildings during summer (June-Sept., M-F noon-1:30pm).

MUSIC AND DANCE

The **Seattle Opera** performs favorites from October to August in newly opened **McCaw Hall.** The culmination of a 10-year renovation project, the new Opera House reopened in 2003, flaunting a glass facade, as well as decked out lobbies, a modernized auditorium, and a new cafe. Opera buffs should reserve well in advance, although rush tickets are sometimes available. (☎389-7676; www.seattleopera.com. Ticket office is located at 1020 John St., one level below the 13 Coins Restaurant parking lot. Students and seniors can get half-price tickets 1½hr. before the performance at the ticket office. Open M-F 9am-5pm; tickets from $35.) The **Pacific Northwest Ballet** also performs at McCaw Hall. In 2005, look for a trio of Stravinsky compositions (Feb. 3-13), *The Merry Widow* (Mar. 17-27), three pieces by prominent American choreographers (Apr. 14-24), and *Silver Lining* (Jun. 2-12), which will honor the retirement of the company's founding artistic directors. (☎441-2424; www.pnb.org. Half-price rush tickets available to students and seniors 30min. before showtime. Tickets from $15.) The **Seattle Symphony** performs in the recently-built **Benaroya Hall,** 200 University St. at 3rd Ave., from September to June. (☎212-4700, tickets 215-4747; www.seattlesymphony.org. Ticket office open M-F 10am-6pm, Sa 1-6pm. Tickets from $15, most from $25-39; ages 60 and older half-price; students $10 day of show. Call ahead; ticket availability varies by season.) Even if you won't be hearing the symphony, drop by the concert hall to take in glass chandeliers and a Rauschenberg mural. (☎215-4895. Tours Tu and F noon and 1pm. Free.) Free organ concerts attract crowds on the 1st Monday of the month at 12:30pm. The University of Washington offers its own program of student recitals and concerts by visiting artists. The World Series showcases dance, theater and chamber music (tickets $25-40). Some lectures and dances are cheaper ($5-10). Contact the **Meany Hall** box office, 4001 University Way. Half-price student tickets are available 30min. before show at the box office. (☎543-4880; www.meany.org. Open Oct.-May M-F 10am-6pm; June-Sept. M-F 10:30am-4:30pm.)

THEATER

The city hosts an exciting array of first-run plays and alternative works, particularly by talented amateur groups. Rush tickets are often available at nearly half-price on the day of the show (cash only) from **Ticket/Ticket** (p. 179).

The Empty Space Theatre, 3509 Fremont Ave. N (☎547-7500; www.emptyspace.org), 1½ blocks north of the Fremont Bridge. Comedies in the small space attract droves. Season runs Oct. to early July. In celebration of 35 years, the 2005 season will show five shows and add the Kitchen Series, 4 workshops of new plays in between the main shows. Tickets $20-40. Under 25 $10, previews $22. Half-price tickets 30min. before curtain. Box office open on show days Tu-Su noon-5pm, non-show days Tu-F noon-5pm.

Seattle Repertory Theatre, 155 Mercer St. (☎443-2222; www.seattlerep.org), the wonderful Bagley Wright Theatre and Leo T. Kreielsheimer Theatre share one building but have their own stages in the Seattle Center. Contemporary and classic productions (including Shakespeare). Tickets $15-45 (cheaper on weekdays), ages 65 and older $32, under 25 $10. Rush tickets 30min. before curtain $20. Box office open daily noon-8pm during season (Sept.-June).

Northwest Asian American Theatre, 409 7th Ave. S (☎340-1445; www.nwaat.com), next to the Wing Luke Asian Museum. Young space features pieces by Asian Americans and hosts the **Northwest Asian American Film Festival** (www.nwaaff.org) in late Sept. Tickets $25, ages 65 and older and under 12 $15. Open M-F 10am-6pm.

CINEMA

Seattle is a cinematic paradise. Most of the theaters that screen non-Hollywood films are on Capitol Hill and in the U District. On summer Saturdays, Fremont **outdoor cinema** begins at dusk at 670 N 34th St., in the U-Park lot by the bridge, behind the Red Door Alehouse. Enter as early as 7pm for a good seat to catch live music that starts at 8pm. **TCI Outdoor Cinema** shows everything from classics to cartoons for free at Gasworks Park. (☎694-7000. Live music 7pm-dusk.) Aspiring independent filmmakers or actors/actresses should check out the Alibi Room for readings (see **Nightlife,** below). To see what's playing in town, call ☎443-4567 (moviefone).

The Egyptian, 801 E Pine St. (☎323-4978), at Harvard Ave. on Capitol Hill. This Art Deco art-house is best known for hosting the **Seattle International Film Festival** in the last week of May and 1st week of June. The festival's director retrospective often features a personal appearance by the director in question. Festival series tickets available at a discount. $9, ages 65 and older $6. (☎324-9997; www.seattlefilm.com.)

Grand Illusion Cinema, 1403 NE 50th St. (☎523-3935; www.grandillusioncinema.org), in the U District at University Way. Plays rare international films and frequently revives old classics and hard-to-find films. One of the last independent theaters in Seattle. $7.50, ages 65 and older and under 12 $5, matinees $5.

The Harvard Exit, 807 E Roy St. (☎323-8986), on Capitol Hill, at the north end of Broadway. Excellent classic and foreign films. Converted women's club has a 1920s lobby with grand piano and an enormous antique projector. $9, ages 65 and older $6.

SPORTS

Seattleites cheered when the beloved home team, the **Mariners,** moved out of the Kingdome, where in 1995 sections of the roof fell into the stands. The "M's" are now playing baseball in the modern **Safeco Field,** at 1st Ave. S and S Royal Brougham Way, under an enormous retractable, presumably collapse-proof roof. Saving the game from frequent rain-outs is simply a matter of pushing a single button labelled "Go." (☎622-4487; www.mariners.org or www.ticketmaster.com. Tickets from $7.) Seattle's football team, the **Seahawks,** are perennial NFC West contenders whose new stadium, the recently-dubbed **Qwest Field,** is one of the most modern in the world. (☎628-0888; www.seahawks.com. Tickets from $20.)

On the other side of town and at the other end of the aesthetic spectrum, the sleek **Key Arena** in the Seattle Center hosts Seattle's NBA basketball team, the **Supersonics.** (☎628-0888; www.supersonics.com. Tickets from $11.) The men now share their turf with their female counterparts, the **Seattle Storm.** (☎628-0888; www.storm.wnba.com. Tickets from $10.) The **University of Washington Huskies** football team reigns supreme at scenic Husky Stadium on Union Bay. Call the Athletic Ticket Office (☎543-2200; www.gohuskies.com) for Husky tickets and prices.

▨ NIGHTLIFE

Seattle has moved beyond beer to a new nightlife frontier: the cafe-bar. The popularity of espresso bars in Seattle might lead one to conclude that caffeine is more intoxicating than alcohol, but often a diner by day brings on a band, breaks out the disco ball, and pumps out the microbrews by night. Many locals tell tourists that the best spot to go for guaranteed good beer, live music, and big crowds is Pioneer Square, where UW students dominate the bar stools and one cover gains you access to almost a dozen establishments; the neighborhood, however, also has a reputation for being unsafe at night. You may prefer to go to Capitol Hill or up Rte. 99 to Fremont, where the atmosphere is usually more laid-back than in the Square. Wherever you go, but especially downtown, stay alert—Seattle is a big city, and has the homelessness and crime that come with size.

DOWNTOWN

▨ **The Alibi Room,** 85 Pike St. (☎ 623-3180; www.alibiroom.com), across from the Market Cinema, in the Post Alley in Pike Place. A remarkably friendly local indie filmmaker hangout, with a bookshelf of scripts at the entrance for your perusal. Bar with music open all week. Downstairs dance floor open F and Sa. Mediterranean style cuisine; brunch Sa-Su. No cover. Open daily 11am-3pm and 5pm-2am.

Club Noc Noc, 1516 2nd Ave. (☎ 223-1333; www.clubnocnoc.com). Casual and spacious, with exposed brick walls, lots of red lighting, and a real dance floor, Club Noc Noc embraces patrons from goths to frat boys. The DJs are uniformly talented and range from synth pop and goth to hip-hop. Drink specials feature Pabst Blue Ribbon (M $0.50, Su $0.25) and an outstanding 5-9pm happy hour ($1 for well drinks and more PBR). Cover varies from free to $5. Open M-F 5pm-2am, Sa-Su 5pm-5am.

BELLTOWN

Often regarded as having the best nightlife in the city, Belltown lies just north of downtown and south of Seattle Center. In the process of becoming more upscale, Belltown retains its liveliness, hot bar and music scene, and a few rough edges.

▨ **Rondezvous,** 2322 2nd Ave. (☎ 441-5823; www.jewelboxtheater.com). Once the home the city's underbelly of punks and drunks, this dive bar has been made swankier, with a new window-filled front and rich drapes, but maintains the character that makes it one of the hotspots of the downtown scene. The Jewel Box Theater in the back shows mainstream films and cabaret. Open daily 3pm-2am.

Sit & Spin, 2219 4th Ave. (☎ 441-9484). A true split personality, combining club and cocktail bar in the back with a cafe and laundromat in the front. This joint sports linoleum floors and low couches and tables, and takes itself about as seriously as you'd expect from a bar with washing machines humming in the background. The cafe's burgers ($4.75) and beers ($2.25-5) are perfect for this chill but popular hangout. Occasional cover for music ($5). Open M-Th and Su 11am-midnight, F-Sa 11am-2am.

Crocodile Cafe, 2200 2nd Ave. (☎ 441-5611; www.thecrocodile.com), at Blanchard in Belltown. Cooks from scratch by day (breakfast is the specialty) and features quality live music by night (Tu-Sa). Proudly young and hip, with a sign outside that warns patrons to leave their "sexism, racism, and general bigotry" at the door. Shows usually start 9pm; some require advance ticket purchase, available through TicketWeb (www.ticketweb.com). 21+ after 9pm. Cover $6-22. Cafe open Tu-Sa 11am-11pm, Su 9am-3pm; club open Tu-Sa 8am-2am, Su 9am-3pm.

Shorty's Coney Island, 2222 2nd Ave. (☎ 441-5449; www.shortydog.com). Taking the dive bar atmosphere to a new level with Coney Island style hot dogs ($2.75-4), carnival decor, and an arcade, Shorty's is nothing if not unique. Keep it real with a beer ($3-6) or a whisky. Open daily noon-2am.

PIONEER SQUARE

Pioneer Square provides a happening scene, dominated by twentysomethings, frat kids, and cover bands. A number of the area bars participate in a joint cover (F-Sa $10, M-Th and Su $5) that will let you wander from bar to bar to sample the bands. These venues are listed below. **Larry's Blues Cafe,** 209 1st Ave. S (☎624-7665; www.larrysbluescafe.com), a smaller venue, features great blues and jazz nightly (no cover weekdays). Not part of the Pioneer Square joint cover because it's often free, **J & M Cafe and Cardroom,** 201 1st Ave. (☎292-0663; www.jandmcafeandcardroom.com) is in the center of Pioneer Square.

■ **Bohemian Cafe,** 111 Yesler Way (☎447-1514), pumps reggae every night. The cafe, bar, and stage are all adorned with art from Jamaica. Live shows 6 nights per week, often national acts on weekends. Happy hour 4-7pm. Part of the joint cover. Open M-Th and Sa 4pm-2am, F 3pm-2am.

Contour, 807 1st Ave. (☎447-7704; www.clubcontour.com). Intimate and elegant, the large paintings, swanky statues, and wide windows make a decadent late night dance spot antidote to frat parties. Happy hour M-F 4-8pm, Sa-Su 2-8pm with $2 food menu, $2 beer, and $3.50 well drinks. Cover ranges from free to $12. Open M 3pm-2am, Tu-Th 11:30am-2am, F 11:30am-5am, Sa 2pm-5am, Su 2pm-2am.

Last Supper Club, 124 S Washington St. (☎748-9975; www.lastsupperclub.com), at Occidental. An oasis of mellow class in a row of frat parties, with two dance floors; DJed with everything from 70s disco (F) to funky house, drum & bass, and trance (Su). Cover varies, about $9-15. Open W-Su 5pm-2am.

The Central, 207 1st Ave. S (☎622-0209; www.centralsaloon.com). Originally a saloon and later one of the early venues for grunge, its newest incarnation is as a music hangout for bikers. Live rock 6 nights a week at 9:30pm. Tu open mic. Part of the joint cover. Open daily 11:30am-2am, kitchen closes 8pm.

CAPITOL HILL

East off of Broadway, Pine St. is cool lounge after cool lounge. Find your atmosphere and acclimatize. West off of Broadway, Pike St. has the clubs that push the limits (gay, punk, industrial, fetish) and break the sound barrier.

■ **Linda's Tavern,** 707 E Pine St. (☎325-1220). A quirky post-gig local scene, with pool tables, a giant buffalo head, and Southern comfort foods. On M and Th nights a live DJ spins jazz, alternative, and old rock. Expanded food and booze on weekends. No cover. Open daily 4pm-2am; happy hour nightly 7-9pm.

■ **Neighbours,** 1509 Broadway (☎324-5358; www.neighboursonline.com). Enter from the alley on Pike. A gay dance club for 20 years and fixture in the now prevalent gay scene, Neighbours prides itself on techno slickness. Frequent drag nights and special events. Open Tu, W, and Su 4pm-2am, Th 4pm-3am, F-Sa 4pm-4am.

Barca, 1510 11th Ave. (☎325-8263; www.barcaseattle.com). Eurotrash at its finest, with plush decor, mood lighting, and tight pants everywhere you look. A mezzanine vodka bar ($2-6) completes the package. Open daily 4pm-2am.

Garage, 1134 Broadway (☎322-2296; www.garagebilliards.com). Gimmicky but fun, this 14-lane bowling alley is intentionally vintage, often crowded, and a refreshing contrast to the average bar or dance scene. Great outdoor patio. Pool $5 per hr., lanes $10 per hr. Open daily 3pm-2am. Happy hour daily 3-7pm with $2.50 pints and $3 wells.

FREMONT AND BALLARD

■ **Fu Kun Wu @ Thaiku,** 5410 Ballard Ave. (☎706-7807). Designed in the spirit of a Chinese apothecary, this unique spot sits in the back of Thai joint Thaiku. The herbal cocktails, infused with teas and roots, claim to provide a range of healthful benefits; don't miss the Yojito, a Mojito with herbs that render it so strong they only allow one per person (cocktails $7, $5 during daily happy hour 5-7pm, when the restaurant's appetizers are $3). Music is anything from live jazz to techno. Open daily 5pm-midnight.

Fremont Dock, 1102 N 34th St. (☎633-4300; www.fremontdock.com). While a dive bar seems uncharacteristic of deliberately hip Fremont, the dark and smoky Dock seems more genuine than much of the neighborhood. Beer ($2.50) and apple pie ($2.75) are an unlikely but popular pairing. M happy hour, Su ladies night. Open daily 7am-2am.

Suite G, 513 N 36th St. (☎632-5656). Unpretentious to a point (its name is simply the name of the suite), Suite G is a casual hangout with a friendly staff and salad instead of fries. Smokers reign, and live music of all sorts enlivens the mood (Th-Sa 9pm; cover $3-5). Specialty drinks (martinis are the best) average $6. Open daily 11:30am-2am.

Tractor Tavern, 5213 Ballard Ave. NW (☎789-3599; www.tractortavern.com). The bar and BBQ are simple and decent enough, but the Tractor's live music selection that sets it ahead. Almost every night you'll find alternative country, rockabilly, folk, groove, jazz, straight-up rock bands, and anything else you've never heard of. The quirky clientele alone make the Tavern worth a visit. Open daily 9:30pm-2am.

🎧 WATERWAYS AND PARKS

Due to the foresight of Seattle's settlers and the architectural genius of the Olmsteds, the city enjoys an unending string of verdant parks and pristine waterways.

LAKE UNION. Sailboats fill Lake Union, situated between Capitol Hill and the University District, and the **Center for Wooden Boats,** home of the **Maritime Heritage Museum,** boast the ability to teach you how to sail in under 30min. and can supply you a boats once you've learned, with a moored flotilla of new and restored craft for rent. *(1010 Valley St. ☎382-2628; www.cwb.org. Free. Open daily 11am-8pm. Rowboats weekdays $13 per person, $19 for two, weekends $20/$30, catboats from $16, sloops from $24.)* The lake makes for an intimate kayaking spot too, with city views and abundant houseboats; rentals available at **Northwest Outdoor Center.** *(2100 Westlake Ave. ☎281-9694, www.nwoc.com. Single $11 per hour, $38 per day; doubles $14 per hour, $46 per day.)* 🖾**Gasworks Park,** at the north end of Lake Union, fills the grounds of a retired oil-refining facility, necessitating frequent EPA checks; still, the reclaimed park has one of the best lakeside and skyline views around and some of the most spirited city musicians providing a beat to the beauty. Fittingly, the park hosts a **4th of July Fireworks show** and is a celebrated kite-flying spot. *(Take bus #26 from downtown to N 35th St. and Wallingford Ave. N.)* **Gasworks Park Kite Shop** provides for the high-fliers. *(3420 Stone Way. ☎633-4780. Open W-Sa 10am-5pm, Su 11am-5pm.)* **Urban Surf** rents surfboards, in-line skates, snowboards, and kiteboards. *(2100 N Northlake Way, opposite park entrance. ☎545-9463; www.urbansurf.com. Boards $18 per day. Skates $7 per hr., $18 per day. Open M-F 10am-7pm, Sa 10am-5pm, Su 11am-5pm.)*

🖾**GREEN LAKE.** Now a city hotspot for strolling, biking, and skating, this lake was eagerly bought up for development during early settlement in the 1800s. In 1910, under the direction of the more famous Olmsted's nephew, John C., a beautification project lowered the lake's water level by 7 ft. to open more shoreline as park land. The tinkering with natural shorelines and streams led to chronic stagnation in the lake that remains today. Still, the picturesque 2¾ mi. paved trail close to the lakeshore bustles on sunny summer days like a California beachfront. The 3¼ mi. unpaved outer trail is closer to cars than the lake, and so less claustrophobic. Sailors and windsurfers take to the water, while birdwatchers find plenty to spy on land. A great place for the sporty to see and be seen. *(Between E Green Lake Dr. N and W Green Lake Dr. N. ☎684-4075. Open dawn-dusk. Parking in three lots: at Latona Ave. N and E Green Lake Way N, 7312 W Green Lake Way N, and 5900 W Green Lake Way N.)*

MARYMOOR PARK. A favorite biking spot for those fleeing the city, Marymoor Park is a swath of open grasslands dotted with sports fields and trails but embedded in the ever expanding suburban sprawl of Redmond. The **Sammamish River Trail,** popular for biking, running, and horseback riding, starts in the park and extends nearly 10 mi. to Bothell Landing. Also home to the Marymoor Climbing Structure, a.k.a. **Big Pointy,** a 45 ft. structure that's a treat for those who don't want to wait in line at REI. Also hosts open air concerts in its amphitheater in the summer, attracting big name folk and rock acts. *(6046 W Lake Sammamish Pkwy. NE, south off Rte. 520. ☎296-2966. Concerts: ☎628-0888; www.concertsatmarymoor.com.)*

ALKI BEACH. The site of original European settlement to the area, this 2½ mi. stretch of beach in West Seattle (across the West Seattle Bridge) brims with bikers, walkers, rollerbladers and especially teenagers on sunny summer afternoons. In the fall and winter it makes for a calming stormy walking spot. Alki is far enough from the heart of the city to offer spectacular views, particularly from **Duwamish Head** at the north end and from **Alki Point and Light Station,** 3201 Alki Ave. SW, maintained by the Coast Guard, at the tip of the point.

DISCOVERY PARK. Across the canals and west of the locks lie the 534 bucolic acres of Discovery Park at 36th Ave. W and W Government Way on a lonely point of the Magnolia District, south of Golden Gardens Park. Grassy fields and steep, eroding bluffs provide a haven for birds forced across Puget Sound by bad weather around the Olympic Mountains. The park is also prime strolling territory for Seattleites; there is an extensive series of trails popular for joggers, including a 2¾ mi. Loop Trail that circles the park. A **visitors center** is right by the entrance. The popular beach and lighthouse are also open for exploration, but only via free **shuttle** from the visitors center. The **Daybreak Star Indian Cultural Center** at the park's north end is operated by the United Indians of All Tribes Foundation as a social, cultural, and educational center. *(Open daily 6am-11pm. Bus #24 or 33. Visitors center: 3801 W Government Way. ☎386-4236. Open Tu-Su 8:30am-5pm. Free guided tours Memorial Day-Labor Day Sa-Su 9am and 11am. Spring and fall, guided bird walks upon request. Beach: open June-Sept. Sa-Su 11:45am-4:30pm. Donation requested. Cultural Center: ☎285-4425; www.unitedindians.com. Open M-F 9am-5pm, Sa 10am-noon, Su noon-5pm. Free.)*

WOODLAND PARK AND WOODLAND ZOO. Woodland Park is mediocre, but the zoo has won a bevy of AZA awards (the zoo Oscars, if you will) for best new exhibits. The African Savanna and the Northern Trail exhibits are both full of zoo favorites: grizzlies, wolves, lions, orangutans, giraffes, and zebras; the Elephant Forest, where the large animals lounge in a Thai logging village and forest pool is worth checking out as well. *(5500 Phinney Ave. or 601 N 59th St. N I-5 50th St. exit or N 50th St. Bus #5 from downtown. ☎684-4800; www.zoo.org. Park open daily 4:30am-11:30pm. Zoo open daily May to mid-Sept. 9:30am-6pm; mid-Mar. to Apr. and mid-Sept. to mid-Oct. 9:30am-5pm; mid-Oct. to March 9:30am-4pm. $14, ages 65 and older $11, 6-17 $9.)*

⚑ OUTDOOR ACTIVITIES

🚲 BIKING. Biking, for commuting and recreation alike, is very popular in Seattle. The city prides itself on 30 mi. of bike-pedestrian trails, 90 mi. of signed bike routes, and 16 mi. of bike lanes on city streets. Almost 10,000 **cyclists** compete in the 190 mi. **Seattle to Portland Classic (STP)** race in late June or early July. Call the

bike hotline (☎522-2453; www.cascade.org) for info. On **Bicycle Saturdays/Sundays** from May to September, Lake Washington Blvd. is open to cyclists exclusively from 10am to 6pm; though the schedule is subject to change, it is usually the second Saturday and third Sunday of each month. Call the **Seattle Parks and Recreation Activities Office** (☎684-4075; www.cityofseattle.net/parks) for info.

Most bike stores in the area have the Bicycle and Pedestrian Program's bikers map of the area so you can create your own route; some tried and true options follow. For 5 mi. between Madrona and Seward Parks, **Lake Washington Boulevard** offers a calm pedal and great views. The **Elliott Bay Trail** starts at Pier 70 and winds for 1½ mi. along the waterfront to Elliott Bay Marina. The trail up **Blue Ridge,** also a short jaunt of only 2 mi., delivers spectacular views of Puget Sound and, weather permitting, the Olympic Mountains. (Follow Aurora Ave. N to N 105th St. This becomes N Holman Rd.; turn right onto 15th Ave. NW and follow to NW 110th St.)

The **Burke-Gilman Trail** makes for a longer ride or jog, running from the University District along Montlake Blvd., then along Lake Union and all the way west to Chittenden Locks and Discovery Park. The **Alki Trail** wanders for 8 mi. along the beachfront from Seacrest Marina to Lincoln Park, with views of both the Sound and the skyline. A bit farther afield, the **Sammamish River Trail** provides a rural respite along the river for almost 10 mi. from Bothell Landing to Marymoor Park.

Mountain bikers will have a bit harder time finding options within the city limits, but **Saint Edward State Park** in Kenmore at the north end of Lake Washington, with 3000 ft. of shoreline and over 10 mi. of trails, acts as a consolation prize. (Go north on I-5 to the 145th St. exit and head east. Turn left on Bothell Way and travel north to 68th Ave. in Kenmore. Park is 1½ mi. on the right.)

🚶 **HIKING.** Unplanned hiking is easy throughout the parks that scatter the city, including those listed above; for advice and general references, try the Outdoor Recreation Information Center at REI in the city (see **Equipment Rental,** p. 178).

The closest area for hiking, and therefore also the most crowded surrounds 4167 ft. **Mount Si,** one of the most climbed mountain in the state. Just an hour from downtown Seattle, hikers can reach the **Tiger Mountain State Forest,** home to both Mt. Si and **Tiger Mountain.** The **Mount Si Trail** is almost a rite of passage for locals in the area; the difficult 8 mi. round-trip takes most of the day, and brings you to **Haystack Basin,** the false summit. Don't try climbing higher unless you have rock-climbing gear, though. (Take I-90 east to SE Mt. Si Rd., 2 mi. from Middle Fork.)

One of the most popular trails on Tiger is **Tradition Lake Loop**, an easy 2½ mi. walk from the scenic **High Point** trailhead, where, on a good day, there are views of Mt. Rainier, the Olympic Mountains, and Seattle. Cross the Snoqualmie River Bridge to the trailhead parking lot. A 4hr. hike (5½ mi. round-trip) leads to the summit of West Tiger Mountain (2522 ft.). Take I-90 to Tiger Mountain State Forest. From the Tradition Plateau trailhead, walk to Bus Road Trail and then to West Tiger Trail. If you parked outside the gated lot, stay for sunset. For additional info, check out *55 Hikes around Snoqualmie Pass*, by Harvey Manning.

🏞 DAYTRIPS FROM SEATTLE

THE EASTSIDE. Seattleites leave the city en masse to play in this bikers', picnickers', and suburbanites' paradise rolled into one, a scant 20min. from downtown barring traffic. With the Internet boom came Range Rovers and outdoor shopping plazas littering the landscape. Expanses of East Sound land were transformed into "campuses," town-like complexes with residential and office areas—witness **Microsoft,** which has nearly consumed the suburb of Redmond. Still, green space remains, particularly in **Marymoor Park** (see above). Rapid growth has had its benefits, though. Once covered in strawberry fields, downtown **Bellevue** now offers **Bellevue Square,** a sunlight-filled, sprawling urban shopping mall, and a few choice ethnic restaurants tucked among the chains. The lakefront suburb of Medina is home to Microsoft founder Bill Gates, among others high rollers. The July **Bellevue Jazz Festival** attracts both local cats and national acts. The small, contemporary **Bellevue Art Museum** was once prized by the community, but has closed due to lack of revenue; there is a strong movement afoot to revive it. *(Head east across Lake Washington on one of 2 floating bridges, I-90 or Rte. 520, to reach the Eastside.)*

JIMI HENDRIX'S GRAVE. Rock pilgrims trek 15 mi. south of the city to the grave of Seattle's first rock legend, **Jimi Hendrix,** to pay homage to the greatest guitarist who ever lived. Jimi's grave is in Greenwood Cemetery, in the town of Renton. Plan on spending some time driving down labyrinthine streets. Once you find the cemetery, look for the grave toward the back, just in front of the sun dial. *(Bus #101 from downtown to the Renton Park 'n' Ride, then switch to #105 to Greenwood Cemetery. Drivers take the Sunset Blvd. exit from Rte. 405—follow Sunset Blvd., not Park—turn right onto Branson, and right again on NE 4th. The Cemetery is on a hill, next to a McDonald's.)*

MUSEUM OF FLIGHT. Seven miles south of Seattle at Boeing Field is the **Museum of Flight.** The huge structure enshrines flying machines, from canvas biplanes to chic fighter jets, under a three-story roof. Tour Eisenhower's old Air Force One, try a realistic flight simulator, or explore the red barn where William E. Boeing founded the company in 1916. Photographs and artifacts trace the history of flight from its beginnings through the 30s. *(9404 E Marginal Way S. Take I-5 south to Exit 158 and turn north onto E Marginal Way S and follow for ½ mi. Bus #174. ☎764-5700; www.museumofflight.com. Open M-Su 10am-5pm, 1st Th of month, 10am-9pm. Free tours every 30min., 10am-3:30pm. $12, ages 65 and older $11, 5-17 $7.50. Free after 5pm on 1st Th of the month.)*

BOEING. The Seattle area is surrounded by the vast factories of **Boeing.** Once the city's most prominent employer, the title has since been usurped by Microsoft, especially since Boeing's headquarters moved to Chicago. Boeing still holds claim to the largest covered structure in North America, located at the facilities in Everett about 30 mi. (25min.) north of the city, where 747s, 767s, and 777s are made. **Public tours** let you see just how large pieces are moved and assembled. Arrive early; the limited tickets often run out in the summer. The tour includes a theater show and a short walk through the facilities. *(Take I-5 north to Exit 189 and then go west on Hwy. 526 and follow the signs. ☎800-464-1476; www.boeing.com. Tours M-F 9am, 11am, 1pm, and 3pm. $6.50, ages 65 and older or under 16 $4. Ticket reservations $10.)*

DAYTRIP: SNOQUALMIE AND EAST

The town of **Snoqualmie,** just 30 mi. east of Seattle, is the hub for the Snoqualmie River drainage, and the location of the most accessible hiking within Seattle's reaches. Even with much of the area's wilderness ravaged by clearcuts, the trails and mountains, including both Mt. Si and Tiger Mtn., continue to lure the active away from the city. The breathtaking **Snoqualmie Falls** springboards the town into the perfect escape for those looking to leave the big city.

Just outside of the town are the astounding Falls. Formerly a sacred place for the Salish, the 270 ft. wall of water has generated electricity for Puget Power since 1898. Five generators buried under the falls continue to work hard, providing energy for 1600 homes. The spring is the best time to visit, when the falls are swollen with melt-off. The falls can be viewed from the vista spot above the falls or from below via the steep hike down to the base. The view from below is stunning; just be prepared for a substantial trek back. (Take the Snoqualmie Parkway exit from I-90.) The surrounding **Snoqualmie Valley** has hiking, biking, kayaking, rafting,

WASHINGTON

and fishing; ask at the **Snoqualmie Valley Chamber of Commerce** for information on local events and recreation in Preston, Snoqualmie, Fall City, and North Bend. (Take I-90 east to North Bend, Exit 31. ☎ 425-888-4440; www.snovalley.org.)

The exits along I-90 east of the city contain several hidden treats. Swim, water-ski, or play volleyball at **Lake Sammamish State Park,** to the west of Snoqualmie, a weekend hot spot on the lake's eastern shores. (Take I-90 15 mi. east of Seattle to Exit 15 and follow the large brown signs.) Farther east the road rises into mountains offering fantastic day hikes. You can really take your pick—for information, contact the **Issaquah Chamber of Commerce** (☎ 425-392-7024; www.issaquahchamber.com), at 155 NW Gilman in downtown Issaquah, just past the State Park, which sells maps ($5-6) and can help set you up with a route.

Overshadowed by the nearby Tiger Mtn. St. Forest is **Olallie State Park,** just east of North Bend. For easy, scenery-heavy hiking, this is the place; while power plants have taken some of the water from the rivers and falls, they've replaced them with well-maintained trails. Follow the signs at Exit 34 to the **Twin Falls Trail** (2½ mi. round-trip, easy). This trail passes through an area of temperate rainforest; highlights include giant moss-covered trees and a spectacular view of one of the twin falls. The trail continues along a new bridge over a 125 ft. wide gorge.

Heading further east of Snoqualmie, the hikes from the valley up to the peaks along the ridge are innumerable. From the west, the options include the trail up to **McClellan Butte,** a steep hike the whole way up to the 5100 ft. summit (9 mi. round-trip, difficult), off Exit 42. Try the hikes up to **Bandera Mountain** (7 mi. round-trip, moderate), where burned areas do little to negate the view of Mt. Rainier, or the popular **Talapus** and **Olallie Lakes** (4 mi. round-trip, easy), both off Exit 45. At Exit 47, you'll find numerous trailheads: to the much-used **Pratt Lake** up on the ridge (11 mi. round-trip, moderate); to **Granite Mountain,** a steep 3800 ft. hike in just 4 mi. (8½ mi. round-trip, difficult); to heavily-trodden alpine **Annette Lake** (7 mi. round-trip, moderate); and to the **Denny Creek Trail,** which leads a moderate 4½ mi. to Melakwa Lake via Snowshow Falls and Hemlock Pass. Just off Denny Creek Rd. is the half-mile stroll to the impressive 75 ft. **Franklin Falls.**

If you like your hiking with a high creepiness factor, consider trekking underground for 2¼ mi. through the **Snoqualmie Tunnel,** best accessed from the Keechelus Lake trailhead at Exit 54. Indisputably eerie, this 1912 tunnel is dark, perpetually cool, and always windy, requiring layers and a tolerance for a ghostly howling sound. If you make it through to the east side, you'll see where the cooled air meets the warm outside and blows out as steam, drawing comparisons to a slumbering monster or dragon deep inside the mountain.

Those who want to get off their feet and onto a bike will find abundant options as well; while most trails are closed to mountain bikers, gravel, Forest Service, and fire roads are plentiful and offer opportunities for spontaneous outdoor exploration. For something a little more structured, bank on the **John Wayne Pioneer Trail** in Iron Horse State Park, ideal for beginners. Put-ins for the trail include Lake Keechelus, Easton, Lake Annette, and McClellan Butte.

▶ DAYTRIP: BREMERTON

Nosing into Puget Sound between the Olympic Peninsula and Seattle, the Kitsap Peninsula's deep inlets seem a natural spot to park a fleet of nuclear-powered submarines. The instant you set foot in **Bremerton,** you see that is exactly what happened. (Washington State Ferries ☎ 206-464-6400 or 800-808-7977; www.wsdot.wa.gov/ferries. A regular ferry runs between downtown Seattle and Bremerton about a dozen times daily. (1hr.; $6.50, car and driver $13.) For maps and local information, head to the **Bremerton Area Chamber of Commerce,** 301 Pacific Ave. (☎ 360-479-3579; www.bremertonchamber.org. Open M-F 9am-4pm.)

WASHINGTON

The **Bremerton Naval Museum,** 402 Pacific Ave., is sure to please any Navy buff, replete with WWII photos, 10 ft. models of ships, and a 14th-century basket from Korea believed to have been used as a launching weapon. (☎360-479-7447. Open M-Sa 10am-5pm, Su 1-5pm. Donations appreciated.)

Behind the museum, explore the destroyer **USS Turner Joy,** the ship that fired the first American shots of the Vietnam War. It is managed by the Bremerton Historic Ships Association. (USS Turner Joy: ☎360-792-2457. Self-guided tours $8, ages 65 and older $7, under 12 $6, military with ID free; buy tickets at Turner Joy gift shop. Gift shop open daily 10am-4:30pm; Turner Joy open 10am-5pm.)

🗗 DAYTRIP: TACOMA

Tacoma, founded as a sawmill town in the 1860s, was called "The City of Destiny" when it was designated the western terminus of the first railroad to reach the Northwest. In the 20th century, however, Seattle became the industrial and cultural hub of the region. Recently, Tacoma has begun to emerge from Seattle's shadow. In July 2002, Tacoma opened the Museum of Glass to showcase the city's native and internationally renowned glassblower, Dale Chihuly. The Museum of Glass is linked to the Washington State History Museum and the Tacoma Art Museum by the Chihuly Bridge of Glass across I-5.

Tacoma is Washington's third largest city and lies on **I-5,** 32 mi. (30min.) south of Seattle and 28 mi. (30min.) northeast of Olympia. Take Exit 133 from I-5 and follow the signs to the city center. There are several public transportation options for getting to Tacoma; **SoundTransit** runs two of these out of the same station. (☎398-5000; www.soundtransit.org) The **Sounder** commuter train runs from Tacoma in the morning, and from Seattle in the evening (1hr.; $4 round-trip). Pick up a schedule booklet at either end. SoundTransit also runs buses to **Portland** (8 per day, $22) and **Seattle** (8 per day, $5). Get the scoop on Tacoma at the **Visitor Information Center,** 1119 Pacific Ave., 5th floor (☎253-627-2846 or 800-272-2662; open M-F 8:30am-5pm), or from the desk in the back of the History Museum gift shop (see below; open M-Sa 10am-4pm, Su noon-5pm). The superb *Pierce County Bicycle Guide Map* shows bike routes and lists trails near Mt. Rainier.

MUSEUM OF GLASS. In 2002, the much anticipated, $63 million Museum of Glass and International Center for Contemporary Art opened its doors to visitors. The highlight inside is the "hot shop," an amphitheater and glassblowing studio where visitors can watch art-in-action. The outdoor draw is the 500 ft. long Chihuly Bridge of Glass, displaying 1700 works by renowned glass artist Dale Chihuly. *(1801 E Dock St. ☎253-284-4750 or 866-468-7386; www.museumofglass.org. Open General Day-Labor Day M-Sa 10am-5pm, Su noon-5pm, 3rd Th of the month 10am-8pm; Labor Day-Memorial Day W-Sa 10am-5pm, Su noon-5pm, 3rd Th of the month 10am-8pm. $10, ages 62 and older and students $8, children $4. Free 3rd Th of the month 5-8pm.)*

POINT DEFIANCE PARK. The 698 acre park is a wonderful place to pass time on a warm day, but it's a secret everyone knows about. The park is excellent for both active and visual pursuits. A 5 mi. driving and walking loop passes all the park's attractions, offering postcard views of Puget Sound and access to miles of woodland trails. In spring, the park is bejeweled with flowers; a rhododendron garden lies nestled in the woods along the loop. **Owen Beach** looks across at Vashon Island and is a good starting place for a ramble down the shore or a paddle. If you don't have your own kayak, you can rent one at the **Don's Ruston Market** booth set up right on the beach. (☎253-759-8151. The main building is at 5102 N Winnifred St. in Ruston. M-F singles $10 per hr., $45 per day; doubles $15/$55; Sa-Su singles $10/$50; doubles $19/$60. Booth open daily noon-7pm.) The park's prized possession is the **Point Defiance Zoo and Aquarium.** The zoo boasts more than 5000 animals, including penguins, puffins, polar bears, beluga whales, and sharks. The meticulously restored **Fort Nisqually** was built by the British Hudson Bay Company in 1832 as they expanded their trade in beaver pelts. The series of 19th century cabins contains museum-like exhibits on the lives of children, laborers, and natives. *(Park: take Rte. 16 to 6th Ave., go east on 6th Ave., then head north on Pearl St. ☎305-1000. Open daily from dawn until 30min. after dusk. Zoo: 5400 N Pearl St. ☎404-3678 or 591-5337; www.pdza.org. Open daily Apr. 9:30am-5pm; May-Sept. 9:30am-7pm; Oct.-Mar. 9:30am-4pm. $8.75, ages 62 and older $8, 4-13 $7. Fort: ☎591-5339. Open daily June-Aug. 11am-6pm; Sept.-Apr. W-Su 11am-4pm. $3, seniors $2, ages 5-12 $1.)*

WASHINGTON STATE HISTORY MUSEUM. The shiny $40 million museum houses interactive exhibits on Washington's history through the 1800s. A sprawling model train on the 5th floor is a highlight for children and railroad buffs. *(1911 Pacific Ave. ☎888-238-4373; www.washingtonhistory.org. Open Tu-W and F-Sa 10am-5pm, Th 10am-8pm, Su noon-5pm. $7, ages 62 and older $6.50, students $5, children under 5 free. Free Th 4-8pm.)*

SOUTH PUGET SOUND

Stretching from Admiralty Inlet to Whidbey Island, the unusually deep Puget Sound runs a full 100 mi. up to the Straits of Juan de Fuca and Georgia. The Sound was originally discovered by George Vancouver, who generously decided that an island was good enough for him and granted the naming rights to his second lieutenant Peter Puget. Sharing the seas with the shipping trade and frequenting the harbors of Seattle, Tacoma, Everett, and Port Townsend, modern US Navy submarines and battleships are now based in Bremerton. The Alaska Marine Highway also ends its voyage here in the Sound. The southern part of the Sound is home to urban escapes like Bainbridge and Vashon Island, as well as Seattle's smaller yet still hip neighbor Olympia, the state capital.

BAINBRIDGE ISLAND   ☎206

Bainbridge Island, a short and lovely 35min. ferry ride from downtown, has a slightly more suburban feel than its neighbors in Puget Sound, thanks to a trend of wealthy Seattleites building their dream homes on the island's 45 mi. of coastline. While this means that less of the beachfront is open for public access than on some of the other islands, Bainbridge nevertheless maintains beautiful state parks, a flourishing wine business, a strong arts community, and excellent biking opportunities. The steep prices for lodging may keep you from spending the night, but Winslow's renowned restaurants are reason alone to spend a day on the island.

▐ TRANSPORTATION. Bainbridge Island lies west of **Seattle,** nestled against the **Kitsap Peninsula** from Port Orchard to Poulsbo. You can drive onto the northwest corner of the island from Poulsbo on **Route 305,** which then stretches southeast across the island to the ferry terminal in **Winslow,** the island's urban center in Eagle Harbor on the eastern side of the island. **Washington State Ferries** run from downtown Seattle to Winslow. (☎464-6400 or 888-808-7977; www.wsdot.wa.gov/ferries. 35min., over 20 ferries daily from 5am-1am; $6.45, $13 per car.) **Kitsap Transit** services Rte. 305, including the ferry terminal and the parks. Bus #90 runs from Poulsbo to Winslow. (☎697-2877 or 800-501-7433; www.kitsaptransit.org. Buses run M-F 4:45am-9pm, Sa 9am-6pm, Su 10:30am-6pm. $1.) **Bainbridge Taxi Service** runs around the island. (☎842-1021. $2 base, $1.75 per mi. 24hr.)

▐ PRACTICAL INFORMATION. The Bainbridge **Chamber of Commerce,** 590 Winslow Way E, doles out maps and advice. (☎842-3700; www.bainbridgechamber.com. Open M-F 9am-5pm, Sa 10am-3pm.) Pharmacy needs are serviced by **The**

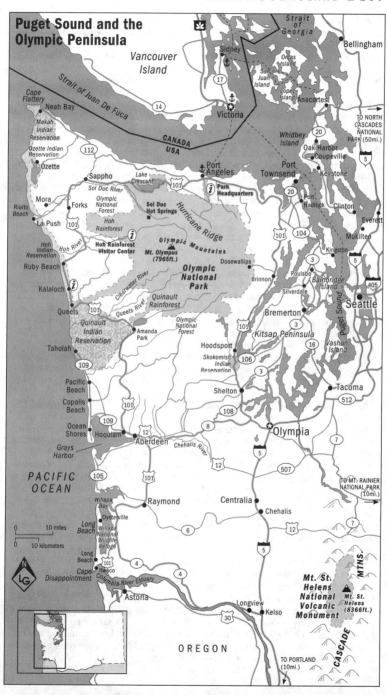

Puget Sound and the Olympic Peninsula

Strait of Georgia

Vancouver Island

Bellingham

Sidney

Orcas Island

San Juan Island

Lopez Island

Anacortes

Cape Flattery

Neah Bay

Strait of Juan De Fuca

14

CANADA
USA

17

Victoria

TO NORTH CASCADES NATIONAL PARK (50mi.)

Whidbey Island

20

Oak Harbor
Coupeville

5

Makah Indian Reservation

112

Ozette Indian Reservation

Ozette

Sappho

Lake Crescent

Port Angeles

101

Park Headquarters

Port Townsend

Keystone

20

Port Hadlock

Clinton

Everett

Sol Duc River

Olympic National Forest

Sol Duc Hot Springs

Mora

Forks

104

Mukilteo

Rialto Beach

La Push

101

Hoh Rainforest

Hurricane Ridge

101

Kingston

5

405

Hoh River

Hoh Rainforest Visitor Center

Olympic Mountains

Mt. Olympus (7965ft.)

Dosewallips

Poulsbo

Bainbridge Island

Seattle

Hoh Indian Reservation

Ruby Beach

Clearwater River

Olympic National Park

Brinnon

Silverdale

Puget Sound

Kalaloch

Quinault Rainforest

Bremerton

3

Queets

101

Queets River

Olympic National Forest

Kitsap Peninsula

16

Vashon Island

Quinault Indian Reservation

Amanda Park

Hoodsport

101

Taholah

109

Skokomish Indian Reservation

106

3

Pacific Beach

Shelton

Tacoma

512

Copalis Beach

101

108

Ocean Shores

109

8

Olympia

7

Hoquiam

Aberdeen

12

Chehalis River

Grays Harbor

PACIFIC OCEAN

105

12

5

507

TO MT. RAINIER NATIONAL PARK (10mi.)

101

Raymond

Centralia

Willapa Bay

Oysterville

Chehalis

Long Beach

Willapa National Wildlife Refuge

6

12

7

Long Beach

Cape Disappointment

101

Ilwaco

4

4

5

Columbia River Estuary

Astoria

Longview

Kelso

Mt. St. Helens National Volcanic Monument

Mt. St. Helens (8366ft.)

30

CASCADE MTNS.

OREGON

TO PORTLAND (10mi.)

0   10 miles
0   10 kilometers

WASHINGTON

Medicine Shoppe, 124 Winslow Way W (☎842-1634; open M-Sa 9am-7pm, Su 11am-4pm). The **police** are at 625 Winslow Way E (☎842-5211). The **Virginia Mason Winslow Clinic,** 380 Winslow Way E, is open 24hr. (☎842-5632). The **library,** 1270 Madison N, has unlimited free **Internet** access. (☎842-4162; www.krl.org. Open M-F 11am-7pm, Sa 10am-5pm, Su 1-5pm.) The **post office** is at 170 Winslow Way E. (☎842-9341. Open M-F 8:30am-5pm, Sa 10am-1pm.) **Postal Code:** 98110.

▐▔▌ ACCOMMODATIONS AND FOOD. Fay Bainbridge State Park ❷, 15446 Sunrise Dr. NE, on the northern tip of the island off Rte. 305, provides both the only camping and one of the best areas on the island; its 1400 ft. beach shore looks out across Puget Sound to downtown Seattle and, on a clear day, to Mt. Rainier. The beach has firepits and abundant driftwood for perching on, which somewhat makes up for the crowded, wind-exposed sites. (☎360-321-4559, reservations 888-226-7688, available May 15-Sept. 15. 46 sites $16, hiker/biker $8, RV sites $22. Open daily Mar.-Oct.; Nov.-Feb. Sa-Su.) Those not willing to fork over the cash for a deluxe **B&B** will be hard pressed to find other indoor options, especially within a reasonable price range; most double occupancy rates start from $90. **Our Country Haus ❺,** 13718 Ellingsen Rd. NE, is a bargain for Bainbridge. (☎842-8425; www.ourcountryhaus.com. Singles $85, doubles $115.)

Groceries are at **Town and Country Market,** 343 Winslow Way E. (☎842-5710. Open M-Sa 8am-7pm, Su 10am-5pm.) The fresher stuff is available in Winslow at the **Bainbridge Island Farmers' Market.** (☎855-1500; www.bainbridgefarmersmarket.com. Apr.-Sept. on Th and Sa 9am-noon.) The best soups and sandwiches around are at **Annie's Place ❶,** 100 Winslow Way W, set back from the road. Their tomato mozzarella ($5.75) and tuna salad ($5.25) are standouts. (☎842-1808. Open M-F 10:30am-5pm, Sa noon-4pm.) To get your fill of burgers ($5-7) and all-day breakfast ($3-8), head to the **Streamliner Diner ❶,** 397 Winslow Way E. (☎842-8595. Open daily 8am-9pm.) **Islay Manor ❷,** 4569 Lynwood Center Rd., previously Ruby's, changed their name but kept the red-colored walls; French-countryside offerings will fill you up. Lunch $5-8, dinner $8-12. (☎780-9303; www.rubysonbainbridge.com. Open M-Th 11am-7pm, F-Sa 11am-9pm, Su noon-8pm.)

◐▟ SIGHTS AND OUTDOOR ACTIVITIES. The reason many Seattleites venture to Bainbridge is to visit the **Bainbridge Island Vineyards & Winery,** 682 Hwy. 305, half a mile south of the ferry terminal, where European-style wines are grown and sold and you can explore a museum; two free tastings await at the end. (☎842-9463; www.bainbridgevineyards.com. Open W-Su noon-5pm.)

Other than Fay Bainbridge State Park, there are two prime pieces of nature awaiting exploration. On the south shore, **Fort Ward State Park** has yet to be fully developed and currently lacks full access to its beachfront; for the best views of the over 4000 ft. of rocky shores, walk or bike along Pleasant Beach Rd. (closed to cars). Keep a lookout for birds, especially around **Orchard Rocks,** offshore on the southernmost end, which is a designated marine park. This is also a popular area for kayaking and scuba diving; rentals are available from **Exotic Aquatics,** 187 Ericksen Ave. NE. (☎842-1980; www.exoticaquaticsscuba.com. Kayaks $13 per hour, $35 per half day, $50 per full day; double kayaks $20/$50/$65. Scuba rentals $50 full package; individual items available. Dive charters available, $65 for a 2-tank dive.) A more serene and unique experience is to be found at **Bloedel Reserve,** 7571 NE Dolphin Dr., a 150-acre plot of second-growth forest, gardens, ponds, and meadows set aside by an old logging family. To preserve the quiet of the land, the number of people allowed in at any time is limited, so reservations are required; allow at least 2hr. for a complete visit, including a tour of the old mansion overlooking Puget Sound. (☎842-7631; www.bloedelreserve.org. $10, ages 65 and older and 5-12 $8, under 5 free. No picnicking. Open W-Su 10am-4pm.)

The best way to see Bainbridge is on a **bike.** Pedaling along Rte. 305 quickly brings ferry travelers the 7 mi. to Fay Bainbridge St. Park. More challenging is the hilly 30 mi. **Bainbridge Island Loop** around the island's circumference. Following the signs from the ferry counter-clockwise around the island, this route travels windy back roads and is the path for the **Chilly Hilly,** an annual ride in late February to mark the opening of bike season. More intrepid explorers can head to the visitors center, pick up a map, and set out on their own adventure. **B.I. Cycle** at the Bike Barn, 71 Olympic Dr. off Hwy. 305 just west of the ferry terminal, offers rentals, maps, and advice (☎855-1770; www.b-i-cycle.com. Bikes from $18 per hour, $42 per day. Open Memorial Day-Labor Day M-F 10am-7pm, Sa-Su 10am-5pm.)

VASHON ISLAND   ☎206

Although it's only a 25min. ferry ride from Seattle and an even shorter hop from Tacoma, Vashon (VASH-on) Island remains largely unnoticed by most Seattle tourists. For an island, this artists' colony (pop. 10,800) has surprisingly few beaches open to the public, but what it lacks in shorelines, it makes up for with an unpretentious feel and rolling hills seemingly designed for hiking and biking. Vashon is the perfect place for a one-day trip or a multi-day exploration.

▣ TRANSPORTATION. Vashon Island stretches between **Seattle** and **Tacoma** on its east side and between **Southworth** and **Gig Harbor** on its west side. The town of **Vashon** lies inland on the northern end of the island; ferries stop at both the south and north ends of the island. **Washington State Ferries** (☎464-6400 or 888-808-7977; www.wsdot.wa.gov/ferries) runs ferries to Vashon Island from three different locations. Ferries from **Fauntleroy** in West Seattle and **Southworth** in the Kitsap Peninsula take cars and walk-on passengers. (Fauntleroy ferries 20min., over 30 ferries daily 4am-2am. Southworth ferries 10min., over 25 ferries daily 4am-2:30am. Both $3, car and driver $10-13.) A third ferry departs from **Point Defiance** in Tacoma and arrives in Tahlequah. (15min.; $3, car and driver $10-13.) To get to the Fauntleroy terminal on the mainland from Seattle, drive south on I-5 and take Exit 163A (West Seattle/Spokane St.) down Fauntleroy Way. To get to Point Defiance in Tacoma, take Exit 132 off I-5 (Bremerton/Gig Harbor) to Rte. 16. Get on 6th Ave. and turn right onto Pearl St.; follow signs to Point Defiance Park and the ferry.

Seattle's **King County Metro** services the downtown ferry terminal, Fauntleroy ferry terminal, and Vashon Island landing. Buses #54, 116, 118, and 119 run between Seattle and Fauntleroy. Bus #54 picks up at 2nd and Pike St. Save your transfer for the connection on Vashon. Buses #118 and 119 service the island's east side from the north ferry landing through Vashon to the south landing. The island is in a different fare zone than Seattle. (☎553-3000 or 800-542-7876; http://transit.metrokc.gov. 30min., buses every 30min. 5:15am-1:40am. One zone $1.50. Between zones $2. See also Seattle's **Public Transportation,** p. 177.)

▣ PRACTICAL INFORMATION. The **Thriftway** (see **Food,** below) provides maps, as does the **Chamber of Commerce,** 17232 SW Vashon Hwy. (☎463-6217; www.vashonchamber.com. Open Tu-Sa 10am-3pm.) **Joy's,** 17318 Vashon Hwy., has laundry facilities. (☎463-9933. Wash $1.50, dry $0.25 per 8min. Open M-F 7am-8:30pm, Sa-Su 8am-8pm.) Other services include: **Vashon Pharmacy,** 17617 Vashon Hwy. (☎463-9118; open M-F 9am-7pm, Sa 9am-6pm, Su 11am-1pm) and the **police,** 19021 Vashon Hwy. (☎463-3618). The **library,** 17210 Vashon Hwy., has free **Internet** access for 30min. (☎463-2069; www.kcls.org. Open M-Th 11am-8:30pm, F 11am-6pm, Sa 10am-5pm, Su 1-5pm.) The **post office** is at 1005 SW 178th St. (☎800-275-8777. Open M-F 8:30am-5pm, Sa 10am-1pm.) **Postal Code:** 98070.

WASHINGTON

ACCOMMODATIONS AND FOOD. The ■Vashon Island AYH Ranch Hostel (HI) ❶, 12119 SW Cove Rd., 1½ mi. west of Vashon Hwy. at the sign, is an oasis just 30min. away from Seattle. This wacky frontierland packed with teepees, old covered wagons with tiny cots inside, and log-cabin bunkhouses, provides the perfect place for a quiet weekend away from the city, to dump a car so you can ferry to downtown Seattle, or even just to poke around and see the unusual accommodations. For $9, you can set up your tent in their meadow; it is the only camping on the island. A nature walk winds though four wooded acres; easy access to another 100 acres call for hiking and biking. (☎463-2592; www.vashonhostel.com. Free pancake breakfast. Free 1-gear bikes, mountain bikes $6 per day. Sleeping bag $2. 24hr. check-in. Full hostel open May-Oct., private double open year round. $13, nonmembers $16. Teepee and covered wagons also $13/$16. Private double $45/ $55; $10 per extra person; children half price. Shuttle to the morning ferry $1.25.) The hostel's B&B, **The Lavender Duck** ❹, 16503 Vashon Hwy., just north on Vashon Hwy., has pleasant, themed rooms and a beautiful living room and kitchen. (☎567-5646. Check in at the hostel. $70.) The B&B scene is downright scarce compared to most Seattle-area islands, but beds can still be found; expect to pay at least $75.

Campers and hostelers will find their food haven at the large, offbeat **Thriftway,** downtown at 9740 SW Bank Rd., set back at the corner of Bank and Vashon Hwy. The bulk food section is a camper's dream. All buses from the ferry terminal stop there. (☎463-2100. Open daily 8am-9pm.) The **Stray Dog Cafe** ❷, 17530 Vashon Hwy., boasts a diverse menu, from crepes to quiche to mac and cheese. The homemade soups ($2.50-4.25) and grilled sandwiches ($6-7.50) are not to be missed. (☎463-7833. Open M-F 8-11am and 11:30am-2:30pm, W-F 5:30-9pm, Sa 8am-3pm and 5:30-9pm, Su 8am-4pm.) **Fred's Homegrown Restaurant** ❷, 17614 Vashon Hwy. SW, serves heaping breakfasts ($3-7). (☎463-6302. Open daily 7am-9pm.) **Bishop's Cafe and Lounge** ❷, 17618 Vashon Hwy., has plenty of meals for meat-lovers (M burger mania $4.25) and options for the night owl in all of us: video games, pool, nightly special drinks, and pints. (☎463-5959; www.bishopscafe.com. Restaurant open daily 10am-10pm, bar open 11am-2am.)

SIGHTS AND OUTDOOR ACTIVITIES. If you leave the mainland looking for island activities, you have some worthwhile options on Vashon; accessible beaches are sprinkled around between the copious No Trespassing signs and are becoming even more plentiful as the state buys up more and more land. **Wingehaven Park** hosts probably the most easily located beach less than a mile from the North End Ferry, which also has a beachfront campsite for those on the Cascadia Marine Trail. **Port Heyer Beach** (follow SW Ellisport off Vashon Hwy.) is on a point facing east, perfect for sunrises; across the island is **Lisabeula Park** (take SW 204th St. to 111th Ave. to SW 220th St.) whose beach faces west for sunset viewing, evening strolling, and teenage partying later on. **Maury Island,** connected to the main island by a narrow isthmus, contains some of the best beach options. **Point Robinson Park,** a gorgeous spot for a picnic, is home to **free tours** of the 1885 **Coast Guard lighthouse.** (Take Ellisburg Rd. off the Vashon Hwy. to Dockton Rd. to Pt. Robinson Rd. ☎217-6123. Open summer Sa-Su noon-3:30pm.) The water between the two islands is Quartermaster Harbor, with **Jenson Point** in Burton Acres an ideal place to relax on its calm waters. Follow Vashon Hwy. to Burton Dr.

Vashon Island provides wonderful but strenuous biking, a sometimes-unbalanced relationship celebrated at the **Bicycle Tree,** off the Vashon Hwy. on SW Ellisport. Rd., where a misbehaving little two-wheeler is lodged in a tree. The potential routes around the island are as abundant as your thighs are strong; a loop around the whole island on Vashon Hwy. out to Maury Island will fill a day with hills and easy access to quaint backroads for further exploration. For rentals or routes to insider spots, pick up a map at **Vashon Island Bicycles,** 9925 SW 178th St.

off Vashon Hwy in the south end of town, and chat up owner Jeff. (☎493-6225. Bikes start at $5 per hr. or $20 per day—Jeff recommends renting on Sunday, so you get all of Monday free. Open Tu 10am-5pm, W-Sa 10-6pm, Su noon-4pm.)

Since the water is often obscured from the inner island roads, the ideal way to enjoy the shoreline and waves is in a boat. Courageous kayakers can take to the open waters that surround the island, while most should be content with the calmer water in **Quartermaster Harbor,** where launch sites abound. If you launch from Portage on the isthmus connecting to Maury Island, you can circumnavigate the island in just over 10 mi. Intrepid boaters make the 1½ mi. ocean crossing from the northern tip of the island to paddle around **Blake Island. Vashon Island Kayak Co.,** at Burton Acres Park, Jensen Point Boat Launch, runs guided tours ($65) and rents sea kayaks. (☎463-9257. Open F-Su 10am-5pm. Call and leave a message for weekday rentals. Singles $18 per hr., $58 per day; doubles $28/$80.)

For those wanting to set out on foot, more than 500 acres of woods in the middle of the island are interlaced with mildly difficult hiking trails. The **Vashon Park District,** 17130 Vashon Hwy., can tell you more. (☎463-9602; www.vashonparkdistrict.org. Open daily 8am-4pm.) Count on some culture no matter when you visit—by recent count there are over 300 artists on Vashon.

OLYMPIA   ☎360

Inside Olympia's seemingly interminable network of suburbs lies a festive downtown area known for its art, antiques, liberalism, and irresistible microbrews. Evergreen State College lies a few miles from the city center, and its highly-pierced, tree-hugging student body spills into the mix in a kind of chemistry experiment that gets progressively weirder when politicians—Olympia serves as Washington's capital—join in. Named because of its superb view of the Olympic mountains, the city is also a logical launching pad into Olympic National Park.

▛ TRANSPORTATION

Settled at the junction of **I-5** and **US 101** between **Tumwater** (to the south, I-5 Exit 102) and **Lacey** (to the east, I-5 Exit 108), Olympia makes a convenient stop on any north-south journey. I-5 Exit 105 leads to the **Capitol Campus** and **downtown** Olym-

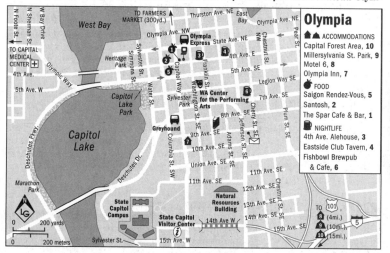

pia. **Capitol Way** divides the city's east and west downtown streets. The west side of downtown borders freshwater **Capitol Lake** and salty **West Bay,** also known as **Budd Bay.** The **4th Avenue** bridge divides the two bodies of water and leads to the city's fast-food-populated section. Navigating Olympia's one-way streets on **bike** or **foot** is easy, and all public buses have bike racks.

Trains: Amtrak, 6600 Yelm Hwy. (☎923-4602 or 800-872-7245). In neighboring Lacey (I-5 Exit 108), but bus #64 runs between downtown and the station. Open daily 8:15am-noon, 1:45-3:30pm, and 5:30-8:30pm. To **Portland** (2½hr., 4 per day, $24-27) and **Seattle** (1¾hr., 4 per day, $17-21).

Buses: Olympia Express runs to downtown **Seattle** ($1.50) and **Sea-Tac Airport** ($2) via **Tacoma** (1hr., M-F 5:50am-6pm, $2). **Greyhound,** 107 7th Ave. SE (☎357-5541 or 800-231-2222), at Capitol Way. Office open daily 8:30am-10pm. To: **Portland** (2¾hr., 7 per day, $24); **Seattle** (1¾hr., 4-6 per day, $8.50); **Spokane** (9hr., 3 per day, $33).

Public Transportation: Intercity Transit (IT; ☎786-1881 or 800-287-6348; www.intercitytransit.com). Reliable, flexible service to most anywhere in Thurston County, even with a bike. Schedules at the visitors center or at the **Transit Center,** 222 State Ave. Open M-F 7:30am-5:30pm. $0.75 per ride. Day passes $1.50. The most useful route is #42, which runs from the Campus to downtown, eastside, and westside (every 15min., 6:45am-5:45pm). Also check out **Olympia Express,** above.

Taxis: DC Cab (☎786-5226). $3.50 base, $2.40 per mi. 24hr.

🛈 PRACTICAL INFORMATION

Tourist Information: Washington State Capitol Visitor Center (☎586-3460; www.ga.wa.gov/visitor), on Capitol Way at 14th Ave., on the south end of the Capitol campus; follow the signs on I-5. Open M-F 8am-5pm; May-Sept. also Sa-Su 9am-4pm.

Outdoor Information: State Natural Resources Building, 1111 Washington St. (☎902-1000 or 800-527-3305), houses the **Department of Natural Resources (DNR)** (www.dnr.wa.gov). The **Fish and Wildlife Office** (☎902-2200; www.wa.gov/wdfw), and the **Washington State Parks and Recreation Commission Information Center** (☎800-233-0321) are on the ground floor. The **Olympic National Forest Headquarters,** 1835 Black Lake Blvd. SW (☎956-2400; www.fs.fed.us/r6/olympic), provides info on forest land. Open M-F 8am-4:30pm. For Olympic National Park info, call ☎565-3000.

Outdoors Equipment: Pick up essentials or go on a buying spree at **Olympic Outfitters,** 407 E 4th Ave. (☎943-1114). Open M-F 10am-8pm, Sa 10am-6pm, Su noon-5pm.

Laundromat: Westside Laundry, 2103 Harrison Ave. NW (☎943-3857), in a strip mall on the west side of town. Wash $1.75, dry $0.25 per 7min. Open daily 9am-10pm.

Police: 900 Plum St. SE (8am-5pm ☎753-8300; 5pm-8am ☎704-2740), at 8th Ave.

Crisis Line: ☎586-2800. 24hr.

Hospital: Capital Medical Center, 3900 Capital Mall Drive SW (☎754-5858). From I-5, take Exit 104 (Hwy. 101) west from downtown.

Internet Access: Olympia Timberland Library, 313 8th Ave. SE (☎352-0595; www.timberland.lib.wa.us), at Franklin St. Up to 1hr. free Internet access. Open M-Tu 10am-9pm, W-Th 11am-9pm, F-Sa 10am-5pm, Su 1-5pm.

Post Office: 900 Jefferson St. SE (☎357-2289). Open M-F 7:30am-6pm, Sa 9am-4pm. **Postal Code:** 98501

🏠🏕 ACCOMMODATIONS AND CAMPING

Rooms in Olympia motels start at prices more accessible to policymakers than budget travelers ($60-80), but options in Tumwater are more affordable. Try **Motel 6 ❸,** 400 W Lee St. (☎754-7320. Singles $44; doubles $52.)

The Olympia Inn, 909 Capitol Way (☎352-8533). A few blocks north of the Capitol building. Clean, spacious rooms are the perfect solution for travelers not on the corporate account. Singles start at $48; doubles at $54. AAA/senior discount $2. ❸

Millersylvania State Park, 12245 Tilly Rd. S (☎753-1519; reservations 888-226-7688), 10 mi. south of Olympia. Take Exit 95 off I-5 N or S, turn onto Rte. 121 N, then take a left at the stop sign. A few secluded sites, most in the back of the park. Some kitchens available. 20-day max. stay. Wheelchair-accessible. 168 sites. $16; RV sites $22; bikers $6. Showers $0.25 per 3min. ❶

Capital Forest Multiple Use Area, 15 mi. southwest of Olympia. Take Exit 95 off I-5. Grab a forest map at the state DNR office (see **Practical Information,** above). 90 campsites spread among 7 campgrounds, administered by the DNR. Free. No showers. ❶

▐ FOOD

Diners, veggie eateries, and Asian quick-stops line bohemian 4th Ave. east of Columbia St. Get groceries at the 24hr. **Safeway,** 520 Cleveland Ave. (☎943-1830), off Capitol Blvd. in Tumwater, a quarter-mile south of the Capitol building. The **Olympia Farmers Market,** 700 N Capitol Way, is a great place to stroll, people-watch, and grab cheap local fruit and fresh baked goods. (☎352-9096; www.farmers-market.org. Open Apr.-Oct. Th-Su 10am-4pm; Nov.-Dec. Sa-Su 10am-3pm.)

The Spar Cafe & Bar, 114 E 4th Ave. (☎357-6444), has been a local icon for beer, burgers ($7-9), and cigars for decades. A national historic monument, still operating to the tunes of live jazz every Sa night. Cafe open M-Th 6am-9pm, F-Sa 6am-11pm, Su 6am-8pm. Bar open M-Th 11am-midnight, F-Sa 11am-2am. ❷

Saigon Rendez-Vous, 117 W 5th Ave. (☎352-1989). Olympia's best Vietnamese spot boasts a huge vegetarian menu ($5-8). Open M-Sa 10:30am-10:30pm, Su noon-9pm. ❶

Santosh, 116 W 4th Ave. (☎943-3442), west of Capitol Way. All-you-can-eat Indian lunch buffet $6.95, regular dishes $8-12. Don't miss the creamy, spicy curry. Open M-F and Su 11:30am-2:30pm and 5-9:30pm, Sa 11am-2:30pm and 5-10pm. ❷

▐ NIGHTLIFE

Olympia's nightlife seems to have outgrown its daylife. Bands like Sleater-Kinney and Bikini Kill and labels like K Records and Kill Rock Stars have made the city a crucial indie pitstop. The daily *Olympian* (www.theolympian.com) lists shows.

Fishbowl Brewpub & Cafe, 515 Jefferson St. SE (☎943-3650; www.fishbrewing.com), 2 blocks south off 4th Ave. With fish painted on outside walls and a small aquarium as the room's centerpiece, this brewpub captures Olympia's love for the sea, art, and beer. The British ales ($3.50) are named after fish. The kitchen, open daily until 11pm, offers sandwiches and pasta ($3.50-7). Open M-Sa 11am-midnight, Su noon-10pm.

Eastside Club Tavern, 410 4th Ave. E (☎357-9985; www.olywa.net/dwight/eastside-club). Old and young come to play pool and sip pints of microbrews; the renovated club pleases those looking to dance. Pints $2.50. Frequent drink specials: M pints $1.75, Th $2. Happy hour daily 4-7pm, pints $1.75. Open M-F noon-2am, Sa-Su 3pm-2am.

4th Avenue Alehouse & Eatery, 210 4th Ave. E (☎786-1444; www.the4thave.com). Townsfolk gather for "slabs" of pizza ($3.75), seafood baskets ($5-6), and one of the 30 regional draft microbrews. Pints $3, $2 during happy hour (5-7pm). Live tunes, from blues to reggae (Th-Sa 9pm). Cover $3-10. Open M-F 11:30am-2am, F-Sa noon-2am.

▐ ▐ SIGHTS AND EVENTS

Olympia's main draw is definitely its political scene, so don't miss the chance to see Washington tax dollars in action. If the Senate floor makes you howl with boredom, unleash your inner beast at Nisqually Wildlife Refuge or at Wolf Haven.

STATE CAPITOL. Olympia's crowning glory is the State Capitol, a complex of state government buildings, carefully sculpted gardens, veterans' monuments, and fabulous fountains, including a remarkable replica of Copenhagen's Tivoli fountain. Get a free tour of the **Legislative Building,** constructed in 1927 and styled after St. Peter's Basilica in Rome. The newly renovated interior, to reopen in January 2005, enshrines a six-ton Tiffany chandelier and six bronze doors depicting the state's history. *(I-5 to Exit 103. Visitors center ☎ 586-3460. Call 586-8687 for more info and wheelchair-accessible options. Free tours depart from the front entrance daily on the hr. 10am-3pm; 11am tour is most in-depth. Open for tourists to explore M-F 8am-5pm, Sa-Su 10am-4pm.)*

NISQUALLY NATIONAL WILDLIFE REFUGE. The **Nisqually National Wildlife Refuge** shelters 500 species of plants and animals by protecting the Nisqually River's estuary and its mix of tidal mudflats, marshes, grasslands, and forest ecosystems, all laced with miles of trails. People come to walk and above all, bird-watch; bald eagles, shorebirds, and Northern spotted owls nest here. The trails are open daily from dawn to dusk and are closed to cyclists, joggers, and pets. The visitors center loans free binocular and info packets—just leave behind an ID. *(Off I-5 between Olympia and Tacoma at Exit 114. ☎ 753-9467; www.nisqually.fws.gov. Visitors center office open W-Su 9am-4pm. Park office open M-F 7:30am-4pm. Park open dawn-dusk. $3 per car.)*

WOLF HAVEN INTERNATIONAL. This sanctuary provides a permanent home for captive-born gray wolves (reclaimed from zoos or illegal owners). During the summer weekly **Howl-Ins** give visitors the chance to make a night of their wolf experience in a fair-like atmosphere replete with music, picnics, arts and crafts, and of course, wolves. *(3111 Offut Lake Rd. 10 mi. south of the capitol. Take Exit 99 off I-5, turn east, and follow the brown signs. ☎ 264-4695 or 800-448-9653; www.wolfhaven.org. Open May-Sept. M and W-Su 10am-5pm; Oct. and Apr. M and W-Su 10am-4pm; Nov.-Jan. and Mar. Sa-Su 10am-4pm. 45min. tours on the hr.; last tour leaves 1hr. before closing. $7, ages 60 and older $6, 3-12 $5. Howl-ins summer Sa evenings, reservations required; $12, ages 3-12 $6.)*

NORTH PUGET SOUND

North from Seattle, the islands get less developed the further they get from easy reach of city-dwellers eager to head for their beach houses on weekends. Nevertheless, Friday afternoons and holiday weekends still cause horrific traffic jams and ferry lines; heading north on I-5 during the week will save you some of the headache and offer a respite from the crowds. Farther north you'll find the counter-culture college town of Bellingham, the winter sports mecca of Mt. Baker, and the port town of Anacortes, gateway to the beautiful San Juan Islands.

WHIDBEY ISLAND ☎ 360

The largest of Puget Sound's string of islands, Whidbey Island, a beach-ringed strip of land, offers peaceful relaxation on the border between the Sound and the San Juan Islands. The varied terrain, with steep sandy cliffs on the wind-strewn western shores contrasting with the gentle protected eastern beaches crowded with wild roses and blackberries, preserves four state parks and historic reserve. The historic town of Coupeville, the first place settled in Puget Sound, in Whidbey's middle, remains a great place to start exploring, while Oak Harbor, northeast of Coupeville, is a much larger town offering chain stores and a Thursday farmers market. The three Whidbey Island Chamber of Commerce locations have maps and info on all six of the island's coastal towns.

TRANSPORTATION. You can drive onto the island along **Route 20,** which heads west from **I-5,** 12 mi. south of Bellingham, at Exit 230. Rte. 20 and **Route 525** meet near Keystone and form the transportation backbone of the island, linking towns and points of interest. **Island Transit** (☎678-7771 or 321-6688; www.island-transit.org) provides free public transportation all over the island and has info on connections to and from Seattle, but no service Sundays. Buses run approx. 6am-8pm. All buses have bike racks. Flag a bus down anywhere that is safe to stop. **Washington State Ferries** (☎464-6400 or 800-808-7977; www.wsdot.wa.gov/ferries) provide frequent service from the mainland to the island. One ferry connects mainland **Mukilteo,** 10 mi. south of Everett and 19 mi. north of Seattle, with **Clinton,** on the south end of the island (20min.; every 30min. from 4:40am-2am; $3.10, car and driver $6.50-7.25, bike $0.90). The other ferry connects **Port Townsend** on the Olympic Peninsula with the **Keystone terminal** near Ft. Casey State Park (see **Accommodations and Camping,** below), at the "waist" of the island. (30min.; approx. every 1½hr. from 6:30am-7:30pm; $2.70, car and driver $7-8.75, bike $0.90.)

PRACTICAL INFORMATION. Visitor information is available at three locations throughout the island: the **Langley South Whidbey** branch, 208 Anthes St. (☎221-5676 or 221-6765; www.whidbey.net.langley; open M-F 8am-5pm), the **Greater Oak Harbor** branch, 32630 Rte. 20 in Oak Harbor (☎675-3535; www.oakharborchamber.org; open M-F 8am-5pm), and the **Central Whidbey** branch, 107 South Main St. Bldg. E in Coupville (☎678-5434 or 678-5664; www.centralwhidbeychamber.com; open M-F 8am-5pm). The **Coupeville Public Library,** 788 NW Alexander, has free **Internet** access. (☎678-4911. M and W 10am-8pm, Tu and Th-Sa 10am-5pm.) **Island County Emergency Services** are located at 840 SE Barrington Dr. in Oak Harbor on the north end of the island (☎678-6116), and the **Coupeville pharmacy** is at 40 Main St. (☎678-8882. Open M-F 9am-6pm, Sa 10am-4pm.) Mail your letters at the **Pony Mailing & Business Center,** 316 SE Pioneer Way. (☎679-5519 or 800-678-5519; www.ponymailing.com. Open M-F 8am-6pm, Sa 10am-4pm.) **Postal Code:** 98277.

ACCOMMODATIONS AND CAMPING. The beautiful **South Whidbey State Park ❶,** amid a dark stand of old-growth forest above a 4500 ft. stretch of beach on Admiralty Inlet, was once a favorite camp of the Skagit and Snohomish tribes. A short, steep trail leads down to the beach, while others, including the Wilbert Trail, a 2 mi. ridge walk, cut through the unique and ancient woods. (☎321-4559, reservations 888-226-7688. 46 sites $16, hiker/biker sites $8, RV sites $22. Open daily Mar.-Oct.; Nov.-Feb. Sa-Su.) Ebey's Landing National Historic Reserve, a Department of the Interior protected area that preserves a large swath of the peninsula while keeping it in private hands, includes abundant beachfront with great views of the islands, the surrounding Olympic Mountains, and Port Townsend. Two state parks lie near Ebey's Landing. **Fort Ebey State Park ❷** lies just north and east off Rte. 20. Built during WWII, it's smaller and more isolated than its fort cousin to the south. The 50 sites are set in a pleasantly wooded area that blooms with rhododendrons in the spring. (☎678-4636 or 800-233-0321. Sites $16, hiker/biker sites $6, RV sites $22. Open daily 6:30am-dusk, booth hours M-Th and Su 6am-7pm; F-Sa 9-10am, 2-4pm, and 6-8pm.) **Fort Casey State Park ❷** sits on a point in the southern tip of the reserve. Its open grassy space and wide spread of beach are home to old bunkers and military paraphernalia. The picturesque day-use area, up on a bluff protecting the water, hosts an interpretive center at the **Admiralty Point lighthouse.** (Open Apr.-Oct. Th-Su 11am-5pm.) The small, slightly crowded camping area is perched on a sand spit that places the 35 sites in the front row for views of the straits. (☎800-233-0321. Sites $16. Showers $0.25 per 3min.) **Deception Pass State Park ❷,** 41229 Rte. 20. at the northernmost point of the island, is the most popular of Whidbey's four state parks, especially on

WASHINGTON

weekends. There are camping facilities, a saltwater boat launch, and a freshwater lake good for swimming, fishing, and boating. The campground, bustling but beautifully situated in great proximity to the beach, is bombarded with jet noise from EA6B Navy attack aircraft from nearby Whidbey Island Naval Air Station in Oak Harbor. (☎675-2417 or 888-226-7688. Reservations suggested. 250 sites. $16, hiker/biker $5, RV sites $22.) To avoid the busier state parks, try **Rhododendron Campground ❶**, 1½ mi. before Coupeville; look for the small and easy to miss tent sign on eastbound Rte. 20/525; if you see the recycling plant you've just passed it. It's a pleasant, quieter area with ballfields and picnic sites. (☎679-7373. 6 primitive sites. $8.) If you prefer a B&B to a tent, the **Anchorage Inn ❹**, 807 North Main Street in Coupeville, offers comfortable Victorian rooms with water views. (☎678-5581; www.anchorage-inn.com. Reservations for summer season a must. $80.)

🞐 FOOD. As much of the island is farmland, roadside stands peddling fresh vegetables or flowers are at every corner, and a short trip down nearly any side road will lead you to the fields. There are five seasonal farmers markets on the island: the **Coupeville Farmers Market** at 8th and Main runs Apr.-early Oct. Sa 10am-2pm (☎678-4288) as does the **South Whidbey Tilth Farmers Market** on Hwy 525 at Thompson Rd. (☎730-1091; www.southwhidbeytilth.org.) If you're struck by a craving for organic beets, head to the **Oak Harbor Public Market**, at Hwy. 20 in the field next to the visitors center. (☎675-0472. June-Sept. Th 4-7pm.) **La Paz ❷**, 8898 Hwy. 525 right off of the ferry dock, is a Baja-style Mexican restaurant in Clinton, replete with loud colors and a fierce following. A tasty seafood taco with rice is $7; heaping nachos ($5.75) are worth sharing or making a lunch. (☎341-4787. Open daily noon-3pm and 5-8pm, F-Sa until 9pm.) **Front Street,** the main drag of seaside Coupeville, Washington's second-oldest town, makes for a nice stroll. At the bakery tucked below the street, **Knead and Feed ❷**, 4 Front St., you can eat a fresh lunch while you watch the waves. Half sandwiches are $3.25; add homemade soup for $6.75. (☎678-5431. Open M-F 10am-3pm, Sa-Su 9am-4pm.) For coffee, a pizza ($5-6), and a great patio view, walk down the stairs to **Great Times Espresso ❶**, 12 Front St. Creative baked goods and lunch menu ($4-6) make this a tasty mid-day option. (☎678-5358. Open M-F 7am-7pm, Sa-Su 8am-7pm.) Finish your meal off with ice cream in a waffle cone ($2.15-4.75) handmade right before your eyes at **Kapaw's Iskreme ❶**, 21 Front St. (☎678-7741. Open daily Apr.-Oct. 10am-7pm.)

🞐 🞐 SIGHTS AND OUTDOOR ACTIVITIES. Whidbey's four state parks are not only the best places to crash for the night, they're the most worthwhile places to explore during the day. The most crowded spot on the island is **Deception Pass Bridge,** the nation's first suspension bridge, connecting Whidbey Island to Fidalgo Island. At the northern tip of Deception State Park, the artful steel creation dramatically spans Deception Pass itself, a thin sliver of water that can be brought to a boil by tides; white-water kayakers come here to test their mettle against the salt-water rapids. Elsewhere in the park, a 27 mi. network of trails weaves around to beaches and stunning lookouts. Of the many shorter trails and nature walks, the 1 mi. round-trip up **Goose Rock Summit** is worth the easy climb from the Deception Pass parking lot for sweeping views of the island and the San Juans across the water. The **Hoypus Point Trail,** a moderate 3½ mi. loop quieter than most trails, wanders through wet old-growth forest. All Whidbey's other parks have trails worth trekking, especially for beach lovers; between Fort Casey and Fort Ebey, 5 mi. of beach lie waiting for a stroll. South Whidbey State Park's dark, ancient forest and calm beach and Fort Ebey's dramatic bluffs are not to be missed.

While bikers may disappointed that the windy, often shoulderless highway that transects the island is not ideal for biking, exploration of nearly any side road yields gentle rolling hills. For aquaphiles, Deception State Park simply begs to be kayaked or canoed. **Cranberry Lake** awaits canoeists, with varied ecosystems all the way around, while the protected waters in Bowman and Cornet Bays are easily accessible through beach launches for kayakers. The 500 ft. narrow **Deception Pass** itself should only be paddled by the most experienced of kayakers as strong currents and gusting winds prevail. Those looking for longer days on the water can make the crossing to Deception and Northwest Island to the west or Strawberry and Hope Island in the east. **Sea Kayak Tours** doesn't rent, but they will take you on a 2hr. guided tour from one of five spots on the island (☎321-4683. $49. Tours leave Apr.-May 10am-2pm; June-Aug. 10am, 2pm and 6pm; Sept.-Oct. 10am-2pm.)

BELLINGHAM   ☎360

Situated between Seattle and Vancouver, Bellingham (pop. 69,850) is a dream city for the outdoor adventurer. Mt. Baker and the North Cascades are just a stone's throw to the east, and Bellingham Bay offers an array of ocean adventures, from kayaking to whale watching. Historic Bellingham was an industrial port city reliant upon rich mineral and timber resources. Today, Bellingham's port still thrives and is home to a large fishing fleet and ferry boats. The town also accommodates Western Washington University (WWU) and its 12,000 students.

■▐ **ORIENTATION AND TRANSPORTATION.** Bellingham lies along **I-5**, 90 mi. north of **Seattle** and 55 mi. south of **Vancouver, BC.** Downtown centers on **Holly Street** and **Cornwall Avenue,** next to the Georgia Pacific pulp mill (Exits 252 and 253 off I-5). **WWU** sits atop a hill to the south. The village of **Fairhaven,** south of Bellingham, is serviced by public transit. **Amtrak** runs two trains per day to Seattle (2½hr., $22) and one to Vancouver, BC (1½hr., $15) from **Fairhaven Station,** 401 Harris Ave., next to the ferry terminal. (☎734-8851 or 800-872-7245. Counter open daily 8:30am-12:30pm and 1-4:30pm.) **Greyhound** is located in the same station. (☎733-5251 or 800-231-2222. Open M-F 8am-6pm, Sa-Su 8am-5pm.) Buses run to Seattle (2hr., 5 per day, $15); Mt. Vernon (30min., 5 per day, $7.50); and Vancouver (2hr., 4 per day, $15). Private shuttles run **ferries** to the nearby San Juan Islands (p. 222). The #1 bus runs from Fairhaven Station to downtown. All downtown routes start at the **Railroad Avenue Mall** between Champion and Magnolia St. (☎676-7433. Runs M-F 6am-7pm, Sa 9:30-5:45pm. $0.50, ages 65 and older $0.25. Buses run every ½hr. or 1hr.) **Taxis** run 24hr. (☎734-8294 or 800-281-5430. $1.80 base rate, $1.10 per mi.)

▐ **PRACTICAL INFORMATION.** Services include a friendly, well-organized **Visitors Info Center,** 904 Potter St. Take Exit 253 (Lakeway) from I-5. (☎671-3990; www.bellingham.org. Open daily 8:30am-5:30pm.) **Fairhaven Bike & Mountain Sports,** 1108 11th St., rents bikes ($20-40 per day), skis ($20-30 per day), snowboards ($30 per day), and snowshoes ($12 per day). (☎733-4433; www.fairhavenbike.com. Open M-Th 9:30am-7pm, F 9:30am-8pm, Sa 10am-6pm, Su 11am-5pm.) **Bellingham Cleaning Center,** 1010 Lakeway Dr., offers washing for $1.50 and drying for $0.25 per 8min. (☎734-3755. Open daily 6am-10pm.) Other services include **police,** 505 Grand Ave. (☎676-6913. Open M-F 8am-5:30pm.); **crisis line,** ☎800-584-3578; and **St. Joseph's General Hospital,** 2901 Squalicum Pkwy. (☎734-5400. 24hr. emergency care.) Access the **Internet** at the **library,** 210 Central Ave., at Commercial St. opposite City Hall. (☎676-6860; www.bellinghampubliclibrary.org. Open M-Th 10am-9pm, F-Sa 10am-6pm; also Sept.-May Su 1-5pm.) Internet access is also available at **The Net Bistro,** 1411 Railroad Ave. (☎733-3133. $3 per hr. Open M-F 10am-7pm, Sa 10am-6pm). The **post office** is at 315 Prospect St. (☎800-275-8777. Open M-F 8am-5:30pm, Sa 9:30am-3pm.) **Postal Code:** 98225.

Bellingham

▲ ■ ACCOMMODATIONS

Bellingham Inn, **4**
Birch Bay Hostel, **1**
Larrabee State Park, **9**

● FOOD
Boundary Bay Brewery &
Bistro, **7**
Casa Que Pasa, **3**
Community Food Co-op, **5**
The Malt Shop, **6**
Old Town Cafe, **2**
Tony's, **8**

🏠🏕 ACCOMMODATIONS AND CAMPING. Bellingham does not have a hostel, but nearby Birch Bay offers the **Birch Bay Hostel ②**, 7467 Gemini St. (☎371-2180; www.biz.birchbay.net/hostel) I-5 exit 266; take 548W 5 mi. and turn on Alderson, then enter Camp Horizon Park. Free Internet access. Open daily for walk-ins Apr. 15-Oct. 30. Reservations needed Nov. 1-Apr. 14. Office open 7:30-9:30am and 5-10pm. Thirty-six beds, four of them double beds. $17, cyclists $15; family suites $42-50. Discounts available for groups of 20 or more. In Bellingham proper you can pick from a strip of budget motels on N Samish Way (2min. off exit 252). The **Bellingham Inn ③**, 202 E Holly St. off I-5 Exit 253, in the heart of Downtown, has queen beds, clean rooms, and cable TV. (☎734-1900. Singles $50; doubles $61.) **Larrabee State Park ①**, on Chuckanut Dr., 7 mi. south of town, offers 14 mi. of trails, bouldering, a boat launch, clamming, and views of the San Juan Islands. (Information ☎902-8844; reservations 888-226-7688. 85 sites, $16; RV sites $22, extra car $10. Free hot showers. Reservations suggested. Park open daily 6:30am-dusk.)

🍴 FOOD. The **Community Food Co-op**, 1220 N Forest St. at Chestnut St., has all the essentials for the healthy eater, plus a tasty cafe and deli (chai $2.45, salad $4.50) in the back. (☎734-8158; www.communityfoodcoop.com. Open daily 8am-9pm; cafe closes at 8pm.) The Saturday **Bellingham Farmer's Market,** on Railroad Ave. between Chestnut St. and Maple St., has vendors selling fresh fruit, vegetables, breads, seafood, and homemade doughnuts. (☎ 647-2060; www.bellinghamfarm-ers.org. Open Apr.-Oct. Sa 10am-3pm.) Feast on huge burritos starting at $3 at **Casa Que Pasa ❶**, 1415 Railroad Ave., which also sports gallery space for local artists and a bar with 77 different types of tequila. (☎ 738-8226; www.barstop.com/casa. Open daily 11am-11pm; tequila bar open until 1am.) For a taste of local brew or a satisfyingly large sandwich, check out the **Boundary Bay Brewery & Bistro ❷**, 1107 Railroad Ave. Pints are $3.50, nachos cost $8.50 and sandwiches start at $7. (☎ 647-5593; www.bbaybrewery.com. Open M-Sa 11am-11pm, Su 4-11pm.) Delectable breakfasts are available all day at **The Old Town Cafe ❶**, 316 West Holly St., which specializes in organic and vegetarian food. Buttermilk pancakes are $4; breakfast specials start at $5. (☎ 671-4431. Open M-Sa 6:30am-3pm, Su 8am-2pm.) A quick meal can be found at **The Malt Shop ❶**, 1135 Railroad Ave., where a "peanut butter burger" is $2.75 and over 48 flavors of ice cream is $2.40. (☎ 715-1555. M-Th 9am-9pm, F-Su 9am-10pm.) **Tony's ❶**, 1101 Harris Ave., is in Fairhaven Village, just blocks from the ferry. This coffee and tea shop serves ice cream, bagels, and a $4.50 espresso milkshake. (☎ 738-4710. Open M-Th 7am-6pm, F-Su 7am-8pm.)

◪ ◪ SIGHTS AND ENTERTAINMENT. The **Whatcom Museum of History and Art,** 121 Prospect St., occupies four buildings along Prospect St., most notably the bright-red former city hall. (☎ 676-6981; www.whatcommuseum.org. Open Tu-Su noon-5pm. Wheelchair-accessible. Free.) The ARCO Exhibits Building, which hosts Northwest-related art, the Syre Education Center (the natural history branch), and the Whatcom Children's Museum make up the rest of the museum. **Big Rock Garden Park,** 2900 Sylvan St., is a little-known three-acre Japanese-style sculpture garden showing mostly contemporary work. Take Alabama St. east and then go left on Sylvan St. for several blocks. The garden also offers concerts; call for a schedule. (☎ 676-6985. Open daily summer 7am-9pm; winter 8am-6pm.)

In the second week of June, lumberjacks from across the land gather for axe-throwing and log-rolling at the **Deming Logging Show.** To reach the show grounds, take Rte. 542 (Mt. Baker Hwy.) 12 mi. east to Cedarville Rd. and then turn left and follow signs. (☎ 592-3051. $6, ages 3-12 $3.) The **Bellingham Festival of Music** attracts symphony, chamber, folk, and jazz musicians from around the world during the first two weeks of August. (☎ 676-5997; www.bellinghamfestival.org. Tickets $19-25; half-price student rush tickets available an hour before showtime.) Also in early August is the two-day **Mount Baker Blues Festival** at Rivers Edge Tree Farm in Deming. (☎ 671-6817; www.bakerblues.com. Festival $50, single day $25.) Memorial Day weekend sees the mother of all relays, the **Ski to Sea Race.** Teams ski, run, canoe, bike, and sea kayak 85 mi. from Mt. Baker to the finish line at Bellingham Bay. Families, friends, and spectators join the participants in a grand parade and festival at the race's conclusion. (☎ 734-1330; www.bellingham.com/skitosea. $25.)

⚠ OUTDOOR ACTIVITIES. The 2½ mi. hike up **Chuckanut Mountain** leads through a quiet forest to a view of the islands that fill the bay. On clear days, Mt. Rainier is visible from the top. The trail leaves from the North Chuckanut Mountain Trailhead off Old Samish Hwy., about 3 mi. south of city limits. From Clayton Beach there is a 1 mi. hike to an excellent vista of the San Juan Islands. From the viewpoint, you can hike the **Fragrance Lake Trail** for a swim (1 mi. from viewpoint to lake). The beach at **Lake Padden Park,** 4882 Samish Way, is also great for a dip; take bus #44 to 1 mi. south of downtown. The park also has tennis courts, playing fields, hiking trails, and fishing off the pier. (☎ 676-6985. Open daily 6am-10pm.) The popular **Rotary Interurban Trail** (great for biking and running) travels 7 mi. from **Fairhaven Park** to **Larrabee State Park** along the relatively flat route of the old Interurban Electric Railway. Breaks in the trees permit glimpses of the San Juan Islands. Several trails branch off the main line and lead into the Chuckanut Mountains or to the coast; maps are available at the visitors center at Larrabee.

MOUNT BAKER   ☎360

Rising 10,778 ft. above sea level, Mt. Baker is the crown jewel of the 1.7 million-
acre Mt. Baker-Snoqualmie National Forest. Mt. Baker hasn't erupted for 10,000
years, but occasionally steam rises from this active volcano. An average yearly
snowfall of 595 in. (49½ ft.) makes for excellent snowboarding and skiing. No high-
speed lifts here; just great bowls, chutes, glades, and cheap lift tickets. During the
summer, hikers and mountaineers challenge themselves on Mt. Baker's trails.

🚍🔁 TRANSPORTATION AND PRACTICAL INFORMATION. To get to this hotbed of outdoor activity, take I-5 Exit 255 just north of Bellingham, to Rte. 542,
known as the Mt. Baker Hwy. Fifty-eight miles of roads through the foothills afford
views of Baker and other peaks in the range. The highway ends at Artist Point
(5140 ft.), with spectacular wilderness vistas. The road closes at Mt. Baker Ski
Area (mile 55) from Oct. to mid-July. For trail maps, backcountry permits, or further info about both the National Forest and National Park, stop by the **Glacier
Ranger Station,** located on Rte. 542 just before the National Forest. (☎599-2714.
Open daily May-Oct. 8am-4:30pm; Oct.-May Sa-Su 8am-4:30pm.)

🏠🏕 ACCOMMODATIONS AND CAMPING. Silver Lake Park ❷, 9006 Silver Lake
Rd., is 3 mi. north of the highway at Maple Falls. The park has 73 sites, 4 mi. of hik-
ing trails, and lake activities. To catch a few of the 17,000 trout stocked yearly in
Silver Lake, a license is necessary. Two-day licenses ($6.50) are available in Maple
Falls. (☎599-2776. Sites $17; RV sites $19.) More primitive and closer to the mountain are **Douglas Fir Campground ❶,** past Glacier at mile 36 off Rte. 542 (Open mid-
May to early Oct. 30 sites, $14), and **Silver Fir Campground ❶,** at mile 46 off Rte. 542.
(☎877-444-6777 or 518-885-3639. Open mid-May to early Sept. 21 sites, $12.) For
more comfort, **Glacier Creek Lodge ❸,** 10036 Mt. Baker Hwy., with its steamy hot
tub, is a fine option for the night. Two-night min. stay on weekends during ski season. (☎599-2991; www.glaciercreeklodge.com. Included breakfast. Reservations
essential Jan.-Feb. and July-Aug. Singles or doubles $48; cabins $75-185.)

❄ WINTER SPORTS. Baker was home to one of the first organized snowboard
races, and boards are wildly popular here. The volcano packs soft powder for
longer than any other nearby ski area, staying open from early November through
May, though the lifts close April 1. The ski area has seven diesel-powered lifts and
some of the lowest lift ticket rates in the Northwest. There is no snow-making or
shaping on the mountain's 1500 vertical feet of runs. Contact the **Mount Baker Ski
Area Office,** 1019 Iowa St., in Bellingham for more info. (☎734-6771;
www.mtbaker.us. Lift tickets Sa-Su and holidays $37, M-F $29; under 16 $28/$23;
ages 60-69 $30/$25; ages 70 and older $10; under 7 free.) In the winter many trails
become impromptu cross-country ski trails and snowshoe tracks.

🥾 HIKING. Many roads and trails are covered in snow well into the summer so
call ahead to check which trails are accessible. In June, you can access the Glacier
Overlook along **Heliotrope Ridge** (Forest Rd. 39 off Hwy. 542). This 3 mi. trail is the
starting point for mountaineers heading up Baker and offers hikers an excellent
view of the mountain. The **Lake Ann Trail** (5 mi., multi-day) is one of the favorites in
the area. This steep trail leads 5 mi. to the lake of the same name, then continues
to the Lower Curtis Glacier. **Skyline Divide,** on Forest Rd. 37 off Hwy. 542, is a great
day-hike that provides stunning views of the North Cascade range (3½ mi.) Hikers
can make the inevitable Robert Frost references along the **Fire and Ice Trail,** a picturesque half-mile loop beginning on Rte. 542. The first part of the trail is wheelchair-accessible. For a hike up to a beautiful, remote lake, head up to **Tomyhoi Lake
Trail** (4 mi., full day). Take Forest Rd. 3065 north from the highway as far as it goes.

MOUNTAINEERING. If you're looking to climb in the North Cascades, considerable experience in mountaineering and glacier travel is necessary. Check out Fred Beckey's *Cascade Alpine Guide: Climbing and High Routes* or contact the **American Alpine Institute,** 1515 12th St., in Bellingham. (☎ 671-1505; www.mtnguide.com. Open M-F 9am-5:30pm.) Both provide information on routes, and the American Alpine Institute provides experienced guides and a variety of organized trips. (3-day Mt. Baker summit $495, 6-day introductory Alpine course $990; private instruction also available starting at $295 per day for one climber.)

DAYTRIP: MT. BAKER-SNOQUALMIE NATIONAL FOREST

The 1.7 million acre **Mt. Baker-Snoqualmie National Forest** spans more than 140 mi. from the Washington-Canada border to Mt. Rainier National Park. The Mt. Baker Scenic Byway (Rte. 542) in the northern part of the forest, is a pleasant 24 mi. drive through gorgeous, mostly untouched wilderness. A more southern approach is from Anacortes; take **Route 20** via Sedro-Woolley to reach nine-mile long **Baker Lake,** which provides ample space for water lovers seeking a place to fish, boat, or just picnic. Both Mt. Baker and **Mount Shuksan** loom in the near distance, only two of the many dauntingly large peaks in the backdrop to an inviting lakefront and an extensive series of trails. There are six Forest Service-maintained **campsites ❷** along the lake—**Horseshoe Cove** has the best swimming beach. (Campsite updates ☎ 856-5700; reservations 877-444-6777 or www.reserveusa.com. Reservations recommended in the busy summer months. Sites $16, RV sites $22. **Maple Grove ❶,** on the east side of the lake, accessible only by boat or foot, is free. **Panorama Point** and **Park Creek** sites are only open mid-May to mid-Sept.)

Numerous short hikes scatter the area; for full information and maps, stop at one of the information or visitors centers or pick up the annual *Visitors Information Guide to the North Cascades.* Some beautiful options include the trail up **Dock Butte,** a moderate 3 mi. round-trip hike to an almost perpetually snow-covered peak with a stunning mountain view (take Baker Lake Rd. to Forest Rd. 1230.) The 5 mi. round-trip hike to **Watson Lake** is an easy route to a series of alpine lakes actually in the adjacent Noisy-Diosbud Wilderness (from Baker Lake Hwy. turn right onto Forest Rd. 1107.) The **Baker River Trail,** also easy at 6 mi. round-trip, meanders along the river into lush old growth forest (at the end of Baker Lake Rd.) Or, to just get a sense of what the ecosystem looked like before being butchered by heavy logging, stroll on the **Shadow of the Sentinels Nature Trail,** an easy half-mile interpretive trek 14 mi. down Baker Lake Rd.

ANACORTES ☎ 360

As the hub of Washington State Ferries' transportation to the San Juan Islands and Sidney, BC, Anacortes serves mainly as a stopover for island travelers. To get there from Seattle take **I-5** North to Mt. Vernon, then pick up **Route 20** west toward Anacortes. Rte. 20 will take you right to **Commercial Avenue.** Follow signs to continue on to the ferry. Rte. 20 will eventually lead into **Ferry Terminal Road** about 5 mi. outside the city center. If you miss your ferry or are looking to spend the night in Anacortes, you can stay in one of the many cheap motels lining Commercial Ave. **The Gateway Motel ❸,** 2019 Commercial Ave, is a reasonable deal with rooms starting at $50 per night (☎ 293-2655). For something a little nicer, try the **Anacortes Inn ❹,** 3006 Commercial Ave. (☎ 293-3153; www.anacortesinn.com. June-Oct. singles from $72; doubles from $77. Oct.-May $62/$65.) **Esteban's Taqueria ❶,** 2520 Commercial Ave. is a fast and filling pre-ferry fix with many vegetarian options. Burritos from $4.95. (☎ 588-1288. Open daily 11am-10pm.) **Daddio's ❶,** 2120 Commercial Ave., blends a 50s diner with a modern-day pizzeria and makes a fine milkshake ($4). Two slices with drink $4.50.(☎ 588-1987. Open daily 10:30am-10:30pm.)

SAN JUAN ISLANDS ☎ 360

With hundreds of tiny islands and endless parks and coastline, the San Juan Islands are an explorer's dream. The islands enjoy nothing less than perfect weather: between May and September the average daily high temperature is in the upper 60s to low 70s, the sun shines almost every day, and only one inch of rain falls each summer month in this "rain-shadow" of the Olympic Mountains. The scattered small towns showcase each island's individuality. Tourists storm the islands in July and August; early June and September tend to be slightly less packed. The *San Juanderer* has tide charts and ferry schedules, and is free on ferries or at visitors centers, or can be read online at www.gosanjuans.com. A trip to the San Juan Islands requires thinking ahead as the info you need may be available only in Seattle; be sure to book early if you are planning a summertime visit.

⊀ INTER-ISLAND TRANSPORTATION

Washington State Ferries (☎ 206-464-6400 or 888-808-7977; www.wsdot.wa.gov/ferries) has frequent daily service to **Lopez** (40min.), **Orcas** (1½hr.), **San Juan Island** (1-2hr.), and **Shaw** (1hr.) from **Anacortes;** check the schedule available at visitors centers in Puget Sound. Travel time to the islands depends on the number of stops. To save on fares, travel directly to the westernmost island on your itinerary, then return: eastbound traffic travels for free. The ferries are packed in summer, so call ahead to ask when to arrive. Generally, you should get there at least 1hr. (2hr. on weekends) prior to departure. (Anacortes to Friday Harbor: passengers $9-12, vehicles $30-44. Westbound inter-island: passengers free, vehicles $13-16. Cash and credit cards accepted in Anacortes; inter-island ferries cash only.)

   Victoria Clipper (☎ 800-888-2535; www.victoriaclipper.com), departs **Seattle's** Pier 69 daily for San Juan Island, arriving at Spring St. Landing in **Friday Harbor** (2½hr., 2 per day, round trip $43-$53, ages 1-11 $27-$32). **Island Commuter** (☎ 734-8180 or 888-734-8180; www.islandcommuter.com) departs **Bellingham** for **Friday Harbor** (2¼hr., 1 per day) and islands on the way ($29, round-trip $39, ages 6-12 $15/$20, under 6 free; bikes $5). **Kenmore Air** (☎ 800-543-9595; www.kenmoreair.com) flies to San Juan from Seattle (4-5 times per day; one-way $98-111, round-trip $163-199). The **Bellingham Airporter** (☎ 866-235-5247; www.airporter.com) runs shuttle buses between **Sea-Tac** (p. 176) and **Anacortes** (10 per day; $31, round-trip $56).

SAN JUAN ISLAND ☎ 360

Home to a National Historic Park and Lime Kiln State Park, the only designated whale watching park in the world, San Juan Island is the island most popular as a tourist destination despite being the farthest from Anacortes. Ferries drop off passengers in Friday Harbor, the largest town in the archipelago. San Juan Island is the easiest island to explore on a budget since the ferry docks right in town, and the roads are good for cyclists, and a shuttle bus services the island.

   ▐ **TRANSPORTATION.** With bicycle, car, and boat rentals within blocks of the ferry terminal, Friday Harbor is a convenient base for exploring San Juan. Miles of poorly marked roads access all corners of the island. It's wise to carefully plot a course on the free map available at the visitors centers, real estate offices, and gas stations. **San Juan Transit** (☎ 378-8887 or 800-887-8387; www.sanjuantransit.com), travels from Friday Harbor to Roche Harbor on the hour and will stop upon request. ($5, return trip $8; from Friday Harbor to Westside $5/$8; day pass $10, 2-day pass $17. $17 tours depart Friday Harbor at 11am and 1pm. Call ahead for reservations.) **San Juan Taxi** (☎ 378-3550; available daily 6am-midnight) charges $4 base, $2 for 2nd person, $1 per person after that, $1 per mi. after the 1st mi.

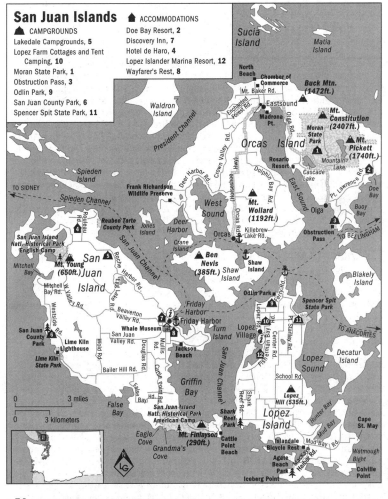

San Juan Islands

▲ CAMPGROUNDS

Lakedale Campgrounds, **5**
Lopez Farm Cottages and Tent
    Camping, **10**
Moran State Park, **1**
Obstruction Pass, **3**
Odlin Park, **9**
San Juan County Park, **6**
Spencer Spit State Park, **11**

♠ ACCOMMODATIONS

Doe Bay Resort, **2**
Discovery Inn, **7**
Hotel de Haro, **4**
Lopez Islander Marina Resort, **12**
Wayfarer's Rest, **8**

WASHINGTON

🛈 PRACTICAL INFORMATION. The **Chamber of Commerce**, 1 Front St. 2a, is upstairs on the corner of Front St. and Spring St. Stop in for a map and information on tours. (☎378-5240 or 888-468-3701; www.sanjuanisland.org and www.guideto-sanjuans.com. Open Apr.-Nov. M-F 9:30am-4:30pm, Sa 10am-2pm. Call for low-season hours.) For **outdoors information,** visit the **San Juan National Historic Park Information Center,** on the corner of First St. and Spring St. which, provides information on the historic buildings of American Camp and British Camp. (☎378-2240; www.nps.gov/sajh. Open daily 8:30am-4:30pm.) A host of companies offer **tours**; shopping around (especially looking at fliers at the tourist office) pays dividends. **San Juan Boat Tours,** on Spring St., docks a block from the ferry and has a 66-passenger boat with speakers to pick up the orcas' chat. (☎800-232-6722; www.whale-watch.com. 3hr., departs daily late May-early Sept. at noon; $39, children $29.) **Sea Quest Expeditions,** a non-profit education, research, and conservation group, runs kayaking tours daily all year. Call to arrange trips. (☎378-5767 or 888-589-4253; www.sea-quest-kayak.com/quest.htm. Daytrip $65; half- and multi-day trips available.) **Crystal Seas Kayaking** (☎378-7899; www.crystalseas.com) also runs tours from $49 for 3hr. to $800 for six days. **Susie's Mopeds,** on the corner of First St. and A St., rents mopeds to those with a driver's license. (☎378-5244, 800-532-0087; www.susiesmopeds.com. $20 per hr. or $60 per day. Also rents scootcars, $40 per hr. or $120 per day and convertible SUVs for $40 per hr. or $120 per day. Open daily 9am-6pm.) **Island Bicycles,** 380 Argyle Ave. (☎378-4941; www.islandbicycles.com) rents bikes starting at $7 per hr. or $35 per day. **Sail-In Laundromat** is located on East St. behind the waterfront strip. Wash $3, dry $0.25 per 5min. (Open daily 7am-8pm.) The **police** can be found on 135 Rhone St. (☎378-4151), at Reed St. **Friday Harbor Drug,** 210 Spring St., is the local **pharmacy.** (☎378-4421. Open M-Sa 9am-7pm, Su 10am-4pm.) To determine whether it's safe to go to the beach, call the **Red Tide Hotline** at ☎800-562-5632. **Inter-Island Medical Center,** 550 Spring St., at Mullis Rd., provides **medical services.** (☎378-2141. Open M-F 8:30am-4:30pm, Sa 10am-1pm.) The **Crisis Line** is ☎378-2345. 24hr. The **San Juan Island Library,** 1010 Guard St., provides visitors with 30min. of free emailing or 1hr. general **Internet** use. (☎378-2798; www.sanjuan.lib.wa.us. Open M, W, and F 10am-6pm, Tu and Th 10am-8pm, Sa 10am-5pm, Su 1-5pm.) The **post office** is on 220 Blair Ave., at Reed St. (☎378-4511. Open M-F 8:30am-4:30pm.) **Postal Code:** 98250.

ACCOMMODATIONS AND CAMPING. The popularity of San Juan and its few budget accommodations makes finding a cheap bed challenging. The campgrounds are wildly popular; reservations are imperative. While beautiful, the B&Bs are also prohibitively expensive; contact **San Juan Central Reservation** (☎800-722-2939; www.sanjuanisland.com) for help. If you miss out on hosteling and camping options, your best bet may be to take the ferry back to Anacortes where a number of (relatively) cheap motels line Commercial Ave. Prices can be less than half of those on the island. **Wayfarer's Rest** ❷, 35 Malcolm St., a 10min. walk from the ferry up Spring onto Argyle St. and turn left at the church. This house-turned-hostel has beautiful homemade driftwood bunks, a comfortable living area with TV, a patio and garden, a full kitchen, and two cats. Coin showers, washers, and dryers (showers $0.25 per 1½ min; $2 wash, $2 dry). (☎378-6428; www.rockisland.com/~wayfarersrest. Bike rental $15 per day. Check-in 2-9pm. Bunk room $22; private room and cabins from $55.) **San Juan County Park** ❶, 380 Westside Rd., 10 mi. west of Friday Harbor, along the bay, offers twenty sites perched on a bluff with a fantastic sunset view. (☎378-1842; www.co.san-juan.wa.us/parks. Open daily 7am-10pm. Reservations can be made up to 3 months in advance. There is a $6 reservation fee, and sites fill up fast in July and Aug. Sites $6; vehicle sites $23.) **Lakedale Campgrounds** ❶, 4313 Roche Harbor Rd., 4 mi. from Friday Harbor, just west of Egg Lake Rd., has lakeside sites. (☎378-2350 or 800-617-2267; www.lakedale.com. Reception 8am-10pm. Reservations suggested, but campers can almost always find spots. Fishing permits $4.50 per day, non-campers $8.50 per day. Boat rental $5-7 per hour. Open Mar. 15-Oct. 15; cabins year-round. Hiker/biker sites $9 per person; vehicle sites $26, plus $5.75 per person after the second person; 4-person tent cabins from $45. Showers $2 for 5min.) The **Hotel de Haro** ❹, 248 Reuben Memorial Dr., was built in 1886 and overlooks a busy harbor and beautiful formal garden. Its guest book has signatures of Teddy Roosevelt and others, and some locals claim that it's haunted. (☎378-2155 or 800-451-8910; www.rocheharbor.com. Oct.-May starting at $69, May-Sept. $85.)

FOOD. Both the quality and quantity of food at **King's Market,** 160 Spring St., will trick you into thinking you're on the mainland; once you see the bill, however, reality will strike. (☎378-4505. Open summer M-Sa 7:30am-10pm, Su 7:30am-9pm.)

Plan ahead to avoid missing a meal; many cafes and restaurants close early. **Vic's Drive Inn ❶,** 25 2nd St., has the cheapest burger in Friday Harbor ($2). Sandwiches start at $4. (☎378-8427. Open M-F 7am-7pm, Sa 7am-2pm.) **Hungry Clam Fish and Chips ❷,** 130 First St., serves up excellent fresh beer-battered Alaskan Cod. (☎378-3474. Open daily Memorial Day-Labor Day 11am-9pm; Labor Day-Memorial Day 11am-7pm.) **Front Street Ale House ❷,** 1 Front St., serves cold brews from the San Juan Brewing Co., located just next door. San Juan local microbrews taste fantastic after a long day of biking or paddling. Pints $4.25. Appetizers ($6-8), sandwiches ($7-9), and burgers ($6-12) complement the local beers. (☎378-2337. Open M-Th and Su 11am-11pm, F-Sa 11am-midnight.) **Thai Kitchen ❸,** 42 First St., next to the Whale Museum, provides diners with a patio for flower-sniffing or star-gazing. Try the fresh lime juice with the popular pad thai. (☎378-1917. Open for lunch Tu-Sa 11:30am-2pm, dinner daily 5-9pm.) **Blue Dolphin Cafe ❷,** 185 First St., is a local favorite for a hearty breakfast or lunch. Daily specials (from $7) are a good bet if you've got a few extra bucks. (☎378-6116. Open daily 5am-2pm.) The **San Juan Donut Shop ❷,** 209 Spring St., feeds ferry travelers with bottomless coffee ($1.50) and fresh donuts ($0.75), and also offers more substantial fare such as omelettes ($6), sandwiches ($7.50), and burgers. (☎378-2271. Open daily 6am-3pm.)

◪ **SIGHTS.** Driving around the 35 mi. perimeter of the island takes about 2hr.; on bike, it makes for the perfect day-long tour. The **West Side Road** traverses gorgeous scenery and provides the best chance to sight **orcas** from three resident pods. To begin a tour of the island, head south and west out of Friday Harbor on Mullis Rd. (Bikers may want to do this route in the opposite direction, as counterclockwise climbs around the island are more gradual.)

The **Whale Museum,** 62 First St. N, has a collection of artifacts and whale skeletons as well as modern tools used for whale research. There is even a phone booth where you can listen to the sound of orcas, dolphins and walruses. Local whale art adds a colorful backdrop to the experience. Call their whale hotline at ☎800-562-8832 to report sightings and strandings. (☎378-4710 or 800-946-7227; www.whale-museum.org. Open daily May-Sept. 10am-5pm; call for winter hours. $6, ages 65 and over $5, students and ages 5-18 $3, under 5 free.)

In the mid-19th century American and British troops came to the brink of war after the slaughtering of a pig brought a border dispute centering on the San Juans to a head. Two national historic parks preserve a living memory of tensions between the British and American camps co-occupying the island. The American army built its barracks on Cattle Point, located on southeastern San Juan Island, south from Friday Harbor. Today, **American Camp** is the more elaborate of the park's two halves. The **visitors center** explains the history of the curious conflict, while a self-guided trail leads from the shelter to an excellent view of Mt. Baker at the Redoubt. (☎378-2240. Open daily June-Aug. dawn-11pm; Sept.-May Th-Su. visitors center open daily June-Aug. 8:30am-5pm; Sept.-May Th-Su 8:30am-4:30pm.) The hike to the top of Mt. Finlayson is slightly longer and rewards its travelers with views, on a clear day, of Mt. Baker to the east, Mt. Rainier to the southeast, the Olympics to the south, and British Columbia to the west. **English Camp,** on Roche Harbor Rd. at the island's north end, exhibits a greater number of historic buildings and contains one of Washington's largest Big Leaf Maple trees. The Bell Point trail is a pleasant 2 mi. loop. During the summer on Saturday afternoons, the two camps alternate re-enacting Pig War-era life. (Open daily June-Aug. 9am-5pm. Walks June-Sept. Sa 11:30am. Re-enactments June-July 12:30-3:30pm. Free.)

◪ **OUTDOOR ACTIVITIES.** Tourism on San Juan Island is centered around whales. The San Juan Islands are home to three pods of orcas, dubbed J, K, and L. San Juan Island receives the majority of whale watching attention due to the

WASHINGTON

HOTEL DE HORROR

In 1886, John S. McMillin built the Hotel de Haro in Roche Harbor on San Juan Island to entertain guests coming to purchase lime from his Tacoma and Roche Lime Company. It has since been a stopover for many distinguished Americans, including President Theodore Roosevelt, whose signature is prominently displayed in the guestbook.

But it's not visits from long-dead presidents that make the hotel worth a second look. According to local legend, the de Haro has sheltered guests both human and supernatural. One story claims that the ghost of a young woman jilted by her fiancé roams the halls. Other accounts warn of the McMillin mausoleum, built as a memorial and final resting place for the family. A brief walk through the woods near the hotel brings you to the mausoleum, where an eerie dining room configuration is set up. Each chair, with a single column behind it, holds the ashes of one family member. Legend says that one of the sons did not make it into the crypt. He was disowned for marrying against his father's will, and his chair was removed. When the son died, the column behind where his chair had been crumbled. Today, all that remains are the ashes of five family members and the destroyed column of the sixth; visitors to the mausoleum at dusk have claimed to see the McMillin family assembled in their places.

whales' travel patterns through the **Haro Strait.** In summer, whales are seen daily from **Lime Kiln Point State Park,** along West Side Rd. More determined whale watchers might prefer a cruise; see **San Juan Boat Tours,** p. 223. Keep in mind that San Juan has almost as many whale-watching boats as it does whales, and whale watching can sometimes feel like whaleboat watching. When choosing a company, ask about boat size; smaller boats usually get closer to the whales. Kayak tours will also seek out orcas; see **Sea Quest Expeditions** and **Crystal Seas Kayaking,** p. 223.

The island provides several laid-back hiking trails and picturesque beaches, both relaxing options for the afternoon. If the sky is clear, the half-mile jaunt down the road to **Cattle Point** offers views of the distant Olympic Mountain. **South Beach** provides a stretch of dazzling shoreline. Also in the south, **Eagle Cove** and **Grandma's Cove** are considered two of the finest beaches on the island. In the northeast the somewhat difficult to find **Reuben Tarte** beach offers more secluded waters and a good place to launch a kayak. (Take Roche Harbor Road to Rouleau Rd. Make a right onto Limestone Pt. Rd. and another right onto San Juan Dr.) Heading east from West Side Rd., Mitchell Bay Rd. leads to a steep half-mile trail to **"Mount" Young,** a tall hill within viewing range of Victoria and the Olympic Range. The gravel False Bay Rd., heading west from Cattle Point Rd., runs to **False Bay,** where **bald eagles** nest. During spring and summer, nesting eagles are visible at low tide along the northwestern shore.

ORCAS ISLAND   ☎ 360

Mt. Constitution overlooks much of Puget Sound from its 2407 ft. summit atop Orcas Island (ORK-us)—this high point is one of the best 360° marine viewpoints in North America. A small population of retirees, artists, and farmers dwells here in understated homes surrounded by green shrubs and the bronze bark of madrona trees. With a commune-like campground and resort and the largest state park in Washington, Orcas Island has the best budget tourist facilities in the San Juans. Unfortunately, much of the beach is occupied by private resorts and closed to the public. Moran State Park offers a relaxing wilderness experience while Eastsound provides a movie theater, several restaurants, a museum, and shopping.

■■ **ORIENTATION AND PRACTICAL INFORMATION.** Orcas is shaped like a horseshoe, leading residents to call the series of main roads that traverse the island the **Horseshoe Highway.** The ferry lands on the southwest tip at **Orcas Village. Eastsound,** the main town, is at the top of the horseshoe, 9 mi. northeast.

Olga and **Doe Bay** are another 8 mi. and 11 mi. down the eastern side of the horseshoe, respectively. Pick up a map in one of the shops at the ferry landing. San Juan Island houses the more official tourist facilities, but the **Chamber of Commerce,** 254 North Beach Rd. offers some guidance. (☎376-2273; www.orcasisland.org. Open M-Sa 10am-2pm.) **Dolphin Bay Bicycles,** near the ferry, rents bikes for $30 per day, $70 for 3 days. (☎376-4157; www.rockisland.com/~dolphin.) **Eastsound Sporting Goods,** 1 Main St., Templin Center #4, caters to all your outdoor equipment needs and rents fishing rods for $10 per day. Provides two-day fishing ($8.60) and crabbing permits ($13). (☎376-5588. Open mid-June to Sept. M-Sa 9:30am-8pm, Su 10am-4pm; Oct.-May M-Sa 9:30am-5pm, Su 10am-4pm.) The pharmacy is **Ray's,** Templin Center #3, in Eastsound at North Beach Rd. (☎376-2230, after-hours emergencies 376-3693. Open M-Sa 9am-6pm.) Log on for free at the **library,** at Rose and Pine St. in Eastsound. (☎376-4985; www.orcaslibrary.org. Open M-Th 10am-7pm, F-Sa 10am-5pm. The **post office** is at 221 A St., in Eastsound. (☎376-4121. Open M-F 9am-4:30pm.) **Postal Code:** 98245.

▐▜ ACCOMMODATIONS AND CAMPING. B&Bs on Orcas charge upwards of $85 per night; call the chamber of commerce for advice. Camping is the cheapest option on Orcas. Reservations are important during summer. **Moran State Park ❶,** on Horseshoe Highway (Olga Rd.) is 15 mi. from the ferry landing. Follow Horseshoe Hwy. straight into the park, 14 mi. from the ferry on the east side of the island. The most popular camping in the islands, but sites are often reserved months in advance (you can reserve as early as 9 months prior to your stay). At Cascade Lake, you can rent rowboats and paddle boats ($12-15 per hr.) (Ranger ☎376-2326, reservations 888-226-7688. 151 sites. About 12 sites are open year-round. Hiker/biker sites $10; vehicle sites $16. Pay showers $0.50 per 3min.) **Obstruction Pass ❶** is only accessible by boat or on foot. Turn off the Horseshoe Hwy. just past Olga and head south (right) on Obstruction Pass Rd. Follow the gravel road marked Obstruction Pass Trailhead to the trailhead and parking lot for access to nice pebble beaches on the Sound. (9 sites, $10.) **Doe Bay Resort ❸** is off Horseshoe Hwy (Olga Rd.) on Pt. Lawrence Rd., 5 mi. east of Moran State Park. A former commune and then Human Potential Center, this retreat keeps the old feeling in its guise as vacation spot thanks to the treehouse, vegetarian **cafe ❷,** and co-ed clothing-optional hot tub and sauna ($10 per day). Office open 11am-9pm; cafe open M 8am-noon, Th 5-9pm, F-Su 8am-noon and 5-9pm. (☎376-2291. Dorm beds $25; camping $35; private rooms start at $55; yurts $75.)

▐ FOOD. Essentials can be found in Eastsound at **Island Market,** 469 Market St. (☎376-6000. Open M-Sa 8am-9pm, Su 10am-8pm.) **Orcas Homegrown Market** offers a large selection of groceries, medicines, and vegan cheeses. Their deli and seafood specials make for a great meal; most specials are $6-7 and there are always vegetarian options. (☎376-2009. Open daily 8am-9pm.) For loads of fresh local produce, the **farmers market** is in front of the museum. (Open Sa 10am-3pm.) **Cafe Jama ❷,** in Eastsound Sq. on N Beach Rd., is perhaps the only place you'll find a Sunday *New York Times* on Orcas Island. The cafe serves Northwest breakfast (specialty coffees and homemade muffins) as well as a variety of tasty $7-9 lunch options: soups, salads and sandwiches. (☎376-4949. Open M-Th and Su 9am-3pm, F-Sa 8:30am-4pm.) Portions are large and the salsa is fresh at **Chimayo ❷,** in Our House Building on North Beach Rd. Design your own burritos and tacos ($5-9), or get two tacos for $3.75. (☎376-6394. Open M-F 11am-7pm, Sa 11am-3pm. **Lower Tavern ❷,** at the corner of Horseshoe Hwy. and Prune Alley, is one of the few cheap places open after 5pm. Dig into burgers and fries from $7 and drink one of seven beers on tap; pints $2.75-4. (☎378-4848. Kitchen open M-Sa 11am-9pm, Su noon-7pm. Bar open M-Th 11am-midnight, F-Sa 11am-1am, Su noon-7pm. Happy hour M-F 4:30-6:30pm.) Those who visit **Roses Bread and Specialties ❷**, 382 Prune Alley, will be rewarded with a huge selection of cheeses (starting at $6 per lb.), fresh bread (from $2), and sweet baked goods. If you aim to make a gourmet picnic lunch for Moran State Park, Roses will provide all you need, or they'll make the lunch for you, with sandwiches $7-10. (☎376-5805. Open M-F 10am-6pm, Sa 9am-6pm.)

◙ SIGHTS. The **Orcas Island Historical Museum,** 181 North Beach Rd., is composed of six clustered homesteads constructed between the 1880s and the 1890s. The museum exhibits Lummi and Samish Native American artifacts and explores early colonial life on the islands. (☎376-4849. Open Tu-Su 1-4pm, F 1-7pm. $2, students $1.) The **Rosario Resort,** 1400 Rosario Rd., is home to the mansion of Robert Moran, an industrialist and politician who donated the land that is now Moran State Park. The mansion totals 35,000 sq. ft. and cost $2.5 million when it was built in 1905. The fine Honduran Mahogany woodwork is worth a look, as is the 1905 organ, the largest built in a private home. For the deep-pocketed, the Rosario also rents rooms at exorbitant prices. (☎376-2222; www.rosario.rockresorts.com. Open 6am-11pm. Free access to the mansion.)

⚔ OUTDOOR ACTIVITIES. Travelers on Orcas Island don't need to roam with a destination in mind; half the fun lies in rambling around, although those who stray too far from designated trails will often find themselves on private property. The trail to **Obstruction Pass Beach** is the best way to clamber down to the rocky shores. Taking up the majority of Orcas' eastern half, **Moran State Park** is the last large undeveloped area on the San Juans, making it a star outdoor attraction. This is a must-see during even a brief sojourn on the island. Ample trails, steep mountains, and several lakes create a landscape with diverse options for outdoor activity.

With 5252 acres, Moran offers over 30 mi. of **hiking** and **biking** trails. Find a good map and detailed trail descriptions in the free *Treasure in the San Juans: Your Guide to Moran State Park*, available at the registration station. (☎376-2326. Open daily mid-June to Labor Day 10am-9:30pm; Labor Day to mid-June 10-11:30am and 4-5:30pm.) Biking in Moran State Park is restricted, with a few of the trails off limits to bikers June-Sept., so be sure to check with the ranger or contact Wildlife Cycles for information (☎376-4708). **Cold Springs Trail** (4¼ mi. one-way, 1 day), goes from the North End Campground up to the summit of Mt. Constitution. A road also runs to the summit for those who don't want to make the difficult trek. 2000 ft. gain. **Mountain Lake Trail** (4 mi. loop, 2-3hr.) starts from the cabin near Mountain Lake campground and loops around Mountain Lake, the larger and more secluded of the park's two big lakes. This mellow trail is great for a hike or a run.

Within the park, two freshwater lakes are accessible from the road, and rowboats and paddleboats can be rented at **Cascade Lake,** just inside the park entrance. ($12-15 per hr., available daily July-Labor Day, May-June M and F-Su, 10am-7pm.) Anglers also hit Moran's water with glee; both Mouton and Cascade Lakes are stocked with silver cutthroat, rainbow trout, and eastern brook trout. On salt water, Orcas offers spectacular kayaking, with a wide variety of conditions and far fewer crowds than San Juan Island. **Shearwater Adventures** runs fascinating **sea kayak tours** and classes, and their store in Eastsound is a great information source for experienced paddlers. (☎376-4699. 3hr. tour with 30min. of dry land training $49. Full-day and multi-day trips available.) **Crescent Beach Kayak,** on the highway (Crescent Beach Rd.) 1 mi. east of Eastsound, rents kayaks for paddling the mellow waters of the East Sound. Also offers tours and training for beginners. (☎376-2464. $18 per hr., $50 per half-day. Open daily 9am-7pm.)

LOPEZ ISLAND   ☎ 360

Smaller than either Orcas or San Juan, "Slow-pez" lacks some of the tourist facilities of the larger islands; still, what it lacks in size it more than makes up for in lethargy. This island is a blessing for those looking for solitary beaches, bicycling without car traffic, rolling farmland, and a small-town atmosphere.

🖪 🔃 ORIENTATION AND PRACTICAL INFORMATION. Lopez Village, the largest town, is 4¼ mi. from the ferry dock off Fisherman Bay Rd. To get there, follow Ferry Rd., which becomes Fisherman Bay Rd. about 2 mi. from the ferry landing, and then take a right onto Lopez Rd., the first street after Lopez Center (before the Chevron station). An excellent free map of the island is available at the **Chamber of Commerce,** which also serves as the visitor center, in Lopez Village across from the Bay Cafe, or at most Lopez businesses. (☎468-4664; www.lopezisland.com. Open W-Sa 11am-3pm.) Lopez is great for cycling and kayaking, and rentals of both are available at **Lopez Bicycle Works** and **Lopez Kayak,** 2845 Fisherman Bay Rd., both south of the village next to the island's Marine Center. (☎468-2847; www.lopezbicycleworks.com, www.lopezkayaks.com. Bicycle Works open daily Apr.-Oct. 10am-6pm. Kayak open daily May-Oct. 10am-5pm. Bikes $7 per hr., $30 per day. Single kayaks $12-25 per hr., $40-60 per day; doubles $20-35 per hr., $60-80 per day. 2hr. and day-long trips available.) **Lopez Island Pharmacy** is at 157 Village Rd. (☎468-2616. Open M-F 9am-6pm, Sa 10am-5pm.) The **library,** 2225 Fisherman Bay Rd., has free **Internet** access. (☎468-2265. Open M and Sa 10am-5pm, W 10am-9pm, and Tu and Th-F 10am-6pm.) A 24hr. **ATM** is available at Islands Bank (45 Weeks Rd.). For a taxi, call **Angie's Cab.** (☎468-2227. Open 6am-11pm.) Keep it so at **Keep It Clean,** south of the winery. (Wash $2, dry $0.25 per 5min. Open M-F 8:30am-7pm, Sa-Su until 5pm.) Other services include: **Lopez Island Clinic,** ☎468-2245, and the **post office,** on Weeks Rd. (☎468-2282. Open M-F 8am-4pm.) **Postal Code:** 98261.

🛏 🍴 ACCOMMODATIONS AND FOOD. When spending the night on Lopez, camping is the only bargain. Luckily, there are many great sites to pitch a tent. **Spencer Spit State Park ❶,** on the northeast corner of the island about 3½ mi. from the ferry terminal, has seven sites on the beach, 30 nicely secluded wooded sites up the hill, two group sites, and a bunkhouse. Spencer Spit offers good **clamming** in the late spring, unless there is red tide (☎800-562-5632; permit required). The park is closed Nov.-Mar. (☎468-2251; reservations 888-226-7688. Reservations necessary for summer weekends. Open until 10pm. Sites $16; bunkhouse $22.) Voted one of the 10 best places to woo by MSNBC, **Lopez Farm Cottages and Tent Camping ❷,** just north of town on Fisherman Bay Rd., is an agrarian dreamland with free morning coffee and showers that open to the sky. Each campsite has a hammock and chairs. (☎468-3555 or 800-440-3556; www.lopezfarmcottages.com. Sites open May-Oct. $28 for double occupancy; cottages $99-150 depending on time of year. Min. age 14.) **Odlin Park ❶** is close to the ferry terminal, 1 mi. south along Ferry Rd., and offers running water, a boat launch, and baseball diamond as well as nice beaches and pleasant walks. (☎468-2496; reservations 378-1842. 29 sites. Hiker/biker sites $11; forest sites $16, beach sites $19. Boat mooring $8.) If you're looking for a roof, a relatively cheap option is the **Lopez Islander Marina Resort ❺,** on Fisherman Bay Road, which offers 30 rooms with mini-refrigerators and color TV. (☎468-2233; www.lopezislander.com. Rooms from $90.)

Although Lopez doesn't boast the selection of restaurants that the other two islands do, a good meal is easy to find. You can play boules while brown-bagging in the grassy park adjacent to the **Village Market,** which has a complete meat and produce department. (☎468-2266. Open daily 8am-8pm.) Across the street, **Holly B's ❷** offers fresh pastries, bread, and pizza. Try the french bread baked with caramelized onions and brie. Bargain breads go for $2, pastries for $1-4. (☎468-2133; www.lopezisland.com/holly/hollyb.htm. Open M and W-Sa 7am-5pm, Su 7am-4pm.) **Vortex Juice Bar and Good Food ❷,** located in the Old Homestead with Blossom Natural Foods in Lopez Village, is great for a vegetarian meal. You'll smell the wraps and burritos (from $6.50), and homemade soups and salads ($4.50-6.50) from the street. (☎468-4740. Open M-Sa 10am-7pm.) Big portions, good beer ($3.25-3.50), and old pictures of the island make **Bucky's ❷,** across from Village Market, a good stop for a bite. (☎468-2595. Burgers $6.25. Open daily 9am-9pm.) The **farmers market** showcases Lopez Island arts and crafts, as well as jams, baked goods, and potted plants. (Open Sa 10am-2pm.)

⚠ 🖸 SIGHTS AND OUTDOOR ACTIVITIES. Lopez is attractive to many for the total lack of things to do—the opportunity to spend the day exploring at a snail's pace is a large part of the island's appeal. The small **Shark Reef** and **Agate Beach County Parks,** on the southwest end of the island, have tranquil and well-maintained hiking trails. Gaze in wonder at the waves crashing against the rocky beaches at Shark Reef Park, or stroll down Agate's calm and deserted shores. The 2 mi. round-trip hike to **Iceberg Point** promises dramatic ocean scenery. For an agrarian adventure, a free copy of the *Guide to Farm Products on Lopez Island* at the Chamber of Commerce will lead you to sheep, cattle, and fruit and vegetable farms. **Lopez Island Vineyards,** 724 Fisherman Bay Rd., San Juan's oldest vineyards, permits visitors to sample all of their wines for $2 per person. (☎468-3644; www.lopezislandvineyards.com. Open Apr.-June and early Sept.-Dec. F-Sa noon-5pm; July-early Sept. W-Sa noon-5pm; year-round by appointment.)

Lopez Island is ideal for **biking.** The car traffic is minimal and the scenery is top notch. Pick up a copy of the *Bicyclists' Touring Companion for the San Juan Islands* to plan out your route ($4, available at bike shops throughout the San Juans). Circling the island in a day is definitely an attainable goal. For the more aquatically inclined, a two-day **clamming/crabbing** permit is available at the **Islands Marine Center** on Fisherman Bay Rd. for $14. (☎468-3377; islandsmarine-center.com. Open M-Sa 8:30am-5pm.) Odlin Park and Spencer Spit State Park are known to have some of the best clamming and crabbing in all of Washington.

OLYMPIC PENINSULA

Due west of Seattle and its busy Puget Sound neighbors, the Olympic Peninsula is a remote backpacking paradise. Olympic National Park dominates much of the peninsula and prevents the area's timber industry from threatening the glacier-capped mountains and temperate rainforests. The towering peaks form the most dramatic feature of the park, covered in snow from the water-laden winds and drastically carved out by ancient glaciers. But the mountains have competition, and with the pick of three ecosystems—rainforest, beach, or mountain—outdoors enthusiasts have a full plate. Outside of the park, a smattering of Indian reservations and logging and fishing communities lace the peninsula's coastline along US 101. To the west, the Pacific Ocean stretches to a distant horizon along rugged but easily-accessible beaches; to the north, the Strait of Juan de Fuca separates the Olympic Peninsula from Vancouver Island; and to the east, Hood Canal and the Kitsap Peninsula isolate this sparsely inhabited wilderness from Seattle's sprawl.

OLYMPIC NATIONAL PARK ☎ 360

AT A GLANCE	
AREA: 896,000 acres.	**GATEWAYS:** Forks, Port Angeles, Port Townsend.
CLIMATE: Fair summers (65-75°F), mild winters (30-40°F). Heavy precipitation.	**CAMPING:** 14-day camping limit.
FEATURES: Olympic National Forest, Hoh Rainforest, Olympic Mountain Range, 57 mi. of protected beach, Hoh, Queets, and Quinault River valleys.	**FEES AND RESERVATIONS:** $10 entrance fee for car, $5 for hikers and bikers. Permit registration fee $5, individual nightly fee $2.

Olympic National Park (ONP) is certainly the centerpiece of the Olympic Peninsula, sheltering one of the most diverse landscapes of any region in the world.
With glacier-encrusted peaks, river valley rainforests, and jagged shores along the
Pacific Coast, the park has something to offer everyone. Roads lead to many corners of Olympic National Park, but with over 90 percent of the park roadless, they
only hint at the depths of its wilderness. A dive into the backcountry leaves summer tourists behind and reveals the richness and diversity of the park's many
faces. Many try to make this trip in a day or two, but beware: the breadth of the
park makes it difficult to fully experience in under three or four days.

✦ ORIENTATION

The entire **Olympic Mountain Range** is packed into the peninsula's center, where
conical peaks wring huge quantities of moisture from heavy Pacific air. An annual
12 ft. of rain and snow is common. At altitudes above 3500 ft. snow can linger as
late as June. The mountains steal so much water that some areas that sit just
below in the western "shadow" are among the driest in Washington.

Temperate rainforests lie on the west side of ONP, along the coast, and in the **Hoh,
Queets,** and **Quinault River valleys,** where low valleys claim the ocean moisture
before it slides up the mountains' sides. Moderate temperatures, loads of rain, and
summer fog support an emerald tangle dominated by giant Sitka spruce and Western Red cedar. The rest of the park is populated by lowland forests of Douglas-fir
and hemlock, with silver fir at higher elevations. Ancient Native American **petroglyphs** along Ozette Lake and boxy offshore bluffs called **sea stacks** lend a sacred
quality to the coastline beaches. Swaths of **Olympic National Forest (ONF)** and private land separate these seaside expanses from the rest of the park. The park's
perimeters are well-defined but are surrounded by **Forest Service** land, **Washington
Department of Natural Resources (DNR)** land, and other public areas. It's important
to remember that the ONP and ONF are maintained by separate organizations.
Their usage, purposes, facilities, rules, and regulations differ accordingly.

Each side of the park has one major settlement—**Port Townsend** in the east, **Port
Angeles** to the north, and **Forks** in the west. The size of the towns and the services
they offer decline as you go west, as does the traffic. The park's eastern rim runs
up to Port Townsend, from which the much-visited northern rim extends westward. Along a winding detour on Rte. 112, off US 101 westward, the tiny town of
Neah Bay and stunning **Cape Flattery** perch at the tip of the peninsula; farther south
on US 101, the town of Forks is a gateway to the park's rainforested western rim.
Separate from the rest of the park, much of the peninsula's coastline is gorgeous.

July, August, and September are the best months for visiting Olympic National Park,
as roads and trails become saturated with snow in early fall, though calming beach
walks remain accessible in spring and fall. Much of the backcountry remains snowed-

in until late June, and only summers are relatively rain-free. The Park Service runs free interpretive programs such as guided forest hikes, tidepool walks, and campfire programs out of its ranger stations. For a schedule of events, pick up a copy of the *Bugler* from ranger stations or the visitors center (see below). Erik Molvar's *Hiking Olympic National Park* ($15), available at local bookstores and some ranger stations, is a great resource for hikers, with maps and step-by-step trail logs for over 585 mi. of trails. Although it lacks coverage of coastal areas and can be slightly outdated, Robert Wood's comprehensive *Olympic Mountains Trail Guide* ($19) is the classic book for those planning to tackle the backcountry. *Custom Correct* maps ($3.75) provide detailed topographic information on various popular hiking areas. Because of the density of ranger stations and adequate signs, however, visitors who are sticking to park campgrounds will have little need to purchase additional literature.

▣ TRANSPORTATION

The peninsula provides more transportation options than you might expect for a place so remote. Hwy. 101 forms an upside-down "U", passing through almost every small town. A combination of roads also heads straight west from Olympia, allowing one to bypass the park and then head north on 101, skipping the crowds and going straight to the rainforest. Local buses link Port Townsend, Port Angeles, Forks, and Neah Bay, cost $0.50-1, and accommodate bicycles. From there, rides can be cobbled together to get farther into the park. Van lines, ride-sharing, and taxis are all options from the cities; the best place to start is at a visitors center or hostel. When combined with buses, bicycling can move a traveler around quickly, as the sides of the park are only 50-60 mi. long. Be aware, though: the stretch of Hwy. 101 that runs along Lake Crescent is poor for bikers. Roads into the park are accessible from US 101 and serve as trailheads for over 600 mi. of hiking.

Actually getting to the peninsula to begin the trip requires a bit of planning. A ferry is probably the fastest bet and can work well for those driving too. For more info, contact **Washington State Ferries** (☎888-808-7977); **Greyhound** (☎800-231-2222); **King County Transit** in Seattle (☎800-542-7876; http://transit.metrokc.gov); **Pierce Transit** in Tacoma (☎206-581-8000; www.piercetransit.org); **Intercity Transit** in Olympia (☎800-287-6348; www.intercitytransit.com); or **Kitsap Transit** in Kitsap and Bainbridge (☎360-373-2877; www.kitsaptransit.org). For bus service on the peninsula, contact **Jefferson Transit** in Port Townsend (☎360-385-4777; www.jeffersontransit.com); **Clallam Transit** in Port Angeles (☎800-858-3747; www.clallamtransit.com); **Grays Harbor Transit** in Aberdeen (☎800-562-9730; www.ghtransit.com); **West Jefferson Transit** in the southwest (☎800-436-3950); or **Mason Transit** in the southeast (☎800-374-3747; www.masontransit.org). The hostels on the peninsula know the terrain and will help visitors navigate around the park.

▣ PRACTICAL INFORMATION

Park Headquarters (☎565-3000). Staffed daily summer 7am-midnight; winter 7am-5:30pm.

Tourist Information: Olympic National Park Visitors Center, 3002 Mt. Angeles Rd. (☎565-3130; www.nps.gov/olym/home.htm), off Race St. in Port Angeles (p. 240). ONP's main info center. Contains extensive exhibits and plays a 12min. movie that gives an overview of the park. The info center distributes an invaluable free **park map,** also available at park entrances. Open daily May-early Sept. 9am-5:30pm; late Sept.-Apr. 9am-4pm. **Park Headquarters,** 600 E Park Ave. (☎565-3000), in Port Angeles, is an administrative office but can answer questions the rangers can't by phone. Open M-F 8am-4:30pm. For the many local **ranger stations,** see specific regions below.

Olympic National Park

▲ CAMPING

Altaire, **5**
Dosewallips, **10**
Elwha Valley, **3**
Fairholm, **2**
Heart o' the Hills, **4**
Hoh Rain Forest, **7**
Lena Lake, **11**
Minnie Peterson, **8**
Mora Campground, **6**
Salt Creek County Park, **1**
Staircase, **12**
Willaby, **13**
Willoughby Creek, **9**

WASHINGTON

Strait of Juan de Fuca

Dungeness Nat'l Wildlife Refuge

Old Towit

Sequim

TO PORT TOWNSEND (31 mi.)

TO PORT ANGELES

Agnew

Dungeness

TO 101 (11 mi.)

TO 101 (5 mi.)

Hamma Hamma River

Freshwater Bay

Ediz Hook

Port Angeles

Olympic N.P. Visitor Center

Lake Aldwell

Mt. Deception (7788ft.)

West Fork

Dosewallips River

Duckabush River

Lake Cushman

East Beach

Lake Crescent

Joyce

1

Mt. Angeles (6454ft.)

Hurricane Ridge Information Center

Obstruction Peak (6450ft.)

Hayden Pass

Olympic National Forest

4

Lake Mills

Elwha River

3

Olympic Hot Springs

Whiskey Bend

High Divide

Mt. Anderson (7321ft.)

Enchanted Valley

Fairholm

2

Storm King Information Station

Marymere Falls

5

Mt. Olympus (7965ft.)

Glacier Meadows

Low Divide

Skokomish River

North Fork Skokomish River

East Fork Quinault River

Olympic Mountains

Olympic National Park

Sol Duc River

Sol Duc Falls

Sol Duc Hot Springs

Hoh Rain Forest Visitor Center

7

North Shore Rd.

South Shore Rd.

USFS

13

Lake Quinault

Olympic National Forest

Clallam Bay

Sekiu

Pysht

112

113

Sappho

Bogachiel River

8

9

Quinault River

Clearwater River

Olympic National Forest

TO MAKAH MUSEUM & NEAH BAY (13mi.), CAPE FLATTERY (17mi.)

Hoko-Ozette Rd.

Ozette

Ozette Indian Reservation

Dickey Lake

Ozette Lake

Sol Duc River

USFS/NPS Information Station

Forks

101

Hoh River

TO ABERDEEN (53mi.)

101

Quinault Indian Reservation

Wedding Rocks

Cake Rock

Hole-in-the-Wall

Rialto Beach

First Beach

La Push

Second Beach

Third Beach

Quileute Indian Reservation

6

Oil City

Hoh

Hoh Indian Reservation

Ruby Beach

Beach 6

Beach 4

Beach 3

Beach 2

Beach 1

Kaloch Information Station

Kalaloch

Quinault

PACIFIC OCEAN

WASHINGTON

N

0 5 miles

0 5 kilometers

Backcountry Information: Olympic National Park Wilderness Information Center (☎565-3100; www.nps.gov/olym/wic), behind the visitors center, provides trip-planning help and information. The center also provides backcountry reservations. Pay the ONP wilderness user fee here or at any ranger station. Quota area permits, on areas where only a specific number of people are allowed in the backcountry at a time, must be purchased at the appropriate ranger stations. Open daily Apr.-June 8am-4:30pm; June-Sept. Th-Sa 7:30am-8pm, M-W and Su 7:30am-6pm; Oct.-Mar. hours vary.

Fees and Reservations: $10 per car; $5 per hiker or biker. Charged at Hoh, Heart o' the Hills, Sol Duc, Staircase, and Elwha entrances. Covers seven-day access to the park; keep the receipt. Backcountry users must pay a $5 permit fee as well as $2 extra per person per night to rangers. The National Forest requires a Northwest Forest Pass to park ($1 per day). **Fishing:** Fishing within park boundaries requires a license except along the Pacific. A booklet listing park's regulations is available at stations upon request.

Park Weather: ☎565-3131. 24hr.

⛺ CAMPING

Competition for sites on the peninsula can get fierce, but there's plenty of room to go around between all the front country sites and the endless backcountry nooks. It just takes a little driving to uncover all the treasures of hidden sites. In addition to numerous national park sites, there is a network of state and county sites and several hostels well spaced across the peninsula.

FRONT COUNTRY CAMPING. Ask at the Olympic National Forest Headquarters in Olympia (p. 212) about ONP campgrounds within its boundaries (sites $8-12). ONF maintains six free campgrounds in the Hood Canal Ranger District and other campgrounds within its boundaries; sites at **Seal Rock, Falls View,** and **Klahowya** can be reserved. (☎800-280-2267; www.reserveusa.com. Open daily 8am-midnight. Sites $8-12.) In addition to **Fort Worden** and **Fort Flagler,** there are four **state parks** on the peninsula. (Reservations ☎800-452-5687. Hiker/biker sites $6; sites $14; RV sites $20.) **Dosewallips** (☎796-4415) and **Lake Cushman** (see **Eastern Rim,** below) are to the east. **Sequim Bay** is northeast of Sequim. (☎683-4235. Table and stove at each site.) Most **drive-up camping** is first come, first served.

BACKCOUNTRY CAMPING. Whether in rainforest, high country, or along the coast, backcountry camping in the park requires a **backcountry permit.** Park offices maintain **quota limits** on backcountry permits for popular spots, including **Lake Constance** and **Flapjack Lakes** in the eastern rim (see below); **Grand Valley, Badger Valley,** and **Sol Duc** in the northern rim (p. 240); **Hoh** in the western rim (p. 246); and the coastal **Ozette Loop.** Make **reservations** in advance as these areas have quotas for a reason and tend to fill up, especially in the Ozette area, where reservations are required. Contact the Wilderness Info Center to secure a spot. Backpackers should prepare for varied weather conditions. Even in the summer, parts of the park get very wet; pack appropriately for the weather. **Giardia,** a nasty diarrhea-inducing bacterium, is common in the area's water. Water purification tablets are available at the visitors center and outfitters. (For more information, see **The Great Outdoors,** p. 69.) **Black bears** and **raccoons** pose another hazard; when issuing permits, ranger stations instruct hikers on keeping food out of reach. (Also see **The Great Outdoors,** p. 63.) Mountain lions are also a concern; ranger officials will give you advice on how to maximize your safety. Above 3500 ft., **open fires** are prohibited; below 3500 ft., maps and signposts indicate whether they are allowed. Before any trip, inquire about **trail closures;** winter weather often destroys popular trails.

EASTERN OLYMPIC PENINSULA

The area of the peninsula most accessible from Puget Sound urban centers, the Olympic's eastern edge suffers from a heavy traffic of weekend cabin-renters and daytrippers. Still, the eastern edge of the park houses some fun (and generally dry) trails. The draw for many is Port Townsend, the town that serves as the peninsula's social capital. "PT," with its combination of quaint Victorian ambiance and a lively population of locals and visitors, is the one settlement west of Olympia that doesn't qualify as "sleepy," making it a welcome change of pace for travelers who have been taking advantage of the park's solitude for a little too long.

PORT TOWNSEND   ☎360

Set apart from the rest of the Olympic Peninsula on Quimper Peninsula, its own finger of land into the Strait of Juan de Fuca, Port Townsend is the local cultural hot spot. During the late 1800s, the city's predominance in the entire state of Washington seemed secure. Every ship en route to Puget Sound stopped here for customs inspection, and speculation held that the bustling port would become the capital of the new state. Simultaneously, the most striking stretches of waterfront were claimed by the government in the form of three forts. When rumors circulated that rail would connect the town to the east, wealthy families flocked to the bluffs overlooking the port, constructing elaborate Victorian homes and stately public buildings. But the railroad passed by; the "inevitable New York" was left a ghost town, perched on the isolated northeast tip of the Olympic Peninsula and made to subsist by paper-milling and logging. In the 1970s, Port Townsend's neglected Victorian homes were discovered by artists and idealists who turned the town into a vibrant, creative community. Now the business district is restored and an official national landmark, and the town takes advantage of its 19th-century feel to entice those heading to the park onto Rte. 20 and into town. Two of the remaining original forts, Flagler and Worden, are being gradually reclaimed by the surrounding nature, making them ideal for exploration.

🔷🔽 ORIENTATION AND PRACTICAL INFORMATION

Port Townsend sits at the terminus of **Route 20** on the northeastern corner of the Olympic Peninsula. It can be reached by **US 101** on the peninsula, or from the Kitsap Peninsula across the Hood Canal Bridge. **Kitsap County Transit** meets every ferry and runs to Poulsbo. From Poulsbo, **Jefferson County Transit** runs to Port Townsend. The ferry also crosses to Keystone on Whidbey Island (p. 214). Ferries dock at **Water Street**, west of touristy downtown, along Water and **Washington Street,** where restaurants, hotels, and motels are located. Laid-back uptown, with a small business district of its own, is four steep blocks up, on **Lawrence Street.**

Local Transportation: Jefferson County Transit (JCT; ☎385-4777; www.jeffersontransit.com). Buses run between Ft. Worden and downtown, and also connect to Port Angeles and Seattle. $0.50; seniors, disabled travelers, and ages 6-18 $0.25; extra-zone fare $0.25; children under 6 free. Day passes $1.50. A **shuttle** runs between downtown and the Park 'n' Ride lot, right next to the Safeway. There is usually ample parking in town, although usually limited to 2hr. **Washington State Ferries (☎**464-6400 or 800-808-7977; www.wsdot.wa.gov/ferries) provides the service that connects to Whidbey Island's Keystone (30min.; approx. every 1½hr.; $2.70; car and driver $7-8.75; bike $0.90).

Taxis: Peninsula Taxi, ☎385-1872. $2 base plus $1.75 per mi. 24hr.

WASHINGTON

Tourist Information: Chamber of Commerce, 2437 E Sims Way (☎385-2722 or 888-365-6978; www.ptchamber.org), lies 10 blocks southwest of town on Rte. 20, well marked by signs. Open M-F 9am-5pm, Sa 10am-4pm, Su 11am-4pm.

Equipment Rental: P.T. Cyclery, 100 Tyler St. (☎385-6470; www.olympus.net/ptcyclery), rents mountain bikes starting at $9 per hr., $20 half-day, $35 per day; make sure to get there early on weekends; they sometimes run out of bikes. Ages 100 and older free. Maps $1.75. Open M-Sa 9am-6pm.

Police: 607 Water St. (☎385-2322), at Madison.

Crisis Line: ☎385-0321 or 800-659-0321. 24hr. **Sexual Assault Line:** ☎385-5291.

Pharmacy: in **Safeway,** 442 W Sims Way (☎385-2860). Open M-F 8:30am-7:30pm, Sa 8:30am-6pm, Su 10am-6pm.

Hospital: Jefferson General, 834 Sheridan Ave. (☎385-2200), off Rte. 20 at 7th St.

Internet Access: Library, 1220 Lawrence St. (☎385-3181; www.ptpl.lib.wa.us). Free Internet access, 15min. drop-in, up to 1¼hr. by appointment. Open M-W 11am-8pm, Th-Sa 11am-6pm. Also at **Cyber Bean,** 2021 E Sims Way (☎385-9773; www.cyberbeancafe.com). 10min. free with purchase, $6 per 15min. Open M-F 8:30am-6pm, Sa-Su 8:30am-2:30pm.

Post Office: 1322 Washington St. (☎385-1600). Open M-F 9am-5pm, Sa 10am-2pm. **Postal Code:** 98368.

ACCOMMODATIONS AND CAMPING

Port Townsend is a B&B mecca; many of the historic Victorian homes now offer rest to weary travelers. If you're looking to splurge, the striking **Ann Starrett Mansion ❺,** built in 1889, offers rooms starting at $110 (see **Sights,** below).

Olympic Hostel (HI) (☎385-0655; www.olympichostel.org), in Ft. Worden State Park, 1½ mi. from town. Follow the signs to the park at W and Cherry St. A converted WWII barracks, the Olympic offers nice clean beds, but the biggest attractions are the surrounding park (over 400 acres) and beaches. Laundry, tennis courts, frequent concerts, trails, and free pancake breakfast. Check-in 5-10pm, check-out 9:30am. Book ahead, especially in summer. $14; nonmembers $17. ❶

Fort Flagler Hostel (HI) (☎385-1288), in Ft. Flagler State Park, on **Marrowstone Island,** 20 mi. from Port Townsend. Take Rte. 20 to Rte. 19 south, go 3 mi., and turn left on Rte. 116 for 9 mi. into the Park. The hostel is an old military building right by the beach. Check-in 5-10pm, lockout 10am-5pm. Call if arriving late. Book ahead, especially on weekends. Open Mar.-Sept. $14, nonmembers $17, hikers/bikers $2 off. ❶

Fort Flagler State Park (☎385-1259, reservations 800-233-0321). Camping in the same island park as the hostel, revered as one of the most picturesque sites in the state. Some sites on the beach's tidal flat are in a fairly crowded, less-than-private setup; others are on stunning bluffs overlooking Kilisut Harbor. Book ahead to ensure a spot. 115 sites. Running water, utility sites. Hiker/biker $6; tents $16; RVs $22. ❷

Fort Worden State Park (☎385-4730, reservations 800-233-0321; www.fortworden.org). Beachfront camping that's only slightly less picturesque than Ft. Flagler, also with a crowded beach section along with an upper area in the woods. 80 sites, 30 full utility. Hiker/biker $6; tents $16; RVs $22. ❷

Water Street Hotel, 635 Water St. (☎385-5467 or 800-735-9810; www.waterstreethotelporttownsend.com), is a recently renovated Victorian building with fabulous views of the water and Port Townsend streets. $50-135, low-season $45-100. ❸

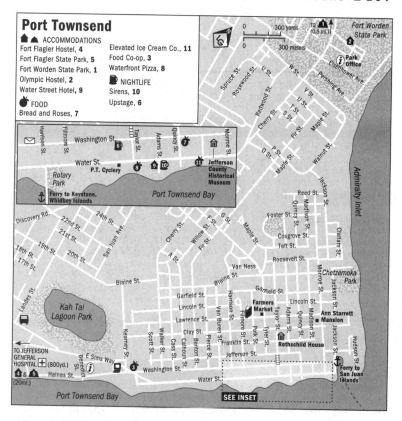

Port Townsend

▲ ■ ACCOMMODATIONS
Fort Flagler Hostel, 4
Fort Flagler State Park, 5
Fort Worden State Park, 1
Olympic Hostel, 2
Water Street Hotel, 9

● FOOD
Bread and Roses, 7

Elevated Ice Cream Co., 11
Food Co-op, 3
Waterfront Pizza, 8

■ NIGHTLIFE
Sirens, 10
Upstage, 6

🍴 FOOD

The **Food Co-op,** 414 Kearney St., is in an old bowling alley. Every Wednesday from 3:30-6pm there is a farmers market in the parking lot. (☎385-2883. Open M-Sa 8am-9pm, Su 9am-7pm.) Also try the **Uptown Farmers Market,** at Tyler and Lawrence St. (☎379-6957; www.ptfarmersmarket.org. Open May-Oct. Sa 9:30am-1:30pm and June-Sept. W 3:30-6:30pm). **Safeway,** 442 Sims Way (☎385-2860), is open 24hr.

🍴 **The Elevated Ice Cream Co.,** 627 Water St. (☎385-1156; www.elevatedicecream.com), ironically on the ground floor. This local icon serves unique flavors of creamy homemade ice cream in classic glass dishes. Single scoop $2. The sweetshop next door satiates the sweet tooths who prefer non-frozen fare. Open daily 10am-10pm. ●

Bread and Roses, 230 Quincy St. (☎385-1044). This friendly bakery serves baked goods, sandwiches ($3-7), and muffins in a gorgeous garden. Open M-Sa 6:30am-5pm, Su 6:30am-4pm. ❷

Waterfront Pizza, 953 Water St. (☎385-6629), offers little historic ambiance but churns out a darn good pizza on sourdough crust (12 in. pie $8-14). 12 in. focaccia $4. Open M-Th and Su 11am-10pm, F-Sa 11am-11pm. ❷

👁 SIGHTS

Port Townsend is full of huge Queen Anne and Victorian mansions, many of which now serve as B&Bs. The **Ann Starrett Mansion,** 744 Clay St., is renowned for its frescoed ceilings and spiral staircase. (☎385-3205 or 800-321-0644; www.starrettmansion.com. Tours daily noon-3pm. $2.) If posh estates tickle your fancy, make sure to visit PT in mid-September for the **Homes Tour,** an annual event when some of the town's most stunning historic homes open their doors for the curious to poke around. (☎385-2772; www.ptguide.com/homestour. $16, advance sales $13.)

Point Hudson, where Admiralty Inlet and Port Townsend Bay meet, is the hub of a small shipbuilding area and forms the corner of Port Townsend. Check out boatbuilders crafting sea kayaks and sailboats. North of Point Hudson are several miles of **beach** and the beautiful **Chetzemoka Park,** a (guess what) Victorian park, manicured with endless flowerbeds and a water view, at Garfield and Jackson St.

Fort Worden State Park is a sprawling complex most easily accessed through the gates at W and Cherry St. (☎344-4400. Open daily 6:30am-dusk.) In the 1900s, Ft. Worden was part of the "Triangle of Fire," a defense for Puget Sound formed by **Worden, Fort Flagler** across the bay, and **Fort Casey** on Whidbey Island. Ft. Worden re-entered service in 1981 as the set for the film *An Officer and a Gentleman.* Three museums are on the grounds. The 1904 **Commanding Officer's Quarters** is stuffed with Victorian furniture and maintained as though the family had just stepped out, with children's toys askew and cutlery set for dinner. (☎344-4452. Open daily June-Aug. 10am-5pm; Mar.-May and Sept.-Oct. Sa-Su 1-4pm. $1.) The **Puget Sound Coast Artillery Museum** features enough weaponry, photographs, and uniforms to satisfy any military craving. (☎385-0373. Open daily Apr.-Sept. 10am-4pm. $2.) Sealife lives above the Ft. Worden pier at the **Marine Science Center.** (☎385-5582; www.ptmsc.org. Open M and W-Su 11am-5pm. $3, children $2.)

🎵 ENTERTAINMENT

Port Townsend's music scene is surprisingly lively. **Sirens,** 823 Water St., hosts live folk and blues (F-Sa) on the deck, which has a great view. (☎379-1100. Happy hour 4-6pm. Occasional cover. Open M-Th 4pm-2am, F-Sa noon-2am.) **Upstage,** 923 Washington St., supports music from classical to country from Thursday to Saturday. (☎385-2216; www.upstagerestaurant.com. Cover $5-14. Open daily 4pm-midnight.) The **Rose Theatre,** 235 Taylor St., is a fine arthouse theater that claims to make the best popcorn in the Northwest. (☎385-1089; www.rosetheatre.com. $6.50, ages 65 and older $5.50, under 12 $4.50; matinees $5.50.)

Every summer, the **Centrum Foundation** (☎385-5320 or 800-733-3608; www.centrum.org) sponsors festivals in Ft. Worden Park, including the **Port Townsend Blues Festival** (tickets $24) at the beginning of August, the **Festival of American Fiddle Tunes** (tickets $17) in early July, and **Jazz Port Townsend** (tickets $24-32) the third week of July. The **Port Townsend Writers' Conference** in July is one of the finest in the Northwest. Guest-readings and lectures cost $5-6. Port Townsend's biggest gathering is the **Wooden Boat Festival** (☎385-3629), held the first weekend after Labor Day. It is organized by the **Wooden Boat Foundation,** 380 Jefferson St. (☎385-3628; www.woodenboat.org), an institute that supports lessons and races.

🏕 OUTDOOR ACTIVITIES

PT's appeal as a destination doesn't end with its mansions and military relics; today, the coastline beckons kayakers as its forts are slowly reclaimed by nature and trails open to land explorers. All three former fort state parks—Ft. Flagler, Ft.

WASHINGTON

Worden, and Old Ft. Townsend—protect miles of shoreline that now boast prime strolling and boat launch sites. One picturesque place to paddle for the day is in the calm waters of **Kilisut Harbor** off the shore of Marrowstone Island, reachable from the launch from Fort Worden. Also pleasant is the kayak all the way around **Indian Island;** although there are no permitted landing spots, the 12 mi. circumnavigation includes a stunning narrow passage between the island and both the mainland and Marrowstone Island (launch from Indian Island State Park, at the island's southern end). The town's history as a swanky sailing center remains today, with plenty of harbor and cruising space for aspiring sailors.

Narrow, winding roads prevent road **biking** from being as enticing as the area would suggest, but mountain biking routes make up for the loss. Check at local biking stores like P.T. Cyclery (see **Equipment Rental,** p. 236) for advice and maps.

ELSEWHERE ON THE EASTERN PENINSULA

NEAR HOODSPORT. The first info area on US 101 coming in from Olympia is the **Hood Canal Ranger Station,** just off the highway in Hoodsport. (☎877-5254. Open daily summer 8am-4:30pm; winter M-F 8am-4:30pm.) This station is run jointly between the forest and park services, so the rangers can answer questions about almost any destination on the peninsula. The station's turn-off also leads to two of the peninsula's most popular destinations. The first, **Staircase Campground ❶,** is a camping and hiking area on Lake Cushman and is a major hub 16 mi. northwest of Hoodsport. An easy 2 mi. loop passes by the namesake rapids. Take a left after 9 mi. on Rte. 119 and follow the signs. (☎877-5491. RV accessible. 56 sites, $10.) The other much sought-out place is the summit of **Mount Ellinor,** also past the station. Follow Rte. 119 for 9 mi. to Forest Rd. 24, turn right, and continue to Forest Rd. 2419, following signs to Upper/Lower Trailhead. Look for signs to the Upper Trailhead along Forest Rd. 2419. Once on the mountain, hikers can choose either the challenging 6¼ mi. round-trip path or an equally steep but shorter journey to the summit. Those hiking on the mountain before late July should dress for snow.

HAMMA HAMMA RECREATION AREA. Fourteen miles north of Hoodsport and 8 mi. west off Forest Rd. 25 lies the Hamma Hamma Recreation Area. Most head for the easy 6 mi. round-trip hike to **Lena Lake,** one of the most popular lakes on the Olympic Peninsula and a frequent stopover for climbers continuing on to the 7000 ft. summit of The Brothers. Unfortunately, the popularity has left the scenic area with clear signs of visitation, although it remains a serene snowshoe route. From Lena Lake, trails lead to Upper Lena Lake and The Brothers Wilderness; escape the crowds on the **Upper Lena Lake Trail,** a difficult 14 mi. round-trip up 2800 ft. from the lower lake toward impressive views and less-trampled wildflowers. The **Hamma Hamma Campground ❶,** at the Lena Lake Trailhead, has 15 sites. ($10.) For backcountry camping, try **Lena Lake Campground ❶,** located on the west shore of Lena Lake, which offers 29 free sites with compost toilets but no water.

North of the Hamma Hamma off Forest Rd. 31, hike a moderate 12 mi. round-trip to **Royal Lake** for a breathtaking waterfall, summertime wildflowers, and views of the second-highest peak in the Olympics, **Mount Deception.** Free permits, available at all the ranger stations, are required for backcountry camping.

QUILCENE. The **Quilcene Ranger Station** (☎765-2200), 30 mi. north of Hoodsport, can answer questions about the national forest. (Open daily 8am-4:30pm; closed Sa-Su winter.) Nearby, the **Mount Walker Viewpoint,** 5 mi. south of Quilcene on US 101, is a popular destination. A one-lane gravel road leads 4 mi. to the lookout, the highest viewpoint in the forest accessible by car. The road is steep, has sheer drop-

WASHINGTON

LOVELY LILACS

Agrotourism has long bloomed in Europe, where a history of farm stays has allowed rural communities to transition into tourist industries. A decade ago, 30 farmers and dreamers in Sequim, along the northern coast of the Olympic peninsula, hatched a scheme to bring their town similar success. The Lavender Festival was born in 1997, and in 2004 there were eight farms harvesting fields of 60-70 varieties of the fragrant purple crop. The festival has done more than transform a few farmers' bank accounts—it has reshaped the identity and future of the eager small town. Lavender now dominates the economic scene: Harvest-your-own farms create an activity for a family afternoon; nurseries send visitors home with their own crop; stores stock an abundance of lavender-enriched soaps and oils boasting the herb's healing and cleansing powers; local menus feature marinades, pastries, and ice cream infused with the delicate flavor.

The culmination of this communal obsession is, of course, the festival itself, held for three days in mid-July. The town overflows with visitors come to tour the farms, browse in the Street Fair, listen to the constant live music, or take in one of the many events: including a 5K run, sailboat rides, a lavender hoedown, and a big band dance. (☎360-681-3035 or 877-681-3035; www.lavenderfestival.com.)

offs, and should not be attempted in bad weather or with a temperamental car. Picnic on the east side while gazing at 7743 ft. **Mount Constance.**

Those wanting to set off on foot in the area will be disappointed at how much over-logging they will inevitably encounter. Still, memorable trails can be found: the quick but challenging 3½ mi. round-trip hike to the old fire lookout at the peak of **Mount Zion** serves up breathtaking views of both the Hood Canal and Puget Sound (follow Forest Rd. 28 to Forest Rd. 2810 to the marked trailhead); meanwhile, the steep 11 mi. round-trip **Mount Townsend Trail** is for the more ambitious. The trailhead is on Forest Rd. 2760, off Penny Creek Rd. in Quilcene, and guides strong thighs to views of Seattle and Mt. Rainier on a clear day.

NORTHERN OLYMPIC PENINSULA

On the north side of the peninsula, the mountains creep toward the shore, leaving only a thin strip of land settled by people. Much of the peninsula is only available via side roads off US 101. The north strikes a good balance between the isolation of the west and the traffic of the east—solitude can be found, yet transportation is still easy to figure out, especially when using Port Angeles as a base. The north gives the right balance for someone with only a day or two to see the park, or who is looking to recover from a stint in the isolation of the western section of the park.

PORT ANGELES   ☎360

Port Angeles is the "gateway" to the Olympic National Park. The administrative headquarters and main info center are both located here. As US 101 turns west on the peninsula, the traffic thins as only those headed to ONP are left. Port Angeles (PA) is the final stop, the point where the weekend traffic drops off and those here to explore remain. PA's charm lies in its surroundings, all competing for most alluring: the formidable mountains to the south, the Strait of Juan de Fuca and Vancouver Island to the north, and Puget Sound and the Pacific coast only a stone's throw away. Though not a destination city, the park headquarters, transportation connections, a small, walkable downtown, and the addition of a new hostel and several good places to eat make Port Angeles at least as much a place to recharge batteries and rest aching muscles as it is a place to pass through.

☐ TRANSPORTATION

Buses: Olympic Bus Lines, 221 N Lincoln (☎417-0700 or 800-457-4492; www.olympicbuslines.com), in the Doubletree Hotel parking lot. To **Seattle** (2½hr., 3 per day, $29 one-way, $49 round-trip) and **Sea-Tac Airport** (3hr., 3-5 per day, $43 one-way, $58 round-trip). **Olympic Van Tours (OVT;** ☎452-3858) runs from the Olympics to **Hoh Rainforest** ($32) and **Hurricane Ridge** ($20). OVT also shuttles to trailheads.

Ferries: Two different vessels (one passengers-only) shuttle across the straits: one to **Victoria** on the **M.V. Coho** from 101 E Railroad Ave. (☎457-4491; www.cohoferry.com), runs Mar.-Jan. The Coho does not take reservations, so call ahead to find out how early to arrive. (1½hr.; up to 4 per day in high season; $9, bicycle $4, with car $36, children $4.50). **Victoria Express,** 115 E Railroad Ave. (☎800-633-1589; www.victoriaexpress.com), has passenger-only service and does take reservations. (1hr.; $16, ages 5-11 $9, under 5 free). US and Canadian citizens crossing into Canada, children included, need valid proof of citizenship. Other internationals should check their own visa requirements. (See **Essentials,** p. 21.) Day parking lots line Railroad Ave. near the docks ($7-10 per day).

Public Transportation: Clallam Transit System, 830 W Lauridsen Blvd. (☎800-858-3747 or 452-4511; www.clallamtransit.com), serves **Port Angeles** and **Clallam County** as far as **Neah Bay** and **Forks,** from the transport center on Railroad Ave. at Oak St., a block west of the ferry. Operates M-F 5:30am-11pm, Sa 8am-11pm. Downtown $0.75, ages 65 and older $0.25, 6-19 $0.50; day pass $2; $0.25 per zone passed.

Taxis: Peninsula Taxi (☎385-1872). $2 base plus $1.75 per mi. 24hr.

Car Rental: Evergreen Auto Rental, 808 E Front St. (☎452-8001). From $36 per day plus $0.20 per mi. after 100 mi. Must be 21 or older with proof of insurance. Open M-F 8am-5pm, Sa 9am-5pm.

☑ PRACTICAL INFORMATION

Tourist Information: Chamber of Commerce, 121 E Railroad Ave. (☎452-2363 or 877-465-8372; www.portangeles.org), near the ferry. Ask for a guide to the town's art for a walking route. Open daily 10am-4pm, dependent on volunteers; winter closed Sa-Su.

Outdoor Information: The **Olympic National Park (ONP) Visitor Center,** 3002 Mt. Angeles Rd. (☎565-3130), is just outside of town. Open daily 8:30am-5:30pm; see p. 230 for details. **Port Brook and News,** 104 E 1st St. (☎452-6367), has maps and advice on the region. Open M-Sa 9am-9pm, Su 10am-5pm.

Equipment Rental:

Olympic Mountaineering, 140 W Front St. (☎452-0240; www.olymtn.com), rents sturdy gear (external frame pack $18 per day, internal pack $22 per day) with lower rates during the week and as the demand wanes toward the low-season. Offers guided hiking and climbing trips in the ONP (from $150 for 2 people). The shop also features an indoor climbing wall, free with your own gear. Open M-Sa 9am-6pm, Su 10am-5pm.

Brown's Outdoor Store, 112 W Front St. (☎457-4150; www.brownsoutdoor.com), rents at low daily rates. Packs $12 per day, tents $12 per day. Call ahead as gear is often snatched up. Open M-Sa 9:30am-6pm, Su noon-4pm.

Sound Bikes & Kayaks, 120 E Front St. (☎457-1240; www.soundbikeskayaks.com), rents bikes from $9 per hr., $35 per day. Leads half-day kayak trips for $40, kayak rentals alone $12 per hr. Open M-Sa 9am-5:30pm.

Laundromat: Peabody Street Coin Laundry, 212 Peabody St. at 2nd St. Look for the big Maytag Laundry sign. Wash $1.75, dry $0.25 per 10min. 24hr.

Police: ☎452-4545. 24hr.

Sexual Assault Crisis Line: Safehome, 1914 W 18th St. (☎452-4357).

Pharmacy: Safeway (☎457-0599; see **Food,** below).

Medical: CliniCare, 621 E Front St. (☎452-5000), urgent care clinic open 24hr. **Olympic Memorial Hospital, 939** Caroline St. (☎417-7000) at Washington St. Open 24hr.

Internet Access: At the **library,** 2210 S Peabody St. (☎417-8501; www.nols.org.) Unlimited free Internet access. Open M and W noon-8pm, Tu and Th-Sa 10am-5pm.

Post Office: 424 E 1st St. (☎452-9275). Open M-F 8:30am-5pm, Sa 9am-noon. **Postal Code:** 98362.

ACCOMMODATIONS AND CAMPING

Countless motels are found in PA, and, keeping in mind that cleanliness is proportional to price, you can pay what you will. The least expensive motels line US 101 west of town, so cruise First St. to price-shop. Winter rates drop $5-15. West on US 101, halfway between Port Angeles and Lake Crescent, a 6 mi. spur road leads south into the park to two **campgrounds** along the waterfall-rich Elwha River: **Elwha Valley ❶** (40 sites) and the nearby **Altaire ❶** (30 sites). Both have access to fishing on the river and farther on at Lake Mills. (☎452-9191. $10.)

Thor Town Hostel, 316 N Race St. (☎452-0931; www.thortown.com), a friendly refuge 7 blocks east of the city center and 1 mi. north of the ranger station. This "work-in-progress" hostel is located in a renovated house; if you want the feel of staying in someone's home, this is your place. Linens and towels provided. Laundry $1. Bike rentals ($8 per day) and bus info. Dorms $12; private rooms $28. ❶

Heart o' the Hills Campground, just after the park entrance, overflows with vacationers poised to take Hurricane Ridge by storm, so get there early to claim a site. The campground has no RV sites or showers but offers plenty of giant trees, fairly private sites, and drinking water. Wheelchair-accessible. 105 sites, $10. ❶

Salt Creek County Park (☎417-2291), west on US 101 to Rte. 112 and down Camp Hayden Rd., sits on a bluff overlooking the Strait of Juan de Fuca. Thirty of the sites are crowded and open on a hill but have a stunning view of the water, while 60 are more secluded. Access to tidal pools and beach. Sites $14. Showers $0.25 for 1½min. ❶

Portside Inn, 1510 East Front St. (☎452-4015 or 877-8588; www.portsideinn.com) is slightly ahead in terms of the price-grime curve. Nice rooms, cable, free Internet access. Small pool. Singles start at $45, usually $53 in peak season; doubles $61. ❸

FOOD

There are plenty of seafood restaurants in town—finding a cheap one is the trick. Picnickers can try **Safeway,** 110 E 3rd St., at Lincoln St. (☎457-0788. Open 24hr.)

Crazy Fish, 229 W 1st St. (☎457-1944). Lively and funky, this brand new Mexican fish joint is the hit in town. The fish tacos (2 for $6) and sides from the classic chips and salsa to the oddball mac and cheese wedges ($4) are guaranteed to brighten your day. Theme nights include M DJed ladies night, Tu $2 taco/$2 tequila night, and live music every Sa. Open M-Sa 11am-2am. ❶

Thai Peppers, 222 N Lincoln St. (☎452-4995). Keeping PA natives and visitors happy. Indulge your craving for a classic Thai menu, but remember the seafood is excellent. Lunch specials $6, dinners $8-10. Open M-Sa 11am-2:30pm and 4:30-9pm. ❷

India Oven, 222 N Lincoln St. (☎452-5170). Before (or after) catching the ferry to Victoria, fill up at the $7 lunch buffet, or grab food to go (large portion $5.95, small $3.95). Entrees $8-14. Open daily 11am-10pm. ❷

Bella Italia, 118 E 1st St. (☎457-5442), offers good classic Italian fare. Lasagna ($10) and spaghetti ($7) please hungry vegetarians while meat-lovers get carnivorous with the sausage red sauce pasta ($9). Open M-Sa 11am-10pm, Su 10:30am-10pm. ❷

WASHINGTON

👁 🏔 SIGHTS AND OUTDOOR ACTIVITIES

The main draw of Port Angeles is the National Park, which looms behind the town in the form of Mt. Angeles. Nevertheless, there are several places to enjoy outside of the park if a change of pace is what you are looking for.

The **Fine Arts Center and Sculpture Park,** 1203 E Lauridsen Blvd., near the national park visitors center, has exhibits by Northwest artists in a small space. The surrounding five acres display contemporary sculptures along paths that wind through the heavily wooded park. (☎457-3532; www.olympus.net/community/pafac. Gallery open Tu-Su 11am-5pm, outside art open daylight hours year-round. Both free.) Take US 101 east about 4 mi. and turn left. A 5 mi. (2hr.) trail leads out on the 7 mi. **Dungeness Spit,** the world's longest natural sand spit, extends 6 mi. into the Strait of Juan de Fuca. The trail winds all the way to **New Dungeness Lighthouse,** once at the tip of the spit, now a half mile from the end. (☎683-9166; www.newdungenesslighthouse.com. Open 9am until 2hr. before sunset.) Over 200 species of birds inhabit this area, part of the Dungeness National Wildlife Refuge. Offshore, indigenous crabs, clams, seals, and sea lions populate the waters. The Dungeness Spit also houses a small **campground ❶** at the **Dungeness Recreation Area.** Many of the very private sites, separated by trees, have beautiful water views. (☎683-5847. Sites $10. Showers $0.25 per 2min.) Nearby, the **Olympic Game Farm,** 1423 Ward Rd. off Woodcock St., is a retirement home for the most privileged of animals: characters in low-budget children's films. Drive by zebras, llamas, rhinos, and bears, or take a guided walking tour. (☎683-4295 or 800-778-4295; www.olygamefarm.com. Open M-F and Su 9am-5pm, Sa 9am-6pm for driving; 10am-3pm for walking. Driving tour 4 mi.; $9, children $7. Walking tour 1hr.; $10/$8. Both driving and walking $15/$12.)

The stand out attraction of PA is **Hurricane Ridge,** which boasts the best drive-up views of the park's interior. Clear days promise splendid views of Mt. Olympus and Vancouver Island against a foreground of snow and indigo lupine. RVs and tourists crowd the ridge by day, but seclusion can be found at dawn. To get there, take Race Rd. south from US 101 and turn right after the ONP visitors center.

While most come to the ridge just to gawk, getting out on your feet is the best way to take in the views without the chatter of families and rangers. Until July, walking on the ridge usually involves snow-stepping. On weekends from late December to late March, the Park Service organizes free guided **snowshoe walks** atop the ridge. (Contact the visitors center. Walks Sa and Su 2pm. $12 per person.) Three paved interpretive trails leave from the parking lot and offer gentle strolls among the meadows. The most dramatic is **High Ridge** (½ mi. loop, 30min.) with access to a view north from **Sunset Point.** More moderate hiking is found up **Hurricane Hill** (3¼ mi. round-trip) for more secluded panoramic views, or along **Klahhane Ridge** (7½ mi. round-trip, 5hr., moderate) which leads 2¾ mi. on flat ground, and then turns for 1 mi. of tough switchbacking to actually get to Klahhane. Get a friend to drive you up to the ridge, where three trails descend dramatically into nearby valleys: **Wolf Creek** and the trail off of Hurricane Hill pass through meadows to descend steep switchbacks to the Elwha Valley, while the **Little River Trail** drops down to Little River Road (8 mi. one-way, all 3 easy downhill, difficult uphill).

Of course, not all the hiking in the area conveniently leaves from a picturesque parking lot. **Switchback Trail,** not for the faint-hearted or weak-kneed, starts at a small parking lot a few miles below the ridge and climbs a steep 1600 ft. over 1½ mi. up to Klahhane Ridge. There, it connects to the Klahhane Ridge Trail and the Heather Park Trail, which lead more gradually off the ridge (3 mi. one-way, very difficult). **Gravelly Obstruction Point Road** leads 7 mi. from the Hurricane Ridge parking lot to trailheads that offer longer treks. The **Lillian Ridge Trail** heads into Grand Valley, past three alpine lakes to **Grand Pass** where peaks loom overhead in every direction (16 mi. round-trip, moderate). From the same trailhead, the **Grand Ridge Trail** sets out on a dramatic ridge-walk to Deer Park (15 mi. round-trip, moderate).

LAKE CRESCENT. One of the few picturesque spots US 101 passes, this massive blue-green oasis in the north-central region of the peninsula has long been a source of awe. Native legend explains that Storm King Mountain, in the heat of a fierce dispute between tribes, threw part of himself into the Lyre River Valley to stop the war, creating Lake Crescent. For long after, the lake was revered and feared as sacred. Today, the lake offers brisk swimming, blissful picnicking, and frequent sunshine. **East Beach** is a prime swimming spot with a gentle sandy beach located, surprisingly, at the eastern most tip of the lake. **Storm King Ranger Station** (a.k.a. Morgenroth Cabin) is on a small peninsula in the center of the lake and offers all of the usual services. (☎928-3380. Open daily May-Sept. 10am-5pm.)

At the west end of the lake, just past the Fairholm General Store, there is a small road that heads to **Fairholm Campground ❶,** which has beautiful moss-covered trees, picnic and beach areas, and sites right on the lakeshore. Wheelchair-accessible. (☎928-3380. Open year-round. 87 sites, $10.) The **Lake Crescent Lodge,** next to the Storm King Station, rents rowboats. (☎928-3211; www.lakecrescentlodge.com. Rentals 7am-8pm. $9 per hr., $20 half-day, $30 full day.) Trout **fishing** is popular on the water, but only catch-and-release is allowed (no permit required).

The lake also acts as a popular trailhead for routes heading up the steep slopes crowned with giant old growth trees and scattered with huge plunging waterfalls. From the Storm King Ranger Station, the **Marymere Falls Trail** departs from the Barnes Creek Trail to gently climb up to the 100 ft. falls back in the forest (2 mi. round-trip, easy). From the same trailhead, the **Mount Storm King Trail** reaches the peak with a view of the lake (6¼ mi. round-trip, difficult). This trailhead can also be used as the input for a longer trip up to the **Aurora Ridge Trail** that peaks 4600 ft. Sourdough Mountain and passes alpine Eagle Lakes before winding back down to US 101 (23 mi. one-way, difficult; give at least 3 days).

SOL DUC HOT SPRINGS. Just west of the tip of Lake Crescent, a road turns south and follows the Sol Duc River south for 12½ mi. into a large green valley. At the end lies an oasis for tired travelers—hot baths in the **Sol Duc Hot Springs Resort.** The hot springs are in the National Park. Natural spring water is filtered into three man-made mineral pools. To avoid the hot water and sulfur smell, jump in the large chlorinated swimming pool. (☎327-3583; www.northolympic.com/solduc. Open daily late May-Sept. 9am-9pm; late March to mid-May 9am-7pm. $11, ages 4-12 $7.65, twilight rate (last 2hr.) $7. Suit, locker, and towel rental available.)

Hiking in the area is also good; to get information and permits, stop at the **Eagle Ranger Station,** just before the springs. (☎327-3534. Open daily summer 8am-4:30pm). With its location, it is no surprise that the **Sol Duc Hot Springs Campground ❶** often fills by 3pm. (☎327-3534. Picnic sites. 78 sites, $12.) With trails leaving the resort, ranger station, and **Sol Duc Trailhead** (at the end of the road, 1 mi. from the campground), Sol Duc is a good leaping-off point, (or better yet given the hot baths, return point). **Lover's Lane Trail** (6 mi. loop, easy) departs the resort and leads to Sol Duc Falls. The lazy or busy just go from the Sol Duc trailhead and make it there in 1½ mi. (1hr.). Continuing past the falls, **Canyon Creek Trail** leads a challenging 3 mi to camping at **Deer Lake ❶** (18 sites, $10). This trip can be either a one-day jaunt or the first day of the notorious **High Divide Loop,** which first climbs into the alpine past Seven Lakes Basin. Next, it teeters along the steep ridge that separates the Hoh and Soleduck drainages, with wildflowers and breathtaking views at hikers' toes. Finally, it hits the 5474 ft. summit of Bogachiel Peak before it passes Heart Lake and joins with the Appleton Pass Trail to drop back down to the trail head. (19 mi. difficult. Allow at least 3 days; snow often covers the trail until July so check with a ranger for info and only proceed on snow with experience and an ice axe). For those with less time but equal craving for challenge, **Mink Lake** climbs 1500 ft. through a dense forest to a mountain lake (5 mi. round-trip, difficult). After this hike, feel no guilt about pampering yourself in a hot spring.

NEAH BAY AND CAPE FLATTERY   ☎ 360

At the westernmost point on the Juan de Fuca Strait and well away from the National Park is **Neah Bay,** the only town in the **Makah Reservation.** The community has recently become famous for its revival of its gray whale hunt and its preservation of artifacts found in 500-year-old Makah village. Gorgeous **Cape Flattery** is the most northwestern point in the lower 48. James Cook gave the Cape its name in 1778, because it "flattered us with the hopes of finding a harbor." Flattery got them nowhere; the nearest port is Port Angeles, 50 mi. away.

You can reach Neah Bay and Cape Flattery by an hour-long detour from **US 101.** From Port Angeles, **Route 112,** a National Scenic Byway, leads west 72 mi. to Neah Bay. From the south, **Route 113** runs north from Sappho to Rte. 112. **Clallam Transit System** runs from Port Angeles; take bus #14 from Oak St. to Sappho (1¼hr.), then #16 to Neah Bay. (☎452-4511 or 800-858-3747; www.clallamtransit.com. 4-5 times per day. $1, seniors $0.50, ages 6-19 $0.85; all-day pass $2)

🏠🍴 ACCOMMODATIONS AND FOOD. If you're eager to spend a night on a Native American reservation, try the few motels and campgrounds here. **Hobuck Beach Campground ❶** is 3 mi. northwest of Neah Bay—follow signs to Ocean Beaches. (20 sites, $10.) If not camping, it's still worth a stop for a picnic or some surfing. The **Cape Motel ❷,** on Rte. 112, offers small but clean rooms and the option of roughing it in a rustic shanty or tentsite. (☎645-2250. Office open 7:30am-10pm. Sites $12; shanty singles $18, extra person $7; rooms $55-75;)

Neah Bay doesn't offer many dining options. Everyone sells salmon, meaning most people will bargain to get you to buy theirs. Pick up some to grill or smoke for a sandwich. Grab picnic materials at **Washburn's General Store** next to the mediocre cafes on Front St. (☎645-2211. Open M-Sa 8am-9pm, Su 8am-7pm.)

◰ SIGHTS. The **Makah Cultural and Research Center,** in Neah Bay on Rte. 112, is just inside the reservation, opposite the Coast Guard station. The center presents beautiful artifacts from the archaeological discoveries of the perfectly preserved coastal village of Ozette exposed in 1970 by tidal erosion. After the excavation of tens of thousands of valuable pieces of the tribe's history, the site was closed in 1981. (☎645-2711; www.makah.com/mcrchome.htm. Open daily June to mid-Sept. 10am-5pm; mid-Sept. to May W-Su 10am-5pm. $5, seniors and students $4, under 5 free. Free tours W-Su at 11am.) The Makah Nation, whose recorded history is 2000 years old, lives on this land. During Makah Days, in the last weekend in August, Native Americans from around the region come for canoe races, dances, and bone games (a form of gambling). Visitors are welcome; call the center for details.

Cape Flattery can be reached through Neah Bay, 8 mi. further northwest. Pick up directions at the Makah Center, or just take the road through town until it turns to dirt. Follow the "Marine Viewing Area" sign once you hit gravel and continue for another 4 mi. to a small circular parking area, where a trailhead leads half a mile to Cape Flattery. At 3pm, a free, short guided hike leaves from the trailhead. You'll know you're close to the amazing views of **Tatoosh** and **Van-**

couver Island when you hear the sound of Tatoosh's bullhorn. The road is excruciatingly bumpy, but the end of the hike reveals a dramatic cliff overlooking ocean stretches crashing against the rocks, and Tatoosh Island waiting offshore. To the south, the Makah Reservation's **beaches** are solitary and peaceful; respectful visitors are welcome to wander. The most common stretch of sand to visit is **Shi Shi Beach,** a 7 mi. round-trip stroll along headlands and down to the secluded and beautiful beach.

Outside the reservation, to the south, day hikers and backpackers populate the walking sections of the 57 mi. of coastal wilderness at **Ozette Lake,** a dislocated section of the national park 21 mi. off Hwy. 112. The 9 mi. boardwalk loop that begins at the lake is especially popular; the boardwalks alone are a marvel, where cedar shakes cut from old-growth red cedar form the attractive walkways. One heads toward a wild stretch of sand spotted with sea stacks at **Cape Alava,** the other to a sublime beach at **Sand Point.** A 3 mi. hike down the coast links the two legs, passing ancient native petroglyphs. The entire area is mostly prairie and coastal forest, but presents plenty of sand to slog through. Overnighters must make permit reservations in advance; spaces fill quickly in summer. The **Ozette Ranger Station** has further info. (☎963-2725. Open intermittently.) Call the visitors center outside of PA at ☎565-3100 for permit reservations.

WESTERN OLYMPIC PENINSULA

Alternating between rainforest, clear cuts, and dramatic coastline, US 101 traces a manic path through a truly stunning landscape. Travelers who drive the distance to this side of the peninsula will be rewarded with seclusion and natural beauty.

FORKS   ☎360

Between ONP's northern and western rims lies the logging town of Forks. Once the king timber town in the region, Forks both embraces and mourns its historic legacy. Lying 2hr. west of Port Angeles, Forks offers the widest selection of amenities on the western peninsula. Visit during the summer if possible; Forks gets more rain than any other city or town in Washington. If you're passing through town or grabbing a bite to eat, visit the **Forks Timber Museum.** (☎374-2531. Open M-Su 10am-4pm, logging and mill tours M, W, and F at 9am.) Check out forestry research in action at the **Olympic Natural Resources Center,** just south of the Logging Museum. Students and faculty from the University of Washington (and beyond) use this research facility to experiment with forest management techniques.

Clallam Transit (☎452-4511 or 800-858-374; www.clallamtransit.com) on #14 serves Forks from **Port Angeles** (M-F 7 per day; $1.25, disabled, seniors, and ages 6-19 $1). The **Forks Chamber of Commerce,** south of town, offers advice and maps, as well as tours through a real saw mill. (☎374-2531 or 800-443-6757; www.forkswa.com. Open M-F 9am-5pm; May-Sept. also Sa 10am-2pm.) The **Department of Natural Resources Main Office,** just off US 101 on the north side of Forks, right next to Tillicum Park, hands out maps of the peninsula. Since tourists who actually stop are a rarity, the DNR is happy to help. (☎374-6131; www.dnr.wa.gov. Open M-F 8am-4:30pm.) Free **Internet** access is at the **library** on 224 S Forks Ave. (☎374-6402; www.nols.org. Open M, Tu, and W noon-8pm, Th-Sa 10am-5pm.) The **police** are in the City Hall on E Division. (☎374-2223. Open daily 6am-6pm.) The **hospital** (☎374-6271) is just west of US 101 on Bogachiel Way. The **post office** (☎374-6303) is at Spartan Ave. and A St. Open M-F 9am-5pm, Sa 10am-noon. **Postal Code:** 98331.

Twenty miles south of Forks on US 101, between Hoh Rainforest and Kalaloch, you'll find the **Rainforest Hostel ❶,** 169312 US 10; follow hostel signs off US 101. Family rooms and dorms are available, as are outside trailers for couples or people allergic to the resident dog and cat. The hostel also has laundry ($2), snacks, ride-sharing, and bus info. (☎374-2270; http://fp1.centurytel.net/rainforesthostel. Morning help with clean-up required. Beds $12; family rooms $1 plus $12 per adult, $6 per child. Hiker/biker sites $6.) In Forks you'll find a row of budget motels. **Bagby's Town Motel ❸**, 1080 S Forks Ave., has small comfortable rooms and a garden stuffed with wicker furniture. (☎374-6231; www.bagbystownmotel.com. Singles $37-43; doubles $47-55.) Off the highway, grab groceries and coffee at **Forks Thriftway**, 950 S Forks Ave. (☎374-6161. Open M-Su 8am-10pm.) The **Raindrop Cafe ❷**, 111 E A St. at S Forks Ave., serves breakfast until 11am, names its burgers ($3.75-7.50) after clouds and serves seriously delicious $7.50 salads. (☎374-6612. Open May-Sept. M-Sa 6am-9pm, Su 6am-8pm; daily Oct.-Apr. 6am-7pm.)

LA PUSH AND MORA   ☎360

Just 10 mi. west of Forks down US 110, the tiny fishing village of La Push sits on one of the longest stretches of wild beach accessible in the country. Sea stacks loom just offshore, while waves crash against rugged patches of rocky beaches scattered with beautiful driftwood. Nearby, Mora provides a quiet beach and campsite that doubles as a trailhead for beach hikes. The sunsets over the water and dewy mornings will make you want to grab your tent and stay here for days.

Mora Campground ❶ is a sprawling 95-site campground that sees quite a bit of traffic from beach-goers. The mostly secluded sites are deep in the verdant forest but only a short walk from the water. (☎374-5460. Sites $10.) **Beach camping ❶** is permitted and common both north and south of the **Mora Ranger Station** but requires a permit ($5, plus $2 per person). The areas open to camping are south of Third Beach and north of Oil City and are clearly designated with signs. Before you go, pick up a required overnight permit, a park map, a tide table, and the useful *Olympic Coastal Strip Info* brochure at a ranger station. Set up camp well above the highest line of tidal debris. Indoor accommodations are springing up as the town shifts its economy from salmon harvesting to tourism. The **La Push Ocean Park Resort ❸**, along Hwy. 110 before the road comes into the marina, offers everything from a small motel to cabins to RV sites. All motel rooms have a kitchenette; swankier digs or an ocean view costs up to $220. (☎374-5267 or 800-487-1267; www.ocean-park.org. Rooms from $55.) **Three Rivers Resort ❶**, 7764 La Push Rd. along the road between Forks and La Push doesn't have the view that Ocean Park does, but offers cheaper cabins and tent sites for when Mora is full. (☎374-5300; www.northolympic.com/threerivers. Sites $10; RV sites $16; cabins from $59.)

Good food options are scarce around La Push. Fresh salmon is everywhere and makes a real beach experience all the more authentic. Otherwise, plan before you come and pick up some takeout or picnic wares in Forks.

The peninsula boasts some of the most stunning beaches around, and some of the most classically picturesque are right here. Mora lies just 1½ mi. from the crown jewel of **Rialto Beach**, where a parking lot allows you to drive right up to wild beauty. Sea stacks lurk offshore, while the beach is windy and steeper than usual, making for constantly dramatic surf. Miles of sand stretch in either direction, calling out to be strolled. Most people meander the 1½ miles to **Hole-in-the-Wall**, where the waters have carved a tunnel into the rocky headlands. The beach is also a perfect jumping-off point for beach backpackers as 17 mi. of secluded beach snakes up to **Shi-Shi Beach**, and a popular hike continues 1½ mi. on to **Sand Point** (18½ mi. one-way, moderate). Camping is allowed anywhere north of Ellen Creek with an overnight backcountry permit, available at ranger stations. Three beaches dot the landscape south of La Push; **First, Second**, and **Third Beaches** each have their own character and are all accessible by short hikes from the clearly marked parking lots along Hwy. 110. Third Beach's small waterfall and tidal pools are the setting-off point for the longer hike down the coast towards the south, 17 mi. to Oil City near the mouth of the Hoh River; this hike is not just a stroll down the sand, as rocky outcroppings and steep headlands have to be traversed (17 mi. one-way, moderate; allow about 3 days). To inject some more excitement into your stay, rent a surfboard at the Three Rivers Resort for $12 per hr. or $26 per day (see **Accommodations,** above). Riding the surf is very popular among locals, especially at First Beach where the waves are the most reliably awesome.

HOH RAINFOREST

The place to go to see the western rainforests, Hoh Rainforest sees plenty of guests. The average yearly rainfall in the Hoh Valley is 142 in. (Seattle gets 34 in. annually). The forest seems one dense mess of tangled branches and moss, but the growth is amazing and the 18 mi. drive into the park from US 101 is an enjoyable patchwork of old-growth, wildflowers, and riverbeds. Turn off from 101 onto the Hoh Valley Rd. and drive about 12 mi. to the park entrance booth. Check out the **visitors center** for backcountry permits and assistance in designing a backcountry route. (☎374-6925; www.nps.gov/olym. Open daily mid-June to Labor Day 9am-5pm.) The park maintains 88 sites in its **campground ❶** near the visitors center. (Limited wheelchair access. $10.) A **campground ❶** with 70 backcountry sites lies along the 17 mi. **Hoh River Trail,** which stretches between the visitors center and the Blue Glacier at Mt. Olympus (permit required, $5 plus $2 per person). Two primitive, free campsites are closer to 101: **Minnie Peterson ❶** (7 sites) and **Willoughby Creek ❶** (3 sites). No reservations are available; check to see what's open.

Hikers regularly file into the Hoh parking lot, returning from several popular routes that thread into the park's interior from the rainforest. The Hoh River Trail parallels the Hoh River for 17 mi., an easy three-day trip that traces through old-growth forests and lowlands to **Blue Glacier** on the shoulder of **Mount Olympus.** Shy Roosevelt elk, the ever-contested northern spotted owl, and the gods of ancient Greece inhabit this area. At around the ninth mile, the **Hoh Lake Trail** intersects and heads off into the notorious High Divide area, where multiple days can bring hikers from this river valley over the ridges into the Soleduck drainage; the full hike of the trail is a challenging 17½ mi. to Glacier Meadows, a common base for expeditions up Mount Olympus. Closer by, the ¾ mi. wheelchair-accessible **Hall of Mosses Trail** offers a whirlwind tour of rainforest vegetation. The slightly longer but still easy **Spruce Nature Trail** leads 1¼ mi. through old-growth forest, passing more varied vegetation along the banks of the Hoh River.

LAKE QUINAULT

Less visited than the Hoh Rainforest, Lake Quinault offers its own rainforest and a large, beautiful lake. This lake, at the southwestern corner of ONP, sustains a small enclave of weekend getawayers, anglers, and hikers, many of them bypassing the rest of the peninsula and coming straight north to the lake via Aberdeen. On the southern, more populated side of the lake, the Forest Service operates an info center at the **Quinault Ranger Station,** 353 S Shore Rd. (☎360-288-2525. Open May-Sept. M-F 8am-4:30pm, Sa-Su 9am-4pm; Oct.-Apr. M-F 9am-4:30pm.) On the northern side of the lake, the **Quinault River Ranger Station** offers similar services, but from within the national park, 6 mi. from the highway. (☎360-288-2444. Open daily Apr.-Sept. 8:30am-5pm.) Campers can drop their gear lakeside in **Willaby Campgrounds ❶,** ¼ mi. before the Forest Service Ranger Station along the south shore of the lake. (☎360-288-2213. First come, first served. 24 sites, $14.) Be aware—like the others in the area, it fills quickly. When Willaby's sites are taken, lakesiders camp at **Falls View ❶,** which has less private sites but still lake access. (☎360-288-2213. First come, first served. 30 sites, \$14.) The **Lake Quinault Lodge** (☎360-288-2900 or 800-562-6672; www.visitlakequinault.com), next to the southern ranger station, rents canoes (\$14 per hr.), rowboats (\$12), and kayaks (\$17).

Lake Quinault is surrounded by a great trail network. Stop at either ranger station for a detailed map of trails in the area. The **North Fork** trailhead is 20 mi. up North Shore Rd. and starts one of the park's most popular multi-day hikes, the **Skyline Loop,** which stretches 44 mi. north across the park, finishing at **Whiskey Bend** on the north rim near Elwha campground. The week-long trip is one of the easier ones into the heart of the Olympics, relatively speaking; bear in mind that the trail is rugged at times and impassable until mid-summer. The views, especially at Low Divide, are complemented by 17 campsites along the way (moderate; backcountry permit required, available at any of the ranger stations). A good day option is to hike the last leg of the loop, the **Skyline Ridge Trail,** just south of the North Fork trailhead, where it leads to the Park's largest yellow cedar (13 mi. round-trip, moderate). **Three Lakes Point** is an exquisite summit that often remains covered with snow into July. The moderate hike (7 mi. one-way) from North Fork runs through yellow cedar and prime mossy amphibian habitat. Give the trip several days. **Day hikes** depart the Quinault Ranger Station, including the easy 3 mi. **Quinault Lake Loop** and the generally easy half-mile **Maple Glade Trail.** Many more are found on the north of the lake, as well as in the interior of the park, and the rangers are always waiting to describe the best open options.

PACIFIC COAST

US 101 travels along beautiful coastal shores as it finishes the journey down the western coast and turns eastward. Small towns, phenomenal shellfish, and sparkling beaches beckon. In the heat of July, the coast starts to get crowded with vacationing inlanders, so those in search of solace should consider catching tourist-free warm weather in June or September. The Pacific coast is worth a visit even in the low season, when winter winds make for exciting wave and storm watching.

GRAYS HARBOR   ☎360

From Olympic National Park to the north, US 101 passes Grays Harbor and the industrial cities of Aberdeen and Hoquiam at the mouth of the Chehalis River. The two towns, once deeply embedded in the now largely defunct fishing and timber industries, are in transition towards tourism—or rather, the prime beachfront plus voracious travelers are pushing them towards tourism. The urban areas are still surpassed by the nature that surrounds them, but are playing a good game of catch-up. The adjacent beaches are abundant, with 22 mi. between Moclips and Ocean Shores alone, while south of Westport lies another 19 mi. strip; however, their beauty is occasionally marred by drag racers. (Driving on the beach is legal in Washington from September to April.) Fortunately, the beaches also offer other activities. Westport has begun to support a surfing enclave, while sea kayakers have taken up in the bay. Fishing still has its place here, as evidenced by the numerous charter companies; there's not much price difference (usually \$60-80 for a chartered day), so pick the name that sounds the prettiest and give 'em a call: **Deep Sea** (☎268-9300), **Islander** (☎268-9166), **Travis** (☎268-9140), or **Westport Charters** (☎268-0900). Fishing boats that are now out of commission have been turned into whale watching boats to catch sight of the spring migration of gray whales passing just offshore. People who get really excited about the friendly giants can visit the **Westport Maritime Museum,** 2210

Westhaven Dr., for whale-watching seminars. (☎268-0078; www.west-portwa.com/museum. Seminars run March to May Sa-Su at 10am. Open M-F 8am-5pm, Sa-Su for seminars.) Other wildlife is abundant throughout the area, but the best bet for guaranteed viewing is at the **Grays Harbor National Wildlife Refuge,** in Hoquiam off Hwy. 109; follow the signs. The refuge sits perched on a salt-marsh and mudflat. Shorebirds are most abundant and best seen from the **Sandpiper Trail** (2 mi. round-trip, easy) out to the tip of Bowerman Peninsula. (☎753-9467; http://graysharbor.fws.gov. Open daily dawn-dusk.)

WILLAPA BAY ☎360

Willapa Bay stretches between the Long Beach Peninsula and the Washington mainland just north of the Washington-Oregon border and the mouth of the Columbia River. Home to one of the last unpolluted estuaries in the nation, this is an excellent place to watch birdlife, especially in late spring and early fall. As US 101 passes through Willapa Bay's sparkling sloughs, the quiet forests of Long Island lure seekers of solitude and lovers of wildlife. From the north, stop at the headquarters of the **Willapa National Wildlife Refuge,** just off US 101 on the left, 12 mi. north of the junction between US 101 and Rte. 103 by Chinook. The headquarters offers info on Canada geese, loons, grebes, cormorants, and trumpeter swans. (☎484-3482; http://willapa.fws.gov. Open M-F 7:30am-4pm.) Rangers can give directions and maps to several hiking trails in the region, including **Leadbetter Point** at the tip of the Long Beach Peninsula. Long Island is home to five limited-use **campgrounds ❶,** all inaccessible by car. Reaching the island, although it is only a stone's throw away from the mainland, requires bringing your own canoe or kayak. Because of the difficulty of access, the bulk of tourist traffic is left stranded on the mainland. After reaching the island, hike 2½ mi. along the island's fern-lined main road to pay your respects to the 900-year-old **Ancient Red Cedars.**

LONG BEACH PENINSULA ☎360

The 28 mi. of unbroken sand that is Long Beach Peninsula is a frenzy of kitsch and souvenir shops sporadically broken up by calm forests and beautiful ocean views. Just don't let the vistas deceive you into taking a dip—the water is very cold and carries lethal riptide currents. Accessible by US 101 and Rte. 103, every town has a clearly marked beach access road (unmarked roads end in private property). Fishing, boating, and kite-flying are how residents recuperate from pounding winter storms. Clamming season lasts from October to mid-March (but beware red tide, when the shellfish are contaminated with a potentially-fatal bacteria). The **Short Stop Store-N-Deli,** 4540 Ocean Beach Hwy. in the Shell Station across from the visitors center (☎425-3190), and **Dennis Co.,** on Hwy. 110 between 2nd and Pacific (☎642-3153), sell non-resident licenses (annual license $15, 3-day license $5, plus a small dealer fee) along with a fishing guide and tide tables. For the best advice, head down Rte. 103, where there are numerous bait shops staffed by local experts.

Like most other towns along the bay, **Ilwaco** was nearly devastated when depleted salmon stocks required a shutdown of the fishery for several years. Salmon steaks are plentiful along the waterfront, where the industry is beginning to recover. The **Long Beach Peninsula Visitors Bureau** is 5min. south of Long Beach in Seaview at the junction of US 101 and Rte. 103. (☎642-2400 or 800-451-2542; www.funbeach.com. Open M-Sa 9am-5pm, Su 9am-4pm.) **Pacific Transit** sends buses from Long Beach as far north as Aberdeen. (☎642-9418; www.pacifictransit.org. $0.85; exact change required.) Buses run up and down the peninsula all day; get schedules at post offices and visitors centers. (local service Sa-Su only).

WASHINGTON

The **Boulevard Motel ❸,** 301 Ocean Blvd., offers cottages, a motel with ocean views from the top floor, and a pool with a mermaid mural. (☎642-2434 or 888-454-0346. Singles from $50, reduced rates in winter.) Other cheap lodging at **Sand-Lo Motel ❸,** 1910 N Pacific Hwy. (☎642-2600. Summer rooms from $50.) The best sandwiches in town are at **Surfer Sands ❷,** 311 S Pacific Way, a shack on the side of Hwy 110. The Turtle ($6) is a turkey sandwich on steroids; packed with cranberry sauce, cashews, raisins, provolone, and fresh greens on thick slices of fresh bread. (☎642-7629. Open daily Apr.-Sept. 10:30am-11pm; Oct.-Mar. M-F 10:30am-8pm.) The **Be Bop Diner ❷,** 110 S. Pacific Way, is a retro 50s-style eatery with old fashioned burgers ($5-8), fabulous chowder ($3-5), and award-winning BBQ. (☎642-4751. Open M-Sa 11am-10pm, Su 11am-7pm.) For the best meal around, head down Hwy. 103 in Ocean Park to historic **Oysterville.** The star draw of this tiny, white-washed town is **Oysterville Sea Farms ❸,** at 1st and Clark St., which raises and sells its namesake mollusk; unfortunately, you've got to cook them yourself, but they're ready with lots of suggestions. If you're not up to the task and willing to fork over some cash, there are lots of other places in town that do serve the salty morsels. (☎665-6585; www.oysterville.net. Open daily 10am-5pm.) For entertainment, head to **Marsh's Free Museum,** 409 S Pacific Way, home to a mechanical fortune teller, Jake the petrified alligator-man, and honky-tonk souvenirs. (☎642-2188; www.marshsfreemuseum.com. Open, ironically, whenever tourists bring money.)

If you want to catch the sea's bounty yourself, **Pacific Salmon Charters** leads 8hr. fishing tours. (☎642-3466 or 800-831-2695; www.pacificsalmoncharters.com. From $70. Opens daily at 5:30am; tours leave between 6am and 8am.) During the third week in August, flyers from Thailand, China, Japan, and Australia compete in the spectacular **Washington State International Kite Festival** (www.kitefestival.com).

COLUMBIA RIVER ESTUARY ☎ 360

Several miles south of Long Beach on Washington's southern border, Cape Disappointment guards the Columbia River Estuary. Over the last 300 years, almost 2000 vessels have been wrecked, stranded, or sunk at Cape Disappointment, and even today the Coast Guard is kept busy during the frequent squalls in the area. **Fort Columbia State Park** lies on US 101 northwest of the Astoria Megler Bridge, 1 mi. east of Chinook on the west side of the highway. An interpretive center showcases numerous artifacts of the Chinook people as

THE HIDDEN DEAL

CLAMMING UP

Food on the Olympic Peninsula often seems limited to, at best, picnic munchies. Luckily, there is a more exciting option; for only $5 for one day or $15 for three, visitors to the peninsula's beaches can dig up razor clams. While the clams can be found at many beaches along the coast, the Long Beach peninsula, from Oysterville to Leadbetter Point, is known as the best digging spot. Contact the Department of Fish and Wildlife for info on clamming seasons and regulations (☎360-586-6129; wdfw.wa.gov).

Head to the beach at least 2hr. before low tide. The clams hide just inches below the surface of the sand; when they sense trouble, they retract their necks, leaving "shows" on the beach. Stomping on the sand will force the clams to show; marching in a circle is the best way to avoid backtracking.

After spotting a clam, the key is to dig it up before it burrows deep into the sand. Beginners should use a clam gun, a 3 ft. tube open at one end and closed at the other with a small hole and a handle. Push it into the sand and place a thumb over the small hole, then pull it out of the sand, hopefully with a tube full of sand and a clam. To free your hands, carry clams in a net attached to a belt around the waist. Before cooking, clams should be cleaned by dipping them in boiling water, removing the shell, and cutting off the siphon tube.

well as of the white soldiers and features the **Commanding Officer's Quarters,** furnished as in the early 1900s to recreate life at the fort. (☎ 777-8221. Open daily Memorial Day-Sept. 10am-5pm.)

Three miles southwest of Ilwaco, at the southern tip of the Peninsula, **Cape Disappointment State Park ❷** offers camping and a mega dose of Lewis and Clark. The park was the dynamic duo's final destination—apparently, they weren't thrilled—and now boasts two lighthouses and a well-pruned campground packed with RVs. The sites fill up quickly in summer. (☎ 642-3078, reservations 800-452-5687. Open daily dawn-dusk. 240 sites, $16; RV sites $22; cabins and yurts sleep 4 for $45. Reservation fee $6.) Abutting the park is the **Lewis and Clark Interpretive Center,** hovering above the ruins of Fort Canby. Inside, a winding display documents their expedition from Missouri to their arrival at the mouth of the Columbia. (☎ 406-727-8733; www.fs.fed.us/r1/lewisclark/lcic. Open daily 10am-5pm.) The **North Head Lighthouse,** built in 1898, is accessible by a gravel path in the northwest corner of the park, off Hwy. 103; the path has great views down the breakers. Lighthouse enthusiasts gleefully take the guided tours. (☎ 642-3078. Tours $1, on request May-Sept.) The **Cape Disappointment Lighthouse,** built in 1856, is the oldest lighthouse in the Pacific Northwest. In the southeast corner of the park, its distinctive red light can be reached by walking up a steep hill from the Coast Guard station parking lot, or by following a narrow, fairly steep trail from the interpretive center. For a magnificent beach-level view of both lighthouses, drive past **Waikiki Beach** on the North Jetty. Waikiki is a solitary spot for winter beachcombing and ship watching. If you just can't get enough of the hometown explorers, the moderate **Discovery Trail,** which runs 8¼ mi. from Ilwaco to Long Beach, displays artifacts commemorating Lewis and Clark's discovery of the Pacific Ocean, including a gray whale skeleton and a 20 ft. bronze tree.

CASCADE REGION

Sprawling in the rain shadow of the Cascades, the hills and valleys of the Columbia River Basin foster little more than sagebrush, tumbleweed, and tiny wildflowers among unirrigated dunes. Where the watershed has been tapped, however, a patchwork of farmland yields bumper crops of fruit and wine. Seeking the best of the region, travelers take high alpine routes through the Cascades, where dry hills give way to green beauty in the mountains. The Cascades are most accessible July through September. Many of the mountain passes are snowed in during the rest of the year, making access difficult and anything beside skiing and snowshoeing just about impossible. Mt. Baker, Mt. Vernon, Mt. Rainier, Mt. Adams, and Mt. St. Helens are accessible by four major roads. The North Cascades Scenic Hwy. (Rte. 20) is the most breathtaking and provides access to North Cascades National Park. Scenic US 2 leaves Everett for Stevens Pass and descends along the Wenatchee River. Rte. 20 and US 2 are often traveled in sequence as the Cascade Loop. US 12 approaches Mt. Rainier National Park through White Pass and provides access to Mt. St. Helens from the north. I-90 sends four lanes from Seattle to the ski resorts of Snoqualmie Pass and eastward to Spokane and beyond. From the west the state is accessible by bus on I-90 and US 2, and the train parallels I-90. Rainstorms and evening traffic can slow hitching; locals warn against thumbing Rte. 20.

NORTH CASCADES NATIONAL PARK ☎ 360

Over half a million acres of vertical rock peaks with tenacious glaciers clinging to their sides and cascades of water pouring through their valleys make the North Cascades National Park one of the wildest places left in the country. The park is a part of the Cascades Range—named for its innumerable waterfalls—that stretches from northern California into British Columbia and is often called the "Alps of North America." These dramatic pinnacles rise abruptly from the neighboring deep glacial valleys, creating some of the most complex and challenging mountaineering in the continental US. With over 93 percent of the park designated part of the Stephen Mather Wilderness, the area protects lush alpine meadows, over 300 of the about 600 US glaciers outside of Alaska, and abundant wildlife, including the grizzly bear and northern grey wolf. More impressive still, the park combines with adjacent wilderness areas—Mt. Baker and Noisy-Diosbud Wilderness Areas to the west, Glacier Peak Wilderness to the south, and Pasayten and Lake Chelan-Sawtooth Wilderness Areas and Liberty Bell Primitive Area to the east—to create a block of over a million acres, protected from all but human feet. While these boundaries will mean little to those on foot, it is important to know on what land you are treading as different agencies have varying rules.

AT A GLANCE	
AREA: 504,781 acres	**GATEWAYS:** Marblemount, Stehekin.
CLIMATE: Lush temperate rainforest in summer; heavy snow and rain autumn through spring.	**CAMPING:** Many campgrounds and backcountry options (p. 255).
FEATURES: Ross and Diabolo Lakes, Hart's Pass, extensive backcountry.	**FEES AND RESERVATIONS:** Passes required for parking, $5 per day, $30 per year. Free backcountry passes, required for camping, are available at certain ranger stations.
HIGHLIGHTS: Driving the North Cascades Scenic Highway, Desolation Peak Trail.	

⊞ ORIENTATION

The park itself consists of four sections: **North Unit, South Unit, Ross Lake National Recreation Area,** and **Lake Chelan National Recreation Area.** The North Unit reaches up to the Canadian border and is the most remote area of the park, accessible mainly by trails coming from near **Mount Baker** or from **Hozeman,** a small camp just south of the Canadian border. The South Unit, pocked by glaciers, is accessible from trails leaving Rte. 20 along both its north and east sides, making it an inviting wilderness to explore. Ross Lake National Recreation Area, running along Rte. 20 and north along Ross Lake, contains the park's main throughway and thus sees most of the park's recreation. Finally, the Lake Chelan National Recreation Area at the park's southernmost tip protects the beautiful wilderness around Stehekin and the northern tip of Lake Chelan, accessible only by boat, by plane, or on foot.

⊏ TRANSPORTATION

To reach North Cascades National Park from the west, take I-5 to Burlington and take the Rte. 20 exit. Coming from the east, take Rte. 20 west from Twisp. The park and its surrounding recreation areas are always open, but access is limited by snow, ice, and avalanche danger in winter. Rte. 20 is partially closed from mid-November to mid-April due to winter conditions. Two gravel roads enter the park itself: the **Cascade River Road** out of Marblemount and the **Stehekin Valley Road.** There is no car access to the Stehekin Valley. It is very difficult to access the park via public transportation. **Greyhound** runs buses along I-5 and as far east as Wenatchee, where the Chelan County Link bus system connects to Lake Chelan. From the lake you can take a ferry to Stehekin Landing in Lake Chelan National Recreation Area. For more information about ferry travel to **Stehekin,** see p. 260.

Many people tend to view the North Cascades as a scenic drive along **Route 20,** also known as the **North Cascades Scenic Highway.** Weaving its way through the craggy peaks and lush valleys of the Cascades, Rte. 20 is a blissful driving experience. Spectacular vistas await at every turn, and a string of small towns scattered along the road provide services. Still, the looming mountain peaks, christened names like Mount Terror, Damnation Peak, Mt. Despair, and Forbidden Peak by those daring enough to scale them, continually remind visitors of the rugged wilderness just past the dashboard. Rte. 20 runs east-west through northern Washington, traveling through the spectacular scenery of Mt. Baker-Snoqualmie National Forest, North Cascades National Park, and Okanogan National Forest.

⚡ PRACTICAL INFORMATION

North Cascades National Park and the Ross Lake and Lake Chelan National Recreation Areas are all managed as one entity—the North Cascades National Park Service Complex. The **North Cascades National Park Headquarters Information Station** is located in Sedro-Woolley, a logging hamlet nestled in the rich farmland of the lower Skagit Valley and the westernmost town of note on Rte. 20. It is also home to the **Mt. Baker-Snoqualmie National Forest Headquarters,** which borders the western side of the park. (For information on daytrips to Mt. Baker National Forest, see p. 221.) Northwest Forest Passes, required for parking, are sold here; see **Fees and Reservations,** above. (810 Rte. 20, near the intersection with Rte. 9. ☎856-5700; www.nps.gov/noca. Open daily 8am-4:30pm; closed Sa-Su mid-Oct. to May.) The **Chelan Ranger Station** in Chelan near the lake is an office of the Wenatchee National Forest and offers information on the Lake Chelan National Recreation Area. (☎509-682-2549. Open daily 7:45am-4:30pm; closed Sa-Su Sept. to mid-June.)

Visitor Information:

■ **North Cascades Visitors Center and Ranger Station** (☎386-4495, ext. 11), at mile 120 in Newhalem, has an extensive display on the area's ecosystems found at each elevation, featuring films, photos, and preserved animals, a visually stunning (and melodramatic) 25min. film on the park's history and legacy, interactive maps and models, and numerous interpretive trails. Open daily summer 8:30am-6pm; winter Sa-Su 9am-4:30pm.

Marblemount Wilderness Information Center (☎873-4500, ext. 39; www.marblemount.com), 1 mi. north of West Marblemount on a well-marked road. The best resource for backcountry trip-planning in the North Cascades. The Center has updates on trails and weather and is the most convenient place to pick up free but required backcountry permits (see **Camping,** below). They also sell the Northwest Forest Pass required for parking at trailheads (see **Fees and Reservations,** above). Open July-Aug. M-Th and Su 7am-6pm, F-Sa 7am-8pm; in winter call ahead. There are **no major service stations** for 69 mi. east of Marblemount.

Golden West Visitor Center and Ranger Station (☎856-5700, ext. 340, then 14), just by the passenger ferry landing at Stehekin Landing at Lake Chelan. General and trail information, free required backcountry permits (for certain park entrances only), and a gallery showcasing local artists. Open daily 8:30am-4pm.

Glacier Public Service Center (☎599-2714), just east of Glacier on Hwy. 542. On the road to North Cascades trailheads, this US Forest Service Station that provides the free backcountry pass as well as information on the history of Mt. Baker National Forest. Open daily 8am-4:30pm.

Hospital: The nearest medical facilities are in **Sedro-Woolley,** 1971 Rte. 20, about 60 mi. from the heart of the park (☎856-6201). **Newhalem** and **Marblemount** have volunteer fire departments trained in emergency medical services. Park rangers are also all trained in emergency first aid.

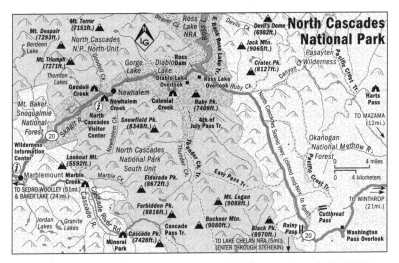

Post Office: In **Marblemount,** 60096 Rte. 20. Open M-F 8am-noon and 12:45-4:30pm. **Postal Code:** 98267.

CAMPING

Backcountry camping requires a **permit,** free from ranger stations and visitor centers. (☎873-4500, ext. 39.) Permits must be picked up in person no earlier than the day before trip date and are on a first-come, first-served basis.

There are campsites available at two parks along Hwy. 20 in the Marblemount area: **Rockport State Park** and **Howard Miller Steelhead Park ❶.** Geared towards RVs, Rockport is embedded within old-growth Douglas-firs, providing a sublime spot to rest for the night. (☎853-8461 or 800-233-0321. 62 utility sites, $22.) Howard Miller Steelhead, a city campground with numerous amenities, includes a playground, Adirondack shelters (three-sided wooden buildings), and free showers. (☎853-8808. 15 sites, $20; 44 utility sites, $26.) More remote options are on Cascade Road, including at **Cascade Island ❶.** (☎902-1000. 15 tent sites; free.) Others are **Marble Creek** and **Mineral Park ❶,** both free National Forest campsites. (Marble Creek: ☎856-5700. 24 sites, no utility hookups, RVs up to 31 feet allowed. No water. Open mid-May to mid-Sept. Mineral Park: ☎856-5700. 5 sites. No water.)

The National Park Service-run ■**Colonial Creek Campground ❶** lies nestled along the shore of Diablo Lake, with turquoise waters lapping at the foot of some sites; all spots are shaded by a lush and verdant canopy. Take a frigid dip in the lake waters, or explore for an afternoon of fishing or boating. Easy access to numerous trails. Nightly naturalist talks are hosted in the site's impressive amphitheater. (☎856-5700. 162 sites, $12. Open mid-Apr. to mid-Oct.) **Goodell Creek Campground ❶,** at mile 119 just west of Newhalem, is a small but beautiful area with leafy sites suitable for tents and small trailers and a launch site for whitewater rafting on the Skagit River. The drive to the site also presents a glimpse of the striking southern Pickett Range. (☎856-5700. 21 sites, $10. Water shut off after Oct., when sites are free.) **Newhalem Creek Campground ❶,** at mile 120, shares a turn-off with the visitors center. It is a larger facility geared toward RV folk. (☎856-5700. 111 sites. $12.)

On the edges of the park at the eastern end of Hwy. 20 are three Forest Service-maintained campsites: **Lone Fir, Klipchuck,** and **Early Winters ❶**. Small and modest, with only 28, 46, and 13 sites respectively, they are still a welcome change from the larger sites at the park's heart. (Campsite updates ☎856-5700; reservations 877-444-6777 or www.reserveusa.com; recommended in summer. $14.)

There are four remote Forest Service sites along Harts Pass Rd.: **Ballard, River Bend, Harts Pass,** and **Meadows.** These fairly primitive, out-of-the-way sites offer a chance to rough it not far from the road; the first three have only a half dozen sites, while Meadows boasts just 14, making them quiet as well. (☎856-5700. $5.)

⚠ OUTDOOR ACTIVITIES

While most people encounter the park via the North Cascades Hwy., there are ample opportunities for on-foot exploration as well. As amazing as the views seem from the car, you can't experience the mountains' flavor from a vehicle, so make sure to hop out and explore the area's hiking trails. Those determined to penetrate the park should allot a stout pair of boots and plenty of time. A park this daunting demands multi-day hiking, and the Marblemount Info Center is the authority on backcountry trekking (see **Practical Information,** p. 254.) There's no shortage of day hikes, either; ask at Marblemount for a trail suggestion to fit your specific need.

DAY HIKING AND SCENIC DRIVING. The best short hiking in the Marblemount area is the moderate 4 mi. climb through wildflower meadows in spring to a viewpoint on **Sauk Mountain.** (On Forest Rd. 1030 off Hwy 20, approx. 3hr.) In Newhalem, take the brief but breath-taking **Sterling Munro Trail** for 300 yd. to a view of the rugged southern Pickett Range. The trail leads directly from the North Cascades Visitors Center (see **Practical Information,** p. 254) and should not be missed.

While the mountains of the park are surely its main attraction, along the stretch of road past Newhalem the lakes created by dams earlier in the century come in a close second, providing a stunning contrast to the foreboding peaks with their surreal aqua waters, and are much more accessible than the seemingly close peaks. The **Gorge Overlook Trail** is an easy half mile to an impressive view of Gorge Lake, while both **Diabolo** and **Ross Lakes** have designated **overlooks** just off the side of Rte. 20 that include multiple explanatory plaques and signs. For a more private overlook of Ross Lake, there is a 1½ mi. round-trip hike from the highway to the dam. From Colonial Creek Campground, the **Thunder Knob Trail** takes hikers to the over 7000 ft. lookout over Diabolo Lake in a short but steep 3½ mi. round-trip. These lakes beg to be seen from the water, and that's an urge you shouldn't resist. Boat rentals are available at **Ross Lake Resort** (p. 257), or in towns to the east (Mazama, Winthrop, and Twisp) and west (Sedro-Woolley).

The stretch of road from **Ross Lake,** near the Eastern border of North Cascades National Park, to **Winthrop,** in the Okanogan National Forest, is the most beautiful section of Rte. 20. The frozen creases of a mountain face stand before you. Snow and granite rise on one side of the road, sheer cliffs plummet on the other. Leaving the basin of Ross Lake, the road begins to climb, revealing the craggy peaks of the North Cascades. Unsurprisingly, this end of the drive also boasts some of the most popular scenery out of the car as well. The **Pacific Crest Trail** (p. 3) crosses Rte. 20 at **Rainy Pass** (mile 157) on one of the most scenic and difficult legs of its 2500 mi. course from Mexico to Canada. From the Rainy Pass parking lot there are numerous well-maintained day hikes into the picturesque surroundings; many can be hiked in sneakers, provided the snow has melted (about mid-July). The most heavily trodden path is the **Rainy Lake Nature Trail,** an easy 1¾ mi. round-trip that takes visitors to a lakeside picnic area facing a waterfall and the impressive Lyall Glacier. Another easy longer day trip is the hike to **Lake Ann** and **Maple Pass,** bringing you first to the lake, stocked with trout for your fishing pleasure, then after another 2 mi. to outstanding views from the pass at 6800 ft. (6¼ mi. round-trip).

Only slightly farther east is the overlook at **Washington Pass** (mi. 162), rewarding visitors with one of the state's most dramatic panoramas, an astonishing view of the red rocks exposed by **Early Winters Creek** in **Copper Basin,** and one of the few spots that really reveals the contrast of the wet western and drier eastern climates.

▣ INTENSIVE OUTDOOR ACTIVITIES FOR EXTENDED STAYS

If you have the time and inclination to devote more than a couple days to the North Cascades, consider the following outdoors options. Even the shorter routes may require you to probe deeper into the park than the average traveler. While the beauty of some trails means that no amount of remoteness can keep the crowds away, for the most part the North Cascades holds the promise of a unique nature experience. Your persistent search for that perfect trail will be rewarded by blissful multi-day hikes deep in the glacier-carved wilderness, where your own two feet and a humble water taxi are the only ways in and out.

MARBLEMOUNT TO NEWHALEM AND AREA. Cascade Road stretches 22 mi. from the bridge in Marblemount from Mt. Baker-Snoqualmie National Forest into the South Unit of the national park. The ultimate destination for most heading this way is the ever popular and ever crowded **Cascade Pass Trail.** One of the original routes of Native Americans into the mountains, today the trail continues to Stehekin Valley Rd. The hike gains 1700 ft. of elevation to a 5400 ft. summit overlooking **Johannesburg Mountain** and the glacier that hangs from its face, regularly dripping chunks of ice. Further trails lead from the peak, such as those to **Sahale Glacier, Doubtful Lake,** and **Mixup Peak.** (7½ mi. round-trip, moderate to difficult.)

Just west of Newhalem on Rte. 20 is the moderate 10½ mi. round-trip hike to **Thornton Lakes,** a series of alpine lakes in a high meadow below the peak of Mt. Triumph. **Thunder Creek Trail** is among the most popular hikes in the area. The 1½ mi. round-trip hike through old-growth forest begins at Colonial Creek at mile 130 of Rte. 20. (Easy.) A more challenging variation is the 3¼ mi. **Fourth of July Pass Trail** beginning 2 mi. into the Thunder Creek trail and climbing 3500 ft. toward views of glacier-draped Colonial and Snowfield peaks. (Moderate to difficult.)

DIABOLO AND AREA. There are hikes around the reservoir for those waiting for the ferry or just looking for a view of the turquoise beauty have many options to choose from. The **Diabolo Lake Trail** begins from near the dock and heads east to Ross Dam via a trail that slowly climbs above the bank for an easy 7½ mi. round-trip hike. This can be a one-way trip if you want to see the lake multiple ways by walking and then taking the tugboat back down the lake. **Stetattle Creek Trail,** also an easy 7 mi. round-trip, provides a gentle walk through the woods along the reservoir starting at Stetattle Creek bridge. More challenging routes include the climb 4000 ft. up **Sourdough Mountain,** where views of the whole valley await those with strong quads. (7 mi. round-trip. Difficult.) Also, along Hwy. 20, between Diabolo and the Colonial Creek Campground, is the popular but steep **Pyramid Lake** hike, leading to the lake and its namesake mountain. (4¼ mi. round-trip. Moderate.)

ROSS LAKE AND AREA. Although Ross Lake is one of the most beautiful spots in the park, and surely along the scenic drive, it is also one of the least accessible. In order to reach the trails and campsites along its shores, you have to walk or take a boat; rentals, portaging, and a **water taxi service** are available though **Ross Lake Resort** (☎386-4437; www.rosslakeresort.com. Canoe $24 per day, kayak $31 per day. Water taxi: $25 to $70 per boat carrying up to 6 people one way, depend-

WASHINGTON

ing on trailhead; call for reservations. $25 for truck portage). The **Seattle City Light boat** runs from the Diabolo Dam up the lake daily to where a truck can shuttle you to Ross Lake (☎206-684-3030; www.ci.seattle.wa.us/light/tours. Boat $10 round-trip; truck $6 round-trip. Boat leaves daily June-Sept. at 8:30am and 3pm.) The shortest route to walk is the **Ross Dam Trail,** a moderate 2½ mi. trail from Rte. 20 to a landing near the dam; the hotel is another 1½ mi. along the path.

Once you've found your way to the lake, the most stunning—and thus most popular—day hike from the area is the **Desolation Peak Trail** (difficult, 9½ mi. round- trip). The trail can be accessed via water-taxi to either the Desolation Landing or the Lightning Creek Campground, adding a 4 mi. trip to the trail-head. The trail climbs almost 4500 ft. in less than 5 mi. to the peak where Ross Lake lies at your feet and Hozomeen Mountain and Jack Mountain stare back at you; in the spring, the meadow is covered in wildflowers. Ross Lake also serves as the input point for many of the park's most celebrated multi-day hikes; the trails openings change annually due to weather, be sure to check with a ranger for seasonal information.

HARTS PASS AND AREA. Just 19 mi. up from Mazama, a side road leads past the intimidating glacially carved **Goat Wall** to **Harts Pass** where it crosses the Pacific Crest Trail. The road, originally constructed in the 1890s in the heat of mining fervor in the area, now climbs for an additional steep 3 mi. to **Slate Peak Lookout.** At 7440 ft. tall, it is the highest point you can drive to in the state. The location of an early warning station constructed in WWII and later used as a radar station in the Cold War, the peak was flattened, opening the area to what remain spectacular views of mountains as far as the eye can see. Although slightly off the main throughway of Rte. 20, Harts Pass is well worth the detour.

Hiking in the area ranges from jaunts to mammoth undertakings, and nearly every route is malleable depending on which exact trails you choose; head to the Methow Valley Visitors Center in Winthrop for maps, further suggested itineraries, and trail updates (☎996-4000). Two easier options to see more of the view from the pass are the **Windy Pass Trail,** which follows the Pacific Crest Trail along meadows overlooking mountain vistas to Windy Pass. (7 mi. round-trip; begins 1½ mi. up Slate Peak Rd. from Hart's Pass; easy) and the hike south down the PCT along ridges to **Grasshopper Pass.** (11 mi. round-trip, trailhead at Harts Pass. Easy.) Harts Pass, situated in a portion of the National Forest between the National Park and the Pasayten Wilderness, is a prime put-in point for an endless array of longer backpacking loops. One good loop to consider is the **Monument Creek Trail,** which follows the creekbed to a ridge with stunning views. (51 mi. round-trip, allow at least 6 to 7 days; trailhead at Lost River off Harts Pass Rd. Moderate.)

CHELAN ☎509

The serpentine body of Lake Chelan (sha-LAN), the state's deepest and bluest body of water, undulates some 55 mi. southeast through Wenatchee National Forest and the Lake Chelan National Recreation Area toward the Columbia River and US 97. Here, the fertile mountains of North Cascades National Park transform into the bone-dry brown hills and apple orchards that surround the town of Chelan. Unfortunately, the town itself is touristy—the economy is structured around family tourism that usually involves renting a house for an extended stay. There is little in the town to draw the budget traveler—the real attraction of Chelan is at the docks, where several ferries leave for the beautiful wilderness farther up the lake.

⚡🛈 ORIENTATION AND PRACTICAL INFORMATION. The town of Chelan rests on the southeast end of Lake Chelan, along Hwy. 97, 190 mi. (4hr.) west of Spokane. **US 97** cuts through the town along the lake and becomes its main street, **Woodin Avenue.** Look out for speed traps near the lake.

Link, the local bus service, runs on Rte. 21 and 31 hourly between the Chamber of Commerce and Wenatchee. (☎662-1155; www.linktransit.com. 1¼hr., M-F 6am-6pm, $0.50-1.) **Northwest Trailways** (☎800-366-3830, or through Greyhound 800-231-2222) departs Wenatchee for Seattle (3½hr., 2 per day, $27) and Spokane (3½hr., 1 per day, $27). For ferry service, see **Stehekin,** p. 260. The **Chamber of Commerce,** 102 E Johnson St., off Manson Hwy., has info on the town. (☎682-3503 or 800-424-3526; www.lakechelan.com. Open summer M-F 9am-5pm, Sa-Su 10am-3pm; winter M-F 9am-5pm.) The **Chelan Ranger Station,** 428 W Woodin Ave., on the lake, is the place to buy maps ($4) or Northwest Forest Passes ($5) for parking. (☎682-2549. Open daily June-Sept. 7:45am-4:30pm; Oct.-May M-F 7:45am-4:30pm.) **Chelan Boat Rentals,** 1210 W Woodin Ave., is one of the shops that rents small fishing boats ($23 per hr.), jet skis (from $35 per hr., $125 per day), and kayaks ($15 per hr.) from its lakeside location. (☎682-4444. Open daily 9am-9pm.) Get clean at **Town Tub Laundry,** near the Pennzoil station on the east end of Woodin Ave. (Wash $1.75, dry $0.25 per 10min. Open daily 8am-9pm.) **Electrik Dreams,** 246 W Manson Rd., ste. 1, provides **Internet** access for $9 per hr. (☎682-8889. Open M-Th 11am-10pm, F-Sa 11am-9pm.) In an emergency, contact the **police,** located at 207 N Emerson St. (☎682-2588). A 24hr. **crisis line** is at ☎662-7105, and there's a 24hr. **pharmacy** at **Safeway,** 106 W Manson Rd. (☎682-4087. Open M-F 9am-7pm, Sa 8am-6pm, Su 10am-6pm.) A **hospital** is at 503 E Highland St. (☎682-3300. Open 24hr.) The **post office** is at 144 E Johnson St. (☎682-2625. Open M-F 8:30am-5pm.) **Postal Code:** 98816.

🛏🏕 ACCOMMODATIONS AND CAMPING. Most Chelan motels and resorts are rather pricey; since the area is so tourist dependent, prices fluctuate with demand both seasonally and daily. The **Apple Inn ❹,** 1002 E Woodin Ave., boasts a hot tub, pool, and shuttle service. (☎682-4044 or 800-276-3229; www.appleinnmotel.com. Singles and doubles $59. Winter $45.) **Mom's Montlake Motel ❸,** 823 Wapato Ave., south off Woodin Ave. on Clifford, as the large sign on Woodin directs you, is a summertime mom-and-pop operation with clean, microwave- or kitchen-equipped rooms. (☎682-5715. Singles $49; doubles $59.) Most campers head for **Lake Chelan State Park ❷,** a grassy but crowded campground 9 mi. up the south shore of the lake with a beach, swimming area, small store, picnic sites, boat launch, playing fields, and jet ski rentals. (☎687-3710, reservations 800-452-5687. Reservations recommended Apr.-Sept. Bus #21. Sites $16; RV sites $22.) **Twenty-Five Mile Creek State Park ❷** is a smaller, but no less crowded, site; it boasts a beach, boat launch, and small store. (☎687-3610 or 800-452-5687. Reservations recommended Apr.-Sept. 63 sites, $16; 23 RV sites, $22.) Campers are free to pitch tents anywhere in the national forest, but may only light fires in established fire rings.

🍴 FOOD. The cheapest food in Chelan is at local fruit stands, although a few good places can be found slightly outside of town on E Woodin Ave. **Safeway,** 106 W Manson Rd., has groceries. (☎682-2615. Open daily 6am-11pm.) **Bear Foods** (a.k.a. Golden Florin's General Store), 125 E Woodin Ave., provides health food, offering every organic, natural, or local food and herbal remedy you desire. (☎682-5535. Open M-Sa 9am-6pm, Su noon-5pm.) Behind the unassuming facade of **▧Local Myth ❷,** 122 Emerson St., Art and the gang create mind-blowing pies from whole-wheat dough and fresh ingredients. The combination of pizzas ($7 and up), calzones ($6-9), and friendly conversation is unbeatable. (☎682-2914. Open Tu-Sa 11:30am-9pm.) **Flying Saucers ❶,** 116 S

WASHINGTON

Emerson, has specialty mocha coffee ($3), chai tea, cinnamon rolls (all $2), and atmosphere galore in a converted 50s diner. (☎682-5129. Open summer M-Sa 7am-6pm; winter M-F 7am-4pm.)

📍 DAYTRIP FROM CHELAN: GRAND COULEE DAM

As the climate warmed 18,000 years ago, a small glacier blocking a lake in Montana gave way, releasing catastrophic floodwaters that swept across eastern Washington, gouging out layers of soil and exposing the layers of granite and basalt below. As the warming continued, this phenomena occurred dozens of times. Each washout carved massive canyons, called coulees, into a region now known as the Channeled Scab Lands, which composes most of the striking, mesa-filled country south of the dam across its largest canyon, the Grand Coulee. Other evidence of these periodic floods scatters the landscape, from the largest boulders in the world transported by water to hill-size ripple marks across the plains.

From 1934 to 1942, 7000 workers (81 of whom died in accidents) toiled on the construction of the Grand Coulee Dam, a local remedy for the agricultural woes of the drought and the Great Depression but a travesty for conservationists and Native Americans. Nearly a mile long, this behemoth is the world's largest solid concrete structure and irrigates the previously parched Columbia River Basin, all while generating more power than any other hydroelectric plant in the US. The amount of concrete used to construct Grand Coulee would be enough to construct a 6 ft. wide sidewalk around the globe at the equator. The Columbia River, raised 350 ft. by the dam, forms both Franklin D. Roosevelt Lake and Banks Lake, where "wetsiders" from western Washington flock for swimming, boating, and fishing.

The dam looms at the junction of Rte. 174 and Rte. 155, about 75 mi. east of Chelan and 90 mi. west of Spokane. The **Visitor Arrival Center,** on Rte. 155 just north of Grand Coulee, is filled with various displays on the construction, operation, and legacy of the dam, as well as four free educational films on the dam and the geology of the area that show at 2hr. intervals throughout the day. A free guided tour of the third and newest power plant, including an elevator ride up the face of the dam, begins every 30min. between 10am and 5pm (contact the visitors center for more info). On summer nights, a cheesy yet technically amazing 36min. laser show chronicles the structure's history on the spillway of the dam. Watch from the visitors center for guaranteed sound (and arrive at least an hour early to beat the crowds), or park at Crown Point Vista off Rte. 174 and tune in to 90.1FM. (☎633-9265. Open daily Memorial Day to July 31 8:30am-11pm; Aug. 8:30am-10:30pm; Sept.-Nov. and Feb.-May 9am-5pm. Laser show daily Memorial Day to July 10pm; Aug. 9:30pm; Sept. 8:30pm. Free.) If you plan to spend the night after the light show, head to the only federal campground in the area, **Spring Canyon Campground** ❶, 6 mi. east of the dam. (Off Rte. 174. Reservations ☎800-444-6777 or www.reserveusa.com. Free ranger-guided activities for children; short Bunchgrass Prairie Nature Trail. Picnic, water front and boat launch area. 79 sites, $10.)

STEHEKIN ☎509

Stehekin (steh-HEE-kin) comes from a Native American word meaning "To pass through," a name the valley home of this isolated village has earned as the easiest route from the harsh Northern Cascades to the parched eastern desert to its south. Occupying the wetter, quieter, more welcoming northern end of Lake Chelan, its main connection to the rest of the world is a stunning 50 mi. ferry route; the only other options are hiking in via a five-day trail along the lake or from the north on the Pacific Crest Trail, or float-planing in. Despite its inaccessibility, Stehekin shouldn't be overlooked; the isolation has preserved a wild, beautiful place. With McGregor Mountain looming and total silence just a 5min. walk out of the tiny settlement, Stehekin is will captivate the outdoorsy for days on end.

■ **INTERCITY TRANSPORTATION.** Three **ferries** traverse the lake in summer. The ferries proceed along a stunning shoreline where mountain goats and brown bears roam as the jagged white-tipped Cascades slowly come into view from behind the smaller peaks: this view alone makes the ride worthwhile. All ferries are operated by the **Lake Chelan Boat Company,** 1418 W Woodin Ave., (☎ 682-2224 or reservations 682-4584; www.ladyofthelake.com) about 1 mi. west of downtown Chelan. *The Lady of the Lake II,* a 350-person ferry, makes one round-trip to Stehekin per day. (4hr., 8:30am, $28.) This ferry also picks up from Fields Point, 16 mi. up South Shore Rd. near **Twenty-Five Mile Creek State Park** (9:45am; parking $3 per day, $17 per week) and from the port of Holden Village, a religious retreat community. You can request that the ferry stop at Manson, Prince Creek, or Moore Point campgrounds along the Lakeshore Trail (see **Outdoor Activities,** p. 262). Arrange in advance to be picked up, then flag them down with a bright article of clothing. The smaller *Lady Express* makes an express trip to Stehekin (2½hr. with a 1hr. layover, departs 8:30am, $47). A combination ticket for the *Lady Express* or *Lady of the Lake II* to Stehekin and back runs $47, allowing for 3hr. in Stehekin. A new high-speed catamaran, the *Lady Cat,* makes two round-trips per day (1¼hr., 7:45am and 1:30pm, $92). Book ferry tickets in advance on summer weekends; they will not accept credit cards on the day of travel. Only the *Lady Express* runs in winter; check online or call for schedules.

▐ **LOCAL TRANSPORTATION.** Stehekin itself is small enough that two legs and 2min. are all one needs to cross it—transport isn't a problem. Getting farther up the road to trailheads and campsites can be an issue, though. **Discovery Bikes** rents well-maintained two-wheelers (☎ 884-4844; www.stehekindiscoverybikes.com. $3.50 per hr., $10 per half-day, $15 per day.) The **Stehekin Lodge Store** also rents bikes. (☎ 682-4494; www.stehekin.com. $12 per day.). From mid-May to mid-Oct., a **shuttle** leaves from the ferry and runs up Stehekin Valley Rd. to High Bridge campground (45min., 4 per day: 8:15am, 11:15am, 2:15pm, 5:15pm). The $6 National Park Service (NPS) shuttles continue on to Bridge Creek campground (30min.) and Glory Mountain (1hr.) from July to mid-Oct., or as far as the road is driveable. From mid-May to mid-June, the NPS shuttle runs to High Bridge upon request. (☎ 856-5700, ext. 340. Reservations recommended.)

▐▐ **CAMPING AND FOOD.** The Park Service maintains 12 **campgrounds** along the Stehekin River off Stehekin Valley Rd. All except the area closest to Stehekin are geared toward the hiker. **Purple Point ❶,** a 5min. walk from the ferry landing, is unique in its amenities: it has water, bathrooms, and free showers. All need reservations, except Purple Point which cannot be reserved. The folks at the ranger station will help you figure out how to get there. A free **permit** is required for backcountry camping and hiking. (Permits available at the **visitors center;** call ☎ 360-856-5700, ext. 340., then ext. 14, or visit www.nps.gov/noca.) The **Stehekin Valley Ranch ❹** offers more expensive lodging than camping, but still keeps it rustic in canvas tent cabins with no plumbing or electricity. (☎ 800-536-0745 or 682-4677. $65-75, ages 4-12 $50-60; price includes meals and transportation.) A delicious **dinner ❸** at the Ranch costs about $14 for non-guests. (☎ 682-4677. Reserve ahead. Office open M-F 9am-5pm; dinner served 5:30-7pm.) The **Lodge Restaurant ❸,** at the landing, serves three meals a day in a oversized log cabin. (☎ 682-4494. Breakfast 7:30-9:30am, $4-12; lunch 10:30am-2:30pm, $4-8; dinner 5-8pm, $6-17. Visit the

Lodge store to make reservations.) Up the road, the **Stehekin Pastry Company ❶** lures hikers out of the hills for sticky buns. (Open daily June-late Sept. 8am-5pm; late May to mid-June and late Sept.-early Oct. Sa-Su 8am-5pm.)

⚠ OUTDOOR ACTIVITIES. Some short, scenic day hikes surround the landing. The simple ¾ mi. **Imus Creek Trail** is an interpretive hike that offers great views of the lake, starting behind the Golden West Visitor Center. (Easy.) The moderately steep **Rainbow Loop Trail** offers stellar valley views. The moderate 4½ mi. trail begins 2½ mi. from Stehekin; the shuttles run to the trailhead four times a day, but it's close enough to walk. From Purple Creek, take a right turn to reach the switchbacks of the steep 15 mi. round-trip **Purple Creek Trail.** The 5700 ft. climb is tough, but the rewards include glimpses of nearby glaciers. The long but fairly easy 17¼ mi., 2- to 3-day **Lakeshore Trail** begins by the Visitor Center and follows the north shore of Lake Chelan to Prince Creek (where the ferry can stop), never rising more than 500 ft. above the lake but offering splendid views of surrounding peaks.

An unpaved road and many trails probe north from Stehekin into **North Cascades National Park** (p. 252). Three hikes begin at High Bridge. The first trail is the short **Coon Lake Trail**, an optimal spot for bird-watching. (Moderate.) The mellow **Agnes Gorge Trail** is the second trailhead on the left, 200 yd. beyond the bridge, and travels a level 2½ mi. through forests and meadows with views of 8115 ft. Agnes Mountain. (Easy.) Behind the ranger cabin, the **McGregor Mountain Trail** is a strenuous straight shot up the side of the mountain, climbing 6525 vertical ft. over 8 mi. and ending with unsurpassed views of the high North Cascades peaks. (Very difficult.) The last half mile is a scramble up ledges. This extremely challenging trail is often blocked by snow well into July; check at the visitors center before starting out. The shuttle to Bridge Creek provides access to the **Pacific Crest Trail,** which runs from Mexico to Canada. The North Cascades portion of this trail has been called its most scenic by many who have completed the journey. (Moderate to difficult.)

The **Rainbow Falls Tour,** in Stehekin, is a guided bus tour that coincides with ferry arrival times (9am, 10:45am, 12:30pm, 2:45pm). It zooms through the valley and its major sights: the Stehekin School, the last one-room schoolhouse in the state; the Stehekin Pastry Company; and Rainbow Falls, a misty 312 ft. cataract. ($7, ages 6-11 $4, under 6 free. Tickets available only on ferries.) The NPS rangers also lead numerous free activities, including a guided walk on the Imus Creek Trail walk. check at the Golden West Visitor Center for a program schedule.

LEAVENWORTH   ☎ 509

Leavenworth is a true experiment in tourism. After the town's logging industry collapsed and the railroad switching station moved to nearby Wenatchee, Leavenworth needed a new schtick. Desperate officials launched "Project Alpine" in 1964, a gimmick to transform the town into a German village: zoning and building codes necessitated Bavarian-style buildings, waiters learned about bratwurst, polka blasted over the loudspeakers, and German beer flowed. Decades later, Leavenworth's unique feel and prime wilderness location still attract swarms of visitors.

🔳🔽 ORIENTATION AND PRACTICAL INFORMATION. Leavenworth is near Washington's geographic center, on the eastern slope of the Cascades. To get there from Seattle, follow I-5 north to Everett (Exit 194), then US 2 east (126 mi., 2½hr.) The **Chamber of Commerce/Visitor Information Center,** 220 9th St. at Commercial St., provides pamphlets and brochures. (☎548-5807; www.leavenworth.org. Open M-Th 8am-5pm, F-Sa 8am-6pm, Su 10am-4pm; winter M-Sa 8am-5pm.) Wash up at **Wash Works Laundromat,** 907 S Wenatchee Ave. (☎662-3582. Open daily 8am-10pm. Wash $1.50, dry $0.25 per 10min.) In an emergency, contact the

police at ☎664-3900 or the **Cascade Medical Center,** 817 Commercial St. (☎548-5815). The **North Central Regional Library System,** 700 Hwy. 2, has free **Internet** access. (☎548-7923; www.ncrl.org. Open M-Tu and Th noon-8pm; W and F 9:30am-5pm.) The **post office** is at 960 US Hwy. 2 (☎548-7212 or 800-275-8777. Open M-F 9am-5pm, Sa 9-11am.) **Postal Code:** 98826.

▢▢ ACCOMMODATIONS AND FOOD. Leavenworth's booming tourist industry has generated a niche for dozens of faux-Bavarian lodgings; unfortunately, there's no confusing exchange rate to hide the high prices of these vacation-oriented hotels. Indulge in the fabulous location of **Bindlestiff's Riverside Cabins ❹,** 1600 Hwy. 2. Eight private cabins rest just feet from the beautiful Wenatchee River where you can watch the rafters drift by, borrow the BBQ, and grill on your own private porch. (☎548-1685; www.bindlestiff.com. One- and two-room cabins $69-89.) The centrally-located **Linderhof Motor Inn ❹,** 690 Hwy. 2, has cozy rooms with hand-crafted furniture , an outdoor hot tub and swimming pool, and included continental breakfast. (☎548-5283 or 800-828-5680; www.linderhof.com. Singles $55-69; doubles $69-84.) Camping is also available at seven different sites out of town on Icicle Creek Rd., which heads southwest out of town off Rte. 2. The closest site, **Eightmile ❶,** is—surprise—8 mi. out at a National Forest campground. (45 sites, $11.) The other sites range from 9½ mi. to 19 mi. out, and all have fewer than 20 sites, with the exception of **Johnny Creek ❶,** 12½ mi. up the road, with 65 sites ($10). For more info, contact the Leavenworth Ranger District.

Predictably, Leavenworth's food mimics German cuisine; surprisingly, it often succeeds. German wurst booths are tucked between buildings everywhere. Other delectable nibbles include the cinnamon rolls ($1.75), pie ($4-8), cookies ($1.15), and other pastries of ▧**Homefires Bakery ❶,** 13013 Bayne Rd. (☎548-7362; www.homefiresbakery.com. Open M and Th-Su 9am-5pm.) Try also **The Cheesemonger's Shop ❷,** 333 Front St., offering cheeses from all over the globe to fit any palate and nearly any budget. Prices start at $6, and go up and up. (☎548-9011 or 877-888-7389; www.cheesemongersshop.com. Open M-Sa 9am-6pm.) There are more pubs serving up goulash and wieners than you can imagine; one worth trying is **Andreas Keller Restaurant ❷,** 829 Front St. The menu spans traditional German cuisine with lunch sandwiches like a Bratwurst Ruben ($8) and Chicken Oktoberfest Style ($9). (☎548-6000; www.andreaskellerrestaurant.com. Open M-W and Su 10:30am-8:30pm; Th-Sa 10:30am-11pm. Live Bavarian music Jan.-June M and F-Su 6pm-closing; June-Jan. nightly 6pm-closing.)

◙▢ SIGHTS AND EVENTS. Leavenworth is its own sight; the town's transformation has been a huge success, as evidenced by the more than 1.5 million Americans who visited in 2000. Tasty pretzels and schnitzel complement the experience of walking down the street and taking in the impressively authentic-looking businesses, the ridiculous-looking McDonald's, and the pleased and confused tourists. The visitors center has a brochure, "Leavenworth Then and Now: A Walk Through Time," with pictures and explanations of local buildings' histories. While visitors on any weekend can almost be guaranteed a celebration of some sort, there are some that stand out, keeping the locals festive and the visitors returning. **Icefest,** in mid-January, is a full winter festival, with sleigh rides and a dog sled competition, while mid-May brings **Maifest** with a parade and live music and dance, including the Maipole Dance. (☎548-5807; www.leavenworth.com. Dog sled $5 entry fee.) The tradition of the town's first festival continues the last weekend in September as **Autumn Leaf** celebrates the foliage with family fun. (☎548-6348; www.autumnfestival.com). No Bavarian town—contrived or otherwise—would be complete without its own **Oktoberfest,** held during the first two weekends in October. (☎548-7021; www.oktoberfestleavenworth.com.)

WASHINGTON

ON THE MENU

EASIER THAN PIE

It doesn't take much time in central and eastern Washington to realize that the region is apple crazy. The biggest apple obsession is easily found in the Wenatchee Valley, where the apple is not only the city's symbol but also plays a substantial role in the local economy. Tourists come from all over to buy the fresh apples at all the local stands, take tours of the orchards, and attend cider tastings. Residents feast on aplets, candy treats made from slow-cooked apple puree, combined with walnuts and coated in powdered sugar. To make your own aplets, you will need:

2 pkg. unflavored gelatin
1¼ cups applesauce
2 cups sugar
½ cup finely chopped walnuts
1½ tsp. vanilla
powdered sugar

Mix gelatin with ½ cup applesauce and let stand for 10 min. Put sugar and remaining applesauce in a saucepan. Bring to a boil. Stir in gelatin-applesauce mixture and cook over low heat for 15min., stirring frequently. Add walnuts and vanilla; mix well. Pour into a greased 8x8 in. pan.
After you've let the pan stand overnight, cut the aplets in squares and toss the squares in a paper bag of powdered sugar, shake well, and serve.

⚄ OUTDOOR ACTIVITIES. When you've had your fill of tourist-watching and sausage-scarfing, embark on an adventure via Leavenworth's extensive hiking, biking, and climbing opportunities. Surrounded by the Wenatchee National Forest, the area's real draw is the Alpine Lakes area, also home to the Icicle Valley and some great skiing. The **Leavenworth Ranger District,** 600 Sherborne St., has extensive information on trails and permits. (☎548-6977. Open M-F 9am-4pm, Sa noon-4pm.) Almost all hiking requires a permit, either from trailheads or from a ranger. Some more popular areas are on advance-reservations lists, including the Enchantments and the Stuart and Colchuck Lakes area. Further details can be found in *100 Hikes in Washington's Alpine Lakes Wilderness* ($17).

Icicle Creek Canyon, with **Icicle Ridge** to the north and the 9415 ft. rock face of **Mount Stuart** to the south, stretches south from Leavenworth into the eastern core of the Alpine Lakes Wilderness. Throughout this area are some of the most coveted spots in Washington's backcountry; however, much of the valley was altered by wildfires in the summer of 1994. The resilient area has recovered quickly, leaving new trees and wildflowers in place of old stands of trees; still, be aware that trails may not be what someone who hasn't been there in 10 years says. Icicle Rd. leads out of town on the south end off Hwy. 2. Adventures (as well as campsites, above) can be found off the road in every direction. Some of the most prominent trails are the **Icicle Ridge Trail** (26 mi. one-way, moderate to difficult), which begins just 1½ mi. down the road and is the main trail that connects all the trails on the northern side of the road. The trail immediately climbs to the ridge, where it follows it all the way to Stevens Pass, passing grand views and bountiful alpine wildflower fields. Day hikers should not be intimidated by the trail; the **Lake Edna Trail,** a moderate 10 mi. round-trip, and **Fourth of July Creek Trail,** a difficult 10½ mi. round-trip, both climb to the ridge trail from further down Icicle Rd. The trail is also an easy jumping-off point for longer hikes north into the Chiwaukum Mountains along such trails as Chiwaukum Creek Trail and Frosty Creek Trail.

East of Mt. Stuart, the mystical **Enchantment Basin,** a chain of backcountry lakes framed by sharp rock peaks, attracts backpackers willing to trudge up to the 7000 ft. basin and climbers ambitious to try their hand at its jagged spires, the Cashmere Crags. The **Snow Lake Trail,** 4 mi. off Icicle Rd., a moderate 13 mi. round-trip hike for day visitors, is the primary put-in to the area. This trail itself does not require the advance permit, so it can serve as a substitute when the only slightly more grand Enchantments are all booked up. After upper Snow Lake, the trail's name changes to the **Enchantment Lakes Trail** as it climbs over endless switchbacks into the Enchantment Basin; the round-trip is an arduous 29 mi.

Continuing west along Rte. 2 into the Alpine Lakes Wilderness, the next prominent swath of wild backcountry is found in the Stevens Pass Corridor. This area is just too rugged to be tamed, and an extensive network of trails for the abundant day hikers to the solitude-seeking week-long expeditioner prove it. The most popular day hike in the area is **Wallace Falls,** a moderate 7 mi. round-trip trek to see the 250 ft. falls visible from the road in winter. Also try the hike up **Tonga Ridge,** an easy 9¼ mi. round-trip from Foss River Rd. 68 off Rte. 2, winding through meadows and enormous fall blueberry patches; and the **Necklace Valley,** with its string of bauble-named lakes (Jade, Jewel, Emerald, Opal, etc.), a more difficult 15 mi. round-trip up into the alpine area shadowed by mountain cirques.

SKIING AND SNOWSHOEING. Cross-country skiers will find they've met their match when they arrive in Leavenworth in the winter. The extensive network of local trails is maintained by the **Leavenworth Winter Sports Club;** they groom and sell passes to 23km of trails. (☎548-5115. $8, under 12 free. Open daily 8am-4pm.) 6½ mi. of these trails are at the Leavenworth golf course, 4¾ mi. are along the Icicle River Trail south of town, and 3 mi. are at the Leavenworth Ski Hill, the best place for beginners. Snowshoers will find numerous local trails and roads open to their exploration during the winter's heavy snowfall, including the last 5 mi. of **Icicle Road** and **Chiwaukum Creek Trail,** off Chiwaukum Creek Rd., 12 mi. north of the town on Rte. 2. The **Stevens Pass Ski Area** taught Seattleites to ski. Its large mix of terrain across an 1800 ft. vertical drop attracts families, skiers, and snowboarders. Trails range from beginner trails to the infamously steep Seventh Heaven. (☎206-821-4510; www.stevenspass.com. Open daily Nov. to Apr. 9am-10pm. $49, ages 62 and older $34, 7-12 $31.)

MOUNT SAINT HELENS ☎360

After two months of mounting volcanic activity, Mt. St. Helens erupted with a cataclysmic blast on May 18, 1980, transforming what had been a perfect mountain cone into a crater 1 mi. wide and 2 mi. long. The force of the ash-filled blast crumbled 1300 ft. of rock and razed forests, strewing trees like charred matchsticks in the process of moving a cubic mile of debris. Ash from the crater rocketed 17 mi. upward, circling the globe and blackening the region's sky for days. Debris from the volcano flooded Spirit Lake and choked the area's watersheds. Today, Mt. St. Helens is made up of the middle third of the Gifford Pinchot National Forest, as well as the Mt. St. Helens National Volcanic Monument. The monument is part National Park and part laboratory, encompassing most of the area affected by the explosion. Parts of the monument are off-limits to the public due to experiments, and hikers are obliged to keep to the handful of trails through such areas.

ORIENTATION

To make the **western approach** (p. 268), the most popular and worthwhile of the approaches, take Exit 49 off **I-5** and use **Route 504,** otherwise known as the **Spirit Lake Memorial Highway.** The relatively-new 52 mi. road has wide shoulders and astounding views of the crater. This is the quickest and easiest day trip to the mountain, and includes the Mt. St. Helens Visitor Center, the Coldwater Ridge Visitor Center, and the Johnston Ridge Observatory. A **southern approach** (see p. 269) on **Route 503** skirts the side of the volcano until it connects with

WASHINGTON

AT A GLANCE	
AREA: 110,000 acres.	**GATEWAYS:** Randle, Cougar.
CLIMATE: Overcast with threat of snow in winter, dry and sunny in summer.	**CAMPING:** Several options in the Sifford Pinchot National Forest.
FEATURES: Mt. St. Helens National Volcanic Monument, Gifford Pinchot National Forest.	**FEES AND RESERVATIONS:** Some ares require a **Monument Pass,** a one-day, multi-site ($6) or single-site ($3) pass. The **Northwest Forest Pass** ($5 per day, $30 per year) will likely cover the other areas. Climbing requires a separate permit ($15). See **Practical Information.**
HIGHLIGHTS: Climbing the volcano's crater, exploring the Ape Cave lava tube, viewing the devastated Spirit Lake.	

Forest Service Road 90. From there, **Forest Service Road 83** leads to lava caves and the Climber's Bivouac, a launch pad for forays up the mountain. Views from the south side don't show the recent destruction, but the green glens and remnants of age-old lava and mud flows make up for it with great hiking and camping. To make a **northern approach** (p. 270), take **US 12** east from I-5 (Exit 68). The towns of Mossyrock, Morton, and Randle along US 12 offer the **closest major services** to the monument. From US 12, **Forest Service Road 25** heads south to Forest Rd. 99, which leads 16 mi. into the most devastated parts of the monument. Travelers can stop by the majestic Spirit Lake and marvel at the huge expanses of blown-down forest. Although the monument itself contains no established **campgrounds,** a number are scattered throughout the surrounding National Forest. See approaches for listings of campgrounds. As always, a ranger will help you find the prime camping spots.

▮ PRACTICAL INFORMATION

Entrance Fee: There are 2 main types of fees associated with Mt. St. Helens. The 1st is the **Monument Pass**—this one-day, multi-site pass allows access to almost every center on the western approach, as well as Ape Cave. It can be purchased as a multi-site pass everywhere it is needed ($6, ages 5-15 $2, under 4 free), or it can be purchased as a single site pass, which allows access to only 1 area ($3, ages 5-15 $1, under 4 free). Areas of the monument that do not require a Monument Pass most likely require the 2nd fee, a **Northwest Forest Pass,** which will take care of the entire northern approach, as well as most of the southern area ($5 per day, $30 annually). Climbing the mountain requires a separate permit (see **Outdoor Activities,** p. 262).

Tourist Offices: There are 9 visitors centers and info stations, listed below by approach. Those on the western approach are by far the most informative, particularly if you're interested in what happened in 1980 as opposed to outdoor activities available today.

Publications: *The Volcano Review,* free from visitors centers and rangers contains a map, copious info, and activity schedules (www.fs.fed.us/gpnf/mshnvm). The *Road Guide to Mount St. Helens* ($6), available at the visitors centers, is more thorough.

Forest Service Information: Gifford Pinchot National Forest Headquarters, 10600 NE 51st Circle, Vancouver, WA (☎891-5000, recording 891-5009; www.fs.fed.us/gpnf). Info on camping and hiking within the forest. Additional **ranger station** and **visitor information** at **Randle,** 10024 US 12 (☎497-1100) north of the mountain on US 12.

Monument Headquarters, 42218 NE Yale Bridge Rd., Amboy (☎449-7800), 4 mi. north of Amboy on Rte. 503. This is *the* place to call or write for any questions prior to the trip: road conditions, permit availability, access, etc. Open M-F 8am-5pm.

Radio: 530 AM. Road closures and ranger hours. In winter only.

Mt. St. Helens, Mt. Rainier, and Vicinity

ACCOMMODATIONS
Cowlitz River Lodge, **10**
Hotel Packwood, **11**
Mt. St. Helens Motel, **16**
Paradise Inn, **8**
Shade Tree Inn, **24**
Whittaker's Bunkhouse, **4**

CAMPING
Beaver Bay, **21**
Camp Muir, **3**
Camp Schurman, **2**
Cougar, **20**
Cougar Rock, **7**
Eco Park, **15**
Guler-Mt. Adams County Park, **26**
Iron Creek, **13**
Ohanapecosh, **9**
Peterson Prairie, **25**
Seaquest State Park, **14**
Sunshine Pt., **6**
Swift, **22**
Takhlakh Lake, **18**
Trout Lake Creek, **23**
White River, **1**

FOOD
Club Cafe, **12**
Highlander, **5**
Jack's Restaurant, **19**
KJ's Bear Creek Cafe, **27**
Papa Pete's Pizza, **17**
Time Out Pizza, **28**

WASHINGTON

TO SEATTLE (40mi.)
TO TACOMA (2mi.)
TO PORTLAND (9mi.)
TO GLENWOOD & 24 (16mi.)

169
162
161
410
165
122
508
12
505
504
706
7
131
25
99
503
90
83
23
141
205
84
123

Carbonado
Kapowsin
Carbon River Entrance
Crystal Mountain Resort
Sunrise
Wonderland Trail
Mt. Rainier (14,411ft.)
White River Entrance
Mt. Rainier National Park
Ex Nihilo Sculpture Garden
Elbe
Nisqually Entrance
Ashford
Paradise
Longmire
Ohanapecosh R.
Grove of the Patriarchs
Ohanapecosh Entrance
Alder Lake
Mineral Lake
Tatoosh Wilderness
Packwood
GOAT ROCKS WILDERNESS
Salkum
Morton
Randle
Mayfield Lake
Mossyrock
Cowlitz R. Lake
Riffe Lake
Cowlitz R.
COWLITZ VALLEY
Cispus R.
Forest Learning Center
Spirit Lake Memorial Hwy.
Mt. St. Helens Visitors Center
Silver Lake
Coldwater Lake
Coldwater Ridge Visitor Center
N Fork Toutle R.
S Fork Toutle R.
Mt. St. Helens National Volcanic Monument
Johnston Ridge Observatory
Spirit Lake
Windy Ridge Interpretive Site
Mt. St. Helens (8366ft.)
Gifford Pinchot National Forest
Pacific Crest Trail
Mt. Adams Wilderness
Mt. Adams (12,276ft.)
Climbers' Bivouac
Ape Cave
Apes Headquarters
Pine Creek Info. Station
Cougar
Lewis R.
Swift Reservoir
Indian Heaven Wilderness
Wind R.
Trout Lake
Yale
Yale Lake
Monument Headquarters
Ariel
Lake Merwin
Amboy
BZ Corner
Husum
White Salmon R.
Battle Ground
Columbia River Gorge National Scenic Area
Carson
White Salmon
Bingen
Hood River
Vancouver
OREGON

0   10 miles
0   10 kilometers

WESTERN APPROACH: ROUTE 504

🖩 VISITORS CENTERS. Mount Saint Helens Visitor Center, opposite Seaquest State Park, is a great introduction to the explosive events of 1980. A detailed description looks at the events leading up to the eruption in increments of years, then months, days, and finally, seconds. Learn how a volcano works before you see its aftermath. Also offers a 1mi. hike through 2500-year-old wetlands. (☎274-2100. Open daily 9am-6pm. 25min. film shows at 5 and 35 after the hour.) The Weyerhaeuser Lumber Company-sponsored **Forest Learning Center,** just inside the blast zone on the west side of the mountain, houses interesting exhibits on logging and the reforestation of the surrounding timber downed by the explosion. A riveting 5min. video, composed mainly of news footage on the eruption, plays on loop. (☎414-3439. Open daily May-Oct. 10am-6pm. Does not require a monument pass.) The **Coldwater Ridge Visitor Center,** 43 mi. east of Castle Rock on Rte. 504, has a superb view of the crater along with trails leading to **Coldwater Lake.** Emphasis on the area's recolonization by living things through exhibits, a short film, and a ¼ mi. trail. Check out this visitors center if only to see the robotic ranger mannequin (her lips, eyes, eyebrows and neck move, but the rest of her is white and frozen in place) lecture a bunch of model visitors on the importance of staying on the trail. Picnic areas, talks, and a gift shop and snack bar. (☎274-2131. Open daily 10am-6pm; call for winter hours.) The **Johnston Ridge Observatory,** at the end of Rte. 504, features geological exhibits and the best view from the road of the steaming lava dome and crater. It is also home to the best relief map in the park, complete with lights to illustrate the landslides and mudflows that followed the eruption. The center is named for David Johnston, a geologist who predicted the May 18, 1980 eruption, stayed to study it, and was killed. A fantastic 16min. widescreen film features a digital recreation of the blast that fills in the space between the famous stills depicting the eruption. (☎274-2140. Open daily May-Oct. 10am-6pm.)

🖩📶 ACCOMMODATIONS AND FOOD. The only non-camping options close to the park are a few expensive motels that cluster around I-5 Exit 49, near the intersection of Rte. 504. Despite high prices, they book solid in the summer. Try the **Mount Saint Helens Motel ❹,** 1340 Mt. St. Helens Way NE in Castle Rock, 5 mi. from the Mt. St. Helens Visitor Center on Rte. 504. Enjoy free local calls, fridge, TVs, morning coffee, and laundry facilities. (☎274-7721. Singles $60, doubles $80; low-season $45/$65.) Just 28 mi. from the Johnston Ridge Visitors Center is the **Eco Park ❶,** mile 24 on the Spirit Lake Hwy. This "tent & breakfast" offers quiet campsites, flush toilets, and even a motion-activated paper towel dispenser. Grab a hearty breakfast at the cafe on your way out. (☎274-6542; www.ecoparkresort.com. Sites $15. Open May-Sept.) **Seaquest State Park ❷,** opposite the Mt. St. Helens Visitor Center, is easy to reach off I-5, and the closest large campground to the park. (☎274-8633, reservations 888-226-7688. Reservations essential. Wheelchair-accessible. 92 sites, $16; 16 full RV sites, $22; 4 primitive walk-in sites, $5. Pay showers.) If your coolers and stomachs are empty, Castle Rock is the best place to refuel. Supermarkets and convenience stores lie on the west side of Hwy. 5, while fast-food joints and a few restaurants sit on the east. Papa Pete throws a mean and inexpensive pizza at **Papa Pete's Pizza ❷,** 1163 Mt. St. Helens Way NE. A pizza big enough for two costs $12-15. (☎274-4271. Open daily 10am-11pm.)

🥾 HIKING. The 1hr. drive from the Mt. St. Helens Visitor Center to Johnston Ridge offers spectacular views of the crater and rebounding ecosystem, with plenty of opportunities to park the car and walk along short, well-marked trails. The **Boundary Trail** (3 mi. to the Lake) leads from the Johnston Ridge Observatory to Spirit Lake, and continues 52 mi. to Mt. Adams. (Moderate to difficult.)

SOUTHERN APPROACH: ROUTE 503

⃟ VISITORS CENTERS. Pine Creek Information Station, 17 mi. east of Cougar on Forest Rd. 90, shows a short film on the eruption. This info station is the only place in the south of the park with free water. (☎ 360-449-7800. Open daily mid-June to Sept. 9am-6pm.) **Apes Headquarters,** at Ape Cave on Forest Rd. 8303, is 3 mi. north of the Rd. 83/Rd. 90 junction (15min. from Cougar). Rangers rent lanterns ($3.50) and guide 45min. lantern walks into the 1900-year-old lava tube. On the weekends arrive early to snag a spot. Dress warmly—the cave is 42°F. (Open daily late May-Sept. 10am-5:30pm. Tours daily 10:30am-4:30pm, every hour on the half-hour.)

⃟ CAMPING. Swift Campground ❶, 30min. east of Cougar on Rd. 90 and just west of the Pine Creek Information Station, has spacious sites on Swift Reservoir. It is one of the most popular campgrounds in the area. Sites go on a first come, first served basis. (☎ 503-813-6666. 93 sites, $12.) **Cougar Campground ❶** and **Beaver Bay ❶,** 2 and 4 mi. east of Cougar respectively, are along Yale Lake. Cougar Lake has 45 sites that are more spread out and private than Beaver Bay's 78 sites. ($15 for up to 5 people, then $2 per person up to 8 people, $5 per extra car at Cougar.)

⃟ OUTDOOR ACTIVITIES. For **caving,** head to the famous **Ape Cave,** 5 mi. east of Cougar just off of Forest Rd. 83. The cave is a broken 2½ mi. lava tube formed by an eruption over 1900 years ago. When exploring the cave, wear a jacket and sturdy shoes, and take at least two flashlights or lanterns (rangers recommend three). The Lower Cave's easy travel attracts most visitors, but the Upper Cave offers a more challenging scramble over rubble and lava breakdown. Budget 1¼hr. for the Lower Cave, 3hr. for the Upper Cave. A Monument Pass is required. Rangers lead cave explorations every day (see **Apes Headquarters,** above), as well as rent lanterns. (Rentals $3.50 each, and stop at 4pm.) Apes has no free water.

Hiking is plentiful in this area. A quarter-mile before Ape Cave on Forest Rd. 83 is the easy **Trail of Two Forests,** a lava-strewn, wheelchair-accessible boardwalk path above the forest floor. A beautiful forest has emerged from the volcanic remnants of a thousands-of-years-old eruption. Forest Rd. 83 continues 9 mi. farther north, ending at **Lahar Viewpoint,** the site of mudflows that followed the eruption. On Forest Rd. 83, 11 mi. northeast of its junction with Rd. 90, the **Lava Canyon Trail #184** hosts a range of challenges: an easy, wheelchair-accessible 30min. stroll yields views of the **Muddy River Gorge** and **Waterfalls;** a more difficult route leads 3 mi. to the site of a now-defunct footbridge over Lava Canyon. Only the brave should venture farther; the trail then continues along a cliff and down a 25 ft. ladder to reach the canyon floor. Be wary of the water, which rushes faster than it looks.

The recently reshaped Mt. St. Helens draws hordes of **climbers** eager to gaze into the crater to see the source of so much power. It is now the most climbed mountain in the Northwest. The biggest challenge to climbing an otherwise very easy route is getting a permit. Between May 15 and October 31, the Forest Service allows 100 people per day to hike to the crater rim. $15 permits are required to climb anywhere above 4800 ft. ($30 for an annual pass; reservations still required). Reserve in person or write to the Monument Headquarters (see **Practical Information,** p. 266). Fifty permits per day may be reserved in advance after February 1. Write early; weekends are usually booked by March, and weekdays often fill up as well. Those without reservations can enter a 6pm lottery (get there 15min. early to enter the lottery) for the next day's remaining permits at **Jack's Restaurant and Country Store,** 13411 Louis River Rd., on Rte. 503 5 mi. west of Cougar. (I-5 Exit 21. ☎ 231-4276. Open M-Th and Su 6am-8pm, F-Sa 6am-9pm.)

MOUNT SAINT HELENS, THE RIGHT WAY. The monitor ridge route up Mt. St. Helens is one of the most popular routes in the cascades. But most people don't do it right, trudging through slushy snow and the glaring reflective heat of a massive snowfield after an 8am or 9am start.

Instead, try to be hiking by 4am. This will undoubtedly seem like an infuriatingly bad idea when the alarm goes off at 3:30am, but by 5am, when you see the incredible red glow of the sun rising behind Mt. Adams, you'll understand. As you move up towards the treeline, you'll also see the dramatic pyramid of Mt. Hood, its eastern flank glowing red and, on a clear day, you'll even notice the distant form of California's Mt. Shasta.

Climbing above the treeline (don't miss the wooden trail markers on the ridge to your left as you exit the trees), you'll remain in St. Helens' shadow, which will keep you at a reasonable temperature and the snow below your feet crisp and easy to move on. Reach the summit between 7:30am and 10am and you'll have ample time to chill out and enjoy the views of nearby Mt. Rainier as well as the humbling summit crater. On the way down, the soft snow will make for forgiving plunge-stepping as you watch the foolish masses inch up through stifling heat.

Although not a technical climb, the route up the mountain is a steep pathway of ash strewn with boulders. Often, the scree on the steep grade is so thick that each step forward involves a half-step back (5hr. up; 3hr. down). The view from the lip of the crater, encompassing Mt. Rainier, Mt. Adams, Mt. Hood, Spirit Lake, and the lava dome directly below, is magnificent and humbling. If you are climbing early in the season, stay back from the heavily corniced **crater edge.** Although no one has died yet, people have been known to poke through to their armpits, and it's only a matter of time before someone goes all the way. Bring sunglasses, sunscreen, sturdy climbing boots, foul-weather clothing, plenty of water, and gaiters to keep boots from filling with ash. Snow covers parts of the trail as late as early summer, making an ice axe a welcome companion. Free camping (no water) is available at the **Climber's Bivouac ❶,** the trailhead area for the **Ptarmigan Trail #216A,** which starts the route up the mountain. The trail is located about 4 mi. up Rd. 83. Note: entry into the crater is strictly prohibited.

In winter, the southern area of Mt. St. Helens houses **SnoParks** along Rte. 90 and Rte. 83, connected by semi-groomed trails, popular with cross-country **skiers** and snowshoers. Pick up a pass—available in Cougar and Randle—before heading out. Another SnoPark can be found along Rd. 25, accessible only from Randle.

NORTHERN APPROACH: US 12

⛰ VISITORS CENTER. Windy Ridge Interpretive Site is at the end of Forest Rd. 99 off Forest Rd. 25, 1¼hr. from Randle. Rangers give 30min. talks about the eruption in the outdoor amphitheater before the stunning backdrop of the volcano. Talks every hour on the half-hour between 11:30am-4:30pm. It's also the starting point of an 8 mi. (one-way) hike through the Pumice Plains to the Johnston Ridge Observatory. The route to Windy Ridge is lined with several viewpoints looking onto the area most damaged by the eruption. Stopping is worth the extra time. The site has no phone—call the **Cowlitz Valley Ranger Station** (☎ 497-1100) for information.

⛺ CAMPING. Iron Creek Campground ❷ is the closest campsite to Mt. St. Helens and has good hiking and beautiful forest. All 98 sites can fill up on busy weekends. (Reservations ☎ 877-444-6777, strongly recommended in summer. Sites $14-28.)

WASHINGTON

⚡ HIKING. Independence Pass Trail #227 is a 3½ mi. hike with overlooks of Spirit Lake and superb views of the crater and dome. (Moderate.) A serious hike continues past the intersection with **Norway Pass Trail,** running through the blast zone to the newly reopened **Mount Margaret Peak.** Considered the best hike in the park, the trail is 8 mi. (7hr.) to the peak and back. (Difficult.) Farther west, **Harmony Trail #224** provides a steep hike (2 mi. round-trip) to Spirit Lake. (Moderate to difficult.) Spectacular **Windy Ridge** is the exclamation point of Rd. 99. From here, a steep ash hill grants a view of the crater 3½ mi. away. The **Truman Trail** (7 mi.) meanders through the Pumice Plain, where flows sterilized the land. The area is under constant scrutiny by biologists, so stay on the trail. (Easy to moderate.)

MOUNT ADAMS   ☎ 509

At 12,276 ft., Mt. Adams is the second highest peak in Washington but, because access is limited, one of the least visited. Overlooked throughout its history, it was named after the second US president by Lewis and Clark only because other volcanos Hood, Rainier, and Baker had already been claimed for British admirals. Still, Mt. Adams' lack of fame works to the advantage of those seeking solitude on its rugged volcanic terrain. The access issues arise from the fact that the eastern half is in the Yakama Indian Reservation, putting that side of the mountain off-limits. This is compounded by the fact that nearly every trailhead on the western half is on a dirt road, many of which are covered by snow and closed into the summer.

⚡ ORIENTATION AND PRACTICAL INFORMATION. The Mt. Adams District is formed by the southern third of the Gifford Pinchot National Forest, as well as the Mt. Adams Wilderness. The entire area is most accessible from the south, by following Hwy. 141 north from Hood River via White Salmon. One can also approach from the north, along Forest Rd. 23 (this road is largely unpaved and usually blocked with snow until June or July). **Amtrak** (☎800-872-7245) is also an option, stopping 20 mi. away in Bingen at the foot of Walnut St., with routes from Portland (1¾hr., $9-20) and Spokane (5¾hr., $29-64).

If you're coming from the south, your last stop before heading into the great unknown should be Trout Lake, found on Hwy. 141. Trout Lake's main draw is the **Mount Adams District Ranger Station,** 2455 Hwy. 141, whose rangers dispense advice, permits, detailed topographic maps of the area for ($4), and $5 hiking trail guides. (☎395-3400. Open daily Memorial Day-Labor Day; Labor Day-Memorial Day M-F 8am-4:30pm.) Trout Lake also has a gas station and **General Store,** 2383 Hwy. 141, which sells a small supply of food and essentials. (☎395-2777. Open daily summer 8am-8pm; winter 8am-7pm.) Another option is to pick up provisions on your way up Hwy. 141, at a grocery store in **BZ Corner,** or any of the other towns.

Get info on the area in White Salmon, at the **Mount Adams Chamber of Commerce Information Center,** just west of the toll bridge from Hood River on Rte. 14. (☎493-3630; www.mtadamschamber.com. Open M-F 9am-12:30pm and 1:30-5pm.) Equipment rental is best in Hood River (see **Columbia River Gorge,** p. 99). For road conditions, call ☎360-905-2958. The **police** are at 170 NW Lincoln in White Salmon (non-emergency ☎493-1177) and the **post office** is at 2393 Hwy. 141 in Trout Lake. (☎395-2108. Open M-F 8:30am-12:30pm and 1-5pm.) **Postal Code:** 98650.

⚡ ACCOMMODATIONS AND FOOD. The Mt. Adams area is packed with places to pitch a tent. The best plan is to stop at the ranger station and tell them what you want to do; they will tell you the best site to use as a base. The closest site to Trout Lake is the **Guler-Mount Adams County Park ❶,** less than a mile out of town and one of the few areas with showers. To get there, take a left at the post office and follow the signs. (40 sites, $10; with electricity $14.) Another large pay area near Trout

Lake is **Peterson Prairie ❶**; head about 5 mi. past Trout Lake on Hwy. 141 to the point where Hwy. 141 ends and continue straight on Forest Rd. 24 for another 3 mi.; look for signs. (30 sites, $15.) On the way, check to see if there is room at **Trout Lake Creek ❶**, a forest-pass-only site just off Hwy. 141; take a right on Forest Rd. 88 and follow the signs. Both sites put you near the Ice Caves, which are ¼ mi. off Hwy. 141 to the south and worth a quick stop. Perhaps the best camping is 1hr. north of Trout Lake, in the Takhlakh Lake area. There are several different spots, but the best is ◪**Takhlakh Lake Campsite ❶**, which offers amazing views of Mt. Adams presiding over the lake and is a spectacular vantage point for alpenglow on Adams at sunset. (Sites $15.) To get there, take the Mt. Adams Rec. Hwy. out of Trout Lake and then take Forest Rd. 23 for 1hr. until you see signs—call the ranger station to ask about road openings.

The one budget option that will put a hard roof over your head is found in Glenwood, a 16 mi. drive from Trout Lake. To get there, take the Mt. Adams Rec. Hwy. out of Trout Lake and take the first right—a small sign will say Glenwood. Look for the small but friendly **Shade Tree Inn ❸**, 105 E Main St. A motel with attached restaurant, convenience store, laundromat, and excellent views of the mountain from a back balcony. ☎364-3471 or 800-519-4715. Reception and store open daily 7am-9:30pm, restaurant 7am-7pm. Singles $49; doubles $59.)

Get basic foods at **BZ Corner Grocery,** on the left when going north on Hwy. 141 in the town of BZ Corner, about 10 mi. south of Trout Lake. (☎493-2441. Open M-Sa 6am-9pm, Su 7am-8pm.) In Trout Lake, **KJ's Bear Creek Cafe ❶**, 2376 Hwy. 141 at the fork of Hwy. 141 and the Mt. Adams Rec. Hwy., has pipin' hot breakfasts ($4-5) and burgers ($5) that will give you something to look forward to as you wander through the wilderness. (☎395-2525. Open daily summer 6am-8pm.) Just south of the Trout Lake school is **Time Out Pizza ❶**, 2295 Hwy. 141, which serves pizza (medium $12) and $5 burgers. (☎395-2767. Open M-F 11am-7pm, Sa-Su noon-8pm.)

◪◪ **HIKING AND MOUNTAIN BIKING.** The absolute best resource in the Mt. Adams area for hiking is the ranger station: supplement the rangers' advice with the **Forest Services Trail Guide** ($5). Hiking is rewarding—most trails meander in and out of broken-up lava flows and occasionally open up onto good views. If you're driving, many trailheads require a **Northwest Forest Pass** ($5 per day, $30 annually; available at the ranger station). The area can get very dry in the summer, so be sure to bring adequate water; also note that **compasses don't work in lava beds** due to the abundance of underground mineral deposits. A long thaw leaves many trails closed through spring, and bugs can make summer very uncomfortable.

The 3¾ mi. one-way **Killen Creek/High Camp Trail** winds its way through thick forest up to the camp used by climbers taking the North Cleaver route up Mt. Adams. Offers an impressively up close and personal view of the mountain from the High Camp, as well as a panoramic view of the Cascades, including Mt. Rainier and Mt. St. Helens (elevation change 2200 ft.) The half-mile trail to **Sleeping Beauty Peak** starts off at a small trailhead on the left side of Forest Rd. 8810-040, about a quarter-mile from the Forest Rd. 8810 junction (see directions to Trout Lake campground, above). Other hiking options abound in the Adams area. For multi-day hikes, the most popular is the **Round-the-Mountain Trail.** It does not actually go around the mountain, but rather stretches 8 mi. to the south of Mt. Adams, eventually ending at the border of the Yakama Indian Reservation. This area is closed to hikers lacking tribal permission, so most parties turn around at this point, yielding a two- to three-day 16 mi. journey (permits to use Yakama land are available from rangers at Bird Lake campground, off the trail on the southeast side). Mountain biking is permitted on many of the trails in the National Forest. Bikeable trails are clearly marked and are listed in the free trail guide available at the ranger station.

CLIMBING. Mt. Adams is laced with at least a dozen mountaineering routes, including the very popular **South Spur** and **Mount Adams Summit Route.** All routes require crampons and an ice axe year-round; crevasses are dangerous, and experience climbing glaciers is absolutely necessary. In addition, climbers should stop at the ranger station to register and purchase a **Cascade Volcano Pass** ($10 for trips on M-Th, $15 for a trip that includes either F, Sa, or Su), required for all parties going higher than 7000 ft. up the mountain. Get climbing info at ☎ 891-5015.

◪ RAFTING AND KAYAKING. Three rivers pour off the flanks of Mt. Adams through volcanic rock and down to the Columbia River. The **White Salmon River** has several classic runs. The Class III-IV section, from BZ Corner to Husum, dives into a craggy gorge with lichen-draped old-growth trees and crumbling lava cliffs. The **Farmlands Run** courses through a beautiful dark canyon, whose flat rim belies the raging Class IVs (two V+) below. Immediately downstream of the Farmland's last rapid lurks the Class V-VI **Green Truss** section, where the Gorge Games' races are held on its sometimes lethal waterfalls. A Class II+ section from Husum down to Northwestern Lake is a popular after-work run.

Other nearby boating options include the **Klickitat River,** famed for its columnar basalt formations and isolated, roadless sections, as well as the **Wind River.** For extreme kayakers, the **Little White Salmon River** has the best paddling in the Northwest. But it's no cakewalk: veterans estimate that only 10 percent of runs finish without mishap. For rafters, guiding companies line Hwy. 141 around BZ Corner, taking patrons to most rivers in the area. **River Drifters** (☎ 800-972-0430; www.riverdrifters.net) has lots of options. Two companies operate out of White Salmon—**Zoller's Outdoor Odysseys** (☎ 800-366-2004; www.zooraft.com) and **All Adventures** (☎ 877-641-7238; www.alladventures.net). **River Riders,** in Hood River, also has competitive prices (☎ 800-448-7238; www.riverrider.com). A day of rafting can cost anywhere between $45 and $70.

▤ BIRD-WATCHING, HUNTING, AND FISHING. Though the prolific elk population in the area around Glenwood is conducive to hunting, marksmen beware: the beasts are protected in the nearby Conboy Lake Wildlife Refuge. The elk are familiar with its boundaries and are known to gloat from inside at frustrated hunters. Duck and other fowl can be hunted from within the refuge, however, and many of the streams in the area are fishable for trout and bullheads. Pick up the *Sport Fishing Rules* and *Big Game Hunting Seasons and Rules* guides at local stores for info on all the details and seasons. For those who prefer to merely observe wildlife, the refuge is home to nesting sites of rare Sandhill cranes, and guided bird-watching trips leave the ranger station every Friday morning. Bird-watching is reputed to be best around the first spring break-up in March or April.

MOUNT RAINIER NATIONAL PARK ☎ 360

At 14,411 ft., Mt. Rainier (ray-NEER) presides over the Cascade Range as the point from which the rest of the state is measured. The Klickitat native people called it Tahoma, "Mountain of God," but Rainier is simply "the Mountain" to most Washington residents. Perpetually snow-capped, this dormant volcano draws thousands of visitors from all around the globe. Rainier only has itself to blame for the clouds that mask the mountain for at least 200 days per year, frustrating those who come solely to see its distinctive summit. The mountain is so big it creates its own weather by jutting into the warm, wet air and pulling down vast amounts of rain and snow. Its sharp ridges, steep gullies, and 76 glaciers combine to make Rainier an inhospitable host for the thousands of determined climbers who attempt its

WASHINGTON

summit each year. Non-alpinists can explore the old-growth forests and alpine meadows of Mount Rainier National Park. With over 305 mi. of trails through wildflowers, rivers, and hot springs, Mt. Rainier has options for all nature lovers.

AT A GLANCE	
AREA: 235,625 acres.	**GATEWAYS:** Ashford, Packwood.
CLIMATE: Characterized by random stormy weather.	**CAMPING:** Extensive backcountry options, see p. 276. Requires a permit.
FEATURES: Dramatically diverse terrain, large backcountry, cross-country skiing.	**FEES:** $10 per car, $5 per hiker. Permits good for 7 days. Backcountry permits free, available at ranger stations and visitors centers.
HIGHLIGHTS: Climbing, hiking trails, Silver Falls during snowmelt.	

⌐ TRANSPORTATION

To reach Mt. Rainier from the northwest, take I-5 to Tacoma, then go east on Rte. 512, south on Rte. 7, and east on **Route 706.** This road meanders through the town of **Ashford** and into the park by the Nisqually entrance, which leads to the visitors centers of **Longmire** and **Paradise.** Rte. 706 is the only access road open year-round; snow usually closes all other roads from November through May. Mt. Rainier is 65 mi. from Tacoma and 90 mi. from Seattle; call a ranger station for road updates.

Gray Line Bus Service, 4500 W Marginal Way, Seattle (☎206-624-5208 or 800-426-7532; www.graylineofseattle.com), has buses that run from Seattle to Mt. Rainier daily May to mid-Sept. (1-day round-trip $54, under 12 $27). Buses leave from the Convention Center at 8th and Pike St. in Seattle at 8am and return at 6pm. The trip up takes 3½-4hr. (with a few stops at picturesque viewpoints) and allows 2½hr. at Paradise. **Rainier Shuttle** (☎569-2331) runs daily between Sea-Tac Airport and Ashford (2hr., 2 per day, $37) or Paradise (3hr., 1 per day, $46).

All major roads offer scenic views of the mountain, with numerous roadside lookouts. The roads to Paradise and Sunrise climb farther onto the sloped side of the mountain and are especially picturesque. Stevens Canyon Rd. connects the southeast corner of the national park with Paradise, Longmire, and the Nisqually entrance, revealing superb vistas of Rainier and the Tatoosh Range. The summer draws hordes of visitors, making parking very difficult at many of the visitors centers and trailheads throughout the afternoon hours.

Rainier weather changes quickly, so pack warm clothes and cold-rated equipment. Before setting out, ask rangers for mountain-climbing, hiking, and equipment recommendations. Group size is limited in many areas, and campers must carry all waste out of the backcountry. Potable water is not available at most backcountry campsites. All stream and lake water should be treated for giardia with tablets, filters, or by boiling it before drinking. For more information on preparing for the outdoors, see **Water Purification and Transport,** p. 69.

🛈 PRACTICAL INFORMATION

The section of the Mt. Baker-Snoqualmie National Forest that surrounds Mt. Rainier on all but its southern side is administered by **Wenatchee National Forest,** with headquarters at 301 Yakima St. in Wenatchee. (☎509-662-4314; www.fs.fed.us/r6/wenatchee.) The **Gifford Pinchot National Forest** (☎425-750-5000), to the south, has headquarters at 6926 E Fourth Plain Blvd. in Vancouver, WA. The **Packwood Ranger**

Station is nearest, at 13068 US 12. (☎494-0600; www.fs.fed.us/gpnf. Open daily 10am-5pm.) A free brochure and the *Tahoma News* are distributed at park entrances and ranger stations and are useful sources for maps, hiking, and safety.

Visitor Information:

Longmire Wilderness Information Center (☎569-4453, backcountry reservations only), 6 mi. east of the Nisqually entrance in the southwest corner of the park, is the best place to plan a backcountry trip. Open daily late May-early Oct. 7:30am-4pm.

The Jackson Memorial Visitors Center (☎569-2211, ext. 2328) at Paradise at 5400 ft., has 360 degrees of windows, an information desk, exhibits on the mountain, and a predictably expensive and greasy cafeteria; chicken strips and fries ($6.75) or a burger ($7.25) will satisfy your artery-destroying cravings. The building's heat-inefficient design and the stress of snow on the roof has led to plans for construction of a new visitors center to begin in 2005; the current building should remain open until 2007 or 2008. Permits available. Open daily 10am-6pm.

White River Wilderness Information Center (☎663-2273), off Rte. 410 on the park's east side, on the way to Sunrise, is also very good for information. Open late May-Sept. W 7:30am-4:30pm, Th 7:30am-7pm, F 7am-7pm, Sa 7am-5pm.

The Wilkeson "Red Caboose" Ranger Station (☎829-5127) is at the Carbon River entrance and is the largest of the ranger stations scattered throughout the park; for particular locations, pick up the free park map at any entrance. These stations all distribute backcountry permits. All are open M-Th 8am-4:30pm, F 8am-7pm, Sa 7am-7pm, Su 8am-6pm.

The Park Headquarters, (☎569-2211; www.nps.gov/mora) is the best place to call with inquiries. Open M-F 8am-4:30pm.

Equipment Rental: Rainier Mountaineering, Inc. (☎888-892-546; www.rmiguides.com), in Paradise across from the Paradise Inn and in Ashford next to Whittaker's Bunkhouse. Expert RMI guides lead summit climbs, seminars, and special programs (a three-day summit course rings up at $770). Rents ice axes ($15), crampons ($15), plastic mountaineering boots ($24), packs ($26), and helmets ($10), all by the day. Open daily May-Sept. 7am-8pm; Oct.-Apr. M-F 9am-5pm.

Climbing: Glacier climbers and mountain climbers intending to scale above 10,000 ft. must register in person at Paradise, White River, or Wilkeson Ranger Stations to be granted permits. $15 per person per day. Annual pass $25.

Hospital: The nearest medical facilities are in **Morton** (40 mi. from Longmire) and **Enumclaw** (5 mi. from Sunrise). **Tacoma General Hospital,** 315 Martin Luther King Way (☎253-552-1000), has 24hr. emergency facilities.

Internet Access: See **Whittaker's Bunkhouse,** below. $3 per 30min.; $5 per hr.

Post Office: In the **National Park Inn,** Longmire (☎569-2275). Open M-F 8:30am-noon and 1-5pm. Also located in the **Paradise Inn** (see below). Open M-F 9am-noon and 12:30-5pm, Sa 8:30am-noon.

Postal Code: Longmire 98397, Paradise 98398.

ACCOMMODATIONS

Longmire, Paradise, and Sunrise offer expensive accommodations. For an affordable bed, stay in Ashford or Packwood. Alternatively, camp and convince yourself that your tent has a roof and heating, and is a hostel.

Hotel Packwood, 104 Main St. (☎494-5431; www.packwoodwa.com), in Packwood 20min. south of Ohanapecosh or 1hr. south of Nisqually. Charming since its founding in 1912. A sprawled-out, very dead grizzly graces the parlor. Singles and doubles in every imaginable configuration $29-49. Private bath extra. ❸

Whittaker's Bunkhouse (☎569-2439; www.whittakersbunkhouse.com), 6 mi. west of the Nisqually entrance. Owned by Lou Whittaker, a long-time RMI guide. View his accomplishments (he was in the first party to climb the north face of Everest) in the photos hanging from nearly every wall. Hot tub and espresso bar, but no kitchen or bedding in dorms. Book ahead. Spacious co-ed dorms with bath $30; 1-2 person private rooms $75; 3-4 person rooms $100. ❷

The Cowlitz River Lodge, 13069 US 12 (☎494-7378; www.escapetothemountains.com), on the east end of Packwood right across from the Packwood Information Center. The Lodge offers very nice rooms for a decent price. Covered outdoor hot tub, cable, included continental breakfast. Singles $54; doubles $67. ❹

Paradise Inn (☎569-2413; reservations ☎569-2275), in Paradise. Built in 1917 from Alaskan cedar. Large dining facility with exquisite-looking–and expensive–food (dinner entrees $19-36). Open late May-Oct. Very popular during the summer; book ahead. Small singles and doubles from $75, extra person $12. ❹

☒ CAMPING

Backcountry camping requires a **permit,** free from ranger stations and visitors centers. (☎569-4453. Reserve ahead.) Inquire about trail closures before setting off. Hikers with a valid permit can camp at well-established trailside, alpine, and snowfield sites (most with toilets and water source). Fires are prohibited except in backcountry campgrounds. Camping in national forests outside the park is free. Avoid eroded lakesides and riverbanks; flash floods and debris flows are frequent. Campfires are prohibited in National Forest campgrounds, except during the rainy season; check with ranger stations for details.

There are six campgrounds within the park. For reservations, apply in person at the visitors centers; from April to September, call ☎800-365-2267 (international ☎301-722-1257) or visit http://reservations.nps.gov. National Park campgrounds are wheelchair-accessible, but have no RV sites or showers. Coin-op showers are available at **Jackson Memorial Visitors Center,** in Paradise (see above). Alternatively, the **Packwood RV Park** has pay showers for $3 at the corner of Main St. and US 12 in Packwood. **Sunshine Point** ❶, a quarter-mile beyond the Nisqually entrance, is a quiet site to the south by a glacial river. It's also the only place to head in the peak of summer if you didn't make a reservation. (Quiet hours 10pm-6am. Open year-round. 18 sites, $10.) **Cougar Rock** ❶, 2¼ mi. north of Longmire in the southwest is large and often crowded, but sits in the shadow of a great view of the peak. (Quiet hours 10pm-6am. Open May-Sept. Reservations required late June-Labor Day. 173 individual sites, $15; in winter $12; 5 group sites for 12 or more, $3 per person.) **Ohanapecosh** ❶, 11 mi. north of Packwood on Rte. 123, in the southeast, provides secluded sites with great scenery. (Open May-Sept. Reservations required. 205 sites, $15; in winter $12.) About 150 ft. outside of the Ohanapecosh entrance, a dirt road descends from the highway and turns into a T. Either fork takes you to free camping spots just down the road. **White River** ❶, 5 mi. west of White River on the way to Sunrise in the northeast, opens later than other sites, but is the main camping area for the Sunrise-side visitors. (Open late June-Sept. 112 sites, $10.)

☒ FOOD

The general stores in the park sell only last-minute items like bug repellent (well worth it). An extra state-park tax is charged, so stock up before you arrive. **Blanton's Market,** 13040 US 12 in Packwood, is the closest supermarket to the park and has an ATM in front. (☎494-6101; www.blantonsmarket.com. Open M-Th and Sa-Su 7am-8pm, F 7am-9pm.) **Highlander** ❷, in Ashford, serves standard pub fare in a single dimly-lit room with a pool table. Burgers $6-9. (☎569-2953; www.the-highlander.com. Open daily 7am to anytime between 10pm and 2am; restaurant closes at 9pm.) **Club Cafe** ❷, 13016 Hwy. 12, is in Packwood. A small, down-home diner, where omelettes always elicit oohs and ahhs. (☎494-5977. Open daily 7am-7pm.)

⚡ OUTDOOR ACTIVITIES

Rainier's moody weather makes it a tricky destination. Clouds and freezing rain can sweep in at any time, making the fireplace at **Paradise Inn** the mountain's most attractive destination. In the winter, huge volumes of snow close most of the park (almost 70 ft. fell at Paradise in 2002), and trails often remain snow-covered well into summer. But in sun or shade (which actually sometimes dramatically enhances the mountain's profile), once on the trail, the mountain's rewards are abundant, revealing perhaps the most glorious scenery in the state.

🏔 HIKING. There are far too many hiking trails to list—Rainier is Washington's most versatile area, with space for summer National Park tourists, the most rugged winter explorers, and everyone else. One option is a **ranger-led interpretive hike,** which touches on everything from area history to local wildflowers. Each visitors center conducts hikes, and most of the campgrounds have talks and campfire programs; the most interesting, varied, and inevitably full are those at Paradise.

The heavily visited Paradise, perched on the side of the southern slope, is the setting-out point for the most-used trails in the area. The hike to ⬛**Camp Muir** (9 mi. round-trip), the most popular staging ground for a summit attempt, is also a challenging day hike, beginning on **Skyline Trail,** a scenic 6 mi. loop reaching its peak at 7000 ft. Panorama Point. From the point, summiters and ambitious day hikers head north on **Pebble Creek Trail** to Camp Muir. The latter half of the hike to Muir is covered in snow throughout the year; only those skilled in snow travel with the proper equipment should attempt it. Along the road up to Paradise is the **Comet Falls** trailhead, a more moderate 5½ mi. round-trip hike to the namesake 320 ft. falls and then to a goat-filled alpine meadow.

Trails also begin at the Sunrise parking lot on the other side of the mountain. The two most popular routes are the short 3 mi. round-trip stroll along **Sunrise Rim** and the moderate 5½ mi. round-trip **Fremont Lookout Trail,** with views over the whole Cascade range and branches leading off to Grand Peak and Burroughs Mtn.

Along the Ohanapecosh River on the southeast side of the park, trails are out of sight of the mountain but traverse through the lush ecosystems in its shadow. A beautiful, easy 3 mi. round-trip half-day hike wanders by **Silver Falls** (a sight to behold during the spring snowmelt), then up to the **Grove of the Patriarchs,** whose stately cedars and ancient Douglas-firs leave the woods dark and peaceful. This is a popular cross-country skiing and snowshoeing route in the winter. A trail leads to the falls from Ohanapecosh campground, and a shorter route begins at a pull-off on the west side of Rte. 123, just south of the intersection with Rte. 706. The Grove can be accessed just inside the Ohanapecosh entrance.

The undeniable behemoth of all the park's routes is the infamous ⬛**Wonderland Trail,** 94 mi. of challenging terrain that circumnavigates the whole mountain. Arguably more difficult than the mountain ascent, the route passes through every type of scenery imaginable: picture dark forests, bright snowfields, rushing rivers, and rocky moraines. A full hike of the route requires experience and careful planning; be sure to spend plenty of time at a ranger station before setting out.

CLIMBING. A trip to the summit of Rainier requires substantial preparation and expense. The ascent involves a vertical rise of more than 9000 ft. over 9 mi. and usually takes two days with an overnight stay at ⬛**Camp Muir** on the south side (10,000 ft.) or **Camp Schurman** on the east side (9500 ft.). Each camp has a ranger station, rescue cache, and toilet. Permits cost $30 per person. Only experienced climbers should attempt the summit, and no one should try going solo; novices can be guided to the summit with the help of **Rainier Mountaineering, Inc.** after a day-long basic climbing course. For details, contact Park Headquarters or RMI (see **Practical Information,** p. 275).

METHOW VALLEY

Time stands still in the Methow (met-HOW) Valley, stretching 56 mi. along the Methow River and North Cascades Hwy. 20 from Mazama to Pateros. Sunny weather in summer and annual winter dumpings of dry powder make the Valley a prime destination for retirees, those seeking a simpler life, and outdoor recreationists. If some of the "Old West" heritage is a shade too contrived for your liking, head for the hills, forests, and rivers for miles of isolated wilderness bliss.

WINTHROP   ☎509

Originally a mining town, Winthrop was hand-picked by beloved Boston-bred founding father Guy Waring in 1891 for its location at the fork of the Chewuck and Methow Rivers. In 1972, Winthrop business owners decided to reinvent the ranching-centered town and restore it to its roots with an Old West motif. Although it boasts barely more than 400 year-round residents, Winthrop's unique look and feel attract over a half million tourists each year, making much of it beyond the budget of an independent traveler. But inexpensive wilderness opportunities abound nevertheless, as Winthrop's location makes it the hub for a wealth of outdoor activities at the heart of the serene Methow Valley.

◼ TRANSPORTATION

Winthrop lies at the fork of the Chewuck and Methow Rivers along North Cascades Hwy. 20. No public transportation comes to the town, but **Mountain Transport,** 94 Bridge St., inside Methow Adventures, runs shuttles throughout the area. Buses run from Winthrop to Twisp, Mazama, or Sun Mountain Resort ($10 one-way). Shuttles also run from the four airports in the region: Okanagan ($25 one-way, $45 round-trip), Wenatchee ($49/$98), Spokane ($75/$145), and Seattle-Tacoma ($87/$174). They also offer shuttles to local mountain bike trailheads starting at $10 and to hiking trailheads for $1.95 per mile. (☎996-8294; www.mountaintransporter.com.) If you prefer to have your own set of wheels, **Winthrop Mini Storage,** 29 Horizon Flats Rd., rents cars. (☎996-2218 or 996-8222; www.winthropstorage.com. Rentals start at $50 per day, $0.20 per mile over 100 per day. Weekly rates available. Must be 18 or older. Open M-Sa 9am-noon.)

◼ PRACTICAL INFORMATION

Tourist Office: The **Methow Valley Visitors Center** (☎996-4000), just outside of town on Hwy. 20, oversees the maintenance of many of the area's trails. They have extensive information and updates on trail conditions, and also provide required free permits for anyone traveling in wilderness backcountry and sell Northwest Forest Service passes for parking at trailheads ($5 per day or $30 for an year-long pass). Open M-Sa 8am-5pm.

Outdoor Information: along with the visitors center, **Methow Valley Sports Trail Association,** 209 Castle Ave., (☎996-3287 or 800-682-5787; www.mvsta.com) also maintains numerous trails in the area—particularly biking and cross-country trails—with an eye to environmentally-conscious recreation. Open daily 8:30am-4pm.

Equipment Rental: Winthrop Mountain Sports, 257 Riverside Ave (☎996-2886 or 800-719-3826; www.winthropmountainsports.com). Mountain bikes from $20 per day; winter rentals include cross-country skis ($28 per day) and snowshoes ($16 per day). Open summer M-F

9am-6:30pm, Sa 9am-7pm, Su 9am-6pm; call for winter hours. **Methow Adventures**, 94 Bridge St., in addition to renting fly fishing rods ($15 per day) and mountain bikes ($25 and up per day) also runs the shuttle service (see **Transportation,** above) and acts as a middle man for guided tours in the area. Mention *Let's Go* and receive a discount. (☎996-8294 or 866-METHOW1/638-4691; www.methowadventures.com. Open M-Sa 8:30am-5pm.)

Laundromat: Pine-Near RV Park, 350 Castle Ave., (☎996-2391; www.pinenear.com) offers laundry services to all, wash $1.25, dry $0.50 per 8min. Open 24hr.

Hospital: **Country Clinic**, 1116 Hwy. 20 (☎996-8180). Open 24hr.

Internet Access: Winthrop Community Library, 509 Hwy. 20, (☎996-2685; www.ncrl.org) provides 1hr. free. Open M 12:30-6pm and 6:30-8pm, Tu 10am-noon and 1-6pm, W-Th 12:30-6pm, Sa 1:30-4:30pm.)

Post Office: 1110 Hwy. 20 (☎996-2282. Open M-F 8am-4:30pm.) **Postal Code:** 98862.

CAMPING AND ACCOMMODATIONS

Winthrop overflows with expensive hotels and resorts catering to the booming tourist industry. The posh destination of the area is the **Sun Mountain Lodge,** where rates start at $140 per night. If that seems a bit out of your price range, never fear—there are also a dozen National Forest **campsites** within 20 mi. of Winthrop's trails, including eight off Rte. 51 to the north ($5 per night). **Falls Creek,** 11 mi. north, is the closest, and has a quarter-mile side trail to Falls Creek Falls; **Chewuch** is the newest with 16 sites. No reservations available for any sites. Check at the ranger station or the visitors center for a map and complete listing of the sites.

Pearrygin Lake State Park, 561 Bear Creek Rd. (☎996-2370, reservations 888-226-7688), 4 mi. northeast of Winthrop. This popular family destination overlooks the pristine Pearrygin Lake. Offerings include a lakefront swimming area with a boat launch and fishing pier, a volleyball area, and over a dozen picnic tables. 53 tent sites $16; 30 utility sites $22. Free showers. Reservations recommended in summer. Open Apr.-Oct. ❷

Big Twin Lake Campground, 210 Twin Lakes Rd. (☎996-2650; www.methownet.com/bigtwin). This private campground has been bringing people to the shores of Big Twin Lake, a 90-acre lake stocked with rainbow trout, for over 100 years. Lots of waterfront activities; rent rowboats ($15 per day) or paddleboats ($5 per hr.) Tent sites $14; RV sites $20; additional people over 2 $3 each. ❶

The Virginian, 808 Hwy. 20 (☎996-2535; www.methow.com/~virginian). On a large property with waterfront space, this log cabin-themed resort offers the lowest prices around. Gas BBQs, hot tub, and a pool; for families there is a kid's Western dress-up room. Singles $45; doubles $65; 4-person cabins with kitchenette $80. ❸

Mount Gardner Inn, 611 Hwy 20 (☎996-2000; www.mtgardnerinn.com). This small inn under friendly new ownership is just walking distance from downtown Winthrop and offers a picnic area in the back, rooms overlooking the river, and great coffee in the morning. Wireless Internet. Closed Nov. and Mar. Singles $49; doubles $69. ❸

FOOD

Winthrop's food is primarily tourist- and family-oriented, with over-priced chicken fingers everywhere you turn. Avoid the largest burger joints and you'll find some cheap local eats with real character. Groceries can be found at **Red Apple Market,** 920 Hwy. 20. (☎996-2525; www.winthropredapple.com. Open daily 8am-9pm.)

THE LOCAL STORY

OUT OF THE FLYING PLANE, INTO THE FIRE

Smokejumper(s) are firefighters who parachute from planes to combat blazes. Let's Go spoke with **Scott Wicklund,** a smokejumper based out of Winthrop, WA.

Q: A lot of people would say this is an insane job. How would you respond?

A: People would say this is an insane job because they don't realize all the safety precautions that go into it. It seems crazy because you're jumping out of a perfectly good airplane... into a forest fire! But the reality is that you've got a perfectly good parachute and you know fire behavior. So you land in a place where you're safe from any sort of fire activity, and take the proper measures to control the fire.

Q: How did you decide to do this?

A: I guess growing up my mom said, "Don't get dirty; don't play with fire." I found a job that paid me to do both.

Q: Any memorable stories?

A: The weirdest thing that ever happened to me? One time I landed in an 80 ft. tree, but the parachute didn't catch on the branches. I slid down the side of the tree, picking up speed until I basically knew I was going to break my leg in about half a second. All of a sudden, the parachute catches on a branch and I was just hanging there barely a foot away from the ground. Hanging there perfectly fine...which was a great feeling.

Java Man, 94 Bridge St. (☎996-2182). Join the locals at the cozy counter for strong espresso ($1.25). Giant hot dogs ($3) are popular, but it's the burritos ($6) that really please—they could feed two, but you won't want to share. Open M-Sa 6:30am-4pm. ❷

Boulder Creek Deli, 80 Bridge St. (☎996-3990). Offering sandwiches ($5-6) from around the world, this deli's best selection is the calzone ($4.75), featuring artichokes, olives, and feta cheese. Open M-W and F 8am-3pm, Th and Sa 9am-5pm. ❷

Winthrop Brewing Co., 115 Riverside Dr. (☎996-3183; www.winthropbrewing.com). Take your pick from the many year-round and seasonal brews on tap here, but don't forget to order some of the simple but savory cuisine it accompanies. Sample the onion rings ($5), indulge in the best burgers in town ($6-8), or treat yourself to a hearty bowl of the gourmet chili ($9). Open daily 11:30am-10pm. ❷

👁 💡 SIGHTS AND EVENTS

The Shafer Museum pays tribute to Winthrop's pioneer history, displaying hundreds of artifacts in a reconstructed settlers' town. At the center of the self-guided tour is "The Castle," Winthrop founder Guy Waring's original house he built for his wife. (On Castle Ave. off of Bridge St. ☎996-2712; www.winthrop-washington.com/winthrop/shafer. Admission by donation. Open June-Sept. M and Th-Su 10am-5pm). Winthrop is also home to the ■**North Cascades Smokejumpers Base,** the birthplace of smokejumping, the dangerous practice where firefighters parachute into forest fires as the first line of defense. Free tours guided by smokejumpers themselves give insider access to the history as well as the equipment and the planes. (23 Intercity Airport Rd., running parallel to Hwy. 20 in between Winthrop and Twisp. ☎997-2031. Open June-Oct. 10am-5pm. Call ahead during low season for a tour.) The annual **Rhythm and Blues Festival** in mid-July includes a street dance, jam session, and shade tent with misting to cool down. (☎360-629-8027; www.winthropbluesfestival.com. $55 for a weekend; $65 at the gate, $40 Sa, $30 Su.) The first week in August is the **Methow Music Festival,** with a classical focus. (☎996-6000; www.methowmusicfestival.org. $22 per concert, students $10, under 18 free.)

🏔 OUTDOOR ACTIVITIES

Winthrop is the gateway to numerous hiking, biking, and equestrian trails, both around the immediate area and leading into the expansive forests and **Pasayten Wilderness.** The most extensive system in the local region is the **Sun Mountain Trail System,** maintained by the local resort. With over 25 mi. of trails looping around Patterson Mtn. and Patterson Lake, those looking for a day of walking, biking, or horseback riding will find options to occupy them from an hour to the whole day.

📷 **DAY HIKES. Pearrygin Lake State Park,** just 5 mi. north of Winthrop, offers a respite from the dry scenery for those looking to swim, fish, hike, or bike (see **Accommodations,** p. 279). This area also lies adjacent to one portion of valley's extensive **Methow Wildlife Area** that offers its own set of trails; hike to **Cougar, Davis,** or **Campbell Lakes** and keep a look out for deer, moose, weasels and badgers, or the hundreds of species of birds native to the area. Hunting and fishing are allowed in the area; check with the rangers for guidelines. Within the same area are the **Rendezvous Huts,** five small cabins scattered through the mountainside and accessible by trails maintained by the Methow Valley Sports Trails Association. (☎ 866-638-4691 or 800-422-3048; www.methow.com/huts. Rates start at $20; $25 in winter.)

Other areas for popular day hikes include **Tiffany Mountain,** with a dramatic steep north face but smooth south side for a gentle hike (a 19 mi. drive up Boulder Creek Rd. to an easy to moderate 3½ mi. ridge walk to the summit, gaining 1500 ft., approx 2hr. each way). The **Cedar Creek Trail** reaches Cedar Creek Falls after an easy 1¾ mi., then continues for 7½ mi., becoming more moderate where it connects with the North Lake Trail from the Twisp River area. **Cooper Glance Lake** lies 4 mi. from the trailhead, a short way for walkers and horses to reach a stunning view of much of the Pasayten Wilderness. Other trail options abound in the area, such as those to **Buck Lake** (1-5 mi. trails), to **Goat Peak** (drive 12 mi. to the end of Rte. 52, past Goat Wall Overlook, to the last 1½ mi. of steep hiking to the vista, approx 1-2hr.), and along the **Methow River** (Big Valley Trail, an easy 5 mi. one-way hike, or Methow Community Trail, up to 11 mi., easy to moderate).

📷 **MULTI-DAY HIKES.** Those seeking a longer adventure need look no further than the **Pasayten Wilderness,** at points less than 25 mi. north of Winthrop. The options are endless; some of the popular inputs into the wilderness are the **Billygoat Trail** and the **Thirtymile Meadows.** The **Chewuch Trail,** an 18 mi. scenic valley trail following the river through lodgepole pine forests towards subalpine and meadow areas, is perhaps the most popular. The trail also offers connections to the Remmel Lake and Cathedral areas and can also be used as to connect to the popular Four

Q: Describe the feeling of crashing.
A: You jump out of the airplane, you see the meadow below that you're supposed to be going for, and you're aiming for that; then the wind picks up, and you know you're not going to make it. At that point you start looking for some shorter trees to land in, so you're not hung up too high off the ground. Then you try and cap that tree with your canopy so you're hung up well; they train you to do that. But there's still a bit of chaos. At that point you don't know exactly what's going to happen. A lot of times it's a soft landing, because you go in there and the canopy catches the tree perfectly. Other times, your feet get kicked out from underneath you, you're upside-down and falling, you're not sure that your canopy hung up, your heart's racing a million miles per hour, and then *jerk,* you're hanging.

Q: What's the injury rate like?
A: I have never been injured jumping. We might get 2 or 3 sprained ankles, maybe a blown ACL, maybe a broken femur, maybe a broken wrist every year.

Q: Is this a team effort?
A: It is every day. The first thing you do after you land is check with your partner and make sure he's okay. We always jump two people at a time.

Q: Do you recommend the job?
A: Yeah, I'd recommend it to anyone who likes having adventures but doesn't want to make a whole lot of money.

Point Lake and Tungeten Mine areas. The Chewuch River offers plentiful fishing holes and access to numerous side trails. Along the trail are also the trailheads of the **Lake Creek Trail** and popular **Andrews Creek Trail.** The 34 mi. trail created by Andrews Creek and Chewuch River is a moderate 5-6 day loop into the Pasayten. Andrews Creek was the site of a devastating forest fire in 2001 that took the lives of four firefighters, now remembered by the **Thirtymile Memorial** 4 mi. into the trail. Again hit by a forest fire in 2003, the area was closed in 2004 for repairs.

OTHER SUMMER ACTIVITIES. Biking options in the valley are too many to name—abundant country roads and numerous trails are open to bikers, and trails are available for every ability. Trails range from those along rivers to journeys into the mountains, like the **Cedar Creek** route. A guide to some of the best, *Methow Valley Mountain Bike Routes*, is available throughout the area for $3.50.

For horseback guides, sign up with **Chewack River Guest Ranch,** 588 E Chewuch, with rates starting at $25 for a 1hr. ride (☎996-2497; www.chewackranch.com). If a bucking bronco is not your style, **Paysaten Llama Packing** offers backcountry tours on a different sort of mount. Full-service trips complete with meals, hikes, and fishing are offered June-Oct.; drop camps, where llamas and guides drop you in the wilderness with all gear and supplies, are also available. (☎996-2326; www.mtllama.com. $125, sleeping bag or tent rental $10 per day.)

To indulge your curiosity about fly fishing, Ben Dennis is your man to call at the **Fly Rod Ranch,** 494 Rendezvous Rd. He'll give you basic instruction starting at $25 for a half-hour lesson, or guide a trip, complete with transport, instruction, and food, starting at $175 for a half-day. (☎996-2784; flyrodranch@mymethow.com.)

CROSS-COUNTRY SKIING. In winter, Winthrop becomes a cross-country skier's mecca, as the valley's average 3 ft. of powdery snow turns all the country roads and bike paths into ski trails. The **Methow Valley Sports Trail Association** grooms 175km of trails in the valley, making the area the second-largest cross-country ski trail system in the country. The trails are in three areas: around the Rendezvous Huts, outside nearby Mazama, and at the Sun Mountain Trails. (☎996-3287 or 800-682-5787; www.mvsta.com. Day pass $15, 3 days $35. The association provides info on conditions as well as maps; see **Outdoor Information,** p. 278.)

TWISP   ☎509

The largest town in the valley, with around 1000 permanent residents and a large summer influx, Twisp stands out not for its size but for its thriving arts population and access to numerous trails along the Twisp River and into the surrounding wilderness. With an enthusiastic sense of community, Twisp is home to a professional theater, numerous relocated coastal residents, and more than one cowboy poet, all of whom bring their talents to this welcoming town. Only beginning to feel the overflow from Winthrop's rampant tourism, Twisp's economy is still inwardly directed, leaving its numerous hiking, biking and cross-country skiing trails mostly to locals and the savvy *Let's Go* reader.

ORIENTATION AND PRACTICAL INFORMATION. Twisp lies at the confluence of the Methow and Twisp Rivers, 2 mi. north of where Hwy. 153 ends at Hwy. 20, 9 mi. south of Winthrop. The closest public transportation is through Wenatchee, 91 mi. south of Twisp. **Mountain Transport,** 94 Bridge St. inside Methow Adventures in Winthrop, also runs shuttles throughout the area; (see Winthrop's **Transportation,** p. 278). (☎996-8294; www.mountaintransporter.com. The tourist office is at the **Chamber of Commerce and Information Center,** on Hwy. 20 at 4th St. and has free Internet. (☎997-2926; www.twispinfo.com. Open M-F 8am-5pm.) Con-

WASHINGTON

tact the **police** at 118 S Glover St. (☎997-6112). For **medical services,** head to the **Twisp Family Clinic,** 541 E 2nd Ave. (☎997-2011). Find **Internet** access at the tourist office and **Twisp Library,** located in the same building on Hwy. 20 at 4th St. (☎997-4681; www.ncrl.org. Open M and W 10:30am-noon and 12:30-5:30pm, Tu 12:30-5pm, Th 12:30-5pm and 6-8pm, Sa 9:30am-12:30pm.) The **post office** is at 205 S Glover St. (☎997-3777. Open M-F 9am-4:30pm.) **Postal Code:** 98856.

ACCOMMODATIONS AND CAMPING. Twisp is one of the biggest towns in the area, but still has an economy less directed at tourism than others in the Methow Valley. The most affordable bet for accommodations is one of the eight National Forest **campsites ❶** within 25 mi. of Twisp. Heading east on Twisp River Rd., the closest option is **War Creek** campsite, 15 mi. out. Also in that direction are **Blackpine Lake, Mystery, Poplar Flat, South,** and **Roads** campsites. **J.R.** and **Loup Loup** are about 12 mi. west of Twisp on Hwy. 20. All cost $5 per night except Blackpine Lake and Poplar Flat, which are $8. Open May-Sept. Check at the visitors center for a map and complete listing of the sites. **Riverbend RV Park ❷,** 19961 Hwy. 20, has a grocery store, free wireless Internet, and two buildings solely for meetings and indoor recreation. (☎997-3500 or 800-686-4498; www.riverbendrv.com. 25 quiet riverfront sites $18; over 90 RV utility sites $22. Showers $0.75 per 8min.) **Sportsman Motel ❸,** 1010 E Hwy. 20, ½ mi. west of Twisp, offers large rooms equipped with kitchenettes and couches. You can sit outside on your own mini-front lawn in your very own lawn furniture while you make dinner. (☎997-2911. Singles start at $49; doubles at $59.) **Idle-A-While Motel ❹,** on Hwy. 20 in Twisp, stands out with its bright yellow buildings and features a hot tub and sauna, movie rental, a tennis court, and fully furnished cabins with kitchenettes. 10% discount to AAA members, free morning coffee. (☎997-3222; www.methow.com/~idlewile. Singles start at $58; doubles $64, all prices up to 20% less in the winter months.)

FOOD. Twisp's taste for high art overflows into its taste for high cuisine. The town is scattered with a mix of pubs, bakeries, and gourmet restaurants with wildly varying prices. Groceries can be rustled up at **Hank's Harvest Foods,** just east of town on Hwy. 20. (☎997-7711. Open M-Sa 8am-9pm, Su 8am-8pm.) Local farms offer their produce at the **Methow Valley Farmers Market,** 313 E Hwy. 20, in the Community Center parking lot. (Apr.-Oct. Sa 9am-noon.) **Twisp River Pub ❸,** 201 Hwy. 20, hangs local art on its walls, hosts local singers at its open mic Sa nights, and is the hub of the local artist scene. Features house-brewed beers from the Methow Valley Brewing Company. Try the nachos ($6), the fish and chips ($9), or indulge in one of the larger main entrees ($10-16). (☎997-6827; www.methowbrewing.com. Open daily 11am-11pm.) **Cinnamon Twisp Bakery ❶,** 116 North Glover St., will lure you in with its aroma, and the freshly baked breads and desserts will keep you wanting more. Whole loaves run $3-4, while deli sandwiches are $4-7. Save room for a soft cookie overflowing with chocolate, nuts, or toffee ($1-2), or the signature cinnamon twisp ($1.75), a crispy braided version of a cinnamon roll. (☎997-5030; www.cinnamontwisp.com. Open M-Sa 7am-4pm.)

ARTS AND ENTERTAINMENT. At the heart of Twisp is a thriving arts population, evidenced by the **Confluence Gallery and Art Center,** 104 Glover St., which hosts local art shows. (☎997-2787; www.confluencegallery.com. Open M-F 7am-4pm, Sa 8am-3pm.) **The Merc Playhouse,** 101 S Glover St. is an old warehouse, home to the town's professional summer theater since 1999. (☎997-7529; www.themercplayhouse.com. Shows run early June-early Sept. W, Th, and Su $15, F-Sa $17.) **Made in the Methow,** 108 N Glover St., is a gift shop and community kitchen supporting the cooking and crafts of local artists. (☎997-7482. Open W-Sa 10am-5pm.) **Cascadia,** in the Community Center on Hwy. 20 at 4th St., is a local music organization hosting lessons and concerts. (☎997-0222; www.methownet.com/cascadia. Concerts $12, seniors and students $10, under 6 free.)

⚐ **HIKING.** The majority of Twisp's outdoor offerings lie off Twisp River Rd. in the **Twisp River Recreational Area** that lies along the boundary of the 145,668-acre **Lake Chelan-Sawtooth Wilderness.** Hikers can enjoy a wide spectrum of trails in the area, ranging from short loops and hikes to opportunities for ventures deep into the mountains. Day hike options in the area include the 10 mi. **Twisp River Trail,** meandering along the bank; **Lookout Mountain,** a 6½ mi. climb (or drive and 1¼ mi. hike) from Blackpine Lake, with a wide, well-maintained trail open to hikers, bikers, and horses, and views to the surrounding mountains; and the 14 mi. loop up along **Blue Buck Trail,** over rugged **Starvation Mountain,** and back along the raging Lightning Creek. Trails also lead to the abundant mountain lakes in the region, including North, Slate, Louis, Williams, Scatter, and Campbell Lakes.

For longer expeditions, the **War Creek Trail, South Creek Trail,** and **Copper Pass Trail** (which connects to the **Pacific Crest Trail** 12 mi. in) are just some of the trails that head straight into the wilderness. These paths climb through 8000-10,000 ft. peaks, finally reaching their destinations in or near Stehekin on Lake Chelan. A popular longer loop begins at **Eagle Creek Trail,** climbs 7 mi. to Eagle Pass where it intersects with the **Summit Trail** that leads towards Stehekin, and, after 1 mi., to **Oval Creek Trail,** where it returns to the original trailhead.

OTHER SUMMER ACTIVITIES. Many trails in the area are open to mountain bikes, and numerous roads weave alongside rivers and mountains, giving vistas worth pedaling for. These include Twisp River Trail, Lookout Mountain Trail, and Blue Buck Trail, as well as the popular route from **Beaver Creek Road,** through **Pipestone Canyon,** and to **Campbell Lake.** Contact the visitors center for a trail map and more detailed information. The area also caters to adventurers seeking experiences on the water or on horseback. **Osprey River Adventures** guides paddlers down the waters of the Methow River. (☎997-4116 or 800-997-4116; www.methow.com/osprey. $70 per day, under 12 $60. For face to face information, visit Methow Adventures in Winthrop, p. 279.) If the local deer aren't enough animal contact for you or you just want to meet Twisp's cowboy poet face to face, spend the day with **Walking D Ranch Adventures,** 20088 Hwy 20, on a scenic ride through the valley. (☎997-1015; www.cowboypoet.com. 1hr. ride $25, 2hr. $35, 3hr. $45.)

⚐ **SKIING.** In the winter, locals avoid the lines and prices at larger resorts and do their skiing at "The Loup," or **Loup Loup Nordic Ski Area.** Twelve mi. east of Twisp on Hwy. 20, the Loup has just 10 trails and a vertical drop of 1240 ft., but boasts an extensive cross-country ski area with over 25km of groomed trails for every ability level. (☎826-2720; www.skitheloup.com. $25, ages 13-21 $22, 9-12 $16, under 9 $12. Ski rental package $18 per day, snowboard package $26 per day. Tube hill with its own lift runs all day. $8 per day, $6 half-day. Cross-country trails $5. Open depending on conditions, approximately Nov.-Mar.)

YAKIMA VALLEY

With the moisture from the Pacific Ocean trapped by the Cascades, central Washington enjoys mild, dry summers and almost 300 days of sunshine each year. Dubbed the "Fruit Bowl of the Nation," the Valley is the state's agricultural hub, as evidenced by the many roadside stands hawking produce. The climate is also kind to grapes, leading to the recent emergence of dozens of wineries. The Yakima and Naches Rivers lure fly fishers and rafters and offer plentiful biking opportunities.

YAKIMA ☎509

A large sign on east I-82 welcomes visitors to Yakima (YAK-ih-muh), the "Palm Springs of Washington." Containing some of the planet's most fertile fruit lands, Yakima is a large rural town par excellence. Thanks to an active conference center, affordable accommodations abound; thanks to the budding wineries and fabulous Mexican food brought in by local workers, tasty and affordable food is plentiful. The fishing is excellent, so while the open desert may not beckon hikers, the area is perfect for a lazy day by the river. Yakima is an attractive place to wash up, grab a meal, hook a few wily trout, and then push on in the morning.

⚡🔃 ORIENTATION AND PRACTICAL INFORMATION. Yakima is on I-82, 145 mi. (2½hr.) southeast of Seattle and 145 mi. (2½hr.) northwest of Pendleton, OR. The Yakima Valley lies southeast of the city, along I-82. Southeastern downtown, especially near the fairgrounds, can be dangerous at night. Numbered streets line up to the east of the railroad tracks, numbered avenues to the west. **Greyhound,** 602 E Yakima Ave. (☎457-5131 or 800-231-2222), stops in Yakima on the way to Portland (4½hr., 1-2 per day, $34) and Seattle (3½hr., 3 per day, $24). (Open M-F 7:45am-5pm; Sa 8am-4:30pm; Su and holidays 10:30-11am and 2:30-4:30pm.) **Yakima Transit** (☎575-6175; www.ci.yakima.wa.us/services/transit), based at 4th St. and Chestnut Ave., near the clock, runs local buses. ($0.50, ages 62 and older $0.25, 6-17 $0.35. Day pass $1.50. Runs M-F 5am-7pm, Sa 8am-7pm.) The **Yakima Valley Visitor and Convention Bureau,** 10 N 8th St. (☎575-3010 or 800-221-0751; www.visityakima.com), is in the convention center; follow the blue signs from Rte. 82. (Open Apr.-Oct. M-F 8am-5pm, Sa 9am-5pm, Su 10am-4pm; Nov.-Mar. M-F 8am-5pm.) Wash clothes at **K's,** 602 Fruitvale St. (☎452-5335. Open daily 7am-9pm. Wash $3.75, dry $0.25 per 10min.) **Emergency services** include the **police,** 200 S 3rd St. (☎575-6200), at Walnut Ave.; a 24hr. **crisis line** ☎575-4200.; and the **Providence Medical Center,** 110 S 9th Ave. (☎575-5000), at W Chestnut Ave. The **post office** is at 205 W Washington Ave. (☎800-275-8777), at 3rd Ave. (Open M-F 8:30am-5:30pm, Sa 9am-3pm.) **Postal Code:** 98903.

🛏🏕 ACCOMMODATIONS AND CAMPING. Yakima is overflowing with reasonably priced, run-of-the-mill motels, and the best way to find a cheap room is to comparison shop on 1st St. (I-82 Exit 31). The most accessible camping around is at the **Yakima Sportsman State Park ❷,** 3 mi. south of the city off Exit 34 on I-82, where sites, including 16 with full utility hookups, cluster in lush shade along the Yakima River. (☎902-8844, reservations 888-226-7688. 64 sites. Tentsites $16, RV sites $22. Showers $0.50 per 3min.) Cheap and pleasant **Forest Service campgrounds ❶** lie along the Naches River on Hwy. 410, about 30 mi. west of town on the way to Mt. Rainier. Most sites with drinking water cost $6-18. (Ranger info ☎653-2205.) A list of other sites is available from the visitors center or the **Naches Ranger Station,** 10061 Hwy. 12, in Naches, 16 mi. from town on Hwy. 12. (☎653-2205. Open M-F 7:45am-4:30pm, Sa 7am-noon; closed Sa-Su low-season. Front foyer with materials open 24hr.) **Red Apple Motel ❸,** 416 N 1st St. is friendly and affordable with cable, laundry, and pool. (☎248-7150. Reception 7am-1am. Singles M-F $37, Sa-Su $47; doubles $42/$53.) **Cedars Inn ❸,** 1010 E A St., has large rooms, a pool, and included continental breakfast. (☎452-8108. Singles $41; doubles $51.)

🍴 FOOD. The **Yakima Valley Fresh Produce Guide,** distributed at the visitors center and at regional hotels and stores, lists local fruit sellers and fruit stands, common on the outskirts of town, particularly on 1st St. and near interstate interchanges (look for several off I-82 Exit 37). In summer, the **Yakima Farmers Market** (☎457-5765; www.yakimafarmersmarket.org) closes off 3rd and Yakima Ave. in front of the Capitol Theater on Sundays from 9:30am-2:30pm. Cheap Mexican eats are all over town, but the gourmet version is worth it at ◨**Santiago's ❷**, 111 E Yakima Ave, where portions are piping hot, spicy, and enormous; tacos Santiago, with steak, cheese, guac, and olives, is the house specialty and big enough for two ($8). Make sure not to fill up on the unlimited complimentary tortilla chips and home-made salsa first. (☎452-1644; www.santiagos.org. Open M-F 11am-2pm and 5-11pm.) **Grant's Brewery Pub ❷**, 32 N Front St., at A St. in the old train depot, is a comfortable, family-style pub with microbrewery; try their fish and chips ($8.25) if you haven't already caught your own that day. The pub has live jazz, blues, and folk bands some weekends. (☎575-2922; www.grants.com. Open M-Th 11:30am-11pm, F-Sa 11:30am-midnight, Su 2-8pm; kitchen closes 1-2hr. earlier.)

◧◨ **SIGHTS AND EVENTS.** The Yakima Valley is the heart of Washington wine country. The vineyards just east of the Cascades benefit not only from mineral-rich soil deposited by ancient volcanoes but also a rain shield that keeps the land dry and easily controlled by irrigation; the number of **wineries** in the Yakima Valley has recently exploded to more than 40, leaving all of them competing for attention and visitors. For a complete list of wineries, pick up the **Wine Tour guide** at visitors centers or call the **Yakima Valley Wine Growers Association** (☎800-258-7270; www.yakimavalleywine.com). **Sagelands Vineyard,** 71 Gangle Rd., in Wapato, 10min. south of Yakima, is the closest vineyard, as well as the classiest. From I-82 Exit 40, head east, and look up for the sign and vineyards on the hills above. Specializing in Cabernet and Merlot, Sagelands boasts an upscale tasting room trumped only by the panoramic view. (☎877-2112; www.sagelandsvineyard.com. Open daily June-Oct. 10am-5pm; Apr.-May Sa-Su 10-5pm. 4 free 1 oz. servings.) The nearby town of **Zillah** lays claim to eleven wineries, including the smaller **Bonair Winery,** 500 S Bonair Rd., framed by the silhouette of Mt. Adams, which boasts blue-ribbon Chardonnay ($11) and affordable Sunset Pinks ($8). Head east from I-82 Exit 52, turn left at the BP gas station onto Cheyne, left again onto Highland Dr., then left once more onto Bonair Rd. (☎829-6027; www.bonairwine.com. Open daily Mar-Nov. 10am-5pm; Dec.-Feb. Sa-Su 10am-5pm or by appointment.) Those who prefer beer can take a gander at the **Yakima Brewing and Malting Co.,** 1803 Presson Pl., where Bert Grant's creations are made at the first US microbrewery to open after Prohibition. (☎575-1900; www.grants.com. Reservations recommended for the free tour. Open M-F 10am-6pm.) The ten-day **Central Washington State Fair,** held in late September, includes agricultural displays, cattle and horse shows, local crafts, rodeos, and big-name entertainers. (☎248-7160; www.fairfun.com.)

🗲 OUTDOOR ACTIVITIES. Yakima's arid landscape provides unique outdoor opportunities for Washington nature explorers. The **Yakima River** has been praised as one of the premier fly fishing locales in the state, especially for Rainbow trout. From the headwaters above Easton down to Ellensburg, the water flows "gin clear", making it great for wading; later in the river it gets murkier and wider, making floating while fishing the best tactic. The best spot is the 20 mi. canyon stretch from Ellensburg to Yakima, where cliffs and bighorn sheep preside above the waters in the cooler months. Put-ins are abundant, and fishing is allowed all year, although wading is easiest in fall, when water is still warm but not as fast.

Bikers will also find the area almost perfectly suited to their desires, with endless dry roads weaving through the farm country. In the city, the **Yakima Greenway,** 10 mi. of paved pathway through three parks and two lakes, is perfect for an afternoon ride or stroll. Rentals are available at **Sagebrush Cycles,** 5110 Tieton Dr. (☎972-1330. Rentals start at $8 per hour, $22 per day. Open M-Sa 9am-6pm.)

The **Indian Painted Rocks** lie just 3 mi. north of town on Powerhouse Rd., off 40th Ave., also accessible from Rte. 12. Occasional native paintings of suns and faces dot the wall, but the attraction for climbers is the unique surface of tubular rock.

Cowiche Canyon, just minutes from downtown, hosts an easy 6½ mi. round-trip hike along Cowiche Creek, over numerous boardwalk river crossings, and along the canyon walls. Drive west on Summitview Ave. off 40th Ave. for 6½mi. and turn right on Weikel Rd.; the trailhead and parking lot are down ¼ mi. on the right. Rattlesnakes have been spotted here in the summer months, so keep your eyes and ears alert. For information on rattlesnake safety, see **The Great Outdoors,** p. 62.

In winter, **White Pass** beckons skiers and boarders just 50 mi. west of Yakima on Hwy. 12. A vertical drop of 1500 ft., 5 lifts, and 6hr. of night skiing make the resort, just 12 mi. from Mt. Rainier National Park, an inexpensive and less-crowded winter option. (☎672-3100; www.skiwhitepass.com. Open daily 8:45am-4pm; night skiing F-Sa 4-10pm. Lift tickets $28-38, ages 65-72 and 7-12 $19-25, over 73 and under 6 free. Night skiing $17.) No lifts in summer, but hiking and mountain biking abound. Contact the **Naches Ranger District** (☎653-2205) for more info.

ELLENSBURG   ☎509

Just 40 mi. north of Yakima, Ellensburg maintains its Western roots with its famous Labor Day rodeo and affinity for Western art, although the historic city center has steered clear of most of the kitsch that could accompany this personality. Instead, the quirky central blocks continue to resist encroachment from the modernity of the expanding city around them.

◗◗ ORIENTATION AND PRACTICAL INFORMATION. Ellensburg is on I-90, 36 mi. north of Yakima and 75 mi. south of Wenatchee. **Main Street** runs north-south through the center of historic downtown, while numbered avenues run east-west, the numbers increasing as you go north. Major intercity transportation runs locally to Yakima and Wenatchee. **Ellensburg Rodeo and Chamber of Commerce,** 609 N Main St., hands out info and maps and sells rodeo tickets. (☎925-3138 or 888-925-2204; www.visitellen.com. Open June-Sept. M-F 8am-5pm, Sa-Su 10am-2pm; Oct.-May M-F 8am-5pm, Sa 10am-2pm.) Wash clothes at **Model Cleaners and Coin-op,** 7071 3rd Ave. (☎962-3157. Open daily 7am-10pm. Wash $1.50, dry $0.25 per 7½min.) Emergency services include the **police,** 100 N Pearl St. (☎962-7280), and the **Kittitas Valley Community Hospital,** 603 S Chestnut St. (☎962-9841). Free **Internet** access is available for 30min. at the **Ellensburg Public Library,** 209 N Ruby St. (☎962-7250; www.ellensburglibrary.org. Open M-Sa 9am-4pm, Su noon-3pm.) The **post office** is at 100 E 3rd Ave. (☎800-275-8777. Open M-F 9am-5:30pm, Sa 10am-2pm.) **Postal Code:** 98926.

◗◗ ACCOMMODATIONS AND CAMPING. Ellensburg doesn't offer the same cheap motel accommodations of Yakima, but it does have many guest ranches, B&Bs, and motels, all of which are especially hard to get into during the rodeo in early September. **Harold's Motel ❸,** 601 N Water St., lets you relax away from the central hubbub with an outdoor pool and cable. (☎925-4141. Singles $43; doubles $51.) **Nites Inn ❸,** 1200 S Ruby St., sits on a spacious green property. (☎933-7100. Singles $47; doubles $55.) Campers can find privately-run RV sites on the periphery of town or head out to the abundance of small **campgrounds ❶** maintained by the Wentachee National Forest scattering the landscape; for locations or information pick up the listing at the visitors center or call the Cle Elum Ranger District (☎674-4411). Few have RV hookups, and most range from free to $10. The **Yakima River RV Park ❶,** 791 Ringer Loop, Exit 109 off I-90 down Canyon Rd. for 2 mi., offers 40 scenic RV sites and sites for tenters. (☎925-4734; www.yakimarv.com. Tent sites $10; RV sites from $15.)

◘ **FOOD.** Ellensburg's fruit and wines are overshadowed by its southern neighbor Yakima, although the town is doing its best to put itself on the culinary map. From May to October, the **Kittitas County Farmer's Market** (☎ 899-3870; www.kcfarmersmarket.com) lords over the corner of 4th and Pearl St. on Saturday from 9am-1pm. For a smoothie and a cheap sandwich, head to **Billy Mac's Juice Bar ❷**, 115 W 4th Ave.; juices and smoothies run $2.75-4 and veggie-based sandwiches start at $5.75. (☎ 962-6620. Open M-Sa 9am-5pm, Su 11am-3pm.) The **Sisters Tea Company ❷**, 311 N Main St., combines the town's antiquey feel—unmatched tables and settings and abundant lace—with a fresh menu and live music every Th 7-9pm. Decadent salads include the $8 White River salmon salad. (☎ 962-4832. Open daily 11am-3pm.) The **Starlight Diner ❷**, 402 N Pearl St., serves tasty lunches and dinners like crab and clam chowder ($6) and pineapple chicken salad. (☎ 962-6100. Open M-Th 11am-2pm and 5-8pm, F-Sa 11am-2pm and 5-10:30pm.)

◙ ▣ **SIGHTS AND EVENTS.** During the ▨**Ellensburg Rodeo,** on five days around Labor Day weekend, the town is taken over by a whole horde of gung-ho spectators and cowboys vying for $100,000. The country fair is held simultaneously to provide a distraction for the less rip-roarin'. During the festivities, new inductees are added to the **Ellensburg Rodeo Hall of Fame,** while the mementos and photos remain on display at the Chamber of Commerce. (609 N Main St. ☎ 962-7831 or 800-637-2444; www.ellensburgrodeo.com. Tickets $12-48 depending on the event.)

Another unique local attraction is Central Washington University's **Chimpanzee and Human Communication Institute** (p. 57), a pioneer in primate communication research. Home to chimps versed in sign language, the institute offers 2hr. "Chimposiums" for those interested in forging a lingual link between man and beast. (☎ 963-2244; www.cwu.edu/~cwuchci. Chimposiums Mar.-Nov. Sa 9:15 and 10:45am, Su 12:30 and 2pm. Reservations recommended. $10, students $7.50.)

Jazz in the Valley is a three-day festival in late July that fills the town's historic area with live music and enthusiastic crowds. (☎ 925-3137 or 888-925-2204; www.jazzinthevalley.com. 3-day pass $30.)

▨ **OUTDOOR ACTIVITIES.** West of Ellensburg, the dry plateau of the Yakima Valley meets the Cascades, combining lakes and rivers with a Ponderosa forest and creating beautiful, largely-untouched wilderness. There are abundant exploring options, whether on foot, bike, or by water. Day excursions around the town are pleasant, but it takes a little more initiative to really get a feel for the landscape. **Manatash Ridge** borders the town to the south and offers ample hiking opportunities; **Manatash Lake** (8¾ mi. round-trip, moderate), trots along Lost Lake, then climbs up a plateau to the lake and then another, steeper climb up onto the ridge. To get there, follow Main St. south to where it becomes Canyon Rd.; turn right onto Umptanum Rd., then 2 mi. later right onto Manatash Rd. The best state park in the area is the 1600 acre **Iron Horse State Park,** home to the **John Wayne Pioneer Trail,** stretching more than 100 mi. from Cedar Falls in the Cascades to the bank of the Columbia River along an old railroad bed. Open to hikers, cyclists, equestrians, cross-country skiers, and snowshoers, the trail provides access to valley views, mountain trails, sagebrush desert, and farmlands. Camping options are easy to find the whole way at the four campgrounds or in the backcountry. Trailhead options abound; two near the town are off I-90 Exits 106 and 109.

Adventures on the Yakima River are a popular treat; **Rill Adventures** rents rafts and kayaks for non-guided exploration, or for a price, will lead you for a day. (10471 Throp Hwy. ☎ 964-2520 or 888-281-1561; www.rillsonline.com. Kayak $40 per day, two-person $50 per day. Rafts from $60 for four-person raft. Guided tours from $75 per person. Open M-Sa 8am-8pm, Su 10am-6pm.) Ellensburg's combina-

THE PACIFIC NORTHWEST SHRUB-STEPPE

A Vanishing Ecosystem

Visitors to the Pacific Northwest imagine a land of evergreen trees and soft mists of rain, brilliant blue mountains and saltwater bays. But these images tell only one side of the region's story. Those who venture east of Seattle over the Cascade Mountains will find open, arid space, rolling hills and long, languid plains. Scattered shrubs and warm colors of sun, golds and browns, replace the dense cool green of trees. While 37 in. of precipitation falls annually in Seattle, less than 7 in. reaches the Tri-Cities (Richland, Pasco, Kennewick) in the lower Columbia Basin.

Officially, this dry land goes by the name of shrub-steppe, a vast treeless plain that is part of one of the largest natural grassland areas in North America. Sagebrush is the dominant shrub species in the lower Columbia Basin. It belongs to the sunflower family, the species Artemisia, named for the Greek goddess Artemis. Sagebrush is a common, low-growing plant with silvery leaves that digs its tap root deep and holds on to water. It grows in a community with other shrubs, such as rabbitbrush, greasewood, and hopsage; drought-resistant perennial grasses; wildflowers; and a moss and lichen crust. Together, these plants combine to make up the shrub-steppe ecosystem.

Before European settlement in the 1880s, shrub-steppe vegetation covered almost 90 percent of the Columbia Basin. Today, it occupies less than 32 percent, creating a much different landscape than the one Lewis and Clark observed nearly 200 years ago. Urbanization, irrigated agriculture, and wildfire have led to the rapid disappearance of sagebrush, which is considered the "old-growth forest" of eastern Washington.

As sagebrush disappears, so do bird species that depend on it for food and shelter such as the sage thrasher and sage sparrow. Burrowing owls and long-billed curlews, which nest on the ground surrounding sagebrush, also are affected, as are sage grouse. In part, destruction of the shrub-steppe ecosystem is related to the appearance of arid land and what it communicates.

The Tri-Cities, the hottest and driest region in the state, is a good place to explore the shrub-steppe, especially in spring when wildflowers such as balsamroot, lupine, and phlox turn local hillsides yellow, purple, and pink.

For a close-up view of these native species, drive to the Rattlesnake Slope Wildlife Recreation area. Bluebunch wheatgrass, as well as Sandberg's and Cusick's bluegrass cover the slopes. To get there from Richland, take Hwy. 240 to Hwy. 225. Turn left, and drive 4 mi. toward Benton City, past Horn Rapids Park on the Yakima River.

In spring, look for horned larks and long-billed curlews along the roadside and red-tailed hawks perched on power poles. Continue driving until you see a parking lot with a sign for the recreation area on the right side of the road. Follow one of the two trails that climb into the hills through large patches of cheatgrass, an alien, annual grass that has recently invaded the dry lands of western states.

Another place to explore native shrub-steppe plants in spring is the Horse Heaven Hills. Bluebunch wheatgrass and Sandberg's bluegrass are common here. Purple sage, rosy balsamroot, and fleabane can be found across the rocky crest of the hills. Look for big sagebrush, three-tip sagebrush, and winterfat.

To get to the Horse Heaven Hills from Richland, take I-82 west toward Benton City to Exit 96. Turn left under the freeway, and drive through Kiona. Turn right onto McBee Rd. Follow the gravel grade slowly to the top of the hills (about 3 mi. from the freeway). Park near the gravel pit and walk across the road to view wildflowers on north-facing slopes and the rocky ridge top. On the way up McBee grade you might hear a western meadowlark sing its liquid flute-like tune or see this yellow-breasted bird perched on a sagebrush or fence post.

Other shrub-steppe birds a visitor might see near the Horse Heaven Country in summer are Swainson's hawks, ferruginous hawks, horned larks, and lark sparrows. These birds are a few of the more than 200 species that inhabit the Tri-Cities area at some time during the year. Western kingbirds, horned grebes, and American white pelicans also can be seen along local waterways—the Columbia, Yakima, and Snake rivers. Thousands of western Canada geese migrate to the Columbia River each fall.

In addition to birds, about 42 species of mammals can be found as well as five kinds of amphibians, 12 species of reptiles, 44 species of fish, and hundreds of insect species.

The Tri-Cities also is the site of the Hanford Reach National Monument, which encompasses native shrub-steppe lands as well as the Hanford Reach of the Columbia River, the last free-flowing stretch of the river. The National Monument, managed by the U.S. Fish and Wildlife Service, was created in 2000 to preserve "an irreplaceable natural legacy."

In a further development, a Hanford Reach Interpretive Center is expected to open in Richland in 2006. For more information, call the Fish and Wildlife Service at ☎ 509-371-1801.

Georganne O'Connor co-authored Northwest Arid Lands: An Introduction to the Columbia Basin Shrub-Steppe. *She has written for* Northwest Magazine, Washington Magazine, *and* Washington Wildlife. *Her most recent project involves editing a book on the Ice Age floods that shaped eastern Washington state.*

THE HIDDEN DEAL

ROCKHOUNDING

Second in rarity only to rubies and colored diamonds, Ellensburg Blue Agate is found literally one place on earth. The sky blue stone is believed to have formed below Green Canyon before the glacial ages, and it is found now only in occasional outcroppings in an area bordered by Reecer Creek Rd. and Hwy. 97, just a few miles north of Ellensburg. The stone is not formed in large blocks, but individual stones are found on the ground and below the top layers of pastures, creek beds, and sagebrush.

Much of the land in the area where the stones have been found is privately owned, and while many of the owners have been known to let people search on their land, **Rock'n'Tomahawk Ranch,** 2590 Upper Green Canyon Rd., is a less risky spot to spend the day searching. Visitors can go rockhunting with a $5 daily permit. (☎ 962-2403. Reservations required.) Ellensburg Blue jewelry is available at numerous locations throughout the store and in the surrounding area; the largest selection is found at **Kim Khap Gems & Jewelry,** 108 Main St., which will also set the stones you find in jewelry of your choice. (☎ 925-4900. Open M-Sa 9am-6pm; Su noon-5pm.)

tion of mountains and desert sun make it an ideal place for both road and mountain **biking.** A guide to the best mountain biking in the area is available at the visitors center; these include bikes to Manastash Creek and Blewett.

EASTERN WASHINGTON

Lying in the Cascade's rain shadow, the hills and valleys of the Columbia River Basin at first glance appear to foster little more than sagebrush and tumbleweeds. But where the construction of dams and canals has made irrigation possible, the desert has bloomed into a land of bountiful fruit and high-quality wines. Where there is water, the contrast between these glimmering lakes and rivers and the rest of the landscape is striking. Sunshine fills the days and attracts sun-starved "wetsiders" from rainy Western Washington. The calm beauty and dry, hot air of the region invite a pleasant and lazy vacation of wine-tasting and apple-munching.

SPOKANE   ☎ 509

Spokane (spoe-KAN) may have peaked when the 1974 World's Fair came to town; parks, department stores, and skyways sprang up in preparation for a promising future that never quite arrived. Today, cafes catering to the college crowd from Gonzaga and nearby Eastern Washington Universities along with 50s-style burger joints make for a suburban atmosphere, and the remains of Spokane '74 slumber in Riverfront Park. During the summer it can feel a bit empty; however, the surrounding wilderness, particularly Mt. Spokane State Park, provides plenty of opportunities to enjoy the dry climate and diverse terrain. Think of Dad when stopping in Spokane—the city was the first to celebrate Father's Day in 1910.

▐ TRANSPORTATION

Spokane is 280 mi. east of Seattle on I-90, between Exits 279 and 282. A grid of alternating one-way streets, avenues run east-west parallel to the **Spokane River,** while streets run north-south. The city is divided north-south by **Sprague Avenue** and east-west by **Division Street.** South of Sprague, avenues are numbered, increasing further from the river. Downtown is the quadrant north of Sprague Ave. and west of Division St., between I-90 and the

Spokane

▲▲ ACCOMMODATIONS
Clinic Center Inn, 11
Ramada Limited
  City Center Inn, 6
Riverside State Park, 1

🍎 FOOD
Dick's, 10
Frank's Diner, 9
High Nooner Gourmet
  Sandwiches, 3
The Onion, 2

🍸&★ NIGHTLIFE &
      ENTERTAINMENT
Dempsey's Brass Rail, 5
Satellite Diner & Lounge, 7
Trick Shot Dixie, 8

river. An extensive local bus system has its hub at the **STA Plaza** (Spokane Transit Authority), 750 Sprague Ave (☎328-7433; www.spokanetransit.com. Plaza open M-Sa 5:30am-12:15am, Su 5:30am-10pm).

Trains: Amtrak, 221 W 1st Ave. (☎624-5144 or 800-USA-RAIL/872-7245), at Bernard St. Counter open daily 10pm-5:30am. All trains depart 1-3am. 1 train per day to **Portland** ($35-75) and **Seattle** ($30-79).

Buses: Greyhound, 221 W 1st Ave. (☎624-5251 or 800-231-2222), at Bernard St., in the same building as Amtrak. Ticket counter open daily 8-11am, 4:30-6:30pm, and 12:30-2:30am. Buses to: **Portland** (8-10hr., 3 per day, price varies depending on season and availability, approx. $40) and **Seattle** (6hr., 5 per day, $30). Also serves Missoula, Billings, and Chicago. **Northwestern Trailways** (☎838-5262 or 800-366-3830) shares the same counter and terminal, serving much of WA, including Seattle, plus other cities such as Boise. Prices vary.

Taxis: Anytime-Anywhere Taxi Service (☎536-1666 or 866-765-6500). **Spokane Cab** (☎568-8000). Base fare $4.10, $2.12 per mi. Both run 24hr.

Car Rental: Dollar Rent-A-Car, 2405 N. Division (☎458-2619; www.dollar.com). Compacts start at $20 per day, $120 per week. Unlimited mileage within the state. 21 or older with credit card; under-25 surcharge $15. Open M-F 7am-6pm, Sa 8am-4pm, and Su 9am-3pm.

▣ PRACTICAL INFORMATION

Tourist Office: Spokane Regional Convention and Visitors Bureau, 201 W Main Ave. (☎747-3230 or 888-SPOKANE/776-5263; www.visitspokane.com). Exit 281 off I-90. Offers free Internet access and local phone calls. Open May-Sept. M-Sa 9am-5pm, Su 10am-3pm; Oct.-Apr. M-F 9am-5pm.

Equipment Rental: Mountain Gear, 2002 N Division St. (☎325-9000 or 800-829-2009; www.mgear.com) rents canoes ($50 per day), sea kayaks ($45 per day), and recreational kayaks ($30 per day). Winter rentals include snowboard ($45 per weekend), skis ($45 per weekend), and tele skis ($30 per weekend). Free climbing wall to those with their own gear. Open M-F 9:30am-8pm, Sa 9:30am-6pm, Su 11am-5pm.

Laundromat: Otis Hotel Coin-Op, 110 S Madison St. (☎624-3111), at 1st Ave. Wash $1, dry $0.25 per 20min. Open daily 7am-7pm.

Police: 1100 W Mallon Ave. (☎456-2233).

Crisis Line: ☎838-4428. 24hr.

Medical Services: Rockwood Clinic, 400 E 5th Ave. (☎838-2531 or 459-1577), at Sherman St. Open daily for walk-ins 8am-8pm.

Internet Access: Spokane Library, 906 W Main Ave. (☎444-5300; www.spokanelibrary.org). Free unlimited Internet and wireless. Open M-Tu noon-8pm, W-F 10am-6pm. Also see the **Visitors Bureau,** above.

Post Office: 904 W Riverside Ave. (☎800-275-8777). Open M-F 6am-5pm. **Postal Code:** 99210

▣▣ ACCOMMODATIONS AND CAMPING

Numerous motels are sprinkled among the chains at all the outskirts of downtown, including along I-90, Rte. 2, and Division Ave.

Riverside State Park (☎465-5064; www.riversidestatepark.org), 6 mi. northwest of downtown. Take the Maple St. Bridge north and turn left at the brown park sign; follow signs to Rte. 291 (Nine Mile Rd.), turn left onto Rifle Club Rd. and follow to the park. 16 standard sites with picnic table ($16) and 15 utility hookup sites ($22) in a sparse Ponderosa forest near the river. Parking $5. Showers $0.25 per 3min. Access to hiking, biking, equestrian trails, canoeing, and rafting. ❷

Clinic Center Inn, 702 S McClellan St. (☎747-6081; www.cliniccenterinn.com). McClellan runs north-south starting at 2nd; follow south up hill. In the medical district, offering spacious, attractive, hospital-clean rooms. AC, cable, and free continental breakfast; $5 surcharge for pets. Singles $38; doubles $46. ❸

Ramada Limited City Center, 123 S Post St. (☎838-8504 or 800-210-8465). Convenient downtown location and immaculate rooms make up for the occasional rumbling of the nearby 1st Ave. overpass. Cable, microwave/refrigerator, and complimentary continental breakfast; shuttle to the airport. Singles $50; doubles $60. ❹

▣ FOOD

The **Spokane Farmers Market,** corner of 2nd and Division, sells produce, baked goods, and fresh fish (☎487-6432; www.spokanefarmersmarket.homestead.com. Open May Sa 8am-1pm; June-Oct. W and Sa 8am-1pm) Groceries are at **Safeway,** 1617 W 3rd St. (☎624-8852. Open 24hr.)

▨ **Frank's Diner,** 1516 W 2nd Ave. (☎747-8798), at Walnut St., operates out of a 1906 observation railroad car, complete with lace curtains, 50s music, and friendly staff. Warm without being kitschy, serving heaping, speedy breakfast food all day long ($4-8). Open M-W and Su 6am-8pm, Th-Sa 6am-9pm. ❷

The Onion, 302 W Riverside Ave. (☎624-9965), at Bernard St., serves juicy burgers with a huge variety of toppings ($8-10) and huckleberry shakes ($3) to throngs of locals. Open daily 11am-around 11pm, depending on business. ❷

High Nooner Gourmet Sandwiches, 237 W Riverside Ave. (☎838-5288) offers sandwiches loaded with fresh ingredients. Try the "Unforgettable Nooner"—turkey, bacon, avocado, tomato, sprouts, and signature cream cheese ($6). Open M-F 10am-3pm. ❷

Dick's, 10 E 3rd Ave. (☎747-2481), at Division St. Look for the colorful panda sign near I-90 declaring "Burgers by the bagful." Fast food taken to a whole new level—customers eat in their parked cars or at picnic tables and pay 1950s prices (burgers and fries $0.63 each; shakes $0.93). Open M-Th 8am-midnight, F-Sa 8am-1am, Su 9am-11pm; mid-June to Aug. open 1hr. later. Cash only. ❶

👁 SIGHTS

▓MANITO PARK. One of the most beautiful spots in Spokane, this park boasts six distinct areas of lovingly-maintained flowerbeds. Take a moment to relax amid the calm pools of the **Nishinomiya Japanese Garden,** smell the 150 varieties of blooming roses on **Rosehill** in late June, listen to concerts in the elegant **Duncan Garden,** peruse the **Lilac Garden,** or sniff around in the **David Graiser Conservatory** and the **Joel Farris Perennial Garden.** *(4 W 21st Ave. From downtown, go south on Bernard St. and turn left on 21st Ave. Park open summer 4am-11pm; winter 5am-10pm; buildings open 8am-dusk. Free.)*

NORTHWEST MUSEUM OF ARTS AND CULTURE. The Mac, as it is fondly known, has become the crown jewel of Spokane's cultural offerings. Focusing on local artists, five galleries display both visiting exhibits and works from the museum's own collections; also home to a cafe, an outdoor amphitheater, the adjacent Cowles Center for research, and the Campbell House, a vintage 1898 residence. *(2316 W 1st Ave. ☎456-3931; www.northwestmuseum.org. Open Tu-Sa 11am-5pm. $7, students and ages 62 and older $5, children ages 5 and under free. First F of the month admission by donation.)*

RIVERFRONT PARK. The centerpiece of downtown, the park is Spokane's civic center and the perfect place for a pleasant stroll. Developed for the 1974 World's Fair, the park's 100 acres are divided down the middle by the rapids that culminate in **Spokane Falls.** Riverfront's **IMAX Theater** houses a five-story movie screen and a small amusement park. On the park's edge lies the historic **Carousel,** hand carved by Charles Loof of Coney Island carousel fame. Scattered throughout are **sculptures,** including the prominent "The Joy of Running Together" in honor of the annual 7½ mi. (12km) Lilac Bloomsday race in early May, which hosts over 60,000 runners (www.bloomsdayrun.org). Centrally located **Serendipity Cycles** rents bikes. The park hosts **Pig Out in the Park** in early September, a five-day food festival with free entertainment. *(Park: 507 N Howard St., just north of downtown. ☎456-4386; www.spokaneriverfrontpark.com. IMAX: ☎625-6686. Open daily 11am-9pm. $7. Carousel: Open M-Th and Su 11am-8pm, F-Sa 11am-10pm. $2. A 1-day pass, $15, covers both, plus a ferris wheel, park train, sky ride, and more. Cycling: Open daily June-Aug. 10am-9pm.)*

🎭 ENTERTAINMENT

Known for locally produced shows, the **Civic Theater,** 1020 N Howard St., has a downstairs space for experimental productions. (☎325-1413; www.spokanecivictheatre.com. Musicals $18, plays $15.) The **Spokane Interplayers Ensemble,** 174 S Howard St., is a resident professional theater troupe. (☎455-7529; www.interplayers.com. Season runs Sept.-June Tu-Sa. $20, students $10, seniors 20% off.)

Spokane Symphony Orchestra makes its home at the **Opera House,** 334 W Spokane Falls Blvd. The opera house also hosts traveling **Broadway shows** and special performances. (☎326-3136; www.spokanecenter.com. Box office open M-F 10am-5pm. Orchestra: ☎624-1200; www.spokanesymphony.com. Symphony tickets $11-13.)

🔊 NIGHTLIFE

For local happenings, pick up the *Spokesman-Review* (www.spokesmanreview.com) "Weekend" section, or look for the *Inlander* (www.inlander.com), a free magazine on the weekly goings-on in the area, available at the library.

Dempsey's Brass Rail, 909 W 1st Ave., has a hot dance floor, raucous karaoke (M, W 8pm), and free Internet access by the bar. Drag Diva shows (F-Sa) and rainbow themed decor—including the beer taps, ceiling gauze, and even straws—make Dempsey's "the place to be gay." Happy hour 3-7pm daily; $3 domestic pitchers. (☎747-5362; www.dempseysbrassrail.com. Kitchen serves dinner daily 3-8pm. Open M-Th and Su 3pm-2am, F-Sa 3pm-4am.) **Trick Shot Dixie,** 321 W Sprague Ave., has lots of space, and lots of people to fill it. Ride the mechanical bull made from a real hide, try their house BBQ, or throw back the favorite Lynchburg Lemonade ($5). Each night has a theme (Tu, blues; W, ladies night; Th, country karaoke; F-Sa, live acoustic and electric music; Su, salsa), and every night there are bottle tossing, bar-dancing bartenders. (☎624-4945. Open M-F and Su 11am-2am, Tu-Sa 11am-4am. Food served 11am-10pm.) **Satellite Diner & Lounge,** 425 W Sprague Ave., lets you choose between the diner half—a great place to people-watch until 4am over biscuits and gravy ($3.25) or the Satellite scramble (with ham and sausage, $6.50)—and the smoky bar half. Quench your thirst with microbrews ($3) and nightly specials ($1 Jell-O shots on Th). Happy hour daily 6-8pm. (☎624-3952. Open M-F 7am-4am, Sa-Su 6pm-4am; bar closes at 2am.)

🏔 OUTDOOR ACTIVITIES

■**MOUNT SPOKANE STATE PARK.** Only 30 mi. northeast of the city lies the largest state park in Washington, offering 14,000 acres of outdoor options. Best known for its **Ski and Snowboard Park** (☎238-2220; www.mtspokane.com), the mountain boasts 35 trails, five double chair lifts, and a 2065 ft. vertical drop, as well as night skiing W-Sa (8-10pm). For nordic skiers, there are over 30 mi. of trails for varying ability levels. The park offers ample opportunities for snowshoeing, backcountry skiing, and snowmobiles (50 mi. of specially designated trails). All activities require a Sno-Park permit ($9). Summer brings hiking, biking, and horse riding to the park's many trails. Loops range in distance and difficulty. Try the 1½ mi. moderate **Entrance Loop Trail** for snowshoeing or a brief stroll, the easy 5 mi. **Day Mountain Loop** to see rocky open meadows (no bikes), or the moderate 4½ mi. **Hay Ridge Loop,** with scenic stream crossings and picnic areas. **Mount Kit Carson** is also a popular and easily accessible destination. Don't miss the 1934 Vista House at the peak of Mt. Spokane. Drive, hike, or in the winter take the chairlift for 360-degree views of lakes, evergreen mountains, and farm fields. (☎238-4258 or 238-4025 for snow report. At the end of State Rd. 206, 15 mi. east of Rte. 2. Follow 395N/2E out of the city to 206. Camping available in summer at the Bald Knob Campground. 12 sites with fire grates, $15. Open daily summer 6am-dusk; winter 8am-10pm. $6 maps of park available at park office. Alpine weekday tickets $26, under 15 $20, ages 70 and older, $10; weekends $33, under 15 $27, ages 70 and older $15; under 6 always free. Student Pack of 5 tickets $99 with ID. Parking $5.)

RIVERSIDE STATE PARK. Covering nearly 10,000 acres around the Spokane River, the park offers a chance to experience nature while barely leaving the city. The scenic **Centennial Trail** runs 37 mi. from Nine Mile Dam all the way to the Idaho border, paved for the benefit of summer hikers, bikers, and in-line skaters and winter cross-country skiers and sledders alike. The locals favor the **Bowl and Pitcher** area, with a 1936 suspension bridge across the namesake rapids—the giant, smooth rock outcroppings require an imagination to see the resemblance. Countless unmarked equestrian and walking trails wind around the area, providing close views of both the river and elevated vistas. Other highlights include the smaller **Deep Creek Canyon**, with vertical volcanic rocks suitable for climbing, evidenced by the few established routes, and the **Indian Painted Rocks**, off Rutter Pkwy. For camping details see above. (*9711 W Charles Rd. ☎ 465-5064; www.riversidestatepark.org. Parking $5 throughout park. Centennial Trail: ☎ 624-7188; www.spokanecentennialtrail.com.*)

COLUMBIA STATE PARK. The new and ever-growing **Columbia Plateau Trail** (currently 23 mi., with expansions planned of up to 130 mi. to East Pasco, along the banks of the Snake River) creates a scenic passage through open wild-flower littered grasslands, verdant rolling hills, and sparse Ponderosa forests. A wide and mostly flat trail with four trailheads for hikes, bikes, or rides of many lengths. The 3¾ mi. section from the northernmost trailhead at Fish Lake to Cheney is paved for the use of road bikes and in-line skaters. From Cheney to Amber Lake, a 15½ mi. stretch passes through the **Turnbull National Wildlife Refuge,** providing a more remote feeling and ample chance for wildlife sightings, especially of the many birds native to the area. This area is accessible by car via a 5 mi. section of Mullinix Rd. through the refuge. Sparkling **Amber Lake** also hosts free public fishing (planted sterile rainbow trout; 2 trout limit) and a boat put-in. (*Follow I-90 S to 904, exit for Cheney. Follow until signs for trailheads at Cheney-Spokane Rd., Cheney-Spangle Rd., and Mullinix Rd. respectively; 16-38 mi. from Spokane depending on trailhead. ☎ 646-9218 or 549-3551. Also accessible by local bus #65 from downtown Spokane to Cheney. Trail facilities open 8am-dusk. Parking $5 at all trailheads. No overnight camping. Turnbull National Wildlife Refuge: office at 26010 S Smith Rd., Cheney. ☎ 235-4723; www.spokaneoutdoors.com/turnwild.*)

CLIMBING. Along the Spokane River by the Upriver Dam are the **Minnehaha Rocks,** or John Shields Park, a small granite outcropping. With many bolted top anchors, the area offers a variety of top-rope and lead climbs for many ability levels. Other climbing options abound in the area, including at **Riverside State Park,** above, and farther afield. For an indoor option, check out **Wild Walls Climbing Gym**'s impressive granite-like wall with 50 top-rope routes, as well as several sport lead routes and a bouldering cave. (*202 W 2nd Ave. ☎ 455-9596; www.wildwalls.com. $12, belay check $5, lead check $10. Refresher course $15. Rentals: harness/belay device $3; shoes $5; package $6. Open M-F noon-10pm, Sa 10am-10pm; Su 10am-7pm.*)

WALLA WALLA ☎ 509

Tucked away in the southeastern corner of the state near the Oregon border, "the town so nice they named it twice" is known primarily for its binary moniker and its sweet onions. Walla Walla, established by settlers in the early 1800s, is also home to Whitman College, the first university founded in the region. While the town itself only holds about a day (or less) of entertainment, it's a good place to spend the afternoon or night en route to local wilderness options like the Blue Mountains in the nearby Umatilla National Forest (p. 166).

■: ⁊ ORIENTATION AND PRACTICAL INFORMATION. Walla Walla and its neighbor, **College Place,** lie just south of **Route 12,** at the terminus of **Highway 125,** which becomes 9th Ave. in town. Downtown is centered around the intersection of **East Main** and **1st Street.** In the downtown area, streets running northwest-southeast are numbered increasing as they go southwest. Streets running south-west-northeast use tree names, in no particular order.

Get information on the entire valley at the **Walla Walla Chamber of Commerce,** 29 E Sumac St., off 2nd Ave. near the post office. (☎525-0850; www.wwcham-ber.com. Open M-Sa 9am-5pm, Apr.-Oct. also Su 9am-5pm.) The **Ranger Station,** 1415 W Rose St., between Avery and Erin St., has information on the nearby Umatilla National Forest. (☎522-6290; www.fs.fed.us/r6/uma. Open M-F 8:30am-5pm.) For laundry, head to **TNT Suds,** 929 S 2nd Ave. (☎525-9810. Wash $1.50, dry $0.25 per 8min. Open 6am-last wash 8:30pm.) The **police** are at 15 N 3rd Ave, at City Hall (☎527-4434), and **medical services** are available at **Walla Walla General Hospital,** 1025 S. 2nd Ave. (☎527-8000), conveniently located near the laundromat so you can get out those tough blood stains. Log in at **library,** 238 E Alder St. Free **Internet** access on one computer. (☎527-4550; www.wal-net.walla-walla.wa.us. Open M-Tu noon-8pm, W 10am-8pm, Th-Sa 10am-5pm.) The **post office** is at 128 N 2nd Ave. (☎800-275-8777. Open M-F 8am-5pm, Sa 10am-2pm.) **Postal Code:** 99362.

🔃 **ACCOMMODATIONS AND FOOD.** Lewis and Clark Trail State Park ➊, 36149 Hwy. 12, 26 mi. northeast of Walla Walla, has 24 shady, secluded sites. (☎520-9242. Sites $15.) **Budget Inn ➌,** 305 N 2nd Ave., has spacious rooms just three blocks from downtown. Rooms come with nice couches and large tables. (☎529-4410. Singles starting at $44.) The **Capri Motel ➌,** 2003 Melrose St., has clean rooms that are a throwback to the 70s. It makes up for its location—a few miles from downtown—with low rates. (☎525-1130. Singles $35; doubles $45.) Walla Walla has a ton of cheap fast food on Isaacs St. and between Walla Walla and College Place. Downtown, along Main St. is packed with cafes. Groceries are available at **Safeway,** 215 E. Rose (☎529-3711. Open daily 5am-1am.) **Tony's Sub Shop ➋,** 1068 Isaac St. in a converted mechanic's garage, serves up quick and tasty subs, from the classic meatball sub to a "Gutt Bomb." 6 in. sub $3.75, 12 in. $6. (☎829-5516; www.tonyssubshop.com. Open M-Sa 6am-9pm, Su 8am-7pm.) **Merchants Ltd. ➋,** 21 W Main St., serves deli sandwiches and coffee in European-style sidewalk seating. (☎525-0900. Free wireless Internet access. Open M 5:30am-5pm, Tu and Th-F 5:30am-6pm, W 5:30am-8pm, Sa 5:30am-4:47pm.) The 75-year-old **Pastime Cafe ➋,** 215 W Main St., still serves pasta ($9-11) and burgers ($6) in a friendly diner atmosphere. (☎525-0873; www.walla-walla.com/pastime. Open M-Sa 6:30am-10pm.)

🎡 **SIGHTS AND ENTERTAINMENT.** Each spring, a rainbow of 50 hot air balloons rises up from the Walla Walla County Fairgrounds in the **Hot Air Balloon Stampede.** Antique cars, food, and music round out the festivities. The Stampede runs May 13-15 2005. (☎877-998-4748; www.wwchamber.com.) Given that Walla Walla is in the Columbia River drainage, you might expect the **Walla Walla Valley Spring Release Weekend** to celebrate the first time the water is let over the dam in early May. Not so in Washington, where that weekend celebrates the release of a new vintage of wines. Winemakers come from all over the valley to share the new vintage. (☎526-3117; www.wallawallawine.com.) Catch a show at Whitman College's **Harper Joy Theatre.** Shows run for four or five days about once a month, Oct.-May. (Schedule at www.whitman.edu/theatre. Tickets $10, students $6.) The **Walla Walla Symphony,** at 46 South Park on the Whitman College Campus, is the longest continuously running symphony orchestra west of the Mississippi. (☎529-8020; www.wwsymphony.com. Tickets start at $12, students $10, under 18 $6.)

⚠️ OUTDOOR ACTIVITIES. When the snows come, Walla Wallans hit the slopes at two ski mountains within an hour of town. **Bluewood,** in the Blue Mountains, has 24 runs just 52 mi. from town. (☎ 382-4725; www.bluewood.com. All-day pass $32, students $28, ages 65 and older and 6-14 $25. Open late Nov.-early Apr. W-Su 9am-4pm.) **Spout Springs,** on the way to Enterprise and the Wallowa Mountains, leaves the lights on for night skiing. (☎ 541-566-0320; www.skispoutsprings.com. All-day pass $25, ages 12-17 $20, 5-11 $15. Night skiing $18/$15/$12. Open daily late Nov.-early Apr. 9am-9pm.)

BRITISH COLUMBIA

> **BC FACTS AND FIGURES**
> **Capital:** Victoria. **Area:** 947,796 sq. km. **Population:** 4,177,400.
> **Motto:** *Splendor Sine Occasu* (Splendor Without Diminishment).
> **Bird:** Steller's Jay. **Flower:** Pacific dogwood. **Tree:** Western Red Cedar.
> **Holiday:** BC Day (Aug. 1) **Sales Tax:** 7% PST plus 7% GST. **Drinking Age:** 19.

Before Europeans plunked themselves down for frontier lives in the huge territory now known as British Columbia, tribal nations (including the Kwakwaka'wakw, Nuu-cha-nulth, and Coast Salish) had already developed complex societies all across the land. Eventually, gold was discovered north and east of Vancouver in 1858, bringing in a flood of prospectors. Vancouver blossomed into the metropolis it is today on account of the Canadian Pacific Railroad, which made the town its western terminus in 1886.

Today, residents swear backwards and forwards that BC is the most beautiful place on earth, and most visitors come to that opinion. It's easy to see why. Small, developed communities surround the metropolitan areas, and breathtaking wilderness is never more than a short drive away. Vancouver's location on the mainland side of the Strait of Georgia affords immediate access to the Gulf Islands and Vancouver Island. Sechelt Peninsula, north along the mainland, is less developed than its surroundings and boasts amazing diving, kayaking, and hiking amid the largest trees and most beautiful waters in Canada. Inland from the ocean, mile upon mile of forests, rugged mountain ranges, and coursing rivers carve out an outdoors paradise in the beautiful Okanagan Valley. Approaching the border with Alberta, the Canadian Rockies loom up before you, encompassing several national parks and enough open space to leave the tourists far behind.

HIGHLIGHTS OF BRITISH COLUMBIA

EDUCATE yourself in Vancouver's famous **Museum of Anthropology** (p. 309).

SKI to your heart's content at the world-class ski resort **Whistler Blackcomb** (p. 318).

SOAK away your sorrows in **Radium Hot Springs** in Kootenay National Park (p. 384).

LEAP off a legal bungee-jumping bridge in **Nanaimo** on Vancouver Island (p. 341).

CHILL with the Haida on **Moresby Island** in Gwaii Hanaas National Reserve (p. 411).

SCUBA DIVE in the clear, undisturbed waters off the **Sechelt Peninsula** (p. 315).

VANCOUVER   ☎ 604/778

The largest city in the province and the third-largest city in Canada, on paper Vancouver may sound like an overwhelming, over-bustling metropolis. But while Vancouver's size is evident in its mind-blowing mix of sights, restaurants, and cultural events, the city's residents know that the British Columbian wilderness is just a short drive, hike, or paddle away. It's a difficult fact to ignore—surrounded on

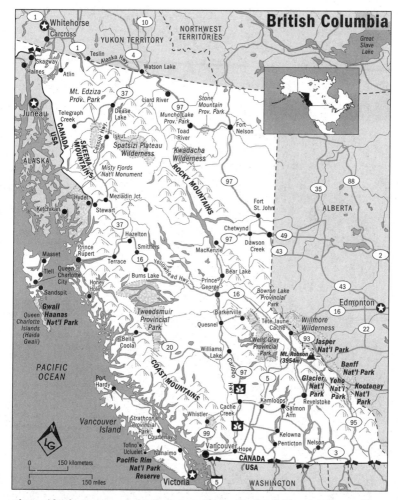

British Columbia

three sides by water and closely hemmed in by the Coast Mountain Range, Vancouver can never stray too far from its humble logging-town roots, no matter how urban the city may become. This mix of big-city benefits with easily-accessible outdoors adventure makes for a unique destination for the budget traveler.

As befits a port city, Vancouver has been routinely invaded by waves of immigration from across the Pacific. Thousands of Chinese immigrants (whose work at the turn of the century made the completion of the Trans-Canada railroad possible) settled at the line's western terminus, founding the city's Chinatown; the Cantonese influence is so strong that it is often referred to by its nickname, "Hongcouver." You'll find Asian flavor in everything from peaceful manicured gardens to raucous annual festivals to, of course, the city's cuisine in North America's third largest Chinatown. The city's other major cultural influence is its youth culture. A self-perpetuating trend among young Canadians from all points east to

BRITISH COLUMBIA

Vancouver Overview

⚑ ACCOMMODATIONS
UBC Lodgings, **15**
Vancouver Hostel
Jericho Beach, **3**

▲ CAMPGROUNDS
Capilano RV Park, **1**
Hazelmere RV Park
and Campground, **18**
Parks Canada, **17**
Richmond RV Park, **16**

🍴 FOOD
Belgian Fries, **9**
Benny's Bagels, **13**
The Excellent Eatery, **12**
Hon's Wun-Tun House, **2**
Mexican BBQ, **10**

Mongolian Teriyaki, **11**
The Naam, **7**
Sophie's Diner, **6**
WaaZuBee Cafe, **5**

🍸 NIGHTLIFE
The King's Head, **4**
Koerner's Pub, **14**

Skytrain

NORTH VANCOUVER

Burrard Inlet

Stanley Park

English Bay

DOWNTOWN

GASTOWN

CHINATOWN

STRATHCONA

RENFREW

GRANVILLE

MT. PLEASANT

FAIRVIEW

KITSILANO

POINT GREY

SEE DOWNTOWN VANCOUVER MAP

500 meters
500 yards

migrate here has resulted in a city with thriving nightlife and cafe culture. The University of British Columbia (UBC), with its campus just outside downtown Vancouver, feeds nearly 40,000 students into the city's population.

From the hip neighborhood of Gastown to the therapeutic walks of Stanley Park, Vancouver's diversity, location, and worldly yet laid-back atmosphere keeps its residents friendly and the tourist influx constant. The city's hospitality will be tested in 2010 when the Winter Olympics come to town; still, Vancouverites should have no trouble keeping their trademark cool and convincing the world of their fortunate status as denizens of one of the most exciting cities on the west coast.

PHONE CODES In 2001, Vancouver switched to 10-digit dialing. All the old numbers will remain 604, but new numbers will have the area code 778. Should you encounter problems, confirm the area code of the number you are trying to reach at www.addthecode.com.

 # INTERCITY TRANSPORTATION

Flights: Vancouver International Airport (☎604-207-7077; www.yvr.ca), on Sea Island, 23km south of the city center. A **visitors center** (☎604-207-1598) is on level 2. Open daily 8:30am-11:30pm. To reach downtown, take bus #424 and transfer to the 98 B-line, heading downtown. An **Airporter** (☎604-946-8866 or 800-668-3141) bus leaves from airport level 2 for downtown hotels and the bus station. (4 per hr.; 6:30am-midnight; $12, seniors $9, ages 5-12 $5.) Airport code: YVR.

Trains: VIA Rail, 1150 Station St. (☎888-842-7245, US 800-561-3949; www.viarail.com) runs eastbound trains. Open M, W, Th, and Sa 8:30am–6pm; Tu, F, and Su 9am-7pm. 3 trains per week to eastern Canada via **Edmonton** (23hr., $288) and **Jasper** (17hr., $215).

Buses: Greyhound Canada, 1150 Station St. (☎604-683-8133 or 800-661-8747; www.greyhound.ca), in the VIA Rail station. Open daily 5am-12:15am. To **Banff** (14hr., 5 per day, $116); **Calgary** (15hr., 5 per day, $133); and **Jasper** (2 per day, $116). **Pacific Coach Lines,** 1150 Station St. (☎604-662-8074; www.pacificcoach.com), runs to **Victoria** every time a ferry sails (3½hr., $30, includes ferry). **Quick Shuttle** (☎940-4428 or 800-665-2122; www.quickcoach.com) makes 8 trips per day from the Holiday Inn on Howe St. via the airport to: **Bellingham, WA** (2½hr.; $22, $17 with student ID), **Seattle** (4hr.; $33, $22 with student ID), and the **Sea-Tac (Seattle-Tacoma) airport** (4½hr.; $41, $29 with student ID). **Greyhound USA** (☎800-229-9424 or 402-330-8552; www.greyhound.com) goes to **Seattle** (3-4½hr., $25).

Ferries: BC Ferries (☎888-BC-FERRY/223-3779; www.bcferries.com) connects Vancouver to the **Gulf Islands,** the **Sechelt Peninsula,** and **Vancouver Island.** Ferries to the **Gulf Islands, Nanaimo** (3 hr.; 4-8 per day; $10, low-season $8.25; cars $38, reservation required) and **Victoria** (1½hr.; 8-16 per day; $11; bikes $2.50; car $36) leave from the **Tsawwassen Terminal,** 25km south of the city center (take Hwy. 99 to Hwy. 17). To reach downtown from Tsawwassen by bus (1hr.), take #640 "Scott Rd. Station," or take #404 "Airport" to the Ladner Exchange, then transfer to bus #601. More ferries to **Nanaimo** (1½hr., 8 per day, same cost as from Tsawwassen) and the **Sechelt Peninsula** (fare charged only from Horseshoe Bay to Langdale; 40min.; 8-10 per day; $8-9.50, ages 5-11 half price, car $24-34; slightly cheaper in low-season) depart the **Horseshoe Bay Terminal** (☎604-985-7777; www.westvancouver.net) at the end of the Trans-Canada Hwy. in West Vancouver. Take the "Blue Bus" #250 (50min.) or #257 express (40 min.), departing every 30min. from Georgia St., to get there from downtown. Reservations strongly encouraged for all ferries, especially in the summer.

⚓ ORIENTATION

Vancouver lies in the southwestern corner of mainland British Columbia. It is divided into distinct regions, mostly by waterways. South of the city flows the Fraser River and to the west lies the Georgia Strait, which separates the mainland from Vancouver Island. **Downtown** juts north into the Burrard Inlet from the main mass of the city and **Stanley Park** goes even further north. The **Lions Gate** suspension bridge over Burrard Inlet links Stanley Park with North and West Vancouver (West Van), known collectively as the **North Shore;** the bridges over **False Creek** south of downtown link downtown with **Kitsilano** ("Kits") and the rest of the city. West of Burrard St. is the **West End. Gastown** and **Chinatown** are just east of downtown. The **University of British Columbia (UBC)** lies to the west of Kitsilano on Point Grey, while the **airport** is on Sea Island in the Fraser River delta tucked between S. Vancouver and Richmond to the south. **Highway 99** runs north-south from the US-Canada border through the city along **Oak Street,** through downtown, then over the Lions Gate bridge. It joins temporarily with the **Trans-Canada Highway** (Hwy. 1) before splitting off again and continuing north to Whistler (see p. 317). The Trans-Canada enters from the east, cuts north across the Second Narrows Bridge to the North Shore, and ends at the Horseshoe Bay ferry terminal. Most of the city's attractions are grouped on the peninsula and farther west.

Vancouver is a major point of entry for heroin, with an active street trade in this drug and marijuana; there is a high addict population. While incidences of armed assaults, armed robbery, and murder are low by US standards, the rates for crimes are higher than in most other Canadian cities. Walking around by day is generally safe most anywhere and downtown is relatively safe at night on main streets. The area east of Gastown, especially around **Hastings** and **Main Street,** should be avoided late at night if possible.

▣ LOCAL TRANSPORTATION

If you're on the outskirts of Vancouver with a car, consider using the **Park n' Rides.** These are cheap or free parking lots at major transit hubs where you can leave your car for the day and take public transit into town. From the southeast, exit Hwy. 1 at New Westminster and follow signs south about 2km for the Pattullo Bridge. The lot is over the bridge and to the right, on the corner of Scott Rd. and King George Hwy. Park for $1 per day and take the **SkyTrain** downtown.

Public Transit: Transit timetables are available at public libraries, city hall, community centers, and **Vancouver Travel Infocentre** (see **Practical Information,** p. 303). The pamphlet *Discover Vancouver on Transit* lists bus numbers for every major site in the city. **Coast Mountain Buslink** (☎ 604-953-3333; www.translink.bc.ca) is the bus system that covers most of the city and suburbs, with direct transport or easy connections to airport and the ferry terminals (see **Intercity Transportation,** above). The city is divided into 3 zones for fare purposes. Riding in the **central zone,** which encompasses most of Vancouver, costs $2. During peak hours (M-F before 6:30pm), it costs $3 to travel between 2 zones and $4 for 3 zones. During off-peak (after 6:30pm) hours, all zones are $2. Ask for a **free transfer** (good for 1½hr.) when you board buses. **Day passes** $8 are sold at all 7-Eleven and Safeway stores, SkyTrain stations, and HI hostels. Seniors and ages 5-13 for 1 zone or off-peak $1.50; 2 zones $2; 3 zones $3; day pass $6. Bikes can travel on the rack-equipped #404/#601 combination to the Tsawwassen ferry terminal. **SeaBus** and **SkyTrain:** Same contact information as the buses, above. Included in the normal bus fare. The SeaBus shuttles passengers across Burrard Inlet from the foot of Granville St. downtown (Waterfront SkyTrain station) to **Lonsdale Quay** at the foot of Lonsdale Ave. in North Vancouver. The SkyTrain is a light rapid transit system, with a 28km track from Vancouver to **Burnaby, New Westminster,** and **Surrey** in 40min. 20 stations with service every 5min. **Bikes** may be brought on board the Sea-Bus, and on the SkyTrain during off-peak hours (9:30am-3pm and 6:30pm-close).

Taxis: Yellow Cab, ☎604-681-1111 or 800-898-8294. **Vancouver Taxi,** ☎604-871-1111. **Black Top Cabs,** ☎604-731-1111. All three $2.56 base, $1.39 per km, $6 per 15min. in traffic. 24hr.

⁊ PRACTICAL INFORMATION

LOCAL SERVICES

Tourist Office: 200 Burrard St., plaza level (☎604-683-2000; www.tourismvancouver.com), near Canada Place. BC-wide info on accommodations, tours, and activities. Courtesy phones for making hotel reservations. Open daily 8:30am-6pm.

Travel Outfitter: The Travel Bug, 3065 W Broadway (☎604-737-1122; www.travelbugbooks.ca). Everything you need to get around. 10% HI discount on accessories. Open M-Tu 10am-6pm, W-F 10am-7:30pm, Sa noon-5pm, Su noon-5:30pm.

Tours: The Gray Line, 255 E 1st Ave. (☎879-3363 or 800-667-0882; www.grayline.ca). Narrated bus tours. The Double Decker Bus stops at over 20 sights. Unlimited use for 2 days $30; students and ages 62 and older $29, 5-12 $17. Buses run every 30min. 8:30am-4:30pm.

Equipment Rental: Stanley Park Cycle, 766 Denman St. (☎604-688-0087), near Stanley Park. Mountain bikes or 21-speed from $3.50 per hr., $11 per 5hr. or $14 per day. Open daily 8:30am-9pm. The immensely popular and knowledgeably staffed **Mountain Equipment Co-op (MEC),** 130 W Broadway (☎604-872-7858; www.mec.ca), rents tents ($12-21 per day), sleeping bags ($8-15 per day), and kayaks ($10-55 per day). Open M-W 10am-7pm, Th-F 10am-9pm, Sa 9am-6pm, Su 11am-5pm.

Laundry: Davie Laundromat, 1061 Davie St. (☎604-682-2717), $2.50 per wash and dry. Open daily 8am-6:30pm.

BGLT Services: The Centre, 1170 Bute St. (☎684-5307; www.lgtbcentrevancouver.com), offers counseling and information. Open M-F 9am-5pm. *Xtra West* (www.xtra.ca) is the city's gay and lesbian biweekly, available here and around Davie St. in the West End.

Weather: ☎604-664-9010; www.weatheroffice.ec.gc.ca.

Road Conditions: Talking Yellow Pages ☎604-299-9000. Select #7623.

EMERGENCY AND COMMUNICATIONS

Police: 312 Main St. (☎604-717-3321), at Powell.

Crisis Center: ☎604-872-3311. 24hr. **Rape Crisis Center:** ☎604-255-6344. 24hr.

Pharmacy: Shoppers Drug Mart, 2979 W Broadway (☎604-733-9128), and 1125 Davie St. (☎604-669-2424). 24hr.

Hospital: Vancouver General Hospital, 855 W 12th Ave. (☎604-875-4111). **UBC Hospital,** 2211 Westbrook Mall (☎604-822-7121), on the UBC campus.

Internet Access: at the **library,** 350 W Georgia St. (☎604-331-3600; www.vpl.vancouver.bc.ca). Free Internet access. Open M-Th 10am-9pm, F-Sa 10am-6pm, Su 1-5pm. Free email at 20 other branches; check White Pages or website.

Post Office: 349 W Georgia St. (☎604-662-5725). Open M-F 8am-5:30pm. **Postal Code:** V6B 3P7.

⌐ ACCOMMODATIONS

Greater Vancouver B&Bs are a viable option for couples or small groups (singles from $45, doubles from $55). **HI hostels** are a good bet for clean and quiet rooms; some non-HI options can be seedy or rowdy.

DOWNTOWN AND WEST END

▨ **Vancouver Hostel Downtown (HI),** 1114 Burnaby St. (☎604-684-4565 or 888-203-4302), in the West End. Sleek and clean 225-bed facility in a quiet neighborhood between downtown, the beach, and Stanley Park. Library, kitchen, Internet ($4 per hr.), lockers, laundry ($3 per load), rooftop patio. Free pub crawls M, W; frequent tours of Granville Island. Travel agency in the lobby. Reception open 24hr. Oct.-May dorms $20; June-Sept. $26; nonmembers $24/$29; private doubles $59/$63, nonmembers $68/$72. Reservations recommended Jun.-Sept. ❷

▨ **SameSun Hostel** 1018 Granville St. (☎604-682-8226 or 888-844-7875; www.samesun.com), on the corner of Nelson, next to Ramada Inn. Ask the hostel for a $5 refund on your $8 taxi fare from the train station. Funky, laid-back, technicolor hangout in an area with great nightlife. Internet, pool table, free lockers (bring your own lock) laundry ($2 per load). Dorms for HI, ISIC, other hosteling members $23, nonmembers $27; doubles $53/$60, with bath $60/$65. ❷

C&N Backpackers Hostel, 927 and 1038 Main St. (☎ 604-682-2441/604-681-9118 or 888-434-6060; www.cnnbackpackers.com), 300m north on Main St. from the train station. At the 1038 location, cheap meal deals with the **Ivanhoe Pub** ($2.50 breakfast all day) make living above the bar a bargain, but across the street is a quieter location. Kitchen, laundry ($1 per wash or dry), bikes ($10 per day). Reception open 8am-10:30pm, no curfew. May-Sept. dorms $16, $90 per week; doubles $40, $240 per week. Monthly rates available in winter. ❷

GASTOWN

Cambie International Hostel, 300 Cambie St. (☎604-684-6466 or 877-395-5335 www.cambiehostels.com). Free airport pickup 10am-8pm. The Cambie offers easy access to the busy sights and sounds of Gastown (including those of the bar downstairs) in one of the older buildings in the neighborhood. No kitchen, but continental breakfast included, with an option to upgrade for $2. Common room, Internet access ($4 per hr.), and laundry ($2 per load). Pool tables in the pub. 24hr. reception. July-Sept. dorms $22; singles $43. Oct.-May dorms $19; singles $40. ❷

KITSILANO AND ELSEWHERE

Vancouver Hostel Jericho Beach (HI), 1515 Discovery St. (☎604-224-3208 or 888-203-4303), in Jericho Beach Park. Follow 4th Ave. west past Alma, bear right at the fork, or take bus #4 from Granville St. downtown to the intersection of Discovery and NW Marine. Practically on the beach with a great view across English Bay. 280 beds in 14-person dorm rooms. 10 4-bed family rooms. Cafe (breakfasts around $6, dinner $7-8), kitchen, TV room, free linen. Laundry $2.50 per load. Parking $3 per day. Bike storage free for guests. Open May-Sept. $19, nonmembers $23; family rooms $50-60. Reservations imperative mid-June to early July when rates increase to $20/$24. ❷

UBC Lodgings, 5959 Student Union Blvd. (☎604-822-1000; www.ubcconferences.com), at Gage Towers on the UBC campus. Bus #4 or #10 from city center. Northeast from bus loop, in the 17-story towers behind the student center. Standard dorm singles. TV lounges, shared microwave and fridge, pubs and food on campus. Internet access $10 per day. Free linen. Laundry $2.50 per load. Open May-Aug. Singles $24-84. 10% HI or ISIC discount. ❷

Downtown Vancouver

ACCOMMODATIONS
Cambie Int'l Hostel, **6**
C&N Backpackers Hostel, **14**
SameSun Hostel, **10**
Vancouver Hostel Downtown, **8**

🍴 FOOD
The Dish, **9**
La Luna Cafe, **2**
Samurai Sushi, **7**
Subeez Cafe, **11**
Superior Tofu, **12**

NIGHTLIFE
Atlantis, **15**
The Blarney Stone, **5**
The Irish Heather, **4**
Odyssey, **13**
Shine, **1**
Sonar, **3**

🏕 CAMPING

Capilano RV Park, 295 Tomahawk Ave. (☎604-987-4722; www.capilanorvpark.com), at foot of Lions Gate Bridge in North Van. Reception open daily 8am-9pm. 2-person sites $28-30; full RV sites $46 and up (10% off with auto club membership). Swimming pool, laundry, showers. ❷

Richmond RV Park, 6200 River Rd. (☎604-270-7878 or 800-755-4905; www.richmondrvpark.com), near Holly Bridge in Richmond, a 30min. drive from Vancouver. Follow the Westminster Hwy. west into Richmond from Hwy. 99, turn right on No. 2 Rd., then right on River Rd. Limited privacy. Open Apr.-Oct. 2-person sites $17; RV sites $25 and up. 10% AAA/CAA discount. Showers. ❷

Hazelmere RV Park and Campground, 18843 8th Ave. (☎604-538-1167; www.hazelmere.ca), in Surrey, a 45min. drive from downtown. Close to the US/Canada border. Off Hwy. 99A, head east on 8th Ave. Quiet sites on the Campbell River, 10min. from the beach. 2-person sites $23, additional person $3, under 7 free; full RV sites $31. Showers $0.25 per 5min. ❷

ParkCanada, 4799 Hwy. 17 (☎604-943-5811), in Delta 30km south of downtown, near Tsawwassen ferry terminal. Take Hwy. 99 south to Hwy. 17, then go east for 2.5km. The campground, located next to a waterslide park, has a pool. 2-person sites $19; RV sites $21 and up; additional person $2. Free showers. ❷

◘ FOOD

The diversity and excellence of Vancouver's international cuisine makes the rest of BC seem positively provincial. Vancouver's **Chinatown** and the **Punjabi Village** along Main and Fraser, around 49th St., both serve cheap, authentic food. Every type of world cuisine, from Vietnamese noodle shops to Italian cafes to succulent-yet-cheap sushi, is represented along **Commercial Drive,** east of Chinatown.

Restaurants in **downtown** compete for the highest prices in the city. The **West End** caters to diners seeking a variety of ethnic cuisines (check out the globe-spanning lineup on Denman St.), while **Gastown** lures tourists fresh off the cruise ships. Many cheap establishments along Davie and Denman St. stay open around the clock. Dollar-a-slice, all-night **pizza places** pepper downtown. For groceries in Kits, stop at **Buy-Low Foods,** at 4th and Alma St. (☎604-222-8353. Open daily 9am-9pm.) Downtown, **SuperValu** is at 1255 Davie St. (☎604-688-0911. Open 24hr.)

WEST END, DOWNTOWN, AND GASTOWN

▧ **Subeez Cafe,** 891 Homer St. (☎604-687-6107), at Smithe, downtown. Serves hipster kids in a cavernous setting. Features an eclectic menu, including vegetarian gyoza ($7.50), organic beef burgers ($10), and breakfast anytime. A lengthy wine list, large bar, and home-spun beats (DJs W, F, and Sa 9pm-midnight). Weekly specials. Entrees $7-15. Open M-F 11:30am-1am, Sa 11am-1am, Su 11am-midnight. ❸

▧ **The Dish,** 1068 Davie St. (☎604-689-0208), prides itself on creative dishes with fresh, natural ingredients. Vegetarian sandwiches and entrees are available, including the roasted veggie wrap ($5) and the lentil stew on rice ($6.50). Carnivores will not be disappointed with their deli-style sandwiches ($5-6) and entrees like curry chicken on rice ($6.50). Open M-Sa 7am-10pm, Su 9am-9pm. ❷

La Luna Cafe, 117 Water St. (☎604-687-5862), in Gastown. Loyal patrons swear by the coffee, roasted on site. Cheap, satisfying sandwiches ($3.95-6) and homemade soups ($4). Internet access $1 per 15min. Open M-F 7:30am-5pm, Sa 10am-5pm. ❶

Samurai Sushi House, 1108 Davie St. (☎604-609-0078). A range of cheap sushi options makes this Japanese restaurant a backpackers' favorite. Lunch specials include salad, soup, and sushi for $7. Open M-Th and Su 11am-midnight, F-Sa 11am-1am. ❷

COMMERCIAL DRIVE AND EAST VANCOUVER

Mongolian Teriyaki, 1918 Commercial Dr. (☎604-253-5607). Diners fill a bowl with their choice of four types of meat, veggies, sixteen sauces, and noodles, and the chefs cook everything up and serve it with miso soup, rice, and salad for only $4 (large bowl $5.95). Take-out menu. Open daily 11am-9:30pm. ❶

WaaZuBee Cafe, 1622 Commercial Dr. (☎604-253-5299), at E 1st St. Sleek, metallic decoration, ambient music, huge murals, and an enormous wine list accompany the inventive food. Brunch includes Belgian waffles and other classics ($5-8). Entrees like spinach and ricotta agnoilotti pasta run $11-16. Chicken, lamb, beef, tuna and veggie burgers $9-11. Open M-F 11:30am-1am, Sa 11am-1am, Su 11am-midnight. ❸

Belgian Fries, 1885 Commercial Dr. (☎604-253-4220). Way beyond ketchup: from what CBC Montreal calls the "Best Poutine in BC" (fries topped with curds and gravy, $4.80) to WAR fries (topped with peanut saytay and mayonnaise, $5.50), Belgian Fries has your topping. Deep fried Mars bars $3.30. Open-daily 11:30am-10pm. ❶

Mexican BBQ, 1859 Commercial Dr. Serves free-range organic chicken ($6 per quarter) in a very laid-back setting. Customers can spin the Wheel of Chicken Fortune for prizes including "I tell you a joke" and "a big hug". Burritos $4, crepes $4. Open daily 7am until the chickens are gone (usually around 6:30pm). ❶

KITSILANO

🖾 **The Naam,** 2724 W 4th Ave. (☎604-738-7151; www.thenaam.com), at MacDonald St. Bus #4 or 7 from Granville Mall. One of the most diverse vegetarian menus around, with great prices to boot. Beautifully presented entrees such as Crying Tiger Thai stir fry ($9) and several kinds of veggie burgers (under $7); Tofulati dairy-free ice cream $3.50. Live music nightly 7-10pm. Open daily 24hr. ❷

🖾 **Benny's Bagels,** 2505 W Broadway (☎604-731-9730). Benny's can start, end, or continue your day with beer ($3 per glass), bagels ($1.35, $6 fully-loaded), and sandwiches and melts ($5.50-7.50). Wireless Internet access $5 per hr., $7 per 4hr. Open M-Th and Su 7am-1am, F-Sa 24hr. ❷

The Excellent Eatery, 3431 W Broadway (☎604-738-5298). This popular spot provides candlelight, sushi, and Warhol-inspired pop art. Reserve 1 of 2 canopied booths. Sushi $3.50-6. Mango-tuna-avocado sushi $5. Open daily 4:30-11:30pm. ❶

Sophie's Diner, 2695 W 4th Ave., Serves a wide array of burgers ($7-10), including a Wild Salmon Burger ($12) and a large selection of milkshakes ($5). Open M-Th and Su 9am-12:30am, F-Sa 9am-10pm. ❷

CHINATOWN

The prettiest are usually the priciest in Chinatown and adjacent **Japantown.** For guaranteed good food, stop in restaurants that are crowded with locals. Lively afternoons make this a better place for lunch than dinner.

🖾 **Hon's Wun-Tun House,** 268 Keefer St. (☎604-688-0871). This award-winning Cantonese noodle-house is the place to go (bowls $4-8). Over 300 options make

IN RECENT NEWS

CANNABUSINESS

At an estimated $1.1 billion, British Columbia's buds generate half as much annual revenue as the province's logging industry. (Most of this money is generated by exports—95% of Canadian marijuana is exported to the US.) Despite the illegality of the drug, public marijuana smoking is commonplace at certain "Vansterdam" cafes.

What's the source of such seeming herbal impunity? It may be that Vancouver authorities don't seem to treat small-time pot smoking as seriously as their US counterparts. But their hands-off attitude may soon be official: in July 2004, Prime Minister Paul Martin and the liberal party introduced a bill to decriminalize the possession of small amounts of marijuana for personal use, making it the equivalent of a parking violation. Despite the currently inhospitable law, the cannabis business is going strong. For a connoisseur's perspective and news on further legalization efforts, tune in to the mind-altering www.cannabisculture.com or www.pot-tv.net. Educate yourself on the issues by visiting the BC Marijuana Party Bookshop and HQ at 307 W Hastings St., which has literature, clothing, and paraphernalia galore. (☎604-682-1172; www.bcmarijuana-party.com. Open M-Th 10:30am-6pm, F-Sa 10:30am-7pm, Su 11am-6pm.)

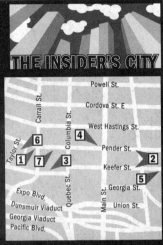

VANCOUVER CHINATOWN

Savvy tourists should take a break from downtown's hotspots and experience the bustling urban scene of Chinatown, Vancouver.

1 Gawk at the impossibly narrow **Sam Kee Building**, said to be the narrowest in the world.

2 Barter, bicker, and haggle at the **Chinatown Night Market**. Open June-Sept. F-Su 6:30-11:30pm.

3 Let the tranquil **Dr. Sun Yat-Sen Classical Chinese Garden** (☎604-689-7133) ease your stress.

4 Recognize the history of Chinese Canadians at the **Winds of Change Mural**.

5 Choose from hundreds of meals at **Hon's Wun-Tun House** (☎604-688-0871). Open Su-Th 8:30am-9pm; F-Sa 8:30am-10pm. Cash only.

6 Visit the huge **Western Han Dynasty Bell**.

7 Explore the exhibitions at the **Chinese Cultural Center** (☎604-658-8865).

reading the menu take almost as long as eating from it. Attentive service. Open M-Th and Su 8:30am-9pm, F-Sa 8:30am-10pm. Cash only. ❷

Superior Tofu, Ltd., 163 Keefer St. (☎604-682-8867; www.superiortofu.com). This deli-style vegetarian restaurant's menu is based around their homemade tofu and soy milk. Tofu pudding $2.50, fried tofu $3. Open 5:30am-6pm daily. ❶

◎ SIGHTS

DOWNTOWN

▧**VANCOUVER ART GALLERY.** This gallery is host to fantastic temporary exhibitions and a varied collection of contemporary art and design from the west coast. *(750 Hornby St. in Robson Square. ☎604-662-4700; www.vanartgallery.bc.ca. Open Apr.-Oct. M-Su 10am-5:30pm, Th 10am-9pm; call for hours Nov.-Mar. $15, seniors $11, students $10, under 12 free; Th 5-9pm pay-what-you-can; 2-for-1 HI discount.)*

CHINATOWN

The neighborhood bustles with restaurants, shops, bakeries, and **the world's narrowest building** at 8 W Pender St. In 1912, the city expropriated all but a 1.8m (6 ft.) strip of Chang Toy's property in order to expand the street; he built on the land anyhow, and today the building is a symbol of Chinatown's perseverance. The serene **Dr. Sun Yat-Sen Classical Chinese Garden** maintains imported Chinese plantings, carvings, and rock formations in the first full-size authentic garden of its kind outside China. *(578 Carrall St. ☎604-662-3207; www.vancouverchinesegarden.com Open daily May to mid-June 10am-6pm; mid-June to Aug. 9:30am-7pm; Sept. 10am-6pm; Oct.-Apr. 10am-4:30pm. Admission to part of the garden is free, while another section is $8.25, students $5.75, seniors $6.75, children under 5 free, family four-pack $18. Tours every hr. 10am-6pm.)* Don't miss the sights, sounds, smells, and tastes of the weekend, when vendors set up stands selling nearly anything at the **night market** along Keefer St. East of Main. *(Open F-Su 6:30-11pm.)* Chinatown itself is relatively safe, but its surroundings make up some of Vancouver's more unsavory sections. *(Chinatown is southeast of Gastown. Bus #22 north on Burrard St. leads to Pender and Carrall St., in the heart of Chinatown.)*

GARDENS

The city's temperate climate, which includes ample rain most months of the year, allows floral growth to flourish. Locals take great pride in their private gardens, and public parks and green spaces also showcase displays of plant life.

■ **VANDUSEN BOTANICAL GARDEN.** Some 55 acres (22 hectares) of former golf course have been converted into an immense garden showcasing 7500 species from six continents. An international **sculpture** collection is interspersed with the plants, while more than 60 species of birds can be seen in areas such as the Fragrance Garden, Children's Garden, Bonsai House, Chinese Medicinal Garden, or the Elizabethan Maze, which is planted with 3000 pyramidal cedars. Daily tours given at 2pm; alternatively, follow a self-guided tour tailored to show the best of the season. The Flower and Garden Show is the first weekend of June. *(5251 Oak St. at W 37th. From downtown take #17 Oak bus and get off at West 37th and Oak. ☎604-257-8665; www.vandusengarden.org. Free parking. Wheelchair-accessible. Open daily June-Aug. 10am-9pm; mid-Aug. to Sept. 10am-8pm; Oct.-Mar. 10am-4pm; Apr. 10am-6pm; May 10am-8pm. Apr.-Aug. $7.50, ages 65 and older $5.20, 13-18 $5.70, 6-12 $3.90, under 6 free, family four-pack $17. Call for Sept.-Mar. rates.)*

BLOEDEL FLORAL CONSERVATORY. Go from tropics to desert in 100 paces inside this 43m diameter triodetic geodesic dome, constructed of Plexiglas bubbles and aluminum tubing. The conservatory, maintained at a constant 18°C (65°F), is home to 500 varieties of exotic plants and 150 birds. Located inside beautiful Queen Elizabeth Park, whose elevation also affords views of downtown Vancouver. *(Center of Queen Elizabeth Park one block east of Cambie and 37th Ave., 1km east of VanDusen. ☎604-257-8584. Open Apr.-Sept. M-F 9am-8pm, Sa-Su 10am-9pm; daily Oct., Feb.-Mar. 10am-5:30pm; Nov.-Jan. 10am-5pm. $4.10, ages 65 and older $2.90, 13-18 $3.10, 6-12 $2, under 6 free.)*

UNIVERSITY OF BRITISH COLUMBIA (UBC)

The high point of a visit to UBC is the breathtaking ■ **Museum of Anthropology.** The high-ceilinged glass and concrete building houses totems and other massive carvings, highlighted by Bill Reid's depiction of Raven discovering the first human beings in a giant clam shell. *(6393 NW Marine Dr., bus #4 or 10 from Granville St. Museum. ☎604-822-5087 or 604-822-3825; www.moa.ubc.ca. Open Jun.-Sept. M and W-Su 10am-5pm, Tu 10am-9pm. $9, students and ages 65 and older $7, under 6 free, family 6-pack $25; Tu after 5pm free.)* Across the street caretakers tend to **Nitobe Memorial Garden.** Consistently rated in the top five North American Shinto gardens, the Nitobe is a peaceful spot designed for walking meditation. *(☎604-822-9666; www.nitobe.org. Open daily mid-Mar. to mid-May 10am-5pm; mid-May to Aug. 10am-6pm; Sept.-Oct. 10am-5pm. $3, ages 65 and older $1.75, students $1.50, under 6 free.)* The **Botanical Gardens** are a collegiate Eden encompassing eight gardens in the central campus, including the largest collection of rhododendrons in North America. *(6804 SW Marine Dr. ☎604-822-9666; www.ubcbotanicalgarden.org. Same hours as Nitobe Garden. $5, ages 65 and older $3, students $2, under 6 free. Dual ticket for both Nitobe and the Botanical Gardens, $6.)*

STANLEY PARK

Established in 1888 at the tip of the downtown peninsula, the 1000-acre **Stanley Park** is a testament to the foresight of Vancouver's urban planners. The thickly wooded park is laced with cycling and hiking trails and surrounded by an 10km **seawall** promenade popular with cyclists, runners, and rollerbladers. *(☎257-8400. To get to the park, take the #19 bus. A free shuttle runs between major destinations throughout the park on the half-hour, late June-Sept. 10am-6:30pm.)*

■ **VANCOUVER AQUARIUM.** The aquarium, on the park's eastern side not far from the entrance, features exotic aquatic animals with a focus on the British Columbia coastline. BC, Amazonian, and other ecosystems are skillfully replicated. Dolphin and beluga whales demonstrate their advanced training and intelligence by drenching gleeful visitors in educational wetness. The new Wild Coast exhibit allows visitors to get a close-up view of marine life including otters and seals. Outside the aquarium, an **orca fountain** by sculptor Bill Reid glistens blackly. (☎604-659-3474; www.vanaqua.org. Open daily July-Aug. 9:30am-7pm; Sept.-June 10am-5:30pm. Shows every other hour from 10am-5:30pm. $17, students and ages 65 and older and 13-18 $13, 4-12 $9.50, 3 and under free.)

WATER. The **Lost Lagoon,** brimming with fish, birds, and the odd trumpeter swan, provides a utopian escape from the skyscrapers. **Nature walks** start from the **Nature House,** underneath the Lost Lagoon bus loop. (Walks ☎604-257-8544. 2hr. Su 1-3pm. $5, under 12 free. Nature House open June-Aug. F-Su 11am-7pm.) The park's edges boast a few restaurants, tennis courts, a cinder running track with hot showers and a changing room, swimming beaches staffed by lifeguards, and an outdoor theater, the **Malkin Bowl** (☎604-687-0174). For warm, chlorinated water, take a dip in the **Second Beach Pool.** (Next to Georgia St. park entrance. Pool ☎604-257-8371. $4.40, ages 65 and older $3.10, 13-18 $3.30, 6-12 $2.25. Towels $2, lockers $0.25. Call for hours.)

FALSE CREEK AND GRANVILLE ISLAND

GRANVILLE ISLAND BREWING COMPANY. Canada's first microbrewery offers daily tours of the facility, including top-notch free samples. (Under the bridge at the southern tip of the island. ☎604-687-2739. Tours daily noon, 2pm, and 4pm. $9.75, students and seniors $8.75, includes samples of 4 brews and a souvenir glass. Store is open M-Th and Su 10am-7pm, F-Sa 10am-8pm.)

▣ ENTERTAINMENT

MUSIC, THEATER, AND FILM

The renowned **Vancouver Symphony Orchestra** (☎604-876-3434; www.vancouversymphony.ca) plays September to May in the refurbished **Orpheum Theatre** (☎604-665-3050), at the corner of Smithe and Seymour. In summer, you can take a tour of the opulent theater ($5). The VSO often joins forces with other groups such as the **Vancouver Bach Choir** (☎604-921-8012; www.vancouverbachchoir.com).

Vancouver has a lively theater scene. The **Vancouver Playhouse Theatre Co.** (☎604-873-3311), on Dunsmuir and Georgia St., and the **Arts Club Theatre** (☎604-687-1644; www.artsclub.com), on Granville Island, stage low-key shows, often including local work. **Theatre Under the Stars** (☎604-687-0174; www.tuts.bc.ca), in Stanley Park's Malkin Bowl, puts on outdoor musicals in the summer. The world-famous improvisational theater company **Theatresports League** performs competitive improv, comedies, and improv jam sessions at the Arts Club New Revue Stage on Granville Island. Shows Th 7:30pm, F 8pm and 10pm, Sa 8pm, 10pm, and 11:45pm. (☎604-687-1644; www.vtsl.com. Open M-Sa 9am-7pm. W-Th $15, students $12. F-Sa 8pm and 10pm shows $17, students $13. Sa 11:45 pm show $10.)

The **Ridge Theatre,** 3131 Arbutus, shows arthouse, Indie, European, and vintage film double features. (☎604-738-6311; www.ridgetheatre.com. $5, seniors and children $4.) The **Hollywood Theatre,** 3123 W Broadway, shows a mix of arthouse, documentaries, and second-run mainstream double features for less than the other theaters around downtown. (☎604-515-5864; www.hollywoodtheatre.ca. $6, M $4, ages 65 and older and 13 and under $3.50.)

SPORTS

One block south of Chinatown on Main St. is **BC Place Stadium,** at 777 S Pacific Blvd. home to the Canadian Football League's BC Lions and the world's largest air supported dome. (☎604-669-2300; www.bcplacestadium.com. Tickets from $15.) The NHL's **Vancouver Canucks** call nearby **GM Place** (www.canucks.com/gm) home. Tickets for both are often available as late as game day. The **Vancouver Canadians** play AAA baseball in Nat Bailey Stadium, at 33rd. Ave. and Ontario, opposite Queen Elizabeth Park, offering some of the cheapest sports tickets going (tickets from $8). For tickets and info call **Ticketmaster** at ☎ 604-280-4400 or visit www.ticketmaster.ca.

✺ FESTIVALS AND ANNUAL EVENTS

As with almost everything else, buying tickets in advance for these festivals often results in drastically reduced prices.

Alcan Dragon Boat Festival, late June. (☎ 604-696-1888; www.adbf.com). Traditional food and dance from around the world and dragon boat racing on False Creek. $10, seniors and youth $8, family $20.

Vancouver International Jazz Festival Late June-early July. (☎ 604-872-5200 or 888-438-5200; www.jazzvancouver.com). Draws over 500 performers and bands for 10 days of jazz, from acid to swing. Free concerts in Gastown, at the Roundhouse on Davie St., and around Granville Island. Other events range from $10-60.

Vancouver Folk Music Festival, third weekend of July (☎ 604-602-9798 or 800-985-8363; www.thefestival.bc.ca). Performers from around the world give concerts and workshops in July. Very kid-friendly. $40-55 per day, $130 for the weekend. Ages 13-18 $25-30/$65, 3-12 $12/$7, under 2 and over 65 free.

Celebration of Light, late July-early Aug. (☎ 604-738-4304; www.celebration-of-light.com). Pyrotechnicians light up the sky over English Bay on Sa and W nights. Thousands gather to watch, closing off downtown streets and crowding Kitsilano beaches.

Holy Pride! Late July-early Aug. (☎ 604-687-0955; www.vanpride.bc.ca). This is Vancouver's gay and lesbian festival. Events include dances, parties, games, music, and a parade. Tickets and info from Ticketmaster (see **Sports,** above) or Little Sisters Bookstore, 1328 Davie St. (☎ 604-669-1753; www.littlesistersbookstore.com).

Vancouver International Film Festival, late Sept.-early Oct. (☎ 604-683-3456; www.viff.org). This event showcases movies from over 50 countries, with particular emphasis on Canadian films, East Asian films, and documentaries. $6-8.

Vancouver International Comedy Festival, late July-early Aug. (☎ 604-683-0883; www.comedyfest.com). Comics from all over the world converge on Granville Island in late July for 11 days of chortles and antics. Expect to pay big for larger acts, and much less for the unknowns. $10 and up.

◪ NIGHTLIFE

Vancouver's nightlife centers around dance clubs playing beats and DJs spinning every night. Local pubs are scattered throughout the city's neighborhoods. The free weekly *Georgia Straight* (www.straight.com) publishes club and event listings, restaurant reviews, and coupons. *Discorder* (http://discorder.citr.ca) is the unpredictable monthly publication of the UBC radio station CITR. Both are available in local cafes, and *Georgia Straight* can be found around town in bins.

GASTOWN

▨ **The Irish Heather,** 217 Carrall St. (☎ 604-688-9779; www.irishheather.com). The 2nd-highest seller of Guinness in BC, this true Irish pub and bistro serves up memories of the Emerald Isle to a clientele of local regulars. Full 20 oz. draughts ($6.10), mixed beer drinks ($6.50), and bangers and mash or fish and chips will keep those eyes smiling. Lots of veggie dishes, too. Entrees $13-16. Live music Tu-Th 8pm-close. Open M-Th noon-11pm, F-Sa noon-midnight.

Sonar, 66 Water St. (☎604-683-6695; www.sonar.bc.ca). People crowd onto this popular beat factory's large dance floor. A long line can form on weekends, but a visit to www.clubvibes.com will get you on the guestlist. International DJs spin house (W), techno (F), and hip-hop (Sa). Open W 9pm-2am, F-Sa 9pm-3am.

Shine, 364 Water St. (☎604-408-4321; www.shinenightclub.com), in the basement. Named the "sexiest club in Canada" in 2001 by *Flare Magazine*, this ultra-hip club draws in crowds with its sleek decor and nightly drink specials. M electro-funk, Tu hip-hop, W reggae, Th 80's, F and Sa hip-hop/pop, Su house (Su is also gay night). Beer and mixed drinks $6-8. Cover $3 weekdays, $10 weekends. Open M-Tu 10pm-2am, W-Th 9pm-2am, F-Sa 9pm-3am, Su 9pm-2am.

The Blarney Stone, 216 Carrall St. (☎604-687-4322). For a more raucous Irish experience, join the mostly university crowd for live music by Killarney, a Celtic-rock band that has played here four nights a week for 20 years. Cover F-Sa $7. Open W-Sa 7pm-2am.

Atlantis, 1320 Richards St. (☎604-662-7707; www.atlantisclub.net). Near the South end of Richards St. Candlelit dining booths, a large dance floor, and one of the most advanced stereo and light systems in Vancouver. Long lines can form on weekends, but getting on the guest list is as easy as emailing info@atlantisclub.net. Hip-hop and top 40, cover W-Th $5, F-Sa $12. No sneakers, no caps. Open W-Sa 9pm-2am.

Odyssey, 1251 Howe St. (☎604-689-5256; www.theodysseynightclub.com). Embark on a high-energy journey at this large gay club downtown. Male go-go dancers spice it up F, male strippers appear on Th and Sa. Su and W Drag Night, and "gay bingo" raises money for charity on Tu. Mixed drinks run around $7, $3-6 cover. Open M-Th and Su 9pm-2am, F-Sa 9pm-3am.

KITSILANO

The King's Head, 1618 Yew St. (☎604-738-6966), at 1st St., in Kitsilano. Cheap drinks, cheap food, relaxing atmosphere, and a great location near the beach. Bands play acoustic sets nightly at 9pm on a tiny stage. Daily drink specials. $3.50 pints. Open M-F 9am-1am, Sa 8am-1am, Su 8am-midnight.

Koerner's Pub, 6371 Crescent Rd. (☎604-822-0983), in the basement of the Graduate Student Building on UBC campus. Owned and operated by the Graduate Student Society, this is the place to meet a smart and sexy special someone. Mellow M with live music and open jam. Pints $5. Open M-F noon-1am, Sa 4pm-1am.

◪ BEACHES

Vancouver has kept its many beaches clean. Follow the western side of the Stanley Park seawall south to **Sunset Beach Park,** a strip of grass and beach extending all the way along **English Bay** to the Burrard Bridge. The **Aquatic Centre,** 1050 Beach Ave., at the southeast end of the beach, is a public facility with a sauna, gym, and 50m indoor pool. (☎604-665-3424. Call for public swim hours, generally M-Th 9am-4:20pm and 8-10pm, F 9am-4:20pm and 8:20-9pm, Sa 10am-9pm, Su 1-9pm. $4, ages 65 and older $2.40, 13-18 $3, 6-12 $2.)

Kitsilano Beach ("Kits"), across Arbutus St. from Vanier Park, is another local favorite for tanning and beach volleyball (the water is a bit cool for swimming). For fewer crowds, more kids, and free showers, visit **Jericho Beach** (head west along 4th Ave. and follow signs). A cycling path at the side of the road leads up a steep hill to the westernmost end of the UBC campus. West of Jericho Beach is the quieter **Spanish Banks;** at low tide the ocean retreats almost a kilometer, allowing for long walks on the flats. Most of Vancouver's 31km of beaches are patrolled daily by lifeguards from late May to Labor Day between 11:30am and 9pm.

OUTDOOR ACTIVITIES

Three mountains on the North Shore provide a stunning backdrop to the city's sky-line, bringing the locals out year-round. In winter, all three offer night skiing and heavier snow than mountains farther from the ocean. Their size and impact on your wallet are much smaller than Whistler, a 2hr. drive north on Hwy. 99 (see p. 317). In summer, all offer hiking and beautiful views of the city from the top.

GROUSE MOUNTAIN. The ski hill closest to downtown Vancouver has the crowds to prove it. Take bus #236 from the North Vancouver SeaBus terminal, which drops passengers off at the Super Skyride, an aerial tramway open daily from 9am-10pm. The slopes are lit for skiing until 10:30pm from mid-November to mid-April. (☎604-984-0661; snow report 986-6262; www.grousemountain.com. Lift tickets $42, ages 65 and older and 13-18 $30, under 13 $18, family 4-pack $99; night passes at a reduced rate. Tramway $27, ages 65 and older $24, 13-18 $15, 5-12 $10.) The very steep and well-travelled 2.9km Grouse Grind Trail is a popular hiking trail among Vancouverites in the summer; it charges straight up 853m to the top of the mountain and takes a recommended 2hr. but rewards its hikers with a beautiful view of downtown and beer ($5). The Skyride back down costs $5.

CYPRESS BOWL. Cypress Bowl in West Vancouver provides a less crowded ski alternative. It boasts the most advanced terrain of the local mountains on its 23 runs, at prices close to Grouse Mtn. Go west on Hwy. 1 and take Exit 8 (Cypress Bowl Rd.). A few minutes before the downhill area, the 16km of groomed trails at Hollyburn **cross-country ski area** are open to the public. In summer, the cross-country trails have excellent **hiking** and **berry-picking.** (☎604-922-0825; snow report 604-419-7669; www.cypressbowl.com. Discount tickets at Costco supermarkets.)

MOUNT SEYMOUR. Take bus #211 from the Phibbs Exchange at the north end of the Second Narrows Bridge to **Mount Seymour Provincial Park.** Trails leave from Mt. Seymour Rd., and a paved road winds 11km to the top. The Mt. Seymour ski area has the cheapest skiing around. Its marked terrain is also the least challenging, although the spectacular backcountry is preferred by many pro snowboarders. (☎604-986-2261; www.mountseymour.com. Lift tickets $34, ages 65 and older $24, 13-18 $28, 6-13 $18, under 6 free.)

WILDLIFE ADVENTURES

The Lower Mainland of British Columbia hosts a huge variety of wild critters, including mule deer, black bears, wolves, cougars, and more than a few bird species. The **Guide-Outfitters Association of British Columbia,** 7580 River Rd., Ste. 250, Richmond, BC (☎604-278-2688; www.goabc.org) is a BC-wide information and contact clearinghouse for hunters. Those interested in importing firearms into Canada should consult the Canadian government's **Firearms Centre** (☎800-731-4000; www.cfc-ccaf.gc.ca). Indian Arm is an ideal spot for fishing, diving, and kayak-camping. The **Deep Cove Canoe and Kayak Center,** 2156 Banbury Rd., in North Vancouver, offers 2hr. canoe and kayak rentals for $28/32 or 2hr. twin rentals for $40/44. 3hr. introductory lessons for novices are $60 65, and overnight kayak trips are $75 for 24hr. or $106 for a double kayak. (☎929-2268; www.deepcove-ekayak.com. Reservations suggested in summer. Apr.-Oct. 9am-9pm.)

DAYTRIPS FROM VANCOUVER

LIGHTHOUSE PARK. The gorgeous **Lighthouse Park** is easily one of the most serene, pleasant places in Vancouver. Numerous trails, including an easy 3km loop that covers most of the park (plan to spend a couple hours walking it), criss-cross the old-growth conifer forest inside the park's 185 acres. To reach numerous pic-nic spots with breathtaking views of the bay and downtown Vancouver, walk down the path toward the lighthouse, hang a left at the buildings, and follow the Pine Shore trail. Some **rock climbing** can be found on the small cliffs at Juniper Point on the west side of the park. *(Head across Lions Gate Bridge from Stanley Park and west along Marine Dr. for about 10km through West Van. 50km round-trip from downtown; blue bus #250 goes right to the park's entrance. For a park map stop by the West Van. Parks & Community Services Office at 750 17th St., 2nd floor. ☎604-925-7200. Open M-F 8:30am-4:30pm.)*

EAST OF NORTH VAN. East of the North Vancouver city center, sea otters and seals ply pleasant **Indian Arm Provincial Park** off the town of **Deep Cove.** A few km west at the end of Dollarton Hwy. lies **Cates Park,** whose calm cool waters are pop-ular for swimming and scuba diving (free public showers and changing areas). This area's location makes for a good bike trip out of Vancouver. Trails leave from Mt. Seymour Rd., and a paved road winds 11km to the top for access to hiking and biking with a great view. See also **Outdoor Activities,** p. 313. *(Bus #210 from Pender St. to the Phibbs Exchange on the north side of Second Narrows Bridge. From there, take bus #211 or 212 to Deep Cove. Bus #211 also leads to Mt. Seymour Provincial Park.)*

REIFEL BIRD SANCTUARY. Reifel Bird Sanctuary is on 850-acre Westham Island. The marshland supports 265 bird species, and spotting towers are set up for extended bird-watching. March and April or October and November are the best months to visit—migratory birds stop through the park on their journey. *(Westham Island lies northwest of the Tsawwassen ferry terminal and 16km south of the city. ☎604-946-6980; www.reifelbirdsanctuary.com. Open daily 9am-4pm. $4, ages 60 and older and 2-14 $2.)*

LYNN CANYON. An idyllic setting that provides easy hiking for city escapists. Unlike the more famous Capilano (below), the suspension bridge here is free, uncrowded, and hangs 50m above the canyon (the actual bridge is also older, con-structed in 1912). The park is 250 hectares, but it joins a conservation range and a regional park and serves as a starting point for far more trails than Capilano; sev-eral are 10-20min., but longer hiking trails (up to 20km) are also plentiful. Swim-ming is not recommended; many have died over the years from the treacherous currents and falls. *(SeaBus to Lynn Canyon Park, in North Vancouver. Take bus #229 from the North Vancouver SeaBus terminal to the last stop (Peters Rd.) and walk 500m to the bridge. ☎604-981-3149. Open May-Sept. 10am-9pm; Oct.-Apr. 10am-dusk.)*

GOLDEN EARS PROVINCIAL PARK. Thick green green moss clings to the trees that grow from the impossibly steep canyon walls in this conifer rainforest. The lower third of the park features hiking trails with great views of the impassible ridges to the North, with difficulties ranging from the easy but spectacular 1hr. walk to the Lower Falls to a two-day backpacking climb through a snowfield to the Golden Ears. Camping on large, level, forested sites is available from Easter to Thanksgiv-ing in a large campground by the beach on Alouette Lake. Reservations recom-mended on weekends. *(Reservations ☎800-689-9025. Sites $22; hiker/biker sites free. Showers. Parking $5 per day. End of Fern Cr. From downtown, drive East on Hwy 7, out of Vancou-ver to Maple Ridge. Turn left (north) on 232 St. for 3km, then turn right (east) on Fern. Open 7am-11pm Easter-Thanksgiving.)*

CAPILANO SUSPENSION BRIDGE. You and every other Vancouver tourist will enjoy crossing the precarious Capilano Bridge. Although the original bridge was built in 1889--this bridge is the fourth to cross at this point--it remains awe-inspir-ing, spanning 137m and swaying 70m above the river. A few short trails meander through the surrounding old-growth forest. Guided tours every 15min. May-Oct. *(3735 Capilano Rd. North Van. 10min. from town. Drive through Stanley Park, over the Lions Gate Bridge, north 1km on Capilano Rd. From Hwy. #1 take Exit 14 and go north 5km. Or take bus*

#246 from downtown to Ridgewood stop and walk 1 block north to park. ☎ 985-7474; www.cap-bridge.com. Open daily May-Oct. 8:30am-dusk; Nov.-Apr. 9am-5pm. May-Sept. $22, seniors and students $14, ages 13-16 $11, 6-12 $5.50, under 6 free. Nov.-Apr. $17, $13, $8.60, $4. CAA, AAA 20% discount; HI members get student rate.)

SECHELT PENINSULA ☎ 604

Tucked between the Strait of Georgia and Porpoise Bay, Sechelt (SEE-shelt) is one of BC's greatest secrets. Only 1½hr. by road and ferry from downtown Vancouver, this quiet and isolated seaside paradise remains miles away from city life in attitude, lifestyle, and even climate. The region offers world-class kayaking, hiking, scuba diving, biking, and even skiing.

■ ⓘ **ORIENTATION AND PRACTICAL INFORMATION.** Sechelt is the largest community on the Sunshine Coast, 27km west of the **BC Ferries** Langdale Ferry Terminal (☎ 886-2242 or 888-223-3779; www.bcferries.com). The fare on the ferry between Langdale and Horseshoe Bay is only charged on the way from the mainland to Sechelt (40min.; 8-10 per day; $8-9.50, under 12 $4, car $25; low season slightly cheaper). **Malaspina Coach Lines** (☎ 877-227-8287) runs to Vancouver (2 per day, $21 including ferry fare). **Sunshine Coast Transit System** (☎ 885-6899) buses run from Sechelt to the ferry terminal ($1.50, students and seniors $1). **National Tilden,** on Wilson Creek, rents cars. (☎ 885-9120. From $51 per day; $0.25 per km over 100km; winter rates start at $44.) **Sunshine Coast Taxi** is at ☎ 885-3666. The **visitors center** is located at 5790 Teredo St. in the Seaside Center, off the highway. (☎ 885-1036 or 877-633-2963. Open M-Sa 9:30am-5:30pm, Su 10am-4pm; closed Su Sept.-May.) **On The Edge Bike Shop,** 5644 Cowrie St., rents mountain bikes. (☎ 885-4888; www.ontheedgebiking.com. Bikes with front suspension $15 per 4hr., $30 per day, or with full suspension, $30/$60. Snowshoes $15 per day, cross-country skis $20 per day. Open M-Sa 9am-6pm, Su 9am-5pm.) **Sechelt Coin Laundry** is on Dolphin St. at Inlet Ave. (☎ 885-3393. Open daily 9am-9pm. Wash $1.75, dry $0.25 per 5min.) **Saint Mary's Hospital** (☎ 885-2224) is on the highway at the east end of town. The **Sechelt Public Library,** 5797 Cowrie St., has **Internet** access for $1 per 30min. (☎ 885-3260; www.secpl.scrd.bc.ca. Open Tu 10am-5pm, W-Th 11am-8pm, F and Su 1-5pm, Sa 10am-4pm.) The **post office** is on Inlet Ave. at Dolphin St. (☎ 885-2411. Open M-F 8:30am-5pm, Sa 8:30am-12:30pm.) **Postal Code:** V0N 3A0.

⌂ ⓘ **ACCOMMODATIONS AND CAMPING.** Most of Sechelt's accommodations are pricey, but deals can be found at ▧**The Upper Deck Hostel ❷,** 5653 Wharf Rd. In downtown Sechelt, towards Porpoise Bay PP. Offers clean dorm and private rooms. Internet access ($4 per hr.), lounge, laundry ($5 per load), full kitchen, lounge, 800 sq. ft. sun deck. (☎ 885-5822; www.wuts.nu/upperdeck. Dorm beds $20; singles $35-60.) **Eagle View B&B ❸,** 4839 Eagle View Rd., 5min. east of Sechelt. Take Bay Rd. from the highway. Has rooms with private bath, sitting room with TV/VCR and video collection, an ocean view, included tea and biscuits, and delightful hosts. (☎ 885-7225. Singles $50; doubles $70.)

The provincial parks in the area cover beautiful coastal rain forest and feature many pristine beaches. The family-oriented **Porpoise Bay Provincial Park ❷,** 4km north of Sechelt along Sechelt Inlet Rd./E Porpoise Bay Rd., offers a forested campground with toilets, showers, firewood, playground, and a lovely beach and swimming area. (Reservations ☎ 800-689-9025. Wheelchair-accessible. 84 sites $20; hiker/biker sites by the water $10. Gate closed 11pm-7am.) For more seclusion, **Roberts Creek Provincial Park ❶,** 11km east of Sechelt, has large, level private sites amid old-growth Douglas-firs. (24 sites, $14. Firewood.) **Smuggler Cove Provincial Park ❶,** named after the smugglers who picked up unemployed Chinese laborers for passage to America after the completion of the Canadian-Pacific railroad, has five primitive, free walk-in sites (no water). The sites are accessible by boat, and the cove is an excellent base for kayaking. Head west out of town towards Halfmoon Bay and turn left on Brooks Rd., which leads 3.5km to a parking area. The campsite is an easy 1km along a flat, well maintained trail through a large swamp.

⊡ **FOOD. Claytons,** in the Trail Bay Centre, is the place to go for groceries. (☎885-2025. Open M-Th 9am-7pm, F 9am-9pm, Sa 9am-6pm, Su 10am-6pm.) **The Gumboot Garden Cafe ❷,** 1059 Roberts Creek Rd., 10km east of Sechelt in Roberts Creek, serves delicious meals with organic ingredients. Lunch and breakfast favorites include fries and miso gravy ($3.50) and Thai salad with chicken, salmon, or tofu ($6-7). A rotating dinner menu is uniformly excellent and always includes vegan options. (☎885-4216; www.thegumboot.com. Open M-W 8am-10pm, Su 8am-6pm.) In Sechelt, the **Old Boot Eatery ❸,** 5530 Wharf St., serves up generous portions of Italian food and local hospitality in a southwestern setting. Pasta entrees $10-15. (☎885-2727. Open summer M-Sa 11am-9:30pm; winter 11am-9pm.) **Wakefield Inn ❷,** on the highway (number 6529) 5min. west of Sechelt, dishes out pub fare and live music with a great view of the ocean and live music on weekends. Burgers $7-10, pints $5-6. (☎885-7666; www.ssc-biz.com/wakefieldinn. Music F-Sa 9pm-1am.)

◨ ⚲ **SIGHTS AND OUTDOOR ACTIVITIES.** The eight wilderness marine parks in the warm, calm waters of **Sechelt Inlet** make for fantastic sea kayaking and canoeing and offer free **camping ❶** along the shore. **Pedals & Paddles,** at Tillicum Bay Marina, 7km north of town (north of Porpoise Bay), rents vessels. (☎885-6440; www.pedalspaddles.com. Single kayaks $27 per 4hr., doubles $56; canoes $25. Full-day single kayaks $38, doubles $72; canoes $45.) The intersection of Sechelt and Salmon Inlets is home to the **S.S. Chaudiere artificial reef,** the third largest wreck dive in North America. Its warm waters (because of the unique tidal flows, the Sechelt inlet can reach 75°F in August) have earned it the title of the "No. 1 Shore Dive in North America" from Scuba Press. **Suncoast Dive Center** rents equipment, dispenses advice, gives lessons, and charters boats (☎740-8006; www.suncoastdiving.com. Regular rental $45 per day; full rental $75 per day; 1 day charter $95). On the other side of the peninsula, **Pender Harbor** offers equally impressive diving; Jacques Cousteau considered this site second only to the Red Sea.

Skookumchuck Narrows (from the Chinook words for "strong water," also known as **Sechelt Rapids**) is a popular destination by water or by land to view tidal rapids. During peak tidal flow, the water rushes at up to sixteen knots through the narrows. Waves standing 1.5m and enormous whirlpools form at peak tides. Visitors should plan around a tidal schedule (available at the trailhead or **Info center** ☎885-1036 or 877-633-2963)—the rapid only forms twice a day. To get there, drive 54km west to **Earl's Cove** and then 4km towards **Egmont** (about 1hr.). From the parking area, it's an easy, well-maintained 4km walk to four viewing sites.

Dakota Bowl and **Wilson Creek,** 4km east of Sechelt, have hiking and free cross-country skiing trails. From Sechelt, turn left on Field Rd. and drive 8km to the trailhead. Sechelt's lumber legacy has left it with an extensive system of former logging roads suitable for hiking and mountain biking. The intermediate **Chapman Creek Trail** passes under huge Douglas-firs en route to **Chapman Falls.** The trailhead is at the top of Havies Rd., 1km north of the Davis Bay Store on Hwy. 101, or access at Brookman Park on the highway. The **Suncoaster Trail** extends over 40km from **Homesite Creek,** near Halfmoon Bay northwest of Sechelt, through the foothills of the **Caren Range,** home of Canada's oldest trees (some as old as 1835 years).

Indoors, the **Sunshine Coast Arts Centre,** on Trail Ave. at Medusa St., showcases local talent in a log building. (☎885-5412; www.suncoastarts.com. Open July-Aug. Tu-Sa 10am-4pm, Su 1-4pm; Sept.-June W-Sa 11am-4pm, Su 1-4pm.

Admission by donation.) They also organize the Hackett Park Crafts Fair, held during the Sechelt's big event, the **Sunshine Coast Festival of the Written Arts,** devoted to showcasing Canadian authors through readings during the second weekend in August. Panels are held in the **botanical gardens** of the historic Rockwood Centre, and tickets ($12 per event, weekend pass $225) go early. (☎885-9631 or 800-565-9631; www.writersfestival.ca. Grounds open daily 8am-10pm.) The **Roberts Creek Community Hall** (☎886-3868 or 740-9616), on the corner of the highway and Roberts Creek Rd., attracts musicians throughout the summer, playing anything from reggae to Latin funk. Tickets ($10-20) are available at the **Roberts Creek General Store** (☎885-3400).

ALONG THE SEA TO SKY HWY.

Winding around the steep cliffs on the shore of Howe Sound from Horseshoe Bay to Squamish and then continuing inland to Whistler, the Sea to Sky Hwy. (Hwy. 99) is one of the loveliest, most dangerous, and best loved drives in British Columbia. Sinuous curves combine with brilliant vistas of the Sound and Tantalus Range. Be sure to check for periodic road closures; the highway is currently being widened between Vancouver and Whistler in preparation for the 2010 Winter Olympics.

VANCOUVER TO WHISTLER ☎604

Numerous provincial parks line the rocky drive to Whistler, providing excellent hiking and climbing opportunities. One worth stopping for is **Shannon Falls,** just off the highway, 3km past the mining museum. The park affords an easy 2min. walk (350m) to a spectacular view of a 335m waterfall, the third highest in BC. Steep but well-maintained trails from the falls make for difficult **day hiking** up to the three peaks of the **Stawamus Chief** (11km round-trip), the second-largest granite monolith in the world, which bares a 671m wall of solid granite. The face of the Chief is a popular destination for expert climbers. **Squamish Hostel (HI) ❷,** 38220 Hwy 99. immediately to the east of Hwy. 99 after entering town, is a common base for those tackling the local geography. In summer, the hostel is packed with wandering climbers, as the region between Squamish and Whistler boasts over 1300 excellent routes. (☎892-9240 or 800-449-8614 in BC. Shower, large kitchen, linen. $18, nonmembers $20; private rooms $60.) At **Eagle Run,** a viewing site 4km north of the hostel along the Squamish River, thousands of **bald eagles** make their winter home along the rivers and estuaries of Squamish Valley.

   Alice Lake Provincial Park has four lakes in the shadows of the Tantalus Mountains, providing excellent swimming and boating opportunities in the summer. A pristine **campground ❷** lies off of Hwy. 99, 13km north of Squamish. Reservations are a must in summer. (☎800-689-9025. Hot water, firewood, free showers. $22.)

   Nearby **Garibaldi Park** contains many stunning hikes around its dormant volcanic peaks, including a moderate 18km round-trip trail up to **Garibaldi Lake.** Nine primitive backcountry campgrounds provide further access to the backcountry, including Black Tusk and Cheakamus Lake, 25km north of Squamish. ($5 hiker/biker sites. Self-registration at the trailhead.) The **BC Parks District Office** in Alice Lake Park has trail maps. (☎898-3678. Open M-F 8:30am-4:30pm.) The **BC Forest Service office,** 42000 Loggers Ln., has maps of local logging roads and primitive campgrounds. (☎898-2100; www.for.gov.bc.ca/dsq. Open M-F 8:30am-4:30pm.)

   Brandywine Falls Provincial Park, 45km north of Squamish, offers an easy 10min. walk to the spectacular 70m **Brandywine Falls** and a 2hr. return hike to the **Cal-Cheak Suspension Bridge.** The park also has 15 cramped drive-in campsites ($14).

WHISTLER
☎ **604**

Whistler is among the top destinations in the world for skiers and snowboarders, and for good reason: over 7000 skiable acres make it the largest ski area on the continent. The mountains are part of Garibaldi Provincial Park, and it takes little effort to get off the beaten path. When the snow melts, bikes (the primary recreation on the summer slopes), boots, horses, and rafts fill in for skis, and bundled up ski junkies are replaced by heavily armored teenagers on mountain bikes. The town itself, with its quaint, uniform buildings, looks a bit like a theme park, and its establishments earn it a deserved reputation as an overpriced, outdoor mall.

ORIENTATION AND PRACTICAL INFORMATION

Whistler is 125km north of Vancouver on the beautiful (if dangerously twisty and perpetually under construction) Hwy. 99. Some travelers report that hitching a ride from Horseshoe Bay to Whistler is easy, but *Let's Go* does not recommend hitchhiking. Services are located in **Whistler Village,** most of which is pedestrian-only. **Whistler Creek,** 5km south on Hwy. 99, offers a smaller collection of accommodations and restaurants. The first thing to do upon arriving in town is obtain a map, free at the visitors center in the Village.

Buses: Whistler Sky to Ski (☎932-5031 or 800-661-8747; www.whistlerbus.com). To **Vancouver** from the **Village Bus Loop** (2½hr., 6 per day, $18). The Activity Centre sells tickets. The **Whistler Snow Shuttle** (☎888-224-6673; www.moosenetwork.com). The Snow Shuttle has door-to-door service from downtown Vancouver (not the airport) to anywhere in Whistler while the slopes are open, including the HI, which is somewhat of a walk from the bus loop. (2½hr., by reservation only, $25.)

Taxi: Whistler Taxi (☎932-3333; www.whistlertaxi.com).

Visitor Information: at the **Tourist Office, Chamber of Commerce,** and **Info Centre** (☎931-3977; www.mywhistler.com), by the bus loop on Gateway Dr., provide maps and booking services. Open daily 9am-6pm. Alternatively, call **Whistler Blackcomb** (☎932-3434 or 800-766-0449; www.whistlerblackcomb.com).

Laundry: Laundry at Nester's, 7009 Nester's Rd. (☎932-2960). Wash $2.25, dry $0.25 per 4min. Open 8:30am-8:30pm.

Weather Conditions: ☎866-218-9690.

Police: 4315 Blackcomb Way (☎932-3044), in the Village.

Telecare Crisis Line: ☎866-661-3311.

Medical Services: Whistler Health Care Center, 4380 Lorimer Rd. (☎932-4911).

Internet Access: Whistler Public Library (☎932-5564; www.whistlerlibrary.ca), between Main St. and Northlands Blvd. Free, but long waits. Open M-Tu and Th 10am-8pm, F-Su 10am-5pm.

Post Office: In the Market Place Mall, (☎932-5012). Open M-F 8:30am-5:30pm, Sa 8:30am-12:30pm. **Postal Code:** V0N 1B4.

ACCOMMODATIONS AND CAMPING

Whistler offers great hostels and campgrounds. The Forest Service office in Squamish (see p. 317) has maps for other camping options.

Whistler Hostel (HI), 5678 Alta Lake Rd. (☎932-5492). The Rainbow Park bus runs to the Village ($1.50). The hostel has a beautiful lakeside setting to go with its kitchen, piano, ski lockers, pool table, Internet, and sauna. Bikes $24 per day. Canoes free on Alta Lake. Check in 8-11am and 4-10pm. Only 32 beds, so reserve ahead. Bunks $20; nonmembers $24; under 13 half-price; under 6 free. Private rooms $10 extra. ❷

The Fireside Lodge, 2117 Nordic Dr. (☎932-4545; www.firesidelodge.org), 3km south of the Village. Caters to a more sedate crowd than most hostels. The spacious and spotless cabin, filled with funky, angular bedrooms, comes with lounge, sauna, coin laundry ($1.50 per load), an extensive and lively game room, storage (bring your own lock), mammoth kitchen, and free parking. 24 bunks. Check-in 3:30-8:30pm. Dec.-Apr. $30; May-Nov. $21. Private rooms from $80. ❷

The Southside Lodge Hostel, 2102 Lake Placid Rd. (☎932-3644; www.snowboardwhistler.com) on Hwy. 99 by the Husky gas station 4km south of the village. Less than 200m from the Whistler Creek lifts, the Southside features in-room washrooms, televisions, and refrigerators. A shared full kitchen is also available. Reception open 4-6pm. Rooms Dec.-Apr. $35; May-Nov. $25. Private rooms $60. ❸

Shoestring Lodge, 7124 Nancy Greene Dr. (☎932-3338; www.shoestringlodge.com), 1km north of the Village. Cable, private bath, laundry, and Internet. The strip club and pub next door can lead to late-night ruckus outside. Free shuttle to slopes Dec.-Apr. Check-in 4pm, check-out 11am. Dec.-Apr. 4-person dorm $24-31; doubles $80-125. Apr.-Dec. $16-19/$50-75. ❸

FOOD

Cheap food is scarce in the Village with the exception of the **IGA** supermarket in the Village North. (☎938-2850. Open daily 9am-9pm.) Pubs, prolific in the Village, are the most affordable places to find food (meals usually around $10, pint $5).

The Wildwood Bistro, 4500 Northlands Blvd. (☎935-4077; www.wildwoodrestaurants.ca) at the tennis club. Despite its yuppie name and setting, the Wildwood is very affordable by Whistler standards. Serves breakfast until 3pm (2 eggs, sausage, and homefries $6) and large sandwiches ($6-9) in the afternoons. Daily pint specials (usually around $3.50). Open daily 7am-9pm. ❷

Hoz's Pub, 2129 Lake Placid Rd. (☎932-5940; www.hozpub.com). Hoz's features burgers ($7-10), and nightly specials on more advanced pub food, like pasta and grilled chicken ($10-15). Pints $5-7. Open daily 11am-midnight. ❷

Moguls Coffee House, 4208 Village Square (☎932-4845). Right on the Village Square, this tasty late-night option serves up delectable home-baked goods ($2-3) and sandwiches ($6-8). Open daily 6:30am-2:30am. ❷

OUTDOOR ACTIVITIES

WINTER SPORTS. Thirty-three lifts (15 of them high-speed), three glaciers, over 200 marked trails, a mile (1609m) of vertical drop, and unreal scenery make **Whistler Blackcomb** a top destination for skiing and snowboarding. Parking and lift access for this behemoth are available at six points, but Whistler Creekside offers the shortest lines and the closest access for those coming from Vancouver. A **lift ticket** is good for both mountains and, depending on the time of year, costs $71 per day with better deals for longer trips. (☎932-3434 or 800-766-0449; www.whistlerblackcomb.com.) A **Fresh Tracks** upgrade ($15), available every morning at 7am, provides a basic breakfast in the mountaintop lodge on Blackcomb along with the chance to begin skiing as soon as the ski patrol has finished avalanche control. **Cheap tickets** ($61) are often available at 7-Elevens in Vancouver, and rates are sometimes cheaper (around $45) early or late in the season. Glacier skiing is open on Blackcomb until August ($45). While Whistler offers amazing alpine terrain and gorgeous bowls, many **snowboarders** prefer Blackcomb for its windlips, natural quarter-pipes, and 16-acre terrain park. Endless **backcountry skiing** is accessible from resort lifts and in Garibaldi Park's **Diamond Head** area. Equipment rentals are available through Whistler Blackcomb or **Affinity Sports,** located next to Moguls Coffee House on the Village Square (☎932-6611; www.affinityrentals.com).

BRITISH COLUMBIA

The BC Parks office in Alice Lake Park (p. 317) has avalanche info. Avalanches kill people every year, and there are no patrols outside resort boundaries. Always file trip plans and stay within the limits of your experience.

SUMMER ACTIVITIES. While skiing is God in Whistler and lasts until August on the glaciers, life goes on in the summer as the **Whistler Gondola** (M-F and Su 10am-5pm, Sa 10am-8pm; $25) continues to whisk sightseers to the top of the mountain, providing access to the resort's extensive **hiking trails,** and Fitzsimmons and Garbanzo Lifts do the hard work for bikers, who enjoy the extensive **mountain bike park.** ($39, open M-Tu, Th, and Su 10am-5pm, W, F, and Sa 10am-8pm.) There are also many free mountain biking trails in the area outside the resort. Hiking trails tend to be short day hikes, with lengths ranging from 20min. to 5-6hr. and most trails taking less than an hour to complete. **Wedge Rafting** makes regular guided **whitewater rafting** trips down four area rivers. (☎888-932-5899; www.wedgerafting.com. $51-110, depending on the river.) **Zip-trek** offers a unique **eco-tour** of the rainforest at Whistler's base via a series of zip-lines and platforms suspended from the trees. (☎935-0001; www.zip-trek.com. Tickets sold inside Carleton Lodge, in Whistler Village. $98, ages 65 and older $78, 15 and under $78, family 4-pack $299.) **Canadian All-Terrain Adventures,** also in Carleton Lodge, gives 2-4hr. **off-road tours** around the Whistler area. (☎938-1616; www.canadiansnowmobile.com. $59-89).

NORTH OF WHISTLER

■ **JOFFRE LAKES PROVINCIAL PARK.** For a fantastic **day hike** 65km north of Whistler, a rugged trail climbs 400 meters, occasionally through moraine, to the three glacially-fed **Joffre Lakes.** The trail is 11km round-trip and affords spectacular views of **Joffre Peak, Slalok Mountain,** and **Tzsi Glacier.** There are primitive campsites for backpackers at the upper lake. (No water, no campfires. 5.5km from the trailhead.) Joffre Lakes is accessible only in summer. Look for the entrance 32km north of Pemberton.

■ **STEIN VALLEY PROVINCIAL PARK.** Stein Valley attracts backpackers with its arid, sunny weather and well-maintained walk-in campsites every 4km in the lower valley. Wide tracts of undeveloped wilderness stretch throughout the upper valley. The easy-to-follow trail in climbs along the roaring Stein River for 20km before turning backpackers loose into an unlimited, unmaintained, unpatrolled backcountry. **Camping ❶** is free. To get to Stein Valley from Lytton, cross the Fraser River at the reaction ferry (5min., crossings on demand daily 6am-10pm, free) and drive 8km up the dirt road on the other side before turning left on Stein Valley Rd. The park is at the end of the road. The **Visitors Centre,** 400 Fraser St., in nearby Lytton provides a free trail guide, good for the lower valley, and sells the topographical maps ($9) necessary for an upper-valley expedition. (☎455-2523. Open daily July and Aug. 9am-5pm; Sept.-Jun. 10am-4pm.) Backpackers can stock up on supplies at the **Super Foods,** 208 Main St. (Open M-Sa 9am-6pm, Su 10am-4pm.) Enjoy a last sandwich ($4-6) in civilization at the **Aciaia Leaf Cafe ❶,** 437 Main St. (☎455-2626. Open M-W 6:30am-6pm, Th-F 6:30am-8pm, Sa noon-6pm.)

NAIRN FALLS PROVINCIAL PARK. Thirty kilometers north of Whistler on Hwy. 99, Nairn offers clean but close-spaced **campsites ❶** at the head of the easy 3km round-trip trail to the spectacular Nairn Falls. (Sites $14. Campground open mid-May to Sept. Firewood available for purchase.)

LILLOOET. Little traffic continues north along Hwy. 99 and the drive is eerily remote, passing through the upper Fraser River Canyon, in the process moving from temperate rain forest into a much more arid climate. **Lillooet** ("BC's Little Nugget"), 135km north of Whistler, was originally the starting point for the historic **Cariboo Gold Rush Wagon Trail,** which led 100,000 gold-crazed miners north to Barkerville between 1862 and 1870. The town is small but rich in history. The **Chamber of Commerce** (☎ 256-4364; www.lillooetchamberofcommerce.com) will help you find a place to crash. You can also camp for free next to the beautiful Seton Lake in the **BC Hydro Seton Lake Campground ❶** on Hwy. 99, 3km south of Lillooet. (Gate open 7am-10pm. Firewood available.) In the last weekend in July, the town celebrates its heritage during **Gold Rush Days** with a host of events including a staged train robbery, mock trial, and execution.

FARTHER NORTH. From Lillooet, Hwy. 99 meanders north another 50km, snaking with the Fraser River until it meets Hwy. 97 11km north of **Cache Creek.** The weary can break halfway for trout fishing and swimming in **Crown Lake** beneath the red limestone cliffs of the Pavilion Mountains at **Marble Canyon Provincial Park ❶.** The sites are squeezed in right on the edge of the lake, which is stocked with trout. ($14. Firewood $5.50.)

MARBLE RANGE PROVINCIAL PARK. Marble Range provides a true wilderness experience. The park is "undeveloped" meaning that there are no signs, no maintained trails or campgrounds, no access to water, potable or treatable—and no rangers to find you if something goes wrong. But for those willing to make the compass-guided trek, the alpine meadows and limestone cliffs are spectacular. Another option is to take day trips into the Marble Range while camping from a car. **Downing Lake Provincial Park ❶** on the Clinton-Pavillion Rd., just past the Jesmond intersection, less than 5 mi. from Marble Range, offers lakeside primitive camping for $14. To get to Marble Range from Clinton, take the Clinton-Pavillion Rd. for 8km, turn right on the unpaved Jesmond Rd. for 5km, turn right on an unmaintained, unmarked mining road (look for the back of its stop sign) off of which the unmarked trailheads originate by piles of rocks. The **BC Forest Service** office, 42,000 Loggers Ln., has maps of local logging roads. (☎ 898-2100; www.for.gov.bc.ca/dsq. Open M-F 8:30am-4:30pm.)

VANCOUVER ISLAND

Vancouver Island stretches almost 500km along continental Canada's southwest coast and is one of only two points in Canada extending south of the 49th parallel. The Kwagiulth, Nootka, and Coastal Salish shared the island for thousands of years until Captain Cook's discovery of Nootka Sound in 1778 triggered European exploration and infiltration. The current culture of Vancouver Island bespeaks its hybrid heritage, presenting a curious blend of totems and afternoon teas. The cultural and administrative center is Victoria, BC's capital, on its southernmost tip.

The Trans-Canada (Hwy. 1) leads north from Victoria to Nanaimo, the transportation hub of the island's central region. Once you get out of Victoria and Nanaimo, wilderness takes over and towns shrink in size, creating a haven for hikers, kayakers, and mountaineers. Pacific Rim National Park Reserve, on the island's west coast, offers some of the most rugged and outstanding hiking in North America. On the northern third of the island, crumpets give way to clamburgers, and 4x4 pickups and logging caravans prowl dirt roads.

BRITISH COLUMBIA

VICTORIA   ☎ 250

Although many tourist operations would have you believe that Victoria fell off Great Britain in a neat little chunk, its high tea tradition actually began in the 1950s to draw American tourists. Before the invasion of tea, Fort Victoria, founded in 1843, was a fur trading post and supply center for the Hudson Bay Company. But the discovery of gold in the Fraser River Canyon pushed it into the fast lane in 1858, bringing international trade and the requisite frontier bars and brothels. The government soon followed. Victoria became the capital in 1868.

Clean, polite, and tourist-friendly, Victoria is a homier alternative to cosmopolitan Vancouver. Its namesake British monarch and her era of morals and furniture aside, Victoria is a city of diverse origins and interests. Galleries selling native arts operate alongside new-age bookstores, tourist traps, funky record stores and pawn shops. Double-decker bus tours motor by English pubs while bike-taxis pedal past the markets, museums, and stores that make up the rest of downtown. Victoria also lies within easy striking distance of the rest of Vancouver Island's "outdoor paradise."

▐ TRANSPORTATION

The **Trans-Canada Highway** (Hwy. 1) runs north to Nanaimo, where it becomes Highway 19, stretching north to the rest of Vancouver Island. The **West Coast Highway** (Hwy. 14) heads west to Port Renfrew and the West Coast Trail unit of Pacific Rim National Park Reserve. The **Pat Bay Highway** (Hwy. 17) runs north from Victoria to Swartz Bay ferry terminal and the airport, 30min. from downtown. Driving in Victoria is relatively easy, but parking downtown is difficult and expensive. Victoria surrounds the Inner Harbour; the main north-south thoroughfares downtown are **Government Street** and **Douglas Street.** To the north, Douglas St. becomes Hwy. 1. **Blanshard Street,** one block to the east, becomes Hwy. 17.

Flights: Victoria International Airport (☎953-7533; www.cyyj.ca.com) 22km north of Victoria off Hwy. 17. Flights to: **Vancouver** (20 per day); **Seattle** (10 per day); **Calgary** (5 per day); and **Toronto** (3 per day). The **Akal Airporter** (☎386-2525) runs between the airport and Victoria daily 4am-midnight (30min; shuttle stops every 30 min.; $14-15). Airport code: YYJ.

Trains: E&N Railway, 450 Pandora St. (schedule ☎383-4324, general info and tickets 800-561-8630), near the Inner Harbour at the Johnson St. Bridge. 10% senior discount. Daily service to **Courtenay** (4½hr.; $44, with ISIC $29) and **Nanaimo** (2½hr.; $23, with ISIC $15).

Buses: Gray Line of Victoria, 700 Douglas St. (☎385-4411 or 800-318-0818), at Belleville St., and its affiliates, **Pacific Coach Lines** and **Island Coach Lines,** connect most points on the island. To: **Nanaimo** (2½hr., 6 per day, $19), **Port Hardy** (9hr., 1-2 per day, $95), and **Vancouver** (3½hr., 8-14 per day, $31). Counter open 7am-8pm.

Ferries: Bus #70 runs between downtown and the Swartz Bay and Sidney terminals ($2.75).

BC Ferries (☎888-223-3779; www.bcferries.com). Service to all **Gulf Islands** (see p. 330). Ferries depart **Swartz Bay** to Vancouver's **Tsawwassen** ferry terminal (1½hr.; 8-16 per day; $8.50-11, bikes $2.50, car and driver $26-36). **Washington State Ferries** (☎656-1831, in the US 888-808-7977; www.wsdot.wa.gov/ferries) depart from **Sidney** to **Anacortes, WA.** A ticket to Anacortes allows free stopovers along the eastward route, including the **San Juan Islands** (mid-June to mid-Sept. 2 per day, mid-Sept. to mid-June 1 per day; US$14, bike US$4-6, car with driver US$38-47. Open 7am-10pm.

Victoria Clipper, 254 Belleville St. (☎800-888-2535; www.victoriaclipper.com), runs passenger ferries direct to **Seattle** (2-3hr.; May-Sept. 2-4 per day, Oct.-Apr. 1 per day; US$64-79, ages 65 and older US$58-73, 1-11 US$32-35).

Vancouver Island

TO BELLA COOLA,
PRINCE RUPERT,
ALASKA

Cape Scott
Prov. Park

Holberg

Quatsino
Sound

Port
Hardy

Brooks
Bay

Coal
Harbour

Brooks Peninsula
Marine Park

Port
Alice

Port
McNeill

Malcolm
Island   Sointula

Kyuquot

Nimpkish
Lake

Alert
Bay

Kyuquot
Sound

Fair
Harbour

Telegraph
Cove

Gilford
Island

Esperanza
Inlet

Zeballos

Woss
Lake   Woss

W Cracroft
Island

Nootka
Island

Tahsis

Schoen
Lake
Prov. Park

Sayward

Hardwicke
Island

PACIFIC
OCEAN

Yuquot

Nootka

Nootka
Sound

(19)

W Thurlow Island

E Thurlow Island
Sonora Island

Gold
River

(28)

Hot Springs Cove

Campbell
Lake

Northern
Gulf
Islands

Strathcona
Prov. Park

Campbell
River

Quadra
Island

W Redonda
Island

Clayoquot
Sound

Mt. Washington
(1588m)

(19)

Cortes
Island

Vargas
Island

(19A)

E Redonda
Island

Tofino

Courtenay

Comox

(101)

Long
Beach

Comox
Lake

Cumberland

Powell
River

Buckley
Bay

Denman
Island

Pacific Rim Hwy

Stamp Falls
Prov. Park

(4)

Ucluelet

(19)

Hornby
Island

Texada
Island

Saltery
Bay

Broken Group
Islands

Port
Alberni

(19A)

Barkley
Sound

Qualicum
Beach

Nelson
Island

Bamfield

Alberni Inlet

Coombs

Parksville

Lasqueti
Island

Egmont

(101)

Sechelt
Peninsula

Pacific Rim National Park Reserve

Nitinat

(19)

Nanaimo

Sechelt

Clo-oose

Cowichan
Lake

Gabriola
Island

Gibsons

CANADA
USA

Mesachie
Lake

Lake
Cowichan

Valdes
Island

Horseshoe
Bay

Juan de Fuca
Prov. Park

Port
Renfrew

Chemainus

(18)

Crofton

Southern
Gulf
Islands

Galiano
Island

Duncan

West Coast Hwy

(14)

Sooke

Sidney/   Salt Spring
Swartz   Island
Bay

(99)   (91)

(17)   (99A)

Mayne
Island

Tsawwassen

Sooke Potholes
Prov. Park

(17)

Saturna
Island

Vancouver

Strait of Georgia

Johnstone Strait

Queen Charlotte Strait

Island Hwy

COAST MOUNTAINS

ISLAND   MOUNTAINS

VANCOUVER

Strait of Juan de Fuca

Pender
Islands

CANADA
USA

WASHINGTON

Victoria

0   20 kilometers
0   20 miles

------- Unpaved Road
········· West Coast Trail

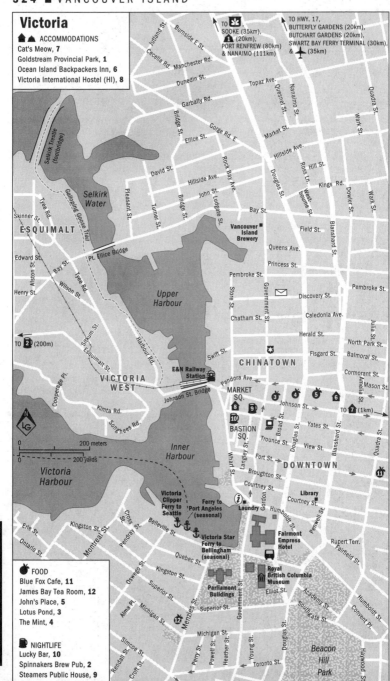

Victoria

🏠▲ ACCOMMODATIONS

Cat's Meow, **7**
Goldstream Provincial Park, **1**
Ocean Island Backpackers Inn, **6**
Victoria International Hostel (HI), **8**

TO 🏕 ,
SOOKE (35km),
🏕 (20km),
PORT RENFREW (80km)
& NANAIMO (111km)

TO HWY. 17,
BUTTERFLY GARDENS (20km),
BUTCHART GARDENS (20km),
SWARTZ BAY FERRY TERMINAL (30km),
& ✈ (35km)

Lutland St.
Cecelia Rd.
Burnside E. St.
Manchester Rd.
Dunedin St.
Topaz Ave.
Quadra St.
Garbally Rd.
Bridge St.
Gorge Rd. E
Quesnel St.
Nanaimo St.
Wark St.
Selkirk Trestle (footbridge)
David St.
Ellice St.
Rock Bay Ave.
Market St.
Hillside Ave.
Ross Ln.
Hill St.
Kings Rd.
Dowler St.
Wark St.
Selkirk Water
Hillside Ave.
John St.
Ludgate St.
Douglas St.
West-bourne St.
Galloping Goose Trail
Tyee Rd.
Pleasant St.
Turner St.
Bridge St.
Bay St.
Skinner St.
ESQUIMALT
Vancouver Island Brewery ■
Field St.
Blanshard St.
Edward St.
Bay St.
Tyee Rd.
Pt. Ellice Bridge
Upper Harbour
Queens Ave.
Princess Ave.
Store St.
Government St.
Pembroke St.
Pembroke St.
Henry St.
Alston St.
Wilson St.
Discovery St.
📫
Skinner St.
TO 2 (200m)
Stadium St.
Esquimalt St.
Harbour Rd.
Chatham St.
Caledonia Ave.
Julia St.
Cooperace Pl.
VICTORIA WEST
E&N Railway Station
Swift St.
Herald St.
Fisgard St.
North Park St.
Balmoral St.
Kimta Rd.
Songhees Rd.
Pandora Ave.
CHINATOWN
🏮
Cormorant St.
Amelia St.
Mason St.
Johnson St.
MARKET SQ.
3
4
5
6
TO 7 (1km)
Quadra St.
Johnson St. Bridge
8
9
Broad St.
Yates St.
Blanshard St.
BASTION SQ.
Trounce St.
View St.
0   200 meters
0   200 yards
Victoria Harbour
Inner Harbour
Wharf St.
Langley St.
Fort St.
DOWNTOWN
11
N
Kingston St.
Cross St.
Belleville St.
Victoria Clipper Ferry to Seattle
Ferry to Port Angeles (seasonal)
Broughton St.
Courtney St.
Gordon
ℹ
Laundry
Courtney St.
Library
Penwell St.
Erie St.
Pendray St.
Montreal St.
Victoria Star Ferry to Bellingham (seasonal)
Humboldt St.
Fairmont Empress Hotel
Rupert Terr.
Ontario St.
Quebec St.
Kingston St.
Oswego St.
Superior St.
🚌
Royal British Columbia Museum
Fairfield Rd.
Simcoe St.
Michigan St.
Menzies St.
Parliament Buildings
Government St.
Elliot St.
Academy St.
Humboldt St.
Convent Pl.
Haywood St.
Alma Pl.
12
Michigan St.
Superior St.
Douglas St.
Southgate St.
Rendall St.
Croft St.
Simcoe St.
Perry St.
Powell St.
Heather St.
Young St.
Toronto St.
Beacon Hill Park

🍴 FOOD
Blue Fox Cafe, **11**
James Bay Tea Room, **12**
John's Place, **5**
Lotus Pond, **3**
The Mint, **4**

🍸 NIGHTLIFE
Lucky Bar, **10**
Spinnakers Brew Pub, **2**
Steamers Public House, **9**

BRITISH COLUMBIA

Black Ball Transport, 430 Belleville St. (☎386-2202; www.northolympic.com/coho), runs to **Port Angeles, WA** (1½hr.; mid-May to mid-Oct. 4 per day; Oct.-Dec. and mid-Mar. to mid-May 2 per day; US$9, car and driver US$35, ages 5-11 US$4.50, bicycle US$4).

Public Transportation: BC Transit (☎382-6161; www.bctransit.com). City bus service with connections at the corner of Douglas and Yates St. Single-zone travel $2; multi-zone (north to Swartz Bay, Sidney, and Butchart Gardens) $2.75; ages 65 and older or 6-18 $1.25/$2; under 6 free. Day passes ($6, ages 65 and older or 6-18 $4) and a free *Rider's Guide* are available at the library, from any driver, or with maps at Tourism Victoria. **Disability Services** for local transit (☎727-7811) is open M-Th and Su 8am-10pm, F-Sa 8am-midnight.

Car Rental: Island Auto Rentals, 850 Johnson St. (☎384-4881) at Quadra. Starting at $20 per day, plus $0.12 per km after 100km. Insurance $13. 21 and over. Chains with comparable rates are located at the bottom of Douglas St. near the Museum.

Taxis: Victoria Taxi (☎383-7111; www.victoriataxi.com) Base rate $2.50, $1.39 per km, $9 per 15 min. in traffic. 24hr.

⚡ PRACTICAL INFORMATION

Tourist Office: 812 Wharf St. (☎953-2033), at Government St. Also a Ticketmaster outlet. Open July-Aug. daily 8:30am-6:30pm; Aug.-July 9am-5pm.

Tours: Grayline, 700 Douglas St. (☎388-6539 or 800-663-8390; www.victoriatours.com). Runs several double-decker bus tours (from $19) through different parts of the city.

Equipment Rental: Cycle BC Rentals, 747 Douglas St. (☎885-2453; www.cyclebc.ca), guarantees the best prices in town. Bikes from $6 per hr., $19 per day; scooters $16 per hr., $45 per day. Motorcycles available. Look for coupons at hostels and hotels. Open daily summer 9am-6:30pm, winter 9am-5pm. **Island Boat Rentals,** 811 Wharf St. (☎995-1661), is opposite the visitors center. Rowboats and single kayaks $15 per hr., doubles $25 per hr., canoes $20 per day. Open daily mid-May to Sept. 10am-8pm; Sept. to mid-May 9am-5pm.

Laundromat and Showers: Oceanside Gifts, 102-812 Wharf St. (☎380-1777). Wash $1.25, dry $1. Showers $1 per 5min. Open daily 7am-9:30pm

Police: 850 Caledonia (☎995-7654), at Quadra St.

Crisis Line: ☎386-6323. 24hr.

Pharmacy: Shoppers Drug Mart, 1222 Douglas St. (☎381-4321). Open M-F 7am-8pm, Sa 9am-7pm, Su 9am-6pm.

Hospital: Royal Jubilee, 1900 Fort St. (☎370-8000).

Internet Access: A free guest pass can be obtained at the **library,** 735 Broughton St. (☎382-7241; www.gvpl.ca). Open M, W, and F-Sa 9am-6pm, Tu and Th 9am-9pm. **Stain Cafe,** 609 Yates St. (☎382-3552; www.staincafe.com), provides access for $3 per hr. Open daily 9:30am-10pm.

Post Office: 621 Discovery St. (☎963-1350). Open M-F 8am-6pm. **Postal Code:** V8W 2L9.

🏠 🏕 ACCOMMODATIONS AND CAMPING

Victoria has an ample supply of budget accommodations. A number of flavorful hostels and B&B-hostel hybrids make a night in Victoria a pleasant experience; many hostels also have discount deals with local expedition and equipment rental companies. More than a dozen campgrounds and RV parks lie in the greater Victoria area. It's wise to make reservations ahead of time in the summer.

■ **Ocean Island Backpackers Inn,** 791 Pandora St. (☎385-1788 or 888-888-4180; www.oceanisland.com), downtown. This colorful hostel boasts a better lounge than many clubs, a fantastic staff, and accommodations comparable to many hotels. Undoubtedly one of the finest urban hostels in Canada. The Victoria Guide on their website is a great and in depth guide to some of the more out of the way places in the city. Pay e-mail and laundry. Limited parking, $5. Reception 24 hr. Check-in after 2pm. Depending on the time of year, dorms, $18-23, students and HI members $18-20; singles $25-36; doubles $22-56. ❷

Victoria International Hostel (HI), 516 Yates St. (☎385-4511), downtown. This quiet, centrally-located hostel has big, spotless barracks-style dorms; foosball; pool; video games; a TV room; and a very helpful info desk. Kitchen, free linen. Storage $3 per week. Provides laundry; wash $2, dry $1.50. Reception 24hr. Dorms July-Sept. $20, nonmembers $24; private rooms $44-48. ❷

The Cat's Meow, 1316 Grant St. (☎595-8878). Take bus #22 to Victoria High School at Fernwood and Grant St. 3 blocks from downtown. This mini-hostel earns its name with quiet dorms, friendly conversation, and a welcoming feline by the name of Egypt. Continental breakfast included. Coin-op laundry, free street parking, discounts on kayaking and whale watching. Dorms $20; private rooms $40-47. ❷

Goldstream Provincial Park, 2930 Trans-Canada Hwy. (☎391-2300; reservations ☎800-689-9025; www.discovercamping.ca), 20km northwest of Victoria. Riverside area with day hikes and swimming. Toilets, firewood. Follow the trail on the other side of the highway to a railway trestle in the woods. Gates closed 11pm-7am. 167 gorgeous, gravelly sites, $20. ❷

◗ FOOD

A diverse array of food awaits in Victoria, if you know where to go. Many **Government Street** and **Wharf Street** restaurants raise their prices for summer tourists. **Chinatown** offers many budget options and extends from Fisgard and Government St. to the northwest. Coffee shops can be found on every corner. Cook St. Village, between McKenzie and Park Sts., offers an eclectic mix of creative restaurants. **Fisherman's Wharf,** at the end of Erie St., has the day's catch. For groceries try **The Market on Yates,** 903 Yates St. (☎381-6000. Open daily 7am-11pm.)

■ **John's Place,** 722 Pandora Ave. (☎389-0711), between Douglas and Blanshard St. Dishing up Canadian fare with Mediterranean flair and a Thai twist. Try your hand at an appallingly large dinner (entrees $10-15) in the presence of greatness (the walls are adorned with the images and autographs of some of North America's finest actors, athletes, and musicians). Extra selections on Thai night (M) and pierogi night (W). Open M-Th 7am-9pm, F 7am-10pm, Sa 8am-4pm and 5-10pm, Su 8am-4pm and 5-9pm. ❸

The Mint, 1414 Douglas St. (☎386-6468) One of the few places you can visit to get a filling meal after a night on the town, The Mint defies traditional late-night eatery expectations with its excellent food, trendy decor, and occasional live music. Vegetarian options abound. Entrees from $9-17. Open daily 5:30pm-2am. ❸

Blue Fox Cafe, 101-919 Fort St. (☎380-1683). Walk 3 blocks up Fort. St. from Douglas St. A local favorite. Breakfast all day, every day; specials until 11am for under $6. Try the "Bubble and Squeak," sautéed veggies and panfries drowned in cheese and baked ($8.25). Open M-F 7:30am-4pm, Sa 9am-4pm, Su 9am-3pm. ❷

James Bay Tea Room & Restaurant, 332 Menzies St. (☎382-8282) behind the Parliament Buildings. A trip to Victoria is improper without a spot of tea. The sandwiches and pastries that accompany tea service ($10) or high tea on Sunday ($14) are a lower-key version of high tea served at the Empress Hotel. Open M-Sa 7am-5pm, Su 8am-5pm. ❸

BRITISH COLUMBIA

Lotus Pond, 617 Johnson St. (☎380-9293). Nestled between Broad and Government St. this vegan establishment serves up affordable and healthy fare. The buffet lunches (pay by weight; half price after 2:30) are a great bargain. Also offers free books on Buddhism. Open Tu-Sa 11am-3pm and 5-9pm, Su 12-3pm and 5-8:30pm. ❷

🔘 SIGHTS

If you don't mind becoming one with the flocks of tourists heading to the shores of Victoria, wander along the **Inner Harbor,** where you can admire street performers on the Causeway or watch the sun set behind neighboring islands.

🔲 ROYAL BRITISH COLUMBIA MUSEUM. You can easily spend a day perusing the thorough exhibits on the biological, geological, and cultural history of the province, including a number of interactive exhibits for all ages. The First Nation exhibit features a totem room and an immense collection of traditional native art. The museum's **National Geographic IMAX Theater** runs the latest action documentaries on a six-story screen. **Thunderbird Park** and its many totems loom behind the museum. *(675 Belleville St. ☎356-7226; www.royalmuseum.bc.ca. Open daily 9am-5pm. $11; students, ages 65 and older or 6-18 $7.70, 6 and under free. IMAX 9am-9pm with museum entrance $19, students $18, ages 65 and older or 6-18 $16, 6 and under $5.*

🔲 BUTCHART GARDENS. The elaborate and world-famous Butchart Gardens, founded by Robert P.'s cement-pouring fortune, sprawl across 50 acres 21km north of Victoria off Hwy. 17. Immaculate landscaping includes the magnificent **Sunken Garden** (a former limestone quarry), the Rose Garden, Japanese and Italian gardens, and fountains. The gardens sparkle with live entertainment and lights at night. Outstanding fireworks on Saturday evenings in July and August draw out the locals. *(Bus #75 Central Saanich runs from downtown at Douglas and Pandora. ($2.75, 1hr.) The Gray Line (☎388-6539) runs a round-trip, direct package including admission ($55, ages 12-18 $44, 5-11 $20; 35min. each way). ☎652-5256 or 866-652-4422; www.butchartgardens.com. Open daily mid-June to Aug. 9am-10:30pm. $21, ages 13-17 $11, 5-12 $2, under 5 free. Low-season hours vary greatly; call ahead for schedule.*

BUTTERFLY GARDENS. Close to the Butchart Gardens, this enclosure devoted to winged insects is maintained at 20-28°C (80-85°F) and 80% relative humidity. Hundreds of specimens of over 35 species float around visitors' heads alongside (non-butterfly-eating) canaries, finches, and cockatiels, while caterpillars munch on the profusion of tropical plants

THE BIG SPLURGE

A SPOT OF TEA

For nearly a century, the grand Fairmont-Empress Hotel has hosted formal afternoon tea, one of England's oldest and most famous traditions. While tea, including many afternoon tea services, can be found throughout Victoria, none have the history nor the majesty of high tea at the Empress. The menu includes fresh fruit topped with Chantilly cream, small tea sandwiches in flavors like carrot and ginger, traditional English scones, a wide selection of freshly prepared pastries, and their "Tea at The Empress" blend, whose ingredients are only known to a group of select insiders.

The menu is, however, only part of the experience. The gorgeous tea lobby is a sight in and of itself, and the dress code—smart casual; shorts, ripped or torn jeans, tank tops, sleeveless shirts, "short" shorts or cut-offs, and running shoes are all forbidden—lends a regal air to the services. The hotel has played host to the rich and famous throughout the centuries, including Edward Prince of Wales, Katherine Hepburn, and Barbra Streisand. The afternoon tea service allows you to join their ranks, even if for just an hour.

The Empress Hotel, 721 Government St. Reservations are required; call ☎389-2727; www.fairmont.com/empress. Afternoon tea service $45-50. Up to 5 seatings from noon-5pm.

thriving in the moist environment. The gardens successfully breed giant Atlas moths, which, with a wingspan of up to 30cm (1 ft.), are the largest species of moth in the world. Perhaps most appealing to the eye, however, are the iridescent hues of the famous morpho butterflies that live the good life in the gardens. *(1461 Benvenuto Ave. ☎652-3822 or 877-722-0272; www.butterflygardens.com. Open daily Mar. to early May and late Sept.-Oct. 9:30am-4:30pm; early May to late Sept. 9am-5:30pm. $6.50, students and ages 65 and over $5.50, 5-12 $3.50.)*

VANCOUVER ISLAND BREWERY. After a few days of hiking, biking, and museum-visiting, a tour of the **Vancouver Island Brewery** is a great way to unwind. The 1hr. tour has 20min. of touring and 40min. of drinking. Or you can just visit the store. *(2330 Government St. ☎361-0007; www.vanislandbrewery.com. 19+. Store open 9am-6pm M-Sa. 1hr. tours F-Sa 3pm year round, more frequent June-Sept. Call for a schedule. $6 for four 4 oz. samples and souvenir pint glass.)*

🎭 ENTERTAINMENT

The **Victoria Symphony Society,** 846 Broughton St. (☎385-6515; www.victoriasymphony.bc.ca), performs regularly under conductor Tania Miller. The highlight of the season is the **Symphony Splash** every BC Day, played on a barge in Inner Harbour. The performance concludes with fireworks and usually draws 50,000 listeners (first Su in Aug.; free). For the last 10 days of June, Victoria bops to **JazzFest.** (☎388-4423; www.vicjazz.bc.ca. Concerts free-$40) **Folkfest** hosts multicultural entertainment with food and dancing at Market Square and Ship's Point. (☎388-4728; www.icafolkfest.com. Late June to early July. Most events $6.)

To experience the cheapest movies available, visit **The Roxy,** 2657 Quadra St., an old airplane hangar turned movie theater. (☎382-3370. $5, seniors $2.50; Tu $2.50.) For off-beat and foreign films, head to the **University of Victoria's Cinecenta** in the Student Union. (☎721-8365; www.cinecenta.com. Bus #4, 26, 11, or 14. $6.75, seniors and students $4.75, Sa-Su matinees $3.75.) July and August bring **free outdoor screenings** of classic movies to the **Boardwalk Restaurant** at the Ocean Pointe Resort on Monday and Tuesday at dusk. Those who wish can reserve at the restaurant and get a table at the front, a good meal (expensive), and free blankets (☎360-5889). The Ocean Pointe Resort is the first right after crossing the blue Johnson St. bridge. Parking and screen are around the back to the right. In June, **Phoenix Theatre** (☎721-8000; www.finearts.uvic.ca/theatre/season) at UVIC, puts on term-time live theater performances ($19-20).

🍺 NIGHTLIFE

English pubs, watering holes and clubs abound throughout town. Live music is available practically every night, and the free weekly Monday Magazine, out Wednesdays and available at hostels, hotels, and most restaurants will keep you updated on who's playing when and where.

Steamers Public House, 570 Yates St. (☎381-4340). Locals and visitors alike dance nightly to live music, from world-beat Celtic to funk. The best Su entertainment in town. Open stage M, jazz night Tu. Cover $3-5 at night, free M-Tu. Open M-Tu 11:30am-1am, W-Su 11:30am-2am.

Spinnakers Brew Pub, 308 Catherine St. (☎384-6613; www.spinnakers.com). Take the Johnson St. bridge from downtown and walk 10min. down Esquimalt Rd., or stick to the waterfront and you'll walk right by it. The oldest brew pub in Canada is a great place to shoot pool and boasts the best view of the Inner Harbor. Beer will run you $3.50-6. Open daily 11am-11pm.

Lucky Bar, 517 Yates St. (☎382-5825; www.luckybar.ca) Across the street from the Victoria International Hostel, this small club has live music almost every night, bringing in some good young rock groups. Beer $5, cover $3-5. Doors open at 9pm most nights.

OUTDOOR ACTIVITIES

The flowering oasis of **Beacon Hill Park,** off Douglas St. south of the Inner Harbour, pleases walkers, bikers, and the picnic-inclined; it borders the gorgeous Dallas Rd. scenic drive, which travels right along the water. The hike or drive up **Mount Douglas,** at the end of Shelbourne St. offers a spectacular view of Victoria and the Island. The **Galloping Goose,** a 100km trail beginning in downtown Victoria and continuing to the west coast of Vancouver Island, is open to cyclists, pedestrians, and horses. Ask for a map, which includes Transit access info, at the Info Centre. The trail is a part of the **Trans-Canada Trail** (still in progress), which will be the longest recreational trail in the world. When it is finished, it will cover 16,000km and stretch from coast to coast.

The **beach** stretches along the southern edge of the city by Dallas St. **Willows Beach** at Oak Bay is particularly nice. Take Fort St. east, turn right on Oak Bay St., and follow to the end. Victoria is a hub for sailing, kayaking, and whale watching tours. The folks at **Westcoast Activities Unlimited,** 606 Johnson St., will help you arrange whatever outdoor activity you choose, free of charge. (☎412-0993; www.activities-unlimited.com. Open daily 8am-7:30pm.) **Ocean River Sports,** 1824 Store St., offers kayak rentals and tours. (☎381-4233 or 800-909-4233; www.oceanriver.com. Open M-Th and Sa 9:30am-6pm, F 9:30am-8pm, Su 11am-5pm. Singles $42 per day, doubles $50. Multi-day discounts available. Tours from $59) Most whale watching companies give discounts, about 10%, for hostel guests. **Ocean Explorations,** 602 Broughton St., runs tours in very fast, very fun, very wet Zodiac raft-boats that visit resident pods of orcas in the area. (☎383-6722; www.oceanexplorations.com. Runs Apr.-Oct. 3hr. tours $70, hostelers and students $60, children $49, less in low season. Reservations recommended. Free pickup at hostels.)

DAYTRIP FROM VICTORIA: SOOKE

The **Sooke Region Museum,** 2070 Phillips Rd., just off the highway, houses a **visitors center** and delivers an excellent history of the area, and has amazing computers to guide you to a room, though many in the area are a bit pricey. (☎642-6351 or 866-888-4748; www.sooke.museum.bc.ca. Open daily July-Aug. 9am-6pm; Sept.-June Tu-Su 9am-5pm. Admission by donation.) The **Sooke Potholes** are a chain of deep swimming holes naturally carved out of the rock in the narrow Sooke River gorge. These popular and sun-warmed waters reputedly host some of the best cliff jumping in the area and draw people from all over ($3 parking fee). North of Sooke, Hwy. 14 continues along the coast, stringing together two provincial parks and their rugged, beautiful beaches. **Juan de Fuca Provincial Park** is home to China Beach and Loss Creek. **China Beach campground ❶** has 78 drive-in sites. (☎391-2300 or 800-689-9025. $14) **French Beach Provincial Park ❶** has tent sites. (☎391-2300 or 800-689-9025. $14) The **Juan de Fuca Marine Trail** starts at China Beach and heads 47km north to Botanical Beach at Port Renfrew. Trails connect beaches with the road, which is still far enough away to keep the seaside wild. The **Galloping Goose** bike and horse trail (see **Outdoor Activities,** above) passes a day-use area and trails heading east and west across the island's southern tip. The **Sooke River Flats Campsite ❶,** on Phillips Rd. past the museum, has open sites with a large picnic area, showers, toilets, and running water. (☎642-6076. Gates locked 11pm-7am. Sites $16, RV sites $18; sani-dump $5 for non-guests.) **Mom's Cafe ❷,** 2036 Shields Rd., in town, caters to locals and visitors alike. Driving from Victoria, turn right after the 2nd stoplight. (☎642-3314. Open daily June-Sept. 8am-9pm; Sept.-June M-Th and Su 8am-8pm, F-Sa 8am-9pm.)

GULF ISLANDS

Midway between Vancouver and Victoria, the Gulf Islands are a peaceful retreat from urban hustle, much less overrun by summer tourists than the nearby San Juans. While the beaches are uniformly rocky with little sand, the islands are known for a contagiously relaxing lifestyle, as well as excellent kayaking and sailing opportunities. BC Ferries visits the chain's five main islands, **Galiano, Mayne, Pender, Salt Spring,** and **Saturna,** at least twice a day.

SALT SPRING ISLAND   ☎250

Named for a dozen brine springs discovered on its northern end, Salt Spring is the largest (185 sq. km) and most populated of the islands, with the widest range of activities and accommodations. Today, the island is a haven for artists whose medium of choice varies from clay to paint to metal to wood. Visitors will enjoy the vibrant downtown of Ganges and peaceful natural areas in the southern regions of the island.

■■ **ORIENTATION AND PRACTICAL INFORMATION.** Life on Salt Spring Island is centered around the small village of **Ganges;** all of the listings below are in Ganges unless otherwise specified. **BC Ferries** (☎386-3431, in BC 888-223-3779), based on **Vancouver Island,** runs two ferries to Salt Spring. One departs Crofton and arrives in Vesuvius (12-15 times per day; $6.50 per person, cars $21 round-trip.) The other ferry leaves from Swartz Bay and arrives in Fulford Harbour, 14.5km south of Ganges (8 per day; $6.50 per person, cars $21 round-trip). Ferries from Vancouver and the other Gulf Islands dock at the Long Harbor wharf, 6km northeast of town. From June-Sept. the **Gulf Island Water Taxi** connects Salt Spring Island to both Mayne and Galiano Islands. W and Sa. (☎537-2510. Runs June-Aug. Departs W and Sa 9am, returns 4:40pm. $20 round-trip, bikes free.) The **Info Centre,** 121 Lower Ganges Rd., is a good starting point to check out the different art and outdoor activities on the island, and will also help travelers find a place to stay. (☎537-5252; www.gulfislands.net. Open July-Aug. daily 9am-6pm; Sept.-Nov. and Mar.-May 10am-4pm, Dec.-Feb. 11am-3pm.) **Silver Shadow Taxi** (☎537-3030) tends to the carless 24hr. (Base rate $2.50, $1.80 per km). **Marine Drive Car Rentals,** 124 Upper Ganges (☎537-6409), next to **Moby's** (see **Food,** below), rents vehicles to those 21 and older starting at $50 per day. Hitching rides is a popular mode of transport on the island, but *Let's Go* does not recommend hitchhiking. The **Bicycle Shop,** 131 McPhillips Ave., rents bikes. (☎537-1544. $5 per hr., $20 per 24hr. Open Tu-F 9:30am-5pm, Sa 10am-4pm.) **New Wave Laundry,** 124 Upper Ganges Rd., is next to Moby's Marine Pub. (☎537-2500. Wash $2, dry $1 per 28min. Open M and Th 8am-8pm, Tu-W 8am-6pm, F 10am-6pm, Sa-Su 9am-6pm. Other services include: **public showers,** beneath Moby's ($1 per 5 min.); **pharmacy,** 104 Lower Ganges Rd. (☎537-5534; open M-Sa 9am-6pm, Su 11am-5pm); **Internet** access at **CorInternet Cafe,** 134 McPhillips Ave. (☎537-9932; $1 per 15min., youths and seniors $0.50 per 15min.; open Tu-Sa noon-6pm) or **Salt Spring Books,** 104 McPhillips Ave. (☎537-2812; $0.10 per min.; open June-Sept. M-Sa 8:30am-6pm, Su 9:30am-6pm; Sept.-June M-Sa 9:30am-6pm, Su 9:30am-5pm); **police,** 401 Lower Granges Rd. (☎537-5555), on the outskirts of town; and the **post office,** 109 Purvis Ln., in the plaza (☎537-2321. Open M-F 8:30am-5:30pm, Sa 8am-noon.) **Postal Code:** V8K 2P1.

⬛⬛ ACCOMMODATIONS AND FOOD. Salt Spring offers a wealth of both food and B&Bs (from $70) despite its small size. The least expensive beds on the island are 8km south of Ganges in the **Salt Spring Island Hostel: Forest Retreat (HI) ❸**, 640 Cusheon Lake Rd.—look for the tree-shaped sign. In addition to two standard dorms in the lodge, the hostel's beautiful 10 acres also hide a tepee, a romantic gypsy caravan for couples and 2 hand-crafted **treehouses** that sleep 2-4. Treehouses are wildly popular and dorm beds are limited, so reservations are essential. Two friendly and feisty goats, a forest trail and a sparkling clean composting toilet add to the charm. (☎537-4149. Office open daily 8:30am-12:30pm and 5pm-8pm. Bike rentals from $15 per day, scooters from $20 per 2hr. Linens $1. Open Mar. 15-Oct. 15. Closed 2005; will reopen 2006. Dorms $17, nonmembers $21; two-person tepees $50; private rooms $60-70; treehouses and caravans $70/$80.) Island bikers will love the overwhelming breakfast at the **Wisteria Guest House ❹**, 268 Park Dr., a short walk from the village. (☎537-5899. mid-May to mid-Oct. singles $75; doubles $85. Mid-Oct. to mid-May singles $55; doubles $65.) ⬛**Ruckle Provincial Park ❶**, 23.5km southeast of Ganges, offers some of the best oceanside campsites in British Columbia. Its 78 walk-in sites on the unsheltered Beaver Point overlook the ocean. 8 RV sites are also available. Gate closed 11pm-7am. (☎391-2300, reservations ☎800-689-9025; www.discovercamping.ca. Free firewood. Sites $14.)

If you want to cook up your own fresh halibut, red snapper, rock cod, or king salmon, check out **The Fishery**, 151 Lower Ganges Rd. (☎537-2457, Tu-Sa 9:30am-6pm, Su 11am-4pm). For all other food needs, head to **Thrifty Foods**, 114 Purvis Ln. (☎537-1522. Open daily 7:30am-9pm.) **Barb's Buns ❶**, 1-121 McPhillips, sells all kinds of baked goods, including spelt bread and delicious chocolate-hazelnut sticky buns ($2.90). Vegetarians will dig the $6 sandwiches. (☎537-4491. Open M-Sa 6am-5:30pm.) The **Tree House Cafe ❷**, 106 Purvis Ln., delivers tasty sandwiches ($6-9) in the shade of an old plum tree and has open-mic Thursdays (7pm) and live music every night June-Sept. (☎537-5379. Kitchen open daily 7am-9pm.) **Moby's ❷**, 124 Upper Ganges Rd., serves up standard pub fare (burgers from $9.50) and a wide selection of brews. (☎537-5559; www.mobyspub.com. Open M-Th 10am-midnight, F-Sa 11am-1am, Su 11am-midnight.)

⬛ SIGHTS. Salt Spring Island is perhaps best known for its resident artists. A self-guided **studio tour** introduces visitors to the residences of 36 artisans around the island; pick up a brochure at the visitors center (see **Tourist Information**, p. 330). The second weekend in June brings **Sea Capers,** a festival highlighted by a boat building competition and a town parade. The century-old **Fall Fair,** held the 2nd weekend of September, draws farmers from all over the islands to display their produce, animals, and crafts with pride. Call the info centre for more information on both festivals. The **Saturday Market**, (www.saltspringmarket.com) held in downtown's Centennial Park from Easter to Thanksgiving, is a smaller version of the fall fair that draws droves of locals and tourists every week.

⬛ OUTDOOR ACTIVITIES. Wallace Island and **Prevost Island** are two excellent kayaking daytrips from Salt Spring. **Sea Otter Kayaking,** on Ganges Harbor at the end of Rainbow Rd., rents boats. They also run 2hr. introductory certification courses ($40), tours including 3hr. sunset ($40) and full-moon trips ($45), and multi-day excursions. (☎537-5678 or 877-537-5678; www.seaotterkayaking.com. Singles $25 per 2hr., $55 per day; doubles $40, $80. 15% discount for hostel guests. Open daily mid-May to Sept.; Sept. to mid-May 9am-5pm. Reservations suggested Sept. to mid-May.) Five of Salt Spring's 10 freshwater lakes are open for swimming (no lifeguards). **Blackburn Lake,** 5km south of Ganges on Fulford-Ganges Rd., is one of the less crowded spots. **Mouat Park** off of Seaview Ave. offers some very easy short hikes and a frisbee golf course. In general, **hiking** and **biking** options are limited on Salt Spring due to the small and residential nature of the islands. **Ruckle**

Provincial Park offers 200 acres of partially settled land and 11km of moderate waterfront trails that offer stunning bay vistas. Watch your step when near farmland; sheep also use these trails. **Mount Maxwell,** 11km southwest of Ganges on Cranberry Rd., offers the best view of the islands and rivals the much heralded view from the top of Mt. Constitution in the San Juan Islands. The trail can be difficult, but there's also a vehicle road to the top.

PACIFIC RIM NATIONAL PARK RESERVE ☎ 250

AT A GLANCE

AREA: 311 sq. km/193 sq. mi.

CLIMATE: Cool, foggy summers, mild but extremely wet winters; heavy precipitation.

FEATURES: The West Coast Trail, Long Beach, the Broken Group Islands, the isolated villages of Ucluelet and Tofino. Excellent surfing, scuba diving, and whale watching.

HIGHLIGHTS: Kayaking in the Broken Group (p. 334), hiking the West Coast Trail (p. 332) or the Nuu-chal-nuth Trail (p. 338).

FEES AND RESERVATIONS: $10-20 camping fee; $90 West Coast Trail fee.

GATEWAYS: Port Renfrew (p. 332), Bamfield (p. 334), Ucluelet and Tofino (p. 336).

Pacific Rim National Park Reserve stretches along a 150km sliver of Vancouver Island's remote Pacific coast. The region's frequent downpours create a lush landscape rich in both marine and terrestrial life. Hardcore hikers trek through enormous old-growth red cedar trees and along rugged beach trails. Long beaches on the open ocean draw beachcombers, bathers, kayakers, and surfers year-round. Each spring, around 22,000 gray whales stream past the park. Orcas, sea lions, bald eagles, and black bears also frequent the area. From October to April, the Pacific Rim area receives 22 rain days per month. In July and August, however, the park is relatively dry. The park is comprised of three distinct geographic regions. The southern portion is home to the West Coast Trail, which connects the towns of Bamfield and Port Renfrew. The park's middle section—the Broken Group Islands—is comprised of 100 islands in Barkley Sound. Finally, the northern region of the park, Long Beach, is northwest of Barkley Sound and bounded by the towns of Ucluelet (yew-KLOO-let) and Tofino. The park's administrative office is in Ucluelet, 2185 Ocean Terrace Rd. (☎726-7721. Open M-F 8am-4pm.)

WEST COAST TRAIL

A winding, 1½hr. drive up Hwy. 14 from Hwy. 1 near Victoria lands you in Port Renfrew. Spread out in the trees along a peaceful ocean inlet, this isolated coastal community of 250 permanent residents is the southern gateway to the world-famous ◼West Coast Trail. The other end of the trail lies 75km north, in Bamfield. Parks Canada recommends that hikers take 5-7 days to travel the entire length of the trail. The route weaves through primeval forests of giant red cedars and sitka spruce, thundering waterfalls, rocky slopes, and rugged beach. The combination of wet weather and slippery terrain over a long distance means that they can also be dangerous. Each year dozens of hikers are evacuated or rescued by park wardens. Most injuries are ankle or knee related, caused by rough and muddy forest trails; on the beach, hikers must be wary of surge channels, narrow crevasses in the ground that amplify the effects of the waves and can suddenly burst with water, knocking hikers into the channel and out to sea. Only experienced backpackers should attempt the trail, and never alone. Excepting weekdays during the shoulder season (May 1-June 15 and Sept. 16-30), the trail is regulated by a strict quota system; reservations are necessary to hike during the peak season from June 15 to September 15 and can be made as early as two months in advance. Reservations are not accepted for the shoulder season. Campsites at the southern end tend to be crowded since there are fewer than in the northern section of the trail. Each regulated day from May 1 to Sept. 30, 60 hikers are allowed to begin the journey from the two trailheads: Pachena Bay in the north and Gordon River in the south (30 from each trailhead; 25 reserved and at least 5 waitlisted). The maximum group is 10 people. For more info on the illustrious trek, call **Tourism BC** (☎800-435-5622) or **Parks Canada** (☎726-7721), or write to Pacific Rim National Park Reserve, Box 280, Ucluelet, BC, V0R 3A0. Hikers pay about $140 per person for access to the trail (reservation fee $25, backcountry camping $90, each of two ferry-crossings $14). Maps, information on the area, and registration info are available at one of the **Trail Information Centres:** in Port Renfrew (☎647-5434), at the first right off Parkinson Rd. (Hwy. 14) once in "town"; or in **Pachena Bay** (☎728-3234), 5km south of Bamfield. (Both open daily May-Sept. 9am-5pm.) David Foster Wayne's *Blisters and Bliss*, available in most bookstores, is an excellent guide to the trail ($11).

[TRANSPORTATION. West Coast Trail Express buses hikers daily from Victoria to Port Renfrew via the **Juan de Fuca** trailhead. (☎888-999-2288; www.trailbus.com. Runs May-Sept.; reservations required May 1-15 and Sept. 15-30; 2¼hr., $35.) Buses also run from Nanaimo to Bamfield (3½hr., $55), Bamfield to Port Renfrew (3½hr., $50), and Port Renfrew or Bamfield to Nitinat (by reservation only, 2hr., $35). Reservations can also be made for beaches and trailheads along the route from Victoria to Port Renfrew. The **Juan de Fuca Express** runs a water taxi between Port Renfrew and Bamfield. (☎755-6578 or 888-755-6578; www.islandnet.com/~jberry/juanfuca.htm. 4½ hr., $85.)

[ ] ACCOMMODATIONS AND FOOD. At the southern side of the trail in Port Renfrew accommodations are plentiful but expensive, generally averaging $80 per night. The **Port Renfrew Info Centre,** on Parkinson Rd. across the street from the turnoff for the entrance to the West Coast Trail, can help you find a place to stay. (☎647-0030. Internet access $4 per hr. Open M-Th 10am-3pm and 5-8pm, F-Sa 10am-3pm and 4-8pm, Su 10am-6pm.) Near Port Renfrew and adjacent to the West Coast Trail registration office lies the **Pacheedaht Campground ❶,** with washrooms and pay showers. (☎647-0090. Sites are first come, first served. Tent sites $15; RV sites $20.) The **West Coast Trail Motel ❸,** on Parkinson Rd., provides hikers with a hot tub to soothe aching muscles. (☎647-5565; www.westcoasttrailmotel.com. May-Oct. singles from $69; Oct.-May from $39.) On the other end of the West Coast Trail, in Bamfield, you can camp at the **Pachena Bay Campground ❶,** adjacent to the registration office. (☎728-1287; www.huuayaht.ca/pachena. Sites $18; RV sites $25.) The **General Store** on the main road into Port Renfrew has basic groceries. (☎647-5587. Open daily mid-June to mid-Sept. 10am-8pm; mid-Sept.to mid-June 11am-5pm.) Almost all of the restaurants in Port Renfrew offer unremarkable fare at average prices. Munch on tasty fish and chips ($9) at the **Lighthouse Pub Restaurant ❸** (☎647-5505), on Parkinson Rd. (Open daily 11am-9pm.)

BRITISH COLUMBIA

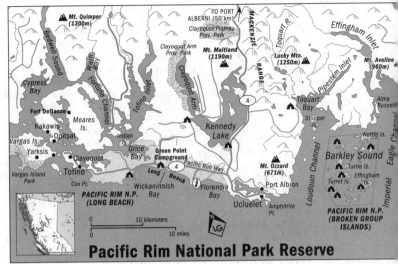

Pacific Rim National Park Reserve

⚠ OUTDOOR ACTIVITIES. If you only want to spend an afternoon roughing it, try the gorgeous **Botanical Beach Provincial Park** in Port Renfrew. Low tide offers the best opportunities for viewing tide pool marine life (info centers will have tide charts). **Botanical Beach** forms one end of the 47km **Juan De Fuca Marine Trail,** connecting Port Renfrew with **China Beach** to the east. The trail can be traveled in four to six days. Compared to the West Coast Trail, the Juan de Fuca has more entrances with a number along Hwy. 19 on the way to Port Renfrew, more forest hiking, and fewer opportunities for beach walks. The Juan de Fuca Trail is also cheaper than the West Coast Trail, with no user fee or registration fee. There are a number of **campsites ❶** along the way; overnight permits are required ($5 per night for a party of 4; self-register at trailheads). For more on the trail, view the **maps** in the Botanical Beach and China Beach parking lots or call BC Parks (☎391-2300).

BROKEN GROUP ISLANDS

The Broken Group's 100 islands stretch across Barkley Sound and make for some great sea kayaking, as well as beautiful **scuba diving.** This is the wettest spot on the island; expect lots of liquid sunshine.

🕎 PRACTICAL INFORMATION. Driving hours of logging roads or traveling by water are the only two ways into **Bamfield.** Gravel roads wind toward Bamfield from **Highway 18** (west from Duncan) and from **Highway 4** (south from Port Alberni). Be sure to watch for logging trucks. **West Coast Trail Express** (see above) runs daily from Victoria to Bamfield (4½hr., $55) and from Nanaimo to Bamfield (3½hr., $55); reservations are recommended. Because Bamfield lies on two sides of an inlet, water transit is necessary to cross town. **Lady Rose Marine Service** (☎723-8313 or 800-663-7192; www.ladyrosemarine.com) operates a passenger ferry from Port Alberni to Bamfield (4½hr., $25) and Ucluelet (5hr., $27). Other services include the **hospital,** 245 Bamfield Blvd. (☎728-3312) and the **post office,** near the Bamfield Inn, by the General Store. (☎800-267-1177. Open M-F 8:30am-4:30pm.) **Postal Code:** V0R 1B0.

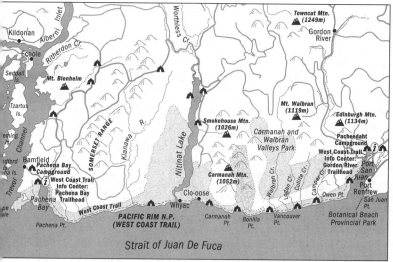

ACCOMMODATIONS AND FOOD. Accommodations are limited; motels and B&Bs are expensive (singles $50-180; doubles $70-180; the majority are at the higher end). **Marie's B&B ❸**, 468 Pachena Rd., has a friendly owner, comfy beds, and large continental breakfast. (☎728-3091; www3.telus.net/marie/bed.htm. Singles $50; doubles $80.) On the mainland, camping is the cheapest option; head to **Pachena Bay Campground ❶** (see above) for tree-rich sites just a short walk from the beach. (☎728-1287; www.hawayaht.ca. Sites $18; RV sites $25.) Eight islands in the archipelago have primitive **campsites ❶** ($5). The **Tides and Trail Market,** 242 Frigate Rd. in Bamfield near the public dock, offers groceries, supplies, and an amazing selection of candy. (☎728-2000. Open M-F 9am-6pm, Su 10am-5pm.)

OUTDOOR ACTIVITIES. The Sound can be dangerous to inexperienced paddlers. A maze of reefs and rocky islands along with large swells, tidal currents, and frigid waters makes ocean travel in small craft hazardous. **Lady Rose Marine Transport** (see **Practical Information,** above) and other operators sail from Ucluelet and Port Alberni to the Broken Group. (3 hr.; one per day M, W, F; round-trip $48.) Parks Canada recommends that kayakers enter through Toquart Bay off of Hwy. 4 between Port Alberni and Ucluelet. For guided trips, contact **Broken Island Adventures** (☎728-3500 or 888-728-6200). For kayak rentals, check with the **Bamfield Kayak Centre** (☎877-728-3535). Several short hiking trails pass through shore and forest at **Pachena Bay, Keeha Beach,** and the **Pachena Lighthouse.**

LONG BEACH

The northern third of Pacific Rim National Park Reserve begins where Hwy. 4 hits the west coast after a 1½hr. drive from Port Alberni. Ucluelet remains quieter than its counterpart Tofino until it floods with travelers accessing both the Broken Group Islands and Long Beach every July and August. Tofino, with its predominantly surfer-dude populace, is an increasingly popular resort destination, attracting backpackers and wealthy weekend-warriors alike.

BRITISH COLUMBIA

■ 🔲 ORIENTATION AND PRACTICAL INFORMATION

The two towns of Ucluelet and Tofino lie 42km apart at opposite ends of the **Pacific Rim Hwy.,** separated by the lovely and trail-laden Long Beach. **Chinook Charters** (☎725-3431) connects Victoria and Nanaimo with Tofino and Ucluelet through Port Alberni. Two buses leave daily in summer from Victoria to Tofino (7hr., $54) via Ucluelet (6½hr., $51). The **Beach Bus,** operated by Tofino Bus, (☎725-2871 or 866-986-3466) connects Tofino with Long Beach and Ucluelet Apr.-Oct. (3 per day; $11 round-trip from either town to Long Beach, $15 round-trip between the towns.) **Lady Rose Marine Services** operates a passenger freighter in summer from Port Alberni to Ucluelet. (☎723-8313 or 800-663-7192; www.ladyrosemarine.com. 5hr; 1 per day M, W, and F, leaves at 8am from Port Alberni and 2pm from Ucluelet; $27.) **Ucluelet Taxi** (☎726-4415) services both towns and everything in between 24hr. A pair of **info centers** guides visitors. The Tofino **Info Centre** is at 1426 Pacific Rim Hwy. (☎725-3414; www.tofinobc.org. Open daily July-Aug. 10am-6pm; Sept.-May Tu-Sa 10am-2pm.) Ucluelet's **Info Centre** is at 100 Main St. (☎726-4641; www.uclueletinfo.com. Generally open daily 10am-5pm; call for hours. Low-season weekends closed.) **Parks Canada** has two **information centers**, one at the Pacific Rim Visitors Centre off the Pacific Rim Hwy. just inside the park (☎726-4212; open daily mid-June to mid-Sept. 9:30am-5pm) and the other farther in at the Wickaninnish Interpretive Centre. (☎726-4701. Open daily 10:30am-6pm.) The **CIBC Bank** is on 301 Campbell St. (**24hr. ATM.** US currency exchange only. Open M-Th 9:30am-4pm, F 9:30am-5pm.) **Stormlight Marine Station,** 390 Main St., rents sleeping bags for $12 per day and tents for $15 per day. (☎725-3342. Open daily 10am-6pm.) **Fiber Options,** at the corner of 4th and Campbell, rents bikes for $6 per hr. or $25 per day. 15% hostel discount. Credit card required. (☎725-2192; www.ecoeverything.com. Open daily June-Sept. 9:30am-9pm; Oct.-May 10am-6pm.) For the **weather,** call ☎726-3415. Other services include: **police,** 400 Campbell St. (☎725-3242. Open M-F 8:30am-4:30pm); **People's Drug Mart,** 460 Campbell St., which houses a pharmacy and a **currency exchange** (☎725-3101; store open daily 10am-9pm; pharmacy open Tu-Su 10am-5:30pm); and a **hospital,** 261 Neill St. (☎725-3212). Get **Internet** access at **Gray Whale Deli,** 1950 Peninsula Ave, in Ucluelet. (☎726-2113. $10 per hr. Open daily 5am-8pm.) In Tofino, head to **Caffe Vincente,** 441 Campbell St. (☎725-2599. $3.75 for 20min. Open 7am-5pm.) The **post office** is at 161 1st St., at Campbell. (☎725-3734. Open M-F 8:30am-5:30pm, Sa 9am-1pm.) **Postal Code:** V0R 2Z0.

🔲🔲 ACCOMMODATIONS AND FOOD

In general, Tofino offers a much wider selection of both accommodations and food, but there are options in Ucluelet and outside the park. There is no free camping, and in the summer both campsites and cheap motels fill up quickly; reservations are a must after mid-May.

IN UCLUELET. Plan ahead; travelers without reservations might get shut out of reasonably priced accommodations and forced into a motel room (singles from $75). For the budget-minded, two hostels have opened in the last two years. **Surfs Inn Guesthouse ❷,** 1874 Peninsula Rd., offers beautifully clean rooms and comfortable wood-frame beds in a charming house on the town's main road (☎726-4426; www.surfsinn.ca. Dorms $24; doubles $43; private double $55. Check in 9am-10pm.) **Gimme Shelter Hostel ❷,** 2081 Peninsula Rd., offers good beds as soon as you enter Ucluelet off Pacific Rim Hwy. (☎726-7416. Dorm beds $18; singles $35.) The Ucluelet info center gives out a pamphlet listing the many B&Bs in town. **Radford's ❸,** 1983 Athlone St. (☎726-2662; www.radfords.ca), off Norah St., is close to town. The owners rent two quaint singles ($45) and a double ($90, $20 per additional guest), and offer fresh muffins, fruit, and a view of the harbor. **Ucluelet Campground ❷,** off Pacific Rim Hwy. in Ucluelet, offers sites in the open. (☎726-4355; www.uclueletcampground.com. June-Sept. $25; May $22; Apr. $20. RV sites $25-30. Showers $2.) The Ucluelet **Co-op,** on Peninsula Rd., provides food basics (☎726-4231. Open M-Sa 9am-7pm, Su 10am-6pm.) ◪**Matterson Tea House ❷,** 1682 Peninsula Rd., has homemade Canadian fare. The delicious sandwiches ($5.50-8) are made on freshly baked bread (☎726-2200. Open daily 7:30am-9pm.) Taste the authentic flavor of the Pacific Northwest in the $9 salmon burgers at **Blueberries Cafe ❸,** 1627D Peninsula Rd. (☎726-7707. Open July-Sept. M-Tu 7:30am-2:30pm, W-Su 7:30am-8:30pm; Oct.-June M-Tu 7:30am-2:30pm, W-Su 5-8:30pm.)

IN AND AROUND THE PARK. While there are several private **campgrounds** between the park and the towns, they average at least $25 to camp and $30 for RV sites. The ones on the Ucluelet side tend to be cheaper. **Parks Canada** (☎726-7721; www.pc.gc.ca) can be contacted year-round for advance information. **Green Point Campground ❶** is the only campground in the park itself and fills up quickly. Green Point has 94 regular sites and 20 walk-ins and is equipped with fire rings. Despite swarms of campers in the summer, it offers hedge-buffered privacy and great beach access. (☎800-689-9025. Reservations essential. Hiker/biker sites cannot be reserved, so arrive at 11am to nab a spot. Hiker/biker sites $14; drive-in sites $20.) The **golf course ❷** in the park often has private gravel sites and pay showers. (☎725-3314. July-Aug. $23; May-June and Oct. $20.

IN TOFINO. ◪**Whalers on the Point Guesthouse (HI) ❷,** 81 West St., voted the best Canadian hostel by HI in 2001, has room for 64. To get there, turn right on 1st St. from Campbell St. and then left on Main St. (follow to West St.). Among the hostel's amenities are a free sauna, billiards, linen, and harborside views. Check inside for HI discounts around town. Internet $6 per hr. (☎725-3443; www.tofinohostel.com. Check-in 7am-2pm and 4-11pm. $22, nonmembers $24-26, private room from $45.) **Tofino Trek Inn ❸,** 231 Main St., provides comfortable beds and a jacuzzi bathtub for the weary traveler as well as fresh baked bread, coffee, and tea in the morning. Internet access $5 per hr. (☎725-2791; www.tofinotrekinn.com. Dorm $35; singles $85.) Shop for groceries at the **Co-op,** 140 1st St. (☎725-3226. Open M-Sa 9am-9pm, Su 10am-6pm.) The **Common Loaf Bake Shop ❶,** 180 1st St., is the best place in Tofino to get a cup of coffee. Wraps from $4.25. (☎725-3915. Open daily mid June-Sept. 8am-9pm; Oct. to mid-June 8am-6pm.) **Breakers ❷,** 131 1st St., serves up delicious burritos ($8-9) and sandwiches. (☎725-2558; www.breakers-deli.com. Open daily 8am-11pm.)

ISLANDS NEARBY. On Vargas Island, 20min. off Tofino, the **Vargas Island Inn ❷** rents guest rooms in a classy lodge and two beach cabins, great for kayakers. (☎725-3309. Tent sites $20; hostel beds $30; private rooms from $40; cabins from $50.) The boat shuttle is free for guests.

⚡ OUTDOOR ACTIVITIES

🏿 **HIKING.** Hiking is a highlight of the trip to the west side of the island. The trails grow even more beautiful in the frequent rain and fog. The **Rainforest Centre,** 451 Main St. in Tofino, has assembled an excellent trail guide (available by donation) for Clayoquot Sound, Tofino, Ucluelet, the Pacific Rim, and Kennedy Lake. (☎725-2560. Open F-Sa noon-5pm.) Park passes (available at park info centers and most parking lots) cost $10 per day; seasonal passes are also available ($45). Long Beach is, fittingly, the longest beach on the island's west coast, and is the starting point for numerous hikes. The **Parks Canada Visitor Centre** and info centers (see **Orientation and Practical Information,** p. 336) provide free maps of nine hikes ranging from 100m to 2.5km in length. On the **Rainforest Trail** (two 1km loops), boardwalks off the Pacific Rim Hwy. lead through gigantic trees and fallen logs of old-growth rainforest. **Bog Trail** (1km loop; wheelchair-accessible) illuminates little-known details of one of the wettest, most intricate ecosystems in the park. You can even view tiny carnivorous plants. **Nuu-Chah-Nulth Trail** (2.5km, one-way) links Wickaninnish Beach with Florencia Bay and provides a glimpse into the culture of the Nuu-chah-nulth people. Outside of the park, the new **Wild Pacific Trail** in Ucluelet provides a number of hikes along the coast with views of Barkley Sound and Pacific Rim Park. In the future, the trail will lead right into the park. Maps and information are available at the visitors center or www.wildpacifictrail.com.

◪ **SURFING AND KAYAKING.** Exceptional **surf** breaks invitingly off **Long Beach** and **Cox Bay** (5km south of Tofino). These two coves funnel large and occasionally dangerous waves; don't forget your wetsuit. **Storm Surf Shop** in Tofino rents everything you'll need. (444 Campbell St. ☎725-3344; www.stormsurfshop.com. Full wetsuits and surfboards each $20 per 4hr., $30 per day.) It is possible to kayak to Meares Island and throughout the sound, although the island is large and the trailhead is extremely difficult to find without a good map or guide. **Pacific Kayak,** at Jamie's Whale Station, provides a map, has the best rates in town, and rents to experienced paddlers. (☎725-3232; www.tofino-bc.com/pacifickayak. Singles $40 per day, doubles $65; 4hr. guided tour $64; multi-day discounts.)

◪ **WHALE WATCHING.** In March and April, gray whales migrate past Clayoquot Sound north of Tofino. Six or seven stay at these feeding grounds during the summer. There are more tour companies than resident whales, and most have comparable prices. **Jamie's Whale Station,** 606 Campbell St., just east of 4th St. in Tofino, is the oldest company in town and runs smooth rides in large boats, but rough-riders choose Zodiacs to ride the swells at 30 knots. Boat-based bear-watching expeditions are also available. (☎725-3919 or 800-667-9913; www.jamies.com. Whale watching $85 per 3hr., students, ages 65 and older or 12-18 $80, under 12 $50. Second branch in Ucluelet.) **Seaside Adventures,** 300 Main St. in Tofino, offers 2-3hr. whale watching trips, bear watching, and a 10% discount if you bring your trusty *Let's Go* guide. (☎725-2292 or 888-332-4252; www.seaside-adventures.com. Family boats $75, ages 65 and older $65, 6-12 $50; Zodiacs $64, ages 65 and older $55, 6-12 $45; bear watch $64, ages 65 and older $59, 6-12 $45.)

HOT SPRINGS. Hot Springs Cove, 1hr. north of Tofino by boat, is one of the least crowded hot springs in all of British Columbia. The Matlahaw Water Taxi, operated by the Hesquiaht First Nation, makes a run or two each day to the cove. (☎670-1110. $45 one-way.) The springs are near a quiet and lush **campground ❷** and a footpath to secluded beaches in the Maquinna Marine Park. (15 sites, $20.) Many whale-watching operations, including Jamie's and Seaside, also run to the cove.

UP ISLAND

To a Victorian, anything north of town is "up island." While not as heavily touristed as the southern tip, the northern reaches of Vancouver Island are among the most pleasant areas in the region, thanks to the beautiful towns, friendly locals, inviting waters, and eminently hikeable Strathcona and Pacific Rim Parks.

NANAIMO

☎250

Primarily a ferry terminal stopover for travelers en route to the rainforests of northern and western Vancouver Island, Nanaimo (na-NYE-moe) appears along the highway as a strip of motels, gas stations, and chain stores. The semi-urban setting lacks some of the natural splendor of Vancouver Island's more secluded locations, but thanks to ample hiking opportunities, some nice beaches and an annual bathtub race, this working man's city attracts its fair share of travelers.

ORIENTATION AND PRACTICAL INFORMATION

Nanaimo lies on the east coast of Vancouver Island, 111km north of Victoria on the **Trans-Canada Highway** (Hwy. 1), and 391km south of **Port Hardy** via the **Island Highway** (Hwy. 19). Hwy. 1 turns into **Nicol Street** and **Terminal Avenue** in Nanaimo before becoming Hwy. 19A. **Nanaimo Parkway** (Hwy. 19) circumvents the town.

Trains: VIA Rail, 321 Selby St. (☎800-561-8630). To **Victoria** (1 per day, $23). No ticket counter; purchase tickets in advance.

Buses: Gray Line (☎384-4411 or 800-753-4371), at Comox Rd. and Terminal Ave., behind Howard Johnson Inn. To: **Port Hardy** (7½hr., 1-2 per day, $83); **Tofino** and **Ucluelet** (4hr., 2 per day, $33); and **Victoria** (2¼hr., 6 per day, $20).

Ferries: BC Ferries (☎888-223-3779), at Departure Bay the northern end of Stewart Ave., 2km north of downtown. To Vancouver's **Horseshoe Bay** (1½hr.; 8 times per day) and Tsawwassen (2hr.; 4-8 per day). $8.50-11, bike $2.50 extra, car and driver $34-41. The **Scenic Ferry** (☎754-7893) runs from the Maffeo-Sutton Park in downtown to Newcastle Island just offshore (on the hr. 10am-6pm; $7). No vehicles are permitted on the island and the passenger ferry runs only April-Labor Day.

Car Rental: Rent-A-Wreck, 227 Terminal Ave. S (☎753-6461). From $33 per day plus $0.16 per km after 150km. Must be 21 or older with major credit card. Free pickup. Open M-F 8am-6pm, Sa 9am-4pm, Su 10am-4pm.

Visitor Info: 2290 Bowen Rd. (☎756-0106 or 800-663-7337; www.tourismnanaimo.com), west of downtown. Head south from Terminal Ave. on Comox Rd., which becomes Bowen Rd., or go north from Hwy. 19 on Northfield Rd. Open daily mid-May to Labor Day 8am-7pm; Labor Day to mid-May M-F 9am-5pm, Sa-Su 10am-4pm.

Laundromat: 702 Nicol St. (☎753-9922), at Robins Rd. in Payless Gas Station. $2.50 per load. 24hr.

Equipment Rental: Chain Reaction, in The Realm at 2 Commercial St. (☎754-3309), rents bikes and in-line skates. Bikes $20 per day, $10 for Nicol St. Hostel Guests; $35 per week. In-line skates $15 per day. Open M-Sa 9:30am-6pm.)

Police: 303 Prideaux St. (☎754-2345), at Fitzwilliam St.

Crisis Line: ☎754-4447. 24hr.

Pharmacy: London Drugs, 650 Terminal Ave. S (☎753-5566), in Port Place Mall. Open M-Sa 9am-10pm, Su 10am-8pm.

Hospital: Nanaimo Regional General Hospital, 1200 Dufferin Crescent (☎754-2141). Open 24hr.

Internet: $1 per hr. at **Literacy Nanaimo,** 19 Commercial St. (☎754-8988). Open M-F 9am-4pm, Sa 10am-4pm, Su noon-4pm. A visitor's Internet pass is $5 at the **library,** 90 Commercial St. (☎753-1154; www.virl.bc.ca.) Open M-F 10am-8pm, Sa 10am-5pm, Su noon-4pm.

Post Office: 650 Terminal Ave. S (☎741-1829), in Port Place Mall. Open M-F 8:30am-5pm. **Postal Code:** V9R 5J9

ACCOMMODATIONS AND CAMPING

Travelers should never be at a loss for a room in Nanaimo. Cheap motels are packed in like sardines along the main drag.

Nicol Street Hostel, 65 Nicol St. (☎753-1188). A quick walk from the ferry, bus station, or downtown. Lots of freebies: Internet, linens, and parking are just a few. Discounts at many downtown establishments. Living room, small tidy kitchen, beautiful artwork in the basement, and laundry facilities. 25 comfortable beds; tent sites and ocean views in backyard. Reservations recommended. Reception 2-11pm. Sites $10; dorms $17; doubles $34-40. ❷

Cosmic Cow Guesthouse, 1922 Wilkinson Rd. (☎754-7150), is a hop, skip, and a jump from the Nanaimo River, 10km south of Nanaimo. From downtown Nanaimo, head south on Hwy. 1 and Nanaimo Pkwy. (#19). Take a left (east) on Cedar Rd. and make a right turn onto Wilkinson Rd. before the bridge. This quiet farmhouse retreat offers solitude, 60 acres of nature trails, bonfires, and free breakfast. Dorms $18, cabins starting at $20. Call to arrange check in and for help in arranging transportation. ❷

The Cambie, 63 Victoria Crescent. (☎754-5323 or 877-754-5323; www.cambiehostels.com) The advantage of The Cambie's central location is offset by its noise. Still, comfortable beds and proximity to nightlife make it a great place for those looking for a night on the town. Laundry. Reception 7:30am-2pm and 6:30pm-1:30am. Dorms $20; Private rooms from $40. ❷

Living Forest Oceanside Campground, 6 Maki Rd. (☎755-1755; www.campingbc.com), 3km southwest of downtown. 193 spacious sites; several amid cedars overlooking the ocean. Sites $17-20; full RV sites $22-24. Showers $1 per 5min. ❷

FOOD

The highway attracts dives and fast-food joints, many open late or 24hr., but off the main road there are many good options. Get groceries from **Thrifty Foods** in the Port Place Mall. (☎754-6273. Open daily 8am-10pm.) The **Farmer's Market** runs on F (10am-2pm) and W (3pm-7pm) at the Pioneer Waterfront Plaza on Front St. in downtown Nanaimo.

Gina's Mexican Cafe, 47 Skinner St. (☎753-5411). A bright pink landmark on Nanaimo's skyline, Gina's offers unique Mexican fare at a great price with excellent service. Experiment with creative items like the Don Juan, a veggie and cheese omelet in a grilled tortilla ($8). Vegetarian options are plentiful, and the margaritas are stellar. Open M-Th 11am-9pm, F 11am-10pm, Sa noon-10pm, Su noon-8pm. ❷

Acme Food Co., 14 Commercial St. (☎753-0042; www.acmefoodco.ca) This trendy eatery in the middle of downtown is a step up from much in the area. Build your own burger (starting at $6.50) or pasta (starting at $8.50), or pick from their own combinations. An extensive martini list and live weekend music. Open daily 11am-midnight. ❷

Pirate Chips, on the corner of Commercial and Victoria Crescent. If you're looking for something deep-fried, this is the place for you. Poutine starting at $4.50. Deep-fried chocolate bars and Oreos from $2.50, deep-fried Nanaimo bar $3.50. Open M-W 11am-midnight, Th-Sa 11am-3am, Su noon-10. ❶

SIGHTS AND EVENTS

The **Nanaimo District Museum,** 100 Cameron Rd., pays tribute to Nanaimo's First Nation communities with an interactive exhibit on the Snuneymuxw (SNOO-ne-moo) and a section on the coal mining origins of the town. (☎753-1821; www.nanaimo.museum.bc.ca). Open daily mid-May to Labor Day 9am-5pm; Labor Day to mid-May Tu-Sa 10am-5pm. $2, ages 65 and older $1.75, under 12 $0.75.) The **Bastion** up the street was a Hudson's Bay Company fur-trading fort, and it fires a cannon every weekday at noon. (Open July-Sept. W-M 10am-4:30pm. Free.)

The multi-day **Marine Festival** is held the last weekend in July, with many events leading up to the actual festival. Highlights include the **Bathtub Race**, organized by the **Loyal Nanaimo Bathtub Society** (☎753-7223; www.bathtub.island.net). Contestants race tiny boats built around porcelain tubs with monster outboards from Nanaimo harbor around Entrance and Winchelsea Islands and finish at Departure Bay. Officials hand out prizes to everyone who makes it and present the "Silver Plunger" to the first tub to sink.

OUTDOOR ACTIVITIES

BUNGEE JUMPING. Adrenaline-junkies from all over the continent make a pilgrimage to the **Bungy Zone**, 35 Nanaimo River Rd. To reach the Zone, take Hwy. 1 south to Nanaimo River Rd. and follow the signs, or take the free shuttle to and from Nanaimo. Plummet 42m (140 ft.) into a narrow gorge (water touches available); variations include a zipline and the Swing. (☎716-7874 or 888-668-7874; www.bungyzone.com. $100, same-day jumps $35, zipline and swing $60. 20% HI discount. **Campsites ❶** $10 per person.)

HIKING. The serene ◪**Newcastle Island Provincial Park**, accessible only by boat, has 756 automobile-free acres filled with hiking trails, picnic spots, and campsites. (☎754-7893. **Scenic Ferries** run only in summer, on the hr. 10am-6pm; $7.) The **Shoreline Trail** that traces the island's perimeter offers great vantage points of Departure Bay. **Petroglyph Provincial Park**, 3km south of town on Hwy. 1, protects carvings inscribed by Salish shamans. A menagerie of animals and mythical creatures decorates the soft sandstone.

WATER SPORTS. The waters of **Departure Bay** wash onto a pleasant, pebbly beach in the north end of town on Departure Bay Rd., off Island Hwy. Jacques Cousteau called the waters around Nanaimo "The Emerald Sea," and they offer top diving opportunities. The **Nanaimo Dive Association**, through **Ocean Explorers** (☎753-2066 or 888-233-4145; www.oceanexplorersdiving.com) helps visitors find charters, lessons, or equipment. **The Kayak Shack**, 1840 Stewart Ave., near the ferry terminal, rents kayaks, canoes, and camping equipment. (☎753-3234; www.thekayakshack.com. Singles and canoes $10 per hr., $40 overnight; doubles $15, $60.)

ON THE MENU

NANAIMO BARS

These gooey, artery-cloggingly rich layered treats were allegedly once sent in care packages from the United Kingdom to hard-working sons in Nanaimo coal mines. They have since become synonymous with this little Canadian town, and are quite a way to finish off a meal (in fact, they're basically a meal in and of themselves). Heart attack in a baking pan—a worthy claim to fame for any small town.

Layer 1: *½ cup butter, ¼ cup white sugar, 1 egg, 1 tsp. vanilla, 1 tbsp. cocoa, 2 cups graham cracker crumbs, 1 cup unsweetened coconut, ½ cup walnut pieces.* Combine butter, sugar, egg, vanilla, and cocoa in the top of a double boiler, over medium heat, and stir until slightly thickened. Combine crumbs and coconut in a bowl, then pour the hot mixture over top. Stir, then press into the bottom of a shallow 6x9 in. rectangular pan. Refrigerate.

Layer 2: *2 tbsp. custard powder, 2 cups icing sugar, ¼ cup room-temperature butter, 3 tbsp. milk.* Blend butter, sugar, milk, and powder until smooth. Spread over first layer.

Layer 3: *5oz. semi sweet chocolate, 1 tbsp. butter.* Melt chocolate and butter in double boiler. Spread the chocolate over layer 2. Refrigerate.

Last Step: Serve. Eat. Enjoy.

HORNBY ISLAND ☎250

In the 1960s, large numbers of draft-dodgers fled the US to settle peacefully on Hornby Island, halfway between Nanaimo and Campbell River. Today, hippie hold-overs of all manners and origins and a similarly long-haired and laid-back younger generation mingle on the island with descendants of 19th-century pioneers. Low tide on Hornby uncovers over 300m of the finest sand in the strait of Georgia. **Tribune Bay,** at the end of Shields Rd., is the more crowded of the two beaches (**Li'l Tribune Bay,** next door, is clothing-optional). The alternative, **Whaling Station Bay,** has the same gentle sands and is about 5km farther north, off St. John's Point Rd. On the way there from Tribune Bay, Helliwell Rd. passes stunning **Helliwell Provincial Park,** where well-groomed trails lead through old-growth forest to bluffs overlooking the ocean.

█ ☎ ORIENTATION AND PRACTICAL INFORMATION. There are two main roads on Hornby: the coastal **Shingle Spit Road** and **Central Road,** which crosses the island from the end of Shingle Spit. The island has no public transit and is hard to cover without a bike or car. On-foot travelers have been known to ask friendly faces for a lift at Denman or on the ferry; *Let's Go* does not recommend hitchhiking. The **Gray Line** (☎753-4371) bus has a flag stop at Buckley Bay on Hwy. 19, where the ferry docks. **BC Ferries** has 15-17 sailings per day from Buckley Bay to Denman and 11-12 from Denman to Hornby. To reach the Hornby ferry, follow Denman Rd. all the way to the end on the other side of the island. (☎335-0323; www.bcferries.com. $4.50-4.75; $15-17 with car.) The **visitors center** is located in the island's **Ringside Market.** (☎335-0313; www.hornbyisland.com. Open daily 10am-3pm.) **Hornby Ocean Kayaks** trans-ports kayaks to the calmest of seven beaches and provides guided tours, lessons, and rentals. (☎335-2726; www.hornbyisland.com/Kayaking. 2½hr. tour $50; rentals $35 per 3hr., $50 per 6hr.) The island's only **24hr. ATM** is at the **Hornby Island Resort** (See **Accommodations and Food,** below). The **post office** is also at the Ringside Market in the Co-op. (Open M-Sa 9:30am-1pm and 1:30-4:30pm.) **Postal Code:** V0R 1Z0.

☎ ◫ ACCOMMODATIONS AND FOOD. At the earthy heart of Hornby sits the grocery-bearing **Co-op** in the Ringside Market. (☎335-1121. Open M-Sa 9:30am-5:30pm.) The colorful market, at the end of Central Rd. by Tribune Bay, is also home to artisan **gift shops,** a beach-gear store, and two budget- and vegetarian-friendly restaurants. Most B&Bs cluster around the **Whaling Station, Galleon Beach, and Sandpiper Beach** areas and cost $65-175 per night, with the majority in the $80-90 range. The **Hornby Island Resort ❷,** right at the ferry docks, is a pub/restaurant/laundromat/hotel/campground. The fare at the resort's **Thatch Pub ❷** is standard, but the view from the outdoor deck is anything but. The **Wheelhouse Restaurant ❷,** with ocean views from a shared deck, has breakfasts ($9), burgers ($7-8.50), and entrees ($8-11). The pub and restaurant serve the same food and drinks at the same prices, but you'll have a waiter and a table of your own at the restaurant. (☎335-0136; www.hornbyisland.com/AllAccom/HornbyResort/HornbyRe-sort.htm. Pub open daily 11:30am-11pm; live jazz every F, 7pm. Restaurant open daily 9:30am-9pm. Apr.-Feb. sites $29; Jan.-Mar. $16. Private rooms from $75-95.) **Tribune Bay Campsite ❶,** on Shields Rd., offers 118 sites a quick walk from the island's popular beach. Showers, toilets, and playground. Reservations are neces-sary July-Aug. (☎335-2359. Hiker/biker sites $20; sites $25, with electricity $28.)

▒ FESTIVALS. For one week in the beginning of August, the Hornby Festival, brings classical music, popular variety, dance and humor to the island. Call the festival office for more info. (☎335-2734; www.hornbyfestival.bc.ca. Mini-pass good for 4 performances $65, ages 65 and older or student $50, full pass $215, ages 65 and older or student $165.)

DENMAN ISLAND ☎250

The ⊠**Denman Island Guesthouse & International Hostel ❶**, 3806 Denman Rd., has a super-relaxed family feel. Features a large kitchen, a cafe next door, and a hot tub. (☎335-2688; www.earthclubfactory.com/guesthouse. Camping $12; dorm beds $20; private rooms $45. Bike rentals $15 per day. Internet $3 per hr. Cafe open daily 9am-1pm and 5-9pm.) You can pitch a tent at beach-side **Fillongley Provincial Park ❶**, just off Denman Rd., halfway to the Hornby Ferry (reservations recommended). The park offers nice beach swimming and a number of short hikes. (☎335-1430. Reservations 800-689-9025. $17) You can camp for free at **Sandy Island Provincial Park, ❶** (also known as Tree Island) at the north end of Denman. To get there, take a hike along NW Rd. from the village center, make a left onto Gladstone Way, and head north toward the island with all the trees. (No campfires; access at low tide only.) The island's two lakes, Graham Lake and Chickadee Lake, offer fine freshwater swimming. The Denman village center, perched above the Buckley Bay ferry terminal, offers crucial amenities. **Denman Island General Merchants** houses the **Visitors Centre** and **Post Office** (**Postal Code:** V0R 1T0. Open 8:30am-4:30pm M-Sa) and sells basic groceries. (☎335-2293. Open M-F 7am-9pm, Sa-Su 9am-9pm.) Next door, the **Cafe on the Rock ❶** serves delicious food at delicious prices. Full vegetarian breakfast $6, homemade pie $4, sandwiches $4. (☎335-2999. Open M-F 8am-8pm, Sa-Su 9am-8pm.)

COMOX VALLEY ☎250

With fine hiking, fishing, skiing, and caving, and the southern regions of Strathcona Provincial Park just a hike away, the tourist season never ends in this self-proclaimed "Recreation Capital of Canada." The area's beaches, trails, extensive cave network, and forested swimming holes could take weeks to explore. Sheltering the towns of Courtenay, Comox, and Cumberland, the Comox Valley boasts one of the highest per-capita concentrations of artists in Canada and offers many free museums and galleries. In addition, the 1989 discovery of the 80-million-year-old "Courtenay Elasmosaur," which swam in the valley back when the valley was a lake, has transformed the region into a minor mecca for paleontologists.

■🔢 **ORIENTATION AND PRACTICAL INFORMATION. Courtenay,** the largest town in the Valley, lies 108km (1hr.) north of Nanaimo on the **Island Highway** (Hwy. 19). In Courtenay, the Island Hwy., heading north, joins **Cliffe Avenue** before crossing the river at 5th St., intersecting with **Comox Road** and then once again heading north. **Gray Line** (☎334-2475) buses run from Courtenay at 2663 Kilpatrick and 27th St. by the Driftwood Mall to Nanaimo (2hr., $20), Port Hardy (5hr., $64), and Victoria (5hr., $40). The **Comox Valley Transit System** connects the valley's three towns. (☎339-5453; www.rdcs.bc.ca/transit. Buses run 7:15am-6:45pm. $1.75, ages 65 and older $1.50.) **BC Ferries** links Comox with Powell River. (☎888-223-3779; www.bcferries.com. 1¾hr.; 4 per day; $8, car $24-27.) The well-organized and informative **visitors center,** 2040 Cliffe Ave. in Courtenay, can help guide your adventure throughout the valley. (☎334-3234; www.comox-valley-tourism.ca. Open daily June-Sept. 9am-5pm; Oct.-May M-Sa 9am-5pm.) **Comox Valley Kayaks,** 2020 Cliffe Ave. beside the visitors center, rents, transports, and leads workshops and full-moon paddles. (☎334-2628 or 888-545-5595; www.comoxvalleykayaks.com. Singles $20 per 2hr., $35 per day, doubles $30-34/$50-63. Multi-day rentals available. Open daily mid-May to Oct. 10am-7pm; Nov. to mid-May by appointment.) Do laundry at **BeNu Laundry,** 339 6th St. Wash $1.75; dry $0.25 for 5min. (☎897-0167. Open M-F 8am-8pm, Sa 9am-5pm, Su 10am-4pm.) Other services include **police,** 800 Ryan Rd., (☎338-1321) and the **hospital,** 2137 Comox Ave. (☎339-2242). For **weather,** call ☎339-5044. **Internet** access is $1 for

30min. at the **library,** 300 6th St. (☎334-3369; www.virl.bc.ca. Open M-F 10am-8pm, Sa 10am-5pm, Su 12:30-4pm.) The **post office** is at 333 Hunt Pl. (☎334-4341. Open M-F 8:30am-5pm.) **Postal Code:** V9N 1G0.

▨▯ **ACCOMMODATIONS AND FOOD.** The ▨**Comox Lake Hostel ❶,** 4787 Lake Trail Rd., about 8km from town, provides access to the hiking, biking, and swimming of Puntledge River Recreation Area (see **Outdoor Activities**) just through the yard, within hiking distance of Strathcona Provincial Park. To get there, take 5th St. toward the mountains to Lake Trail Rd., turn west, and keep going. Free linen, plus kitchen and laundry. Pickup from ferry $6, from bus $3. (☎338-1914; www3.telus.net/hostel. Tent sites $15, dorm beds $20.) The spotlessly clean ▨**Mount Washington Guest House and Hostel ❷** offers rooming right by the ski resort and at a trailhead into Strathcona Provincial Park, with a hot tub to ease the muscles after a long day outdoors. (☎898-8141; www.mtwashingtonhostel.com. Laundry, free linen. Dorm bed $24-30, private room $65-100.) **Riding Fool Hostel ❷,** at the corner of 2nd and Dunsmuir in Cumberland, offers comfortable beds and an open, friendly setting. The hostel is close to great local mountain biking trails and provides bike storage as well as a kitchen and free linen. Take 29th St. Connector across Island Hwy. until it turns into 4th St., then make a right onto Dunsmuir. (☎336-8250 or 888-313-3665; www.ridingfool.com. Dorm beds $18; private rooms $45.) Campers often hit **Kin Beach ❶,** on Astra Rd. past the Air Force base in Comox. To get there, turn left at the four-way stop in front of the base, take your first right and follow it for 5min. (☎339-6365. 18 wooded sites $9.) The **Comox Valley Farmers Market** occurs twice per week: W at 4th St. and Duncan St. in downtown Courtenay and Sa at the Comox Valley Exhibition Grounds. (May-Sept. 9am-noon.) Get groceries at **Safeway** on the corner of 18th St. and Cliffe Ave. in Courtenay. (Open daily 8am-11pm.) The surprisingly hip **Atlas Cafe ❸,** 250 6th St., serves delicious quesadillas ($8-14) and light entrees from a variety of cuisines. (☎338-9838; www.comoxvalleyrestaurants.ca/atlas.htm. Open M 8:30am-3:30pm, Tu-Th and Sa 8:30am-10pm, F 8:30am-11pm, Su 8:30am-10pm.) **Union Street Grill ❸,** 475 5th St., offers upscale burgers ($8-12) and pastas. (☎897-0081; www.comoxvalleyrestaurants.ca/unionstgrill.htm. Open M-Sa 11:30am-9pm.)

◪ **SIGHTS.** The area's largest draw is the **Mount Washington** ski area, on the edge of Strathcona Provincial Park (see below). It's only a 30min. drive to the base of the lifts from Courtenay, so staying in a cheap motel or at one of the hostels near town is a viable way to avoid the mountain's stratospheric prices. The **I-Hos Gallery,** 3310 Comox Rd., displays the work of some of the finest traditional Salish and Kwakwaka'wakw carvers, painters, and metalworkers on northern Vancouver Island. (☎339-7702; www.ihosgallery.com. Open daily Mar.-Dec. 10am-5pm; Jan.-Feb. Tu-Sa 10am-5pm.) The **Cumberland Museum,** 2680 Dunsmuir Ave., displays exhibits on the coal-mining town that in 1920 was home to large Chinese and Japanese communities. (☎336-2445; www.cumberland.museum.bc.ca. Open mid-May to Sept. M-F 9am-5pm, Sa-Su 10am-4pm; Oct. to mid-May closed Su. $3, ages 65 and older $2, 12-18 $1, under 12 free.)

◩ **OUTDOOR ACTIVITIES.** The snowmelt-fed **Puntledge River** at **Stotan Falls,** a long stretch of shallow waters racing over flat rocks, is a great place for **swimming,** but it's a good idea to check the current and depths before wading or jumping. Coming from Courtenay on Lake Trail Rd., turn right at the stop sign onto the unmarked road at the first "hostel" sign. Take the next left at the logging road Duncan Bay Main, cross the pipeline, and then park on either side of the one-lane bridge. The visitors center or Comox Lake Hostel (see **Accommodations,** above) can provide a map. There are also a number of hiking trails (ranging from 600m-5.5km) and mountain biking trails (for experienced and beginning riders) in the Puntledge River Recreation Area. For longer trails through the woods, try breathtaking

Nymph Falls, upriver. From Duncan Bay Main, go left on Forbidden Plateau Rd. to the "Nymph" sign. Mountain bikers can find trail maps at the visitors center or Riding Fool Hostel. ◪**Horne Lake Caves Provincial Park,** 55km south of Courtenay off the Island Hwy. on Horne Lake Rd., offers superb caving tours—a genuinely other-worldly experience—for beginners (1½hr., $17; 3hr., $49), and a 5hr. tour involving crawl ways, rappelling and the ethics of caving. (☎ 248-7829; www.hornelake.com. $139. 15 and older. Bring heavy, non-cotton clothing. Reservations highly recommended.) Hikers can explore two short, highly damaged caves for free.

Skiers and snowboarders hit the slopes just outside the park boundaries at **Mount Washington** to take advantage of 10m of annual snowfall. The mountain is accessible from the Island Hwy. Make a left onto Strathcona Pkwy. and follow signs. In 1998, one of the nearby lodges actually caved in from too much snow, and lifts have been known to close on occasion on account of excess precipitation. (☎ 338-1386, reservations 888-231-1499; www.mtwashington.bc.ca. $47, ages 65 and older and 13-18 $39, ages 7-12 $25, 6 and under free. Night skiing F-Sa 4:30-9pm. $10, 6 and under free.) A lift is open in the summer to satiate the appetites of hardcore mountain bikers and the vista-hungry. ($11, youth and senior $9, under 6 free; with bike $19.) The mountain also offers 40km of cross-country and snowshoe trails; the **Alpine Lodge** has rentals. (Alpine ski package $28; cross-country $17-24; snowboards $37; snowshoes $9.)

CAMPBELL RIVER ☎ 250

A big rock covered with graffiti welcomes visitors to Campbell River, another of BC's many "Salmon Capitals of the World." Jacques Cousteau considered Campbell River's incredible fishing and scuba diving second only to the Red Sea. The number of gas stations and motels along the old Island Hwy. (Hwy. 19A) confirms Campbell River's role as the transportation hub of the island's north. It provides easy access to Strathcona Provincial Park, Port Hardy, and the Discovery Islands.

◪◪ **ORIENTATION AND PRACTICAL INFORMATION.** Campbell River lies 45km north of Courtenay on the **Island Highway** (Hwy. 19). **Gray Line** (☎ 287-7151), at 13th and Cedar, sends buses to Nanaimo (4 per day, $26), Port Hardy (1 per day, $59), and Victoria (4 per day, $45). **BC Ferries** (☎ 888-223-3779; www.bcferries.com) runs to Quadra Island (all day; $5-5.25, ages 5-11 $2.50-2.75; cars $12-13). The **visitors center** is off the Island Hwy. near the Tyee Mall, next to the Marina. (☎ 287-4636 ext. 1; www.visitorinfo.incampbellriver.com. Open daily June-Aug. 9am-7pm; Sept. M-F 9am-6pm, Sa 9am-5pm, Su 10am-4pm; Oct.-Apr. M-F 9am-5pm, Sa 10am-4pm; May M-Sa 9am-6pm. Call ☎ 287-4463 for **weather.** The **police,** on Dogwood St. between Pinecrest Rd.and Merecroft Rd., can be reached at ☎ 286-6221. A **crisis line** is at ☎ 287-7743. The **hospital** is at 375 2nd Ave. (☎ 287-7111). **Shoppers Drug Mart** pharmacy is in the Tyee Mall. (☎ 286-1166. Open M-F 8am-9pm, Sa 9am-6pm, Su 10am-5pm.) The **post office** is in the Tyee Mall (☎ 286-1813. Open M-F 8:30am-5pm.) **Postal Code:** V9W 4Z8.

◪◪ **ACCOMMODATIONS AND FOOD.** B&Bs and motels in Campbell River tend to be a bit expensive (singles $45-70; doubles $60-90), but the visitors center can help you find a bed to sleep in. **Quiet Crescent B&B ❷,** 531 Frederick Crescent, has large rooms, big breakfasts, and offers a backpackers' bar rate. (☎ 286-1076. Backpackers $28; singles $60; doubles $75. Backpacker rooms do not include breakfast or cooking facilities.) The best camping near town is at **Quinsam Campground ❶,** in Elk Falls Provincial Park, 10min. from town on Hwy. 28, with space among firs. (Reservations ☎ 800-689-9025; www.discovercamping.ca. 122 sites, $14.) The **Beehive Cafe ❷,** 921 Island Hwy., has a deck overlooking the water. Breakfast starting from $6, large lunches from $8. The seafood stack sandwich ($10) is an amazing local treat. (☎ 286-6812. Open daily 11am-10pm.) **Super Valu,** in the Tyee Mall, sells groceries. (☎287-4410. Open daily 8:30am-9:30pm.) **Spice Island ❷**, 2269 Island Hwy., offers customized meat, seafood, or tofu dishes at five levels of spiciness. (☎923-0011. Open for lunch Tu-F noon-1:30pm, for dinner Tu-Sa 4:30-around 7:30pm. Tables are few, so calling ahead is recommended.) Sockeye, coho, pink, chum, and chinook **salmon** are hauled in by the boatload from the waters of the Campbell River. The seafood-savvy can reap the fruits of the sea from **Discovery Pier** in Campbell Harbour, and the unskilled can at least buy ice cream and frozen yogurt on the pier ($2.50), which has an artificial reef to attract fish. (Fishing $2; rod rentals $2.50 per hr., $6 per half-day.) One-day **fishing licenses** ($7.50-11, salmon $6.50 extra) are available at the visitors center or at local sports outfitters.

■ ⚠ **SIGHTS AND OUTDOOR ACTIVITIES.** The **Quinsam River Salmon Hatchery,** 4217 Argonaut Rd. off Hwy. 28, offers free tours to see a wealth of natural resources. (☎287-9564. Open daily 8am-4pm.) **Scuba** gear rentals can be pricey and require proper certification, but **Beaver Aquatics,** 760 Island Hwy., offers a nifty $25 **snorkeling** package that includes suit, mask, snorkel, and fins; they also have a $50 full dive package. (☎287-7652; www.connected.bc.ca/~baquatics. Open M-Sa 9:30am-5:30pm.) Beaver only supplies equipment, so if you have charter needs, give a call from 10am-6pm to **Abyssal Charters** (☎285-2420; www.abyssal.com) for some guided, bubble-blowing, spear-gunning, underwater good times.

QUADRA ISLAND   ☎250

Quadra boasts pleasing landscapes that rival her southern Gulf Island cousins, a European history that is older than that of most settlements on Vancouver Island, and a thriving First Nation community around Cape Mudge. The 🟥**Kwagiulth Museum and Cultural Centre,** 37 Weeway Rd., in the village of Cape Mudge just south of Quathiaski Cove, houses a spectacular collection of potlatch regalia which was confiscated by the government in the early 20th century and returned in 1988. (☎285-3733. Open M-Sa 10am-5pm. $3, seniors $2, children $1. Tours $1 extra.) Quadra is a 10min. ferry ride from Campbell River (see p. 345). **BC Ferries** sail to Quadra every hour on the half hour from Campbell River (see **Orientation,** above). **Quadra Credit Union** (☎285-3327. **24hr. ATM**) and a **visitors center** with maps of island trails and rental info await at the first corner of Harper Rd., across from **Quadra Foods,** which will satisfy your grocery needs and sell you a **fishing license.** (☎285-3391. Open daily 9am-9pm. Licenses $7.50-11 per day, $6.50 extra for salmon.) Call the **police** in Quathiaski Cove (☎285-3631) in an **emergency.** World-weary sojourners can relax at the 🟥**Travellers' Rural Retreat ❷,** run by remarkable and friendly hosts. Ask for a tour of Jim's driftwood sculptures. (☎285-2477. The hostel is nestled amid unmarked logging roads; call for directions or pick-up. Singles $16.) **Heron House ❷,** 646 Maple Rd., provides comfortable beds, spectacular views and a friendly host, just a short hike from Rebecca Spit Provincial Park. (☎285-3876. Dorm beds $20; private boathouse $55.) Several minutes down Heriot Bay Rd. from the beauty of **Rebecca Spit Provincial Park** and Heriot Bay, the **We Wai Kai Campsite ❶** lies on the water. (☎285-3111. Open May 15-Sept. 15. Sites $19-21; RV sites $25. Coin showers, laundry.) **Heriot Bay Inn Fireside Lounge ❷,** Heriot Bay Rd., near the Cortes Ferry, is one of the few restaurants on the island, with a decent pub scene on the weekends. (☎285-3322. Burgers $6-8, beer $4.50. Open daily 7am-9pm.) **Spirit of the West** rents kayaks and runs guided trips that explore Quadra Island's wildlife-rich shores and beyond. (☎285-2121 or 800-307-3982; www.kayakingtours.com. Singles $40 per 8hr., $50 per day; doubles $55/$75. Full-day tour $89, including a huge lunch; sunset tour $89 with snack; 4-day kayaking trip also available.) **Island Cycle,** in the same building, rents bikes. (☎285-3939; www.quadraisland.ca/islandcycle. $14 per 2hr., $25 per day.)

STRATHCONA PROVINCIAL PARK ☎250

Elk, deer, marmots, and wolves all inhabit Strathcona's over 2000 sq. km; it's one of the best-preserved wilderness areas on Vancouver Island and the oldest provincial park in BC. The park spans the land just west of the Comox Valley, reaching north to connect with Campbell River via Hwy. 28. It stretches from sea level to the highest point on Vancouver Island, 2200m Golden Hinde.

◪ ⁊ ORIENTATION AND PRACTICAL INFORMATION. The park is accessible from Courtenay or Campbell River. The two **BC Parks** offices are on **Buttle Lake** (open late June F-Su 9am-4pm), on Hwy. 28 between Gold River and Campbell River, and **Mount Washington/Forbidden Plateau,** outside Courtenay off Hwy. 19. For park info, contact the BC Parks District Manager (☎954-4600).

⁊ ⁊ ACCOMMODATIONS AND CAMPING. The two frontcountry **campgrounds,** with 161 sites between them, are Buttle Lake and Ralph River. Both are on the shores of Buttle Lake and accessible by **Highway 28** and secondary roads (follow the highway signs). **Buttle Lake ❶,** 50km from Campbell River (about 45min. of scenic but winding driving), has comfortable sites, a playground, and sandy beaches on the lake ($14). Less crowded **Ralph River ❶,** 75km (1½hr. drive) west of Campbell River, provides convenient access to the park's best hiking trails ($14). Five smaller marine campsites are accessible only by trails (pick up a map at the park entrance, $5). The **Ark Resort ❶,** 11000 Great Central Lake Rd., just west of Port Alberni off Hwy. 4, rents two-person canoes ($140 for 4 days) for the 35km water journey to the Della Falls trailhead (see **Hiking,** below) or provides a water taxi for $95 per person round-trip. (☎723-2657; www.arkresort.com. Sites $22; RV sites $33; rooms $65.) For outfitting and outdoor guidance on the doorstep of the park, **Strathcona Park Lodge ❷,** 30km from Campbell River on Hwy. 28, offers equipment rental and guides. The lodge has roomy lakefront houses and a dining hall. (☎286-3122; www.strathcona.bc.ca. Single kayaks $9 per hr., $37 per day; doubles $14/$53; 17 ft. sailboats $20/$70. Dining hall open late June-early Sept. 7-9am and noon-2pm $10; 5:30-7pm $17; 6-9pm a la carte.)

▨ HIKING. The park offers a great variety of trails of all lengths and difficulties. Visitors who wish to explore Strathcona's **backcountry areas** must camp 1km from main roads and at least 30m away from water sources; campfires are discouraged. Those entering the undeveloped areas of the park should notify park officials of their intended departure and return times and should be well equipped (maps and rain gear are essential). Be sure to check back in with wardens upon your return.

Karst Creek Trail (1.3km loop, 45min.). Leaves from the Karst Creek day-use area and passes limestone sinkholes and waterfalls. Easy.

Lower Myra Falls Trail (1km one-way, 20-40min.) starts 1km past Thelwood bridge at the south end of Buttle Lake at a marked parking area. The trail features a walk through old-growth forest and a steep hill with loose rock on the way to the immense, pounding falls. Moderate.

Elk River Trail (11km one-way, 4-6hr.). This popular trail starts just before Drum Lakes along Hwy. 28; follow signs to trailhead on the left. A campsite at 9km has bear food caches. The trail gains 600m in elevation as it follows an old elk trail to Landslide Lake, where part of Mt. Colonel Foster fell into the water. Moderate.

Phillips Ridge (6.5km one-way, 2-5hr.). Trailhead at the parking lot just south of the campsite along the highway. The trail leads to Arnica Lake and wildflower-strewn alpine meadows, passing 2 waterfalls and ascending 700m along the way. Difficult.

BRITISH COLUMBIA

PORT MCNEILL AREA   ☎250

The protected waters and plentiful fish of Johnstone Strait provide a fine summer home for orca pods. Mainland and island settlements near Port McNeill provide for beautiful quiet waterside trips. The fascinating native and local history adds to the splendor of the area. Port McNeill is the best base for exploring the surrounding hot spots of **Telegraph Cove, Alert Bay,** and **Sointula.**

⑦ PRACTICAL INFORMATION. Gray Line (☎956-3556) runs one bus per day to Port McNeill from Victoria (9hr., $93). **BC Ferries** (☎956-4533 or 888-223-3779; www.bcferries.com) runs from Port McNeill to Sointula on Malcolm Island (30min.) and Alert Bay (45min.; 6 per day; round-trip $6-6.25, car $14-16, free between islands). **Visitors centers** are stationed at 351 Shelley Crescent in Port McNeill (☎956-3131; www.portmcneill.net. Open June-Sept. 9am-5pm) and 118 Fir St. in Alert Bay. (☎974-5024. Open daily June-Sept. 9am-6pm; Sept.-June M-F 9am-5pm.) The **police** station is at 2700 Paddington Crescent (☎956-4441). The **hospital** is at 2750 Kingcome Pl. (☎956-4461) in Port McNeill.

IN TELEGRAPH COVE. With a permanent population of 6 people, this old sawmill town and fish saltery 25km south of Port McNeill has become a resort town. Turn left south of town on the Island Hwy.; over the last 5km it becomes an unpaved road. **Telegraph Cove Resort ❷** provides cabins in the old town buildings and a 125-site campground. (☎928-3131 or 800-200-4665; www.telegraphcoveresort.com. Sites $20, with electricity $24; RV sites $25; cabin rooms $80-175). The resort's **Killer Whale Cafe ❹**, decorated in yellow cedar and stained glass, is the only restaurant in town, and the prices show it. (☎928-3155. Dinner from $15. Open daily 8am-2:30pm and 4-10pm.) **Stubbs Island Whale Watching** runs tours in the M.V. Lukwa, the longest-running whale watching service in the area. (☎925-3185 or 800-665-3066; www.stubbs-island.com. 1pm departures $70, ages 65 and older and 1-12 $60, 9am departures all $60). **North Island Kayaks** in Port Hardy (see below) will pick up and drop off in the cove.

IN ALERT BAY. Tiny Cormorant Island and the town of Alert Bay are home to a rich repository of native culture. The cultural legacy of several groups of the Kwak-waka'wakw peoples (ka-kwak-QUEW-wak; formerly known as the Kwakiutl or Kwagiulth) sets the fishing village apart from its aquatourist siblings. By the Big House stands a 173 ft. **totem pole,** the tallest in the world. Two kilometers north of the ferry terminal, the pole towers over the ◪**U'mista Cultural Centre,** which houses an astonishing array of Kwakwaka'wakw artifacts which were repatriated decades after Canadian police pillaged a potlatch. U'mista means "the return of a loved one taken captive by raiding parties." (☎974-5403; www.umista.org. Open daily June-Sept. 9am-5pm; Oct.-May M-F 9am-5pm.) The **Sun Spirit Hostel and Guesthouse ❷,** 549 Fir St. in Alert Bay, is a welcome spot to play piano and whale watch from the spacious living room while chatting with the friendly hosts. (☎974-2026. Internet $9 per hr. Dorm beds $19, cash only.) The budget-mindful eschew island restaurants for the hardtack at **ShopRite,** 99 Fir St. (☎974-2777. Open M-Sa 9am-6pm, Su 10am-5pm.) The **Old Customs House ❷,** across the street from the visitors center, provides an expansive menu, and a filling meal can be had for less than $10. (☎974-2282; www.alert-bay.com/customs. Open daily 10am-9pm). **Seasmoke** whale watching offers great tours in a 40 ft. sailboat made homey by fresh baked goods and a friendly staff. (☎974-5225 or 800-668-6722; www.seaorca.com. 5hr. tour $75, ages 11 and under $60). **Alert Bay Ecological Park** offers great short hikes and prime opportunities for bald eagle and raven sightings.

IN SOINTULA. On the coast of Malcolm Island, the quiet town of Sointula (Soyn-TU-la, pop. 876) is a modern artists' and fishing haven originally established to be a utopian community based on farming, fishing, and forestry. (Sointula is Finnish for harmony.) The town relishes its history, and there are stories and signs of its past throughout. **Bere Point Regional Park,** whose beach is frequented by orcas, offers beautiful camping with a view of the coastal range. (☎956-3301. 11 sites. Reservations are essential.) The aptly named **Beautiful Bay Trail** (5km one-way) runs from Bere Pt. along the coast to Malcolm Pt. and offers great views.

PORT HARDY   ☎250

Port Hardy, an idyllic logging and fishing community, is the southern terminus for the BC Ferries route up the Inside Passage. The northernmost major town on the island, it has a vested interest in tourism. You will be welcomed by a chainsaw-carved sign, erected for the 1500 passengers who sleepily disembark the ferry every other night. These transients join a surge of fishermen preparing for unpredictable fall fisheries on the west coast of BC and a growing indigenous population drawn from more remote towns by the lures of schooling and employment.

TRANSPORTATION. Port Hardy, on Vancouver Island, is perched 36km north of Port McNeill and 238km (2½hr.) north of Campbell River on **Highway 19.** The main drag, **Market Street,** runs through the shopping district and along a scenic seaside path. **Gray Line** (☎949-7532), opposite the visitors center on Market St., runs to Victoria (10hr., $104) via Nanaimo (7hr., $84) each day at 9am and when the ferry arrives. **BC Ferries** (☎949-6722 or 888-223-3779; www.bcferries.com) depart 3km south of town at Bear Cove, for Prince Rupert (every other day May-Sept.; winter every Sa and 2nd W $55-76, ages 5-11 $28-38, car $128-178). The Discovery Coast Passage route between Port Hardy and Bella Coola runs Tu and Sa from mid-June to mid-Sept. ($107, ages 5-11 $54, car $213). Booking at least one month ahead for cars is suggested. **North Island Taxi** (☎949-8800) services the ferry from all over town for $5.25 per person, $6.50 to the airport.

ORIENTATION AND PRACTICAL INFORMATION. To reach the **visitors center,** 7250 Market St., follow Hwy. 19 to its end and take a right on Market St. (☎949-7622; www.ph-chamber.bc.ca. Open mid-May to Labor Day M-F 8:30am-7pm, Sa-Su 9am-5pm; Labor Day to mid-May M-F 9am-5pm. The **Port Hardy Museum** (see **Sights and Outdoor Activities,** below) also has in-depth info on the region. The **CIBC bank,** 7085 Market St., has a **24hr. ATM.** (☎949-6333. Open M-Th 10am-4pm, F 10am-6pm.) The **Port Hardy Adventure Center,** 8635 Granville St., rents bikes (☎949-7707; www.adventurecenter.ca. $5 per hr, $25 per day. Open daily 10am-5pm.) For all else, there's **Jim's Hardy Sports,** in the Thunderbird Mall. (☎949-8382. Open M-Sa 9:30am-6pm, Su noon-5pm.) Do laundry at the **Shell Station** on Granville St. (☎949-2366. Wash $1.75; dry $0.25 per 7min. Open 24hr.) **Internet** access is $2 per hr. at the **library,** 7110 Market St. (☎949-6661. Open Tu 10am-6pm, W and F noon-5pm, Th noon-5pm and 6-8pm, Sa 10am-2pm.) The **police** are at 7355 Columbia St. (☎949-6335) and the **hospital** is at 9120 Granville St. (☎949-6161). The **post office** is at 715 Hall St. (☎800-267-1177. Open M-F 8:30am-5pm.) **Postal Code:** V0N 2P0.

FOOD. Stock up on groceries before the long ferry ride or trip down the island at **Glenway Foods,** 8645 Granville St. (☎949-5758. Open M-Sa 9am-9pm.) The burger is this town's budget meal, and one of the best is $6.50 at **I.V.'s Quarterdeck Pub ❷,** 6555 Hardy Bay Rd., on the fishing dock. The pub's great vegetarian fare, including delicious sandwiches ($5-8) is balanced by F prime rib night ($15 with all the trimmings) and $0.25 wings on W and Su. (☎949-6922; www.quarterdeckresort.net/pub. Open daily 11am-midnight.) The **Oceanside Restaurant & Pub ❶,** 6435 Hardy Bay Rd., just down from I.V.'s at the Glen Lyon Inn, has a terrific view and serves

$0.25 wings on W and F. (☎949-7115. Open daily 6:30am-9pm.) Breakfast at **Snuggles Restaurant ❶,** 4965 Byng Rd., by the Quatse River Campground is delicious and affordable. (☎949-7494. Breakfast starting at $5. Open daily 7:30am-9:30pm.)

🏠🏕 ACCOMMODATIONS AND CAMPING. The visitors center will reserve B&B rooms at no charge. Accommodations can fill up quickly the night before ferries leave and the night they arrive, so book ahead. (☎949-7622.) The 🌊**Dolphin House B&B ❸,** 297 Harbor Rd. in Coal Harbor, is a short excursion (20min.) from Port Hardy. This secluded establishment offers incredible ocean views, beautiful sculptures, an array of outdoor activities, proximity to native villages, charming hosts, and a delicious Northwest breakfast. Take Island Hwy. 19 to Coal Harbor Rd., turn right at the coffee shop in town, and head past the whale bones. (☎949-7576; www.mondaytourism.com/dolphin. Sauna, hot tub, and beach access. Free pickup from ferry, bus station, airport. Singles $50; doubles $60.) The proprietors of **Hudson's Home B&B ❹,** 9605 Scott St., provide all the TLC and large custom breakfasts you can handle, as well as a hot tub, Internet access, and pickup and drop-off from the bus station. (☎949-5110; www.bbcanada.com/hudsonshome. Singles $60; doubles $80.) **Bonita B&B ❸,** 9310 Elk Drive, offers guests privacy and their own sparkling kitchens. (☎949-6787; www.bbcanada.com/5406.html. Singles $50; double $65-70.) Quiet, wooded sites can be found at **Quatse River Campground ❶,** 8400 Byng Rd., just minutes from Snuggles Restaurant (see **Food,** above), or a 25min. walk from town. (☎949-2395; www.quatsecampground.com. May-Sept. $14; RV sites $18. Oct.-Mar. $10; RV sites $15. Laundry, free showers.) The campground shares its grounds with (and financially supports) a nearby fish hatchery. (☎949-9022. Open 8am-4pm. Tours are best Sept.-Nov.)

👁🔦 SIGHTS AND OUTDOOR ACTIVITIES. The **Port Hardy Museum and Archives** is at 7110 Market St., beneath the library. The museum's sea-creature remnants, 19th-century Cape Scott pioneers' personal effects, and 8000-year-old tools from Hardy Bay merit a visit. (☎949-8143; www.northislandmuseums.com. Open May 15-Sept. Tu-Sa 10am-3:30pm; Oct.-May 14 W-Sa 10am-3pm. Donation requested.) A 15min. drive from town brings picnickers to the hard sand of **Storey's Beach,** a good place to put in a kayak, stroll along the rocky shore, or take a (chilly) swim. Turn left off the Island Hwy. when driving out of town onto Byng Rd. and then take a left on Beaver Harbour Rd. to the water. Nearby, the **Copper Maker,** 114 Copper Way, commissions some of the finest Kwakiutl carvers in the region. From Byng Rd., turn left onto Beaver Harbour Rd., right on Tsak'is Way, and right again. (☎949-8491; www.calvinhunt.com/gallery.htm. Call for hours.) Farther down Tsak'is Way, a ceremonial and community **bighouse** overlooks the sea from the heart of Fort Rupert village, a site inhabited by the Kwakiutl for thousands of years. **Petroglyphs** adorn rocks near **Fort Rupert;** the museum can give advice on locating them at low tide. At the north end of the village stands the decaying stone chimney of Fort Rupert, an outpost built in 1849 by the Hudson's Bay Company.

A map of logging roads from the visitors center will allow you to explore the **geological curiosities** of the region's limestone bedrock, or just to get out into the woods: Devil's Bath sinkhole, the Vanishing and Reappearing Rivers, and several explorable caves are all located toward **Port Alice** (40min. from town). **Vancouver Island Nature Exploration** runs cave tours in the area. (☎902-2662; www.nature-exploration.com. 2-3hr. tour $90, 4-5hr. $160, 5-7hr., $240. Reservations required.) **North Island Kayak** at the **Port Hardy Adventure Center,** 8635 Granville St., offers rentals, guided tours, and instruction. (☎949-7707 or 877-949-7707; www.kayakbc.ca. Open daily 10am-5pm. Canoes $7 per hr., $40 per day; single kayak $10/$55; double $14/$75. Sunset trips $39-119.) The Port Hardy area is known for some of the world's best **cold-water diving. Sun Fun Divers** (☎956-2243; www.sunfundivers.com)

rents gear ($75 first day, $25 second day) and runs full-day trips ($114 per person) out of Port Hardy and Port McNeill. **North Island Diving and Water Sports,** at Market and Hastings St. also does rentals and charters. (☎949-2664; www.northisland-diver.com. Open daily mid-June to mid-Sept. 9am-6pm; mid-Sept. to mid-June Tu-Sa 10am-5pm; full setup around $100. Single dive charter in Hardy Bay $50.)

INTERIOR BRITISH COLUMBIA

From the jagged snow-capped Rocky Mountains, the Fraser River courses and hurtles its way through 1300km of canyons and plateaus on its journey toward a land more arid than the Pacific. The sweeping agricultural basin in the middle of BC, between the Rockies and the Coast Range mountains, sees much more sun than the coast and is a vacation hot spot for city-slickers and backcountry adventurers alike. The Rockies form the boundary that was finally breached by rail lines to unite Canada, and the mountains still constitute a large part of western Canada's identity. Today they are home to hugely popular national parks and thousands of square kilometers of hiking, climbing, and camping. Bus and train routes cross the interior and pass by various means through the mountains.

FRASER RIVER CANYON

In 1808, Simon Fraser enlisted the help of native guides to make the perilous expedition down the river from Mt. Robson to Vancouver. Today's route from Cache Creek to Hope on the Trans-Canada Hwy. (Hwy. 1) makes his trailblazing seem like a distant dream. Up close, the canyon is a good place to feel small, with 200km of pounding rapids below and pine sprouting out of near-vertical rock walls above.

In quiet Hope, travelers will find a tranquil town despite its fame as the Chainsaw Carving Capital. Hope's location at the intersection of several highways ensures easy arrival and departure. The Trans-Canada Hwy. (Hwy. 1) originates in Vancouver, passes through Hope, and then bends north to Yale and eventually Cache Creek, where it meets the Cariboo Hwy. (Hwy. 97; see p. 389). Hwy. 7 runs west along the north bank of the Fraser River to Vancouver. The Crowsnest Hwy. (Hwy. 3) winds east through breathtaking country like Manning Provincial Park, through Kootenay Country to Nelson, and over Crowsnest Pass into Alberta. The Coquihalla Hwy. (Hwy. 5) is a toll road ($10) running north to Kamloops, is preferred by those heading to the Rockies in a hurry—it's nearly three hours faster.

HOPE ☎604

Buses arrive in Hope at the **Greyhound** station, #1, 800 3rd Ave, in the back of Midtown Laundromat. (☎869-5522. Open M 8am-1pm, Tu-F 8am-3pm, 4-9pm, Sa 8am-noon, Su 8am-3pm, holidays 8am-1pm.) Buses run north on the Coquihalla to Kamloops (2½hr., 3 per day, $32), then east to Banff (10½hr., 3 per day, $94), Calgary (12hr., 3 per day, $116), and Jasper (8½hr., 2 per day, $93); north on Hwy. 1 along the Fraser Canyon to Cache Creek (2¾hr., 2 per day, $27); east on Hwy. 3 to Penticton (3½hr.; 2 per day, 1 on Sa; $37) and points east; and west to Vancouver (2½hr., 8 per day, $22). **Gardner Chev-Olds,** 945 Water Ave., rents cars. (☎869-9511. $40 per day, 7th day free. $0.13 per km after 100km. Must be 25 or older with credit card. Open M-Sa 8am-6pm.) For biking, hiking, fishing, and hunting needs, stop by

Cheyenne Sporting Goods, 267 Wallace St. (☎869-5062. Open M-Sa 8:30am-5:30pm.)
The **Visitors Centre,** 919 Water Ave., provides the riveting, self-guided **Rambo Walking Tour** (First Blood was filmed here) in addition to sharing info on Fraser River Canyon and Manning Park. (☎869-2021 or 800-435-5622; www.destinationhopeandbeyond.com. Open daily July-Aug. 8am-8pm; June M-F 9am-5pm, Sa-Su 8am-6pm; Sept.-May M-F 8am-4pm.) Ask about the **Carving Walking Tour** through downtown, which runs through Memorial Park in the town's center. The **police** are located at 690 Old Hope-Princeton Way (☎869-7750), and the **post office** is at 777 Fraser St. (☎869-9019; Open M-F 8:30am-5pm.) **Postal Code:** V0X 1L0. **The Blue Moose Cafe,** 322 Wallace St., offers **Internet** access ($.10 per min, free Bluetooth wireless) and a variety of coffee ($1.65), smoothies ($4), and beer ($4). (☎869-0729; www.bluemoosecafe.com. Open M-F 8am-10pm, Su 9am-10pm.)

There's a wide selection of motels in downtown Hope. On the outskirts of town, **Holiday Motel ❸,** 63950 Old Yale Rd., offers an outdoor swimming pool, playground, volleyball court and fire-pit. (☎869-5352. Rooms with cable TV start at $40. Tent sites $19; RV sites $22; both include showers.) Campers can head for the big trees at the spacious and secure **Coquihalla Campsite ❶,** 800 Kawkawa Lake Rd., off 6th Ave., on the east side of town along the banks of the Coquihalla River. Party animals may want to consider other campsites–the front gate at Coquihalla closes at 11pm. (☎869-7119 or 888-869-7118. Open Apr.-Oct. 122 sites, $17; river sites $20; RV sites $23.) Shop for groceries at **Buy and Save Foods,** 489 Wallace St. (☎869-5318. Open daily July-Aug. 8am-10pm; daily Sept.-June 8am-9pm.) Locals feast on generous portions of homemade cherry pie ($3.50 per slice) at the **Home Restaurant ❷,** 665 Old Hope Princeton Hwy. (☎869-5558. Open daily 6am-11pm.)

AROUND HOPE   ☎604

Seven hikes begin in or near Hope. The lush **Rotary Trail** (20min.) on Wardle St., is a casual walk with views of the Fraser and Coquihalla Rivers. **Mount Hope Lookout** (45min.) offers an impressive view of the town and surrounding area. This trail continues past the Lookout to become the **Mount Hope Loop** (4 hr. round trip; challenging). (Hike begins at intersection of Hwy. #1 and Old Hope Princeton Way, off the dirt road behind the picnic tables.) Pause for a pleasant diversion at **Kawkawa (a.k.a. Suckers) Creek,** off Union Bar Rd., enhanced in 1984 to aid the late summer and mid-fall salmon spawning. The boardwalk along the creek leads to a swimming hole and picnicking spot. **Manning Provincial Park** (☎800-330-3321), 30min. east of Hope on Hwy. 3, has more extensive hiking options with over 70,000 hectares of cedar rainforest and flowering alpine meadows. April through September, campers have access to four **campgrounds ❶** throughout the park: **Lightning Lake Campground, Coldspring, Mule Deer,** and **Hampton.** September through April campers have two campgrounds, **Lone Duck** and **Cambie.** (350 total sites. Tents $14; RVs $22.) Rent bikes at the Lightning Lake boathouse ($13 per hr.). **Paintbrush Nature Trail** provides a rare opportunity to enjoy subalpine meadows, which bloom late July to early August. (1km, 20 min; wheelchair-accessible.) For a more difficult hike, the **Pacific Crest Trail** passes through Manning at Windy Joe. A parking lot ($3 per day) is on the Gibson Pass Road. (13km one-way).

OTHELLO-QUINTETTE TUNNELS. The **Coquihalla Canyon Recreation Area** is a 10min. drive east of Hope along Kawkawa Lake Rd. Here the **Othello-Quintette Tunnels,** blasted through solid granite, provide mute evidence of the daring engineering that led to the opening of the **Kettle Valley Railway** in 1916. The railway has since been turned into an easy walking path, allowing hikers to walk through the dark tunnels, leading to narrow bridges over whitewater that shoots through the gorge. These tunnels serve as the backdrop to many Hollywood adventure films: First

Southern British Columbia

Blood (Rambo), Shoot to Kill, and Far from Home: Adventures of Yellowdog. To get there, follow the signs right on Othello Rd. off Kawkawa Lake Rd. and right again on Tunnel Rd.; allow 30min. to walk through the tunnels.

LADY FRANKLIN ROCK AND RAFTING. For a closer view of the Fraser River, head 36km east on Hwy. 1 to the town of **Yale.** Take the first right after the traffic light, then follow the gravel road for about 1km to a view of the majestic **Lady Franklin Rock,** which splits the river into two sets of rapids (class III-IV). **Fraser River Raft Expeditions,** south of town, runs full-day whitewater trips almost daily on the Fraser and its tributaries. Travelers can stay in an oversized teepee or in the B&B. (☎863-2336 or 800-363-7238. Rafting with lunch $120. B&B single $60; double $70.)

HELL'S GATE AIRTRAM. When Simon Fraser made his pioneering trek down the river in 1808, he likened one stretch of rapids carrying double the volume of Niagara Falls, 25km north of Yale on Hwy. 1, to the Gates of Hell—where "no human beings should venture." **The Hell's Gate Airtram,** 43111 Hwy. 1, transports the vertigo-immune 500 ft. down into the canyon to a restaurant and viewing deck in four minutes, although acrophobes and budgeteers may prefer the nearby 1km trail and bridge into the gorge and across the river. (☎867-9277; www.hellsgateairtram.com. Open mid-May to early Sept. 9:30am-5:30pm; early Apr. to mid-May and early Sept. to mid-Oct. 10am-4pm. $13, seniors $11, ages 6-18 $9, families $35.)

KAMLOOPS
☎250

T'Kumlups, a Shuswap word meaning "where the waters meet," fits the town well, as Kamloops surrounds the convergence of the North and South Thompson rivers and the heavily traveled Hwys. 5 and 1. Over 200 lakes lie within an hour's drive of town. That, combined with a fine hostel, outdoor live music in the summer, and numerous outdoor adventure opportunities, makes "BC's Adventure Destination" a great base for area daytripping or a good waystation on long highway voyages.

■ 🔃 ORIENTATION AND PRACTICAL INFORMATION. Kamloops lies 356km east of Vancouver and 492km west of Banff, anchoring the junction of the Yellowhead (Hwy. 5) and Trans-Canada (Hwy. 1). **VIA Rail** (☎888-842-7245) trains stop at North Station, 11km north of the city center off Hwy. 5 (the station is only open a half hour before arrival, so book ahead), making three runs per week to Edmonton (15hr., $226) and Vancouver (8½hr., $102). **Greyhound,** 725 Notre Dame Ave. (☎374-1212), leaves Kamloops for Vancouver (4½hr., 7 per day, $54); Jasper (6hr., 3 per day, $60); and Calgary (9hr., 3 per day, $90). **Kamloops Transit System** will get you around in town. (☎376-1216; www.city.kamloops.bc.ca/transportation/transit-buses. $1.50, all-day pass $3.75. Buses run M-Sa 6:30am-11pm, Su 6:30am-5pm.) **Cycle Logical,** 194 Victoria St. (☎828-2810), rents bikes for $25 per day. Kamloops claims to be the geographically largest city in North America; get a free map from the **visitors center,** just off the Trans-Canada Hwy. at Exit #368. (☎374-3377 or 800-662-1994. Open daily mid-May to Sept. 9am-6pm; Oct. to mid-May M-F 9am-5pm.) **McCleaners,** 437 Seymour St. (☎372-9655), is a McLaundry. The **police** station is at 560 Battle St. (☎828-3000) in the city center. Free **Internet** access can be found at the **public library,** 465 Victoria St. (☎372-5145; www.tnrdlib.bc.ca. Open Tu-Th 10am-9pm, M and F-Sa 10am-5pm, Su noon-4pm.) The **post office** is at 217 Seymour St. (☎374-2444. Open M-F 8:30am-5pm.) **Postal Code:** V2C 5K2.

🔳🔲 ACCOMMODATIONS AND FOOD. The excellent 🔳**Kamloops Old Courthouse Hostel (HI) ❶,** 7 W Seymour St., at the intersection of Seymore and 1st, is in fact a turn-of-the-century courthouse. The old courtroom has become a giant common room, the jury box, judge's bench, and witness stand still intact. The tightly packed dorm rooms are in the judge's old chambers. (☎828-7991. Check-in 8am-noon and 5-10pm. 75 beds. Sept.-late June $17, nonmembers $21; late June-Aug. $19, nonmembers $23; private rooms $5 surcharge.) Campers can stay the night 8km east of the city center at **Kamloops View Tent and Trailer Park ❷**, 1-4395 Trans-Canada Hwy. E., which features forty sites, flush toilets, free showers, and laundry. (☎573-3255. Sites $16; full RV sites $25.)

A huge variety of foods lines Victoria St., the main strip downtown. **Amsterdam Pancake House ❷**, 369 Victoria St., serves the best breakfast in town: Dutch-style *pannenkoeken* (somewhere between a crepe and an American pancake) are $5-9 and grilled sandwiches $5-6. (☎377-8885. Open daily 8am-3pm.)

◪ **SIGHTS.** Every night in July and August at 7:30pm there is "Music in the Park," as bands perform in **Riverside Park** on the banks of the Thompson River. **Secwepemc Museum and Heritage Park**, 355 Yellowhead Hwy., is devoted to preserving the heritage of the Shuswap people. It contains the reconstructed remains of a 2000-year-old Shuswap village. Located near the site of a school from which the Canadian government removed native children as late as the 1970s, the museum is a testament to the endurance of the First Nations. (☎828-9801; www.secwepemc.org/museum.html. Open June to Labor Day M-F 8:30am-5pm, Sa-Su 9am-5pm; Labor Day to May M-F 8:30am-4:30pm. $8, ages 60 and older and 16 and under $7.)

◪ **OUTDOOR ACTIVITIES. Sun Peaks**, 1280 Alpine Rd., a 45min. drive north of Kamloops, is a powdery magnet for snowboarders and skiers. The mountain's large vertical drop (881m), annual snowfall (559cm), and 3678 skiable acres served by five chairlifts justify the somewhat pricey tickets. In summer, the lift carries hikers and bikers up to trails and wildflower meadows. (☎800-807-3257; www.sunpeaksresort.com. Hiking $12, seniors and ages 13-18 $11, 6-12 $9; mountain biking $26, ages 65 and older and 13-18 $22, 6-12 $12; winter access $56/$49/$30.) To get to Sun Peaks, take Hwy. 5 north from Kamloops, turn right at Heffley Creek and continue 31km. The **Stake Lake Trails** form a network of cross-country skiing terrain, with a good selection of beginner and intermediate options. Take Exit 366 from Hwy. 1 south of Kamloops, and follow Lac Le Jeune Rd. for 20min. Ask for a map at the visitors center or get one at the hut in winter. (Snow report ☎372-5514. $7 per day, $30 per 5 days. Summer usage for biking or hiking is free.)

For an up-close look at the creatures inhabiting the area surrounding the rails, check the **Wildlife Park**, 15min. east of Kamloops along Hwy. 1, a non-profit organization devoted to rehabilitating local wildlife. (☎573-3242; www.kamloopswildlife.org. $9, ages 65 and older and 13-16 $8, 3-12 $5.) Local climbers head out to **rock climb** at **The Beach**, about 25km west of Kamloops on Hwy. 1. Always in the shade, these 35 easy-to-moderate sport climbs offer a scenic view of Kamloops Lake. **Ropes End Climbing Gym**, 975 B Laval Cres. (☎372-0645; www.ropesendgym.com), has more details. **Ark Park Trout Fishing** (☎573-3878; www.arkpark.com) offers cheap fly-fishing trips starting at $20. Call for transportation info.

CLEARWATER AND WELLS GRAY ☎250

Wells Gray Provincial Park, 12km north of Clearwater, is largely an untamed wilderness—only about a fifth of the park's 540,000 hectacres are accessible by vehicle and developed trails, and the northern half of the park is completely undeveloped. Its unnamed, unclimbed peaks and glaciers require a multi-day backcountry trek to reach and are among the wildest places left in North America.

BRITISH COLUMBIA

■**█ ORIENTATION AND PRACTICAL INFORMATION.** The town of Clearwater, "Gateway to Wells Gray Park," sits on Hwy. 5, 120 km north of Kamloops. **VIA Rail** runs three times per week to Edmonton ($196) and Vancouver ($142). Trains stop by request only; 48hr. advance notice is required. **Greyhound** buses run east to Edmonton (8 hr., 2 per day, $94) and west to Vancouver (7 hr., 2 per day, $69). In an emergency, call the **police** (☎674-2237) or the **hospital** (☎674-2244). For **groceries**, head to Safety Mart, 74 Young St. (☎674-2213. Open M-Th 9am-7pm, F 9am-8pm, Sa 9am-6pm, Su 9am-5pm.) Buy maps of the park ($3) at the **visitors center**, 425 E. Yellowhead Hwy. (☎674-2646; www.ntvalley.com/clearwaterchamber. Open daily Apr.-July and Sept.-Oct. 10am-5pm; July-Aug. 9am-6pm.)

█**█ ACCOMMODATIONS AND CAMPING.** Most accommodations in town are expensive B&Bs, but the **Half-Moon Hostel ❷**, 625 Greer Rd. (☎694-4199; www.halfmoonhostel.com) 3km north of town offers 8 clean bunks and a TV room in a renovated barn for $20 per night. In Wells Gray, **backcountry camping ❶** is $5 per person. Those who lack the equipment or time for a backcountry expedition can stay with the RVs in one of the park's four vehicle-accessible **campgrounds ❶**, which offer spacious and clean primitive sites ($14).

█**. OUTDOOR ACTIVITIES.** For most, the highlight of the park is Helmcken Falls, a spectacular 143m waterfall accessible either by an easy 3km hike or a five-minute drive. The southern half of the park is mostly accessible by canoe and backpack; maintained campgrounds dot the Clearwater, Azure, and Murtle Lakes. While much of the park requires a canoe or kayak to explore, the Trophy Mountains in the southeastern corner have easily accessible backcountry camping above the treeline; the hiking is moderate, thanks to a forest service road that takes hikers to the edge of the treeline. But the elevation comes at a price; weather is much more unpredictable, and snowpacks blanket the trail well into June.

In case you forgot your boat (or anything else), **Clearwater Lake Tours** (☎674-2121; www.clearwaterlaketours.com) rents canoes ($40 per day, reservations recommended in July and August), tents ($10 per day), and even cookware ($3 per day). They also offer guided canoeing and hiking ($250 per day) and a 4hr. power-boat tour of 100km of Clearwater and Azure Lakes, the easiest way to see the rugged interior of the park ($50). **Bearfoot Outdoors,** 425 E. Yellowhead Hwy., under the visitors center, has backpacking supplies and expert advice on planning your trip into the park. (☎674-3503; www.bearfoot.ca. Open daily 9:30am-7pm May-Oct.) **Interior Whitewater Expeditions** (☎800-661-7238; www.interiorwhitewater.bc.ca), in downtown Clearwater, runs **guided rafting** packages inside Wells Gray on the uncrowded and pristine Clearwater River. Prices range from an $80 three-hour trip to a $250 two-day package. **Vavenby Trail Rides** (☎676-9598; www.ntvalley.com/trailrides), 1.2km past the Vavenby Bridge, east of Clearwater on Hwy. 5, provides guided **horseback riding** for $20 per hr., and, in May and June, the opportunity to participate in a real **cattle drive** on their working ranch for $100 per day. In winter, call **Alaskan Husky Adventures** in Clearwater to get your mush on with frighteningly efficient blue-eyed dogs. (☎866-587-0037; www.dogsleddingadventures.com. Prices range from $30 for a one-hour introduction to an $800 24-hour "Iditarod-race-style" package. Open Dec.-Apr.)

SHUSWAP LAKE REGION ☎250

From the dugout canoes of the Shuswap to the RVs of today's vacationers, the warm waters and productive fisheries of the sublime Shuswap Lake have attracted people for centuries. The area is a peaceful place to stay for the night or to stop and enjoy the scenery. Salmon Arm, a bustling metropolis compared to the nearby villages, stands out mainly for its lakefront location and its poster-perfect back-drop of rolling, forested mountains. Beware: if you are going to try and find your way through Salmon Arm off the highway, have a good map—the streets are confusing. The area is rich in camping and fishing opportunities, making it a popular destination for British Columbians looking for a relaxing weekend getaway.

■ 7 ORIENTATION AND PRACTICAL INFORMATION. Shuswap Lake is shaped like a sideways 'H.' Hwy. 1 hugs the northern arm of the lake before dipping south and following the southern arm east from Salmon Arm. The **Salmon Arm Transit System** (☎832-0191) has scheduled ($1.25, M-Sa) and door-to-door service ($1.50, M-F), and the **Salmon Arm Taxi** can be reached at ☎832-2252, 24hr. The **visitors center** is at 200 Trans-Canada Hwy. SW (☎832-6247 or 877-725-6667; www.sachamber.bc.ca. Open May-Sept. M-Su 9am-7pm; Oct.-Apr. M-F 9am-4pm.) **Greyhound** is located at 50 10th St. SW and runs two buses daily to Calgary (7½hr., $75), Vancouver (6½hr., $69), and Jasper (8½ hr., $86). (☎832-3162. Open M-F 7:30am-9pm, Sa 7:30am-4pm and 8pm-9pm, Su 7:30-9:30am, 1-2:30pm, and 8pm-9pm. **Shuswap Laundry**, 330 Ross St., is a laundromat and dry cleaners. (☎832-7300. Open daily 6:30am-10pm. $2 per load.) The **hospital** is at 601 10th St. NE (☎833-3600). Free **Internet** access can be found at the **library,** in Picadilly Pl. Mall on 10th Ave. SW. (☎832-6161; www.checkout.orl.bc.ca. Open M, W-Th, and Sa 10am-5pm; Tu and F 10am-8pm.) The **post office** is at 370 Hudson St. NE. (☎832-3093. Open M-F 8:30am-5pm.) **Postal Code:** V1E 4M6.

▮ ▌ ACCOMMODATIONS AND CAMPING. ▧Squilax General Store and Caboose Hostel (HI) ❷, 10km east of Chase, 8km west of Sorrento on Hwy. 1, sleeps travelers in three decommissioned Canadian National Railway cabooses. All three were specially outfitted for hosteling with kitchenettes and restrooms. Ample lounge space, a traditional sweat lodge, laundry facilities, and use of the hostel's canoe are also part of the package; a pancake breakfast is available for $3. Reception noon-10pm daily. (☎675-2977. 24 beds $16; nonmembers $20. Tent sites by the river $8. Showers.) B&Bs are the way of Salmon Arm; for help finding a cheap one (prices range $45-100), visit or call the visitors center or Chamber of Commerce (see above). Campgrounds in Salmon Arm, especially those on Shuswap Lake, are often crowded and cramped. There are a handful of them on the lake side of Hwy. 1, about 10km west of Salmon Arm. For a peaceful stay, **Herald Provincial Park ❷** is a 27km drive northwest of Salmon Arm following signs off Hwy. 1. The park maintains 119 spacious, clean campsites with a large swimming area and access to day hiking along Margaret Falls. (Reservations ☎800-689-9025. $22. Firewood and hot showers included. See **Entertainment and Outdoor Activities,** below.)

◘ FOOD. The best food deal for miles around awaits at the **Real Canadian Wholesale Club,** 360 Hwy. 1. Even the non-bulk items cost less than at a supermarket. (☎804-0258. Open M-F 9am-9pm, Sa 9am-6pm, Su 10am-5pm.) Farther west on Hwy. 1, **De Mille Fruits and Vegetables,** 3710 10th Ave. SW, markets local produce like incredible sweet corn. (☎832-7550. Open daily June-Sept. 8am-8pm; Oct.-May 8am-6:30pm.) Satisfy your sweet tooth at **Wee Willie's Bakery & Deli ❶,** 160 Lakeshore Dr. (☎832-3888. Open M-F 7:30am-5:30pm, Sa 9am-5:30pm.)

▐ ▊ ENTERTAINMENT AND OUTDOOR ACTIVITIES. The ▧**Recline Ridge Vineyards & Winery,** 2640 Skimikin Rd., is the northernmost vineyard in North America and offers free tours (at 2pm and 4pm) and free tastings of their distinctively light and fruity wines. (☎835-2212; www.recline-ridge.bc.ca. Open daily noon-5pm, or by appointment). **Caravan Farm Theatre,** 8km northwest of Armstrong and 45min. from Salmon Arm, presents top-notch performances during summer. Tickets are

BRITISH COLUMBIA

FIRE SAFETY. The long sunny summer days in interior BC are ideal for hiking and backpacking, but they also dry the pine forests, making conditions ideal for forest fires. Nearly every summer, entire towns are threatened by uncontrolled blazes (in late June 2004, almost every resident of Lillooet was placed on a 15min. evacuation notice). Because of this, many campgrounds and most provincial parks do not allow open campfires, which can easily get out of control. If you are planning on doing much camping in interior BC, consider buying an isobutane gas stove (outdoors stores sell them for $40-70), or—a cheaper option—bringing along a cheap stove ($10-15) and a a tin of petroleum cooking fuel, like Sterno ($4). While sitting around the stove lacks the charm of a campfire, it may often be your only option for a warm supper (not to mention being cleaner, safer, easier, quicker, and better for the environment than an open fire). If you do build a fire, keep it small, and make sure your fire pit is inside an 8 ft. radius clear of flammable material. Those from more humid climates will be amazed at how quickly the dry deadwood can turn into an out-of-control bonfire.

available from the Squilax General Store and Hostel. (☎546-8533; www.caravan-farmtheatre.com. Shows at 8pm, M pay-what-you-can, Tu-Su. $12-20.) The mystery of curds is solved in a tour of **Gort's Gouda Cheese Factory,** 1470 50th St. SW. The tour is short and filled with tasty samples—skip the tour, stock up on bargain cheeses, and watch the cheese-making process, from cow to wax package, through viewing windows. (☎832-4274; www.gortsgoudacheese.bc.ca. Tours $3, mid-June to Aug. M-W and F 10am, store M-Sa 9am-5pm.) For an amazing festival of Native American dancing, visit the **Squilax Pow Wow** in North Shuswap, held on the 3rd weekend in July; call the visitors center for further info.

The area's outdoors attractions revolve around the waterways that surround town, and range from **fishing** for kokanee and rainbow trout in Lake Shuswap to taking a 10min. walk through **Herald Park** (see **Accommodations,** above) and viewing the lovely **Margaret Falls.** When doing the latter, be careful to stay on the path; the habitat is recovering from excessive trampling. Closer to town, many trails are open for hiking, biking, and cross-country skiing. **Skookum Cycle** at the intersection of 4th and Lakeshore in Salmon Arm, rents bikes for $25 per day and skis for $17 per day. (☎832-7368; www.skookumcycle.com. Open M-Sa 9:30am-6pm.) On the banks of Lake Shuswap, you can catch a glimpse of the rare Western grebe and ospreys from the birdblind next to the wharf on the protected shoreline around Salmon Arm. Call Shuswap Lakes Tourism Association (☎800-661-4800) for the date of this year's **Grebe Festival,** held in late May. **Adams River Rafting,** in Scotch Creek, leads 2hr. trips on the reasonably gentle (Class II-IV) **Adams River.** (☎800-440-7238; www.adamsriverrafting.com. $48, under 16 $38; 15% HI discount. Take Hwy. 1 to turnoff, cross the bridge, and continue 16km.) The paths along the river can be hiked or mountain-biked on an 18km round-trip trail. Take Squilax-Anglemont Rd. north across the bridge, just west of the Squilax General Store; the trail heads upriver across the first narrow bridge.

OKANAGAN VALLEY

Known throughout Canada for its bountiful fruit harvests, the Okanagan (oh-kuh-NAH-gan) Valley or "Canada's California," lures visitors with summer blossoms, ample sun, plentiful wineries, and tranquil lakes. The Okanagan Connector (Hwy. 97C) links Vancouver to the valley in a 4hr. drive, making it a popular vacation destination among sun-starved coastal British Columbians. In the winter, Big White and Apex Mountain ski resorts both attract skiers and

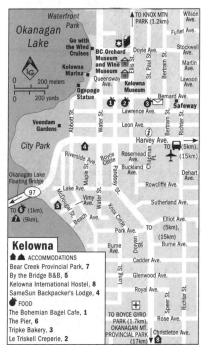

Kelowna

▲ ■ ACCOMMODATIONS
Bear Creek Provincial Park, 7
By the Bridge B&B, 5
Kelowna International Hostel, 8
SameSun Backpacker's Lodge, 4

🍴 FOOD
The Bohemian Bagel Cafe, 1
The Pier, 6
Tripke Bakery, 3
Le Triskell Creperie, 2

snowboarders looking to avoid long lines and pricey lift tickets at Whistler. Travelers looking to earn cash can sign on to pick fruit at one of the many orchards stretching south from Penticton to the US border along Hwy. 97.

KELOWNA ☎ 250

In the heart of the Okanagan Valley, Kelowna (kuh-LOW-nuh) is one of Canada's richest agricultural regions and a popular tourist destination. Kelowna (pop. 103,000) lies on the east shore of 170km long Okanagan Lake, halfway between Penticton to the south and Vernon to the north. The town's fruit stands, acclaimed wineries, and a unique blend of chains and independent shops draw thousands every summer. And in the winter, those not skiing in Whistler find the slopes of Big White Ski Resort equally rewarding.

⌐ TRANSPORTATION

Kelowna lies 400km east of Vancouver, 602km west of Calgary, and 86km north of Penticton on **Highway 97** at the eastern shore of Okanagan Lake. Hwy. 97, **Harvey Avenue** in town, runs east-west across the lake and bisects the town. The floating bridge across the lake is one-of-a-kind in Canada.

Buses: Greyhound, 2366 Leckie Rd. (☎860-3835 or 860-2364), off Harvey Ave. next to the Best Western, runs through Canada including to: **Calgary** (10hr., 3 per day, $85); **Penticton** (1½hr., 6 per day, $12); **Edmonton** (13½ hr., 2 per day, $125), and **Vancouver** (6½hr., 6 per day, $58). Ticket office open daily 7am-7pm, depot 7am-1am.

Public Transportation: Kelowna Regional Transit System (☎860-8121) services town. Runs, depending on the route, M-F 6am-midnight, Sa 8am-midnight, Su 9am-7pm. $1.75, ages 65 and older or under 21 $1.25, under 5 free; day pass $5/$4.50.

Taxis: Kelowna Cabs, 1180 Graham St. (☎762-2222 or 762-4444). $1.65 base, $2.60 1st km, $1.55 per additional km. 24hr.

Car Rental: Rent-A-Wreck, 2787 N Hwy. 97 (☎763-6632) at McCurdy Rd., will supply your means about town. Must have a major credit card and be 19 or older. From $30 per day, $0.12 per km over 100km. Open M-Sa 8am-5pm, Su 9am-4pm.

🛈 PRACTICAL INFORMATION

Tourist Office: 544 Harvey Ave. (☎861-1515; www.tourismkelowna.org). Brochures, bathrooms, and a doggie watering trough. Open May-Sept. M-F 8am-7pm, Sa-Su 9am-7pm; Oct.-Apr. M-F 8am-5pm, Sa-Su 10am-3pm.

Equipment: Sports Rent, 3000 Pandosy St. (☎861-5699; www.sportsrentkelowna.com). Mountain bikes starting at $23, in-line skates $11, kayaks $30, canoes $35, water skis starting at $20 (all daily rates, also offers two-day and weekly rates for all rentals). Weekend packages for downhill, cross-country, and snowboards available. Open daily May-Sept. 9am-6pm; Oct.-Apr. 9am-8pm.

Laundromat: Cullen's Cleaning Carousel, 2660 Pandosy St. (☎763-9992). Wash $1.75, dry $0.25 per 8min. Open M-F 8:30am-8pm, Sa 8:30am-6pm, Su 9am-5pm.

Police: 350 Doyle Ave. (☎762-3300).

Hospital: 2268 Pandosy St. (☎862-4000), 7 blocks south of Harvey Ave.

Forest Fire Report: ☎Dial 0 and ask for Zenith 555 or 800-633-5555.

Internet Access: Okanagan Regional Library Kelowna Branch, 1380 Ellis St. (☎762-2800; www.orl.kelowna.bc.ca), offers 1hr. of free Internet access. Open M and F-Sa 10am-5:30pm, Tu-Th 10am-9pm. The **SameSun Hostel** charges $1 for 10min., and **Kelowna International Hostel** offers 30min. for $1 (see **Accommodations and Camping,** below.)

Post Office: Town Centre Postal Outlet, 101-591 Bernard Ave. (☎868-8480). Open M-F 8:30am-5:30pm, Sa 9am-5pm. **Postal Code:** V1Y 7G0.

ACCOMMODATIONS AND CAMPING

Warm, dry summer days attract thousands seeking beaches and hot trails, so be sure to make reservations (at campgrounds too) or you'll be stuck in a chain hotel. If everything is full, there are numerous inns and chain hotels along **Lakeshore Drive** and **Route 97** in either direction.

Kelowna International Hostel (HI), 2343 Pandosy St. (☎763-6024; www.kelowna-hostel.bc.ca). Only 1 block from the beach in a colorfully painted, restored home, this laid-back hostel is a budget paradise with super-friendly hosts. Comfortable lounge, kitchen, included pancake and coffee breakfast, daily activities, and pick-up from bus station. Laundry $1.25 wash, $1.25 dry. Internet access $1 for 30min. Reception 7am-11pm, checkout 11am. 30 dorm beds. $19 with any hosteling membership, passport, or student card; otherwise $20. Private rooms $40. ❷

SameSun Backpacker's Lodge, 245 Harvey Ave. (☎861-3001 or toll-free 877-562-2783; www.samesun.com). Just across the floating bridge, you'll find this youth hostel featuring keg parties and BBQs ($5 hamburgers) almost every summer night. For daytime fun, join a bike trip to Mission Creek ($20, includes bike rental) or spend the day on the SameSun houseboat ($27 afternoon). Huge kitchen, fresh linens, and laundry facilities. Key deposit $5. Reception 7am-11pm. Call ahead if you'll arrive after-hours. Pickup from bus terminal $10. Dorm beds $20; private rooms $49; prices rise to $24 and $57 June-Aug. ❷

By the Bridge B&B, 1942 McDougall St. (☎860-7518; www.villagenet.ca/bythebridge), at the east end of Okanagan Lake Bridge, minutes from the beach and downtown. Cozy rooms, private baths, and included continental breakfast. Checkout 11am. Singles $49-69; doubles $59-79; triples $79-89; quads $89-99. ❸

Bear Creek Provincial Park, (☎800-689-9025 or 494-6500), 9km north of Hwy. 97 on Westside Rd. Day use/picnic area and camping. Unique features include shaded lakeside sites, 400m of Okanagan lake shore, boat launch, and a walking trail along the creek and waterfront. Lakeside sites go quickly in summer. 122 sites, $22. Campground gate closed to cars 10pm-7am. Free showers, firewood. ❶

FOOD

Kelowna overflows with fresh produce. Find juicy delights at the stands outside town along **Benvoulin Road** and **KLO Road,** or head south on **Lakeshore Drive** to the u-pick cherry orchards. In town, the shelves of **Safeway,** 697 Bernard Ave., are stocked with monster carrots and cucumbers. (☎860-0332. Open daily 8am-midnight.) **Bernard Avenue** is lined with restaurants and cafes.

The Bohemian Bagel Cafe, 363 Bernard Ave. (☎862-3517; www.vtours.com/boh). This cafe features rich breakfast and lunch offerings in a casual and colorful atmosphere right on the main drag. Try the mango-chutney turkey salad ($6.95), homemade bread and soup ($4.75), or a unique sandwich creation (starting at $5). Open Tu-F 7:30am-2:30pm, Sa 8:30am-2:30pm, Su 9am-1pm. ❶

The Pier Marina Pub & Grill, 2035 Campbell Rd. (☎769-4777), just across the floating bridge outside Kelowna. This unassuming joint serves up hot and heaping lunches—calamari ($7), burgers with lots of fixings ($8), and chowder ($5)—along with dinners at a steal, including an $11 12oz. Sirloin steak. Nine beers on tap all the time ($3.75 pint). Ask to sit on the patio for an incredible lake view. Open M-W and Su 11am-midnight, Th-Sa 11am-1am. ❷

Le Triskell Creperie, 467 Bernard Ave. (☎763-5151). This long, narrow restaurant with lace table coverings and Parisian artwork manages to emulate the essence of a sidewalk bistro. Crepes run from $2-4 simple sweet takeout options—sugar, lemon, nutella, and the like—all the way to full and decorative meal crepes ($5-12). Meal fillings include ingredients like eggs, goat cheese, or spinach, while dessert crepes overflow with chocolate sauces, caramel, or fruit ($4-6). Open M-W 9am-2pm, Th-F 9am-2pm and 5-10pm, Sa 10am-2pm and 5-10pm. ❶

Tripke Bakery Konditorei & Cafe, 567 Bernard Ave. (☎763-7666). You'll smell this European style bakery from across Lake Okanagan. Grab a loaf of health bread ($3.15) before taking off for an outdoor adventure. Or try one of their many pastries (cookies $0.39, homemade pretzels $0.75, and cinnamon buns $0.95.) For the hungrier they offer fresh quiche ($4-8), as well as a variety of sandwiches ($5-6) and homemade soups ($3-5). Open M-Sa 8am-5:30pm. ❶

SIGHTS

The sun is Kelowna's main attraction, warming Okanagan parks and beaches for an average of 2000hr. per year. **City Park** and **Waterfront Park,** on the west end of downtown, are popular hangouts for locals and tourists alike. **Boyce Gyro Park,** on Lakeshore Rd. south of the Okanagan Bridge, features beach volleyball. **Kelowna Parasail Adventures,** 1310 Water St. at the docks of Grand Okanagan Resort north of City Park., transforms patrons into kites, floating them high above the lake. (☎868-4838; www.parasailcanada.com. $50, $82 tandem. Open daily May-Sept. 9am-dusk.) Those wishing to splurge can rent small 4- to 8-person boats and jetskis at the **Kelowna Marina,** on the waterfront at the end of Queensway Ave. (☎861-8001; www.kelownamarina.com. Boats $50-100 per hr., jetskis $65 per hr., $170 per 3hr. Requires a $200 insurance deposit while you use the equipment. Open daily May-Sept. 7am-5pm.) Take a skippered sail around the lake with **Go With the Wind Cruises,** on the waterfront along Waterfront Walkway. (☎763-5204; www.gowiththewind.com. 2-4hr. sails, $25 per hr. Open daily May-Sept. 9am-6pm.)

The **Kelowna Museum,** 470 Queensway Ave., houses a wealth of regional artifacts, including those of the Okanagan and other First Nations; they also show temporary exhibits recognized as the best in the region. (☎763-2417; www.kelownamuseum.ca. Suggested donation $2, child $1. Open Tu-Sa 10am-5pm.)

LOCH NESS LITE

First reported in 1872, the sea monster Ogopogo is said to have pre-dated the native peoples of the Okanagan Lake area. Now affectionately dubbed "Ogie" by the people of Penticton and Kelowna, the monster was known as "N'ha-a-itk" in the native tongue. The 500 ft. creature has as many descriptions as it has nicknames, sporting either the head of a horse, a bearded goat, or a sheep, depending on whom you talk to. Experts agree that Ogopogo possesses a snake-like body—most Ogopogo sightings so far have been characterized by several humps a few feet apart sticking out of the water.

Between August of 2000 and September of 2001, a search for Ogopogo was conducted, with a prize of $2 million for a verifiable sighting of the monster in Okanagan Lake. To check the results of the hunt, or to join a potential new race for the booty, head to www.ogopogoquest.com. Still not convinced? The website has a 30-second clip of the official documentary on Ogie, "The Legend Hunters," available for purchase online. If you don't become an instant millionaire with a sighting of the *real* Ogopogo, you can still enjoy its image on the signs, sculptures, and blow-up dolls peddled by the good people of Penticton and Kelowna. There is a small statue of Ogopogo in downtown Kelowna, and in 1990 Canada issued a stamp with an artist's rendering of the creature.

Parks Alive!, 101-389 Queensway Ave., is an organization dedicated solely to presenting music and arts in all the parks throughout the summer months; look for an annual schedule and banners for information on the events, including August's free Mozart in the Park (☎ 868-3307; www.parksalive.com or www.okanaganmozartfestival.com.)

OUTDOOR ACTIVITIES

HIKING AND BIKING. While Kelowna's main attraction is Okanagan Lake, surrounding areas offer excellent opportunities for terrestrial fun. Ponderosa pines dominate this hot and dry landscape. You'll also find bluebunch wheatgrass, bitterroot (a pink flower) and balsamroot (a bright yellow flower). **Knox Mountain,** just north of the city, features many hiking trails as well as a paved road to the summit. Hike, bike, or drive to the top for a spectacular view of Kelowna and Okanagan. While you're there, don't pass up a chance to check out one of the city's natural secrets, **Paul's Tomb.** A secluded gravel beach named for the grave of one of Kelowna's early settlers located there, it's only a 2km walk or bike from either the trailhead at the base of the mountain or the one at the lookout halfway up.

Hikers will also find trail opportunities throughout **Bear Creek Regional Park's** 20km of trails, including a challenging hike that starts at the canyon floor and takes you up to the canyon rim to view the city and lake (9km north of Hwy. 97 on Westside Rd.) Much of the large and popular **Okanagan Mountain Provincial Park** was ravaged by a voracious 2003 wildfire, leaving large portions of the park closed. Ask at the Visitors Center for information on which trails have been re-opened; day hiking and longer backcountry options abound. Bikers can head to **Wildhorse Canyon** in the southern end of Okanagan Mt. Park for technically challenging rides; follow Lakeshore Rd. south from the city.

Another popular biking trail is the **Kettle Valley Railbed** (12-41km, 2-8hr.), which passes through scenic **Myra-Bellevue Provincial Park** and the stunning **Myra Canyon** and then through the only desert in western Canada. To access Myra Canyon from downtown, go east on K.L.O. Rd. (off Pandosy) to McCulloch Rd., follow McCulloch to June Springs Rd., take June Springs to Little White Forest Service Rd., and follow Little White 4.5km to the parking lot. The railbed through Myra stretches 12km, but the bike trail continues all the way to Penticton. (Easy to moderate).

In addition, there are 18 regional parks within a 40km radius of Kelowna, providing everything from picnic areas to swim spots, and in some cases nature and hiking trails. Highlights include the **Mission Creek Regional Park,** with over 12km of hiking trails, many along the raging creek and a connection to the **Mission Creek Greenway,** with 7km of trails leading to the waterfront; and **Glen Canyon Regional Park,** offering hikes along the old concrete flume and one along cliff edges (☎868-5232. Parking for Mission Creek: follow Hwy. 97 east through the city to Leckie Rd., follow that street to its end at the park. Parking for Glen Canyon: Take Hwy. 97 west out of the city, follow to the Westbank exit at Glenrosa Rd. Take the 2nd right, Webber Rd., and the second right off it, Aberdeen Rd. Follow to its end.)

☒ SKIING. In the winter, downhill skiing is the most popular outdoor activity in the Okanagan Valley. **Big White Ski Resort,** on a clearly-marked access road off Hwy. 33, east of town, offers 15 lifts servicing over 100 trails throughout 7355 acres of terrain. With two hostels and plenty of cheap eats surrounding the slopes, Big White is a great place for skiers on a budget. The resort completed a $130 million expansion at the beginning of the 2004 season, adding two new chairlifts and a state-of-the-art terrain park. (☎765-3101, snow report 765-7669; www.bigwhite.com. Open mid-Nov. to late Apr. Day pass $56, ages 13-18 $48. Night skiing 5-8pm, $16. Multi-day discounts. Ski rental $28; snowboard $35.) Those preferring a smaller, less crowded mountain should head to **Crystal Mountain,** with 22 trails and an 800 ft. vertical drop located at the top of Glenrosa Rd., 10min. from the Westbank overpass of Hwy. 97. (☎768-5189, snow report 712-6262; www.crystalresort.com. Open mid-Nov. to mid-Dec. Sa-Su 9am-3:30pm; daily mid-Dec. to mid-Jan. 9am-3:30pm; mid-Jan. to Mar. Th-Su 9am-3:30pm. $34, ages 13-17 $27. Ski rental $26, snowboard $30, snowshoes $15.)

☒ CLIMBING. The area around Kelowna boasts numerous spots for the rock inclined. Along the KVR, in the Myra-Bellevue Provincial Park are the **Boulderfields,** with six main areas, 25 independent walls, almost all of advanced difficulty (rated at least 5.11), earning the area the name "eleven heaven." **Idabel Lake,** lying near Okanagan Falls on Rte. 33 off Hwy. 97, boasts the best bouldering routes in the area. Unfortunately, the most popular climbing in the area at **Kelowna Crags,** by Chute Lake Mountain Park, has been closed since the area was decimated by a 2003 forest fire. When open, the area offers climbs of a range of difficulties, as well as a trail to the top for spectators to see the lake vista and relax in well-worn chairs constructed from stones. (Contact tourist office or Regional Parks Department, ☎868-5232, for information on the park's current status. To get there, follow Lakeshore Ave. to Chute Lake Rd. Follow the road for 2 mi. after it becomes a dirt road, 1 mi. after the sign marking the edge of Kelowna. Parking is on the right.)

☒ WINE AND FRUIT. Over the past few years, the Okanagan Valley has become the center of the British Columbian, and therefore Canadian, **wine** industry. Kelowna and the surrounding area is home to 12 of the valley's more than 25 wineries, all of which offer tastings, and many of which have tours. Contact the Visitors Center or call Okanfana Wine Country Tours at ☎868-9463 for a complete list of tours. Wine and cheese parties are common at the **Okanagan Wine Festival** (☎861-6654; www.owfs.com) for 10 days in early October, for four days at its lesser counterpart in late April, and for three days at the **Icewine Festival** in late January (events $15-65 each.) **Mission Hill,** 1730 Mission Hill Rd., overlooking the west bank of Okanagan Lake, is one of Kelowna's most respected and opulent local wineries. To get there, cross the bridge west of town, turn left on Boucherie Rd., and follow the signs. Offers tours of a unique underground wine cavern, bell tower, and outdoor amphitheater, including a tasting of four wines. (☎768-6448; www.missionhillwinery.com. Open daily 10am-5pm, July-Sept. 10am-7pm. Hour-long tours run daily Oct.-Apr. at 11am, 1pm, and 3pm; May-June and Sept. hourly 11am-4pm; July and Aug. every 30min. 10am-5pm. $5.) The posh **Summerhill Estate Winery** lets you taste five sparklers and join a tour to get a peek into an aging replica of the Cheops pyramid. Take Lakeshore Dr. to Chute Lake Rd. (☎764-8000 or 800-667-3538; www.summerhillwine.com. Open daily June-Aug. 9am-9pm; May-Sept. M-F 9am-5pm, Sa-Su 9am-7pm; tours hourly noon-4pm all year. Free.) For the feel of a smaller, less tourist-oriented winery, **Quail's Gate,** 3303 Boucherie Rd., off Hwy 97 heading west out of Kelowna, also offers an impressive look out onto Okanagan Lake from the west; their tour takes you through fields and aging room, showcasing a strong regional pride and knowledge for the local history. (☎769-4451 or 800-420-9463; www.quailsgate.com. Open daily May-Sept. 9am-7pm; Oct.-Apr. 10am-5pm. Tours daily May-Sept. hourly 11am-4pm. $5.)

Kelowna Land and Orchard, 3002 Dunster Rd., off KLO Rd. on E Kelowna, the town's oldest family farm, offers a 45min. hayride tour that explains farming techniques. The tour finishes at the orchard's farm stand, giving you a chance to browse and munch on delicious produce. (☎763-1091; www.k-l-o.com. Open daily Apr.-Oct. 9am-4pm; call for winter hours. Tours run June-Aug. at 11am, 1pm and 3pm; Apr.-May and Sept.-Oct. at 11am and 3pm; $6.50, students $3, under 12 free.)

If your intention is to become a true connoisseur, head to the **The Wine Museum** and the **British Columbia Orchard Industry Museum,** both housed in the historic **Laurel Packinghouse,** Kelowna's oldest packinghouse and first designated heritage building, at 1302 Ellis St. The Wine Museum displays artifacts for the earliest production of wine, explores the history of wine in the area, and offers free tastings at the museum's extensive wine shop. (☎868-0441; www.kelownamuseum.ca/wm. Admission by donation. Open M-Sa 10am-5pm, Su noon-5pm.) The Orchard Museum explains the process of fruit growing and documents the trade's history in the area, including a model of Kelowna with a 50 ft. model railroad. (☎763-0433; www.kelownamuseum.ca/om. Admission by donation. Open Tu-Sa 10am-5pm.)

PENTICTON ☎250

Indigenous peoples named the region between Okanagan and Skaha Lakes Pentak-tin, "a place to stay forever." Today, Penticton (pop. 41,000) is known more commonly as the "Peach City," complete with a giant peach on the waterfront that would make Roald Dahl proud. Penticton is more than an agricultural mecca, however; the city bustles with tourists and visiting fruit harvesters during the summer months. With the added incentives of endless outdoor adventures along with two inviting waterfronts, Penticton coaxes you to linger past tourist season.

▐ TRANSPORTATION

Penticton lies 395km east of Vancouver and about 60km north of the Canadian-US border at the junction of **Highway 3** and **Highway 97,** at the southern extreme of the Okanagan Valley. **Okanagan Lake** borders the north end of town, while smaller **Skaha Lake** lies to the south. **Main Street** bisects the city from north to south, turning into **Skaha Lake Road** as it approaches Skaha Lake.

Buses: Greyhound, 307 Ellis St. (☎493-4101), runs buses to **Kelowna** (1½hr., 7 per day, $12) and **Vancouver** (6-7hr., 6 per day, $52). Open M-Sa 6am-5pm, Su 7am-5pm.

Public Transportation: Penticton Transit System, 301 E Warren Ave. (☎492-5602), services town and nearby Naramata. $1.50, ages 65 and older and 7-21 $1.20, under 6 free; day pass $3.25/$2.75. Runs M-F 6:15am-7pm, Sa 8:30am-7pm, Su 9am-6pm. Limited night routes run M-Sa 7-10pm. Extended Su hours July-Sept.

Taxis: Courtesy Taxi (☎492-7778). $2 base, $1.40 per km. 24hr.

Car Rental: Rent-a-Wreck, 130 W Industrial Ave. (☎492-4447), rents cars from $35 per day, then $0.12 per km over 100km. Major credit card required. 10% discount for hostelers. Open M-Sa 8am-5pm.

ⓘ PRACTICAL INFORMATION

Tourist Office: Penticton Wine and Information Center, 888 W Westminster Ave. (☎493-4055 or 800-663-5052; www.penticton.org), at Power St. Free Internet and daily free wine tastings in the wine center in the same space. Open daily July-Sept. 8am-8pm; Oct.-June M-F 9am-6pm, Sa-Su 10am-5pm.

Equipment: Skaha Outdoor Sports, 101-399 Main St. (☎493-1216). A great resource for gear and advice. Rock climbing shoes $10 per day (no other climbing equipment rentable); cross-country skis and snowshoes $13 per day. Open M-F 9:30am-6pm, Sa 9:30am-5pm, Su 10am-4pm. **Freedom: The Bike Shop,** 533 Main St. (☎493-0686; www.freedombikeshop.com). Bikes $30 per day, $20 per half day, $5 HI discount; many local bike maps and even more insider knowledge. Open M-Sa 9am-5:30pm.

Laundromat: The Laundry Basket, 976 W Eckhardt Ave., (☎493-7899) next to the golf course. Look for the Maytag Laundry sign. Wash $1.75, dry $0.25 per 5min. Open M-F 8am-6pm, Sa-Su 9am-5pm.

Hospital: Penticton Regional, 550 Carmi Ave. (☎492-4000).

Police: 1101 Main St. (☎492-4300).

Crisis Line: ☎493-6622. **Women's Shelter:** ☎493-7233. 24hr.

Internet Access: Penticton Public Library, 785 Main St. (☎492-0024; www.library.penticton.bc.ca), offers free access. Open M, W, and F-Sa 10am-5:30pm; Tu and Th 10am-9pm; in winter also Su 1-5pm.

Post Office: 56 W Industrial Ave. (☎492-5769). Open M-F 8:30am-5pm. **Postal Code:** V2A 6J8.

🏠 ACCOMMODATIONS AND CAMPING

Penticton is a resort city year-round; cheap beds are rare, and it's essential to make reservations in summer. If possible, avoid the generally expensive yet decrepit hotels that lurk along Skaha Lake Rd. and the appealing but pricey B&Bs and benefit from the beautiful hostel. Campground sites along Skaha Lake are surprisingly costly and often tightly packed. If you're camping, head north to Okanagan Lake Provincial Park for a lakeside site.

Penticton Hostel (HI), 464 Ellis St. (☎492-3992). A large, well-maintained youth hostel with rooftop solar panels for hot water. Only a 10min. walk to the beach. Comfortable lounge, kitchen, TV room with cable, patio, free linen, and laundry facilities ($1 wash, $1 dry). Bike rentals ($24 full day, $18 half day, $10 evening) and information on wine tours, local jobs, and outdoor activities. Reception 8am-noon and 5-10pm. June-Sept. $19, nonmembers $23; Oct.-May $17/$21; private singles (without private bath) $29/$33. Ask about multi-day discounts. ❶

Riordan House, 689 Winnipeg St. (☎493-5997; www.icontext.com/riordan), rents busily decorated rooms with shared bathrooms in a historic Penticton home. Scrumptious "Okanagan breakfast" of fresh muffins and fruit cobbler made from local peaches. Free pickup from Greyhound depot; bike rentals available to guests ($15 per day). Singles $50; doubles with TV/VCR and fireplace $60-95. ❸

Okanagan Lake Provincial Park, (☎494-6500 or 800-689-9025), 24km north of town on Hwy. 97. 168 sites total on two campgrounds (North and South, with a walking trail along the shoreline connecting the two). The North park is more spacious, with a good swimming beach. Reservations recommended. Free firewood and free showers. $22. ❶

FOOD

Find your staples at **Safeway,** 1301 Main St. (☎487-2103. Open 7am-10pm). The **Penticton Farmer's Market,** 100 Block Main St., sells local produce and baked goods. (☎770-3276. In Gyro Park at the corner of Westminster and Main St. Open June-Oct. Sa 8:30am-noon, rain or shine.) You cannot miss **fruits and vegetables** at family stands (look for roadside signs) both north and south of town on Hwys. 97 and 3A.

Il Vecchio Delicatessen, 317 Robinson St. (☎492-7610). Delicious sandwiches at an incredible value. Ask for the "mortadella capicollo," a 2-meat, 2-cheese sandwich for $3.25, try the vegetarian sandwich with sun-dried tomatoes and fresh pickles, or make your own, at an equally low price. Homemade soup $2.15. Open M-Sa 8:30am-6pm. ❶

The Dream Cafe, 67 Front St. (☎490-9012), moved to a larger space to accommodate the audiences for their weekly live music. An intimate, colorful organic oasis with light, fragrant sandwiches and dinners; try the gypsy spring salad rolls ($5.25) or the mango roasted chicken sandwich ($7.25). Open daily 9am-11pm; closed M Nov.-Mar. ❷

Isshin Japanese Deli, 101-449 Main St. (☎770-1141) a local favorite, serving affordable, fresh sushi and heaping noodle dishes. Individual sushi runs from $1-4, but for the best deal, go for the lunchbox special, with 8 pieces of sushi, 4 pieces of tempura, 2 types of fried noodles, and a spinach side ($8). Open M-Th 11:30am-2:30pm and 5-9pm, F 11:30am-2:30pm and 5-10pm, Sa noon-2:30pm and 5-10pm. ❶

◎ SIGHTS

S.S. SICAMOUS AND S.S. NARAMATA. While lounging on the beachfront, you can meander over to the **S.S. Sicamous** and **S.S. Naramata,** restored steel-hulled ships from 1914 that originally transported goods and passengers to the communities along the Okanagan. Self-guided or guided tours (available upon request) offer a window into the leisure and luxury of the early Okanagan Valley; for those truly intrigued, the Sicamous also hosts a musical about life on board the ship. Just adjacent is the small but fragrant and calming **Penticton Rose Garden** in which to sit or stroll. (*1099 Lakeshore Dr.* ☎ *492-0403; www.sssicamous.com. Open daily June-Sept. 9am-9pm; Apr.-May and Oct.-Dec. 15 9am-6pm; Jan. 15-Mar. 9am-5pm. $5. Musical runs July-Aug., W-Sa 7:30, Su 3pm. $19, students $13.)*

SUMMERLAND. Just 12 mi. north of Penticton on Hwy. 20, the town of **Summerland** is home to **ornamental gardens** and the preserved portion of the 1910 **Kettle Valley Steam Railway** today operating as a tourist attraction. The 1½hr. tour provides views of orchards and vineyards, as well as the highest bridge on the original railway. (☎ *494-8422 or 877-494-8424; www.kettlevalleyrail.org. $16, students $14. Tour runs May-June and Sept.-early Oct. M and Sa-Su; July-Sept. M and Th-Su, always departing at 10:30am and 1:30pm. Take Hwy. 97 to Summerland exit. Follow Prairie Valley Rd. to a right on Doherty Ave. Doherty becomes Bathville Rd. which has the station on the right.)*

PENTICTON MUSEUM. Houses the history of Penticton's gold trails and the Kettle Valley Railway, as well as First Nations history. The museum is home to more than 8000 artifacts. (☎ *490-2451. 785 Main St., same building as the library. Suggested donation $2, children $1. Open Sept.-June Tu-Sa; July-Aug. M-Sa, 10am-5pm.)*

▲ OUTDOOR ACTIVITIES

LAKEFRONT. In the summer, the Penticton tourist trade revolves around both **Lake Okanagan** and **Lake Skaha.** Youths tend to gravitate toward Skaha Lake Park to the south and to the popular hot summer afternoon pastime of floating down the Okanagan River canal from Lake Okanagan to Lake Skaha. **Coyote Cruises,** 215 Riverside, rents tubes for $11 and provides a free shuttle for the return. (☎492-2115. Open daily late June-Sept. 10am-6pm, weather permitting.) **Pier Water Sports,** 45 N Martin St., just beyond the Peach on the beach pier, rents more advanced water vessels for those with an active spirit and a few extra bucks. (☎493-8864. Jet skis $83 per hr., canoes $16 per hr., and kayaks $19 per hr.; banana boat rides $10.)

WALKING, HIKING, AND BIKING. Although the lakes are the star attractions, those looking for land-based adventures will not be disappointed. Visit **Munson Mountain,** an extinct volcano with "PENTICTON" spelled out in letters 50 ft. high and 30 ft. wide, by bike, foot, or car for a bird's eye view of the valley. (Take Vancouver Ave. north of town, turn right on Tupper Ave. then left on Middle Bench Rd., to Munson Mt. Rd. The road takes you within minutes of the summit.)

Bikers, walkers, and runners will enjoy dozens of pathways and trails in the city and surrounding hills, many of which offer panoramic views of the lakes. The abandoned tracks of the **Kettle Valley Railway** run through Penticton and along both sides of Okanagan Lake and are the site of the Trans Canada Trail in this area. Traveling north, you'll pass through orchards, vineyards, and wineries, all with a fantastic view of the lake. To access the eastern section of the KVR from downtown, take Vancouver Ave. north to the intersection with Vancouver Pl. Those looking for a day trip from Penticton can travel 21km at a gradual 2% ascent to Glenfir, or 41km to Chute Lake. For a short, moderate hike, follow the trail on the western side of the river channel to Sage Mesa for stunning views. (☎496-5220; www.kettlevalleytrail.com).

Within the city, there are endless options for biking and strolling; particularly scenic routes on Valleyview Rd., along Penticton Creek, and on the trail along the River Channel. Those seeking a more backcountry experience should head to the rugged **Cathedral Provincial Park,** 40 mi. west of Penticton. Inhabiting the area between the wet Cascades and the arid Okanagan Valley, the park contains five major azure lakes, endless jagged peaks, abundant summer wildflowers, and unique rock structures with names like **Smokey the Bear** and **Grimface Mountain.** Sixteen vehicle-accessible campsites lie on the periphery of the park, while three more—at Quiniscoe Lake, Pyramid, and Lake of the Woods—serve the interior. An extensive network of trails centering around Quiniscoe Lake allows for day trips or extended trips alike; fishing is allowed with a permit, and hunting season is from Aug. 25-Apr. 15.

CLIMBING. The **Skaha Bluffs,** southeast of town on Valley View Rd., feature some of Canada's best sport and traditional rock climbing. For hikers and spectators there are trails throughout the park. Check out *Skaha Rock Climbs,* by Howie Richardson for detailed information on climbs. **Skaha Rock Adventures,** 113-437 Martin St., offers guiding and instructional services. (☎493-1765; www.skaharockclimbing.com. Open M-F 9am-5pm. $115 per day of guided climbing.)

SKIING. If you're visiting Penticton in the winter, **Apex Mountain Resort,** off Green Mtn. Rd. west of Penticton on Hwy. 3, offers the best downhill **skiing** in the area. Apex has downhill, cross-country, and night skiing (W and F-Sa 4:30-9:30pm) on over 60 runs with a 2000 ft. vertical drop. They also boast a new halfpipe and terrain park for boarders and an extensive glade area for the truly adventurous. For a $16 round-trip bus ride from Penticton to Apex, contact Tim Horton's Magic Ski Bus (www.apexresort.com/skibus.htm). In the summer, ski slopes transform into a dream come true for mountain bikers. (☎877-777-2739 or 487-4848 for snow conditions; www.apexresort.com. Adult day pass $48, ages 13-18 $39, 8-12 $29; under 7 free; night skiing $12. Rental equipment $29, ages 13-

18 $16, 8-12 $13.) An additional 21km of cross-country trails of all levels, including some with views of Okanagan lake, are just 5km away in the **Carmi** area. (☎492-8721. Follow Carmi Rd. east out of Penticton. Free.)

NELSON ☎250

Like many BC towns, Nelson was born in the wake of a local gold rush and proudly celebrates its mining history. Nowadays, tourism has replaced mining as Nelson's major industry. The town of just over 9000 is a fascinating combination of Canadian and Bohemian culture, charming visitors with its vibrant street culture and proximity to the surrounding beauty of Kootenay Lake and its neighboring mountains. The sport of curling is all the rage, granola devotees eat tofu scrambles for breakfast, and during summer and winter the town is awash with eager hikers and skiers in search of nature at its most extreme. But for all this, Nelson remains a mellow and alternative locale, with a charm independent of its natural splendors.

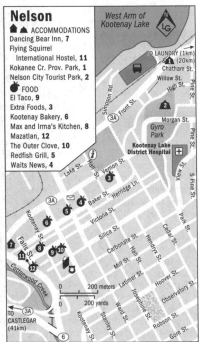

Nelson

West Arm of Kootenay Lake

🏠🏠 ACCOMMODATIONS
Dancing Bear Inn, **7**
Flying Squirrel
   International Hostel, **11**
Kokanee Cr. Prov. Park, **1**
Nelson City Tourist Park, **2**
🍴 FOOD
El Taco, **9**
Extra Foods, **3**
Kootenay Bakery, **6**
Max and Irma's Kitchen, **8**
Mazatlan, **12**
The Outer Clove, **10**
Redfish Grill, **5**
Waits News, **4**

▌ TRANSPORTATION

Nelson lies at the junction of **Highway 6** and **3A,** 620km southwest of Calgary, 460km southeast of Kamloops, and 660km east of Vancouver. From Nelson, Hwy. 3A heads 41km west to Castlegar. Hwy. 6 leads 65km south to the US border, where it becomes Washington's Rte. 31 and continues 110 mi. south to Spokane.

Buses: Greyhound, 1112 Lakeside Dr. (☎352-3939), in the Chako-Mika Mall. Terminal open M-F 7:30-8:30pm, Sa 7:30-11am and 4-8:30pm, Su 7:30-8:30am and 4:30-8:30pm. Runs buses to: **Banff** (13½hr. with a 1-5am layover in Cranbrook, 1 per day, $76); **Calgary** (12hr., 2 per day, $94); **Vancouver** (12hr., 2 per day, $101).

Public Transportation: Nelson Transit Systems (☎352-8201; www.busonline.ca) has 5 bus lines covering the area. Runs M-F 7am-11:30pm, Sa-Su 8:30am-7:30pm. $1-3.

Taxis: Glacier Cabs (☎354-1111). 24hr. $2 base, $2 per km in Nelson.

Car Rental: Rent-a-Wreck, 524 Nelson Ave. (☎352-5122), in the Esso station. Must be 18 or older. $40 per day, $0.12 per km after 200km.

▌ PRACTICAL INFORMATION

Outdoor information is generally available at the **West Kootenay Visitor Centre** (☎825-4723), in Kokanee Creek Provincial Park, 20km east of Nelson on Hwy. 3A. (Open daily 10am-4pm and 7-9pm.) If the West Kootenay Centre is closed, some park information can be obtained from **BC Parks, Kootenay District** at ☎422-4200.

Tourist Office: Visitor Info, 225 Hall St. (☎352-3433; www.discovernelson.com), provides an unusually good map of the city and surrounding area. Open daily May-Aug. 8:30am-8pm; Sept.-Oct. 8:30am-6pm; Nov.-Apr. 8:30am-5pm.

Equipment: The Sacred Ride, 213 Baker St. (☎354-3831), rents front suspension bikes for $35 per day and full-suspension bikes for $55. Maps go for $5, and helpful trail advice is free. Open M-Sa 9am-5:30pm. Gerick Cycle and Sports, 702 Baker St. (☎354-4622; www.gericks.com), rents dual suspension bikes for $40 per 24hr. and features cross-country ski packages for $15 per day. Open M-Th 9am-5:30pm, F 9am-7pm, Sa 9am-5:30pm.

Laundromat: Found at the Esso Station, 524 Nelson St. (☎352-3534). Wash $2-4, dryers free. Open Su-F 7am-9:30pm.

Showers: Nelson City Tourist Park (see Accommodations and Camping, below). $2 for non-campers.

Police: 606 Stanley St. (☎352-2266). Right next to the library.

Hospital: 3 View St. (☎352-3111).

Internet Access: Nelson Library: 602 Stanley St. (☎352-6333; www.library.nelsonbc.net). M, W, and F 1-8pm, Tu and Th 10am-6pm, Sa 11am-6pm. $2 per 30min. The Dancing Bear Inn and the Flying Squirrel Hostel (see Accommodations and Camping, below) both charge $1 per 10 min.

Post Office: 514 Vernon St. (☎352-3538). Open M-F 8:30am-5pm.

Postal Code: V1L 4EO.

ACCOMMODATIONS AND CAMPING

Flying Squirrel International Hostel, 198 Baker St. (☎352-7285 or 866-755-7433; www.flyingsquirrelhostel.com). Superlatives abound here: younger, hipper, cooler. Catering to the more youthful outdoorsy crowd, this happening hostel provides Nelson with a social scene unto itself. With foosball, a full kitchen, laundry, ensuite bath, and free pickup from the bus station, they do it all. Internet access $1 per 10min. Reception 8am-noon and 4-9pm. Check-out by 11am. $20, private rooms from $42. ❷

Dancing Bear Inn (HI), 171 Baker St. (☎352-7573 or 877-352-7573; www.dancingbearinn.com). Dancing Bear offers a more sedate alternative to the party hostel scene at Flying Squirrel; this place just might remind you of grandma's house with its cozy, fire-warmed common room, art-decked and book-covered walls, full supply of board games and movies, immaculately clean hardwood floors, and bountiful hospitality services. Super-helpful staff. Laundry, kitchen, free parking, and Internet access $1 per 10min. Reception 7-11am and 4-10pm. Reservations recommended June-Aug. Dorm rooms $19, nonmembers $22; under 10 half-price. Private rooms $34-45/$40-54. ❷

Kokanee Creek Provincial Park, (☎825-4212; reservations ☎800-689-9025; www.discovercamping.ca), 20km north of town on Hwy. 3A. Shaded, spacious sites with decent privacy are near the lake. Flush toilets. Wheelchair-accessible. 166 sites; half for reservations, $25; half first-come, first-served, $19. ❷

Nelson City Tourist Park, (☎352-7618) on High St., is convenient for camping, backyard-style. Take Vernon St. to its eastern end and follow signs. Flush toilets. Wash $1, dry $.50 for 30min. 40 sites. $15, electricity $18, with water $20; showers free. ❶

FOOD AND NIGHTLIFE

Basic groceries can be found at Extra Foods, 708 Vernon St. (Open M-Sa 9am-9pm, Su 9am-6pm.)

Redfish Grill, 479 Baker St. (☎352-3456), offers an eclectic menu alongside local artwork. Both are in very good taste. Thai-influenced wraps start at $7; burgers run $7-9, and an excellent breakfast of two eggs, bacon and hashbrowns is $4. A limited selection of local brew runs $3-5. Open daily 7am-1am. ❷

BRITISH COLUMBIA

Waits News, 490 Baker St. (☎352-5667) This corner lunch counter serves $4 sandwiches, $5 subs, and the best milkshake in town ($3.75). Open M-Th 5am-10pm, Sa-Su 5am-11pm. ❶

Kootenay Bakery, 295 Baker St. (☎352-2274), caters to the organic, vegetarian, vegan, wheat-free, and gluten-free diet with a wide array of fresh-baked bread ($2-5), pastries ($3-4), sandwiches ($4-6), vegetarian lasagna ($7) and beautiful smoothies ($4). Open M-Th 7:30am-6pm. ❷

The Outer Clove, 536 Stanley St. (☎354-1667). Vegetarians, rejoice! Those who sleep next to them, cringe! This "Garlic Cafe" puts garlic in everything from tapas ($4-8) to ice cream ($2). The garlic yamburger is $11 and the "Orbit Veggie Burger" made with hemp seeds runs $9. For those with problems other than garlic breath, the vampire-killer chili is only $7. Open M-Sa 11:30am-9pm. ❷

Max and Irma's Kitchen, 515 Kootenay St. (☎352-2332; www.maxandirmas-kitchen.com). More chic than its name implies, Max and Irma's makes gourmet 10 in. pizzas in a wood-fired oven ($10-13) and serves enticing sandwiches like vegetarian croque monsieur ($9). Open M-Th and Su 11am-9pm, F-Sa 11am-10pm. ❷

Mazatlan, 198 Baker St. (☎352-1388). Run by the super-friendly Medina family, Mazatlan offers excellent platters ($10-16) of authentic Mexican food. Open M-Th and Su 11:30am-10:30pm, F-Sa 11:30am-midnight. ❷

El Taco, 306 Victoria St. (☎250-2060) An unoriginal but descriptive name, $4 tacos and $5 burritos, and a relaxed courtyard patio make this quick Mexican joint a favorite local hangout. Open M-Th 11am-8pm, F-Sa 11am-11pm. ❶

⚑ OUTDOOR ACTIVITIES

Bordering Nelson on the north, the watery **West Arm** seems huge, but it's just a tiny segment of enormous **Kootenay Lake.** Dolly varden, rainbow trout (up to 14kg according to local legend), and kokanee cruise the lake, while sturgeon up to 1.5m long inhabit the nearby **Kootenay River.** The best time to find the big ones is from October to February. Licenses and bait are available at the **Balfour Dock,** 30min. north of town on Hwy. 3A.

⚐ **HIKING.** Hiking is plentiful in the hills around Nelson. Maps of brief hikes from the city center can be obtained at the **Dancing Bear Inn** (see **Accommodations and Camping,** above). Some of the area's best hiking can be found in **Kokanee Glacier Provincial Park,** which is generally uncrowded because it's so hard to reach. Various entrances off Hwy. 31 (which heads north off Hwy. 3A east of town) are not regularly maintained; these roads are not for the weak-willed driver or the low-riding vehicle and can be closed well into June. For a complete list of trails, check out *Don't Waste Your Time in the West Kootenays* ($18), by Kathy and Craig Copeland, a worthwhile trail guide published by Voice in the Wilderness Press and available at most bookstores.

Old-Growth Trail (1.5km one-way, 1-2hr.) begins 12km up the Kokanee Creek Rd. 20km out of town on Hwy. 31. Pass the Kokanee Creek campground turnoff on your right; the road is an unmarked, easily missable left turn about 500m further on. The trailhead is much better marked on the left. Following the 1km **Cedar Grove Loop,** this trail wanders through a cedar forest and offers views of the surrounding mountains and an old mining tramway. Easy.

Gibson Lake to Slocan Chief Cabin Trail (10km round-trip, 3-4hr.) lies another 4m up Kokanee Creek Rd. at the Gibson Lake Trailhead. If you're parking, wrap your vehicle with chicken wire to prevent porcupine damage. From the trailhead, a 4km trail leads up and across the mountainside to **Kokanee Lake** and continues 3km to the **Kaslo Lake** campground, which consists of 10 sites with good fishing. Another few kilometers and the path reaches the 12-person Slocan Chief cabin below **Kokanee Glacier.** (Campgrounds $5. Cabin $15 per person or $30 for group.) **Do not walk on any glacier without a guide.** Moderate.

Silver Spray Trail (8km one-way, several hr.) On Hwy. 31, take the Woodbury Creek turn-off 10km north of Ainsworth Hot Springs (a few kilometers beyond Woodbury Creek itself) and drive 13km to the trailhead. This trail passes through several avalanche areas and prime grizzly bear feeding zones en route to the Silver Spray Cabin (wood fire-place, sleeps 4-8) and the circa 1920s Violet mine and blacksmith shop. The views of the glacier are simply unbelievable. Difficult.

HOT SPRINGS. Several kilometers northeast of Nelson, at 3609 Hwy. 31, the **Ainsworth Hot Springs** are a source of healing for the rheumatic and source of relaxation for everyone else. The water in the main swimming area hovers around body temperature and contains low levels of 10 allegedly healthful minerals. A second pool contains water coming out of the humid limestone caves, naturally filled with water that reaches 45°C/112°F. It's like the Batcave, only filled with steam and really hot water. Next to the hot pool is what looks like a hot tub, but filled with 10° water, 10 min. melted from the glacier above (40°F). Jumping from pools of radically different temperatures is rumored to be good for the skin. Watching other swimmers jump from pool to pool is rumored to be wildly funny. (☎229-4212 or 800-668-1171; www.hotnaturally.com. Open daily 10am-9:30pm. $7.50, ages 60 and older $6.50, 3-12 $5, family four-pack $20.)

☒ SKIING. The soft powder of **Whitewater Ski Resort,** 12km southeast of town off of Hwy. 6, draws skiers and boarders to two lifts servicing 32 well-maintained runs, some of Canada's best bowls, and 400m of vertical drop. Whitewater has over 12km of groomed cross-country trails and a 15m average snowfall. (☎354-4944 or 800-666-9420, snow report 352-7669; www.skiwhitewater.com. Lift tickets $37, ages 13-18 $28, 7-12 $21, under 7 free. Full package rentals $25 per day.)

VALHALLA PROVINCIAL PARK ☎250

Valhalla stretches up from the enchantingly turquoise and trout-filled waters of Slocan Lake, then continues through a lush and temperate rain forest before arriving at a curtain of craggy alpine peaks. Once a homeland to the Sinixt Indians, who left pictographs on the bluffs above the lake, the park has now been largely given over to pikas, mountain goats, and bears. Residents of nearby New Denver fought for countless years to have this treasure declared a park protected from logging interests before finally achieving success in 1983. Much of the park is accessible only by boat; the only roads to the park leave from the miniscule town of Slocan. Twenty-two separate camping areas, many with bear caches and pit toilets, are spread throughout the park. Motorists and cyclists beware—no mechanized vehicles of any kind, including mountain bikes, are allowed. Dogs must be leashed and are only allowed in certain areas of the park; fires also are allowed only in designated areas and must be made with driftwood from the beaches. Many trails require expert-level route-finding skills; others allow for a less strenuous journey through the amazing scenery. With cars, jet skis, and snowmobiles prohibited for miles, this is truly a paradise where the heroically slain Norseman (or the odd traveler) can rest in peace.

BRITISH COLUMBIA

▣ ▨ ORIENTATION AND PRACTICAL INFORMATION

Valhalla lies on the west shore of Slocan Lake, 150km south of Revelstoke and 286km east of Kelowna. In the south, a bridge from **Slocan** provides access to southern trailheads, most at the end of long and bumpy forest roads. In the north, the town of **New Denver** provides food and shelter to weary wanderers as well as water access to the northern trailheads. The towns are linked by Hwy. 6, which runs north from Nelson. On Tu and Th, a **shuttle bus** (☎877-843-2877) runs from Nelson Mall to Mountain Berry Foods in New Denver, with an optional stop at Slocan ($4). A **water taxi** (☎358-7775) ferries hikers by appointment from Centennial Park in New Denver to any of the lakeside campsites in Valhalla. Back in the 1940s, New Denver was one of many Japanese internment camps set up by the Canadian government during WWII. The **Nikkei Internment Memorial Center,** at 306 Josephine St. just off 3rd Ave., has exhibits on the living conditions and culture of the nearly 20,000 interned Japanese-Canadians. (☎358-7288. Open daily May-Sept. 9:30am-5pm. $4, students and seniors $3, family four-pack $10.)

The **visitors center** is in New Denver, at 202 6th Ave., at Bellevue St. (☎358-2719), offering free guides and information on the park. Open daily June-late Aug. 9am-5pm. For **outdoor info,** visit the folks who led the crusade to preserve Valhalla as a national park, the **Valhalla Nature Centre/Valhalla Wilderness Society,** 307 6th Ave., in the building that says Valhalla Trading Post. The society sells a $4 trail guide and topographic map. (☎358-2333; www.savespiritbear.org. Open May-Oct. M-F 10am-5pm.) If the office seems closed, knock anyway; someone working late may answer. Get **equipment** at **Valhalla Pure Outfitters** on 6th St. (☎358-7755; www.vpo.ca. Open daily May-Oct. 10am-6pm.) To get to the park from New Denver, rent a kayak at **Sweet Dreams Guesthouse** ($70 per day; see **Accommodations**) Reach the **police,** 407 Slocan Ave. south of 6th St. at ☎358-2222, and the **hospital,** 401 Galena Ave., at ☎358-7911. **Post office:** 219 6th Ave. (☎358-2611. Open M-F 9am-5pm, Sa noon-4pm.) **Postal Code:** V0G 1S0.

▨ ▧ ACCOMMODATIONS AND FOOD

Valhalla Park itself is filled with free, well-maintained **backcountry sites ❶**. Convenient but unaesthetic (aside from the view) camping is available at the **municipal campground ❷** at Centennial Park, on the south side of town by the lakeshore between 3rd and 1st Ave. Forty small sites, most filled with RV toting boaters, cluster around showers and a boat launch. (Tents $15, on the water $17, electricity and water $19.) Those who don't wish to camp can stay in luxury at the **Sweet Dreams Guesthouse ❹,** 702 Eldorado Ave. Take 6th Ave. toward the lake and turn left on Eldorado Ave. This B&B is located in a cozy country home with a beautiful view of the lake (Room 4 is famous for its view). Three-course dinners are available by reservation and run about $20. (☎358-2415; www.newdenverbc.com. Breakfast included. Singles $57-75; doubles $109. Multiple-day rates are often available.) Another lodging option is the **Valhalla Inn ❹,** on Hwy. 6 in town, which offers spare but spacious and spotless motel rooms, as well as a restaurant (entrees run $6-15. Open daily 8am-8pm.) and a pub with $4 pints. (☎358-2228. Singles $55; doubles $60, can accommodate up to seven in one room with an initial price of $70 for 2 people, $10 for each additional person.)

Basic supermarket goods can be found at **Eldorado Market,** 402 6th Ave. (☎358-2443. Open May-Sept. M-Sa 9am-6pm, Su 10am-5pm; closed Su Oct.-Apr.) **Ann's Natural Foods,** 805 Kildare St., has a small selection of natural food products. (☎358-2552. Open M-Sa 9am-5:30pm.) Meals abound on 6th Ave., where you can find the renowned **Appletree Cafe ❶**, 210 6th Ave. The tiny cafe is home to a colorful local crowd promising, and honoring its promise of, "up to the minute gossip" and other essential small-town services including home-made soups ($3.50), and build-your-own $6-8 sandwiches. (☎ 358-2691. Open M-F 7am-4pm, Sa 11am-4pm.)

🖉 HIKING

Backpacking in Valhalla is made especially attractive by its quiet solitude and pris-tine backcountry campsites, but explorers of Valhalla's outdoor paradise must take a few important precautions. First off, Slocan Lake, while usually placid and eerily mirror-like, occasionally bears the brunt of winds funneled down the valley. Talk to locals about weather conditions and watch out for "the black line" visible on the water when a squall comes in—if you see it, take cover. The temperate rain-forest of Valhalla is often very wet, and hypothermia is a real concern, even in the summer. Extra layers of warm clothing are a good idea. Additional safety gear is always recommended when camping, and a whistle is particularly handy in Val-halla because it can be heard across the lake. Be aware of the possibility of bear encounters. Most camping areas provide bear-proof food caches, but if none are available, bear-bagging supplies are necessary. Finally, remember that forest roads may be impassable as late as June due to winter-like weather conditions. One popular activity which arose in response to this problem is kayaking along the lake's shore and camping near the beach.

Evans Creek Trail (12.5km one-way, 2-3hr.) Park on the Slocan City side of the Slocan River bridge, walk across, then turn right to walk 200m to the trailhead. The trail passes along the lakeshore and past moss-carpeted waterfalls. A cabin and tent pads are avail-able at the creek; ample fishing and very nice backcountry camping await at Cahill and Beatrice Lakes. Easy to moderate.

Bannock Burn to Gimli Ridge (4km, 2-3hr.) Turn off Hwy. 6 at Slocan City, cross the river, and follow the gravel road 13km south. Turn right onto Bannock Burn Creek log-ging road and go until the parking lot. This unsurpassed hike comes with opportunities for world-class **rock climbing.** Camping allowed along the trail. Moderate to difficult.

Sharp Creek to New Denver Glacier (8km one-way, day-long). The trail begins along the west shore of Slocan Lake, directly across from New Denver, and is accessible only by boat. A very steep climb through several hanging valleys of lush moss, mon-umental cascades, and old-growth forest. There's a campground about halfway up and stunning views of the glacier and surrounding area from the top. Difficult.

🏔 OTHER OUTDOOR ACTIVITIES

Newly constructed trails have made **biking** an increasingly common and popular activity. Pathways have been carved from old rail beds 50km in the direction of Nakusp to the north, and 50km to Kaslo to the east. Fairly flat, these trails offer a relaxing, leisurely, and quiet way to see the West Kootenays. Bike rental is a fairly informal affair usually run from someone's back porch. Ask locally for a map of the trails and rental information; **Sweet Dreams Guest House** (see **Accom-modations**) is a good place to start. Kayaking, though often seen as a means of transportation by locals, is a perfect Slocan Lake recreation unto itself. Count-less inlets are well worth exploration, filled with loons, wrecked ships, and pic-tographs. Winter sports are also available in the area. Cross-country skiing is the primary activity, but snowmobiling has also become popular.

FERNIE
☎ 250

Those willing to go the extra kilometer will be rewarded with the best snow around. A magnet for mountain bikers and snowboarders, Fernie combines the familiarity of small-town life with the commercialism of franchised strip malls, plus the breadth of outdoor activities found in Jasper and Banff. While not as well-known as Banff or Whistler, Fernie has begun to attract the attention of travel guides and snow-lovers alike. During the summer, Fernie offers everything you would expect from a city set in the Rockies: gorgeous hiking, superior mountain biking, and world-class trout fishing. Add to these a range of excellent, cheap hostels, and you have a locale that's destined for discovery.

■⁊ **ORIENTATION AND PRACTICAL INFORMATION.** Fernie is located on Hwy. 3, 1hr. east of Cranbrook and 3½hr. southwest of Calgary. Local services cluster along Hwy. 3 and in downtown Fernie, 5km north of the ski resort. The **visitors center,** with free pamphlets and a few free books, is set beneath a wooden oil rig 1km east of town on Hwy. 3. (☎423-6868; www.fernietourism.com. Open daily July-Sept. 9am-7pm; Oct.-June M-F 9am-5pm.) **Greyhound,** 742 Hwy. 3 (☎423-6871) in the Park Place Lodge, runs two buses per day to Calgary (6½hr.; $55) and Vancouver (18hr.; $128). **Kootenay Taxi** (☎423-4408) runs 24hr. and ferries powder-heads to the slopes in winter ($10 one-way). The **police** are at 496 13th St. (☎423-4404). The **Fernie District Hospital** is at 1501 5th Ave. (☎423-4453). **Fernie Library,** 492 3rd Ave., offers **Internet** access for $5 per hr. (☎423-4458; www.elkvalley.net/library. Open Tu-F 11am-8pm, Sa noon-5pm.) **Raging Elk Hostel** has access for $2 per 20 min. **Ski & See Adventure Lodge** offers free Internet access to guests. **Laundry** is available at **Squeaky's Laundromat** (☎423-6091) on Hwy. 3, east of town next to Taco Time. Wash $3, dry $1. Open 8:30am-10:30pm. The **post office** is at 491 3rd Ave. (☎423-7555. Open M-F 8:30am-5pm.) **Postal Code:** V0B 1M0.

⋔⋌ **ACCOMMODATIONS AND CAMPING.** The ◖SameSun Fernie Backpackers Lodge, ❷** 892 Hwy. 3 (☎423-4492 or 877-562-2783; www.samesun.com) on 6th Ave and Hwy. 3, is an old motel with new bunk beds. Heated outdoor swimming pool, laundry, kitchen, private baths, hot tub, and a slightly more youthful scene than the HI. $20, private rooms from $39. The **Raging Elk Hostel (HI) ❷,** 892 6th Ave., offers both dorm-style lodging and private rooms with a healthy dose of ski culture on the side. In addition to the cozy living quarters, it boasts a large common area, a kitchen, laundry, Internet access, a sauna, a theater-style TV room, and an included pancake breakfast. Reservations are crucial during the ski season Dec.-Apr. (☎423-6811; www.ragingelk.com. Reception daily 8-11am and 5-11pm. During the ski season, $20, non-members $23, private rooms $63-73, ski and stay packages start at $68; in summer $18/$21, private rooms from $43.) **Ski & See Adventure Lodge ❸,** 301 2nd Ave. above the Grand Central Hotel, is the latest addition to the Fernie travel scene. This new European-style hotel offers shared and private rooms, comfortable common areas, and a huge outdoor patio with a hot tub. (☎423-7367; www.enjoyfernie.com. Dec.-late Apr. singles $30-60; Apr.-Dec. $19.) **Mount Fernie Provincial Park ❶,** 3km south of town on Hwy. 3, offers 40 private and shaded sites as well as flush toilets and water for $14.

◖ **FOOD.** Groceries can be found at **Overwaitea Foods** on 2nd Ave. (☎423-4607. Open M-Sa 8am-9pm, Su 8am-8pm.) **The Arts Station ❷,** 1st Ave. and 6th St., is a former train depot that now acts as a staging point for local artists; it also serves homemade soups ($3.50), incredible omelettes ($7), and sandwiches. (☎423-4627;

www.theartsstation.com. Open daily 8am-3pm and 6-10pm.) **Mug Shots Bistro ❷**, 592 3rd Ave., offers Internet access ($1.50 per 15min.) alongside its blueberry pancakes ($4.50) and homemade sandwiches. (☎423-8018. Open M-F 7am-6pm, Sa 8am-5:30pm.) **The Curry Bowl ❷**, 931 7th Ave., offers "enlightened Asian cuisine" including eight varieties of curry ($8-12) and large bowls of noodles for $9. (☎423-2695. Open Tu-F 5-11pm, Sa-Su 4-11pm.) Unwind after snowboarding at **The Grand Central Hotel ❶**, 301 2nd Ave., with $4 pints, Tu $0.45 wings, and Th $0.50 potato skins. (☎423-3343. Open M-Sa noon-2am, Su noon-midnight.)

🎿 SKIING. The engine driving Fernie's expansion is the **Fernie Alpine Resort** and its over 2500 acres of feathery powder. With a 875cm annual snowfall, the Fernie Alpine Resort embarrasses the competition. Over 100 trails serviced by eight lifts are spread out across the Lizard Range, creating a winter wonderland of gullies, ravines, five alpine bowls, a terrain park, and tree-skiing. (☎423-4655, snow report 423-3555; www.skifernie.com. $56; ages 65 and older and 13-24 $45, 6-12 $15.) **Gear Up Sport,** 100 Riverside Way off Hwy. 3, includes ski ($24 per day) and snowboard ($28 per day) rental packages, cross-country skis (from $15 per day), ice climbing gear ($43 per day), and all-important ski pants ($8 per day) among its supplies. (☎423-4556; www.gearupsport.com. Open daily Nov.-Apr. 7am-9pm.)

🏔 OUTDOOR ACTIVITIES. The April thaw, while heralding the end of ski season, also uncovers Fernie's abundant hiking trails. Many trails leave from the Alpine Resort, where free maps are provided. The **Fernie Ridge Walk** (11 mi., at least 8hr.) begins in the parking lot of the ski resort and offers spectacular views of alpine meadows and jagged limestone peaks before returning to the valley floor. Cheaters can take the lift part way up the mountain in the summer ($8, bikes $3), but won't avoid the steep **Snake Ridge** or a 15m/50 ft. fixed-rope climb. (1000m gain. Difficult.) Fernie and the mountain resort offer various trails. **The Guides Hut,** 671 2nd Ave., is happy to recommend equipment and trails and rent skis. (☎423-3650 or 888-843-4885; www.guideshut.com. Open daily in winter 8am-8pm; summer M-Sa 10am-6pm, Su noon-5pm. Ski rentals $30 per day.) The **Bike Base,** 432 2nd Ave., and neighboring **Ski Base** rent trade-ins at great prices. (☎423-6464; www.skibase.com. Full-suspension $40 per day. Open Sa-Th 9:30am-5:30pm, F 9:30am-8pm.) The Elk River and its tributaries provide 180km of world-class **fly-fishing** for bulltrout and cutthroat. Follow the crowd and fish along Hwy. 3 or head off the beaten path and farther along the river. A good start is the **Kootenay Fly Shop and Guiding Company,** 821 7th Ave., which rents rods for $20 per day and sells maps and books for $10-17. (☎423-4483 or 877-423-4483; www.kootenayflyshop.ca. Open daily Apr.-Oct. 8:30am-6pm; Dec.-Mar. M-F noon-6pm.)

REVELSTOKE ☎250

In the 19th century, Revelstoke was a town straight out of a Western, complete with dust-encrusted miners maiming one another amid the gold-laden Selkirk and Kootenay Mountains; in the 21st century, it still retains the feel of its roots. Located on both the Columbia River and the Canadian Pacific Railway, the town was born as a transfer station for boats and trains. Although still largely a stopover for travelers to the Rockies, Revelstoke is finally coming into its own. The first sign of good outdoor opportunities is that the town is empty during the day. Revelstoke's laid-back social life complements the physical rigors of the area. Excellent hostels, free and surprisingly lively outdoor entertainment in the town center, and extensive outdoor pursuits make Revelstoke a particularly welcoming destination.

✠ ⁊ ORIENTATION AND PRACTICAL INFORMATION

Revelstoke is on the **Trans-Canada Highway** (Hwy. 1), 285km west of Banff, 210km east of Kamloops, and 565km east of Vancouver. The town is easily navigated on foot or by bike, hence the lack of traffic and abundance of parking spaces downtown. **Mount Revelstoke National Park** lies just east of town on Hwy. 1.

Buses: Greyhounds depart from 1899 Fraser Dr. (☎837-5874). To get there, turn away from the city center at the traffic lights on Hwy. 1 and take your first left. Open M-F 8am-6pm, Sa-Su 11am-1pm and 3-5pm. To: **Calgary** (6hr., 4 per day, $60); **Salmon Arm** (1½hr., 5 per day, $19); and **Vancouver** (8-10hr., 5 per day, $81).

Taxi: Revelstoke Taxi ☎837-4000.

Tourist Office: Visitors Centre (☎837-3522; www.revelstokecc.bc.ca), located at junction of Mackenzie and Victoria. Open daily July-Aug. 9am-6pm; May-June 9am-5pm. An additional, smaller information center is located at the **Chamber of Commerce,** 204 Campbell Ave. in central Revelstoke (☎837-5345. Open M-Sa 9am-5pm). **Parks Canada** (☎837-7500) sells National Park passes and maps at Boyle Ave. and 3rd St. Open M-F 8:30am-noon and 1-4:30pm.

Bike Rental: High Country Cycle and Sports, 118 Mackenzie Ave. (☎814-0090). $30-45 per day, cross-country skis $16 per day. Open M-Sa 9:30am-5:30pm.

Laundromat: Family Laundry, 409 1st St. W (☎837-3938), just behind the SameSun Lodge. $1.50 for wash, $4 for massive loads, dry $0.25 per 5min. Open M-Sa 8am-6pm, Su 9am-5pm.

Police: 320 Wilson St. (☎837-5255).

Hospital: Queen Victoria Hospital, 6622 Newlands Rd. (☎837-2131). **Ambulance:** ☎837-5885.

Internet Access: Free at the **library,** 600 Campbell Ave. (☎837-5095; www.checkout.orl.bc.ca. Open Tu noon-8pm, W noon-7pm, Th 10am-4pm, F 10am-5pm). Also at **Woolsey Creek Cafe** (p. 377).

Post Office: 307 W 3rd St. (☎837-3228). Open M-F 8:30am-5pm. **Postal Code:** V0E 2S0.

⌂⌂ ACCOMMODATIONS AND CAMPING

▩ **SameSun Backpacker Lodge,** 400 2nd St. W (☎877-562-2783; www.samesun.com). The friendly staff successfully hosts both a lively youth hostel scene and a more sedate older crowd in the private rooms. Several kitchens, full bathrooms, living room with TV, and a constant mellow soundtrack. Free pool table, backyard BBQ, Internet $1 for 10 min. Deals with some local restaurants and the Powder Springs Resort. 24hr. check-in. Dorms $20; singles $43, winter $39; groups of 6 or more $18 per person. ❷

Martha Creek Provincial Park, 22km north of Revelstoke on Hwy 23. Has a beach and a boat launch. The campground tends to be full of RVs, so get there early if you want an isolated spot. Open Apr.-Oct. $14. ❶

Williamson's Lake Campground, 1818 Williamson Lake Rd. (☎837-5512 or 888-676-2267; www.williamsonlakecampground.com), 5km southeast of town on Airport Way. Farther from the highway than competitors, next to a peaceful and popular swimming hole. Laundry and general store. Reception 8am-9:30pm. Open mid-Apr. to Oct. 41 sites, $16; 20 full RV sites, $20. Free showers. ❷

▱ FOOD

The town's local market is **Cooper's Supermarket,** 555 Victoria St. (☎837-4372. Open daily 8am-9pm.) On the east side of town lies **Southside Grocery,** 900 4th St. (☎837-3517. Open daily 9am-9pm.)

 Luna Taverna, 102 2nd St. E (☎837-2499). Titanic helpings of Greek and Mediterranean fare. Entrees like *souvlaki* dish up an appropriate amount of deliciously tender meat after a day on the trail. Appetizers run $6-8, full meals $12-18. Staying at Same-Sun Lodge earns free cheesecake. Open Tu-Sa 11am-2pm and 5-9pm. ❸

Woolsey Creek Cafe, 212 Mackenzie Ave. (☎837-5500), offers meals in a relaxed, toy-strewn atmosphere. Internet access $1 per 10min. Breakfast runs $5-8, lunch and dinner $6-15. $5 pints. Open M-Th and Su 7:30am-11pm, F-Sa 7:30am-midnight. ❷

Chalet Deli and Bakery, 555 Victoria St. (☎837-5552), across the parking lot from Cooper's. This bakery is also a lunch spot with a hot deli, pizza by the slice ($2.50), fresh baked bread (loaves $2), and sandwiches ($4.50). Open M-Sa 6am-6pm. ❶

Main Street Cafe, 317 Mackenzie Ave. (☎873-6888) at 3rd St., serves breakfast ($5-8) and sandwiches ($5-6) at a pleasant downtown patio. Open daily July 8am-9pm; Aug.-June 8am-5pm. ❷

SIGHTS AND ENTERTAINMENT

Revelstoke Railway Museum, 719 W Track St. off Victoria Rd., tells of the construction of the Trans-Canada line, which was completed a few miles from Revelstoke in 1885. Other exhibits include a real steam engine and a full passenger car. (☎877-837-6060; www.railwaymuseum.com. Open daily July-Aug. 9am-8pm; May-June and Sept. 9am-5pm; Apr. and Oct. M-Sa 9am-5pm; Nov. M-F 9am-5pm; Dec.-Mar. M-F 1pm-5pm. $6, ages 60 and older $5, 7-16 $3, under 7 free, family $13.)

The modern mechanical marvels of the **Revelstoke Dam,** one of North America's largest hydroelectric developments 5km north of Hwy. 1 on Hwy. 23, along with the latest in utility company propaganda, are illustrated in a free self-guided audio tour. Wheelchair-accessible. (☎837-6515. Open daily mid-June to mid-Sept. 8am-8pm; May to mid-June and mid-Sept. to mid-Oct. 9am-5pm.)

The town also boasts a **blues festival** during the third weekend in June, a **lumberjack competition** in early July, and a **railroad festival** in August. Call the visitors center for dates. From late June through August, the town's main square fills every night with quality bands from a cappella to ska. Weeknight shows tend to be family-oriented, while weekends rock a little harder.

OUTDOOR ACTIVITIES

SUMMER ACTIVITIES. At **Canyon Hot Springs,** between Mt. Revelstoke National Park and Glacier National Park on Hwy. 1, two swimming pools filled with spring water simmer at 26°C and 40°C (86°F and 106°F) and ease aching muscles. (☎837-2420; www.canyonhotsprings.com. July-Aug. 9am-10pm; May-June and Sept. 9am-9pm. $6.50, ages 60 and older and 4-14 $5.50, under 4 free. Two-person sites $22, with water and electricity $30. Free showers.) The neighboring **Apex Raft Company** runs 2hr. and 4hr. whitewater rafting tours on the Illecillewaet's Class II-III rapids. (☎837-6376 or 888-232-6666; www.apexrafting.com. $74, under 17 $62. From Revelstoke, drive east on Hwy. 1 and turn right at the arrow-shaped Canyon Hot Springs billboard.) A more relaxing aquatic experience can be found with **Natural Escapes Kayaking,** 1115 Pineridge Cres. (☎837-2679; www.naturalescapes.ca. $25 per 2hr., $40 for 2hr. lesson and guided tour.) The 140 bolted routes on Begbie Bluffs offer exceptional **sport climbing** (from the small parking area almost 9km down 23 South from Hwy. 1, the bluffs are a 10min. walk; take the left fork). Rogers Pass and the surrounding peaks offer a limitless amount of year-round opportunity to hone one's **mountaineering** skills. **Glacier House Resort** has a large range of rentals and trips year-round. (☎827-9594; www.glacierhouse.com. Canoe rentals $30 per half-day, $40 per day. Mt. Revelstoke guided day hike $85 per day.)

WINTER SPORTS. Winter in Revelstoke brings 60-80 ft. of powder, and with it excellent **downhill skiing. Powder Springs Resort** (☎800-991-4455; www.catpowder.com) is only 5km outside town and maintains one chairlift and 21 trails with a 1000 ft. vertical drop on the bottom third of Mt. MacKenzie. Tickets cost $28-32, but inquire about economical accommodation packages. The **Powder Springs Inn,** 200 3rd St. W (☎837-5151; www.catpowder.com), offers Ski & Stay packages for as little as $30 per day. The **SameSun Backpacker Lodge** (see **Accommodations and Camping,** above) also offers lift-ticket packages. Parks Canada offers excellent advice and brochures on area nordic trails and world-class backcountry skiing. They also provide info on snowmobiling, as does **Great Canadian Snowmobile Tours,** by Frisby Ridge, 6km north of town on West Side Rd. (☎837-5030 or 877-837-9594; www.snowmobilerevelstoke.com. Snowmobile rentals $210-300 per day.)

MOUNT REVELSTOKE NATIONAL PARK. Adjacent to town, Mt. Revelstoke National Park furnishes convenient and satisfying access to nature with its astounding scenery, and is a favorite of mountain bikers and hikers. Visitors will need a National Parks Permit ($5, ages 65 and older $4.25, under 16 $2.50) that can be purchased at the **Parks Canada Office** in Revelstoke, **Rogers Pass** visitors center in Glacier National Park, or the base of the **Meadows in the Sky Parkway.** The park is too tiny to offer many backcountry opportunities but does boast two backcountry campgrounds, **Eva Lake ❶,** a 6km hike, and **Jade Lake ❶,** a 9km hike. (Each has four sites, $8 per person. Open July-Sept. No pumped water. Jade Lake has a bear pole.) Two boardwalks off Hwy. 1 on the east side of the park access the trails. **Skunk Cabbage Trail** (1.25km, 30min.) leads through acres of stinking perfection: skunk cabbage plants tower at heights of over 1.5m **Giant Cedars Trail** (500m, 15min.) has majestic, over-600-year-old trees growing around babbling brooks. **Meadows in the Sky Parkway** (Summit Rd.) branches off Hwy. 1 about 1.5km east of town, leading to a 1km hike up Mt. Revelstoke to subalpine meadows. A wheelchair-accessible shuttle is available (summer only, 10am-4:20pm). The **Summit Trail** (10km one-way, full-day) leaves from the trailer drop-off parking lot at the base of Summit Rd. and ascends the summit of Mt. Revelstoke, where the weary traveler will be joined by everyone who drove up. **Jade Lake Trail** (9km one-way, full-day) cuts up from the Heather Lake parking lot on Summit Rd. to a series of picturesque jade lakes.

GLACIER NATIONAL PARK ☎250

This aptly named national park is home to over 400 monolithic ice floes that cover one-tenth of its 1350 sq. km. area. The jagged peaks and steep, narrow valleys of the Columbia Range not only make for breathtaking scenery but also prevent development in the park. The park is very hiking-intensive; no roads penetrate its expansive backcountry. An inland rain (although it feels more like snow) forest, Glacier receives significant precipitation every other day in the summer, but the clouds of mist that encircle the peaks and blanket the valleys only add to the park's astonishing beauty. In late summer, brilliant explosions of mountain wildflowers offset the deep green of the forests. In the winter, more literal explosions of Howitzer shells shake the calm of the valleys. Glacier is Canada's prime avalanche research area; scientists fire 105mm shells into mountain sides to create and observe controlled avalanches. This makes winter travel dangerous on almost every level, and consultation with park rangers is necessary. Rogers Pass, the park's main tourist attraction, has quite a history itself, as it was the last great obstacle of nature overcome by the Canadian Pacific Railroad in 1882.

ORIENTATION AND PRACTICAL INFORMATION

Glacier is 350km west of Calgary and 723km east of Vancouver. There are no roads in the park other than the Trans-Canada Highway (Hwy. 1)—all trailheads depart from the highway. **Greyhound buses** stop at Rogers Pass via: Revelstoke (1 hr., 1 per day, $15); Vancouver (9hr., 4 per day, $93); and Calgary (5hr., 4 per day, $54). For details on the park, including trail suggestions, talk to the Parks Canada staff at the **Rogers Pass Information Centre** (☎837-7500) on Hwy. 1 in Glacier, or buy a copy of *Footloose in the Columbias* ($2) at the bookstore. Topographical backcountry maps ($5-13) are also sold. (☎814-5232. Open daily mid-June to mid-Sept. 7:30am-4:30pm; mid-Sept. to mid-June 9am-5pm.) Daily **park passes** cost the same as at Revelstoke (p. 378). In an **emergency,** call the **Park Warden Office** (☎877-852-3100).

CAMPING

Glacier has two newly rebuilt frontcountry campgrounds: **Illecillewaet ❶** (ill-uh-SILL-uh-way-et), 3.5km west of Roger's Pass (wheelchair-accessible, 60 sites open late June-early Oct. $16), and **Loop Brook ❶,** another 3km west on Hwy. 1 (20 sites, open July-Sept. $16) Both offer toilets, kitchen shelters with cook stoves, and firewood. The park has no vehicle-accessible sites until late June; **Canyon Hot Springs** (p. 377) is the closest alternative for drivers. Backcountry campers must purchase a **backcountry pass** ($8 per day) from the Parks Canada office in Revelstoke (☎837-7500) or from the Rogers Pass Information Centre. Food is limited to the convenience-store options at the Rogers Pass gas station and the Rogers Pass Cafe at the inn (lunch and breakfast specials $7.50); stock up in **Golden** or **Revelstoke.**

OUTDOOR ACTIVITIES

HIKING. More than 140km of rough, often steep trails lead from the highway, inviting mountaineers to attempt the unconquerable. While the highway works its way through the park's lush valleys, a majority of the area lies above the treeline, providing for incredibly steep, high altitude, highly beautiful hikes.

Abandoned Rails Trail (1.25km one-way, 1hr.) follows the 1885 Canadian Pacific Railway bed over the top of historic Rogers Pass. Leaves from the information center. Easy.

Copperstain Trail (16km one-way, 6hr.) Beaver River Trailhead, 10km east of the Glacier Park Lodge uphill through alpine meadows. This trail is often combined with the longer Beaver Valley Trail to create a four-day backpacking loop. Moderate.

Balu Pass Trail (10km round-trip, 4hr.) Trailhead is at the west edge of Rogers Centre parking lot, near Rogers Pass info station. The Ursus Major and Ursus Minor peaks provide the best chance of seeing wildlife. (*Balu* is Inuit for bear, while *Ursus* is Latin for it.) This trail is prime bear habitat; check with park wardens before embarking. Difficult.

Hermit Trail (3km one-way, 2hr.) climbs nearly 800m into the Hermit Glacier, hanging high over Rogers Pass. This trail is on the south-facing slope, clear of snow up above the tree-line long before trails on the other side of the valley. Difficult.

Illecillewaet Trails (varies, 1-6.5km one-way). A web of trails built by Swiss guides imported by the railway leave from the campground (see **Camping,** above) and climb to the retreating Illecillewaet and Asulkan Glaciers. Dramatic views of the valley behind and opportunities to extend the hikes to the toes of the glaciers make these trails well worth the rigorous climbs. The **Avalanche Crest,** arguably the most spectacular of Glacier's trails, leaves from here. Difficulty varies.

OTHER ACTIVITIES. While biking and fishing in Glacier are prohibited, the **backcountry skiing** at Rogers Pass and Balu Pass is legendary. Contact the info center for registration and info on areas and avalanche conditions. Glacier also boasts the **Nakimu Caves,** located off the Balu Pass Trail near the info center, an extensive limestone wonderland open only to experienced cavers by special permission of the Park Warden.

YOHO NATIONAL PARK ☎ 250

A Cree expression for awe and wonder, Yoho is the perfect name for this small, superlative-inducing park. It sports some of the most engaging names in the Rockies, such as Kicking Horse Pass, named after Captain John Hector who, struggling to find a mountain pass for the Canadian Pacific Railroad, was kicked in the chest by his horse. The park was created in 1913, allegedly at the instigation of railroad companies, who wanted a scenic place for their passengers to stop and eat so the train wouldn't have to pull the heavy dining cars through the steep terrain. Driving down Yoho's narrow pass on Hwy. 1, visitors can see evidence of geological forces: massive bent and tilted sedimentary rock layers exposed in sharply eroded cliff faces, and natural rock bridges formed by water that has carved away the stone. Beneath these rock walls, Yoho overflows with natural attractions, including the largest waterfall in the Rockies—Takakkaw Falls—and paleontologically illuminating 500-million-year-old fossils.

✈ 🛈 ORIENTATION AND PRACTICAL INFORMATION

The park lies on the Trans-Canada Hwy. (Hwy. 1), next to Banff National Park. Within Yoho, the town of **Field** is 27km west of Lake Louise on Hwy. 1. **Greyhound** (☎800-661-8747) stops for travelers waving their arms on the highway at the Field junction as long as they have cash. (To Calgary, 3½hr., 5 per day, $33). **Hostelling International** runs a shuttle connecting hostels in Yoho, Banff, and Jasper National Parks and Calgary ($8-65). The **visitors center** in Field is on Hwy. 1. (☎343-6783. Open M-F July-Sept. 9am-7pm; Apr.-June and Sept.-Nov. 9am-5pm; Dec.-Apr. 9am-4pm.) Other services include **bike rentals** (see **Equipment Rental** for Banff) and **park pass** sales ($8, senior $5, child $4, groups up to 7 $14. Valid for Glacier and Revelstoke.) In case of **emergency,** call the **Park Warden Office** (☎403-762-4506, non-emergency 343-6142) or the **RCMP** (☎344-2221) in Golden. The **post office** is at 312 Stephen Ave. (☎343-6365. Open M-F 8:30am-4:30pm.) **Postal Code:** V0A 1G0.

🏠 🏕 ACCOMMODATIONS AND CAMPING

With one of the best locations of all the Rocky Mountain hostels, the ◪**Whiskey Jack Wilderness Hostel (HI) ❷**, 13km off the Trans-Canada on the Yoho Valley Rd., perfectly blurs the line between civilization and nature. Located across the valley from **Takakkaw Falls,** one of Canada's most scenic spots, the hostel offers a kitchen, campfires, plumbing, propane light, easy access to Yoho's best high-country trails, and the splendor of the Yoho Valley right from the front porch. (☎866-762-4122. Reception 8-10am and 5-11pm. Reserve through the HI Central Reservations. Open July-Sept. M-Th and Su $21, nonmembers $25; F-Sa $24/$25.)

The four official frontcountry **campgrounds** offer a total of 200 sites, all accessible from the highway. Sites are first come, first served, but only Monarch and Kicking Horse fill up regularly in summer. ❧**Takakkaw Falls Campground ❶** lies beneath mountains, glaciers, and the magnificent falls 14km up curvy Yoho Valley Rd. It offers only pump water and pit toilets; campers must park in the Falls lot and haul their gear 650m to the peaceful sites. (Open late June-Sept. 35 sites, $13.) **Hoodoo Creek ❶**, on the west end of the park, has kitchen shelters, running hot water, flush toilets, a nearby river, and a playground. (Open June- Sept. 106 sites, $13.) **Monarch Campground ❶** sits at the junction of Yoho Valley Rd. and Hwy. 1. (Open early May-early Sept. 46 sites and 10 walk-ins, $13.) **Kicking Horse ❶**, another kilometer up Yoho Valley Rd., has toilets and is wheelchair-accessible. (Open June-Sept. 86 sites, $20. Hot showers.) Reserve the **Stanley Mitchell Hut ❷** through the Alpine Club of Canada. (☎403-678-3200; www.alpineclubofcanada.ca. $26 per person. No walk-ins.) The campground at splendid **Lake O'Hara ❶**, in the east end of the park, can only be reached by a 13km trail or bus. (Bus reservations ☎343-6433, up to 3 months in advance. Round-trip $15. $8 backcountry permit required for camping.)

🍴 FOOD

The most convenient food stop in Yoho, and potentially a sit-all-day stop, is the ❧**Truffle Pigs Cafe and General Store ❷**, on Stephen Ave. in Field, which sells basic foodstuffs, beer, wine, and camping supplies. Local crafts line the walls, and the owners peddle homemade sandwiches ($4.25), breakfast ($4.50-7), burgers ($6.50), and eclectic, delicious $8-15 dinners. (☎343-6462; www.trufflepigs.com. Has the only **ATM** in the area. Open daily 8am-10pm; winter M-Sa 10am-7pm.)

🎿 OUTDOOR ACTIVITIES

HIKING
The park's six **backcountry campgrounds** and 400km of trail make for an intense wilderness experience, with countless quickly accessed trails exhibiting scenery equal to and beyond that of the larger parks. Before setting out, pick up **camping permits** ($6 per person per day), maps, and the free *Backcountry Guide to Yoho National Park* at the visitors center. Whiskey Jack Hostel (see above) is also well stocked with trail information. The park's finest terrain is in the Yoho Valley and is accessible only after the snow melts in late June and early July.

THE LOCAL STORY

BLASTING THE PASS

When the Canadian Pacific Railway was plotting routes for its trans-Canada line in the 1880s, it was faced with the decision of heading north, through the Yellowhead Pass in Jasper, or south, over a steeper pass in the Rockies and an as-yet-undiscovered pass through the Selkirk range, where Glacier National Park sits today. The railroad decided, against the advice of its engineers, to take the southern route, in order to prevent US railroads from making a land grab in southern BC.

To find a pass through Selkirk, Canadian Pacific hired A.B. Rogers, an American engineer. The railroad offered him a $5000 bonus if he found a pass, whose existence many engineers openly doubted. Rogers was known for three things: an immense mustache, superhuman endurance, and an uncontrollable temper resulting in a constant stream of profanity. The men who had ventured into the unknown wilderness with him were kept in constant fear of their boss's unpredictable anger.

Rogers did find his pass, a narrow slot that today bears his name. The Canadian Pacific was completed in 1882 and Rogers received his $5000. He was more interested in glory than money, however, and had the check framed. His check lasted longer than his pass—avalanches closed the route so frequently in winter that the Connaught Tunnel bypassed the area in 1916.

Wapta Falls (5km round-trip). The trailhead is not marked on Hwy. 1 for westbound traffic as there is no left-turn lane. Continue 3km to the west entrance of the park, turn around, and come back east. Highlights include seeing the Kicking Horse River drop 30m. The least ambitious and least spectacular of the Yoho hikes. Easy.

Iceline Trail (via Little Yoho 20km, via Celeste Lake 17km). Starts at the hostel. Takes hikers briefly through forests of alder, spruce, and fir before leading them on an extended trip above the tree line, over glacial moraines, and past the striated rock and icy pools of Emerald Glacier. Moderate.

Emerald Triangle (19.75km round-trip). The route travels through the Yoho Pass (see *Backcountry Guide*) to the Wapta Highline trail, Burgess Pass, and back to the start. Most of the journey is above treeline with breathtaking views over much of Yoho's diverse landscape. Moderate.

Mt. Hunter Lookout to Upper Lookout (13km one-way). Cuts through Yoho's lush lower altitudes but manages a nice view of Kicking Horse and Beaverfoot valleys from two abandoned fire lookouts. Moderate.

OTHER ACTIVITIES

The **Great Divide** is the boundary between Alberta and British Columbia as well as the Atlantic and Pacific watersheds. Here a stream forks with one arm flowing 1500km to the Pacific Ocean, the other flowing 2500km to the Atlantic via Hudson's Bay. It is also the site of the **Burgess Shale**, a layer of sedimentary rock containing the world's most important animal fossils, imprints of the insect-like, soft-bodied organisms that inhabited the world's oceans prior to an intense burst of evolution known as the **Cambrian Explosion.** Discovered in 1909, the unexpected complexity of these 505 million-year-old specimens changed the way paleontologists thought about evolution. Larger, clumsier animals known as humans have since successfully lobbied to protect the shale from excessive tourism. Access is restricted to educational hikes led by the **Yoho-Burgess Shale Foundation** (☎800-343-3006; www.burgess-shale.bc.ca). A full-day, 20km hike costs $70, under 12 $28. A steep 6km loop to the equally old and trilobite-packed **Mount Stephen Fossil Beds** runs $48, under 12 $16. (July to mid-Sept. only. Reservations required.) For easier sightseeing, follow the 14km of the Yoho Valley Rd. to views of the **Takakkaw Falls,** Yoho's most splendid waterfall.

KOOTENAY NATIONAL PARK ☎ 250

Kootenay National Park hangs off the Continental Divide on the southeast edge of British Columbia. Many visitors travel through Kootenay to get to or from Banff on the majestic Banff-Windermere Hwy. (Hwy. 93), the first road to cross the Canadian Rockies. The federal government built the road in 1920 in exchange for the 8km of land on either side that now constitutes the park. Kootenay's biggest attraction is its lack of visitors: unlike Banff and Jasper, Kootenay has not been developed at all. The only civilization is found at the Radium Hot Springs, on the park's western border. The park's stately conifers, alpine meadows, and pristine peaks hide in Banff's shadow, allowing travelers to experience the true solitude of the Canadian Rockies while still in a national park. Visitors to the park will need a Park Pass ($7 per individual, $14 per 2-7 person group, available at the park entrance and transferable to Yoho, Banff, and Jasper National Parks).

■✱ ❼ ORIENTATION AND PRACTICAL INFORMATION

Kootenay lies southwest of Banff and Yoho National Parks. **Highway 93** runs through the park from the **Trans-Canada Highway** in Banff to **Radium Hot Springs** (see **Hot Springs**, p. 384) at the southwest edge of the park, where it joins **High-**

way 95. Greyhound stops once per day at the Esso station, 7507 E Main St. (☎347-9726; open daily 7am-11pm), at the junction of Hwy. 93 and Hwy. 95 in Radium Hot Springs, on the way to Banff (2hr., $22) and Calgary (3½hr., $44). The park information center and Tourism BC Info Centre are both located at 7556 Main St. W in Radium. They offer Internet access ($2 per 15min.), free maps, and a back-country hiking guide. (Parks Canada: ☎347-9505; Tourism BC: 347-9331. Open daily July-Aug. 9am-7pm; Sept.-June approximately 9am-4pm. Tourism BC also open Oct.-May Tu-Sa 10am-4pm.) The Kootenay Park Lodge operates another visitors center 63km north of Radium. (☎403-762-9196. Open daily late May-late Sept. 10am-6pm; Apr. to mid-May and the first week of Oct. 11am-6pm. The Park Administration Office, on the access road to Redstreak Campground, dispenses the backcountry hiking guide. (☎347-9615. Open M-F 8am-noon and 12:30-4pm.) An ambulance can be reached at ☎342-2055. In an emergency, contact the Banff Park Warden ☎403-762-4506 and the police in either Invermere (☎342-9292) or Radium Hot Springs (☎347-9393). Windermere District Hospital is in Invermere, 850 10th Ave. (☎342-9201), 15km south of Radium on Hwy. 95. The post office is on Radium Blvd in Radium Hot Springs. (☎347-9460. Open M-F 9am-5pm.) Postal Code: V0A 1M0.

ACCOMMODATIONS AND FOOD

The Misty River Lodge (HI) ❷, 5036 Hwy. 93, the first left after you exit the park's West Gate, offers bike rentals for $10 per day. (☎347-9912; www.mistyriverlodge.bc.ca. Dorms $17, nonmembers $22; private room with bath $42/$65.) There's also a B&B ❹ upstairs. ($69-79, 10% HI discount.) Downtown, Radium features over 30 other motels, with high-season doubles starting at $40. The park's only serviced campground is Redstreak ❷, on the access road that departs Hwy. 95 near the south end of Radium Hot Springs, which features free showers, firewood, and playgrounds, and boasts 242 sites, including 38 with electricity and 50 additional fully-serviced sites. Arrive early to secure a spot. (Open mid-May to mid-Oct. $22; full RV sites $30.) McLeod Meadows ❷, 27km north of the West Gate entrance on Hwy. 93, offers quiet, unserviced wooded sites on the banks of the very blue Kootenay River, as well as access to hiking trails. (Open mid-May to mid-Sept. 98 sites, $17.) From September to May, seven free winter sites are available at the Dolly Varden ❶ picnic area, 36km north of the West Gate entrance, which boasts free firewood and a shelter. Ask at the visitors centers for details on Crooks Meadow ❶, which is available for groups (75 people max., $4 per person.), and cheap ($8), unserviced camping in the nearby Invermere Forest District.

There is little affordable food in Kootenay, with the exception of a few basic staples at the Kootenay Park Lodge. Radium supports a few inexpensive eateries on Main St. The best selection of groceries and deli sandwiches ($4-6) is at Mountainside Market, 7546 Main St. E. right next to the visitors center. (☎347-9600. Open M-Sa 7:30am-11pm, Su 9am-8pm.)

OUTDOOR ACTIVITIES

The 95km Banff-Windermere Highway (Highway 93) forms the sinuous backbone of Kootenay. Stretching from Radium Hot Springs to Banff, the highway follows the Kootenay and Vermilion Rivers, passing views of glacier-enclosed peaks, dense stands of virgin forest, and green, glacier-fed rivers. The wild landscape of the Kootenay River Valley remains unblemished but for the ribbon of road.

BRITISH COLUMBIA

HOT SPRINGS. The park's main attraction is **Radium Hot Springs,** named after the radioactive element detected there in trace quantities. The crowded complex is responsible for the traffic and towel-toting tourists just inside the West Gate. Natural mineral waters fill two swimming pools—a hot one for soaking at 40°C/104°F and a cooler one for swimming at 27°C/81°F. The hot pool is wheelchair-accessible. (☎347-9485. $6.25, children and seniors $5.25; winter $5.25/$4.75; group and family rates available. Lockers $0.25, towel rental $1.25, swimsuit rental $1.50. Open daily May to mid-Oct. 9am-11pm. Mid-Oct. to Apr., the hot pool is open Su-Th noon-9pm, F-Sa noon-10pm, the cold pool F 6-9pm and Sa-Su noon-9pm.)

🏃 **HIKING.** The **Rockwall Trail** in the north of the park is the most popular backcountry area in Kootenay. All **backcountry** campers must stop at a visitors center (see **Orientation and Practical Info,** p. 382) for the hiking guide, which has maps, trail descriptions, and topographical profiles, as well as a mandatory **wilderness pass.** ($6 per person per night, $38 per year.) A number of short trails lead right off Hwy. 93 about 15km from the Banff border. Two fire roads, plus all of Hwy. 93, are open for **mountain biking,** but Kootenay lacks the extensive trail systems of its larger siblings. Icy water and rock flour from glaciers limit fishing opportunities.

> **Marble Canyon Trail** (750m, 15min.) This popular path traverses a deep limestone gorge cut by Tokumm Creek before ending at a roaring waterfall. Easy.
>
> **Paint Pots Trail** (1.7km, 30min.) 3.3km south of Marble Canyon on Hwy. 93. This partially wheelchair-accessible trail leads to springs rich in iron oxide. Tourist-heavy. Easy.
>
> **Stanley Glacier Trail** (5.5km, 4hr.) Starts 3.5km from the Banff entrance and leads into a glacier-gouged valley, ending 1.8km from the foot of Stanley Glacier. One of the hot springs' most astounding and therapeutic powers is their ability to suck travelers out of the woods, leaving Kootenay's many longer hiking trails uncrowded. Considered the best day hike in the park. Moderate.
>
> **Kindersley Pass** (16.5km round-trip, 5hr.) The two trailheads at either end of the route, Sinclair Creek and Kindersley Pass, are less than 1km apart on Hwy. 93, about 10km inside the West Gate entrance. The trail climbs more than 1000m to views of the Columbia River Valley in the west and the crest of the Rockies in the east. Difficult.

NORTHERN BRITISH COLUMBIA

Northern BC remains among the most remote and sparsely inhabited regions of North America. Averaging one person per 15 sq. km, the land's loneliness and sheer physical beauty are overwhelming. Native peoples have lived here for thousands of years, adapting their lifestyles and culture to patterns of animal migration and the uncompromising climate. White settlers began migrating westward in the early 19th century, attracted by the wealth of natural resources. While furs were lucrative, it wasn't until several gold rushes hit that stampedes rushed in to settle permanently. Since then, the lumber and mining industries have brought a steady flow eager to extract the wealth of the land. Despite some tell-tale signs of logging and mining, the land remains mainly unspoiled. Unfortunately, the area is often blown through by travelers hellbent on Alaska. Their loss—the stark mountains, yawning canyons, roaring rivers, and clear lakes are left all that more pristine for those who will stop to appreciate them.

ALONG THE CHILCOTIN HWY.

WILLIAMS LAKE TO BELLA COOLA ☎ 250

The allure of the Chilcotin Hwy. lies not just in its endpoints at Bella Coola and Williams Lake, but in the rugged and scenic lands along the 457km highway (a 5-7hr. drive). Most of the drive is smooth sailing, but the "Hill" is an unforgettable guardrail-less 21km of gravel (see **Tweedsmuir Provincial Park,** p. 387). Leaving Williams Lake, the Chilcotin Hwy. heads west across the **Fraser River** and climbs briefly before flattening out through forests and pastures dotted with cattle ranches. Warning to unsuspecting travelers, this is open range: cattle at large. Watch for them on roads to avoid unplanned BBQs.

Alexis Creek (km 110), Nimpo Lake (km 300), and Anahim (km 305) all offer gas, cafe, lodging, and a general store. **Bull Canyon Provincial Park ❶,** 8km past Alexis Creek, features great fishing on the Chilcotin River, home to five species of Pacific salmon, as well as steelhead, rainbow, and cutthroat trout. (Two dozen tent sites $14). Lakeside resort turn-offs, with camping and cabins all with comparable prices, are sprinkled along the highway with a concentration worth visiting at **Puntzi Lake.** South of the Chilcotin Hwy., **Tsylos Provincial Park** (sigh-LOSS), the highest point in the Chilcotin Range, boasts the glacier-fed, trout- and salmon-rich Lake Chilko. To reach the **Gwa da Ts'ih campground ❶** on the north side of the park, turn off at Tatla Lake (km 220) and drive 63km on gravel roads. (No reservations. Sites $10.) The best meal around can be consumed around Nimpo Lake at the **Chilcotin's Gate ❷.** Burgers $7-8, sandwich and fries $7, steak dinner $13. (☎742-3720. Open daily June-Sept. 6am-9pm; Oct.-May 7am-7pm.)

Low-priced, convenient camping is across the highway at **Vagabond RVs ❶,** but bring earplugs to sleep through the early morning take-offs of floatplanes—Nimpo Lake is known as the floatplane capital of BC. (☎742-3347. Tent $15, full RV $20, cabins $60 per day. Free shower, coin laundry, fish cleaning facilities, boat and motor rental $50 per day.) **Nimpo Service and Towing** aids the broken-down Chilcotin-traveler (☎742-3484, M-Sa 8am-6pm) or feeds the hungry at the **Country Bakery and Cafe** (open M-F 6am-6pm, Sa 8am-6pm). **Chilko River Expeditions** runs **rafting** expeditions along the Chilcotin and Chilko Rivers from Williams Lake lodging. (☎398-6711 or 800-998-7238; www.chilkoriver.com. From $110 for a daytrip.) Whatever you do and wherever you stay, use enough insect repellent to ward away the clouds of mosquitoes that attach to you the moment you slow down.

PUNTZI LAKE. A 5km turnoff along a gravel road at Chilanko Forks (km 175) leads to the 9km long **Puntzi Lake,** surrounded by several affordable resort options. Summer activities include fishing for kokanee and rainbow trout while watching white pelicans. The friendly owners of **Barney's Lakeside Resort ❶** offer well-kept sites and cabins as well as an option to buy great home-cooked meals. (☎481-1100 or 800-578-6804; www.barneyslakesideresort.com. Sites $14; full RV $18; cabins from $48; boat and motor rental $45 per day.) At **Puntzi Lake Resort ❷,** smiling owners dole out campsites, cabins, and canoe rentals. (☎481-1176 or 800-578-6804; www.puntzilake.com. Sites $17; full RV sites $21; cabins $50-105; canoes $25 per day; boat and motor $49 per day.)

BELLA COOLA ☎ 250

The seemingly lackluster town of Bella Coola, homeland of the Nuxalk Nation, lies at the end of the Chilcotin Hwy. Salmon fishery restrictions and the pull-out of the logging industry in recent years have severely depressed the local economy. Nevertheless, the locals are very friendly and willing to share a story or two, the amazing peaks of the surrounding Coast Mountain Range are a spectacular end to the highway, and although it may take a little looking, there are plenty of sights and activities right in Bella Coola Valley.

◾ TRANSPORTATION. Lately, the town has become increasingly dependent on the tourism from the **BC Ferries'** *Discovery Passage* route, which links Bella Coola with Port Hardy, on the northern tip of Vancouver Island, from mid-June to mid-September. (☎888-223-3779; www.bcferries.com. $107, ages 5-11 $54, under 5 free. Car, driver's ticket not included, $213.) The ferry departs Port Hardy three times a week. On Tuesday, the ferry leaves in the morning, stopping along the mid-coast in McLoughlin Bay and Shearwater before arriving in Bella Coola on Wednesday morning. On Thursday the ferry runs non-stop, arriving later that night. Saturday's ferry makes stops in McLoughlin Bay, Shearwater, Klemtu (where it stops for 4hr.), and Ocean Falls, and deposits you in Bella Coola on Monday morning. All of the mid-coast stops are great places to launch a kayak. If you're taking the ferry away from Bella Coola, leaving M,W, and F mornings, reservations can be made in town at **Tweedsmuir Travel,** on Cliff St. downtown. (☎799-5638. Open mid-June to mid-Sept. M, W, and F 9:30am-4:30pm, Tu and Th 9:30am-5pm, Su 3-5pm; mid-Sept. to mid-June M-F 9:30am-4:30pm).

◾ PRACTICAL INFORMATION. The **visitors center** is located on Mackenzie St. next to the Co-op store, and can provide a guide to nearby hiking trails as well as info on local businesses and sights. (☎799-5202; www.bellacoola.ca. Open daily late May-Aug. 7am-7pm; call for winter hours.) The **Shell Station,** across from the Valley Inn on McKenzie Rd., does repairs and has the only gas in town. (☎799-5616. Open M-Sa 8am-6pm, Su 10am-4pm.) **Sept.** supplies all outdoor needs, including bear spray and topographical maps. (☎799-5553. Open M-Sa 8am-5:30pm; also open mid-June to mid-Sept. Su 2-5pm.) Other services include **police,** 442 Mackenzie St., (☎799-5363; open M-F 8:30am-4:30pm); **hospital,** at Dean Ave and MacKay St., (☎799-5638); and **post office,** at Dean Ave and Cliff St. (☎799-5933; open M-F 8:30am-5:30pm, Sa 9am-1pm). **Postal Code:** V0T 1C0.

◾ ACCOMMODATIONS AND FOOD. Rooms in town are expensive, but the **Bella Coola Motel ❹,** at Burke and Clayton St., has **camping ❶** on its large back lawn, right next to the river. Campers have kitchen access in a cabin on the historic "Hudson Bay Trading Post" site. The rooms offer full kitchens and bathrooms, providing some welcome comfort after the long drive or ferry. (☎799-5323. Singles $60-80; doubles $65-85. Tents $10; RVs $12, no RV sites. Free showers. Canoe rentals $40 per day; bikes $20 per day.) For attractive shaded and forested sites, head to **Gnome's Home Campground and RV Park ❶** in Hagensborg, 16km east of Bella Coola along the highway. An on-site Nature Conservancy Trail allows for exploration of old growth forest and salmon spawns. (☎982-2504; www.gnomeshome.ca. Sites $15; full RV sites $18. Showers $2. Firewood by donation.) The **Co-op,** on Mackenzie St., provides all you need to cook up a feast. (☎799-5325. Open M-Th and F 9am-7pm, Sa 9am-6pm; also open mid-June to mid-Sept. Su noon-5pm.) If you don't want to cook, the **Bay Motor Hotel ❶,** on Hwy. 20 in Hagensborg, has an inexpensive **coffee shop ❶,** a more expensive **restaurant ❸,** and a bustling **pub ❷.** Toonie Tuesdays in the pub offer $2 burgers, fries, and beers. (☎982-2212. All open for food daily 6:30am-9pm; F and Sa to 6:30am-10pm; pub open for drinks until 11pm and F-Sa until midnight.) In Bella Coola, the **Bella Coola Valley Inn ❸** offers deck seating and dinner options ($12-16). (☎799-5316; www.bellacoolavalleyinn.com.

Open daily 6am-9pm.) **Palm Garden Restaurant ❷,** on Cliff St. across from the laundromat, serves Chinese ($8.50-13), Mexican ($7-10) and North American cuisine. (☎799-5989. Open daily 10:30am-8:30pm.)

◪ **SIGHTS.** There are a number of hiking trails available for exploration throughout the valley, and a guide can be picked up at the visitors center. A short 200m past the BC Hydro plant off the logging road that continues past the ferry dock provides an excellent view of **Clayton Falls.** The **Bella Coola Museum,** on Hwy. 20 just outside of town on the way to the ferry, gives a view into the history of the area including a large section on the building of the hill and the final leg of Alexander Mackenzie's journey to the Pacific. (☎799-5767. $2.50, students $2. Open June-Sept. M-F and Su 10am-5pm.)

TWEEDSMUIR PROVINCIAL PARK   ☎250

Established in 1938, the 981,000 hectare Tweedsmuir Provincial Park is the largest of British Columbia's provincial parks. Home to caribou, marmots, fox, deer, black and grizzly bears, and more than its fair share of mosquitoes, the park is separated into two sections, North and South. Tweedsmuir South, with vehicle-accessible campsites, is more easily reached than its northern sister, and boasts hiking trails (though not all well-maintained), wilderness horseback riding, and prime canoeing on the Turner Lake Chain. Visitors are treated to a breathtaking view of 260m Hunlen Falls, multi-colored mountains, and spectacular alpine summits. Despite the beauty of both the North and South sections, however, the park is mostly undiscovered; a hiker could spend days without coming across another adventurer on Tweedsmuir's under-utilized trails.

◪◪ **ORIENTATION AND PRACTICAL INFORMATION.** The trailheads and entrance to Tweedsmuir South lie along the **Chilcotin Highway** between Anahim Lake and Bella Coola. The eastern boundary is at Heckman's Pass, about 365km from Williams Lake, while the western boundary is 50km from Bella Coola. The stretch inside the park is best known for 21km of **"The Hill":** a one-lane, brake-burning, head-turning, windshield-cracking, free-falling, no-barrier, roller-coaster ride with steep (18%) grades and switchbacks notable for their sharpness and susceptibility to avalanches, in addition to undeniably spectacular views of the Coast Range and the valley below. (Road conditions ☎604-660-9770.) For decades, Hwy. 20 ended at **Anahim Lake,** 315km west of Williams Lake. In 1955, frustrated by inaction from a government that said the road to the sea could not, financially and physically, be completed, locals got two bulldozers, borrowed money, and finished the job themselves. The route's alternate name is the "Freedom Highway." Hwy 20 becomes paved again after the hill for the rest of its course through the park. Tweedsmuir North is off of **Highway 16** and is accessible only across the manmade lakes to the north of the park.

    The **BC Parks** office is located at 400-640 Borland St. in Williams Lake and can provide a wealth of information on the Southern region of the park, (☎398-4530. Open M-F 8:30am-noon and 1-4:30pm.) There is also an office on Airport Rd. in **Hagensborg** that has a representative for Tweedsmuir from May-Oct. (☎982-2786).

◪◪ **CAMPING AND ACCOMMODATIONS.** There are a number of resorts and RV parks on both sides of the park boundary. There are two vehicle accessible campsites in Tweedsmuir South. **Atnarko Campground ❶,** located at the base of the hill, has 24 beautiful and mostly private sites while **Fisheries Pool Campground ❶,** has 12 closely packed and open sites. (No reservations. Both $14; Atnarko open June 15-Sept. 15; Fisheries open June 1-Sept. 15.) Both sites offer great access to the spectacular salmon and trout fishing in the Atnarko River. There are a number of primitive wilderness **campsites ❶** throughout the park, both north and south, some of which provide bear caches. The well maintained sites at the Turner Lakes/Hunlen Falls area are $5 per night. **Tweedsmuir Wilderness Camp ❸,** operated by Tweedsmuir Air, provides cabins at Turner Lake, an excellent jumping-off point for paddling the chain. (☎742-3388 or 800-668-4335; www.tweedsmuirair.com/adventures/twc/intro.htm. Cabins $50 per day; canoes $28 per day.)

⚠ OUTDOOR ACTIVITIES. Tweedsmuir offers a number of spectacular trails as well as limitless opportunities for alpine exploration off the trail. *Hikes in Tweedsmuir South Provincial Park,* by Scott Whittemore ($10), is a comprehensive guide to everything available in the park and can be found in most outdoor stores in the area. BC Parks strongly recommends that hikers bring bear spray or bear bangers. Also, in recent years funding cuts have led to less frequent trail maintenance. Many trails have become overgrown and can be hard to follow. This, along with the year-round threat of snowfall in many parts of the park, makes topographical maps a must. There are two main parking lots from which the majority of marked hiking trails leave. All distances and times are one-way unless otherwise noted.

▓ HUNLEN FALLS AND THE TURNER LAKE TRAILHEAD. At the base of "The Hill" lies the Atnarko Tote Rd. This 12km 4WD road deposits travelers at the Hunlen Falls trailhead, from which a number of hikes depart. **Stillwater Lake Trail** is a short 5km hike from the parking lot with views of Stillwater Lake, Mt. Ada, and a variety of wildlife. The most popular option is the moderate 16km **Hunlen Falls Trail,** which provides spectacular views of the large falls. The falls provide access to the **Turner Lake Chain,** a series of seven lakes that can be paddled in about 3-5 days. Many people decide to get to the lakes by float plane; **Tweedsmuir Air** runs flights from Nimpo Lake. (☎742-3388 or 800-668-4335; www.tweedsmuirair.com. Flights from $239.) The **Junker Lake Trail,** a fairly easy 10km trail, leaves from the Turner Lake area and offers views of many of the lakes in the chain. **Ptarmigan Lake Trail** is also available from Turner Lake. This trail goes through an alpine tundra wonderland before arriving at Ptarmigan Lake (12km one way). **Panorama Lakes Loop Route** allows for further exploration of the alpine area and many more lakes, as well as hanging glaciers and snowfields.

RAINBOW RANGE TRAILHEAD. Located at the top of "The Hill," the **Rainbow Range Trail** takes hikers into the alpine and provides views of the incredible pastel-colored rock in shades of red, orange, yellow and purple formed millions of years ago by active volcanoes. The round-trip makes for a good long day hike. From the campsite at the end of the trail there are limitless opportunities for unmarked alpine exploration. The **Crystal Lake Trail** is a 20km route from the same parking lot to Crystal Lake at the base of the rainbow-hued mountains. It offers views of the Coast Mountains and great wildlife viewing opportunities. From Crystal Lake, the short but steep **Boyd Pass Connector** leads down to **Rainbow Cabin,** built originally for a hunting and guiding outfit. It has been refurbished to provide a little warmth after a few days on the trail. The cabin's guestbook is fascinating, particularly the "radio show" written by someone stuck in the cabin due to weather. Also leading from the trailhead is the **Octopus Lake Trail,** an easy 16km trail that leads to beautiful lakeside campsites and views of the Capoose Mountain Range. A good and popular loop can be made with Crystal Lake, Boyd Pass, and Octopus Lake if hikers take the portion of the **Tweedsmuir Trail** that goes from Octopus Lake to Rainbow Cabin. The rock cairns of this trail are hard to follow at points, but it affords spectacular views of the Coast, Capoose, and Rainbow Ranges. Allow no fewer then three days for the entire loop. Be advised: large parts of these trails are through bog and marsh land. You will get wet, and your boots will be soaked for days.

OTHER TRAILS. Other trails include one end of the 25- to 30-day **Alexander Mackenzie Heritage Trail,** reserved for those hikers beyond hardcore and off the deep end. Its 420km stretch from **Blackwater River,** just west of Quesnel, across western British Columbia to **Burnt Creek Bridge** on Hwy. 20, tracing the final leg of Mackenzie's 1793 journey across Canada to the west coast. Mackenzie reached the Pacific more than a decade before Lewis and Clark. The **Valley/Burnt Bridge Loop** is great for people just looking for a short hike. The 1-2 hr. loop is easy to follow and has a viewpoint that displays the Bella Coola River below and the intimidating Mt. Defiance and Mt. Stupendous of the Coast Range.

WILLIAMS LAKE TO QUESNEL   ☎250

Williams Lake is the Cariboo's largest town, but by no means its most appealing. Fortunately, it's easy to leave, with Hwy. 20 meandering 460km west to **Bella Coola** (p. 385) and Hwy. 97 continuing north to the rough-hewn lumber towns of **Quesnel** and **Prince George.** The biggest event in town is the celebration of its cowboy heritage over Canada Day weekend (July 1) with the **Williams Lake Stampede.** Festivities include a rodeo, mountain race, wild cow milking, barn dance, and live music. (☎392-6885 or 800-717-6336; www.williamslakestampede.com. $11-15 depending on which events you attend.) The **tourist office** in town is available on Hwy. 97. (☎392-5025; www.wlake.com. Open daily June-Aug. 9am-5pm; Sept.-May M-F 9am-4pm.) The **library** at the corner of 3rd Ave. N and Proctor St. has free **Internet** access for 30min. (☎392-3630. Open Tu-Th 10am-8pm, F-Sa 10am-5pm.) There is a **pharmacy** at the **Save On Foods,** 730 Oliver St. (☎392-7266. Open M-Th and Sa 9am-6pm; F 8am-9pm; Su 10am-6pm.) Other services include **police,** 575 Borland St. (☎392-6211) and the **Cariboo Memorial Hospital,** 517 N 6th Ave. (☎392-4411). The **post office** is at 28 S 2nd Ave. (☎392-7543). **Postal Code:** V2G 1H6.

The **Slumber Lodge ❸,** 27 7th Ave., has a small indoor pool and cable. (☎392-7116 or 800-577-2244. Singles $50-55; doubles $60-65.) For a cheap thrill, pitch your tent on the **Stampede grounds** in the center of town. To get there, cross the bridge on Hwy. 20 from the junction with Hwy. 97 and take the first right on Mackenzie Rd.; the grounds are on your right. (☎392-6718. Open mid-May to mid-Oct. $12, full RV sites $20.) To escape the bustle, bask on the beach at **Blue Lake Holiday Campground** (☎297-6505); take the turnoff at Blue Lake Rd. 32km north of town and drive 3km up the gravel road. Campsites ($15) and canoes ($5 per hr.) on the bright blue-green lake are at your disposal.

Basics and the rest are available at **Save on Foods,** 730 Oliver St. (☎392-7225. Open daily 8am-7pm.) **Leone's Pizza & Steakhouse ❷,** at the corner of N 3rd Ave. and Oliver St., offers pizza ($10) and entrees ($10) that will satisfy any appetite. (☎389-8299. Open daily 11am-10pm.)

While the city is hardly a hotbed of outdoor activity, there are several parks that are good for picnics, including **Boitano Park** in the center of town. **Scout Island Nature Center,** off Borland Rd., has a few short trails that offer opportunities to see marsh environments and an array of wildlife just outside of the city itself. The info center has information on other **hiking** and **biking** trails in the surrounding area.

The 122km drive north to Quesnel can be a little dull, but those willing to subject their cars to a little gravel can make it more interesting. About 35km north of Williams Lake, the **Soda Creek Townsite Road** splits from Hwy. 97 for 20km of rustic splendor alongside the **Fraser River.** The road returns to the highway several kilometers south of the free **Marguerite Ferry,** which shuttles drivers across the river to a gravel road paralleling Hwy. 97 for the remainder of the trip to Quesnel. (Open May-Oct. 5min., on demand 7-11:45am, 1-4:45pm, and 6-6:45pm.)

QUESNEL   ☎ 250

The town of Quesnel (QUIN-nel), 123km north of Williams Lake and 116km south of Prince George, takes great pride in its gold-driven past and forestry-propelled present. The town itself is an industrial center but provides relatively close access to other options. After being welcomed into town by the world's largest (and purplest) gold pan on the north end of town on Hwy. 97, you're only a 10min. drive from Pinnacles Provincial Park: cross the river on Marsh Rd., then turn right on Baker Dr., and follow it for 5km. Park at the gate and walk 1km to the hoodoos—volcanic rock formations that look like giant sand dribble castles—and impressive views. Every third weekend in July, crowds flock to Quesnel for the wholesome family fun of **Billy Barker Days** (☎ 992-1234; www.quesnelbc.com/billybarkerdays) featuring a rodeo, live entertainment, and a "Crash-to-Pass" demolition derby. The logging industry maintains a strong presence (and odor) in this industrial oasis.

■ ⑦ **ORIENTATION AND PRACTICAL INFORMATION.** Hwy. 97 becomes Front St. in Quesnel and wraps along the river. One block east, the main road, Reid St., parallels Front St. in the "city centre." The **Greyhound** depot is on Kinchant St. between St. Laurent and Barlow. (☎ 992-2231 or 800-661-8747. Open M-F 6am-8pm, Sa 6am-noon and 6-7:30pm, Su 6-10:30am and 6-7:30pm.) Buses run to Prince George (1½hr.; 3 per day, $21) and Vancouver (10hr.; 3 per day, $96). The **visitors center,** 705 Carson Ave., is just off Hwy. 97 at the south end of town. (☎ 992-8716 or 800-992-4922; www.northcariboo.com. Open daily 9am-6pm mid-May to mid-Sept.; mid-Sept. to mid-May Tu-Sa 9am-4pm.) **Safeway,** 445 Reid St., serves as both **market** (☎ 992-6477. Open daily 8am-10pm) and **pharmacy** (☎ 992-6898. Open M-W 9am-6pm, Th-F 9am-9pm, Sa 9:30am-5:30pm.) You'll find free **Internet** access at the **library,** 593 Barlow Ave. on two computers. Reserve in advance. (☎ 992-7912; www.cln.bc.ca. Open Tu-Th 10am-8pm, F-Sa 10am-5pm.) Contact the **police** at ☎ 992-9211. The **post office** is at 346 Reid St. (☎ 992-2200. Open M-F 8:45am-5:15pm.) **Postal Code:** V2J 2M0.

█ ▐ **ACCOMMODATIONS AND FOOD.** One of Quesnel's oldest establishments, the **Cariboo Hotel ❸,** 254 Front St., downtown, still offers up fine rooms with a river view, continental breakfast, cable, and whirlpool bath. Some of the rooms are right above the **pub,** so request rooms 1-3 for a quieter night. (☎ 992-2333 or 800-665-3200. Singles $55; doubles $60. Live music W-Sa. Pub open M-Sa 11am-1am, Su 11am-midnight.) Check for nightly drink and food bargains. A **drive-in liquor store** keeps the pub hoppin'. For more ambience than the cheap RV parks on either end of town, try **Robert's Roost Campground ❷,** 3121 Gook Rd., 8km south of town and 2km off Hwy. 97, which offers elegantly landscaped lakeside sites. Features include coin showers, laundry, playground, and fishing; rowboat and canoe rentals are $5. (☎ 747-2015; www.robertsroost.com. Sites $19; full RV sites $25.)

Pub food can be found throughout Quesnel and south on Hwy. 97. A burlap-bag-ceilinged alternative for any meal, **Granville's Coffee ❶,** 383 Reid St., bakes gigantic ham and cheese muffins ($1.50) and sells heaping sandwiches (under $6) and $5 mac and cheese. (☎ 992-3667. Open M-Sa 7am-10pm; Su 9am-5pm.)

◙ ▲ **SIGHTS AND OUTDOOR ACTIVITIES.** The ▇**Quesnel Museum and Archives,** next to the visitors center, is one of the finest museums in BC. Exhibits and artifacts include rooms of a Cariboo home, a village street, the Royal Bank, logging and mining tools, one of the best collections of rare Chinese artifacts in North America, and Mandy the haunted doll. (☎ 992-9580; www.city.quesnel.bc.ca/museum2004. Open daily June-Aug. 8am-6pm, May 8:30am-4:30pm; Sept.-Apr. Tu-Sa 8:30am-4:30pm.) The long-defunct mining town of **Barkerville,** 90km east of

Quesnel along Hwy. 26, was established in 1862 after Billy Barker found gold on Williams Creek and sparked BC's largest gold rush. For the rest of the 19th century, Barkerville was the benchmark against which the rest of western Canada was measured. Since 1958 the town has been operated as an educational **"living museum,"** housing only residents who run the local B&Bs. (☎994-3332; www.heritage.gov.bc.ca/bark/bark.htm. Open daily 8am-8pm; many displays close at 6pm, late May-Sept. 2-day pass $13, students and ages 65 and older $12, 13-18 $7.25, 6-12 $3.50, under 6 free. 30% off late May to mid-June. Additional fee for shows and stagecoach rides.) Although the brochure asks that you "plan to spend enough time to re-live a century of time," most modern folks find that one day is enough to see it all. If you do decide to stay awhile, services are 8km toward Quesnel in **Wells.** The visitors center has the scoop on mill tours at **West Fraser Lumber.**

Quesnel is the starting point of the 450km **Alexander Mackenzie Heritage Trail,** which retraces the steps of Mackenzie, the first European to cross North America by land. The trail travels to Bella Coola (p. 385), passing through Tweedsmuir (p. 387) on the way. The trip requires extensive planning and about three weeks to complete one-way; it's a good idea to bring along a hiking buddy, since the trail passes through some very remote areas. The visitors center can provide more information on this and other local trails, as can **BC Parks,** 400-640 Borland St. in Williams Lake. (☎398-4530. Open M-F 8:30am-noon and 1pm-4:30pm.)

Anyone traveling between Prince George and Quesnel on Hwy. 97 will live a better life for having stopped at ▣**Cinema Second Hand General Store,** 32km north of Quesnel on Hwy. 97. Cash-strapped road warriors will find everything they need (except an actual cinema) plus a wide variety of things they could never possibly need, like old-fashioned snowshoes and disco LPs. The store also offers **free camping** with a pit toilet. (☎998-4774. Open daily 9am-9pm.)

▣ BOWRON LAKES PROVINCIAL PARK   ☎250

This paddling paradise is located about 85km east of Quesnel; the turnoff is just before the entrance to Barkerville. Follow the gravel road to the lakes about 25km north of Barkerville. The necklace of lakes forms a 116km loop in the heart of the **Cariboo Mountains,** which takes most canoeists 10 days to complete. The loop provides for great lake and river paddling and offers opportunities to view moose, bears, deer, eagles, and more. It costs $60 per person to canoe the circuit and $30 per person to canoe from the west side to Unna Lake (three to four days). Fifty paddlers, including at least four without reservations, are permitted to canoe each day. Reserve a spot through **Super, Natural BC** (☎387-1642 or 800-435-5622. Reservations $18 per canoe.) The **Bowron Lake Lodge ❷** rents canoes and kayaks and also runs a campsite and motel near the lake. (☎992-2733; www.bcadventure/bowron. Canoe and kayak rentals $100-225 for the circuit. Sites $20; motel doubles $65-80. Pay showers and firewood.) **Becker's Lodge ❶** also rents kayaks and canoes and operates a campsite with more privacy than Bowron. (☎992-8864 or 800-808-4761; www.beckerslodge.ca. Boat rentals $130-230 for the circuit. Sites $15, RVs $20.)

PRINCE GEORGE   ☎250

Prince George stands at the confluence of the Nechako and Fraser Rivers, the banks of which play host to the pulp and lumber mills that crowd the valley floor in an impressive display of industrialism. Prince George is a crucial point of transport for goods and services heading in all directions, but even with recent additions to the town—a civic center, a national university, and a Western League hockey team—Prince George is still a stopover, not a destination.

F TRANSPORTATION. Greyhound, 1566 12th Ave. (☎564-5454 or 800-661-8747) is open M-Sa 6:30am-5:30pm and 8pm-midnight; Su 6:30-9:30am, 3:30-5:30pm, and 8:30pm-midnight. Buses run to: Edmonton (11hr., 2 per day, $102); Dawson Creek (6hr., 2 per day, $56); Prince Rupert (10hr., 2 per day, $95); and Vancouver (12hr., 3 per day, $103). **VIA Rail,** 1300 1st Ave. (☎888-842-7245), runs three or four times a week to Prince Rupert (12hr., $103) and Jasper (7½hr., $79).

■■ ORIENTATION AND PRACTICAL INFORMATION. Highway 97 cuts straight through Prince George just to the west of the city center. Highway 16 runs through the city center, becomes Victoria Street in town, and crosses Hwy. 97 to the south of town. Running the width of the city, 15th Avenue, which becomes Patricia St. east of Victoria St., is home to most of the shopping centers and terminates at the east end of downtown. The **visitors center** is on 1300 1st Ave., at Quebec St. (☎562-3700 or 800-668-7646; www.tourismpg.com. Open daily May-Sept. 9am-8pm; Sept.-May Tu-Sa 9am-5pm.) Another center is at the junction of Hwy. 16 and Hwy. 97 beneath a huge "Mr. P.G." logger. (☎563-5493. Open daily May-Sept. 9am-8pm.) **Cariboo Outfitters,** 1222 4th Ave., sells outdoor gear at competitive prices. (☎564-1630. Open M-Sa 9:30am-5:30pm.) **Save on Foods,** in the Parkwood Mall at Victoria and 15th St., sells groceries. (☎564-4525. Open daily 8am-11pm.) The market also has a **pharmacy.** (☎561-0240. Open M-Sa 8am-8pm, Su 10am-6pm.) Get clean at **Whitewash Laundromat,** 231 George St. Wash $1.50, dry $0.25 per 8min. (☎563-2300. Open M-Sa 7:30am-6pm.) In an emergency, call the **police** (☎561-3300) at 999 Brunswick St., or the **hospital,** 2000 15th Ave. (☎565-2000; emergency 565-2444). **Crisis Line:** ☎563-1214. 24hr. **Internet** access is free for 1hr. daily on 12 computers at the **library,** 887 Dominion St. (☎563-9251; www.lib.pg.bc.ca. Open Labor Day-Memorial Day M-Th 10am-9pm, F-Sa 10am-5:30pm, Su 1-5pm; closed Su Memorial Day-Labor Day.) An Internet cafe is inside **London Drugs** in the Parkwood Mall, $3.20 per 30min. (☎561-0011. Open M-Sa 9am-10pm, Su 10am-8pm.) The **post office** is at 1323 5th Ave. (☎561-2568. Open M-F 8:30am-5pm.) **Postal Code:** V2L 3L0.

■■ ACCOMMODATIONS AND CAMPING. During the summer, the **College of New Caledonia Student Residence ❷,** 3330 22nd Ave. (turn off Hwy. 97 west of downtown and take the second right), boasts clean rooms and a young crowd. Rooms include a fridge and microwave. With kitchen, lounge, BBQ, sundeck, and cheap laundry, the price is right. (☎561-5849 or 800-371-8111; www.cnc.bc.ca/res. Linen $6.50. Wash $1.50, dry $0.50. Singles $20, with private bathroom $25. Reception 10am-4pm, 6-10pm.) **University of Northern British Columbia Residence ❷,** 3333 University Way, has clean dorm rooms farther outside of town. (☎960-6434. $20. Linens $9. It's a good idea to call before arriving. Reception 10am-6pm.) To upgrade to a queen bed and cable TV, a good bet is the **Queensway Court Motel ❸,** 1616 Queensway St., one motel over from 17th Ave., close to downtown. Well-kept rooms come with fridges and cable. (☎562-5068. Singles $45; doubles $50.) The **Log House Restaurant and Kampground ❶,** located on the shores of Tabor Lake, pleases with its impeccable grounds, proximity to fishing, and costly German-owned **steakhouse ❹.** To reach this slice of Europe, head out of town on Hwy. 16 E; after 3km, turn right on Old Cariboo Hwy., left on Giscome Rd. and follow the signs (15min. from downtown). Rowboats, canoes, and pedal boat rentals all available. (☎963-9515. Boats $8 per hr. Sites $15; full RV sites $22; teepees $22 per person; cabins with kitchenettes $45.) To secure a B&B room, call the B&B Hotline (☎562-2222 or 877-562-2626; www.princegeorgebnb.com.)

BRITISH COLUMBIA

⚡🍴 FOOD AND NIGHTLIFE. While it is hard to escape Prince George's plague of chains and interchangeable pasta joints, a few alternatives stand out. **Javva Mugga Mocha Cafe ❶**, 304 George St., has reasonably priced sandwiches ($7) and the best coffee in town. (☎562-3338. Open M-Sa 7am-7pm, Su 10am-4pm.) An oasis for the big appetite, **Esther's Inn ❸**, 1151 Commercial Crescent (☎562-4131 or 800-663-6844; www.esthersinn.bc.ca), off Hwy. 97 near 15th Ave., has an all-you-can-eat spread laid out next to a waterfall in the tropical dining area. Main dish theme varies. Lunch $9, dinner M-Th $12, F-Sa $14. (Open for lunch M-Sa 11:30am-2pm, dinner M-Th 6:30-9pm, F 6:30-10pm, Sa 7-10pm, Su 3:30-9pm, brunch Su 7am-2pm.) **The Waddling Duck ❹**, 1157 5th Ave., serves delicious burgers ($8) and upscale entrees (chicken cordon bleu $16) in an English pub atmosphere. (☎561-5550; www.waddlingduck.ca. Open daily 11am-11pm.)

There's no shortage of taps in Prince George. **JJ's Pub**, 1970 S Ospika Blvd. off 15th Ave. heading from Hwy. 97 to UNBC, reminds its loyal Canadian crowd and visitors that "Canadians kick ass." (☎562-2234. Open M-Th and Su 11am-midnight, F-Sa 11am-1am. Pints $5.) Cowboys congregate for pints ($4.50) and live country rock at **Cadillac Ranch**, 1390 2nd Ave., and two-step under disco lights. (☎563-7720. Open M-Th 9pm-2am, F-Sa 8pm-2am.) Clubs and bars teem with college students during the academic year; in summer, twentysomethings line up outside **Sgt. O'Flaherty's**, 770 Brunswick at 7th Ave., under the Crest Hotel. Thursday nights, pints fill up for $3. Live music nightly, except for when the live acts are pre-empted by special events. (☎563-0121. Open M-Sa 4pm-1am.)

🏞 PARKS. Fort George Park, on the banks of the Fraser River off 20th Ave., offers an expansive lawn, beach volleyball courts, picnic tables, and barbecue pits. It also makes a perfect starting point for the 11km **Heritage River Trail,** which wanders through the city and along the Fraser and Nechako Rivers. Across the street from a cluster of industrial logging buildings, **Cottonwood Island Nature Park,** off River Rd., has a few short trails along the river and nice picnic sites. For a bird's eye view of Prince George, scramble up to **Connaught Hill Park,** with picnic tables and ample frisbee-throwing space. To reach the park, scale the yellow metal staircase near the library or take Connaught Dr. off Queensway St. **McMillan Regional Park** is right across the Nechako River off Hwy. 97 N and features a deep ravine with a view of the city from the river's cutbanks. The lush **Forests for the World,** only 15min. away (take Hwy. 97 N, turn left on 15th Ave., right on Foothills Blvd., left onto Cranbrook Hill Rd., and finally left on Kueng Rd.), will pump the fresh woodsy air right back into your lungs. To take advantage of the web of trails, pick up a map at the visitors center. The longer trails at **Eskers Provincial Park** (☎565-6340), off Hwy. 97 (12km north) and 28km down Ness Lake Rd., circle three lakes.

FISHING. With more than 1600 lakes within a 150km radius, fishing is excellent near Prince George. The closest spot is **Tabor Lake,** where the rainbow trout and char all but jump into boats April through July. Tabor is east on Hwy. 16; follow the directions to the Log House Restaurant and Kampground (see **Accommodations and Camping,** above). For a complete listing of lakes and licensing information, contact the visitors center.

◼ EVENTS. Each Saturday, organic produce, baked goods, jams, salsas, and tofu concoctions are available on tables at the **Farmers Market,** Courthouse Plaza on George Ave. (☎563-3383. Open May-Sept. 8:30am-1pm.) **Mardi Gras** (☎564-3737) lasts for 10 days in late February and features such events as snow golf, dog-pull contests, and bed races. **Sandblast** (☎564-9791) sends daredevils down

BRITISH COLUMBIA

the steep, snowless Nechako Cutbanks on the third Sunday in August. Anyone can participate, using almost any contraption: see how well your couch fares against the bikers, if you've got the guts.

ALONG THE YELLOWHEAD HWY.

PRINCE GEORGE TO MT. ROBSON ☎ 250

East of Prince George, the pristine terrain that lines the 319km of road to Mt. Robson gives little indication of the logging that drives the regional economy, thanks to scenic, sightline-wide strips of forest left untouched alongside the route. Lakeside campsites can be found at **Purden Lake Provincial Park ❶**, 59km east of Prince George. (Free firewood. Open May-Sept. Gate closed 11pm-7am. $14. One wheelchair-accessible site.) **Purden Lake Resort ❶** (☎565-7777; www.purden.com), 3km east, offers tent sites ($10), RV sites ($22-24), a cafe (open 7am-8pm), and the last gas before **McBride**, 140km east. Tenters find showers and laundry at the **Beaverview Campsite ❶**, 1km east of McBride. (☎569-2513. $13; partial RV sites $17.)

From McBride, the Yellowhead weaves up the **Robson Valley**, part of the Rocky Mountain trench stretching north-south the length of the province. **Tête Jaune Cache** lies 63km east of McBride, where Hwy. 5 leads 339km south to Kamloops and the Okanagan beyond. **Tête Jaune Lodge ❷** offers no-frills lodging right off the highway. (☎566-9815; www.tetejaunelodge.com. Sites $17, with hookups $20. Free showers.) Just 2km east of the intersection, the diminutive **Rearguard Falls** (a 20min. walk) is the terminus of the Chinook salmon's migration from the Pacific.

As Hwy. 16 continues east, the scenery reaches a crescendo at towering **Mount Robson,** 84km west of Jasper and 319km east of Prince George. Standing 3954m tall, Robson is the highest peak in the Canadian Rockies; after five unsuccessful attempts, mountaineers finally reached its summit in 1913. Less ambitious folk can appreciate the mountain's beauty from the parking lot and picnic site beside the **Mount Robson Provincial Park Headquarters.** (☎566-4325, reservations 800-689-9025. Open daily June-Aug. 8am-8pm; May and Sept. 8am-5pm.) Tenters need go no further than **Robson River Campground ❷** and the larger **Robson Meadows Campground ❷**, both opposite the headquarters. ($17. Free showers.) Five nearby **hiking trails,** ranging from 2km jaunts to 66km treks, are the park's main draws (backcountry camping permit $5 per person per night; under 13 free). The 22km **Berg Lake Trail** (two days; trailhead at the parking lot by Robson River, 2km from the visitors center) is a green, well-maintained path along the milky-blue Robson River past Lake Kinney and **Valley of a Thousand Falls. Berg Lake ❶** is the highest of five backcountry campsites along the route and can be used as a base to explore options from alpine ridge-running to wilderness camping.

PRINCE GEORGE TO TERRACE ☎ 250

As Hwy. 16 winds westward 575km (8hr.) toward Terrace from Prince George, towering timbers gradually give way to the gently rolling pastures and tiny settlements of British Columbia's interior. While many of these towns are easy to blow through on a mad dash to the coast, those willing to take a little time will discover spectacular fishing, pleasant hikes, and a range of other outdoor activities. The lakes are packed with kokanee, char, burbot, and rainbow trout, but make sure to get a fishing license, available at the nearest visitors center. A number of **resorts** with campsites and motel rooms as well as budget **motels** can be found at almost any point along the highway. Campsites run around $15, motel rooms around $50.

Vanderhoof, 100km west of Prince George, prides itself on being the geographical center of BC. **Riverside Campground and RV Park ❶,** at the end of Burrard Ave., off 1st St., offers spacious and private sites a short distance from the town's main drag. Some of the sites line the street and can be loud at night. (☎ 567-4710. $15. Full hook-up RV sites $17.) The campground is home to **Ferland Park** and a bird sanctuary that make for easy yet worthwhile strolls. The **Visitor Information Centre,** 2353 Burrard Ave., has a guide on some of the other area hikes. (☎ 567-2124 or 800-752-2094; www.netbistro.com/tourism/vanderhoof. Open daily 9am-6pm.)

Another 40km brings drivers to the **Fort Fraser/Fraser Lake** area. The last spike in the Grand Trunk Pacific Railroad, Canada's second trans-continental railroad, was driven in Fort Fraser; the **visitors center** sits in a refabbed railroad car just off Hwy. 16. (☎ 690-7739. Open May-Aug. 10am-5pm.) The **Fraser Mountain Lookout Trail,** just west of Fort Fraser heading toward Fraser Lake, is a moderate 4km climb that offers spectacular views of Fraser Lake. **Beaumont Provincial Park ❶,** on Fraser Lake, has 49 roomy sites, clean facilities, a playground, a swimming area, and firewood. It's also a great place to launch a fishing boat. (☎ 565-6340. Sites $14.) A handy guide to local trails is available at the **Fraser Lake Tourist Centre/Museum.** (Open May to mid-Sept. M-Sa 10am-3pm.) **Mouse Mountain Trail** (3km one-way, 1hr.) offers a great view of surrounding lakes as well as ample opportunity for wildlife watching as deer, bears, moose, eagles and many other animals inhabit the area. The **Cheslatta Falls Trail** (1.2km, one-way) brings hikers to a small yet thundering waterfall great for a picnic.

The 139km long **Francois Lake,** 31km south of Fraser Lake on Francois Lake Rd., is home to world-class fishing and a number of resorts. **Birch Bay Resort ❶** has plain tenting sites and beautiful cabins. (☎ 699-8484; www.birchbay.ca. Tenting $15, beach $17; full RV hookup $22. Cabins $50-165.)

Just west of Fraser Lake is BC's **Lake District,** the center of which is **Burns Lake,** 230km west of Prince George, embedded amidst dozens of lakes great for avid anglers, including Francois Lake and Ootsa Lake. The **visitors center,** 540 Hwy. 16, is one of the best run and most helpful along the highway. (☎ 692-3773. Open daily July-Aug. 8am-7pm; May-June and Sept. M-F 8am-7pm.) They have a map and guide to a number of free **Forest Service recreational campsites ❶** in the area, many of which are located on beautiful lakeside beaches. A number of long day hikes leave from the area. **Nellian Lake Trail** is a 15km trail that winds through mixed pine and spruce forest as well as abandoned logging camps and old mill sites. To reach the trailhead, go 17km west of town on Hwy. 16. Turn south on West Palling Rd. and park at km 4. Burns Lake is the best access point to the northern portion of **Tweedsmuir Provincial Park** (p. 387). Access is by boat only across Ootsa Lake.

SMITHERS   ☎ 250

One of the best roadside stops along Hwy. 16, this small town is home to underhyped yet world-class year-round outdoor activities. In winter, the **Smithers Ski Area** at Hudson Bay Mountain, south of town on the Hudson Bay Mountain Rd., has some of the finest powder and least crowded slopes in BC. (☎ 847-2058 or 866-665-4299; www.skismithers.com. Day pass $35, ages 65 and older and 13-17 $25, 7-12 $18. Full ski rental package $22 per day, full snowboard $35 per day.) The trails throughout Hudson Bay Mountain make for hundreds of kilometers of excellent cross-country skiing. **Babine Mountains Provincial Park,** about 26km north of town on Driftwood Rd., turns its trails over to skiers in the winter; there are also designated snowmobiling areas throughout the park. During the rest of the year, hiking trails in both mountains provide opportunities for spotting moose, bear, and other wildlife. The **Joe L'Orsa Cabin,** about

13km from the **Silver King Basin Trailhead,** makes for a good stopping point along overnight hikes ($5). For more information on Babine Park contact **BC Parks** at ☎847-7320. Smithers is also home to a number of rugged mountain biking trails maintained by local riders; contact McBike for more information. **Driftwood Canyon Provincial Park,** on Driftwood Rd. 2km before the entrance to Babine Park, contains plenty of entertainment for the amateur archaeologist, with a short hike leading to a vast fossil bed containing remnants of plants, fish, and birds in the sedimentary rock. Lake Kathlyn Rd. leads 10km west of town to the **Glacier Gulch and Twin Falls** parking lot. From here, a 45min. hike leads to spectacular views of a pair of waterfalls and the glacier from which they flow, and another 3hr. leads to the glacier itself.

The 🏠**Smithers Hostel** ❷, at the corner of Main St. and 13th Ave., north of Hwy. 16, is the only hostel for hundreds of kilometers, but it can stand up to any competition. The friendly owners bring a touch of European charm to the immaculate establishment. A host of freebies—linen, Internet access, coffee, and tea—and a great mountain view sweeten the deal. (☎847-4862; www.smithershostel.com. Laundry $2. Dorms $24; private rooms $50. Reception 8am-10pm.) **Riverside Park Campground** ❶, north on Main St. past 16th Ave., offers well-kept open sites near town. ($8, full hookup $14.) **Alpenhorn Bistro & Bar** ❷, 1261 Main St., serves up pub food (burgers $8) and steaks. (☎847-5366; www.alpenhornbistro.com. Open M-Th and Sa 11:30am-11pm, F 11:30am-midnight, Su 1-10pm.) **Louise's Kitchen** ❷, 1293 Main St., serves Ukrainian-Canadian cuisine. (☎847-2547. Open M-Sa 8am-8pm.)

The Smithers **visitors center** is on the corner of Hwy. 16 and Queen St. (☎847-5072 or 800-542-6673; www.tourismsmithers.com. Open daily 9am-6pm.) **McBike & Sport,** 1191 Main St., has bike rentals ($20 half-day, $25 full day) and offers maps and advice on mountain biking in the area. (☎847-5009; www.mcbike.bc.ca. Open M-Th and Sa 9am-6pm, F 9am-9pm, Su 11am-4pm.) **Valhalla Pure Outfitters,** 1122 Main St., can meet all your other outdoor needs; the extremely friendly staff is overflowing with knowledge and advice on area adventures. (☎847-0200; www.vpo.ca. Open M-Th and Sa 9:30am-6pm, F 9:30am-9pm, Su 11am-4pm.) Get groceries at **Super Valu,** at the intersection of Hwy 16 and Main St. (☎847-9737. Open M-F 8am-9pm, Sa 9am-6pm, Su 8am-7pm.) Pharmaceuticals are at **Northern Drugs,** 1235 Main St. (☎847-2288. Open M-F 9am-9pm, Sa 9am-6pm, Su noon-6pm.) The **hospital** (☎847-2611) is on Columbia Dr. at 8th Ave., and the **police** (☎847-3233) can be found on Park Pl. at Victoria St. The **post office** is on 3rd Ave. between Main St. and King St. (☎800-267-1177. Open M-F 8:30am-5pm.) **Postal Code:** VOJ 2NO.

NEW HAZELTON. The town of **New Hazelton** is 68km past Smithers. The **visitors center,** on Hwy. 16, can give you a map and directions for a driving tour of the area. (☎842-6071. Open daily May-Sept. 8am-8pm.) The **'Ksan Village and Museum,** 7km along Churchill Ave. towards Old Hazelton, displays a rich collection of totem poles, longhouses, and artwork of the Gitskan. Gitskan dancers perform Fridays at 8pm in July and August. (☎842-5544. Tours every 30min. Open daily July-Aug. 9am-6pm; reduced hours in winter. Wheelchair-accessible. $10, seniors and ages 6-18 $6.50.) About 500m farther north is **Old Hazelton,** which retains the charm of an early 1900s frontier outpost. Heading back down Churchill Ave., a left turn about 2km past 'Ksan onto Kispiox Rd. leads to **Kispiox Village,** home to 15 totem poles. Another 44km west of New Hazelton is the junction with the Cassiar Hwy. (Hwy. 37), which leads 733km north to the Yukon Territory and the Alaska Hwy. For info on the Yukon and the Last Frontier, see *Let's Go: Alaska Adventure Guide.* The **Petrocan** sells the last gas before Terrace. (☎849-5793. Open daily 7am-9pm.)

TERRACE
☎250

Terrace was once famous as the site of a World War II army mutiny. Today, Terrace is known for its wildlife. The area is the habitat of the world's largest Chinook salmon (weighing in at 82½ lb.), and the infamous Kermodei bear, a member of the black bear family recognizable by a coat that ranges from light chestnut blond to steel blue-gray in color. Terrace itself is a working-class town, but its backyard is one big wilderness. The locals will tell you all about the great fishing, but rodless hikers can still find peace in the hills and on the curvy banks of the Skeena River.

🔳 PRACTICAL INFORMATION. Terrace is 144km east of Prince Rupert on Hwy. 16 and 91km southwest of the junction of the Yellowhead and the Cassiar Hwy. (Hwy. 37). **VIA Rail** (☎800-842-7245) sends three trains per week to Prince George (10hr., from $56) and Prince Rupert (2½hr., from $16). **Greyhound,** 4620 Keith St. (☎635-3680), also runs twice daily to Prince George (8hr., $80) and Prince Rupert (2hr., $24). **Canadian Tire,** at 5100 Hwy. 16, can get your wheels back in action. (☎635-7178. Open M-F 7am-9pm, Sa 7am-6pm, Su 10am-5pm.)

The **visitors center,** 4511 Keith St., is just east of town off Hwy. 16. (☎635-2063 or 635-0832; www.terracetourism.bc.ca. Open daily mid-May to Aug. 8:30am-5:30pm; Sept. to mid-May M-F 8:30am-4:30pm.) The **24hr. ATM** is in the city center at **Bank of Montreal,** 4666 Lakelse Ave. (☎615-6150). **Richard's Cleaners,** 3223 Emerson St., has washers ($2) and $0.25 dryers. (☎635-5119. Open daily 7am-9pm.) A **market** and **pharmacy** are at **Safeway,** 4655 Lakelse Ave. (☎635-7206. Market open daily 8am-10pm; pharmacy open M-F 9am-9pm, Sa-Su 9am-5pm.) For cheap produce, check out **The Real Canadian Wholesale Club,** behind the visitors center off Hwy. 16. (☎635-0995. Open M-F 9am-9pm, Sa-Su 9am-6pm.) The **hospital** (☎635-2211) is at 4720 Haugland Ave., the **police** are located on 3205 Eby St. (☎635-4911), and the **sexual assault crisis line** is at ☎635-1911. (Staffed daily 8:30am-4:30pm.) An hour of **Internet** access is free at the **library,** 4610 Park Ave. (☎638-8177; www.terracelibrary.ca. Open M 1-9pm, Tu-F 10am-9pm, Sa 10am-5pm, Su 1-5pm; closed Su July-Aug.) The **post office** is located at 3232 Emerson St. (☎635-2241. Open M-F 8:30am-5pm.) **Postal Code:** V8G 4A1.

🔳🔳 ACCOMMODATIONS AND FOOD. Motels in the $45-75 range line the highway outside of the city center. **Kalum Motel ❸,** 5min. west on Hwy. 16, is a bargain. (☎635-2362. Coffeemakers. Singles $47; doubles $50. Kitchenettes $5 extra.) The **Alpine House Motel ❸,** 4326 Lakelse Ave., is removed from noisy downtown. Take the Alternate Route across the one-lane bridge as you enter on Hwy. 16 from the east. (☎635-7216 or 800-663-3123; www.kermode.net/alpinehouse. Singles $45; doubles $55. Oct.-Apr. $10 less. Ask about same-cost rooms with kitchenettes.) **Ferry Island Municipal Campground ❶** lies just east of Terrace on Hwy. 16, with spacious sites and walking trails under big trees. The island's prime fishing spot is a short walk away. The community pool is half-price for Ferry Island campers. (☎615-3000. Firewood. Sites $14; RV sites $16.) **Kleanza Creek Provincial Park ❶** is on an abandoned gold mine, 19km east of the town on Hwy. 16, with sites nestled amid towering evergreens along the rushing creek. (Firewood. Sites $14.)

Terrace offers a welcome break from highway diner cuisine. **Don Diego's ❷,** 3212 Kalum St., is a fun, laid-back joint that serves Mexican, Greek, and whatever's in season. (☎635-2307. Lunch $7-9. Dinner $10-15. Open M-Sa 11:30am-3pm and 5-9pm.) **Haryana's Restaurant ❸,** in the Kalum Motel drive 5min. west of town along Hwy. 16, serves a succulent chicken tikka masala. (☎635-2362, ext. 555. Open M-Th 5-9pm, F 5-11pm, Sa 11am-11pm, Su 11am-9pm.) Burgers ($8), beer (pints $5), and big TVs await at the **Back Eddy Pub ❷,** 4332 Lakelse Ave., next to the Alpine House Motel. While away the time with chess boards and pool tables. (☎635-5336; www.tkp-biz.com/bavarianinn. Open daily 11am-midnight.)

⬛ ⛰ SIGHTS AND OUTDOOR ACTIVITIES. The **Falls Gallery**, 2666 Hwy. 37, just east of town, has an impressive collection of native masks and art. Take the Hwy. 37 turnoff south towards Kitimat, and turn in the driveway before the Volkswagen dealership. (☎638-0438. Open June to mid-Sept. M-Sa 10am-4:30pm, Su noon-4pm; mid-Sept. to May Tu-Sa noon-4pm.)

Gruchy's Beach, in Lakelse Lake Provincial Park, 13km south of Terrace on Hwy. 37 and a 1.5km hike from the parking lot, is big, sandy, and just begs to be picnicked upon, but isn't safe for swimming. The large park **campground ❶,** about 10km south of the beach parking lot, has a number of good swimming spots as well as hikes throughout the park. (☎798-2468. Sites $14.)

The **Terrace Mountain Nature Trail** is a popular climb of moderate difficulty, beginning at Johnstone Ave. in the east end of town. The route (10km, 1½-2½hr.) offers spectacular views of plateaus and the surrounding valley. **Redsand Lake Demonstration Forest,** 26km north on West Kalum Forestry Rd., a well-maintained gravel route found 200m past the Kalum River Bridge west of town off Hwy. 16, offers easy strolls. Three trails meander around beautiful Redsand Lake and through a variety of forested areas. A steep skidder trail awaits mountain bikers who make it up to **Copper Mountain,** but directions to the logging roads that lead up the mountain are complex; pick up a free map at the visitors center.

Anglers can strap on their waders and try their luck on the east shore of **Ferry Island** (see above). Ask for tips and pick up a license at the **Misty River Tackle Shop,** 5008 Agar Ave. (☎638-1369, or 800-314-1369. Open June-Aug. M-Sa 6:30am-10pm, Su 7am-10pm; daily Sept.-May 9am-8pm.) An eight-day angling license for non-Canadians costs $36. Licenses are also sold at tackle shops and hardware stores in town. To find the hottest fishing spots, watch for where the locals clump.

In winter, groomed **cross-country** trails run halfway to Kitimat (about 30km down Hwy. 37) around the breathtaking **Onion Lake. Shames Mountain,** 35km west on Hwy. 16, offers world-class **downhill skiing.** Skiers go nuts every winter on Shames' double chair and handle tow, 18 trails on over 130 acres, and 500m vertical drop. (☎877-898-4754; www.shamesmountain.com. Full day $35, ages 65 and older and 13-18 $25, 7-12 $18. Full ski rental package $22, snowboard package $30.)

PRINCE RUPERT   ☎ 250

In 1910, railway magnate Charles Hays made a covert deal with the provincial government to purchase 10,000 acres of choice land at the western terminus of the Grand Trunk Pacific Railway. When the shady operation was exposed two years later, Hays was already under water—not drowned in his dire financial straits, but in the wreckage of the *Titanic.* The sole fruit of Hays' illegal labors was the town of Prince Rupert, victim of a nationwide naming contest lacking in creativity. Nowadays, the famous Cow Bay waterfront draws many visitors throughout the year with its funky shops, beautiful views, and outdoor opportunities. With exceptional hiking and sea kayaking available in the area, Prince Rupert offers a smooth blend of tasteful urbanism and access to the outdoors.

⬛ TRANSPORTATION

Located on Kaien Island, on the mouth of the Skeena, Prince Rupert is a gateway to southeast Alaska. Both BC Ferries from Vancouver Island and the Alaska Marine Hwy. from Bellingham, WA stop here on their coastal routes, providing access to nearby villages like Metlakatla, and ports farther in the Inside Passage. The only major road into town is the Yellowhead Hwy. (Hwy. 16), known as **McBride Street** within the city. At the north end of downtown, Hwy. 16 makes a sharp left and becomes **2nd Avenue.** At the south end, Hwy. 16 becomes **Park Avenue,** continuing to the **ferry docks.** Avenues run north to south parallel to the waterfront with McBride splitting east from west. Streets run perpendicular and ascend numerically from the waterfront. Many of the city's businesses are located on 2nd and 3rd Ave. **Cow Bay** is to the right upon entering town from the east.

Trains: VIA Rail (☎ 627-7304 or 800-561-8630), at the BC Ferries Terminal. To **Prince George** (12hr., 3 per week, $110).

Buses: Greyhound (☎ 624-5090), 6th St. at 2nd Ave. To **Prince George** (11 hr., 2 per day, $102) and **Vancouver** (24hr., 2 per day, $196). Station open M-F 8:30am-12:30pm and 4-8:45pm, Sa-Su 9-11am and 7-8:45pm.

Ferries: The docks are at the end of Hwy. 16, a 30min. walk from downtown. Ferry-goers may not park on Prince Rupert streets; check with the ferry company or visitors center for paid parking options. **Seashore Charter Services** (☎ 624-5645) runs shuttle buses between the terminal and the hotels and train station for $5, ages 5-12 $3. **Alaska Marine Highway** (☎ 627-1744 or 800-642-0066; www.akmhs.com) runs to **Ketchikan** (6hr., US$55; vehicles US$55) and **Juneau** (26hr., US$145). **BC Ferries** (☎ 624-9627 or 888-223-3779; www.bcferries.bc.ca) runs to **Port Hardy** (15hr.; every other day; $73-103; vehicles $170-242) and the **Queen Charlotte Islands** (6-7hr.; June to mid-Sept. 6 per week, from mid-Sept. to May 3 per week. $20-25; cars $74-90; kayak or canoe $7, bike $6). Reserve for BC ferries at least 2 weeks in advance. If the ferry is full, you can get on the standby list by phone.

Public Transportation: Prince Rupert Bus Service (☎ 624-3343; www.busonline.ca) runs downtown Sa-Th 7am-6:45pm, F until 10:45pm. $1.25, students (up to grade 12) and ages 65 and older $1, under 5 free; day pass $3, ages 65 and older and students $2.50. Buses from downtown leave from 2nd Ave. W and 3rd. St. about every 30min. To reach the **ferry terminal,** take the #52. A bus also runs to **Port Edward** ($1.75/$1.25) and the **North Pacific Historic Fishing Village** ($2.50/$2).

ℹ PRACTICAL INFORMATION

Tourist Office: Prince Rupert Visitor Information Centre, 215 Cow Bay Rd. (☎ 624-5637 or 800-667-1994; www.tourismprincerupert.com), in Cow Bay. Free maps and useful packets on accommodations, attractions, and trails. Open May 15-Labor Day M-Sa 9am-8pm, Su 9am-5pm; Labor Day-May 14 M-Sa 10am-5pm.

Equipment Rental: Far West Sporting Goods (☎ 624-2568), on 3rd Ave. near 1st St., rents bikes. $10 per hr., $30 per day. Open M-W and F-Sa 9:30am-5:30pm, Th 9:30am-8pm. **Eco-Treks** (☎ 624-8311; www.citytel.net/ecotreks), on the dock in Cow Bay, rents **kayaks** and gear. Singles $35 per 4hr., double $50 per 4 hr.; $50/$75 per day. No rentals to novices or soloists. 3hr. guided tours for any ability level leave at 1 and 6pm with safety lessons for novices ($60).

ATM: Banks line 2nd Ave. W and 3rd Ave. W; all have 24hr. ATMs.

Market: Safeway (☎ 624-2412), at 2nd St. and 2nd Ave., offers everything from a florist to a deli. Open daily 8am-10pm.

Laundromat: Mommy's Laundromat, 6th St. between 2nd and 3rd Ave. Wash $1, dry $0.75 per 15min. Open daily 9am-9pm.

Police: 100 6th Ave. (☎ 624-2136).

Hospital: 1305 Summit Ave. (☎ 624-2171).

Internet Access: Library, 101 6th Ave. W (☎ 624-8618; www.princerupertlibrary.ca), at McBride. 1st 30min. free, then $2 per hr. Open M-Th 10am-9pm and F-Sa 10am-5pm.

Post Office: In the mall at 2nd Ave. and 5th St. (☎624-2353). Open M-F 9:30am-5pm. **Postal Code:** V8J 3P3.

⌂⌂ ACCOMMODATIONS AND CAMPING

Most of Prince Rupert's hotels are in the six-block area bordered by 1st Ave., 3rd Ave., 6th St., and 9th St. Everything fills to the gills when the ferries dock, so be sure to call a day or two in advance.

▨ **Andree's Bed and Breakfast,** 315 4th Ave. E (☎624-3666; www.andresbb.com). A spacious 1922 Victorian-style residence overlooking the harbor and city—check out the sunsets from the deck. Singles $55; doubles $70; twins $75. $15 per extra person. ❹

▨ **Eagle Bluff Bed and Breakfast,** 201 Cow Bay Rd. (☎627-4955 or 800-833-1550; www.citytel.net/eaglebluff), on the waterfront in the nicest part of town. Attractively furnished with bright rooms and private deck on the bay. Rooms come with TVs and a common kitchen area. Singles from $45; ensuite bath from $55; doubles from $65/$85. ❸

Pioneer Hostel, 167 3rd Ave. E (☎624-2334 or 888-794-9998; www.citytel.net/pioneer), 1 block east of McBride St. Prince Rupert's only hostel keeps things simple and clean. Microwave, TV, gazebo, and BBQ. Laundry $4. Reservations recommended. Dorms $16; bed in 2-person shared room $22; private room $35. ❷

North Pacific Historic Fishing Village (☎628-3538), at the Cannery Museum in Port Edward. Live for cheap in the renovated cannery workers' quarters. Bunkhouse rooms $15; modest inn rooms with shared bath $45; small 1-bedroom units with kitchens $65; cabins with kitchenettes and private bathrooms $85; family-sized house $100. ❶

Prudhomme Lake (☎638-8490), 20km east of town on Hwy. 16, run by BC Parks. Camp along the shore, under shady trees. Worth the drive to escape the RVs. Fishing and firewood. Sites $14. ❶

Park Avenue Campground, 1750 Park Ave. (☎624-5861 or 800-667-1994), 1km east of the ferry on Hwy. 16. An RV metropolis. Sites $13; RVs $16, with hookups $26. Laundry, free showers. ❶

◖ FOOD

▨ **Cow Bay Cafe,** 201 Cow Bay Rd. (☎627-1212), shares the waterfront corner of Cow Bay with Eagle Bluff B&B. This popular hot spot switches the menu around on a whim but always keeps the lunches ($8-10) and dinners ($12-17) fresh. Extensive wine list. Reservations recommended, especially for dinner. Open Tu noon-2:30pm, W-Sa noon-2:30pm and 6-8:30pm. ❸

▨ **Opa,** 34 Cow Bay Rd. (☎627-4560), upstairs. Sushi bar in an old fishing net loft. Free tea is served in beautiful handspun mugs. Local art and old fishing tools adorn the walls and add to the trendy marine atmosphere. Tuna rolls $3, miso soup $1.50. Open Tu-Th and Sa 11:30am-2pm and 5-9pm, F 11:30am-2pm and 5-9:30pm. ❸

Cowpuccino's, 25 Cow Bay Rd. (☎627-1395). Caffeinate while taking in cow pics from around the world and munching on a colossal muffin ($1.50) or bagel sandwich ($5). Open M-Sa 7am-10pm, Su 8am-8pm. ❶

Rodhos (☎624-9797), on 2nd Ave. near 6th St. Huge menu of pleasing Greek entrees ($14-18), pastas ($8-10), and pizzas ($14 for a loaded medium). Open daily 4pm-1am. Free delivery in town. ❸

Javadotcup, 516 3rd Ave. W (☎622-2822; www.citytel.net/javalodge/java). Internet cafe with speedy computers and lunches ($3.50). Internet access $1.75 per 30min. Open M-Th 7:30am-10:30pm, F 7:30am-11pm, Sa 8am-11pm, Su 7:30am-10pm. ❶

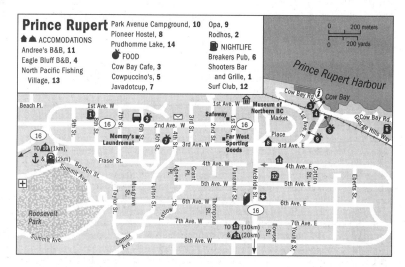

Prince Rupert

♠▲ ACCOMODATIONS
Andree's B&B, 11
Eagle Bluff B&B, 4
North Pacific Fishing
  Village, 13

Park Avenue Campground, 10
Pioneer Hostel, 8
Prudhomme Lake, 14
🍴 FOOD
Cow Bay Cafe, 3
Cowpuccino's, 5
Javadotcup, 7

Opa, 9
Rodhos, 2
🍺 NIGHTLIFE
Breakers Pub, 6
Shooters Bar
  and Grille, 1
Surf Club, 12

🏮 NIGHTLIFE

Drinking establishments in Prince Rupert compete for ferry tourists and fishing boat crews. Come sundown, the town is a-crawl with sealife come to shore. **Surf Club,** 200 5th St., attracts a younger set later in the evening with alternating nights of live music and karaoke. (☎624-3050. Pints $4.50. Open M and Th-Sa 10pm-2am.) **Shooters Bar and Grill** at the Commercial Inn, 901 1st Ave., and **Breakers Pub,** 117 George Hills Way in Cow Bay overlooking the small boat harbor, are full of local color. (Shooters ☎624-6142. Open Su-M noon-midnight, Tu-Th noon-1:30am, F-Sa noon-2am. Breakers ☎624-5990. Open M-Th 11:30am-midnight, F-Sa 11:30am-1am, Su noon-midnight.)

👁 🏔 SIGHTS AND OUTDOOR ACTIVITIES

The **Museum of Northern British Columbia,** 100 1st Ave. at the corner of McBride St., displays haunting Tsimshian artwork. (☎624-3207; www.museumofnorthernbc.com. Open late May-early Sept. M-Sa 9am-8pm and Su 9am-5pm; mid-Sept. to late May M-Sa 9am-5pm. $5, students $2, ages 6-12 $1.) Prince Rupert's harbor has the highest concentration of archaeological sites in North America. Archaeologists have unearthed materials from Tsimshian settlements dating back 10,000 years. The museum occasionally offers archaeological boat tours. **Lax-spa'aws** runs tours of Pike Island and villages throughout the harbor. (☎628-3201; www.pikeisland.ca. Tickets available at museum front desk.) **Seashore Charters** also runs Pike Island ($56) and harbor ($26) tours as well as guided kayaking and city tours. (☎624-5645 or 800-667-4393; www.seashorecharters.com.)

The best time to visit Prince Rupert may be during **Seafest** (☎624-9118), an annual four-day event the second weekend in June. Surrounding towns celebrate the sea with parades, bathtub races, and beer contests. The **Islandman Triathlon** (☎624-6770), a 1000m swim, 35km bike, and 8km run, is also held around the time of Seafestivities; it was won in 1997 by an intrepid *Let's Go* researcher.

A number of attractive small parks line the hills above Prince Rupert. Tiny **Service Park,** off Fulton St., offers views of downtown and the harbor beyond. An even wider vista awaits serious hikers east of town, atop **Mount Oldfield** (8.4km, 5-6hr.)

The trailhead is at Oliver Lake Park, about 6km from downtown on Hwy. 16. The **Butze Rapids Trail** (5km, 2½-3½hr.) teaches walkers about plants and then plants them in front of rushing tidal rapids. The trailhead is across the highway.

Freshwater anglers can enjoy the great **fishing** in the Skeena and pull up big steelhead or salmon. Permits (Canada residents 1-day $6, 3-day $12, 5-day $18; nonresidents $8, $21, $35) and hot spot info are available at **Seashore Charters,** 215 Cow Bay Rd., next to the visitors center.

Prince Rupert is hemmed in by dozens of sandy little islands just waiting to be explored. **Eco-Treks** (see **Equipment Rental,** above) specializes in kayak introductions and rents to experienced paddlers (able to wet exit and enter), who can put in at Cow Bay, paddle north around Kaien Island, and brave the challenging **Butze Reversing Tidal Rapids.** One of the most incredible wilderness experiences in all of BC is the **Khutzeymateen/K'tzim-a-Deen Grizzly Bear Sanctuary.** Hiking is not permitted within the sanctuary, leaving the surrounding wilderness untouched and accessible only to those with a paddle. Access is through the Khutzeymateen River and takes 6-10hr. from Rupert. Unguided access into the river estuaries is prohibited. For more information, contact BC Parks at ☎ 798-2277.

North Pacific Historic Fishing Village, 20min. east of Prince Rupert just outside Port Edward, is a quasi-living village complete with working cannery, exhibits on the fishing and industry of the area, old village buildings, restaurant and lodgings. (☎ 628-3538; www.district.portedward.bc.ca/northpacific. Open daily mid-May to Sept. 9am-6pm. $12, students and ages 65 and older $10, under 18 $8.)

QUEEN CHARLOTTE ISLANDS/ HAIDA GWAII

Nothing in Haida Gwaii is far from rainforest or foggy coast. A full 130km west of Prince Rupert, two principal islands and 136 surrounding inlets form the archipelago known as "the Canadian Galápagos." Graham, the northern island, is home to all but one of the islands' towns and an eclectic population of tree-huggers, tree-cutters, First Nations people, and fishermen. To the south, hot springs steam from mountainous Moresby Island, which contains Gwaii Haanas (Gwaii HAH-nus) National Park Reserve, where the wooden totem poles of the islands' first inhabitants decay. Remote wilderness envelops the kayakers and boaters who approach Haida Gwaii's lonely outcroppings and coves. The Islands' chief employer is the timber industry, edging out the Canadian government. In the 1980s, the Islands attracted attention when environmentalists from around the globe joined the Haida Nation in demonstrations to stop logging on parts of Gwaii Haanas. In 1988 the Canadian government established the Gwaii Haanas National Park Reserve, now managed co-operatively by the government of Canada and the Haida Nation.

❗ EMERGENCY INFORMATION
The Queen Charlotte Islands lack ☎ 911 service. In an emergency, dial the relevant local emergency number, found under **Practical Information.**

📠 TRANSPORTATION

The **BC Ferry** from Prince Rupert docks at Skidegate Landing on Graham Island, which is between **Queen Charlotte City** (4km west of the landing) and the village of **Skidegate** (SKID-uh-git), 2km to the northeast. All of the towns of Graham Island lie along Hwy. 16, which continues north from Skidegate through **Tlell, Port Clem-**

ents, and **Masset.** Be wary of deer while driving—they're everywhere, and they bolt at all the wrong times. Queen Charlotte City is the best bet for food and hostels, while farther north, Tlell and Masset offer hikes and beaches. To the south, Gwaii Haanas is home to **Sandspit** and the Islands' only commercial airport. From Skidegate Landing, 12 ferries per day make the 20min. crossing between the big islands. The lack of public transportation and the exorbitant cost of rental cars bankrupt backpackers, but residents are supposedly generous in picking up hitchhikers. *Let's Go* does not recommend hitchhiking.

QUEEN CHARLOTTE CITY   ☎ 250

Queen Charlotte City's central location and size make it the best base for exploring both main islands. "Size" is relative, however; this community of just over 1000 people is not the city its name claims it to be. Most locals either work the sawmills, the trawlers, for the government, or in the tourist industry.

◗ **TRANSPORTATION.** Towns on the island line one waterfront road; in Queen Charlotte City, that road is **3rd Avenue. BC Ferries** (☎559-4485 or in BC 888-223-3779) docks in Skidegate Landing, 3km east of Queen Charlotte City, leaving for Prince Rupert (6hr.; June to mid-Sept. 6 per week, mid-Sept. 3 per week; $20-25, cars $74-90, kayak or canoe $7, bike $6). Reserve at least 3 weeks in advance for cars; car fares do not include driver. Ferries also run between Skidegate Landing on Graham Island and Alliford Bay on Moresby Island. (20min.; 12 per day; round-trip $5-6; cars $12-13. No reservations.) **Eagle Cabs** run between Charlotte and the ferry terminal for $8-11. (☎559-4461. Open M-W and Su 7am-9pm, Th-Sa 7am-closing. Hours vary.) Get a set of wheels at **Rustic Rentals,** west of downtown at Charlotte Island Tire. (☎559-4641. Must be 21 or older with credit card. Will pick up at the ferry terminal in Skidegate. From $39 per day, $0.15 per km. Office open daily 8am-7pm, but cars available 24hr.) Rentals are also available through **Pioneer Creek Lodging** from $30 per day, $0.15 per km. Reservations are necessary, and cars cannot be taken off-road. Repair that flat tire at **Charlotte Island Tire,** along Hwy. 33; they also provide 24hr. towing. (☎559-4641. Open daily 8am-7pm.)

◙ **PRACTICAL INFORMATION.** The **visitors center,** on Wharf St. at the east end of town, features an ornate 3D map of the islands and a creative natural history presentation. The free *Guide to the Queen Charlotte Islands* has detailed maps. **Mandatory orientations** for visitors to Gwaii Haanas National Park Reserve (see below) are held every day at 7:30pm. (☎559-8316; www.qcinfo.com. Open daily May-Sept. 10am-7pm; call or check the website for hours Oct.-Apr.) **Gwaii Haanas Park Information,** on 2nd Ave. off 2nd St. above city center, runs another **orientation** session daily at 8am. (☎559-8818; www.fas.sfu.ca/parkscan/gwaii. Open M-F 8am-noon and 1-4:30pm.) For registration info, see **Gwaii Haanas National Park Reserve,** p. 411. **Ministry of Forests,** on 3rd Ave. at the far west end of town, has info on Forest Service campsites and logging roads on both islands. Maps, however, are available only from the visitors center and the **Government Agent.** (☎559-6200. Open M-F 8:30am-noon and 1-4:30pm.) Saltwater **fishing licenses** (Canadian residents $12 for one day, non-residents $14, 3-day $18/$27, 5-day $24/$41) are available at **Meegan's Store,** 3126 Wharf St. (☎559-4428. Open daily 9am-6pm; closed Su Sept.-June.) **Freshwater licenses,** as well as Forest Service Recreation maps and topographical maps, are available from the Government Agent (☎559-4452 or 800-663-7867), 1½ blocks west of the city center. **Premier Creek Lodging** (see **Accommodations and Camping,** below) has on-road bikes. $15 per half-day, $30 per full day. **Northern Savings Credit Union,** on Wharf St., has a **24hr. ATM.** Many businesses don't take credit cards. (☎559-4407. Open Tu-Th 10am-5pm, F 10am-5:30pm, Sa 10am-3pm. The only

BRITISH COLUMBIA

other island bank is in Masset. Food is more expensive on the islands; stock up off-island. The only fully-stocked grocery in town is **City Centre Store** in the City Centre Mall. (☎559-4444. Open M-Sa 9:30am-6pm.) **Isabel Creek Store,** 3219 Wharf St. opposite the visitors center, offers organic foods. (☎559-8623. Open M-Sa 10am-5:30pm.) **Laundromat:** 121 3rd Ave., in the City Centre Mall. Wash $1.50, dry $0.25 per 5min. (☎559-4444. Open daily 9am-9pm. At **Premier Creek Lodging,** $4 including soap. In an **emergency,** call ☎559-4421; the **ambulance** is at ☎800-461-9911, and the police are on 3211 Wharf (☎559-4421). A **pharmacy** lies downstairs in the hospital building. (☎559-4310. Open M-Tu and Th-F 10:30am-12:30pm and 1:30-5:15pm, W 1:30-5:15pm.) The **hospital** (☎559-4300) is on 3rd Ave. at the east end of town. **Internet** access is $1 per 30min. at the **library,** 138 Bay St., under the community hall. (☎559-4518; www.virl.bc.ca. Open M and W 10:30am-12:30pm, 1:30-5:30pm, and 6:30-8:30pm, Sa 10:30am-12:30pm and 1:30-5:30pm.) **Premier Creek Lodging,** $2 per 10min. The **post office** is located in the City Centre Mall on 3rd Ave. (☎559-8349. Open M-F 9am-5pm, Sa noon-4pm.) **Postal Code:** V0T 1S0.

▮▾ ACCOMMODATIONS AND CAMPING. ◪**Premier Creek Lodging ❷,** 3101 3rd Ave., offers bunk beds in a creekside cottage behind the main hotel with shared kitchen, bath, common room, and campfire pit. (☎559-8415 or 888-322-3388; www.qcislands.net/premier. Fresh breakfast $6-8. Laundry $4. Bed in hostel $20. Clean rooms in hotel with shared bath $30; single with private bath $65, double $75. Add $10 for kitchenette.) ◪**Dorothy and Mike's Guest House ❸,** 3125 2nd Ave., a beautiful house centrally located up the hill behind the downtown Rainbow Gallery, has a standing hammock chair, library, breakfast, and kitchen use. Call ahead for check-in. (☎559-8439; www.qcislands.net/doromike. Singles $45; doubles $65, loft with private bathroom $70.)

Joy's Campground ❶ is halfway between the ferry terminal and Charlotte. Camping is in Joy's waterfront backyard (which runs alongside 3rd Ave.), and has a spring with drinkable water. To secure space just go to the campground or stop by Joy's Island Jewellers, 3rd Ave., next to Sea Raven Restaurant. (☎559-4666 or 559-8890. Tent sites $5; RV sites $9; with electricity $15. No toilets.) The pleasant and forested **Haydn-Turner Community Campground ❶** is a 5min. drive west of town. Turn left down a short dirt road labeled "campground" as the main drag turns to gravel. (Walk-in beachfront sites $5; 6 tent sites $10. Firewood.)

▯ FOOD. The local bohemian hangout, ◪**Hanging by a Fibre ❶,** on Wharf St. beside the Howler's building, hangs local art on the walls and serves a Starving Artist lunch with bread and soup for $5. (☎559-4463. Lunch served 11:30am-2:30pm. Open M-W 9am-5pm, Th-Sa 9am-9pm, Su 11am-4pm.) **Howler's Bistro ❷,** on 3rd Ave., serves burgers ($9) and sandwiches ($9) and has deck seating overlooking the water. (Open daily 11am-10pm.) **Howler's Pub,** downstairs, is the only pub in town. (☎559-8602; www.qcislands.net/howle. Open M-W and Su 5pm-midnight, Th-Sa 1pm-2am.) **Oceana ❷,** 3119 3rd Ave., provides a huge menu ($11-16) of Chinese cuisine. (☎559-8683. Open daily 11:30am-2pm and 5-10pm.) **Sea Raven ❷,** 3301 3rd Ave., offers an airy, sun-washed dining area and glimpses of the ocean through alder trees. Large seafood selection and the best salmon clam chowder on the island at $4.50 a bowl. Dinner ($15-22) is expensive, but lunch ($8-10) is more reasonable. (☎559-8583; www.searaven.com. Open daily 7am-2pm and 5-9:30pm.)

▣ SIGHTS. Few Haidas survived the smallpox plague that hit the once-thriving villages in the southern islands in late 1800s. Still, the Haida history of 10,000 years on the Queen Charlotte Islands—"Haida Gwaii," which means "Islands of the People"—remains alive today. Six impressive cedar totem poles were raised in June 2001 on **Second Beach,** 1km east of the ferry landing on Hwy. 16, as a symbolic demonstration of the continuation of Haida culture. Traditionally, totem poles were built in Haida villages for a variety of reasons, both spiritual and secular. The local poles represent each of the six southern Haida villages, now in ruins, which can be visited by boat in **Gwaii Haanas Haida Heritage Site** (p. 411). A new heritage center, to be completed by 2006, will sit behind the poles and connect to the museum. This complex also protects a 50 ft. cedar canoe, the **Loo Taa.** Next door, the ▧**Haida Gwaii Museum** at Qay'llnagaay houses totem poles alongside intricate argillite carvings, amazing cedar weavings, and haunting Haida paintings. (☎559-4643. Open June-Aug. M-F 10am-5pm, Sa-Su 1-5pm; closed Su May and Sept.; Oct.-Apr. closed Tu as well. $5, students and ages 65 and older $4, 12 and under free.)

The Haida town of **Skidegate,** known as "the village," lies 1km beyond the museum. This community of 743 people is the nexus of Haida art and culture. Residents are sensitive to tourists and expect that visitors will exhibit discretion and respect concerning local culture and practices. Bald eagles often perch atop the totem pole out front of the **Skidegate Community Hall** near the water, a Haida longhouse built in 1979 according to ancient design specifications. Visitors must get permission from the **Skidegate Band Council Office** (☎559-4496), between the Gwaii Co-op on the main highway, to photograph the cemetery, or to camp and hike in certain areas; ask for details from the receptionist at the **Haida Gwaii Watchmen,** next to the museum. (☎559-8225. Open M-F 9am-noon and 1-5pm.) **Balance Rock** teeters on a roadside beach 1km north of Skidegate. While it looks as if a strong wind could topple this boulder from its precarious perch, a group of brawny loggers once failed in an attempt to dislodge it.

The second to last weekend in July brings **Skidegate Days** to town: three days of fun including dancing, comedy, a fish splitting contest, and an opportunity for anyone to race the Loo Taa war canoe. Contact the visitors center in Queen Charlotte City for more information.

🏃 **OUTDOOR ACTIVITIES.** Queen Charlotte City offers the easiest road access to the west coast of the island. Following 3rd Ave., it becomes gravel; multiple west coast destinations are listed on a sign less than 1km down the road. Multiple forestry recreation sites on Rennell Sound, 27km down feisty lumber roads, provide a true escape. Watch out for the 22% grade as the road dips toward the sound.

Hiking the tangle of local logging roads is easier with a few good maps from the **Tlell Watershed Society** (see **Tlell,** below). Even on a two- or three-day hike, it's important to leave a **trip plan** with the visitors center before setting out. The visitors center issues crucial information on **tides** and **scheduled logging road activity.** It's very dangerous for hikers or 4x4s to vie for trail space with an unstoppable logging truck. For the most part, logging road use is restricted to industrial traffic from M-Sa 6am-6pm. Ignoring this restriction isn't just illegal; it can be deadly. The **Sleeping Beauty Trail** west of town makes for a great day hike with spectacular views of the west coast from the top of Sleeping Beauty Mountain. The trail takes about 2½hr. one way and is fairly steep the whole way up. The visitors center can provide directions to the trailhead and more information.

The **Spirit Lake Trail** network (several loops and 3km of trail, 1-2hr.) departs from a parking lot beside the George Brown Recreation Centre off Hwy. 16, in Skidegate. The network leads up a hillside to the lake (1000m), where it breaks off into various well-maintained and clearly-marked loops. A free guide pamphlet is available at the visitors center. Outfitters rent boats and kayaks, with rates varying according to the length of your journey and your level of experience. **Queen Charlotte Adventures,** 34 Wharf St., offers a $125 guided day paddle of Skidegate Inlet perfect for island newcomers. It'll be tough to concentrate on paddling as otters, seals, salmon, and birds all sidle up alongside to investigate you. (☎559-8990 or 800-668-4288; queencharlotteadventures.com. Kayaks $40 per day, $200 per week.)

TLELL AND PORT CLEMENTS   ☎250

Tlell (tuh-LEL), 40km north of Queen Charlotte City, is a line of houses and farms spread thinly along a 7km stretch of Hwy. 16. Here, the rocky beaches of the south give way to sand and the Tlell River offers fishing and, in July and August, water warm enough for swimming. The quasi-town enjoys some of Graham Island's best beach vistas, plus a population of artisans who earn Tlell a reputation as the Charlottes' hippie zone. Tlell hosts its own Woodstock, **Edge of the World Music Festival,** the second weekend in July. (www.edgefestival.com. Weekend pass $50, day passes $20-$35, ages 65 and older and 13-18 $25/$10-20, under 12 free.)

Port Clements lies 26km farther north. This town of 516 people was once home to the famous Golden Spruce and White Raven, both of which met premature ends in 1997. It is also a center for the island's logging activity and houses a museum on the town's history. Hwy. 16 forks with the well-signed left road leading to Port Clements and becoming Bayview Dr.

🛈 PRACTICAL INFORMATION. The **visitors center,** outdoors information, and flora and fauna displays are put together by the Tlell Watershed Society at **Naikoon Park Headquarters,** right before **Misty Meadows** campground. (Open daily 11am-4pm.) Information on Port Clements is available at the **Port Clements Museum** (see **Sights,** below). Tlell's **bookstore** is in the Sitka Studio (at the end of Richardson Rd.), which shows local art and sells art supplies. (☎557-4241. Open daily 10am-6pm.) **Wrench Tech,** on the Port Clements turnoff, offers some of the only auto service between Queen Charlotte and Masset. (☎557-4324. Open M-Sa 8am-6pm.) Other services include: **emergency/ambulance** ☎800-461-9911; **police** (☎559-4421) in Queen Charlotte City; and the **post office,** on Hwy. 16, 2km south of Wiggins Rd. (Open M-F 2:30-5:30pm.) **Postal Code:** V0T 1Y0.

🛏🍴 ACCOMMODATIONS AND FOOD. Sea breezes and birds singing in the spruces await at 🏠**Cacilia's B&B/Hitunwa Kaitza ❶,** snuggled against the dunes just north of Richardson Ranch on the ocean side of the road. Friendly cats, driftwood furniture, and hanging chairs give character to the common living space. Rooms are skylit and comfortable. (☎557-4664. Grassy tent site and campfire pit near dunes $15. Singles $45; doubles $65.) **Misty Meadows Campground ❶,** in Naikoon Provincial Park, 2km beyond Cacilia's, just south of the Tlell River bridge, has beautiful, spacious, and private campsites suitable for tents or RVs. (Picnic tables, beach access. 14-night max. stay. Sites $12.)

Lunch ($6-10) can be found at **Dress for Less ❶,** 1km south of Richardson Ranch in a pink building. The pink coffee bar is nestled among racks of vintage clothing. There are plenty of local artists' wares and even a deck on which to enjoy your coffee. (☎557-2023. Open daily 10am-5pm.) Turn off for Port Clements, 22km north of Tlell, for a good-sized dinner ($12-18) at a good old diner, the **Hummingbird Cafe ❹,** 2600 3rd Ave. (Open Tu-Su 11am-3pm and 5-8pm.)

📷🥾 SIGHTS AND OUTDOOR ACTIVITIES. One of the most popular trails around Tlell leads to the **Pesuta Shipwreck,** the hulking remains of a 246 ft. lumber barge that ran aground during a gale in 1928. The 2hr. hike to the site leaves from the Tlell River picnic area off Hwy. 16, just north of the river. When the trail branches, follow the "East Beach" sign up the ridge, or walk the whole way at low tide along the river. Hwy. 16 cuts inland just north of Tlell, leaving over 90km of pristine beach exclusively to backpackers. Allow four to six days to reach the road access at the north end of the route, 25km east of Masset. Before setting out on the East Beach hike, register at **Naikoon Provincial Park Headquarters** (☎557-4390), in a brown building on the right side of the highway, just before the Tlell River bridge. **Tlell Watershed Society** leads hikes throughout the island to local secret spots, such as **Pretty John's Hike.** Hikes are on island time, so return time may be later than estimated. (For information, call ☎557-4709; www.tlellwatershed.org.)

Though its shimmering endpoint is no more, the **Golden Spruce Trail** in Port Clements is still a fascinating short hike through old growth forest with very large cedar and spruce trees throughout. Take Bayview Dr. about 6km west of town and look for the signs. A portion of the drive is on active logging roads. If traveling during the week and before 6pm, call Weyerhaeuser (☎557-6810) for information on their logging activity on the road.

Visitors to Port Clements often mistakenly assume that the body of water surrounding town is a lake. It's actually the oceanic **Masset Inlet,** which has some of the least crowded fishing on the islands. Cast right off the docks or head down the rocky shore for total seclusion. **Neat Things,** (☎557-4226), on Bayview Drive at Yakoun St., and other local shops along the Bayview Dr. waterfront can set you up with permits and whatever gear you need.

The **Port Clements Museum,** on Bayview Dr. just before the center of town, has a wide array of logging and mining tools, pictures and artifacts from the town's founders and history, a scrapbook of the saga surrounding the felling of the Golden Spruce, and the stuffed White Raven of Port Clements, which was killed by an electrical transformer. Outside are artifacts too large to fit inside the building, including a Soviet sonar device that washed up on the shore. (Open June to mid-Sept. M-F 11am-4pm, Sa-Su 2-4pm; closed M-F mid-Sept. to May. $2.) Across the street in **Millennium Memorial Park** are the well-protected Golden Spruce saplings.

MASSET ☎250

At mile zero of the Yellowhead Hwy., Masset isn't a showy city. The mixture of loggers, Haida, and hippies leads to the occasional culture clash and a sometimes volatile political scene. Spectacular scenery surrounds the town; the rainforest of Tow Hill and the expansive beachfront of the Blow Hole and North Beach, east of town in Naikoon Provincial Park, more than justify the northward trek.

ORIENTATION AND PRACTICAL INFORMATION. Masset is about 108km (1¼hr. on a good, although narrow and deer-filled, road) north of Skidegate on Hwy. 16. To get downtown, take a left off the highway onto the main bridge, just after the small boat harbor. After the bridge, Delkatla Road is

THE LEGEND OF THE GOLDEN SPRUCE

For years, oddity-seekers drove, biked, hiked, and ran to Port Clements, where the planet's only Golden Spruce basked in singular glory. Due to a rare genetic mutation, the 300-year-old tree contained only a fraction of the chlorophyll present in an ordinary Sitka spruce, causing its needles to be bleached by sunlight. The striking 50m giant glowed fiery yellow in the sun, beaming its way into Haida creation myths and horticulturists' dreams. In January 1997, however, a disgruntled ex-forestry worker arrived at the site with an axe and a mission. To protest the logging industry's destruction of British Columbia's forests, he chopped down the tree. These actions won him no prize for logic, but certainly drew province-wide attention.

While islanders reacted with astonishment at their beloved tree's untimely demise, the University of British Columbia revealed another shocker: there had been not one but three Golden Spruces—two, created in 1977 from clippings of the original, were growing peacefully in the botanical gardens of the UBC Victoria campus. University authorities donated these golden saplings to the Haida nation. Concurrent with the fall of the original Golden Spruce, an albino raven was born on the island, an event that locals took as a sign foretelling a continuation of the Spruce's three-century history.

on the left. **Collision Avenue,** the main drag, is the first right off Delkatla. To reach the campgrounds (see below), continue on Hwy. 16 without crossing the bridge.

Vern's Taxi will get you around. (☎626-3535. Open daily 8am-6pm.) **National,** 1504 Old Beach Rd., at the Singing Surf Inn, **rents cars.** From $30 per day. Must be 25 or older. (☎626-3318. Open M-Sa 7am-9pm, Su 8am-9pm.) **TLC,** on Collision Ave., provides **car repair.** (☎626-3756. Open daily 8am-6pm. 24hr. towing.) The **Tourist Information Centre,** Old Beach Rd., at Hwy. 16, offers history, maps for bird-watching, and an extensive Masset packet. (☎626-3982 or 888-352-9242. Open daily July-Aug. 10am-8pm; Sept.-June M and F-Su 9am-2pm.) The **Village Office** has advice year-round. (☎626-3955. Open M-Th 9am-4pm, F noon-4pm.) **Northern Savings,** Main St. north of Collision Ave., is the only bank and **24hr. ATM** outside Queen Charlotte City. (☎626-5231. Open Tu-Th and Sa 10am-3pm, F noon-5pm.) The **laundromat** is located just north of Collision Ave. on Orr St. (☎626-5007. Open Tu-Sa 9am-9pm. Wash $1.75, dry $1.75.) In an emergency, call the **ambulance** (☎800-461-9911), the **police** (☎626-3991), on Collision Ave., at Orr St., or the **hospital** (☎626-4700; emergency 626-4711). The **clinic** is on Hodges Ave., on the right just over the main bridge into Masset. (☎626-4702 or 626-4703. Open M-Tu and Th-F 8:30am-4:30pm.) A **pharmacy** is at the clinic. (☎626-4701. Open M-Tu and Th-F 10:30am-12:30pm and 1:30-4:45pm, W 1:30-4:45pm.) The **library,** at Collision Ave. and McLeod St., offers 30min. of **Internet** access for $1. It's a good idea to call ahead to reserve a space. (☎626-3663; www.virl.bc.ca. Open Tu 2-6pm, Th 2-5pm and 6-8pm, Sa noon-5pm.) The **post office** is located on Main St. north of Collision. (☎626-5155. Open M-F 9am-5:30pm, Sa 1-4pm.) **Postal Code:** V0T 1M0.

◪◪ ACCOMMODATIONS AND CAMPING. Masset campsites are scenic, cheap, and everywhere. There is free beach **camping ❶** on North Beach, 1km past Tow Hill, 30km east of Masset, in Naikoon Provincial Park. Look for signs marking the end of Indian Reserve property. Call ahead for favored indoor lodging.

Rapid Richie's Rustic Rentals ❸, 18km east of Masset on Tow Hill Rd., offers self-sufficient accommodation on a wild beach, with six airy cabins with water collected from the roof, propane lights, wood or propane heating, kitchen, cookstove, and pit toilets. (☎626-5472; www.beachcabins.com. Sleeps 2-4. Reservations recommended. $40-70 per day for 2; $15 per extra person.) At **Copper Beech House ❹,** 1590 Delkatla Rd., at Collision Ave. by the small boat dock, guests dine off Beijing china, share a bath with carved wooden frogs from Mexico, and snuggle under Finnish comforters. (☎626-5441. Singles $75; doubles $100; Oct.-Apr. garden shed loft $25, or work and stay for free.) **Daisy's RV Park and Campground ❶,** 1440 Tow Hill Rd. about 2km east of town, features large and well-maintained sites. (☎626-5280. Tent sites $15, RV sites with water and electricity $20, full hookups $24.)

◳ FOOD. North Beach is a great spot for crabbing; few amateur fishermen come away emptyhanded. Razor clams can be found as well, but gathering them requires a little more effort and the clams are potentially toxic. Call the **Department of Fisheries and Oceans** (☎626-3316) for safety information before harvesting mollusks. Permits ($7.50 per day) are available at Christie St. behind the visitors center. Lemons and seafood garnishes are sold at **Delmas Co-op,** on Main St., south of Collision Ave. (☎626-3933. Open M-Sa 10am-6pm.)

◪Moon Over Naikoon ❷, 18km on the left on Tow Hill Rd., is a small cafe decorated with whalebones and other beachside finds. Edibles include whole wheat flaxseed bread ($5), melt-in-your-mouth butter tarts ($1), and seafood lunches. (Open M and F-Su 11am-7pm.) **Marj's ❷,** on Main St. next to the post office, is a diner and local hangout where most of the village's problems are solved (or at least discussed) over all-day breakfast ($6-8), burgers ($6-8), NY steaks ($12), and gargantuan slices of fresh pie. (☎ 626-9344. Open daily 7am-3pm.) **Sandpiper Restaurant ❷**, 2062 Collision Ave., offers expensive but hearty seafood dishes. (☎ 626-3672. Open M-Sa 8:30am-9pm.)

🎦 🔍 **SIGHTS AND OUTDOOR ACTIVITIES. Tow Hill,** an incredible outcrop of volcanic basalt columns about 26km east of town, rises out of nowhere at the far end of Agate Beach, and presides over Masset as the area's reigning attraction. Continue 1km past Agate Back Campsite to ✦**Tow Hill Viewpoint Trailhead.** The trail takes about 30min. to ascend on tar paper covered boards leading to a fabulous overlook. On a clear day, miles of virgin beach and even the southerly reaches of Alaska spread out below; slow summer sunsets hang in the horizon for hours. On the way back down (10min.), take a detour to loop past the **Blow Hole** (25min.), a small cave that erupts with 4.6m high plumes of water at mid-tide.

Two less-traveled trails depart from the Tow Hill Viewpoint parking lot: an 11km beach walk to **Rose Spit** (2½-3hr. one-way) at the island's northeast corner, and a 10km hike on the **Cape Fife Trail** (3½-4hr. one-way), which passes through some of the island's most varied vegetation and provides access to the East Coast Beach and the long hiking route out of Tlell (see p. 406). A lean-to at the end of the Cape Fife Trail allows tireless backpackers to link the two routes, exploring the entire island in a 4- to 6-day trek. Inform **Naikoon Park Headquarters** (☎ 557-4390 in Tlell; see p. 406) before multi-day trips, and contact them for advice. Across the Hiellen River, **North Beach** is where Raven discovered a giant clam containing the first men in the Haida creation myth and where clam and crab catchers congregate today.

Closer to town, red-breasted sapsuckers, orange-crowned warblers, glaucouswinged gulls, and binocular-toting bird-watchers converge on the **Delkatla Wildlife Sanctuary,** off Tow Hill Rd. The best paths for observing 113 local species begin at the junction of Trumpeter Dr. and Cemetery Rd. Continue on Cemetery Rd. past the sanctuary to reach **Oceanview Cemetery,** in a lush green forest on the beach.

Fishing in streams near North Beach and off the docks in town is plentiful; just don't forget your permit (available at virtually any store in town). Locals regularly pull up bucketfuls of coho, sockeye, chinook, and halibut in only a few hours. But be courteous—Masset folk don't take kindly to dock-hogs.

SANDSPIT ☎ 250

Sandspit is the only permanent community in Gwaii Haanas. The town sprawls alongside the beach, misting people and bald eagles alike with salty spray. Mother Nature buffets the community with a perpetual west wind and provides sprawling sunsets over a porpoise-filled bay each evening. This well-groomed hub houses the only commercial airport on the islands and serves as a major launching point for kayak and boat trips to Gwaii Haanas National Park Reserve (p. 411).

📭 🔟 **ORIENTATION AND PRACTICAL INFORMATION.** Having a car or bike is handy in Sandspit, since the town is spread over the long **Beach Road** parallel to the seashore. There isn't much traffic on the 13km road between Sandspit and **Alliford Bay,** where the ferry docks. Bringing a bike over on the ferry is free, and the trip to town is an idyllic, easy 1hr. ride along the ocean.

Sandspit Airport is near the end of the spit on Beach Rd. (Airport code: YZP.) **BC Ferries** (☎ 223-3779 or 888-559-4485; www.bcferries.bc.ca) runs between Skidegate Landing on Graham Island and Alliford Bay on Gwaii Haanas. (20min.; 12 per day;

round-trip $5-6, car $12-13, kayak or canoe $2.) **Eagle Cabs** runs a shuttle from the airport to Queen Charlotte City twice per day. (☎559-4461 or 877-547-4461. 1 shuttle Sa. $14. Reservations recommended.)

Tourist and outdoor information is available at the airport. Register and gather trail information or buy maps ($8) here before heading into the park. **Park orientations** are held M and F at 3:30pm, Tu-Th and Sa-Su at 3pm. (☎637-5362; www.sandspitqci.com. Open daily May-Sept. 8am-5pm.) **Budget,** 383 Beach Rd., by the post office, rents autos. (☎637-5688 or 800-577-3228. $50 per day plus $0.35 per km. Must be 21 or older with a credit card.) **Bayview Sales and Services,** at the west end of town, pumps gas and sells propane. (☎637-5359. Open M-F 9am-noon and 3-7pm, Sa 9am-noon and 1-6pm, Su 9am-1pm and 6-8pm.) **The Trading Post,** on Beach Front Rd., before the gas station when heading out of Sandspit, sells fishing licenses and outdoor gear. (Open M-Sa 9am-noon and 1-6pm.) The Sandspit Inn near the airport also provides gear and licenses. The **Supervalu** supermarket, 383 Alliford Bay, in the mini-mall near the spit, carries some produce and sells alcohol. (☎637-2249. Open M-Sa 9:30am-6pm, Tu 9:30am-7:30pm, Su 10am-4pm.) The **ambulance** is at ☎800-461-9911. The **police** (☎559-4421) are in Queen Charlotte City. The **health clinic** is on Copper Bay Rd., in the school building. (☎637-5403. Open M-F 10am-noon.) After hours, call the **Queen Charlotte General Hospital** (☎559-4506). The **post office** is at Beach and Beban Rd. (☎637-2244. Open M-F 9am-5pm, Sa 11am-2pm.) **Postal Code:** V0T 1T0.

🏠🏕 **ACCOMMODATIONS AND CAMPING.** Sandspit rooms are more affordable and less crowded than most on the islands. The ▩**Seaport Bed and Breakfast ❷,** just up the road toward Spit Point, offers island hospitality with guest pickup at the airport. Rooms in two cottages with kitchens and cable TV in common rooms. (☎637-5698. Reservations are essential in summer. Singles $30; doubles $50.) Identical accommodations are provided by the owner's daughter two blocks away on Beach Rd. at ▩**Bayside Bed and Breakfast ❷** (☎637-2433). **Lynn's Place ❸,** on Blaine Shaw Rd., provides clean, comfortable rooms. A well-kept yard with a pond is a great setting to read a book. Kitchen use. (☎637-5654. Singles $40; doubles $65; cottage $110.) **Moresby Island Guest House ❸,** on Beach Rd. next to the post office, is not quite as homey but more economical, offering 10 rooms with shared washrooms, a kitchen, and coin-operated laundry facilities. Make-your-own-breakfast is included, but further kitchen use costs $10. (☎637-5300. Cots $15. Singles $32; doubles from $65.) **501 RV and Tent Park ❶,** 501 Beach Rd., has the only public showers on the island. (☎637-5473. Open daily 8am-9pm. 5 tent sites $10; 10 RV sites $15-20. Showers $1 per 2min.)

Along the west coast of the island, BC Parks and the Forestry Service maintain two campgrounds. The first, at **Mosquito Lake ❶,** about 35km (1hr.) from Sandspit, is every tenter's dream with mossy sites in wooded seclusion. About another 7km down the road, **Moresby Camp ❶** has mowed sites with fewer bugs but lots of loud boat traffic into Gwaii Haanas. Both are free to campers. Follow Alliford Bay Main past the ferry docks to South Bay Main to Moresby Rd. to get there. **Gray Bay,** 20km south of town (30min.), offers a virtually uninterrupted expanse of sand. Twenty primitive forestry **campsites ❶** line the long expanse of the beach and afford tons of privacy. Obtain directions and logging road activity updates at the visitors center. Arrive early on weekends to ensure a spot.

📁 **FOOD.** For a nice, long round of golf ($20) and loaded burgers or veggie burgers ($7-9), head to **Willows Golf Course Clubhouse ❷,** near the end of Copper Bay Rd. (☎637-2388. Open W-Sa 11:30am-9pm, Su 11:30am-5pm.) More pleasant inside than out, **Dick's Wok Restaurant and Grocery ❸,** 388 Copper Bay Rd., serves a heaping plate of fried rice ($10) next to a tank filled with monster goldfish. Dick also offers a small selection of groceries. (☎637-2275. Open daily 5-10pm.) The **Sandspit Inn ❸**, opposite the airport near the spit's end, houses the town's only **pub**. (☎637-5334. Open daily 11:30am-1am. Kitchen closes at 9pm.)

⚠️ 🏕️ OUTDOOR ACTIVITIES AND EVENTS.

Spectacular sunrises and sunsets reward those who wander to the end of the **spit**, where anglers surf-cast for silver salmon. Beachcombers should stay below the tide line, since the spit is airport property. Several trails depart from the road between the ferry docks and the spit. An easy stroll along the **Onward Point Trail** (30min.) leads to a fossil bed, and, in May, to a vantage point for watching migrating grey whales. The **Dover Trail** (2hr.) begins 40m west of the Haans Creek Bridge across from the small boat harbor and passes giant cedars with ancient Haida markings. The **Skyline Loop** runs an hour to the shore over more difficult terrain. Although the trail system is marked, it goes through dense brush and crosses other trails, making the return trip more difficult.

Dirt logging roads lead south and west of town into some bogglingly scenic areas. Those using **logging roads** between 6am and 6pm during the week must check in at the visitors center for active logging status; in winter call Teal-Jones Group (☎637-5323). Ten kilometers past where Copper Bay Rd. turns into gravel are the rocky shores of **Copper Bay,** a haven for bald eagles.

The roads are perfect for **mountain biking.** The closest rentals are in Queen Charlotte City, and bikes are allowed free on ferries. The 24km **Moresby Loop** is a popular route that runs from Sandspit to an old train trellis over Skidegate Lake and on to an abandoned Cumshewa Inlet logging camp. Logging in the area has slowed but locals still celebrate **Logger Sports Day** in July. The festival features pole-climbing, caber-tossing, axe-throwing, and other vigorous lumber-related activities.

GWAII HAANAS NATIONAL PARK RESERVE/HAIDA HERITAGE SITE ☎250

Roadless Gwaii Haanas corrals visitors with its haunting calm. Paddlers who reach the park's lonesome Haida villages, abandoned and rotting in the rainforest, see and hear nothing but mile after mile of quickening water and the steady thrum of ocean pounding the empty shore. Provincially owned Crown land for most of the 20th century, the territory has been disturbed only by sporadic logging and occasional tourist visits to deserted Haida villages. In the mid-80s, the timber industry, the Haida nation, environmentalists, and the provincial government came to heads over land use on the island. In 1988, the federal government interceded, purchasing the southern third of the Queen Charlotte Islands to create a National Park Reserve. A 1993 agreement united the Haida Nation and the Government of Canada in the management of Gwaii Haanas. The Canadian Parks Ministry now patrols the islands, while the Haida Gwaii Watchmen guide visitors with the goal of protecting their cultural heritage.

By air or by sea, each summer a few thousand visitors make the long ocean journey south from Moresby Camp (about 25km). No trails penetrate Gwaii Haanas, and most exploration remains close to the 1600km of shoreline. The seas pound on the rocky west coast, making travel treacherous. On the east coast, the serene waters teem with marine life and birds, peaking in Burnaby Narrows with the highest density of biomass in any intertidal zone in the world. Gaze up to see bald eagle nests in dead trees and paddle silently along shore at dawn to spot the strong-jawed sub-species of black bears unique to Haida Gwaii.

◼◻ ORIENTATION AND PRACTICAL INFORMATION. The islands hold treasures as inspiring as the seascape. Old-growth forest stands tall in **Hik'yah (Windy Bay),** where Haida stood up to loggers. Chains of lakes and waterfalls span Gwaii Haanas. At **Gandll K'in (Hotsprings Island),** three pristine seaside pools steam, soothing ocean-weary muscles.

Haida Gwaii Watchmen share the history of their culture at settlements that, in keeping with Haida tradition, are being permitted to "return to the land." Totem poles slowly decay at **K'uuna (Skedans)** on Louise Island, north of Gwaii Hanaas, and the UNESCO World Heritage site of **Nan Sdins (Ninstints).** Both Haida villages were deserted after late 19th-century epidemics of smallpox and tuberculosis. At **T'aannu (Tanu),** a longhouse village can be envisioned from the depressions and fallen poles. The grave of the recently deceased, famous Haida carver Bill Reid can be visited on the point next to the grave of the anonymous "Charlie."

The number of people who can enter the park without licensed tour operators is limited and those who choose to visit face unique planning and preparation concerns. These experienced kayakers and small craft owners may reserve dates to enter and exit the park by calling **Super, Natural British Columbia.** (In Canada and the US ☎800-663-6000; elsewhere 250-387-1642. Reservations $15 per person.) The park also provides six standby entries daily. All visitors must attend the 1½hr. **orientation session** before they depart: these are held daily from May to Sept. at 8am and 7:30pm at the **Queen Charlotte City visitors center** (p. 403) and at 3pm at the **Sandspit visitors center** (p. 409). Park user fees are $10 per day (under 17 free; $80 max.). Those visiting between Oct. 1 and Apr. 30 do not need to make a reservation or pay a fee. Orientation and registration, however, are still required. For a **trip-planning** package with a list of charter companies, contact **Parks Canada** (☎250-559-8818). Ask the park management about camping locations to avoid traditional Haida sites. Kayakers venturing into the park alone should file a **sail plan** with the **Prince Rupert Coast Guard** (☎250-627-3081) but should know that rescue may not be possible for many hours after a distress incident due to the park's remoteness. Contact **Fisheries and Oceans** (☎559-4413) before eating shellfish. Freshwater fishing is not allowed; saltwater licenses are available in Queen Charlotte City (p. 403).

Weather reports are broadcast on VHF channel 21. Two **warden stations** are staffed from May to September, at Huxley Island (about halfway down the park) and at Rose Harbour (near the south tip of Gwaii Haanas). They can be reached on VHF channel 16. Five **watchmen sites** (VHF 6) are staffed during the same period, and will offer assistance upon request, although their role is not to act as tour guides. To visit a cultural site, contact the watchmen a day in advance as there is a limit on the number of people permitted ashore at each site at any one time.

◪ OUTDOOR ACTIVITIES. To avoid the exposed north portion of Gwaii Haanas and begin your trip in shelter of coastal islands, **Moresby Camp,** on the west side of the island, is a logical place to enter the park. Check with the info center in Sandspit (p. 409) before traveling the potentially hazardous logging roads to this access point. **Bruce's Taxi** will run you down the gravel roads to Moresby Camp. (☎637-5655. 1hr. one-way; $150. Fits 7 people and 2 kayaks; pre-arranged pickup.) **◪Moresby Explorers** (☎800-806-7633; www.moresbyexplorers.com), on Beach Rd. in Sandspit, just west of Copper Bay Rd., will transport kayakers, kayaks, and gear from Sandspit into Gwaii Hanaas or to their float camp at the north edge of Gwaii Haanas to pick up rental kayaks ($20-220 per person round-trip). **Queen Charlotte Adventures** (p. 405), in Queen Charlotte City, offers sea kayak rentals (singles $40 per day, $200 per week) and marine transport ($135 from Queen Charlotte to Juan Perez Sound). A round-trip kayak voyage down the length of the Gwaii Haanas takes two weeks; a guided voyage will run you around $3000. Both Moresby Explorers and Queen Charlotte Adventures run shorter kayaking trips ranging from 5 to 10 days and costing $800-2000.

For those wanting to avoid hassles, **tour operators** guide visitors and take care of all logistics for entering Gwaii Haanas. Guided visitors do not have to make independent reservations or attend an info session. Run by energetic Doug Gould, **Moresby Explorers** offers chartered trips. (Trips $140-160, 2 days with overnight at float camp $360, 4-day trips $900.) **South Moresby Air Charters** (☎ 559-4222) flies over many of the heritage sites.

ALBERTA

> **ALBERTA FACTS AND FIGURES**
> **Capital:** Edmonton. **Area:** 661,185 sq. km. **Population:** 3,224,400.
> **Official Tartan:** Forest green, wheat gold, sky blue, rose pink, oil black.
> **Bird:** Great Horned Owl. **Mammal:** Rocky Mountain Bighorn Sheep.
> **World's Largest Mall:** West Edmonton Mall. **Drinking Age:** 18.

With its wide-open prairie, oil-fueled economy, and conservative politics, Alberta is often called the Texas of Canada by the Yanks to the south. Petrodollars have given birth to gleaming, modern cities on the plains. In 1988, the Winter Olympics temporarily transformed Calgary into an international mecca, and the city hasn't yet stopped collecting tourist interest off the legacy. Calgary is also the stamping grounds for the Stampede, the world's largest rodeo and meeting place for the most skilled cowboys in the West. The capital, Edmonton, has only recently been surpassed in population by Calgary, its hockey rival to the south, and serves as a transportation hub for the stunning national and provincial parks that line the Alberta-BC border.

For outdoor enthusiasts, Alberta is a year-round playground. Hikers, mountaineers, and ice climbers will find a recreational paradise in the Canadian Rockies in Banff and Jasper National Parks and Kananaskis Country. The parks represent Alberta's most consistent draw, and with good reason: the splendor of the Canadian Rockies is unparalleled in North America. The province boasts fossil fields, centers of indigenous Canadian culture, and thousands of prime fishing holes.

HIGHLIGHTS OF ALBERTA

RIDE through breathtaking scenery between Banff and Jasper on the **Icefields Parkway**; best seen from a bike (p. 447).

SWAGGER into town in your hat and spurs for the annual **Calgary Stampede** (p. 425).

DIG for ancient dinosaur bones in the appropriately-named **Badlands** (p. 426).

LEARN time-tested methods for killing tens of thousands of buffalo using only ingenuity and gravity at **Head-Smashed-In Buffalo Jump** (p. 430).

HIT the powder-filled back bowls in the heart of the Rockies at **Lake Louise** (p. 446).

EDMONTON ☎ 780

The provincial capital of Alberta may not lay claim to the amazing scenery of Banff and Jasper, or the spectacle that is the Calgary Stampede, but Edmonton has a variety of other things to offer a wide spectrum of tastes. This popular travel destination hosts the Canadian Finals Rodeo in November, and is home to the world's largest shopping mall. A number of museums attract children and art lovers alike, while the Saskatchewan River valley draws hikers and bikers. A perpetual stream of music, art, and performance festivals brings summer crowds to the self-proclaimed "City of Festivals." Near the shadow of the Rockies, Whyte Ave.'s plentiful food and nightlife offerings help transform Edmonton into an urban oasis.

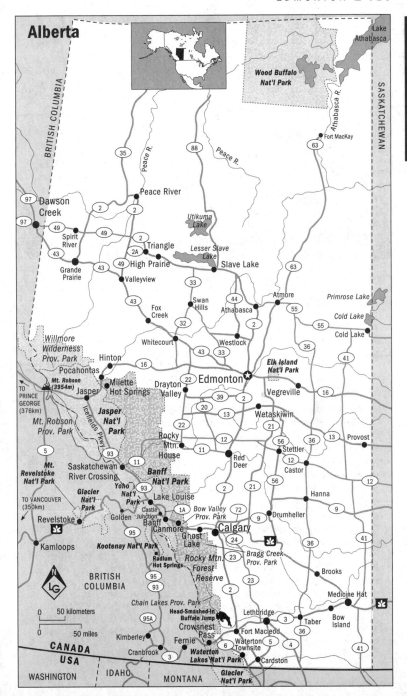

Alberta

ALBERTA

BRITISH COLUMBIA

SASKATCHEWAN

Lake Athabasca

Wood Buffalo Nat'l Park

Athabasca R.

Fort MacKay
63

35
88
Peace R.
Peace R.

97 Dawson Creek
2
Peace River
2

97
49
49
Spirit River
49
2
Triangle
2A
High Prairie
49
43
43
Grande Prairie
Valleyview
43
Fox Creek
32

Utikuma Lake

Lesser Slave Lake
Slave Lake
63

33
Swan Hills
44
Athabasca
55
Primrose Lake
Cold Lake
55
Cold Lake

Willmore Wilderness Prov. Park
Pocahontas
Hinton
16
Whitecourt
43
33
Westlock
2
36
41

Mt. Robson (3954m)
TO PRINCE GEORGE (376km)
Jasper
Milette Hot Springs
Drayton Valley
22
Edmonton
Elk Island Nat'l Park
Vegreville
16

Mt. Robson Prov. Park
Jasper Nat'l Park
39
2
20
13
Wetaskiwin
21
22
56
36
13
Provost

5
Mt. Revelstoke Nat'l Park
Saskatchewan River Crossing
93
11
Banff Nat'l Park
Rocky Mtn. House
11
12
Red Deer
Stettler
12
Castor

TO VANCOUVER (350km)
Glacier Nat'l Park
Yoho Nat'l Park
93
Lake Louise
2
21
56
Hanna
12

Revelstoke
Castle Junction
1A
Bow Valley Prov. Park
72
9
Drumheller
9
41

Kamloops
Banff
95
Canmore
Ghost Lake
Calgary
24

Kootenay Nat'l Park
Radium Hot Springs
Golden
23
Bragg Creek Prov. Park
36
Brooks

BRITISH COLUMBIA
N LG
95
93
Rocky Mtn. Forest Reserve
23
2
Medicine Hat

0   50 kilometers
0   50 miles

Chain Lakes Prov. Park
95A
Head-Smashed-In Buffalo Jump
Crowsnest Pass
Lethbridge
3
Taber
Bow Island

CANADA
USA
Kimberley
Fernie
6
Fort Macleod
5
4
41
Cranbrook
3
Waterton Lakes Nat'l Park
Waterton Townsite
Cardston

WASHINGTON   IDAHO   MONTANA
Glacier Nat'l Park

ALBERTA

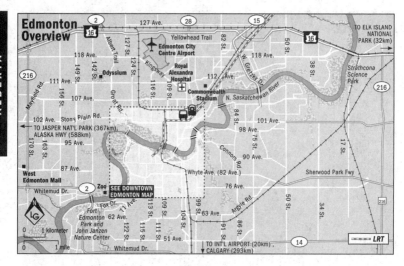

🔲 TRANSPORTATION

The city lies 294km north of Calgary, an easy but tedious 3hr. drive across the prairie on the **Calgary Trail (Highway 2).** Jasper is 362km to the west, a 4hr. drive on Hwy. 16. Edmonton's streets run north-south, and avenues run east-west. Street numbers increase heading west, and avenues increase heading north. The first three digits of an address indicate the nearest cross street: 10141 88 Ave. is on 88 Ave. near 101 St. The **city center** area is actually off-center, at 105 St. and 101 Ave. Most establishments of interest are clustered around **Whyte Avenue** (82 Ave.)

> **Flights: Edmonton International Airport** (☎890-8382; www.edmontonairports.com) sits 29km south of town, a $35 cab fare away. The **Sky Shuttle Airport Service** (☎465-8515 or 888-438-2342) runs a shuttle downtown, to the university, or to the West Edmonton Mall for $13 ($20 round-trip). Airport code: YEG.

> **Trains: VIA Rail,** 12360 121 St. (☎888-842-7245 or 514-871-6000) is a 10min. drive NW of downtown in the CN tower. 3 per week to **Jasper** (5hr.; $145) and **Vancouver** (24hr.; $270). No train service to Calgary.

> **Buses: Greyhound,** 10324 103 St. (☎420-2400). Open daily 5:30am-12:30am. To: **Calgary** (3½hr., 11 per day, $46); **Jasper** (5hr., 4 per day, $57); **Vancouver** (16-21hr., 6 per day, $152); **Yellowknife, NWT** (22-28hr.; 1 per day M-F, fewer in winter; $210). Locker storage $2 per day. **Red Arrow,** 10010 104 St. (☎800-232-1958; www.redarrow.pwt.ca), at the Holiday Inn. Open daily 7:30am-10pm. 10% HI discount. To **Calgary** (3hr., 4-7 per day, $53) and **Fort McMurray** (5hr., 2 per day, $61).

> **Public Transportation: Edmonton Transit** (schedules ☎496-1611, info, including when the next bus will arrive at your stop, 496-1600; www.takeets.com). Buses and **Light Rail Transit (LRT)** run frequently. LRT is **free downtown** between Grandin Station at 110 St. and 98 Ave. and Churchill Station at 99 St. and 102 Ave. Runs M-Sa 5:30am-1:30am, Su 5:30am-12:30am. $2, ages 65 and older or 6-15 $1.75, under 6 free. No bikes on LRT during peak hours traveling in peak direction (M-F 7:30-8:30am and 4-5pm); bikes on 1, 4 and 19 buses only. Info booth open M-F 8:30am-4:30pm.

Taxis: Yellow Cab (☎462-3456). **Alberta Co-op Taxi** (☎425-0954). $2.50 base rate, $0.20 for each 210m after the first, $0.20 per 30 seconds. Both 24hr.

Car Rental: Budget, 5905 104 St. (☎448-2000 or 800-661-7027); call for other locations. From $46 per day, with unlimited km; cheaper city rates—$16 per day with a $.014 per km charge. Must be 21 or older. Ages 21-24 $20 per day surcharge. Must have major credit card. Open M-F 7:30am-6pm, Sa 9am-3pm, Su 9am-2pm.

🛈 PRACTICAL INFORMATION

Tourist Office: Edmonton Tourism (☎496-8400 or 800-463-4667; www.edmonton.com/tourism), at **Gateway Park** on Hwy. 2, at the intersection of Gateway Blvd. and 24th Ave. SW, south of town. Open daily June to mid-Sept. 8am-8pm; mid-Sept. to June M-F 8:30am-4:30pm, Sa-Su 9am-5pm. Also at 9990 Jasper Ave. Open M-F 9am-5pm. **Travel Alberta** (☎427-4321 or 800-ALBERTA/252-3782; www.travelalberta.com) is open M-F 7am-7pm, Sa-Su 8:30am-5:00pm.

Equipment Rental: Mountain Equipment Co-op, 12328 102 Ave. (☎488-6614; www.mec.ca) rents camping equipment (tents $18 per day) and watercraft (canoes $30 per day, kayaks $25 per day). Open M-F 10am-9pm, Sa 9am-6pm, Su 11am-5pm.

Gay and Lesbian Services: Pride Centre, ste. 45, 9912 106 St. (☎488-3234; www.pridecentreofedmonton.org). Open M-F 7-10pm. **Womonspace** (☎482-1794; www.gaycanada.com/womonspace) is Edmonton's lesbian group. Call for a recording of local events.

Police: ☎423-4567.

Crisis Line: ☎482-HELP/4357. **Sexual Assault Centre** ☎423-4121. Both 24hr.

Pharmacy: Shoppers Drug Mart, 11408 Jasper Ave. (☎482-1011) or 8210 109 St. (☎433-2424) by Whyte Ave. Open 24hr.

Hospital: Royal Alexandra Hospital, 10240 Kingsway Ave. (☎477-4111).

Internet Access: Free at the **library,** 7 Sir Winston Churchill Sq. (☎496-7000; www.epl.ca); limited to 1hr. per day for a week. Open M-F 9am-9pm, Sa 9am-6pm, Su 1-5pm. **Dow Computer Lab,** 11211 142 St. (☎451-3344), at the Odyssium (see **Sights,** below); free with admission.

Post Office: 9808 103A Ave. (☎800-267-1177), adjacent to the CN Tower. Open M-F 8am-5:45pm. **Postal Code:** T5J 2G8.

🏠 ACCOMMODATIONS

The hostel is the liveliest place to stay in Edmonton; St. Joseph's College and the University of Alberta provide a bit more privacy. For B&B listings, contact **Alberta B&B Association,** 3230 104A St. (☎438-6048; www.wcbbia.com).

▨ **Edmonton International Youth Hostel (HI),** 10647 81 Ave. (☎988-6836). Bus #7 or 9 from the 101 St. station to Whyte Ave. You'd never know that this hostel is in a renovated convent but for the many private 2-person bedrooms with the dimensions of a nun's cell. Facilities include a kitchen, game room, lounge, laundry, and small backyard. Drinking is allowed until 11pm. The location is unbeatable: just around the corner from the clubs, shops, and cafes of Whyte Ave. Reception open 24hr. $22, nonmembers $25; semi-private doubles $24/$27. Family rooms available. ❷

St. Joseph's College, 89 Ave. at 114 St. (☎492-7681). The rooms here are smaller than those at the university. Library, huge lounges, rec room, and laundry, and close to University of Alberta sports facilities. Call ahead; the 60 dorms often fill up quickly. Rooms available early May to late Aug. Singles $33, with full board $43. ❸

University of Alberta, 87 Ave. The Lister Center, between 116 and 117 St. (☎492-4281). Generic dorm rooms. Dry cleaning, kitchen, high-speed Internet access ($1 for 10min.), convenience store, and buffet-style cafeteria downstairs (Open 7am-7pm, $5-6 meals). Reception open 24hr. Check-in after 4pm. Reservations strongly recommended. Rooms available late May-Aug. Singles $36, $55 with suite kitchen, bath and Ethernet. Weekly and monthly rates available. ❸

☐ FOOD

Edmonton locals tend to swarm into the coffee shops and cafes of the Old Strathcona area along Whyte Ave. (82 Ave.), between 102 and 106 St.

■ **Dadeo's,** 10548 Whyte Ave. (☎433-0930). Cajun food away from the bayou at this funky 50s diner. Spicy dishes make you sweat just right. Gumbo $4.50. M-Tu po'boys $7. Su $4 for a pint or a plate of wings. Open M-Th 11:30am-11pm, F-Sa 11:30am-midnight, Su 10am-10pm. ❷

Cafe Mosaics, 10844 Whyte Ave. (☎433-9702) offers socially and environmentally responsible dining. Breakfast ranges from eggs and hash browns ($5) to the fresh fruit, granola and yogurt bowl ($6). Vegetarian and vegan options available all day, and the coffee is Fair Trade ($1.25). Open M-Sa 9am-9pm, Su 11am-2:30pm. ❷

The Silk Hat, 10251 Jasper Ave. (☎425-1920). The oldest restaurant in Edmonton maintains the smoky feel of days gone by. This greasy spoon diner in the heart of downtown serves a huge array of food, from seafood to veggie burgers ($6.25). Breakfast all day. Happy hour M-F 4-6pm. Open M-F 7am-8pm, Sa 10am-8pm. ❷

Chianti, 10501 Whyte Ave. (☎439-9829). Daily specials, desserts, and coffees accompany a wide variety of pasta, veal, and seafood in a setting that feels much more expensive than it is. Pastas $7-12; veal $10-13. Open daily 11am-11pm. ❸

Kids in the Hall Bistro, 1 Sir Winston Churchill Sq. (☎413-8060), in City Hall. This lunchroom is truly one-of-a-kind. Every employee, from waiter to chef, is a young person hired as part of a cooperative community service project. Various entrees ($5-10) and sandwiches ($5-7). Takeout available. Open M-F 8am-4pm. ❷

☉ SIGHTS

WEST EDMONTON MALL. The $1.3 billion **West Edmonton Mall** engulfs the general area between 170 St. and 87 Ave. No ordinary collection of stores, the **world's biggest mall** is a temple to the capitalist experience, containing water slides and the world's largest indoor wave pool, an amusement park with a fourteen-story roller coaster, miniature golf, dozens of exotic caged animals, over 800 stores, an ice-skating rink, 110 eating establishments, a full-scale replica of Columbus's *Santa Maria*, an indoor bungee jumping facility, a casino, a luxury hotel, a dolphin show, swarms of teenage mall rats, multiple movie theaters, and twice as many submarines as the Canadian Navy. One note of caution: remember where you park. *(Bus #1, 2, 100, or 111. ☎444-5200 or 800-661-8890; www.westedmall.com. Open M-F 10am-9pm, Sa 10am-6pm, Su 11am-6pm. Amusement park open later.)*

FORT EDMONTON PARK. At the park's far end sits the fort proper: a 19th-century office building for Alberta's first capitalists, the fur traders of the Hudson Bay Company. Between the fort and the park entrance are three streets—1885, 1905, and 1920 St.—bedecked with period buildings from apothecaries to blacksmith shops, all decorated to match the streets' respective eras. A real steam train shuttles visitors from the main office to the far end of the park. *(Park: On Whitemud Dr. at Fox Dr. Buses #4, 30, 32, 104, 105, and 106 stop near the park. ☎496-8787; www.gov.edmon-*

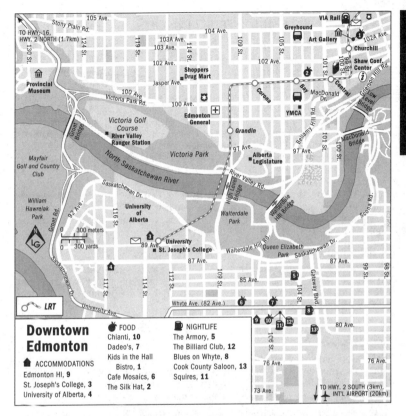

Downtown Edmonton

ACCOMMODATIONS
Edmonton HI, 9
St. Joseph's College, 3
University of Alberta, 4

FOOD
Chianti, 10
Dadeo's, 7
Kids in the Hall Bistro, 1
Cafe Mosaics, 6
The Silk Hat, 2

NIGHTLIFE
The Armory, 5
The Billiard Club, 12
Blues on Whyte, 8
Cook County Saloon, 13
Squires, 11

ton.ab.ca/fort. Open mid-May to late June M-F 10am-4pm, Sa-Su 10am-6pm; daily late June to early Sept. 10am-6pm; rest of Sept. wagon tours only from M-Sa 11am-3pm, Su 10am-6pm. $9, ages 65 and older and 13-17 $6.75, 2-12 $4.50, family $29.)

ODYSSIUM. The reincarnated Space and Science Centre still appeals to the curiosities of all ages with exhibits on the human body and the environment, including a bodily-function themed **Gallery of the Gross** and a hands-on **Crime Lab.** Housed in a building shaped like an alien spacecraft, the largest **planetarium dome** in Canada uses a booming 23,000 watts of audio during its laser shows. Canada's first **IMAX theater** makes the planetarium seem like a child's toy. (11211 142 St. ☎451-3344; www.odyssium.com. Open M-Th and Su 10am-5pm, F-Sa 10am-9pm. Day pass includes planetarium shows and exhibits: $10, students and ages 65 and older $8, 3-12 $7, family $39. General admission and IMAX show $16, students and ages 65 and older $13, 3-12 $11, family $60.)

RIVER VALLEY. From an outdoors perspective, the best part of Edmonton would have to be the longest stretch of urban parkland in Canada. Edmonton's **River Valley** boasts over 50km of easy to moderate paved multi-use trails and 69km of granular and chip trails for hiking and cycling. Any route down the river leads to the linked trail system; pick up a map at the Ranger Station. (12130 River Valley Rd. ☎496-2950. Open daily 7am-1am.)

FESTIVALS AND ENTERTAINMENT

Edmonton proclaims itself "Canada's Festival City" (www.festivalcity.ca); celebrations of one kind or another go on year-round. The **Jazz City International Music Festival** packs 10 days with club dates and free performances by top international and Canadian jazz musicians (☎432-7166; www.jazzcity.ca. June 25-July 3 2005. Concerts $15-90 each, most around $25.). Around the same time is a visual arts celebration called **The Works.** (☎426-2122; www.theworks.ab.ca. Most events free, some $5-10.) In the second weekend of August, the **Folk Music Festival,** considered one of the best in North America, takes over Gallagher Park. Buy tickets early; 4-day passes sell out months in advance. (☎429-1899; www.edmontonfolkfest.org. 4-day passes $110-190, evening passes $40; ages 12-17 $55, evening passes $25. Ages 65 and older and 11 and under free. Adult day passes cheaper if purchased several months in advance.) All the world's a stage in Old Strathcona for the **Fringe Theatre Festival,** when top alternative music and theater pour from parks, stages, and streets. This is the high point of Edmonton's festival schedule, and 500,000 travelers come to the city just to find the Fringe. (☎448-9000; www.fringetheatreadventures.ca. Mid-Aug. Tickets around $10 per play; 10-play pass $80.)

The **Edmonton Oilers,** the local NHL franchise, remain in an extended rebuilding period following their glorious Wayne Gretzky-led Stanley Cup runs of the 1980s. But this is Canada, and even a rebuilding hockey team gains a fierce following. The Oilers play at 11230 110th St. (☎451-8000; www.edmontonoilers.com. $35-147. Season runs Oct.-Apr.)

◪ NIGHTLIFE

Edmonton, like many big cities, has a variety of clubs; like other Alberta cities, many of them are cowboy-themed. The happening clubs are lined up along Whyte (82) Ave. in Old Strathcona. For club listings, see *See Magazine* (www.seemagazine.com), published every Thursday and available in free stacks at cafes.

▨ **Blues on Whyte,** 10329 Whyte Ave. (☎439-5058). Cheap beer ($2.50-3 pints) and live blues and R&B from top-notch performers every night make this gritty biker bar an excellent hangout. Sa afternoon jam 3-8:30pm. 8 oz. glasses of beer for just $1. $3 cover on F and Sa from 8pm. Open daily 10am-3am.

▨ **Cook County Saloon,** 8010 Gateway Blvd. (103 St.) (☎432-2665; www.cookcountysaloon.com). This honky-tonk was voted Canada's best country nightclub by the Canadian Country Music Association in 2001 and eight times before that. W and Th feature $2 highballs until 9pm. Live concerts twice a month. Open W-Sa 8pm-2am.

Squires, 10505 Whyte Ave. (☎439-8594), lower level by Chianti. Popular with the college crowd. Specials include M $3 shots, W $0.17 ribs, Th $2.25 beer and highballs, and F $4 Molson Coldshots. Open daily 5pm-3am.

The Armory, 10310 85 Ave. (☎432-7300). This well-known dance club inside the old Armory building shows Edmonton's younger crowd how to party. Th $0.50 highballs until 10pm, F "Summer of Love" 60s party, Sa top 40/hip-hop. M is ladies' night, with male strippers. $5 cover. Open M and Th-Sa 9pm-3am.

The Billiard Club, 10505 82 Ave. (☎432-0335; www.thebilliardclub.com), 2nd fl., above Chianti. A busy bar packed with a diverse crowd of young up-and-comers and some older already-theres. Perfectly level and smooth pool tables ($10 per hour) and outdoor patio. Open M-Tu 11:30am-1am, W-Th 11:30am-2am, F-Su noon-3am.

ALBERTA

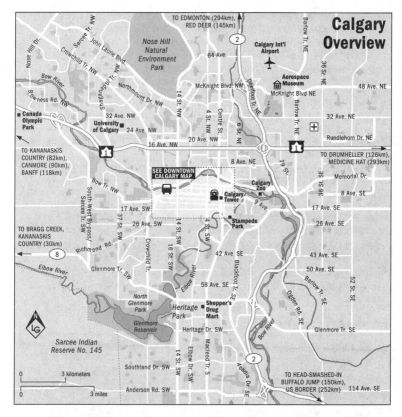

CALGARY ☎ 403

Mounties founded Calgary in the 1870s to control Canada's flow of illegal whiskey, but oil made the city what it is today. Petroleum fuels Calgary's economy and explains why the city has the greatest number of corporate headquarters in Canada outside of Toronto. As the host of the 1988 Winter Olympics, Calgary's dot on the map grew larger; already Alberta's largest city, this thriving young metropolis is growing rapidly. No matter how big its britches, however, the city still pays annual tribute to its original tourist attraction, the "Greatest Outdoor Show on Earth," the Calgary Stampede. For 10 days in July, the entire city dons cowboy duds for world-class bareback riding, country music, and Western art.

◪ TRANSPORTATION

Calgary is 126km east of Banff along the Trans-Canada Hwy. (Hwy. 1). It is divided into quadrants (NE, NW, SE, SW): **Centre Street** is the east-west divider; the **Bow River** splits the north and south. Avenues run east-west, streets north-south. Cross streets can be derived from the first digit of the street address: 206 7th Ave. SW, for example, would be found on 7th Ave. at 2nd St.

Flights: The **Calgary International Airport** (☎735-1200; www.calgaryairport.com) is 17km northeast of the city center. Take Bus #57. Taxi fare from downtown runs $30-40, but an Airport Shuttle (☎509-4799; www.airportshuttleexpress.com) runs from downtown for $14. Call or reserve at least 90min. ahead. Airport code: YYC.

Buses: Greyhound, 877 Greyhound Way SW (☎260-0877 or 800-661-8747). To: **Banff** (1¾hr., 4 per day, $24); **Drumheller** (2hr., 2 per day, $26); **Edmonton** (3½-5hr., 10-11 per day, $46). Free shuttle from Calgary Transit C-Train at 7th Ave. and 10th St. to bus depot (every hr. near the half-hour. 6:30am-7:30pm). **Red Arrow,** 205 9th Ave. SE (☎531-0350; www.redarrow.pwt.ca), goes to **Edmonton** (3hr., 4-7 per day, $53) and points north. 10% HI discount; student and senior rates. **Brewster Tours** (☎221-8242; www.brewster.ca) runs from the airport to **Banff** (2hr., 2 per day, $42) and **Jasper** (8hr., 1 per day, $80). 10% HI discount.

Public Transportation: Calgary Transit, 224 7th Ave. SW (☎262-1000; www.calgarytransit.com). Open M-F 6am-9pm, Sa-Su 8am-6pm. C-Trains free in downtown zone on 7th Ave. S from 3rd St. E to 10th St. W. Buses and C-Trains outside downtown $2, ages 6-14 $1.25, under 6 free. Day pass $5.60, ages 6-14 $3.60. Book of 10 tickets $18, ages 6-14 $10. Runs M-F 6am-12:30am, Sa-Su 6am-11:30pm. Tickets at stops, the transit office, or Safeway stores.

Taxis: Checker Cab (☎299-9999). **Yellow Cab** (☎ 974-1111). Base rate $2.50, $.20 per each 162m after the first, $.20 per 30 seconds. Both are 24hr.

Car Rental: Rent-A-Wreck, 113 42nd Ave. SW (☎287-1444). From $25 per day. Unlimited travel in Alberta. Must be 18 or older with major credit card. Open daily 8am-6pm.

🛈 PRACTICAL INFORMATION

Tourist Office: 220 8th Ave. SW (☎800-661-1678; www.tourismcalgary.com). Open daily June-Sept. 9am-5pm; Sept.-June 9:30am-5:30pm.

Equipment Rental: Outdoor Program Centre, 2500 University Dr. (☎220-5038; www.ucalgary.ca/opc), at U of Calgary, rents tents (from $11 per day), canoes ($23 per day), kayaks ($30 per day), and downhill skis ($21 per day). Open daily 8am-8pm. **Mountain Equipment Co-op,** 830 10th Ave. SW (☎269-2420; www.mec.ca) rents watercraft ($20-50 per day, including all safety equipment and paddles), camping gear ($8-20 per day), rock- and ice-climbing gear ($4-22 per day), and snow sports equipment ($8-35 per day). Both companies have weekend specials. Be prepared to shell out a deposit for nearly the replacement cost.

Laundromat: Hunterhorn Coin Laundry, 6518 4th St. NE (☎630-6575). Wash $2, dry $.25 per 5min. Open daily 7am-10pm.

Gay and Lesbian Services: Gay and Lesbian Community Services Association. (Events and clubs ☎234-9752, counseling 234-8973; www.glcsa.org.)

Weather: ☎299-7878.

Police: 133 6th Ave. SE (☎266-1234).

Pharmacy: Shopper's Drug Mart, 6455 Macleod Trail S (☎253-2424). Open 24hr.

Hospital: Peter Lougheed Centre, 3500 26th Ave. NE (☎943-4555).

Internet Access: At the **library,** 616 Macleod Trail SE (☎260-2600; www.calgarypubliclibrary.com). $2 per hr. Open M-Th 10am-9pm, F-Sa 10am-5pm; mid-Sept. to mid-May also Su 1:30-5pm.

Post Office: 207 9th Ave. SW (☎974-2078). Open M-F 8am-5:45pm. **Postal Code:** T2P 2G8.

ALBERTA

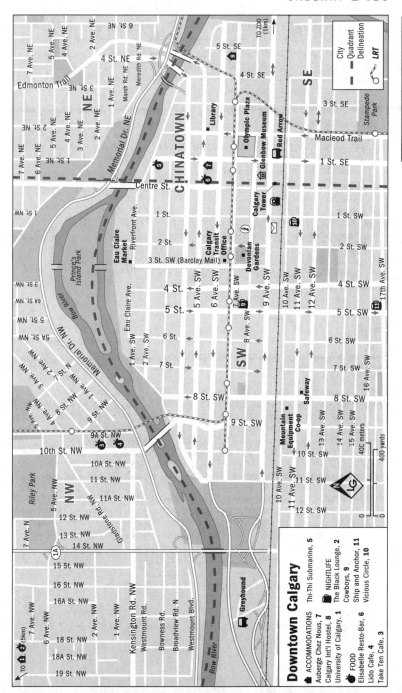

Downtown Calgary

ACCOMMODATIONS
Auberge Chez Nous, 7
Calgary Int'l Hostel, 8
University of Calgary, 1

FOOD
Elisabelle Resto-Bar, 6
Lido Cafe, 4
Take Ten Cafe, 3

Thi-Thi Submarine, 5

NIGHTLIFE
The Black Lounge, 2
Cowboys, 9
Ship and Anchor, 11
Vicious Circle, 10

City
Quadrant Delineation
LRT

▗ ACCOMMODATIONS

Lodging prices skyrocket when tourists pack into the city's hotels for the July Stampede; call well in advance. Calgary's downtown lacks cheap places to sleep; finding a hotel bed for under $100 is virtually impossible. As a result, hostels and alternative accommodations are undoubtedly the way to go.

Calgary Intern+ational Hostel (HI), 520 7th Ave. SE (☎269-8239), near downtown. Walk east along 7th Ave. from the 3rd St. SE C-Train station; the hostel is on the left, just past 4th St. SE. This urban hostel has some nice accessories; the clean kitchen, lounge areas, laundry, and backyard with BBQ are pluses. Information desk, occasional guest activities. Wheelchair-accessible. 120 beds. May to mid-Oct. $29, nonmembers $34; mid-Oct. to Apr. $20/$24. Private rooms $75/$83. ❷

Auberge Chez Nous, 149 5th Ave SE (☎866-651-3387; www.auberge-cheznous.com) This distinctly French-Canadian hostel has large dorm rooms divided into cubicles, offering more privacy than a standard dorm. Reception open 8am-3am. Kitchen, TV room, Internet access ($3 per hour) and laundry ($2) Dorms $25. ❷

University of Calgary, the ex-Olympic Village in the NW quadrant, far from downtown if you're walking. Accessible by bus #9 or a 12min. walk from the University C-Train stop. Offers both standard dorm rooms and rooms with kitchen and bath. Popular with conventioneers and often booked solid. Coordinated through **Cascade Hall,** 3456 24th Ave. NW (☎220-3203). Rooms available May-Aug. only. Singles $36-56. Rates subject to change based on availability; call ahead. ❸

▗ FOOD

Most of the affordable restaurants with good food in Calgary are not found downtown. The cheapest and most satisfying eats are located in ▓Chinatown, concentrated in a four-block area at the north end of Centre St. S and 1st St. SE. Six dollars gets you a feast in any Vietnamese noodle house or Hong Kong-style cafe, many of which don't close until the wee hours. Some budget chow-houses also hide out among the trendy, costlier spots in the popular **Kensington District,** along Kensington Rd. and 10th and 11th St. NW; still others can be found on **17th Avenue** between 2nd St. SW and 14th St. SW. Downtown **Safeway,** 813 11th Ave. SW, sells groceries. (☎800-723-3929. Open daily 8am-11pm.) Restaurants, produce, international snack bars, and flowers grace the plaza-style, upscale **Eau Claire Market** (☎264-6450; www.eauclairemarket.com), at the north end of 3rd St. SW.

▓ **Thi-Thi Submarine,** 209 1st St. SE (☎265-5452). Some people have closets larger than Thi-Thi, but this place manages to pack in 2 plastic seats, a bank of toaster ovens, a line of office workers on lunch break, and the finest Vietnamese submarines in Calgary. Most meaty subs are $5-7; the veggie sub is an unreal $2.25. Open M-F 10am-7pm, Sa-Su 10:30am-5pm. ❶

Elisabelle Resto-Bar, 137 5th Ave. SE (☎232-5499). Elisabelle serves breakfast ($4-6) until 11am and an American bistro-style menu afterwards (entrees $6-8). Nightly drink specials include $3.50 pints and highballs. Open M-F 8am-10pm, Sa 9am-10pm. Has discount deal with Auberge Chez Nous. ❷

Lido Cafe, 144 10th St. NW. (☎283-0131). Lido feels like a bit of an anomaly—a truck-stop-style restaurant in the trendy Kensington area. Breakfast special $3.88, burgers $5. Open M-Sa 8am-9pm, Su 9am-8pm. ❷

Take Ten Cafe, 304 10th St. NW (☎270-7010). Take Ten became a local favorite by offering dirt-cheap, high-quality food. All burgers are under $5.75, and the menu also sports some sizzling Chinese food (under $8) and all-day breakfast ($5). Open M-F 9am-4pm, Sa 8:30am-5pm, Su 8:30-3pm. ❷

🔍 SIGHTS

OLYMPIC LEFTOVERS. For two glorious weeks in 1988, the world's eyes were on Calgary for the Winter Olympics. Over fifteen years later, the world has moved on, but the city still has some exciting facilities whose interest to visitors has long outlasted the two weeks of Olympic stardom. The **Canada Olympic Park**'s looming ski jumps and twisted bobsled and luge tracks are still used as training grounds year-round—ski-jumpers can be seen flying over wet Teflon hills in July. The **Olympic Hall of Fame,** also at Olympic Park, honors Olympic achievements with displays and films. In summer, the park opens its hills, terrain park, and lift to **mountain bikers.** *(A 10min. drive northwest of downtown on Hwy. 1, or the 408 bus runs every 45 min. from the Brentwood C-Train. ☎ 247-5452; www.canadaolympicpark.ca. Open in summer daily 8am-9pm; in winter M-F 9am-9pm, Sa-Su 9am-5pm. $10 ticket includes chairlift and entrance to ski-jump buildings, Hall of Fame, and icehouse. Tour $15; families $45. Open for mountain biking daily May-Oct. 9am-9pm. Roadway pass $9 for cyclists. Front-suspension bike rental $15 per hr., $35 per day.)* The miniature mountain (113m vertical) also opens up for **downhill skiing** in winter. *(Snow report ☎ 289-3700. $30.)* The **Olympic Oval,** an enormous indoor speed-skating track on the University of Calgary campus, remains a major international training facility. Speedskaters work out in the early morning and late afternoon; sit in the bleachers and observe the action for free. *(☎ 220-7890; www.oval.ucalgary.ca. Open Aug.-Mar. Public skating hours vary, so call ahead. $4.75, children and seniors $2.75, family $11, under 6 free. Skate rental under $5.)*

PARKS AND MUSEUMS. Footbridges stretch from either side of the Bow River to **Prince's Island Park,** a natural refuge only blocks from the city center. In July and August, Mount Royal College performs **Shakespeare in the Park.** *(☎ 240-6908; www.mtroyal.ab.ca/shakespeare-in-the-park. Various matinees and evening shows; call for shows and times.)* Calgary's other island park, **Saint George's Island,** is accessible by the river walkway to the east or by car. It houses the large **Calgary Zoo,** which includes a botanical garden and children's zoo. For those who missed the wildlife in Banff and Jasper, the **Canadian Wilds** exhibit has recreated Canadian animal habitats from the prairie to the Yukon. For those who missed the Cretaceous Period, life-sized plastic dinosaurs are also on exhibit. *(Parking is off Memorial Dr. on the north side of the river, and there is a C-train station 20 meters from the front gate. ☎ 232-9300; www.calgaryzoo.ab.ca. Open daily 9am-5pm. $15, seniors $13, ages 13-17 $9, 3-12 $7.50.)*

STAMPEDE. The more cosmopolitan Calgary becomes, the more tenaciously it clings to its frontier roots. The **Stampede** draws over 1.1 million cowboys and tourists each summer in the first couple weeks of July, when the grounds are packed for world-class steer wrestling, bareback and bull-riding, and pig and chuck wagon races. The cowboy mardi gras features livestock shows, a huge midway and casino, a roller coaster, and numerous live country, folk, and rock music shows. The festival spills into the streets from first thing in the morning (free pancake breakfasts all around) through the night. Depending on your attitude, the Stampede will either be an impressive spectacle rekindling the Western spirit or an overpriced, slick carnival where humans assert their hegemony over lesser animals. *(Stampede Park is just southeast of downtown, bordering the east side of Macleod Trail between 14th Ave. SE and the Elbow River. The C-Train features a Stampede stop. Tickets ☎ 269-*

ALBERTA

ALBERTA

9822 or 800-661-1767; www.calgarystampede.com. Midway admission $11, ages 65 and older and 7-12 $6, under 7 free. Rodeo and evening shows $23-67, cheaper rush tickets go on sale at the grandstand 1½hr. before showtime, and Wal-Mart offers discounted tickets.)

 NIGHTLIFE

Calgary has some of the best nightlife in the province; the city overflows with cheap beer and crawls with bars and nightclubs that cater to waves of visitors and young locals. Live music in Calgary ranges from national acts and world-famous DJs to some guy with a guitar. The best areas in town for finding pubs, clubs, and live music are the downtown **Stephen Avenue Walk** (8th Ave. SW), **17th Avenue SW,** and **1st and 4th Street SW.** Last call in Alberta is at 2am and is strictly observed. For listings of bands and theme nights, check *The Calgary Straight* or *Ffwd* (www.ffwdweekly.com). Both come out on Thursday and are free. *Outlooks* (www.outlooks.ca), the city's gay and lesbian events publication, offers information on different bars. All are available at local clubs and cafes.

■ **Cowboys,** 826 5th St. SW. (☎265-0699; www.cowboysniteclub.com) is Calgary's premiere country-western bar. The drink specials are unreal, including the famous Th $0.25 drafts. $7 cover. Open W-Sa 7:30pm-2:30am.

■ **Ship & Anchor,** 534 17th Ave. SW (☎245-3333; www.shipandanchor.com) A popular soccer-oriented pub (during the World Cup, they open at 5am to catch the live action) that has more beers on tap (29) than any other bar in the city. Pints run $4.25-$5.25. Live music W night and an open jam-session on Sa afternoons from 2-6pm. The pub grub is satisfying and cheap (burgers $4-6). Open 11am-3am daily.

Vicious Circle, 1011 1st St. SW (☎269-3951). A very relaxing bar, "The Vish" offers a solid menu of health-conscious bar fare, colored mood lights, and a disco ball, plus pool tables, couches, a constantly changing gallery of eclectic local art, and TV. All kinds of coffee, a full bar, and 140 martinis ($7.60). Summer patio. Happy hour 4-7pm daily and all night Su, live music W. Open M-Th 11:30am-1am, F-Su noon-2am.

The Black Lounge, 2500 University Dr. (☎210-9441; www.su.ucalgary.ca/61.0.html), on the 2nd floor of McEwan Student Center. Operated by the University of Calgary Student Union, the lounge has a large outdoor patio and is a favorite of people living on campus. Pints $3.50. Open M-Sa 11am-11pm.

■ **DAYTRIP: ALBERTA BADLANDS**

Once the fertile shallows of a huge ocean, the Badlands are now one of the richest dinosaur fossil sites in the world. After the sea dried up, wind, water, and ice molded twisting canyons into sandstone and shale bedrock, creating the desolate splendor of the Alberta Badlands. The **Royal Tyrrell Museum of Paleontology** (TEER-ull), with its remarkable array of dinosaur exhibits and hands-on paleontological opportunities, is the region's main attraction. **Greyhound** runs from Calgary to Drumheller (1¾hr., 2 per day, $26), 6km southeast of the museum.

ROYAL TYRRELL MUSEUM OF PALEONTOLOGY. The world's largest display of dinosaur specimens is a forceful reminder that *Homo sapiens* missed out on the first 2½ billion years of life on earth. From the Precambrian to the present, the museum celebrates evolution's grand parade with quality displays, videos, computer activities, and a huge gallery of towering skeletons, including one of only 12 reconstructed Tyrannosaurus rex skeletons in existence. The Cambrian life preserved in the Burgess Shale is recreated at twelve times its original size, and the Cretaceous Garden is a living re-creation of the Jurassic climate. The Predator Room features ferocious dinos and creepy background lighting. *(6km northwest of*

Drumheller, which itself lies 138km northeast of Calgary. Get there by driving east on Hwy. 1 from Calgary, then northeast on Hwy. 9. ☎ 403-823-7707 or 888-440-4240; www.tyrrellmuseum.com. Open daily Victoria Day-Labor Day 9am-9pm; Labor Day-2nd M in Oct. 10am-5pm; 2nd M in Oct.- Victoria Day Tu-Su 10am-5pm. $10, seniors $8, ages 7-17 $6, under 7 free, families $30.)

DIGS. The museum's hugely popular twelve-person **Day Digs** include instruction in paleontology and excavation techniques and a chance to dig in a fossil quarry. The fee includes lunch and transportation; participants must also agree that any finds go to the museum. *(Daily July-Aug.; June Sa-Su. Digs depart 8:30am, return at 4pm. $90, ages 10-15 $60. Reservations required; call the museum.)*

DINOSAUR PROVINCIAL PARK AND BADLANDS BUS TOUR. The Badlands, a UNESCO World Heritage Site, are the source of many finds on display at the Tyrrell Museum; more fossil species—over 300, including 35 species of dinosaurs— were discovered here than anywhere else in the world. The museum's **Field Station,** 48km east of the town of **Brooks** in **Dinosaur Provincial Park,** contains a small museum, but the main attraction is the **Badlands Bus Tour.** The bus chauffeurs visitors into a restricted hotspot of dinosaur finds. Many fossils still lie within the eroding rock. The park's **campground ❶** is shaded from summer heat, and grassy plots cushion most sites. Although it stays open year-round, the campground only has electricity and running water in summer. *(To reach the Field Station from Drumheller, follow Hwy. 56 south for 65km, then take Hwy. 1 about 70km to Brooks. Once in Brooks, go north along Hwy. 873 and east along Hwy. 544. Field Station ☎ 378-4342. Field Station Visitor Centre exhibits $3, seniors $2.50, ages 7-17 $2. Open daily mid-May through Aug. 8:30am-9pm; Sept. to mid-Oct. 9am-5pm; mid-Oct. to mid-May M-F 9am-4pm. Tours $6.50, ages 7-17 $4.25. Reservations ☎ 378-3700. Sites $15, with electricity $18.)*

DINOSAUR-FREE ACTIVITIES. The Badlands also offer a variety of other recreational activities. The staff of **Midland Provincial Park** (☎ 823-1749), located halfway between the Tyrrell Museum and Drumheller, leads free 75min. natural history walking tours, departing from the museum once or twice per day. To see **hoodoos**—towering rock formations capped by boulders—in the making, go 15km east on Hwy. 10 from Drumheller. These limestone columns are relatively young: the stone caps on their tops have not yet eroded away. In **Horseshoe Canyon,** about 20km west of Drumheller on Hwy. 9, **hiking** and **biking trails** wind below the prairie through red rock layers carved into bizarre, rounded formations. Trails located in Dinosaur Provincial Park take hikers over and through the eroded landscape, including the **Coulee Viewpoint Trail** (1km, 45min., moderate) and the **Cottonwoods Flats Trail** (1.4km, 2hr., easy), which weaves around Deer River. Carry plenty of water, and be sure not to hop fences onto private property. Groceries are in Drumheller at **IGA Market,** at N Railroad Ave. and Centre St. (☎ 823-3995. Open 24hr.)

CANADIAN ROCKIES

The national parks of the Canadian Rockies comprise one of Canada's top tourist draws, and with excellent reason. Every year, some five million visitors make it within sight of the parks' majestic peaks, stunning glacial lakes, and many varieties of wildlife. Thankfully, much of this traffic is confined to highway-side gawkers, leaving infinite backcountry trails and mountains where one can escape the flocks of tourists. Of the two most popular parks—Banff and Jasper—the latter feels a little farther removed from the droves of tourists. The hostels that line both parks are among the country's best, and are usually booked up as a result. It's also

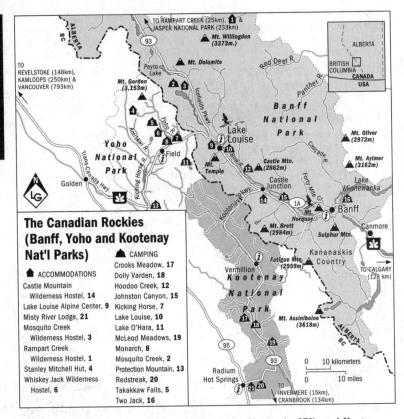

The Canadian Rockies (Banff, Yoho and Kootenay Nat'l Parks)

🏠 **ACCOMMODATIONS**

Castle Mountain
  Wilderness Hostel, **14**
Lake Louise Alpine Center, **9**
Misty River Lodge, **21**
Mosquito Creek
  Wilderness Hostel, **3**
Rampart Creek
  Wilderness Hostel, **1**
Stanley Mitchell Hut, **4**
Whiskey Jack Wilderness
  Hostel, **6**

▲ **CAMPING**

Crooks Meadow, **17**
Dolly Varden, **18**
Hoodoo Creek, **12**
Johnston Canyon, **15**
Kicking Horse, **7**
Lake Louise, **10**
Lake O'Hara, **11**
McLeod Meadows, **19**
Monarch, **8**
Mosquito Creek, **2**
Protection Mountain, **13**
Redstreak, **20**
Takakkaw Falls, **5**
Two Jack, **16**

well worth diving into the quieter Yoho (p. 380), Glacier (p. 378), and Kootenay National Parks (p. 382), as well as Kananaskis Country (p. 429), the locals' free playground that separates Calgary from the Rockies.

▊ TRANSPORTATION

BY CAR, BUS, AND TRAIN. Alberta's extensive highway system makes travel between major destinations easy and provides the traveler with beautiful roadside scenery. The north-south **Icefields Parkway (Highway 93)** runs between **Banff** and **Jasper.** The east-west **Yellowhead Highway (Highway 16)** connects **Edmonton** with **Jasper,** and continues across British Columbia. The **Trans-Canada Highway (Highway 1)** completes the loop, linking **Calgary** with **Banff.** The easiest way to get here is to drive yourself or explore the bus options. **Buses** (Greyhound, Brewster, and Red Arrow) travel all of these routes; VIA Rail **trains** run from **Edmonton** to **Jasper.**

BY BIKE. Icefields Parkway (p. 447) is a popular trail, although the trip is best suited to experienced cyclists. Inquire at the rental shops about returning bikes after one-way trips. The 291km separating Jasper and Banff swells with hundreds of glaciers, dramatic mountain peaks, and fantastic hostels located on and off the highway.

BY TOUR. Without a car, guided bus rides may be the easiest way to see some of the park's main attractions, such as the **Great Divide,** the **Athabasca Glacier,** and the spiral railroad tunnel. **Brewster Tours** offer 9½hr. guided trips on the Icefields Parkway. (☎762-6767; www.brewster.ca. Mid-May to Oct. at 8:10am. $98, child $49. 10% HI discount. A visit to the Columbia Icefields is $27 extra, children $14.) **Bigfoot Tours** runs two-day, 11-passenger van trips between Banff and Jasper with an overnight stop at the **Mount Edith Cavell Hostel.** (☎888-244-6673; www.bigfoottours.com. $175, not including food or lodging. See p. 450.) Jump on/jump off trips connecting Vancouver, Whistler, Kamloops, Jasper, Banff, and Revelstoke in a minimum ten-day trip, make three departures a week May-Oct.; trips east stop at the **Squilax General Store Hostel** and trips west stop at the **Old Courthouse Hostel** in Kamloops ($429 with ISIC or HI membership, $449 without).

KANANASKIS COUNTRY   ☎403

To the southeast of Banff, along Hwy. 40, lie eleven provincial parks that together make up the 4000 sq. km Kananaskis Country. Unmarketed as a vacation destination, "K-Country" is bypassed by almost all tourists in favor of the more well-known Banff and Jasper National Parks, leaving Kananaskis just as spectacular, far more isolated, and without any of the entrance fees. Another side benefit of tourist neglect is the relative deregulation of the park—if you want to hunt, fish, or snowmobile in the Rockies, this is the place to do it. Although K-Country is ideal for finding lonely campsites and serene mountains, isolation produces its own set of hassles: the closest thing to a townsite in Kananaskis is three hotels and a store in Kananaskis Village, there is no bus or train service (the nearest bus stop is Canmore, over 20km to the northeast), the only nightlife you will see takes the form of raccoons and porcupines, and dining out will mean picnicking for the budget traveller. Those with their own vehicles seeking a peaceful, quiet Canadian Rockies experience will find Kananaskis Country unbeatable.

ORIENTATION AND PRACTICAL INFORMATION. The main **visitors center** is located inside the **Bow Valley Provincial Park** at Barrier Lake, 6km south from Hwy. 1 on Hwy. 40. The center offers a very helpful free guide to the parks' facilities and sells trail maps ($1.25), backcountry permits ($6 per party, plus $3 per person per night), and cross-country ski permits. Backcountry permits can also be purchased over the phone at ☎678-3136. (☎673-3985. Open daily 9am-5pm.) There is another major visitors center at **Peter Lougheed Provincial Park,** on Kananaskis Lakes Trail Rd., 35km south of Hwy. 1 on Hwy. 40. (☎591-6322. Open daily 9am-5pm.) The nearest **hospital** is in Canmore and can be reached at ☎678-5536. Environment Canada operates a **weather service** at ☎762-2088. The **post office** is located inside Kananaskis Village, near the Natiska Ski Resort, 25km south of Hwy. 1, and also sells trail maps for all the parks. (☎800-267-1177. Open daily 9am-5:30pm.)

ACCOMMODATIONS AND CAMPING. Accommodations in Kananaskis Country are provided almost exclusively by the thirty-eight maintained campgrounds within the parks. Sites range from $17-22 per night (the free guide to Kananaskis Country available at the visitors center has an index of campsites). Showers and electrical hookups can be found at **Bow Valley ❷** and **Willow Rock ❷,** both within Bow Valley Provincial Park, and free showers are available at **Elkwood ❷** and **Boulton Creek ❷** inside Peter Lougheed Provincial Park. **McLean Creek ❷** at Elbow River Valley Park has electrical hookups and showers. (Reservations for most sites can be made at ☎591-7226 or www.kananaskiscamping.com.) For a warm bed, **Ribbon Creek (HI) ❷** just outside the village, is the best option. The hostel has a huge kitchen, laundry (wash $2, dry $2), a beautiful common room with a fireplace, a firepit, volleyball

THE LOCAL STORY

A HEAD ABOVE THE REST

5700 years ago, plains-dwelling Blackfoot began using gravity to kill whole herds of bison. Disguised as calves, a few men would lure a herd of the short-sighted animals into lanes between stone cairns. Hunters at the rear, dressed as wolves, then pressed forward, whipping the bison into a frenzy. When the front-running bison reached the cliff and tried to stop, the momentum of the stampede pushed their one-ton bodies over the edge. Each year, the communities obtained food, tools, and clothing from the bison's remains.

The particular cliffs of Head-Smashed-In Buffalo Jump were an active hunting site for nearly 8000 years but only earned their modern name at one of the site's final jumps 150 years ago when a thrill-seeking warrior watching the massacre from under the cliff ledge was crushed. Over a century later, the United Nations named Head-Smashed-In a UNESCO World Heritage Site; ten-meter-deep beds of bone and tools make this one of the best-preserved buffalo jumps in North America. (☎553-2731; www.head-smashed-in.com. Open daily May 15 to Labour Day 9am-6pm; low-season 10am-5pm. $6.50, seniors $5.50, ages 7-17 $3; family $15) Head-Smashed-In Buffalo Jump lies 175km south of Calgary and 18km northwest of Fort Macleod, on Secondary Rd. 785 off Hwy. 2.

court, and $2.75 admission to the hot tub at Mt. Kidd RV Park. (☎591-7333. Reception 8-10am and 5-10pm. M-Th, Su dorms $21, non-members $25; F-Sa $24/$28. Private rooms $56-72.)

◐ **FOOD.** Food is best purchased in Canmore before entering the park, but a limited selection of groceries is available at the **Boulton Creek Trading Post** inside Peter Lougheed. (Open daily 9am-8pm.) Another store is **Ribbon Creek Groceries** in Kananaskis Village (☎591-7551. Open Jun.-Sept. 9am-8pm and 10:30pm-2:30am; Oct.-May 9am-6pm.) The three hotels that make up Kananaskis Village all have **restaurants ❹**, but a meal will easily run in excess of $20 per person.

◪ **HIKING.** Kananaskis Country offers an enormous array of outdoor activities. Over 450km of hiking, biking, equestrian, cross-country, and snowmobiling trails provide endless opportunity for backcountry adventure, although not all activities are allowed on all trails or in all parks. The visitors center provides a complete directory. Gillean Dafferns's *Kananaskis Country Trail Guide* ($17), available at any area information center, is a definitive, detailed source of information on longer trails, and rangers at either center will be more than happy to suggest day hikes. The most popular areas for hiking are in the western areas of K-Country. The **Ribbon Creek** trailhead near Kananaskis Village provides access to many spectacular routes, such as the trails leading from Peter Lougheed's **Interlakes** trailhead, including the **Upper Lakes** with views of the Interlakes Valley (16km one-way, moderate). **Three Isle Lakes,** which passes over the Continental Divide through South Kananaskis Pass (13km one-way, moderate) and the **1982 Canadian Mount Everest Expedition,** an interpretive trail capturing the essence of climbing Mt. Everest through views of the Upper and Lower Kananaskis Lakes (2km one-way, easy), are also popular trails.

◪ **SKIING.** Downhill skiing is available at **Nakiska Ski Resort** (☎800-258-7669; www.skinakiska.com), 25km south of Hwy. 1 near Kananaskis Village. The mountain was the site of all downhill competitions in the 1988 Calgary Winter Olympic Games, and while its 325 acres and 775m vertical drop are not nearly as large as Sunshine Village or Lake Louise, it is steep and cheap—lift tickets are only $45, and the above-treeline skiing is as challenging as anything further north.

◪ **OTHER ACTIVITIES.** Many **whitewater rafting** companies compete for business on the Bow and Kananaskis Rivers. **Canmore Rafting Centre** (☎678-4919; www.canmoreraftingcentre.com) offers half-day trips from $59. **Llamas** are available for rental at **XTC Llama Adventures** (☎615-2629; www.xtcllamaadventures.com). Llamas will carry your gear for backcountry camping and fishing (half-day for four people $375, including lunch and transportation from Calgary), or will serve as a caddy on golf courses throughout the region (18 holes $100). **Boundary Ranch** (☎591-7171; www.boundaryranch.com) provides guided horseback tours, including backcountry adventures. Cliffs throughout the park offer excellent **climbing** opportunities. **Barrier Bluffs** has dozens of bolted routes up the wall. The foothills of the **Sibbald Area** in the northeast of K-Country (30min. off Hwy. 1) offer wide expanses of terrain to horseback riders, hikers, and cyclists.

WATERTON-GLACIER INTERNATIONAL PEACE PARK

Waterton-Glacier transcends international boundaries to encompass one of the most strikingly beautiful portions of the Rockies. Both established in 1932, the two parks are connected by a natural unity of landscape and wildlife. The massive Rocky Mountain peaks span both parks, sheltering endangered bears, bighorn sheep, moose, mountain goats, and gray wolves. Perched high in the Northern Rockies, Waterton-Glacier is sometimes called the "Crown of the Continent," and the high alpine lakes and glaciers shine like jewels.offer wide expanses of terrain to horseback riders, hikers, and cyclists.

AT A GLANCE

AREA OF WATERTON: 129,730 acres

AREA OF GLACIER: 1,013,572 acres

CLIMATE: Variable, prone to sudden rain and wind. Mild winters and summers.

FEATURES: Waterton Lake, Lake McDonald, St. Mary Lake

HIGHLIGHTS: Driving the Going-to-the-Sun Road, hiking the Avalanche Lake Trail and the Crypt Lake Trail.

GATEWAYS: Waterton (p. 432), Polebridge (p. 437), St. Mary (p. 436), East Glacier, (p. 436), West Glacier (p. 436), Many Glacier, Apgar, Two Medicine.

WATERTON FEES: $5 per day, ages 65 and older $4.25, 6-12 $2.50, groups of up to seven people $13.

GLACIER FEES: $20 per week per car, $10 for pedestrians and cyclists (including motorcycles); yearly passes $25.

PRACTICAL INFORMATION

Technically one park, Waterton-Glacier is actually two distinct areas, with two distinct entrance fees: the small **Waterton Lakes National Park** in Alberta, and the enormous **Glacier National Park** in Montana. There are several **border crossings** nearby: **Piegan/Carway,** at US 89 (open daily 7am-11pm); **Roosville,** on US 93 (open 24hr.); and **Chief Mountain,** at Rte. 17 (open daily mid- to late May and Sept. 9am-6pm; June-Aug. 7am-10pm). The fastest way to Waterton is to head north along the east side of Glacier, entering Canada through Chief Mountain. Since snow can be unpredictable, the parks are usually in full operation only from late May to early September—check conditions in advance. The *Waterton-Glacier Guide,* provided at all park entrances, has dates and times of trail, campground, and border crossing openings. To find out which park areas, hotels, and campsites will be open when you visit, contact the **Park Headquarters,** Waterton Lakes National Park, Waterton Park, AB T0K 2M0 (☎403-859-2224), or **Glacier National Park,** West Glacier, MT 59936 (☎406-888-7800). Mace and firewood are not allowed into Canada.

WATERTON LAKES NATIONAL PARK ☎ 403

Unlike its neighbors Banff and Jasper to the north, Waterton Lakes never earned a rail link, leaving it unexposed to the early tourists who explored the northern Rockies. Today this legacy holds true. While Banff and Jasper struggle to stand tall under the countless feet that yearly roll them flat, Waterton Lakes National Park is relatively quiet. Here the Rockies rise straight up out of the prairies, creating a stark contrast of color and altitude between the grainy flatness and the granite continental divide. Rich in history, the centerpiece of Waterton townsite is the lofty and aloof chalet-style Prince of Wales Hotel, constructed in 1927. Dominating the town's vistas and posters, the Hotel leads the area's increasing interest in tourism. The town itself is quite expensive, and cheaper alternatives are readily found across the border in East, West, and Many Glacier.

EMERGENCY INFORMATION
Waterton Lakes National Park lacks ☎911 service. In a park emergency, call the warden at ☎589-2636. For town emergencies, call the police at ☎859-2244. For medical emergencies, the nearest hospitals are in Cardston (☎653-4411) or Pincher Creek (☎627-3333).

▐ TRANSPORTATION

Getting to Waterton Lakes requires two bus trips. The closest that **Greyhound** (☎800-661-8747) gets is Pincher Creek. From there, **White Mountain Adventures** (☎678-4099 or 800-408-0005; www.whitemountainadventures.com) runs a $15 shuttle to Waterton townsite. White Mountain also runs once a day each way between Banff and Waterton (8hr., $65). **Waterton Visitor Services** (☎859-2378; www.watertonvisitorservices.com), located on Mt. View Rd. in Tamarack Village Square, offers a shuttle to and from the Chief Mountain Customs on the US border ($20 per person, minimum $50 charge, by reservation only). Shuttles also run to Cameron Lake ($7.50, June-Oct.) at 9am daily and by reservation to Rowe Trailhead ($20 per person, minimum $50). **Waterton Inter-Nation Shoreline Cruise Company** (☎859-2362) runs a boat tour from the Waterton marina to Goat Haunt, Montana. The tour is $23 round-trip or $13 one-way. The same company will shuttle hikers to the Crypt Lake trail head for $13 round-trip.

▮▮ ORIENTATION AND PRACTICAL INFORMATION

Waterton Lakes occupies the extreme southwestern corner of Alberta and forms the northern portion of the Waterton-Glacier International Peace Park. **Highway 5** enters the park from the east and connects it at Cardston with Hwy. 2 heading north to Calgary two and a half hours away. **Highway 6** heads north out of the park to Pincher Creek 50 km away, and south to US Customs at Chief Mountain, Montana. Hwy. 5 extends all the way into **Waterton townsite** on the shores of Upper Waterton Lake. Admission to the park is $5 per day, ages 65 and older $4.25, 6-12 $2.50, groups of up to seven people $13.

Tourist Office: The **Waterton Lakes Visitor Centre** is located across from the Prince of Wales Hotel on the way into town. It houses information primarily on the park but offers limited information on the town. (☎859-5133. Open mid-May to Oct. 8am-7pm.) The **Park Administration Office**, 215 Mt. View Rd., can also provide information. (☎859-2224. Open M-F 8am-4pm.)

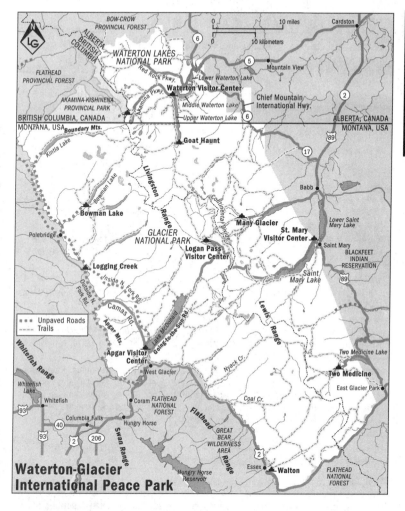

Waterton-Glacier
International Peace Park

Equipment Rental: Pat's, 224 Mt. View Rd. (☎859-2266). Regular bikes are $7 for the first hr., $5 per additional hr., and $34 per day; motor scooters go for $22 for the first hr., $13 per additional hr., and $70 per day. Boat rentals are available at Cameron Lake from **Cameron Lake Boat Rentals**; canoes are $22 for the first hr., $17 per additional hr., cash only. (☎859-2396. Open daily June 15-Sept. 15 7:30am-7:30pm.)

Laundromat: Itussiststukiopi Coin-Op Laundry, on Windflower Ave. Wash $3, dry $0.25 per 5min. Open daily 8am-10pm.

Internet Access: A very slow dial-up Internet connection can be found at **Peace Park Pitas** (see Food, below) for $0.30 per min.

Post Office: On the corner of Fountain Ave. and Windflower Ave. (☎859-2294). **Postal Code:** T0K 2M0.

ALBERTA

ACCOMMODATIONS AND CAMPING

Waterton townsite is as expensive as Banff, with the Prince of Wales Hotel setting the standard on the drive into town. The budget traveller will find relief (and shelter) in the towns hostel or campsites. Information on B&Bs in the extended area can be found at the visitors center. Waterton also offers four seasonal campgrounds, but they fill up quickly and are first come, first served. The park's 13 backcountry campgrounds provide a cheaper, quieter, and more cardiovascularly-challenging alternative. Fees for these are $6 per night, and you can make reservations for a $10 charge up to 90 days in advance by calling ☎859-5133.

Waterton Alpine Hostel (HI), 101 Clemantis Ave. (☎859-2150 or 888-985-6343; www.watertonlakeslodge.com/hostel.html), is run through the pricier Waterton Lakes Lodge and enjoys many of the Lodge's comforts. Comfortable dorm rooms house four bunkbeds while private rooms sleep three. Access to Lodge pool, hot tub, and recreation areas, including tennis courts. Summer $31, non-members $35; family rooms $94/$105. Winter $26/$30; family rooms $90/$100. Pool and shower access $6.50 for non-guests. ❸

Crandell Mountain Campground, along the beautiful Red Rock Parkway north of town, provides 129 unserviced sites for those who value their privacy enough to avoid Waterton townsite. Open mid-May to early Sept. $13. ❶

Belly River Campground, on Hwy. 6 south of town, just before the US border, offers 24 unserviced sites along the river, away from the hubbub of town. Open mid-May to early Sept. $10. Also contains a group campground that charges $2 per person. ❶

Waterton Townsite Campground, located on the south side of town, crams in 95 sites with full hookups and another 143 unserviced sites to create a tent/RV village all its own. Expect big crowds and very little privacy but a location convenient to town. Open May-Oct. $15-23. ❷

Northland Lodge, 408 Evergreen Ave. (☎859-2353), presents the perfect opportunity for a splurge. Built in 1928 by the president of the Great Northern Railway as his private residence, this posh lodge is a bargain even at the price. Provides deluxe beds, patio, fireplace, and a location right next to some of Waterton's finest trails.There are only nine rooms, so reservations are necessary. Breakfast included. Doubles with shared beds start at $101 in summer, $68 in winter. ❺

FOOD

Food, like the mountains and all else, is a bit steep in Waterton. As in all things historical and financial, the **Prince of Wales Hotel** leads the charge with its $25 High Tea daily from 2-4:30pm. For more reasonable eats, hit up **Rocky Mountain Food Mart,** on Windflower Ave. (☎859-2526), for grocery goods. Open daily 7am-9pm.

Peace Park Pitas, (☎859-2582) on the corner of Windflower Ave. and Cameron Falls Dr. serves an original, healthy menu, an excellent alternative to the burger joints. All styles of pita wraps $6-8. Internet access $0.30 per min. Open daily 10am-10pm. ❸

New Franks Restaurant, 106a Waterton Ave. (☎859-2240), serving the cheapest breakfast in town (under $4), delivers the least expensive, and most Asian, food in town. Lunch and dinner entrees are more pricey ($6-9) but still do a fine job on the competition. Open daily 7:30am-10pm. ❷

The Big Scoop (☎859-2346) on Waterton Ave. is packed with tourists after milkshakes ($4) and ice cream, but the $4-6 subs and $3 slices of pizza make for a quick and easy lunch. Open May-Oct. M-Sa 10am-10pm, Su 1:30-10pm. ❶

HIKING

Waterton Lakes is far smaller than its southern sister-park, and the number of trail selections reflects that fact. But the raw steepness of the mountains, rising sheer out of the prairie, the multitude of lakes and waterfalls, and the abundance of passes and peaks to mount make hiking Waterton's premier pastime.

Waterton Lakeshore Trail (13km one-way, 4½ hr.) This popular trail extends the length of the western shore of Upper Waterton Lake from Waterton townsite down to Goat Haunt, MT. Lacking views downwards, the trail makes up for it with views upwards to the surrounding peaks, and, hey, everybody likes crossing international borders on foot. Waterton Inter-Nation Cruise Company (see **Orientation and Practical Information**) offers rides to and from Goat Haunt for one-way hikers. Easy.

Rowe Lakes Trail (11km round-trip, 3-4hr.) A beautiful, more relaxed hike towards nestled lakes and open meadows. Here is one of Waterton's lesser known and less dramatic trails, but one truly wonderful in its scope. The trailhead departs from the Akamina Parkway west of town. Moderate.

Crypt Lake Trail (8.6km one-way, 4hr.) This steeply climbing trail is almost as famous for its spectacular ascent as it is for its incredible finale. After the water shuttle across Upper Waterton Lake (see **Orientation and Practical Information**), the sharp grade eventually must be conquered by a ladder, followed by a tunnel crawl, and concluded by traversing a 240m sheer face. But the lake at the end is surreal in both its colors and surroundings. Perhaps the finest photograph Waterton has to offer. Moderate.

Bertha Lake Trail (11km round-trip, 4hr.) Leaving from the town campground, the trail climbs through the surrounding forests to grand views of Lower and then Upper Bertha Falls. The climb continues onward to Bertha Lake, cradled in a glacial hanging valley. An additional trail extends around the lake. Moderate.

Carthew-Alderson Trail (20km one-way, 6½hr.) Arguably Waterton's most scenic, most popular, and most difficult day hike, Carthew-Anderson covers the full range of Waterton's landscape. The trail cuts from Cameron Lake at the end of the Akamina Parkway west of town back into the townsite. Most hikers take the hiker shuttle (see **Orientation and Practical Information,** above) or use two cars to start at Cameron Lake. The trail climbs steeply to Carthew Ridge, where a jagged, rocky, near-lunar landscape awaits, and then follow the trail down through lake country and forests to the town. Difficult.

OTHER OUTDOOR ACTIVITIES

Outdoor playground that it is, Waterton boasts a full range of activities for those desiring more than the multiple methods of breathtaking that hiking provides. **Fishing** is a favorite sport in Waterton, with lakes housing trout, graylings, pike, and whitefish. The fishing season extends from mid-May through August on Akamina, Cameron, Crandell, Middle and Upper Waterton Lakes. Elsewhere the season is from July to October. Several lakes have zero-fishing policies; check with the visitors center. **Fishing permits** are available at the visitors center at $7 per day and $24 per year. Motorboats are allowed only on Middle and Upper Waterton Lakes. Less exerting water rides are available from the Waterton Inter-Nation Cruise Company (see **Orientation and Practical Information**), which, besides ferrying folks to trailheads, also offers narrated cruises along Upper Waterton Lake.

Land-lubbers can travel at high speeds by **renting bikes** at Pat's (see **Orientation and Practical Information**) and taking them out to one of the bike-friendly trails, including the Snowshoe Trail, the Crandell Lake Trail, the Wishbone Trail, and the Kishinena Forestry Rd. Horse rentals are available at **Alpine Stables** just off the highway into town. Rates start at $25 for one hour and climb to $118 for 8 hours.

ALBERTA

(☎859-2462; www.alpinestables.com. Open daily May-Sept. 9am-5pm.) In winter, traction can be found on one of the park's many **snowshoe** and **cross-country ski trails**. Inquire at the park administration building.

GLACIER NATIONAL PARK ☎ 406

Nearly eight times the size of its Canadian neighbor to the north, Glacier has the same larger-than-life scenery, varied flora and fauna, and endless adventure potential. Perhaps the most renowned attraction of Glacier is the Going-to-the-Sun Road, a breathtaking drive as famous for its incredible views of majestic glaciers and glittering lakes as for its hairpin turns and narrow lanes. But those who leave their vehicles won't be lacking in excitement either—Glacier's seemingly limitless expanse of mountains promises wildlife encounters, thrilling hikes, and rustic backcountry campsites in some of the wildest wilderness in the Northwest.

▐▔ TRANSPORTATION

Amtrak (☎226-4452) traces a dramatic route along the southern edge of the park. The station in **West Glacier** is staffed mid-May to September, but the train still stops at the station in the winter. Trains chug daily to East Glacier (1½hr., $14); Seattle (14hr., $117); Spokane (5hr., $46-59); Whitefish (30min., $7-8). Amtrak's Empire Builder route also runs from East Glacier to Chicago (32hr., $152-198). **Rimrock Stages** (☎800-255-7655; www.rimrocktrailways.com), the only bus line that nears the park, stops in Kalispell at the Kalispell Bus Terminal, 1301 S Main St. (☎755-4011), and goes to Missoula (3hr., 1-2 per day, $21-25) and Billings (8hr., 1 per day, $59-82). Tickets are cheapest if purchased seven days in advance. As in most of the Rockies, a car is the most convenient mode of transport, particularly within the park. **Dollar Rent-a-Car**, 1023 Hwy. 49N (☎226-4432) in East Glacier rents vehicles starting at $56 per day, plus a $10 per day underage fee for those under 26. Must be 21 with a major credit card. Free pickup from the Amtrak station. Unlimited mileage. Open daily May-Oct. 9am-9pm. **Glacier Park, Inc.** (☎892-2525; www.glacierparkinc.com) runs famous red jammer buses on the Going-to-the-Sun Road. (4hr. tours $25, 6hr. $45; children half-price.) **Sun Tours** offers additional tours, guided by members of the Blackfeet Indian Tribe, leaving from East Glacier and St. Mary. (☎226-9220 or 800-786-9220. All-day tour from East Glacier $55, from St. Mary $40.) **The Hikers Shuttle** (☎892-2525; www.glacierparkinc.com) runs on the Going-to-the-Sun Rd. from early July to early September and offers connecting service to Watertown ($8 per person per segment within the park, under 12 $4. To Waterton, $8 from Chief Mountain, $24 from St. Mary Visitors Center, $40 from West Glacier); shuttles run four times per day within the park, twice per day to Waterton. Schedules are available at visitors centers or at www.nps.gov/glac/shuttles.htm.

▞▚ ORIENTATION

There are few roads in Glacier, and the locals like it that way. Glacier's main thoroughfare is the **Going-to-the-Sun Road**, a narrow two-lane road that winds through Logan Pass and is one of the most spectacular drives in America, connecting the two primary points of entry, West Glacier and St. Mary. **US 2** skirts the southern border of the park and is the fastest route from Browning and East Glacier to West Glacier. At the "Goat Lick," about halfway between East and West Glacier, mountain goats traverse steep cliffs to lap up the natural salt deposits. **Route 89** heads north along the eastern edge of the park past St. Mary. Anyone interested in visiting the northwestern section of the park should take the unpaved **Outside North Fork Road** and enter the park through Polebridge—the pothole-ridden **Inside North**

Fork Road takes an hour longer and is often closed for maintenance. While most of Glacier is primitive backcountry, a number of villages provide lodging, gas, and food: St. Mary, Many Glacier, and East Glacier in the east, and West Glacier, Apgar, and Polebridge in the west.

🛈 PRACTICAL INFORMATION

Before entering the park, visitors must pay **admission:** $20 per week per car, $10 for pedestrians and cyclists (including motorcycles); yearly passes to Glacier $25. The accessible and knowledgeable rangers at each of the three visitors centers give the inside scoop on campsites, day hikes, weather, flora, and fauna. **Saint Mary Visitors Center** guards the east entrance of the park. (☎ 732-7750. Open daily July 9am-9pm; May, June and Sept. 8am-5pm.) **Apgar Visitors Center** is located at the west entrance. (☎ 888-7939. Open daily May-June and Sept. 9am-5pm; late June-Aug. 8am-7pm.) A third visitors center graces **Logan Pass,** on the Going-to-the-Sun Road. (Open daily July-Aug. 9am-7pm; Sept. 9am-4:30pm; June 9:30am-4:30pm.) The **Many Glacier Ranger Station** can also help answer important questions. (Open daily mid-May to mid-Sept. 8am-5pm.)

Visitors planning overnight backpacking trips must obtain the necessary **backcountry permits.** With the exception of the **Nyack/Coal Creek** camping zone, all backcountry camping must be done at designated campsites equipped with pit toilets, tent sites, food preparation areas, and food hanging devices. (Open June-Sept. Overnight camping fee $4 per person per night, ages 9-16 $2; Oct.-May no fees. For an additional $20, reservations are accepted beginning in mid-Apr. for trips between June 15 and Oct. 31.) Reservations can be made in person at the Apgar Permit Center, St. Mary Visitors Center, Many Glacier Ranger Station, and in Polebridge, or by writing to Backcountry Reservation Office, Glacier National Park, West Glacier, MT 59936. Pick up a free and indispensable Backcountry Camping Guide from visitors centers or the **Backcountry Permit Center,** next to the visitors center in Apgar, which also has info on Glacier's less-traveled areas. (☎ 888-7857. Open daily July 7am-4pm; May-June and Sept. 8am-4pm.) **Medical Services: Kalispell Regional Medical Center,** 310 Sunny View Ln. (☎ 752-5111), north of Kalispell off Rte. 93. **Post Office:** 110 Going-to-the-Sun Rd., in West Glacier. (☎ 888-5591. Open M-F 8:30am-12:30pm and 1:30-4:45pm.) **Postal Code:** 59936.

🏠 ACCOMMODATIONS AND CAMPING

Staying indoors within Glacier is expensive, but several affordable options lie just outside the park boundaries. On the west side of the park, the small, electricity-less town of ▓**Polebridge** provides access to Glacier's remote and pristine northwest corner. From Apgar, take Camas Rd. north, and take a right onto the poorly-marked gravel Outside North Fork Rd., just past a bridge over the North Fork of the Flathead River. (Avoid Inside North Fork Rd.—your shocks will thank you.) From Columbia Falls, take Rte. 486 north. To the east, inexpensive lodging is just across the park border in **East Glacier.** The distant offices of **Glacier Park, Inc.** (☎ 756-2444; www.glacierparkinc.com) handle reservations for all in-park lodging. **Camping** is available at 13 campsites within the park. Most are open from late May to early September. Fees run from $12 at **Bowman Lake** to $17 at **Saint Mary's. Apgar** is the largest campground (192 sites) and is open the longest (May 7-Oct. 18. $15). No campgrounds within the park have hookups or showers.

▨ **North Fork Hostel,** 80 Beaver Dr. (☎ 888-5241; www.nfhostel.com), in Polebridge; follow the signs through town. The wooden walls and kerosene lamps are reminiscent of a deep woods hunting retreat. Hot showers and beautiful fully-equipped kitchen, but no flush toilets. During the winter, old-fashioned wood stoves warm frozen fingers and toes after skiing or snowshoeing, and thick quilts keep guests warm at night. Internet access $2 per 20min. Call ahead for a pickup from the West Glacier Amtrak station ($30-35). Canoe rentals $20 per day; mountain bikes $15 per day; snowshoes $5 per day; nordic ski equipment $5 per day. Showers $4 for non-lodgers. Linen $2. Check-in by 10pm. Check-out noon. Call ahead, especially in winter. Teepees $10 per person; dorms $15, $12 after 2 nights; cabins $30; log homes $65. ●

Brownies Grocery (HI), 1020 Rte. 49 (☎226-4426), in East Glacier Park. The reception desk is at the grocery store and the hostel occupies the second floor. Travelers can refuel with a thick huckleberry shake ($4) or a vegan sandwich ($5). Kitchen, showers, linens, laundry, and a stunning view of the Rockies from the porch. Key deposit $5. Check-in by 9pm; call ahead for late arrivals. Check-out 10am. Reservations recommended; credit card required. Open May-Sept., weather permitting. Internet access $1.75 per 15min. Tent sites $10. Dorms $13, nonmembers $16; doubles $26/29; family room for 4-6 $38/$41. Extra bed $5. ●

Backpacker's Inn Hostel, 29 Dawson Ave. (☎226-9392), just east of the East Glacier Amtrak station and behind Serrano's Mexican Restaurant, has 14 clean but narrow beds. Hot showers. No kitchen. Sleeping bags $1. Open May-Sept. Rooms $10; private room with queen-sized bed and full linen $20 for 1 person, $30 for 2. ●

Swiftcurrent Motor Inn (☎732-5531), in Many Glacier Valley, is one of the few budget motels in the area. Open early June-early Sept. All cabins are shared bath. 1-bedroom cabins $43, 2-bedroom $53. ❸

◗ FOOD

▧ **Polebridge Mercantile Store** (☎888-5105), on Polebridge Loop Rd. ¼ mi. east of N Fork Rd., has a constant stream of fresh homemade pastries ($1-3) that are as splendid as the surrounding peaks. The Mercantile has been in operation since 1918, before the park existed. Gas, gifts, groceries and pay phones are also available. Open daily June-Sept. 8am-9pm; Oct.-May 8am-6pm. ●

▧ **Northern Lights Saloon** (☎888-5669), right next to the Polebridge Mercantile. The friendly staff and patrons make this saloon an excellent place to order a cheeseburger ($5-6) and all-Montana-brewed cold pints ($3) while sitting on one of the tree trunks this one-room cabin uses as bar stools. Kitchen open June-Sept. M-Sa 4-9pm, Su 9am-noon and 4-9pm; bar open until midnight. ●

▧ **Whistle Stop Restaurant** (☎226-9292), in East Glacier next to Brownies Grocery. Sample homemade delicacies at this restaurant best known for unbelievable deep-fried huckleberry-injected French toast ($7). Open daily mid-May to mid-Sept. 7am-9pm. ❷

Park Cafe (☎732-4482), in St. Mary on Rte. 89, just north of the park entrance, provides sustenance to those who dare to cross the Going-to-the-Sun Road. Incredible homemade pies $2.75 per slice. "Hungry Hiker" special (2 eggs with hash browns and toast) $5. Vegetarian Caribbean burrito $6. Open daily May-Sept. 7am-10pm. ●

◪ HIKING

Most of Glacier's spectacular scenery lies off the main roads and is accessible only by foot. An extensive trail system has something for everyone, from short, easy day hikes to rigorous backcountry expeditions. Stop by one of the visitors centers for maps with day hikes. Beware of bears and mountain lions; if approached by one of the cats, stay put, make eye contact, and throw stones at it. If attacked, fight back. Familiarize yourself with the precautions necessary to avoid an encounter, and ask the rangers about wildlife activity in the area in which you plan to hike.

Hidden Lake Nature Trail (3 mi. round-trip, 2hr.), beginning at the Logan Pass Visitor Center, is a short and modest 460 ft. climb to a lookout of Hidden Lake and a chance to stretch your legs while winding along the Going-to-the-Sun Road. Easy.

Avalanche Lake (4 mi. round-trip, 3hr.) is a breathtaking trail and by far the most popular day hike in the park. Starting north of Lake McDonald on the Going-to-the-Sun Road, this hike climbs 500 ft. to picture-perfect panoramas. Moderate.

Grinnell Glacier Trail (11 mi. round-trip, 7hr.) passes within close proximity of several glaciers and follows along Grinnell Point and Mt. Grinnell, gaining a steady 1600 ft. Trailhead at the Many Glacier Picnic Area. Moderate.

Mount Brown Lookout (11mi. round-trip, 5 hr.) Starts at Lake McDonald Lodge and climbs 4325 ft. to the fire lookout. Mountain goats frequent the treeline and are occasionally quite curious. The top has views of the lake nearly a mile below. Difficult.

Numa Ridge Lookout (12 mi. round-trip, 9hr.) starts from the Bowman Lake Campground, northeast of Polebridge. After climbing 2930 ft., this well-maintained trail ends with sweeping vistas of Glacier's rugged northwest corner from a fire lookout. Difficult.

▓ OUTDOOR ACTIVITIES

▓▐ **BIKING AND HORSEBACK RIDING.** Opportunities for bicycling are limited and confined to roadways and designated bike paths; cycling on trails is strictly prohibited. Although the Going-to-the-Sun Road is a popular **bike route,** only experienced cyclists with appropriate gear, legs of titanium, and nerves of steel should attempt this grueling ride; the sometimes nonexistent shoulder of the road can create hazardous situations. From mid-June to August, bike traffic is prohibited 11am-4pm from the Apgar campground to Sprague Creek and eastbound (uphill) from Logan Creek to Logan Pass. The Inside North Fork Rd., which runs from Kintla Lake to Fish Creek on the west side of the park, is good for **mountain biking,** as are the old logging roads in the Flathead National Forest. Ask at a visitors center for more details. **Glacier Raft Co.** (☎888-5454 or 800-235-6781; www.glacierraftco.com), outside West Glacier, offers adult bike ($29 per day), cross-country ski ($15 per day), and kayak ($75 per day) rentals. (Open daily May-Sept. 7:30am-9pm; Sept.-Dec. 8am-5pm; Dec.-Apr. 9am-4pm.) **Equestrian** explorers should check to make sure trails are open; there are steep fines for riding on closed trails. **Mule Shoe Outfitters** (www.mule-shoe.com) offers 1hr. ($28), 2hr. ($47), 4hr. ($79), and full-day ($150) trail rides May-early Sept. Rides are available at Many Glacier (☎732-4203) and Lake McDonald (☎888-5121).

BOATING. The **Glacier Park Boat Co.** (☎257-2426; www.glacierparkboats.com) provides **boat tours** that explore all of Glacier's large lakes and surrounding peaks. Tours leave from **Lake McDonald** (☎888-5727; 1hr., 4 per day, $10); **Two Medicine** (☎226-4467; 45min., 5 per day, $9.50); **Rising Sun,** at St. Mary Lake (☎732-4430; 1½hr., 5 per day, $12); and **Many Glacier** (☎732-4480; 1¼hr., $13). Children ages 4-12 ride for half price. The tours from Two Medicine, Rising Sun, and Many Glacier provide access to Glacier's backcountry, and there are sunset cruises from Rising Sun and Lake McDonald. **Glacier Raft Co.,** in West Glacier, leads trips down the middle fork of the Flathead River. (☎888-5454 or 800-235-6781; www.glacierraftco.com. Half-day $40, under 13 $30; full-day trip with lunch $65/48.) You can rent **rowboats** ($10 per hr.) at Lake McDonald, Many Glacier, Two Medicine, and Apgar; **canoes** ($10 per hr.) at Many Glacier, Two Medicine, and Apgar; **kayaks** ($10 per hr.) at Apgar and Many Glacier; and **outboards** ($17 per hr.) at Lake McDonald and Two Medicine. Call Glacier Boat Co. for more details.

FISHING. No permit is needed to **fish** in the park, and limits are generally high. Some areas, however, are restricted, and certain species may be catch-and-release. Pick up *Fishing Regulations*, available at visitors centers, for more info. Lake Ellen Wilson, Gunsight Lake, and Lake Elizabeth are good places to sink a line. Outside the park, on Blackfeet land, a special permit is needed, and everywhere else in Montana a state permit is required.

BANFF NATIONAL PARK   ☎ 403

AT A GLANCE	
AREA: 6641 sq. km.	**GATEWAYS:** Banff townsite, Lake Louise.
CLIMATE: Alpine and subalpine.	**CAMPING:** Plentiful options. Most sites are between $10 and $17 per night (see p. 443).
FEATURES: Cave and Basin Mineral Springs, Tunnel and Sulphur Mountain.	
HIGHLIGHTS: Backcountry hiking (see p. 445), winter sports (see p. 446).	**FEES:** $5, seniors $4, ages 6-16 $2.50, family $10.

Banff is Canada's best-loved and best-known natural park, with 6641 sq. km of peaks, forests, glaciers, and alpine valleys. It also holds the title of Canada's first National Park, declared so only days after the Canadian Pacific Railway's completion in 1885. The park's name comes from Banffshire, Scotland, the birthplace of two Canadian Pacific Railway financiers. These men convinced Canada's first Prime Minister that a "large pecuniary advantage" might be gained from the region, telling him that "since we can't export the scenery, we shall have to import the tourists." Their plan worked to a fault, but even streets littered with gift shops and chocolatiers cannot obscure the beauty of the gorgeous wilderness outside the townsite. Outdoors lovers arrive with mountain bikes, climbing gear, and skis, but a trusty pair of hiking boots remains the park's most widely-used outdoor equipment. Banff's natural beauty, along with the opportunities for excitement and laid-back attitude it affords, have turned Banff into one of Canada's youngest towns, with a median age of 29.

▐ TRANSPORTATION

Banff National Park hugs the Alberta side of the Alberta-British Columbia border 128km west of Calgary. The **Trans-Canada Highway** (Hwy. 1) runs east-west through the park, connecting it to Yoho National Park in the west. The **Icefields Parkway** (Hwy. 93) connects Banff with Jasper National Park to the north and Kootenay National Park to the southwest. Civilization centers around the towns of **Banff** and **Lake Louise,** 58km apart on Hwy. 1. The more serene **Bow Valley Parkway** (Hwy. 1A) parallels Hwy. 1 from Lake Louise to 8km west of Banff, offering excellent camping, hostelling, sights, and wildlife. The southern portion of Hwy. 1A is restricted at night in the late spring and early summer to accommodate the wildlife on the road. All listings apply to Banff townsite, unless otherwise specified.

Buses: Brewster Transportation, 100 Gopher St. (☎ 762-6767; www.brewster.ca). Depot open daily 7:45am-9pm. To: **Calgary** (2hr., $42); **Jasper** (5hr., $57); **Lake Louise** (1hr., $14). Ages 6-15 half-price. See **The Rockies,** p. 427, for info on tours to, from, and within parks. **Greyhound** (☎ 800-661-8747) uses Brewster's station. 4 per day to **Jasper** (5 hr., $106), **Lake Louise** (1hr., $14), and **Vancouver** (12½-15hr., $118); 5 per day to **Calgary** (1½hr., $24).

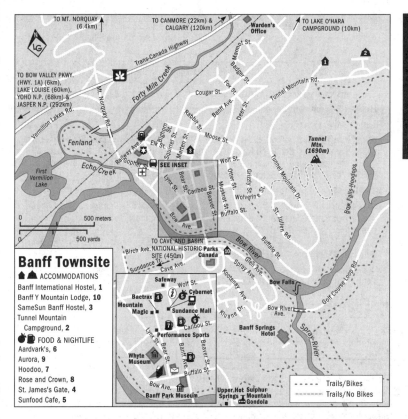

Banff Townsite

🏠🏔 ACCOMMODATIONS
Banff International Hostel, **1**
Banff Y Mountain Lodge, **10**
SameSun Banff Hostel, **3**
Tunnel Mountain
  Campground, **2**

🍴🍺 FOOD & NIGHTLIFE
Aardvark's, **6**
Aurora, **9**
Hoodoo, **7**
Rose and Crown, **8**
St. James's Gate, **4**
Sunfood Cafe, **5**

- - - - - Trails/Bikes
━━━━━ Trails/No Bikes

Public Transportation: Banff Transit runs every 30min. between the Banff Springs Hotel, the RV parking area, and the Banff Hostel on Tunnel Mountain Rd., as well as between the Tunnel Mountain Campground, downtown, and the Banff Park Museum. $1, children $0.50. Runs daily mid-May to Sept. 7am-midnight; late Apr.-early May and Oct.-Dec. noon-midnight.

Taxis: Banff Taxi (☎762-4444). 24hr. **Lake Louise Taxi** (☎522-2020). Runs 6am-2:30pm.

Car Rental: Available from several establishments with rates ranging from $50-60 per day, with 100-150 free km. The visitors center keeps an up-to-date comparison chart.

🛈 PRACTICAL INFORMATION

Tourist Office: Banff Visitor Centre, 224 Banff Ave. Includes **Banff/Lake Louise Tourism Bureau** (☎762-8421; www.banfflakelouise.com) and **Parks Canada** (☎762-1550). Open daily June-Sept. 8am-8pm; Oct.-May 9am-5pm. **Lake Louise Visitor Centre** (☎522-3833), at Samson Mall on Village Rd. Open daily June-Sept. 9am-7pm; Oct.-May 9am-4pm.

Equipment Rental:

Mountain Magic Equipment, 224 Bear St. (☎762-2591; www.mountainmagic.com) is one of the few places in Banff to rent packages for telemarking ($30 per day) and mountaineering ($40 per day). They also offer the usual bike, ski, and snowboard rentals. Open daily 9am-9pm.

Bactrax Rentals, 225 Bear St. (☎762-8177; www.snowtips-bactrax.com), rents mountain bikes for $10-12 per hr., $35-42 per day. Bike tours $20-60 including all equipment. Ski packages from $16-35 per day, snowboard packages $25. 20% HI discount. Open daily Apr.-Oct. 8am-8pm; Nov.-Mar. 7am-10pm.

Wilson Mountain Sports (☎522-3636; www.lakelouisewilsons.com) in the Lake Louise Samson Mall, rents bikes ($15 per hr., $39 per day) and camping and fishing gear. They also offer mountaineering packages ($35 per day) and rock climbing packages ($15 per day). Open daily mid-June to Sept. 9am-9pm; Oct. to Apr. 8am-8pm; May to mid-June 9am-8pm.

Weather: Environment Canada ☎762-2088.

Road Conditions: ☎762-1450.

Police: Banff Police (☎762-2226. Non-emergency 762-2228). On Lynx St. by the train depot. **Lake Louise Police** (☎522-3811. Non-emergency 522-3812). **Banff Park Warden** is the main number for emergencies inside the park (☎762-4506. Non-emergency 762-1470). 24hr. **Lake Louise Park Warden** (☎522-1200).

Hospital: Mineral Springs, 301 Lynx St. (☎762-2222), near Wolf St. in Banff.

Internet Access: Library, 101 Bear St. (☎762-2611; www.bannflibrary.ab.ca). Sign up in advance. Open daily early Sept.-late May 10am-8pm; closed Su late May-early Sept. **Cyber Web** (☎762-9226), 215 Banff Ave. $2 per 15min., $8 per hr., $5 per hr. 9:30pm-close. Open daily 10am-midnight. For laptops, open M-Th 10am-8pm, F 10am-6pm, Sa 11am-6pm, Su 1-5pm. $1 per 15min.

Post Office: 204 Buffalo St. (☎762-2586). Open M-W 8:30am-5:30pm, Th-F 8:30am-7pm, Sa 8:30am-5pm. **Postal Code:** TOL 0C0.

ACCOMMODATIONS

Finding a cheap place to stay in Banff has become increasingly difficult; the number of visitors soars into the millions every year. Townsite residents offer rooms in their homes, occasionally at reasonable rates (Apr.-Oct. $75-140; Oct.-Apr. $60-100). Check the list at the back of the *Banff and Lake Louise Official Visitor Guide,* available free at the visitors centers.

Mammoth **modern hostels** at Banff and Lake Louise anchor a chain of cozier hostels from Calgary to Jasper. **Rustic hostels** provide more of a wilderness experience (some have no electricity or flush toilets), and often have some of the park's best hiking and cross-country skiing right in their backyards. HI runs a **shuttle service** connecting all the Rocky Mountain hostels and Calgary ($8-90). Wait-list beds become available at 6pm, and the larger hostels try to save a few stand-by beds for shuttle arrivals. Beds go quickly, especially during the summer, so make your reservations as early as possible. The hostels below are listed from north to south, and all reservations are made through the southern Alberta HI administration at ☎866-762-4122 or online at www.hostellingintl.ca. Free reservations are held until 6pm, but can be guaranteed until later with a credit card.

Rampart Creek Wilderness Hostel (HI) (☎670-7580), 34km south of the Icefield Centre. Close to several world-famous ice climbs (including Weeping Wall, 17km north), this hostel is a favorite for summer bikers, winter mountaineers, and anyone who likes a sauna after a hard day's hike. Full-service kitchen. A steep climb behind the hostel leads to a hammock with free access to the valley's visual orgy. 2 co-ed cabins with 12 beds each. $20, nonmembers $24; F-Sa $23/$28. ❷

Mosquito Creek Wilderness Hostel (HI) (☎670-7580), 103km south of the Icefield Centre and 26km north of Lake Louise. Across the creek from the Mosquito Creek campground. Close to the Wapta Icefield and a network of hiking trails. Enormous living room with wood stove, wood-burning sauna, kitchen, and pump water. 2 co-ed cabins of 16 beds each. $21, nonmembers $25; F-Sa $24/$28. ❷

Lake Louise Alpine Centre (HI) (☎ 670-7580), 500m west of the info center in Lake Louise townsite, on Village Rd. toward the Park Warden's office. Ranked 4th in the world by HI, and rightly so. More like a resort than a hostel, it boasts a reference library, a stone fireplace, 2 full kitchens, a sauna, and a quality cafe. Internet access $2 per 20min. Hub for mountaineering tours. Check-in 3pm, check-out 11am. Dorms $27-34, nonmembers $31-38; private rooms available. ❸

🏚 **Castle Mountain Wilderness Hostel (HI)** (☎ 670-7580 or 866-762-4122) in Castle Junction, 1.5km east of the junction of Hwy. 1 and Hwy. 93 south, off the connector between Hwy. 1 and Hwy. 1A, almost halfway between Banff and Lake Louise. Castle Mountain offers a smaller, quieter, cheaper alternative to the hubbub of its big brothers. Comfy common area with huge bay windows. A library, collection of games, fireplace, friendly staff, kitchen, laundry, volleyball, and backpack rental ($5). Check-in 5-10pm; check-out 10am. Sleeps 28. M-Th and Su $21, nonmembers $25; F-Sa $24/$28. ❷

Banff International Hostel (HI) (☎ 762-4122), 3km uphill from Banff townsite on Tunnel Mountain Rd. Walk or take Banff Transit from downtown ($1). This huge hostel has 3 lounges and kitchens and space for 215 guests. Laundry. Check-in 3pm, check-out 11am. Reception 24hr. Reservations recommended. $29, nonmembers $33; for better rooms in new building add $1.50. Private rooms $83-125. Bike rental $36 per day. ❷

SameSun Banff Hostel, 499 Banff Ave. (☎ 877-562-2783; www.samesun.com). SameSun lives its motto "play hard" with this hostel, a short walk from Banff's nightclubs and bars, but with Saturday night keggers, who needs to leave? Hot tub, pool table, kitchen, laundry, courtyard, BBQ grill, free pancake mix, and free parking. Reception 7am-midnight. Dorms $31, $28 with student ID. Private rooms $75-89. ❸

Banff Y Mountain Lodge, 102 Spray Ave. (☎ 762-3560; www.ymountainlodge.com). Across the Bow River from downtown. Run by the YWCA, this well-appointed co-ed dorm is clean, if a bit impersonal. Huge common room, kitchen, in-dorm showers, TV room, laundry ($1.75 wash, $1.75 dry), Internet access ($1 per 10 min), lockers ($1), and 24hr. reception. $31, private rooms $70-90. ❸

🏕 CAMPING

A chain of campgrounds stretches between Banff and Jasper. Huge, fully serviced grounds lie closer to the townsites; for more trees, fewer vehicles, and less of a refugee-camp atmosphere, try the sites farther from Banff and Lake Louise. At all park campgrounds, a campfire permit, which includes firewood, is $4 per night. Sites are first come, first served. The sites below are listed from south to north and are wheelchair-accessible but have no flush toilets unless otherwise noted.

Tunnel Mountain Village, 4km from Banff Townsite on Tunnel Mountain Rd. With nearly 1200 sites, this facility is a camping metropolis. Trailer/RV area has 321 full RV sites, Village 2 has 188 sites, and Village 1 houses a whopping 618 sites. Fires allowed in Village 1 only; all villages have showers. Village 2 is open year-round; 1 and 3 open early May-early Oct. $22; electricity $26; full RV sites $30. ❷

Two Jack, 13km northeast of Banff, across Hwy. 1. Open late May-early Sept. The 381 sites in the main area ($17) have no showers or wheelchair access, while the 74 lakeside sites ($22) do. ❷

Johnston Canyon, 26km northwest of Banff on Bow Valley Pkwy. Access to Johnston Canyon Trail (see below). Open early June-late Sept. 140 sites; $22. Showers. ❷

Protection Mountain, 15km east of Lake Louise and 11km west of Castle Junction on the Bow Valley Pkwy. (Hwy. 1A). 89 spacious and wooded sites (14 trailer) in a primitive campground. Open late June-early Sept. Sites $17. ❷

Lake Louise, 1.5km southeast of the visitors center on Fairview Rd. On Bow River, not the lake. Plenty of hiking and fishing awaits nearby. 189 trailer sites with electricity, open year-round; $26. 220 tent sites, open mid-May to Sept.; $22. Showers. ❷

Mosquito Creek, 26km north of Lake Louise. 32 quiet sites next to the creek, with hiking access. Open mid-June to mid-Sept. Sites $13. ❶

Rampart Creek, 147km north of Banff, 34km south of the Icefield Centre, across the highway from Rampart Creek hostel and amazing ice climbing. Open late June-early Sept. 50 sites; $13. ❶

⬛ FOOD

Like everything else in the park, Banff restaurants tend toward the expensive. The Banff and Lake Louise hostels serve affordable meals in their cafes ($3-10). Groceries await at **Safeway,** at Marten and Elk St. just off Banff Ave. (☎762-5378. Open daily 8am-11pm.)

Laggan's Mountain Bakery and Deli (☎522-2017; www.samsonmall.com/laggan-swin.htm), in Samson Mall in Lake Louise. Always crowded with folks after thick sandwiches ($5-6) and fresh-baked loaves ($3). Open daily 6am-7pm. Cash only. ❷

Sunfood Cafe, 215 Banff Ave. (☎760-3933; www.sunfoodcafe.com), 2nd floor of the Sundance Mall. A very relaxed vegetarian cafe hidden upstairs in a touristy mall. Veggie burger with the works $6.50. Daily specials, takeout available. Beer and wine. Open M-Sa 11am-9pm. ❷

Aardvark's, 304A Caribou St. (☎762-5500 or 762-5509). This small pizza place does big business after the bars close. Minimal seating. Small-ish slices of pizza $3. Small pie $7-10; large $15-22; 10 buffalo wings $5. Open daily 11am-4am. ❷

⬛ NIGHTLIFE

Bartenders maintain that Banff's true wildlife is in its bars. Check the paper or ask at the visitors center to find out which nightspots are having "locals' night," featuring cheap drinks. Banff Ave. hosts more bars, restaurants, kitschy gift shops, ATMs and banks than there are mountains. The fun doesn't stop after Saturday night, either: Banff Sundays boast great nightlife.

Rose and Crown, 202 Banff Ave. (☎762-2121; www.banffroseandcrown.com), upstairs on the corner of Banff and Caribou. This British-style pub has ample room for dancing and pool-playing ($1.25). Couch-adorned living room for watching sports and live music every night at 10pm. Happy hour M-F 3:30-6:30pm, Th $13 jugs 9pm-close. Sa $2 cover, Su Jam Night with happy hour 9pm-close. Open daily 11am-2am.

Aurora, 110 Banff Ave. (☎760-5300; www.aurorabanff.com). This neon-lit, ultra-modern club caters to the 25+ crowd with a martini and cigar bar in back. House, hip-hop, and trance dance floor; 5 bars. Tu and Th $0.75 draft and $0.25 wings, F $1.25 highballs for ladies, Su $1.75 highballs and draft. Sa $5 cover. Open daily 9pm-2am.

Hoodoo, 137 Banff Ave. (☎760-8636; www.hoodoolounge.com), down Caribou St. off the Banff Ave. intersection. This trendy club hosts a primarily under 25 crowd, with a constant rotation of DJ's playing house, top 40, and hip-hop. Tu and Su are $6 jug nights. $2 cover F-Sa. Open daily 9pm-2am.

Saint James's Gate, 205 Wolf St. (☎762-9355). A laid-back Irish pub with friendly staff. The bartenders will help you select one of the 32 beers on tap (pints $5.50-$6.50). Live jigs and reels F-Sa complete the Irish ambience. Happy hour daily 5-7pm. Open M-Th and Su 11am-1am, F-Sa 11am-2am.

◎ SIGHTS

Visitors can purchase a "Heritage Pass" to gain admission to all of the following sites for $11, students and ages 65 and older $7.50, family 4-pack $26.

MUSEUMS. The **■Banff Park Museum National Historic Site** is western Canada's oldest natural history museum—when the Canadian Pacific began to "import the tourists", it decided Victorian tourists would like to see the wildlife of the park, only without climbing into the mountains. The museum today is packed with specimens from the park, with rooms of taxidermy dating to the 1860s. *(93 Banff Ave. ☎ 762-1558. Open daily mid-May to Sept. 10am-6pm; Oct. to mid-May 1-5pm. Tours daily in summer 3pm, weekends in winter. $4, ages 65 and older $3.50, children $3.)* The **Whyte Museum of the Canadian Rockies** explores the history and culture of the Canadian Rockies over the last 200 years in the Heritage Gallery, while temporary exhibits focus on local artists and the natural history of the region. *(111 Bear St. ☎ 762-2291; www.whyte.org. Open daily 10am-5pm. $6, students and ages 65 and older $3.50, under 6 free.)*

HOT SPRINGS. Banff National Park was formed by the government to resolve a conflict over the rights to the Cave and Basin Mineral Springs, once rumored to have miraculous healing properties. The **Cave and Basin National Historic Site,** a refurbished bathhouse built circa 1914, is now a small museum detailing the history and science of the site. Five of the pools are the only home of the park's most endangered species: the small Banff Springs snail—*Physella johnsoni.* *(311 Cave Ave. ☎ 762-1566. Open daily mid-May to Sept. 9am-6pm; Sept. to mid-May M-F 11am-4pm, Sa-Su 9:30am-5pm. Tours daily at 11am mid-May to Sept., Sept. to mid-May Sa-Su. $4, ages 65 and older $3.50, 6-18 $3.)* The springs are southwest of the city on Cave Ave. For an actual dip in the hot water, follow the egg smell to the **Upper Hot Springs pool,** a 40°C (104°F) sulfurous cauldron on Mountain Ave. *(☎ 762-1515. Open daily mid-May to mid-Oct. 9am-11pm; mid-Oct. to mid-May M-Th and Su 10am-10pm, F-Sa 10am-11pm. Summer rates $7.50, seniors and ages 3-17 $6.50, families $22. Winter $5.50/$4.50/$15. Swimsuits $1.50, towels $1.25, lockers $0.50.)*

EVENTS. In summer, the **Banff Festival of the Arts** (www.banffmountainfestivals.ca) keeps tourists occupied. A wide spectrum of events, from First Nations dance to opera, are performed from May to mid-August. Some shows are free; stop by the visitors center for a schedule. The **Banff Mountain Film Festival** (☎ 762-6301; www.banffmountainfestivals.ca/festivals/film), in the first week of November, screens films and videos that celebrate mountains and mountaineers.

◤ OUTDOOR ACTIVITIES

A visitor sticking to paved byways will see only a tiny fraction of the park and the majority of the park's visitors. Those interested in the seemingly endless outdoor options can hike or bike on more than 1600km of trails; grab a free copy of the *Mountain Biking and Cycling Guide* or *Dayhikes in Banff* and peruse park maps and trail descriptions at information centers. For still more solitude, pick up *The Banff Backcountry Experience* and an **overnight camping permit** at a visitors center and head out to the backcountry ($8 per person per day, up to $30; $56 per year). Be sure to check with the park rangers at the information center for current weather, trail, and wildlife updates.

LAKE LOUISE TOWNSITE AREA

The highest community in Canada (1530m), Lake Louise and the surrounding glaciers have often passed for Swiss scenery in movies and are the emerald in the Rockies' tiara of tourism. Once at the lake, the hardest task is escaping fellow

THE LOCAL STORY

FLOUR POWER

Passing by the many lakes and streams in the Rockies, you may notice that they have an unusual color. When looking at the swimming-pool turquoise or glowing blue of the water, you might wonder if this is some kind of gimmick perpetuated by the park wardens to bring in the tourists. Many years ago, a visitor to Lake Louise claimed that he had solved the mystery of the beautiful water: it had obviously been distilled from peacock tails. Turns out he was a bit off the mark.

The actual cause of the color is "rock flour." This fine dust is created by the pressure exerted by the glacier upon rocks trapped in the ice; the resulting ground rock is washed into streams and lakes in the glacial meltwater. Suspended particles trap all colors of the spectrum except for the blues and greens, which are reflected back for your visual pleasure. The glacially-fed lakes are too cold to grow murky algae, and the water is free from the dirt sediment that would interfere with their color. This means, however, that the water is usually free of large populations of either fish or swimmers as well—it's pleasing to the eye, but not so nice to the touch.

The floury water is just as safe as any other water in the mountains as long as you filter it first (unfiltered rock flour can cause diarrhea), but only try it as a last resort: you'll have to go through plenty of clogged filters before the water becomes potable.

gawkers at the posh, though aesthetically misplaced, **Chateau Lake Louise.** The chateau's canoe rentals are an unheard-of $30 per hr.

HIKING

If you don't want to succumb to the town's prices, you can view the water and its surrounding splendor from several hiking trails that begin in the neighborhood and climb along the surrounding ridgelines. But with beauty comes crowds; expect masses of tourists (and bears).

Lake Agnes Trail (3.5km round-trip, 2½ hr.), and the **Plain of Six Glaciers Trail** (5½km round-trip, 4hr.) both end at teahouses and make for lovely, if sometimes crowded, day hikes with views down to the Lake. Open daily summer 9am-6pm.

Moraine Lake, 15km from the village, at the end of Moraine Lake Rd. and off Lake Louise Dr. (no trailers or long RVs). Moraine lies in the awesome **Valley of the Ten Peaks,** opposite glacier-encrusted **Mount Temple.** Join the multitudes on the **Rockpile Trail** for an eye-popping view of the lake and valley and a lesson in ancient ocean bottoms (10min. walk to the top). To escape the camera-wielding hordes, try one of the lake's more challenging trails, either **Sentinel Pass** via Larch Valley (6km one-way, 5-6hr.), with stunning views from flower studded meadows, or **Wenkchemna Pass** via Eiffel Lake (10km one-way, full day), which carries hikers the length of the Valley of the Ten Peaks with incredible views in both directions. Moraine packs more scenic punch than its sister Louise; be sure to arrive before 10am or after 4pm to see the view instead of the crowds. In lieu of visiting Moraine, travelers can look at an old Canadian $20 bill; the Valley of Ten Peaks is pictured on the reverse.

Paradise Valley, depending on which way you hike it, can be an intense day hike or a relaxing overnight trip. From the **Paradise Creek Trailhead,** 2.5km up Moraine Lake Rd., the loop through the valley runs 18.3km through subalpine and alpine forests and along rivers (7½hr., elevation gain 880m). One classic backpacking route runs from Moraine Lake up and over **Sentinel Pass,** joining the top of the Paradise Valley loop after 8km. A **backcountry campground** marks the midpoint from either trailhead. Campers aren't the only admirers of the scenery: grizzly activity often forces the park wardens to close the area in summer. Check with the wardens before hiking in this area.

WINTER SPORTS

Winter activities in the park range from world-class ice climbing to ice fishing. Those 1600km of hiking trails make for exceptional **cross-country ski-ing** (**Moraine Lake Road** is left unplowed in the winter and is used for cross-country skiing, as are the backcountry trails), and three allied resorts offer a range of **skiing** and **snowboarding** opportunities from early November to mid-May. All have terrain parks for snowboarders. Shuttles to all the following three resorts leave from most big hotels in the townsites, and Banff and Lake Louise hostels typically have ticket and transportation **discounts** available for guests. Multi-day passes good for all three resorts are available at the **Ski Banff/Lake Louise** office, 225 Banff Ave., lower level, and at all resorts. Passes include free shuttle service and an extra night of skiing at Mt. Norquay. (☎762-4561; www.skibigthree.com. 3-day packages $200, ages 65 and older and 13-17 $178, 6-12 $81.)

Sunshine Mountain (☎762-6500, snow report 760-7669, in Calgary 277-7669; www.skibanff.com). Spreading seven lifts and the world's fastest gondola across three mountains, with the most snowfall (10m) in the area, this mountain attracts loyal followers to its 3168 acres. $60; students under 24 and ages 65 and older and 13-17, $48; 6-12 $20.

Lake Louise (☎522-3555, snow report in Banff 762-4766, in Calgary 244-6665; www.skilouise.com). The 2nd-largest ski area in Canada (4200 skiable acres), with amazing views, over 1000m of vertical drop, and the best selection of expert (double-black) terrain. Some simpler slopes cover the front of the mountain. $58; students under 24 and ages 65 and older $47; 6-12 $19.

Mount Norquay (☎762-4421; www.banffnorquay.com). A steep local's mountain: smaller (200 acres), closer to town, and less manic. Includes draws like F night-skiing and 2-5hr. tickets. ($50; students, ages 55 and older and 13-17 $38; 6-12 $16. Night-skiing $24; students, ages 55 and older and 13-17 $22; ages 6-12 $12.)

SIGHTSEEING

The **Lake Louise Sightseeing Lift,** up Whitehorn Rd. and across the Trans-Canada Hwy. from Lake Louise, goes halfway up **Mount Whitehorn.** (☎522-3555; www.skilouise.com. Open daily June-Sept. 8:30am-6pm; May 9am-4pm. $23, students and seniors $21, ages 6-12 $12, under 6 free. For breakfast at the top, add $2; for lunch, add $6, under 6 $2. Guided hikes ($5) and walks ($3) available at the top.)

BANFF TO JASPER: HIGHWAY 93   ☎780

Hwy. 93 (the Icefields Parkway) began in the Great Depression as a work relief project. The 230km Parkway is one of the most beautiful rides in North America, heading north from Lake Louise in Banff National Park to Jasper townsite in Jasper National Park. Drivers may struggle to keep their eyes on the road as they skirt stunning peaks, aquamarine lakes, and highwayside glaciers, not to mention all the wonders of Rocky Mountain fauna, visible from the safety of a car window.

🛈 **PRACTICAL INFORMATION.** Parks Canada manages the Parkway as a scenic route, so all users must obtain a Park Pass, available at entrance gates and information centers. ($7 per day, seniors $6; $38 per year, $70 for 2-7 persons. Valid at all Canadian national parks.) Free maps of the Icefields Parkway can be found at park visitors centers in Jasper, Lake Louise, and Banff. They are also available at the Icefield Centre, at the boundary between the two parks, 132km north of Lake Louise and 103km south of Jasper townsite. (☎852-6288. Open daily May to mid-Oct. 9am-5pm; July-Aug. 9am-6pm.) Although the center is closed in winter, the Parkway is only closed for plowing after heavy snowfalls. Thanks to the extensive campground and hostel networks that line the Parkway, longer trips between Banff and Jasper National Parks are convenient and affordable. Cyclists should be prepared to face rapidly changing weather conditions and some very steep hills.

⚠ OUTDOOR ACTIVITIES. The Icefields Parkway has 18 trails into the wilderness and 22 scenic points with spectacular views. **Bow Summit,** 40km north of Lake Louise, is the Parkway's highest point (2135m); there, a 10min. walk leads to a view of fluorescent, aqua **Peyto Lake.** The Icefield Centre (see above) lies in the shadow of the tongue of the **Athabasca Glacier.** This gargantuan ice floe is one of six major glaciers that flow from the 200 sq. km **Columbia Icefield,** the largest accumulation of ice and snow in the Canadian Rockies. The icefield's runoff eventually flows to three oceans: the Pacific, Atlantic, and Arctic.

Columbia Icefield Snocoach Tours carry visitors over the Athabasca Glacier in monster-truck-like buses for a 1¼hr. trip. (☎877-423-7433; www.columbiaicefield.com. Open daily mid-Apr. to mid-Oct. 9am-5pm; $30, ages 6-15 $15.) Visitors can also drive close and take a 10min. walk up piles of glacial debris onto the glacier's mighty toe. Dated signposts mark the glacier's speedy retreat up the valley over the last century. The trail onto the glacier is limited to a very small "safe zone," and all hikers are warned that glacial crevices are a very real concern; two people have died on Athabasca in the last decade. For more geological tidbits, sign up for an **Athabasca Glacier Icewalk.** The daily "Ice Cubed" hike provides 3hr. of fun and education on the ice. ($45, ages 7-17 $23.) Sunday and Thursday at 11am, the "Icewalk Deluxe" hike takes the eager out for a 5-6hr. tour higher up on the glacier, though snow may limit these trips to July and August. Contact the Icefield Centre. (☎852-3803. Tours run mid-June to mid-Sept. $50, ages 7-17 $25.)

The **Wilcox Pass Trail** begins 3km south of the Icefield Centre at **Wilcox Creek Campground** (p. 450). After 2.5km, the path reaches a ridge with astounding views of Athabasca Glacier and Mt. Athabasca. Considered one of the best hikes in Jasper, it's 8km to the pass and back, and 11km one-way from the trailhead to a later junction with the Icefields Parkway, requiring either two vehicles or good hitchhiking skills. *Let's Go* does not recommend hitchhiking. The **Parker Ridge Trail** leads 2.5km away from the road and up above treeline, where an impressive view of the **Saskatchewan Glacier** awaits. The trailhead is 1km south of the **Hilda Creek Hostel**'s burned-down remains and 8.5km south of the Icefield Centre.

JASPER NATIONAL PARK ☎780

AT A GLANCE

AREA: 10,878 sq. km.

CLIMATE: Alpine, subalpine.

FEATURES: Columbia Icefields, Maligne Lake.

HIGHLIGHTS: Hiking the 2 Mt. Edith Cavell trails, visiting the Athabasca Glacier.

GATEWAYS: Banff (p. 440), Edmonton (p. 414).

CAMPING: First come, first served (p. 451).

FEES: Day pass $7, ages 65 and older $6, 6-16 $3, groups of up to 7 in the same vehicle $14.

Northward expansion of the Canadian railway system led to further exploration of the Rockies and the 1907 creation of Jasper, the largest of the National Parks in the region. The area went virtually untouristed until 1940, when the Icefields Parkway paved the way for the masses to appreciate Jasper's astounding beauty. The Parkway is popular with cyclists, making for a remarkable, albeit long, bike journey. In summer, caravans of RVs and charter buses line the highway jostling for the chance to take photos of wildlife. Because 40% of the park is above the treeline, most visitors stay near Jasper townsite, smaller and far less crowded than its nearby counterpart, Banff. Every summer, tourists quadruple the town's population to over 20,000, while Jasper's permanent residents struggle to keep their home looking and feeling like a small town. In the winter, crowds melt away and a modest ski resort welcomes visitors to a slower, more relaxed settlement.

TRANSPORTATION

All of the addresses below are in **Jasper Townsite,** near the center of the park at the intersection of **Highway 16,** which runs east-west through the northern reaches of the park, and the **Icefields Parkway** (Hwy. 93), which connects Jasper with Banff National Park in the south. Many bike shops rent one-way between the two parks. Hitching is popular and reportedly easy along the Parkway, but *Let's Go* does not recommend hitchhiking. The two front streets in Jasper hold all the shops and stores, while the hostels and campgrounds are several kilometers out from town.

Trains: VIA Rail, 607 Connaught Dr. (☎888-842-7245). 3 per week to **Edmonton** (5hr., $155), **Vancouver** (17hr., $215), and **Winnipeg** (24 hr., $313). Ticket counter open M 10am-5pm, Tu-W and Su 9am-4:30pm, Th and Sa 10am-5:30pm, F 9:30am-5pm.

Buses: Greyhound (☎852-3926), in the train station. To **Edmonton** (4½hr., 3 per day, $57) and **Vancouver** (10½hr., 2 per day, $116), via **Kamloops** (5hr., 2 per day, $61). **Brewster Transportation** (☎852-3332), in the movie theater, across the street from the train station. To **Calgary** (8hr., $80) via **Banff** (6hr., $57).

Taxis: Heritage Cabs (☎852-5558). 24hr.

Car Rental: Hertz (☎852-3888), in the train station. $50 per day, $0.23 per km after 150km. Must be 24 or older with credit card. Open M, W, and F 9am-7pm, Tu, Th, and Sa-Su 9am-5pm. **Budget,** 638 Connaught Dr. (☎852-3222), in the Shell Station. $23 per day, $0.19 per km after 250km. Open daily 8am-7pm.

Tours: Bigfoot Tours (p. 429) run between Vancouver, Jasper, and Banff.

PRACTICAL INFORMATION

Tourist Office: Park Information Centre, 500 Connaught Dr. (☎852-6176), has trail maps, trail reports, and backcountry permits. Lists local accommodations, homestay and activity options. Free local calls. The attached bookstore sells trail guides. Open daily mid-June to early Sept. 8:30am-7:30pm; early Sept.-late Oct. and late Dec. to mid-June 9am-5pm.

Bank: CIBC, 416 Connaught Ave. (☎852-3391), by the visitors center. Open M-Th 10am-3pm, F 10am-5pm. **24hr. ATM.**

Equipment Rental: Freewheel Cycle, 618 Patricia St. (☎852-3898; www.freewheeljasper.com). High-end mountain bikes $9 per hr., $30 per day, $36 overnight. Snowboards $28 per day. Watch for twin-tip ski demo deals. Open daily summer 9am-9pm; spring and fall 9am-6pm; winter 8am-6pm. **Jasper International Hostel** (see **Accommodations**) rents mountain bikes. $8 per half-day, $15 per day. Snowshoes $8 per day.

Laundromat and Public Showers: Coin Clean, 607 Patricia St. (☎852-3852). Wash $3, dry $0.25 per 15min. Showers $2 per 10min. **Internet** access $2 per 15min. Open daily 7:30am-10pm.

Weather: Environment Canada ☎852-3185. **Road Conditions:** ☎852-3311.

Police: 600 Pyramid Lake Rd. (☎852-4421).

Women's Crisis Line: ☎800-661-0937. 24hr.

Pharmacy: Cavell Value Drug Mart, 602 Patricia St. (☎852-4441). Open daily May-Sept. 9am-11pm; Sept.-May approximately 9am-7pm.

Hospital: Corner of Miette Ave. and Turret St. (☎852-3344).

Internet Access: Soft Rock Cafe (see **Food,** below). $2 for 15 min., $8 per hr. The **library,** 500 Robson St. (☎852-3652; www.jasper-alberta.com), charges $5 per hr. Open M-Th 11am-9pm, F-Sa 11am-5pm. Also available at **Coin Clean** (see **Laundromat**), $2 per 15min.

Post Office: 502 Patricia St. (☎852-3041), across from the townsite green and the visitors center. Open M-F 9am-5pm. **Postal Code:** T0E 1E0.

Jasper Townsite

🍴 FOOD
Bear's Paw Bakery, **2**
Coco's Cafe, **5**
Jasper Pizza Place, **1**
Mountain Foods and Cafe, **4**
Scoops and Loops, **3**

TO JASPER INT'L HOSTEL (4km),
LAKE LOUISE (232km),
BANFF (287km) &
CALGARY (413km)

TO PRINCE GEORGE (377km),
KAMLOOPS (438km) &
VANCOUVER (863km)   Icefields Pkwy.

🏠 ACCOMMODATIONS

The modern Jasper International Hostel, just outside Jasper townsite, anchors a chain of **Hostelling International (HI)** locations throughout the park. The rustic hostels farther into the park offer fewer amenities but lie amid some of Jasper's finest scenery and outdoor activities. HI runs a shuttle service connecting the Rocky Mountain hostels with Calgary. Reservations are necessary for most hostels after the snow melts in June, but wait-list beds become available at 9am. In winter, Jasper International, Athabasca Falls, and Maligne Canyon run normally; guests at other hostels must pick up the key at Jasper International and give a deposit. For couples or groups, a B&B may prove more economical (summer doubles $40-130; winter $30-95). Many are in town near the train station; the park information center and the bus depot can assist with booking.

Jasper International Hostel (HI) (☎852-3215 or 877-852-0781), also known as Whistlers Hostel, is 3km up Whistlers Rd. from its intersection with Hwy. 93, 4km south of the townsite. The hearth of this old ski lodge is constantly surrounded by a gregarious breed of backpackers and cyclists. The hostel sponsors guided hikes or bike rides nearly every day. 88 often-full beds in large rooms. Reception 8pm-midnight. 2 private rooms available for groups of at least 2. 2am curfew. SunDog Tours (☎852-4056; www.sundogtours.com) runs from train station to hostel en route to Jasper Tramway ($3). $20, nonmembers $25. ❷

Maligne Canyon Hostel (HI) (☎852-3215 or 877-852-0781), on Maligne Lake Rd. north of the Maligne Canyon parking lot, 11km east of town off Hwy. 16. Small, recently renovated cabins sit on bank of Maligne River, with access to the Skyline Trail, Maligne Canyon, and Maligne Lake. Manager is on a first-name basis with several local bears. Fridge, payphone, lockers. Check-in 5-11pm. Closed W Oct.-Apr. 24 beds. $13, nonmembers $18. ❶

Mount Edith Cavell Hostel (HI) (☎852-3215 or 877-852-0781), 12km up Edith Cavell Rd., off Hwy. 93A. Cozy quarters in cabins heated by wood-burning stoves. Literally in the shadow of Mt. Edith Cavell, with easy access to the mountain and trails. Propane light, spring water (filter in the kitchen), private wash area, firepit, and the best-smelling outhouses in the park. No electricity. Road often closed until late June, but the hostel is open to anyone willing to pick up the keys at Jasper International Hostel and ski uphill from the highway. Check-in 5-11pm. 32 beds. $13, nonmembers $18. ●

Athabasca Falls Hostel (HI) (☎852-3215 or 877-852-0781), on Hwy. 93 just south of the 93-93A junction, 32km south of the townsite. A hostel in a quiet setting that still has the comforts of town—electricity, e-mail, and ping-pong. However, the only running water around is the beautiful Athabasca Falls, a 500m stroll away. Propane heat. Closed Tu Oct.-Apr. 40 beds in 3 cabins. $13, nonmembers $18. ●

Beauty Creek Hostel (HI) (☎852-3215 or 877-852-0781), on Hwy. 93, 87km south of the townsite. On the banks of the glacier-fed Sunwapta River and 17km north of the Columbia Icefields. Half a kilometer south of the 3.2km Stanley Falls trailhead. Poetry on the outhouse walls and views of the whole valley from the solar shower. Check-in 5-11pm. 22 beds. $13, nonmembers $18. ●

⚑ CAMPING

These government-run campgrounds are listed from north to south. Most are primitive sites with few facilities. All but Pocahontas are first come, first served, and all are popular. Call the park info center (☎852-6176) for details. Fire permits are $4. All campgrounds except Pocahontas also offer kitchen shelters.

Pocahontas, (☎877-737-3703) on Hwy. 16 at the northern edge of the park, 44km northeast of the townsite. Closest campground to Miette Hot Springs. Flush toilets. Open mid-May to mid-Oct. 140 sites, including 10 hiker/biker sites, $17. ❷

Snaring River, on Hwy. 16, 16km north of Jasper Townsite. Right on the river. Come early for choice spots. Open mid-May to late Sept. 66 sites and 10 walk-in tent sites, $13. ●

Whistlers, on Whistlers Rd., 3km south of the townsite off Hwy. 93. This 781-site behemoth is the closest campground to Jasper Townsite and has all the amenities. Public phones, dump station. Wheelchair-accessible. Open early May to mid-Oct. Sites $22; full RV sites $30. Free showers. ❷

Wapiti, on Hwy. 93, 4km south of Whistlers, along the Athabasca River. Plentiful brush separates tenters from RVers. Pay phone, sani-dump, and electric RV site. Wheelchair-accessible. Mid-June to early Sept. 362 sites, $22-26. Early Oct.-early May. 91 sites, $14-17. Coin showers. ❷

Wabasso, on Hwy 93A, 1km south of Edith Cavell Rd. The nearest campsite to Mt. Edith Cavell, Wabasso has 228 wheelchair-accessible sites. Sani-dump and flush toilets. Open late June-early Sept. $17. ❷

Columbia Icefield, 109km south of the townsite. Lies close enough to the Athabasca Glacier to intercept icy breezes and even a rare summer night's snowfall. Difficult and steep access road makes sites tents-only. Pay phones. Open mid-May to mid-Oct. 22 sites and 11 walk-ins, $13. ●

◖ FOOD

Food prices in Jasper often tend toward the outrageous, but cheap options can be found, and lots of places offer good lunch deals. **Super A Foods,** 601 Patricia St., satisfies basic grocery needs. (☎852-3200. Open daily 8am-9pm.) A larger selection and the bakery at **Robinson's IGA Foodliner,** 218 Connaught Dr., is worth the walk. (☎852-3195. Open daily June-Sept. 8am-10pm; Oct.-May 9am-8pm.) **Nutter's Bulk Foods,** 622 Patricia St., offers bulk snacks, vitamins, and fresh $5 sandwiches. (☎852-5844. Open daily 8am-11pm.)

Coco's Cafe, 608 Patricia St. (☎852-4550). A small vegetarian- and vegan-friendly cafe down-town. Homemade items include tasty soups, baked goods, and smoothies ($3.50). Hearty breakfast wraps made with free range eggs are served all day ($5.25). A variety of tasty sand-wiches from $5. Open daily June-Oct. 7am-8:30pm; Nov.-Apr. 7:30am-5pm. ❶

Jasper Pizza Place, 402 Connaught Dr. (☎852-3225). Has draft and bottle beer on its heated rooftop patio. Free delivery in Jasper area (min. order $5). Large wood-oven piz-zas $10-15, sandwiches $4-9, and burgers $7-10. Open daily 11am-midnight. ❷

Mountain Foods and Cafe, 606 Connaught Dr. (☎852-4050). Offers a wide selection of sandwiches ($4.25), salads, home-cooked goodies, and take-out lunches for the trail. Turkey focaccia sandwich and assorted wraps $9. Daily breakfast special of 2 eggs and bacon for $6. Open daily 8am-6pm. ❷

Bear's Paw Bakery, (☎852-3233), on the corner of Connaught and Cedar, has a wide selection of pastries ($1-3), deli sandwiches ($4-5), and excellent coffee ($1.25). Open M-Th 6am-6pm, F-Su 6am-9pm. ❶

Scoops and Loops, 504 Patricia St. (☎852-4333). Not just an ice-cream parlor. Sandwiches ($3-4), sushi ($3-7), and udon ($8). Open M-Sa 10am-11pm, Su 11am-11pm. Cash only. ❷

⚑ OUTDOOR ACTIVITIES

⚐ HIKING. Jasper National Park offers excellent day hiking, with nature writ large and exotic wildlife that includes bears and bighorn sheep. Remember, it's illegal (and unwise) to feed wildlife. Jasper's low treeline gives plenty of scenery for the altitude, and short, aesthetically mind-boggling walks make the postcard-perfect scenery of the Canadian Rockies easily accessible. For more info, stop by the information center for a copy of the free "Summer Hiking" pamphlet and trail condition updates. As a supplement to hiking, the **Jasper Tramway** (☎852-3093; www.jaspertramway.com) will do the hard work for you, just past the hostel on Whistlers Rd., 4km south of the townsite on Hwy. 93. Climbing the first 973m up Whistlers Mountain, the tramway leads to a panoramic view of the park and, on clear days, far beyond it. From the upper station, you can join hikers on the Whistlers Trail for the last 200m elevation gain to the summit. ($24, ages 5-14 $10, under 5 free. Open daily mid-June to July 8:30am-10pm; mid-May to mid-June and Sept. 9:30am-9pm; mid-Apr. to mid-May and Oct. 9:30am-4:30pm.) **SunDog Tours** (☎852-4056; www.sundogtours.com) offers a shuttle from town and tram ride to the top ($24).

Path of the Glacier Loop (1.6km, 45min.) The trailhead is 30km south of the townsite; take Hwy. 93 to 93A to the end of the bumpy, twisty, and often closed (see Mt. Edith Cavell Hostel) 15km Mt. Edith Cavell Rd. One of the two paths features **Mount Edith Cavell,** the glacier-laden peak named after an English nurse executed by the Germans for providing aid to the Allies during World War I. A crowded path leads to the rewarding view of a glacier receding into an iceberg-littered lake littered. Open June-Oct.; no trail-ers or vehicles over 6m long. Easy.

Valley of the Five Lakes (4.2km round-trip, 2-3hr.) From the Valley of the Five Lakes trailhead, south of the townsite on Hwy. 93, just south of the 93A junction. This family-friendly trail passes five lakes, each a different depth and a different shade of brilliant blue. Mountain bikers also use this trailhead to reach the Wabasso Trail. Easy.

Maligne Canyon (2.1km one-way, 1-2hr.) The spectacular but over-touristed Maligne Canyon is 8km east of the townsite on the Maligne Lake Rd. The best way to view the Canyon is by parking at the 5th Bridge parking area, crossing the bridge, and bearing right at every possible opportunity. From the trailhead, the path follows the Maligne River as it plunges through a sculpted limestone gorge, which is often over 10m deep, but less than 5m wide. Be sure to make it to the first Bridge for views of the upper waterfall, where the canyon depth instantly doubles. Along the walk, look for springs pouring into the Canyon. The water flows underground from Medicine Lake, 15km away, making this the longest known underground river in North America. Easy to moderate.

Cavell Meadows Loop (8km, 3-6hr.) Trailhead is same as Path of the Glacier Loop. A more strenuous ascent past the treeline and through a carpet of wildflowers (from mid-July to Aug.), with striking views of the towering north face and the Angel Glacier. Be careful to stay on the trail as steep cliffs make for dangerous slide conditions. 400m gain. Open June-Oct.; no trailers or vehicles over 6m long. Difficult.

Sulphur Skyline Trail (9.6km round-trip, 4-6hr.) This hike enables the hardy to summit a peak in a day and attain views of the limestone Miette Range and Ashlar Ridge. The trail leaves from the parking lot of the Miette Hot Springs. If you have lunch at the peak, guard it from the courageous golden-mantled ground squirrels. Beware afternoon thunderstorms and serious wind gusts at the peak. 700m gain. Difficult.

Whistlers Trail (8km one-way; 3-5hr. up, 2-3hr. down) begins next to the Jasper International Hostel basketball court. The hike passes through three climate zones, so extra layers are a good idea: weather conditions change rapidly at the 2470m summit. Worth the effort; the summit features an incredible 360-degree view of mountain range after mountain range, which you will share with the tram riders. The restaurant at the top serves burgers ($7.50) and beer ($4.25). Taking the tram down is $9, but your knees will thank you. 1240m gain. Difficult.

MALIGNE LAKE. Maligne Lake (mah-LEEN), at the end of the road, is the longest (22km) and deepest (97m) lake in the park. A flotilla of water vessels allows escape from fellow tourists (except those who also rent a boat) and the plastic geraniums of Maligne Lake Chalet. **Maligne Tours,** 627 Patricia St. (☎852-3370; www.malignelake.com), rents kayaks ($85 per day) and leads canoe trips ($15 per hr.) and narrated scenic cruises (90min.; $35, ages 6-12 $18). Free maps to hiking trails are available at the Maligne Tours office or by the lake; bookings for whitewater and sightseeing trips are available at the office. Perhaps the best way to see the lake's scenery is to escape into the surrounding hills on foot. The **Opal Hills Trail** (8.2km round-trip, 4-6hr.), which starts at the northeast corner of the first parking area, winds through subalpine meadows and ascends 460m in only 3km to views of the lake. The truly strong of stamina and mammoth of calf muscle can follow one of the drainages away from the lake at the halfway point of the hike in the high, tundra valley. At the ridge overlooking the valley, follow the rough footpath (avoid trampling the delicate alpine tundra) that leads up to **Opal Peak,** the highest in the vicinity. This is not a maintained trail, and the loose shale makes for dangerous hiking, but the champion of the mountain will be rewarded with a view hard to surpass. **Shuttle service** from Jasper to the area is available from Maligne Tours. (To the canyon $9; to the lake $14; round-trip with cruise $56; 4 per day, 8:30am-4:30pm.)

⊠ MULTI-DAY HIKES. An extensive network of trails weaves through the park's backwoods, providing respite from tourist-land. The trails cover three different ecological regions. The **montane zone,** which includes Jasper townsite, blankets valley floors with lodgepole pine, Douglas-fir, white spruce, and aspen; it hosts elk, bighorn sheep, and coyotes. Subalpine fir and Engelmann spruce share the **subalpine zone** with porcupines and marmots, while fragile plants and wildflowers struggle against mountain goats and pikas in the uppermost **alpine zone.** To avoid trampling endangered plant species, hikers should be especially careful to stay on trails in the alpine area.

Start any foray into the wilderness by visiting the townsite visitors center, where rangers distribute the free *Backcountry Visitors' Guide* and plentiful advice. Overnight hikers need to register and pay the $8 per night fee (reservations can be made for

$12, and a $56 one-year backcountry pass is also available), either at the visitors center or by calling ☎ 852-6177; many also buy *The Canadian Rockies Trail Guide* ($20). Before hitting the trail, ask about road and trail closures, water levels (some rivers cannot be crossed at certain times of the year), and snow levels at high passes. The Icefield Centre (p. 447), on Hwy. 93 at the southern entrance to the park, provides similar services. Longer trails particularly worthy of recommendation include the **Skyline Trail** (45km, 3 days, almost entirely above treeline), **Maligne Pass** (48km, 3 days), **Tonquin Valley** (42km, 3 days), **Jonas Pass** (53km, 4 days), **Athabasca Pass** (51km one-way, 7 days), **North Boundary Trail** (192 km, 10 days), and **South Boundary Trail** (176km, 10 days).

HOT SPRINGS. The **Miette Hot Springs,** 42km north of the townsite on Hwy. 16 and 15km along Miette Hot Springs Rd., blends heat therapy with a panoramic view of the surrounding limestone mountains. Once a rudimentary log bathhouse in 1913, the waters—at 54°C/129°F, the hottest in the Canadian Rockies—are now chlorinated, filtered, and cooled before they arrive in three outdoor swimming pools at temperatures ranging from 39-41°C/102-106°F or 6-22°C/43-72°F. The road to Miette is, sadly, closed after the snow falls. (☎ 866-3939; www.hotspring.ca. Open daily mid-June to early Sept. 8:30am-10:30pm; early May to mid-June and early Sept. to mid-Oct. 10:30am-9pm. $6.25, seniors and children $5.25. Swimsuit $1.50; towel $1.25.)

🎿 **SKIING.** Four meters of snowfall and nine lifts bring plenty of skiing opportunities to the slopes of **Marmot Basin** 19km south of Jasper via Hwy. 93, 93A and the Marmot Basin Rd. The upper half of the slope's 914m vertical drop is above the treeline, creating room for bowls and a modest snowboard park. (☎ 852-3816; www.skimarmot.com. Full-day lift ticket $49, ages 65 and older $38, 13-17 and students up to age 25 $39, 6-12 $20, under 6 free.) Bargain ski rental is available at **Totem Ski Shop,** 408 Connaught Dr. (☎ 852-3078; www.jasper.ca/totems. Open daily June-Dec. 9:30am-10pm; Dec.-June 8am-6pm. Ski package $20; snowboard package and boots $25; cross country skis from $9.50 per day.) **Jasper Source for Sports,** 406 Patricia St., offers ski packages ($20), snowboard packages and boots ($25); cross country skis (from $9.50 per day), and rents ice skates as well as camping and fishing equipment. (☎ 852-3654; www.jasper.ca/sourceforsports. Skates $4 per hr., $10 per day.) Maligne Lake offers cross-country ski trails from late November through May. **Everest Outdoor Stores,** 414 Connaught Dr., also has ski rentals. (☎ 852-5902; www.jaspersports.com/eos_index.htm. Open daily June-Dec. 9:30am-9:30pm; Dec.-June 8am-6pm. Cross-country skis from $9 per day, downhill skis and boots $15-20 per day, snowshoes $12 per day.)

OTHER OUTDOOR ACTIVITIES. Climb Canada leads half-day ($59) and full-day ($89) rock climbing courses. (☎ 852-4161; www.climbcanada.com.) **Peter Amann** teaches 2-day introductory climbing classes for $150 as well as 2-3 day ice climbing classes for $220-300. (☎ 852-3237; www.incentre.net/pamann. May-June and Sept.) Both companies lead ice climbing and mountaineering trips. **Gravity Gear,** 618 Patricia St. (☎ 888-852-3155; www.gravitygearjasper.com), has rentals for mountain adventures and offers multi-day discounts. **SunDog Tours,** 414 Connaught Dr., serves as a reservation service for most local outdoor businesses, as well as providing prices and recommendations for rafting, fishing, horseback riding, wildlife safaris, and most other outdoor pursuits. (☎ 852-4056; www.sundogtours.com. Open daily July-Sept. 8am-9pm; Sept.-June 9am-6pm.) **White Water Rafting** leads two trips on the Athabasca River and one on the faster Sunwapta River. (☎ 852-7238. 2-3½hr. From $49. Register by phone.) **Rocky Mountain River Guides,** 626 Patricia St., offers similar rides. (☎ 852-3777; www.rmriverguides.com. 2-3hr. $45.) Rent boats from **Pyramid Lake Resort,** 7km north of town off Pyramid Ave. from Connaught Dr. (☎ 852-4900. Open daily 8am, last boat out at 8:30pm. Canoes $25 per hr., $75 per day, pedal boats $25 per hr., both $15 per additional hr.)

INDEX

INDEX

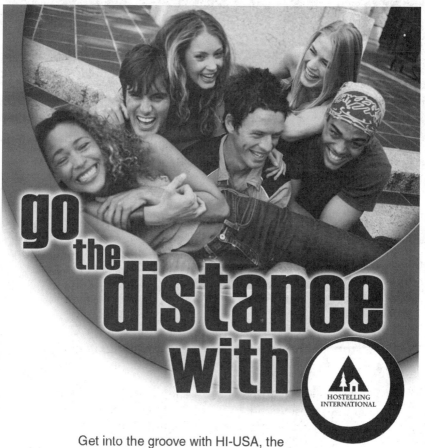

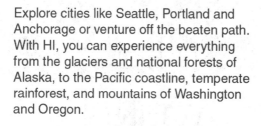

MAP INDEX

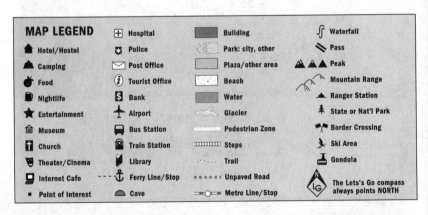

MAP LEGEND

Hotel/Hostel	Hospital	Building	Waterfall
Camping	Police	Park: city, other	Pass
Food	Post Office	Plaza/other area	Peak
Nightlife	Tourist Office	Beach	Mountain Range
Entertainment	Bank	Water	Ranger Station
Museum	Airport	Glacier	State or Nat'l Park
Church	Bus Station	Pedestrian Zone	Border Crossing
Theater/Cinema	Train Station	Steps	Ski Area
Internet Cafe	Library	Trail	Gondola
Point of Interest	Ferry Line/Stop	Unpaved Road	The Lets's Go compass always points NORTH
	Cave	Metro Line/Stop	